THE THEORY OF
PARSING, TRANSLATION,
AND COMPILING

Prentice-Hall
Series in Automatic Computation

George Forsythe, editor

AHO AND ULLMAN, *The Theory of Parsing, Translation, and Compiling,*
  Volume I: *Parsing;* Volume II: *Compiling*
(ANDREE),[3] *Computer Programming: Techniques, Analysis, and Mathematics*
ANSELONE, *Collectively Compact Operator Approximation Theory*
  and Applications to Integral Equations
ARBIB, *Theories of Abstract Automata*
BATES AND DOUGLAS, *Programming Language/One,* 2nd ed.
BLUMENTHAL, *Management Information Systems*
BOBROW AND SCHWARTZ, *Computers and the Policy-Making Community*
BOWLES, editor, *Computers in Humanistic Research*
BRENT, *Algorithms for Minimization without Derivatives*
CESCHINO AND KUNTZMAN, *Numerical Solution of Initial Value Problems*
CRESS, et al., *FORTRAN IV with WATFOR and WATFIV*
DANIEL, *The Approximate Minimization of Functionals*
DESMONDE, *A Conversational Graphic Data Processing System*
DESMONDE, *Computers and Their Uses,* 2nd ed.
DESMONDE, *Real-Time Data Processing Systems*
DRUMMOND, *Evaluation and Measurement Techniques for Digital Computer Systems*
EVANS, et al., *Simulation Using Digital Computers*
FIKE, *Computer Evaluation of Mathematical Functions*
FIKE, *PL/1 for Scientific Programers*
FORSYTHE AND MOLER, *Computer Solution of Linear Algebraic Systems*
GAUTHIER AND PONTO, *Designing Systems Programs*
GEAR, *Numerical Inital Value Problems in Ordinary Differential Equations*
GOLDEN, *FORTRAN IV Programming and Computing*
GOLDEN AND LEICHUS, *IBM/360 Programming and Computing*
GORDON, *System Simulation*
GREENSPAN, *Lectures on the Numerical Solution of Linear, Singular, and*
  Nonlinear Differential Equations
GRUENBERGER, editor, *Computers and Communications*
GRUENBERGER, editor, *Critical Factors in Data Management*
GRUENBERGER, editor, *Expanding Use of Computers in the 70's*
GRUENBERGER, editor, *Fourth Generation Computers*
HARTMANIS AND STEARNS, *Algebraic Structure Theory of Sequential Machines*
HULL, *Introduction to Computing*
JACOBY, et al., *Iterative Methods for Nonlinear Optimization Problems*
JOHNSON, *System Structure in Data, Programs and Computers*
KANTER, *The Computer and the Executive*
KIVIAT, et al., *The SIMSCRIPT II Programming Language*
LORIN, *Parallelism in Hardware and Software: Real and Apparent Concurrency*
LOUDEN AND LEDIN, *Programming theIBM 1130,* 2nd ed.
MARTIN, *Design of Real-Time Computer Systems*
MARTIN, *Future Developments in Telecommunications*
MARTIN, *Man-Computer Dialogue*

THE THEORY OF PARSING, TRANSLATION, AND COMPILING

VOLUME I: PARSING

ALFRED V. AHO

Bell Telephone Laboratories, Inc.
Murray Hill, N.J.

JEFFREY D. ULLMAN

Department of Electrical Engineering
Princeton University

PRENTICE-HALL, INC.

ENGLEWOOD CLIFFS, N.J.

15 14 13 12 11

ISBN: 0-13-914556-7
Library of Congress Catalog Card No. 72-1073

Printed in the United States of America

PRENTICE-HALL INTERNATIONAL, INC., London
PRENTICE-HALL OF AUSTRALIA, PTY. LTD., Sydney
PRENTICE-HALL OF CANADA, LTD., Toronto
PRENTICE-HALL OF INDIA PRIVATE LIMITED, New Delhi
PRENTICE-HALL OF JAPAN, INC., Tokyo

For Adrienne and Holly

PREFACE

This book is intended for a one or two semester course in compiling theory at the senior or graduate level. It is a theoretically oriented treatment of a practical subject. Our motivation for making it so is threefold.

(1) In an area as rapidly changing as Computer Science, sound pedagogy demands that courses emphasize ideas, rather than implementation details. It is our hope that the algorithms and concepts presented in this book will survive the next generation of computers and programming languages, and that at least some of them will be applicable to fields other than compiler writing.

(2) Compiler writing has progressed to the point where many portions of a compiler can be isolated and subjected to design optimization. It is important that appropriate mathematical tools be available to the person attempting this optimization.

(3) Some of the most useful and most efficient compiler algorithms, e.g. LR(k) parsing, require a good deal of mathematical background for full understanding. We expect, therefore, that a good theoretical background will become essential for the compiler designer.

While we have not omitted difficult theorems that are relevant to compiling, we have tried to make the book as readable as possible. Numerous examples are given, each based on a small grammar, rather than on the large grammars encountered in practice. It is hoped that these examples are sufficient to illustrate the basic ideas, even in cases where the theoretical developments are difficult to follow in isolation.

Use of the Book

The notes from which this book derives were used in courses at Princeton University and Stevens Institute of Technology at both the senior and graduate levels. Both one and two semester courses have been taught from this book. In a one semester course, the course in compilers was preceded by a course covering finite automata and context-free languages. It was therefore unnecessary to cover Chapters 0, 2 and 8. Most of the remaining chapters were covered in detail.

In a two semester sequence, most of Volume I was covered in the first semester and most of Volume II, except for Chapter 8, in the second. In the two semester course more attention was devoted to proofs and proof techniques than in the one semester course.

Some sections of the book are clearly more important than others, and we would like to give the reader some brief comments regarding our estimates of the relative importance of various parts of Volume I. As a general comment, it is probably wise to skip most of the proofs. We include proofs of all main results because we believe them to be necessary for maximum understanding of the subject. However, we suspect that many courses in compiling do not get this deeply into many topics, and reasonable understanding can be obtained with only a smattering of proofs.

Chapters 0 (mathematical background) and 1 (overview of compiling) are almost all essential material, except possibly for Section 1.3, which covers applications of parsing other than to compilers.

We believe that every concept and theorem introduced in Chapter 2 (language theory) finds use somewhere in the remaining nine chapters. However, some of the material can be skipped in a course on compilers. A good candidate for omission is the rather difficult material on regular expression equations in Section 2.2.1. One is then forced to omit some of the material on right linear grammars in Section 2.2.2. (although the equivalence between these and finite automata can be obtained in other ways) and the material on Rosenkrantz's method of achieving Greibach normal form in Section 2.4.5.

The concepts of Chapter 3 (translation) are quite essential to the rest of the book. However, Section 3.2.3, on the hierarchy of syntax-directed translations, is rather difficult and can be omitted.

We believe that Section 4.1 on backtracking methods of parsing is less vital than the tabular methods of Section 4.2.

Most of Chapter 5 (single-pass parsing) is essential. We suggest that LL grammars (Section 5.1), LR grammars (Section 5.2), precedence grammars (Sections 5.3.2 and 5.3.4) and operator precedence grammars (Section 5.4.3) receive maximum priority. Other sections could be omitted if necessary.

Chapter 6 (backtracking algorithms) is less essential than most of Chapter 5 or Section 4.2. If given a choice, we would cover Section 6.1 rather than 6.2.

Organization of the Book

The entire work *The Theory of Parsing, Translation, and Compiling* appears in two volumes, *Parsing* (Chs. 0–6) and *Compiling* (Chs. 7–11). (The topics covered in the second volume are parser optimization, theory of deterministic parsing, translation, bookkeeping, and code optimization.) The two volumes form an integrated work, with pages consecutively numbered, and with a bibliography and index for both volumes appearing in Volume II.

Problems and bibliographical notes appear at the end of each section (numbered i.j). Except for open problems and research problems, we have used stars to indicate grades of difficulty. Singly starred problems require one significant insight for their solution. Doubly starred exercises require more than one such insight.

It is recommended that a course based on this book be accompanied by a programming laboratory in which several compiler parts are designed and implemented. At the end of certain sections of this book appear programming exercises, which can be used as projects in such a programming laboratory.

Acknowledgements

Many people have carefully read various parts of this manuscript and have helped us significantly in its preparation. Especially, we would like to thank David Benson, John Bruno, Stephen Chen, Matthew Geller, James Gimpel, Michael Harrison, Ned Horvath, Jean Ichbiah, Brian Kernighan, Douglas McIlroy, Robert Martin, Robert Morris, Howard Siegel, Leah Siegel, Harold Stone, and Thomas Szymanski, as well as referees Thomas Cheatham, Michael Fischer, and William McKeeman. We have also received important comments from many of the students who used these notes, among them Alan Demers, Nahed El Djabri, Matthew Hecht, Peter Henderson, Peter Maika, Thomas Peterson, Ravi Sethi, Kenneth Sills, and Steven Squires.

Our thanks are also due for the excellent typing of the manuscript done by Hannah Kresse and Dorothy Luciani. In addition, we acknowledge the support services provided by Bell Telephone Laboratories during the preparation of the manuscript. The use of UNIX, an operating system for the PDP-11 computer designed by Dennis Ritchie and Kenneth Thompson, expedited the preparation of certain parts of this manuscript.

ALFRED V. AHO

JEFFREY D. ULLMAN

CONTENTS

3   THEORY OF TRANSLATION   212

4   GENERAL PARSING METHODS   281

5   ONE-PASS NO BACKTRACK PARSING   333

O MATHEMATICAL PRELIMINARIES

To speak clearly and accurately we need a precise and well-defined language. This chapter describes the language that we shall use to discuss parsing, translation, and the other topics to be covered in this book. This language is primarily elementary set theory with some rudimentary concepts from graph theory and logic included. For readers having background in these areas, Chapter 0 can be easily skimmed and treated as a reference for notation and definitions.

0.1. CONCEPTS FROM SET THEORY

This section will briefly review some of the most basic concepts from set theory: relations, functions, orderings, and the usual operations on sets.

0.1.1. Sets

In what follows, we assume that there are certain objects, referred to as *atoms*. The term atom will be a rudimentary concept, which is just another way of saying that the term atom will be left undefined, and what we choose to call an atom depends on our domain of discourse. Many times it is convenient to consider integers or letters of an alphabet to be atoms.

We also postulate an abstract notion of *membership*. If a is a member of A, we write $a \in A$. The negation of this statement is written $a \notin A$. We assume that if a is an atom, then it has no member; i.e., $x \notin a$ for all x in the domain of discourse.

We shall also use certain primitive objects, called *sets*, which are not atoms. If A is a set, then its *members* or *elements* are those objects a (not

1

necessarily atoms) such that $a \in A$. Each member of a set is either an atom or another set. We assume each member of a set appears exactly once in that set. If A has a finite number of members, then A is a *finite set*, and we often write $A = \{a_1, a_2, \ldots, a_n\}$, if $a_1, \ldots, a_n$ are all the members of A and $a_i \neq a_j$, for $i \neq j$. Note that order is unimportant. We could also write $A = \{a_n, \ldots, a_1\}$, for example. We reserve the symbol $\varnothing$ for the *empty set*, the set which has no members. Note that an atom also has no members, but $\varnothing$ is not an atom, and no atom is $\varnothing$.

The statement $\#A = n$ means that set A has n members.

Example 0.1

Let the nonnegative integers be atoms. Then $A = \{1, \{2, 3\}, 4\}$ is a set. A's members are 1, $\{2, 3\}$, and 4. The member $\{2, 3\}$ of A is also a set. Its members are 2 and 3. However, the atoms 2 and 3 are not members of A itself. We could equivalently have written $A = \{4, 1, \{3, 2\}\}$. Note that $\#A = 3$. □

A useful way of defining sets is by means of a *predicate*, a statement involving one or more unknowns which has one of two values, *true* or *false*. The set defined by a predicate consists of exactly those elements for which the predicate is true. However, we must be careful what predicate we choose to define a set, or we may attempt to define a set that could not possibly exist.

Example 0.2

The phenomenon alluded to above is known as *Russell's paradox*. Let $P(X)$ be the predicate "X is not a member of itself"; i.e., $X \notin X$. Then we might think that we could define the set Y of all X such that $P(X)$ was true; i.e., Y consists of exactly those sets that are not members of themselves. Since most common sets seem not to be members of themselves, it is tempting to suppose that set Y exists.

But if Y exists, we should be able to answer the question, "Is Y a member of itself?" But this leads to an impossible situation. If $Y \in Y$, then $P(Y)$ is false, and Y is not a member of itself, by definition of Y. Hence, it is not possible that $Y \in Y$. Conversely, suppose that $Y \notin Y$. Then, by definition of Y again, $Y \in Y$. We see that $Y \notin Y$ implies $Y \in Y$ and that $Y \in Y$ implies $Y \notin Y$. Since either $Y \in Y$ or $Y \notin Y$ is true, both are true, a situation which we shall assume is impossible. One "way out" is to accept that set Y does not exist. □

The normal way to avoid Russell's paradox is to define sets only by those predicates $P(X)$ of the form "X is in A and $P_1(X)$," where A is a known set and P_1 is an arbitrary predicate. If the set A is understood, we shall just write $P_1(X)$ for "X is in A and $P_1(X)$."

If $P(X)$ is a predicate, then we denote the set of objects X for which $P(X)$ is true by $\{X \mid P(X)\}$.

Example 0.3

Let $P(X)$ be the predicate "X is a nonnegative even integer." That is, $P(X)$ is "X is in the set of integers and $P_1(X)$," where $P_1(X)$ is the predicate "X is even." Then $A = \{X \mid P(X)\}$ is the set which is often written $\{0, 2, 4, \ldots, 2n, \ldots\}$. Colloquially, we can assume that the set of nonnegative integers is understood, and write $A = \{X \mid X \text{ is even}\}$. $\square$

We have glossed over a great deal of development called axiomatic set theory. The interested reader is referred to Halmos [1960] or Suppes [1960] (see the Bibliography at the end of Volume 1) for a more complete treatment of this subject.

DEFINITION

We say that set A is *included in* set B, written $A \subseteq B$, if every element of A is also an element of B. Sometimes we say that B *includes* A, written $B \supseteq A$, if $A \subseteq B$. In either case, A is said to be a *subset* of B, and B a *superset* of A.

If B contains an element not contained in A and $A \subseteq B$, then we say that A is *properly* included in B, written $A \subsetneqq B$ (or B properly includes A, written $B \supsetneqq A$). We can also say that A is a proper subset of B or that B is a proper superset of A.

Two sets A and B are *equal* if and only if $A \subseteq B$ and $B \subseteq A$.

A picture called a *Venn diagram* is often used to graphically describe set membership and inclusion. Figure 0.1 shows a Venn diagram for the relation $A \subseteq B$.

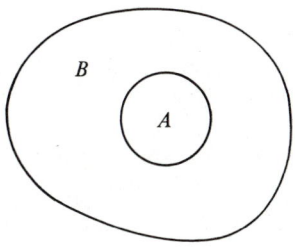

Fig. 0.1   Venn diagram of set inclusion: $A \subseteq B$.

0.1.2. Operations on Sets

There are several basic operations on sets which can be used to construct new sets.

DEFINITION

Let A and B be sets. The *union* of A and B, written $A \cup B$, is the set containing all elements in A together with all elements in B. Formally, $A \cup B = \{x \mid x \in A$ or $x \in B\}$.†

The *intersection* of A and B, written $A \cap B$, is the set of all elements that are in both A and B. Formally, $A \cap B = \{x \mid x \in A$ and $x \in B\}$.

The *difference* of A and B, written $A - B$, is the set of all elements in A that are not in B. If $A = U$—the set of all elements under consideration or the *universal set*, as it is sometimes called—then $U - B$ is often written $\bar{B}$ and called the *complement* of B.

Note that we have referred to the universal set as the set of all objects "under consideration." We must be careful to be sure that U exists. For example, if we choose U to be "the set of all sets," then we would have Russell's paradox again. Also, note that $\bar{B}$ is not well defined unless we assume that complementation with respect to some known universe is implied.

In general $A - B = A \cap \bar{B}$. Venn diagrams for these set operations are shown in Fig. 0.2.

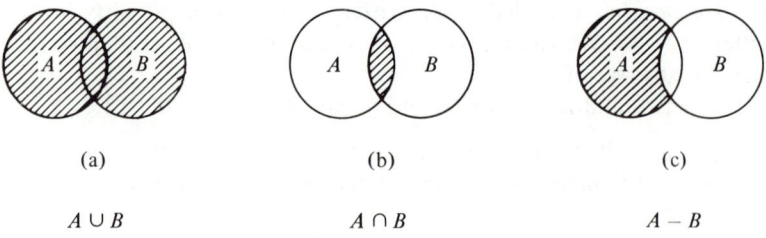

(a)   (b)   (c)

$A \cup B$ $A \cap B$ $A - B$

Fig. 0.2   Venn diagrams of set operations.

If $A \cap B = \varnothing$, then A and B are said to be *disjoint*.

DEFINITION

If I is some (indexing) set such that A_i is a known set for each i in I, then we write $\bigcup_{i \in I} A_i$ for $\{X \mid$ there exists $i \in I$ such that $X \in A_i\}$. Since I may not be finite, this definition is an extension of the union of two sets. If I is defined by predicate $P(i)$, we sometimes write $\bigcup_{P(i)} A_i$ for $\bigcup_{i \in I} A_i$. For example, "$\bigcup_{i > 2} A_i$" means $A_3 \cup A_4 \cup A_5 \cup \cdots$

†Note that we may not have a set guaranteed to include $A \cup B$, so this use of predicate definition appears questionable. In axiomatic set theory, the existence of $A \cup B$ is taken to be an axiom.

DEFINITION

Let A be a set. The *power set* of A, written $\mathcal{P}(A)$ or sometimes 2^A, is the set of all subsets of A. That is, $\mathcal{P}(A) = \{B \mid B \subseteq A\}$.†

Example 0.4

Let $A = \{1, 2\}$. Then $\mathcal{P}(A) = \{\varnothing, \{1\}, \{2\}, \{1, 2\}\}$. As another example, $\mathcal{P}(\varnothing) = \{\varnothing\}$. □

In general, if A is a finite set of m members, $\mathcal{P}(A)$ has 2^m members. The empty set is a member of $\mathcal{P}(A)$ for every A.

We have observed that the members of a set are considered to be unordered. It is often convenient to have ordered pairs of objects available for discourse. We thus make the following definition.

DEFINITION

Let a and b be objects. Then (a, b) denotes the *ordered pair* consisting of a and b in that order. We say that $(a, b) = (c, d)$ if and only if $a = c$ and $b = d$. In contrast, $\{a, b\} = \{b, a\}$.

Ordered pairs can be considered sets if we define (a, b) to be the set $\{a, \{a, b\}\}$. It is left to the Exercises to show that $\{a, \{a, b\}\} = \{c, \{c, d\}\}$ if and only if $a = c$ and $b = d$. Thus this definition is consistent with what we regard to be the fundamental property of ordered pairs.

DEFINITION

The *Cartesian product* of sets A and B, denoted $A \times B$, is
$$\{(a, b) \mid a \in A \text{ and } b \in B\}.$$

Example 0.5

Let $A = \{1, 2\}$ and $B = \{2, 3, 4\}$. Then
$$A \times B = \{(1, 2), (1, 3), (1, 4), (2, 2), (2, 3), (2, 4)\}. \qquad \square$$

0.1.3. Relations

Many common mathematical concepts, such as membership, set inclusion, and arithmetic "less than" ($<$), are referred to as relations. We shall give a formal definition of the concept and see how common examples of relations fit the formal definition.

†The existence of the power set of any set is an axiom of set theory. The other set defining axioms, in addition to the power set axiom and the union axiom previously mentioned, are:
(1) If A is a set and P a predicate, then $\{X \mid P(X) \text{ and } X \in A\}$ is a set.
(2) If X is an atom or set, then $\{X\}$ is a set.
(3) If A is a set, then $\{X \mid \text{for some } Y, \text{ we have } X \in Y \text{ and } Y \in A\}$ is a set.

Definition

Let A and B be sets. A *relation from A to B* is any subset of $A \times B$. If $A = B$, we say that the relation is *on A*. If R is a relation from A to B, we write $a \, R \, b$ whenever (a, b) is in R. We call A the *domain* of R, and B the *range* of R.

Example 0.6

Let A be the set of integers. The relation $<$ is $\{(a, b) \mid a$ is less than $b\}$. We thus write $a < b$ exactly when we would expect to do so.   □

Definition

The relation $\{(b, a) \mid (a, b) \in R\}$ is called the *inverse* of R and is often denoted R^{-1}.

A relation is a very general concept. Often a relation may possess certain properties to which special names have been given.

Definition

Let A be a set and R a relation on A. We say that R is

(1) *Reflexive* if $a \, R \, a$ for all a in A,

(2) *Symmetric* if "$a \, R \, b$" implies "$b \, R \, a$" for a, b in A, and

(3) *Transitive* if "$a \, R \, b$ and $b \, R \, c$" implies "$a \, R \, c$" for a, b, c in A. The elements $a, b,$ and c need not be distinct.

Relations obeying these three properties occur frequently and have additional properties as a consequence. The term *equivalence relation* is used to describe a relation which is reflexive, symmetric, and transitive.

An important property of equivalence relations is that an equivalence relation R on a set A partitions A into disjoint subsets called *equivalence classes*. For each element a in A we define $[a]$, *the equivalence class of a*, to be the set $\{b \mid a \, R \, b\}$.

Example 0.7

Consider the relation of congruence modulo N on the nonnegative integers. We say that $a \equiv b \bmod N$ (read "a is congruent to b modulo N") if there is an integer k such that $a - b = kN$. As a specific case let us take $N = 3$. Then the set $\{0, 3, 6, \ldots, 3n, \ldots\}$ forms an equivalence class, since $3n \equiv 3m \bmod 3$ for all integer values of m and n. We shall use $[0]$ to denote this class. We could have used $[3]$ or $[6]$ or $[3n]$, since any element of an equivalence class can be used as a representative of that class.

The two other equivalence classes under the relation congruence modulo 3 are

$$[1] = \{1, 4, 7, \ldots, 3n + 1, \ldots\}$$
$$[2] = \{2, 5, 8, \ldots, 3n + 2, \ldots\}$$

The union of the three sets [0], [1] and [2] is the set of all nonnegative integers. Thus we have partitioned the set of all nonnegative integers into the three disjoint equivalence classes [0], [1], and [2] by means of the equivalence relation congruence modulo 3 (Fig. 0.3). □

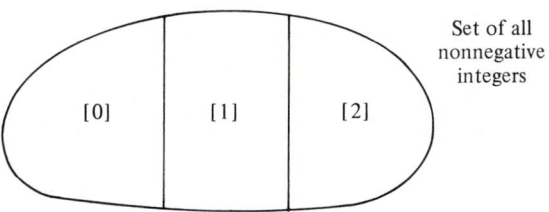

Fig. 0.3   Equivalence classes for congruence modulo 3.

The *index* of an equivalence relation on a set A is the number of equivalence classes into which A is partitioned.

The following theorem about equivalence relations is left as an exercise.

THEOREM 0.1

Let R be an equivalence relation on A. Then for all a and b in A, either $[a] = [b]$ or $[a]$ and $[b]$ are disjoint.

Proof. Exercise. □

0.1.4. Closures of Relations

Given a relation R, we often need to find another relation R', which includes R and has certain additional properties, e.g., transitivity. Moreover, we would generally like R' to be as "small" as possible, that is, to be a subset of every other relation including R which has the desired properties. Of course, the "smallest" relation may not be unique if the additional properties are strange. However, for the common properties mentioned in the previous section, we can often find a unique superset of a given relation with these as additional properties. Some specific cases follow.

DEFINITION

The *k-fold product* of a relation R (on A), denoted R^k, is defined as follows:

(1) $a R^1 b$ if and only if $a R b$;

(2) $a R^i b$ if and only if there exists c in A such that $a R c$ and $c R^{i-1} b$ for $i > 1$.

This is an example of a recursive definition, a method of definition we shall use many times. To examine the recursive aspect of this definition, suppose that $a R^4 b$. Then by (2) there is a c_1 such that $a R c_1$ and $c_1 R^3 b$. Applying (2) again there is a c_2 such that $c_1 R c_2$ and $c_2 R^2 b$. One more application of (2) says that there is a c_3 such that $c_2 R c_3$ and $c_3 R^1 b$. Now we can apply (1) and say that $c_3 R b$.

Thus, if $a R^4 b$, then there exists a sequence of elements c_1, c_2, c_3 in A such that $a R c_1$, $c_1 R c_2$, $c_2 R c_3$, and $c_3 R b$.

The *transitive closure* of a relation R on a set A will be denoted R^+. We define $a R^+ b$ if and only if $a R^i b$ for some $i \geq 1$. We shall see that R^+ is the smallest transitive relation that includes R.

We could have alternatively defined R^+ by saying that $a R^+ b$ if there exists a sequence $c_1, c_2, \ldots, c_n$ of zero or more elements in A such that $a R c_1, c_1 R c_2, \ldots, c_{n-1} R c_n, c_n R b$. If $n = 0$, $a R b$ is meant.

The *reflexive and transitive closure* of a relation R on a set A is denoted R^* and is defined as follows:

(1) $a R^* a$ for all a in A;
(2) $a R^* b$ if $a R^+ b$;
(3) Nothing is in R^* unless its being there follows from (1) or (2).

If we define R^0 by saying $a R^0 b$ if and only if $a = b$, then $a R^* b$ if and only if $a R^i b$ for some $i \geq 0$.

The only difference between R^+ and R^* is that $a R^* a$ is true for all a in A but $a R^+ a$ may or may not be true. R^* is the smallest reflexive and transitive relation that includes R.

In Section 0.5.8 we shall examine methods of computing the reflexive and transitive closure of a relation efficiently. We would like to prove here that R^+ and R^* are the smallest supersets of R with the desired properties.

THEOREM 0.2

If R^+ and R^* are, respectively, the transitive and reflexive-transitive closure of R as defined above, then

(a) R^+ is transitive; if R' is any transitive relation such that $R \subseteq R'$, then $R^+ \subseteq R'$.

(b) R^* is reflexive and transitive; if R' is any reflexive and transitive relation such that $R \subseteq R'$, then $R^* \subseteq R'$.

Proof. We prove only (a); (b) is left as an exercise. First, to show that R^+ is transitive, we must show that if $a R^+ b$ and $b R^+ c$, then $a R^+ c$. Since $a R^+ b$, there exists a sequence of elements $d_1, \ldots, d_n$ such that $d_1 R d_2, \ldots, d_{n-1} R d_n$, where $d_1 = a$ and $d_n = b$. Since $b R^+ c$, we can find $e_1, \ldots, e_m$ such that $e_1 R e_2, \ldots, e_{m-1} R e_m$, where $e_1 = b = d_n$ and $e_m = c$. Applying the definition of R^+ $m + n$ times, we conclude that $a R^+ c$.

Now we shall show that R^+ is the smallest transitive relation that includes R. Let R' be any transitive relation such that $R \subseteq R'$. We must show that $R^+ \subseteq R'$. Thus let (a, b) be in R^+; i.e., $a R^+ b$. Then there is a sequence

$c_1, \ldots, c_n$ such that $a = c_1$, $b = c_n$, and $c_i \, R \, c_{i+1}$ for $1 \leq i < n$. Since $R \subseteq R'$, we have $c_i \, R' \, c_{i+1}$ for $1 \leq i < n$. Since R' is transitive, repeated application of the definition of transitivity yields $c_1 \, R' \, c_n$; i.e., $a \, R' \, b$. Since (a, b) is an arbitrary member of R^+, we have shown that every member of R^+ is also a member of R'. Thus, $R^+ \subseteq R'$, as desired. $\square$

0.1.5. Ordering Relations

An important class of relations on sets are the ordering relations. In general, an ordering on a set A is any transitive relation on A. In the study of algorithms, a special type of ordering, called a partial order, is particularly important.

DEFINITION

A *partial order* on a set A is a relation R on A such that

(1) R is transitive, and
(2) For all a in A, $a \, R \, a$ is false. (That is, R is *irreflexive*.)

From properties (1) and (2) of a partial order it follows that if $a \, R \, b$, then $b \, R \, a$ is false. This is called the *asymmetric* property.

Example 0.8

An example of a partial order is proper inclusion of sets. For example, let $S = \{e_1, \ldots, e_n\}$ be a set of n elements and let $A = \mathcal{P}(S)$. There are 2^n elements in A. Then define $a \, R \, b$ if and only if $a \subsetneq b$ for all a, b in A. R is a partial order.

If $S = \{0, 1, 2\}$, then Fig. 0.4 graphically depicts this partial order. Set S_1 properly includes set S_2 if and only if there is a path downward from S_1 to S_2. $\square$

In the literature the term partial order is sometimes used to denote what we call a reflexive partial order.

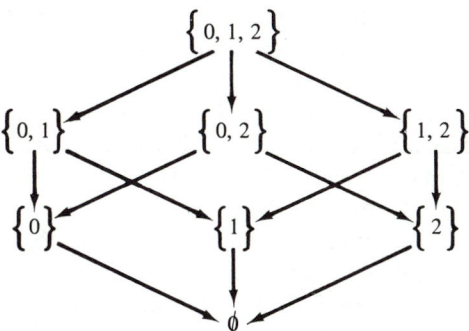

Fig. 0.4 A partial order.

DEFINITION

A *reflexive partial order* on a set A is a relation R such that

(1) R is transitive,
(2) R is reflexive, and
(3) If $a\,R\,b$ and $b\,R\,a$, then $a = b$. This property is called *antisymmetry*.

An example of a reflexive partial order would be (not necessarily proper) inclusion of sets.

In Section 0.5 we shall show that every partial order can be graphically displayed in terms of a structure called a directed acyclic graph.

An important special case of a partial order is linear order (sometimes called a total order).

DEFINITION

A *linear order* R on a set A is a partial order such that if a and b are in A, then either $a\,R\,b$, $b\,R\,a$, or $a = b$. If A is a finite set, then one convenient representation for the linear order R is to display the elements of A as a sequence $a_1, a_2, \ldots, a_n$ such that $a_i\,R\,a_j$ if and only if $i < j$, where $A = \{a_1, \ldots, a_n\}$.

We can also define a reflexive linear order analogously. That is, R is a *reflexive linear order* on A if R is a reflexive partial order such that for all a and b in A, either $a\,R\,b$ or $b\,R\,a$.

For example, the relation $<$ (less than) on the nonnegative integers is a linear order. The relation $\leq$ is a reflexive linear order.

0.1.6. Mappings

One important kind of relation that we shall be using is known as a mapping.

DEFINITION

A *mapping* (also *function* or *transformation*) M from a set A to a set B is a relation from A to B such that if (a, b) and (a, c) are in M, then $b = c$.

If (a, b) is in M, we shall often write $M(a) = b$. We say that $M(a)$ is *defined* if there exists b in B such that (a, b) is in M. If $M(a)$ is defined for all a in A, we shall say that M is *total*. If we wish to emphasize that M may not be defined for all a in A, we shall say that M is a *partial* mapping (function) from A to B. In either case, we write $M : A \longrightarrow B$. We call A and B the *domain* and *range* of M, respectively.

If $M : A \longrightarrow B$ is a mapping having the property that for each b in B there is at most one a in A such that $M(a) = b$, then M is an *injection* (*one-to-one mapping*) from A into B. If M is a total mapping such that for each b in B there is exactly one a in A such that $M(a) = b$, then M is a *bijection* (*one-to-one correspondence*) between A and B.

If $M : A \longrightarrow B$ is an injection, then we can find the *inverse mapping*

$M^{-1} : B \longrightarrow A$ such that $M^{-1}(b) = a$ if and only if $M(a) = b$. If there exists b in B for which there is no a in A such that $M(a) = b$, then M^{-1} will be a partial function.

The notion of a bijection is used to define the *cardinality* of a set, which, informally speaking, denotes the number of elements the set contains.

DEFINITION

Two sets A and B are of *equal cardinality* if there is a bijection M from A to B.

Example 0.9

$\{0, 1, 2\}$ and $\{a, b, c\}$ are of equal cardinality. To prove this, use, for example, the bijection $M = \{(0, a), (1, b), (2, c)\}$. The set of integers is equal in cardinality to the set of even integers, even though the latter is a proper subset of the former. A bijection we can use to prove this would be $\{(i, 2i) | i \text{ is an integer}\}$.   □

We can now define precisely what we mean by a finite and infinite set.†

DEFINITION

A set S is *finite* if it is equal in cardinality to the set $\{1, 2, \ldots, n\}$ for some integer n. A set is *infinite* if it is equal in cardinality to a proper subset of itself. A set is *countable* if it is equal in cardinality to the set of positive integers. It follows from Example 0.9 that every countable set is infinite. An infinite set that is not countable is called *uncountable*.

Examples of countable sets are

(1) The set of all positive and negative integers,
(2) The set of even integers, and
(3) $\{(a, b) | a \text{ and } b \text{ are integers}\}$.

Examples of uncountable sets are

(1) The set of real numbers,
(2) The set of all mappings from the integers to the integers, and
(3) The set of all subsets of the positive integers.

EXERCISES

0.1.1. Write out the sets defined by the following predicates. Assume that
$A = \{0, 1, 2, 3, 4, 5, 6\}$.
(a) $\{X | X \text{ is in } A \text{ and } X \text{ is even}\}$.

---

†We have used these terms previously, of course, assuming that their intuitive meaning was clear. The formal definitions should be of some interest, however.

(b) $\{X \mid X$ is in A and X is a perfect square$\}$.

(c) $\{X \mid X$ is in A and $X \geq X^2 + 1\}$.

0.1.2. Let $A = \{0, 1, 2\}$ and $B = \{0, 3, 4\}$. Write out

(a) $A \cup B$.

(b) $A \cap B$.

(c) $A - B$.

(d) $\mathcal{P}(A)$.

(e) $A \times B$.

0.1.3. Show that if A is a set with n elements, then $\mathcal{P}(A)$ has 2^n elements.

0.1.4. Let A and B be sets and let U be some universal set with respect to which complements are taken. Show that

(a) $\overline{A \cup B} = \bar{A} \cap \bar{B}$.

(b) $\overline{A \cap B} = \bar{A} \cup \bar{B}$.

These two identities are referred to as *De Morgan's laws*.

0.1.5. Show that there does not exist a set U such that for all sets A, $A \in U$. *Hint:* Consider Russell's paradox.

0.1.6. Give an example of a relation on a set which is

(a) Reflexive but not symmetric or transitive.

(b) Symmetric but not reflexive or transitive.

(c) Transitive but not reflexive or symmetric.

In each case specify the set on which the relation is defined.

0.1.7. Give an example of a relation on a set which is

(a) Reflexive and symmetric but not transitive.

(b) Reflexive and transitive but not symmetric.

(c) Symmetric and transitive but not reflexive.

Warning: Do not be misled into believing that a relation which is symmetric and transitive must be reflexive (since $a\,R\,b$ and $b\,R\,a$ implies $a\,R\,a$).

0.1.8. Show that the following relations are equivalence relations:

(a) $\{(a, a) \mid a \in A\}$.

(b) Congruence on the set of triangles.

0.1.9. Let R be an equivalence relation on a set A. Let a and b be in A. Show that

(a) $[a] = [b]$ if and only if $a\,R\,b$.

(b) $[a] \cap [b] = \varnothing$ if and only if $a\,R\,b$ is false.†

0.1.10. Let A be a finite set. What equivalence relations on A induce the largest and smallest number of equivalence classes?

0.1.11. Let $A = \{0, 1, 2\}$ and $R = \{(0, 1), (1, 2)\}$. Find R^* and R^+.

0.1.12. Prove Theorem 0.2(b).

---

†By "$a\,R\,b$ is false," we mean that $(a, b) \notin R$.

0.1.13. Let R be a relation on A. Show that there is a unique relation R_e such that

(1) $R \subseteq R_e$,

(2) R_e is an equivalence relation on A, and

(3) If R' is any equivalence relation on A such that $R \subseteq R'$, then $R_e \subseteq R'$.

R_e is called the *least equivalence relation* containing R.

DEFINITION

A *well order* on a set A is a reflexive partial order R on A such that for each nonempty subset $B \subseteq A$ there exists b in B such that $b \, R \, a$ for all a in B (i.e., each nonempty subset contains a smallest element).

0.1.14. Show that $\leq$ (less than or equal to) is a well order on the positive integers.

DEFINITION

Let A be a set. Define

(1) $A^1 = A$, and

(2) $A^i = A^{i-1} \times A$, for $i > 1$.

Let A^+ denote $\bigcup_{i \geq 1} A^i$.

0.1.15. Let R be a well order on A. Define $\hat{R}$ on A^+ by:
$(a_1, \ldots, a_m)$† $\hat{R}$ $(b_1, \ldots, b_n)$ if and only if either

(1) For some $i \leq m$, $a_j = b_j$ for $1 \leq j < i$, $a_i \neq b_i$ and $a_i \, Rb_i$, or

(2) $m \leq n$, and $a_i = b_i$ for all i, $1 \leq i \leq m$.

Show that $\hat{R}$ is a well order on A^+. We call $\hat{R}$ a *lexicographic order* on A^+. (The ordering of words in a dictionary is an example of a lexicographic order.)

0.1.16. State whether each of the following are partial orders, reflexive partial orders, linear orders, or reflexive linear orders:

(a) $\subseteq$ on $\mathcal{P}(A)$.

(b) $\subsetneqq$ on $\mathcal{P}(A)$.

(c) The relation R_1 on the set H of human beings defined by $a \, R_1 \, b$ if and only if a is the father of b.

(d) The relation R_2 on H given by $a \, R \, b$ if and only if a is an ancestor of b.

(e) The relation R_3 on H defined by $a \, R_3 \, b$ if and only if a is older than b.

0.1.17. Let R_1 and R_2 be relations. The *composition* of R_1 and R_2, denoted $R_1 \circ R_2$ is $\{(a, b) \, | \, \text{for some } c, \, a \, R_1 \, c \text{ and } c \, R_2 \, b\}$. Show that if R_1 and R_2 are mappings, then $R_1 \circ R_2$ is a mapping. Under what conditions will $R_1 \circ R_2$ be a total mapping? An injection? A bijection?

†Strictly speaking, $(a_1, \ldots, a_m)$ means $(((\ldots(a_1, a_2), a_3), \ldots), a_m)$, according to the definition of A^m.

0.1.18. Let A be a finite set and let $B \subseteq A$. Show that if $M: A \longrightarrow B$ is a bijection, then $A = B$.

0.1.19. Let A and B have m and n elements, respectively. Show that there are n^m total functions from A to B. How many (not necessarily total) functions from A to B are there?

*0.1.20. Let A be an arbitrary (not necessarily finite) set. Show that the sets $\mathcal{P}(A)$ and $\{M \mid M$ is a total function from A to $\{0, 1\}\}$ are of equal cardinality.

0.1.21. Show that the set of all integers is equal in cardinality to
      (a) The set of primes.
      (b) The set of pairs of integers.
Hint: Define a linear order on the set of pairs of integers by $(i_1, j_1) R (i_2, j_2)$ if and only if $i_1 + j_1 < i_2 + j_2$ or $i_1 + j_1 = i_2 + j_2$ and $i_1 < i_2$.

0.1.22. Set A is "larger than" B if A and B are of different cardinality but B is equal in cardinality to a subset of A. Show that the set of real numbers between 0 and 1, exclusive, is larger than the set of integers. *Hint:* Represent real numbers by unique decimal expansions. In contradiction, suppose that the two sets in question were of equal cardinality. Then we could find a sequence of real numbers $r_1, r_2, \ldots$ which included all real numbers r, $0 < r < 1$. Can you find a real number r between 0 and 1 which differs in the ith decimal place from r_i for all i?

*0.1.23. Let R be a linear order on a finite set A. Show that there exists a unique element $a \in A$ such that $a R b$ for all $b \in A - \{a\}$. Such an element a is called the *least element*. If A is infinite, does there always exist a least element?

*0.1.24. Show that $\{a, \{a, b\}\} = \{c, \{c, d\}\}$ if and only if $a = c$ and $b = d$.

0.1.25. Let R be a partial order on a set A. Show that if $a R b$, then $b R a$ is false.

*0.1.26. Use the power set and union axioms to help show that if A and B are sets, then $A \times B$ is a set.

**0.1.27. Show that every set is either finite or infinite, but not both.

*0.1.28. Show that every countable set is infinite.

*0.1.29. Show that the following sets have the same cardinality:

      (1) The set of real numbers between 0 and 1,
      (2) The set of all real numbers,
      (3) The set of all mappings from the integers to the integers, and
      (4) The set of all subsets of the positive integers.

**0.1.30. Show that $\mathcal{P}(A)$ is always larger than A for any set A.

0.1.31. Show that if R is a partial order on a set A, then the relation R' given by $R' = R \cup \{(a, a) \mid a \in A\}$ is a reflexive partial order on A.

0.1.32. Show that if R is a reflexive partial order on a set A, then the relation $R' = R - \{(a, a) \,|\, a \in A\}$ is a partial order on A.

0.2. SETS OF STRINGS

In this book we shall be dealing primarily with sets whose elements are strings of symbols. In this section we shall define a number of terms dealing with strings.

0.2.1. Strings

First of all we need the concept of an alphabet. To us an *alphabet* will be any set of symbols. We assume that the term symbol has a sufficiently clear intuitive meaning that it needs no further explication.

An alphabet need not be finite or even countable, but for all practical applications alphabets will be finite. Two examples of alphabets are the set of 26 upper- and 26 lowercase Roman letters (the *Roman alphabet*) and the set $\{0, 1\}$, which is often called the *binary alphabet*.

The terms *letter and character* will be used synonymously with *symbol* to denote an element of an alphabet. If we put a sequence of symbols side by side, we have a *string* of symbols. For example, 01011 is a string over the binary alphabet $\{0, 1\}$. The terms *sentence* and *word* are often used as synonyms for *string*.

There is one string which arises frequently and which has been given a special denotation. This is the *empty string* and it will be denoted by the symbol e. The empty string is that string which has no symbols.

CONVENTION

We shall ordinarily use capital Greek letters for alphabets. The letters a, b, c, and d will represent symbols and the letters t, u, v, w, x, y, and z generally represent strings. We shall represent a string of i a's by a^i. For example, $a^1 = a$,† $a^2 = aa$, $a^3 = aaa$, and so forth. Then, a^0 is e, the empty string.

DEFINITION

We formally define *strings over an alphabet* Σ in the following manner:

(1) e is a string over Σ.
(2) If x is a string over Σ and a is in Σ, then xa is a string over Σ.
(3) y is a string over Σ if and only if its being so follows from (1) and (2).

There are several operations on strings for which we shall have use later on. If x and y are strings, then the string xy is called the *concatenation* of x

---

†We thus identify the symbol a and the string consisting of a alone.

and y. For example, if $x = ab$ and $y = cd$, then $xy = abcd$. For all strings x, $xe = ex = x$.

The *reversal* of a string x, denoted x^R, is the string x written in reverse order; i.e., if $x = a_1 \cdots a_n$, where each a_i is a symbol, then $x^R = a_n \cdots a_1$. Also, $e^R = e$.

Let x, y, and z be arbitrary strings over some alphabet Σ. We call x a *prefix* of the string xy and y a *suffix* of xy. y is a *substring* of xyz. Both a prefix and suffix of a string x are substrings of x. For example, ba is both a prefix and a substring of the string bac. Notice that the empty string is a substring, a prefix, and a suffix of every string.

If $x \neq y$ and x is a prefix (suffix) of some string y, then x is called a *proper* prefix (suffix) of y.

The *length* of a string is the number of symbols in the string. That is, if $x = a_1 \cdots a_n$, where each a_i is a symbol, then the length of x is n. We shall denote the length of a string x by $|x|$. For example, $|aab| = 3$ and $|e| = 0$. All strings which we shall encounter will be of finite length.

0.2.2. Languages

DEFINITION

A *language* over an alphabet Σ is a set of strings over Σ. This definition surely encompasses almost everyone's notion of a language. FORTRAN, ALGOL, PL/I, and even English are included in this definition.

Example 0.10

Let us consider some simple examples of languages over an alphabet Σ. The empty set $\varnothing$ is a language. The set $\{e\}$ which contains only the empty string is a language. Notice that $\varnothing$ and $\{e\}$ are two distinct languages. □

DEFINITION

We let Σ^* denote the set containing all strings over Σ including e. For example, if A is the binary alphabet $\{0, 1\}$, then

$$\Sigma^* = \{e, 0, 1, 00, 01, 10, 11, 000, 001, \ldots\}.$$

Every language over Σ is a subset of Σ^*. The set of all strings over Σ but excluding e will be denoted by Σ^+.

Example 0.11

Let us consider the language L_1 containing all strings of zero or more a's. We can denote L_1 by $\{a^i \mid i \geq 0\}$. It should be clear that $L_1 = \{a\}^*$. □

CONVENTION

When no confusion results we shall often denote a set consisting of a single element by the element itself. Thus according to this convention a^* = $\{a\}^*$.

DEFINITION

A language L such that no string in L is a proper prefix (suffix) of any other string in L is said to have the *prefix (suffix) property*.

For example, a^* does not have the prefix property but $\{a^i b \mid i \geq 0\}$ does.

0.2.3. Operations on Languages

We shall often be concerned with various operations applied to languages. In this section, we shall consider some basic and fundamental operations on languages.

Since a language is just a set, the operations of union, intersection, difference, and complementation apply to languages. The operation concatenation can be applied to languages as well as strings.

DEFINITION

Let L_1 be a language over alphabet Σ_1 and L_2 a language over Σ_2. Then $L_1 L_2$, called the *concatenation* or *product* of L_1 and L_2, is the language $\{xy \mid x \in L_1 \text{ and } y \in L_2\}$.

There will be occasions when we wish to concatenate any arbitrary number of strings from a language. This notion is captured in the closure of a language.

DEFINITION

The *closure* of L, denoted L^*, is defined as follows:

(1) $L^0 = \{e\}$.
(2) $L^n = LL^{n-1}$ for $n \geq 1$.
(3) $L^* = \bigcup_{n \geq 0} L^n$.

The *positive closure* of L, denoted L^+, is $\bigcup_{n \geq 1} L^n$. Note that $L^+ = LL^* = L^*L$ and that $L^* = L^+ \cup \{e\}$.

We shall also be interested in mappings on languages. A simple type of mapping which occurs frequently when dealing with languages is homomorphism. We can define a homomorphism in the following way.

DEFINITION

Let Σ_1 and Σ_2 be alphabets. A *homomorphism* is a mapping $h : \Sigma_1 \longrightarrow \Sigma_2^*$. We extend the domain of the homomorphism h to Σ_1^* by letting $h(e) = e$ and $h(xa) = h(x)h(a)$ for all x in Σ_1^*, a in Σ_1.

Applying a homomorphism to a language L, we get another language $h(L)$, which is the set of strings $\{h(w) \mid w \in L\}$.

Example 0.12

Suppose that we wish to change every instance of 0 in a string to a and every 1 to bb. We can define a homomorphism h such that $h(0) = a$ and $h(1) = bb$. Then if L is the language $\{0^n 1^n \mid n \geq 1\}$, $h(L) = \{a^n b^{2n} \mid n \geq 1\}$. ☐

Although homomorphisms on languages are not always one-to-one mappings, it is often useful to talk about their inverses (as relations).

DEFINITION

If $h: \Sigma_1 \longrightarrow \Sigma_2^*$ is a homomorphism, then the relation $h^{-1}: \Sigma_2^* \longrightarrow \mathcal{P}(\Sigma_1^*)$, defined below, is called an *inverse homomorphism*. If y is in Σ_2^*, then $h^{-1}(y)$ is the set of strings over Σ_1 which get mapped by h to y. That is, $h^{-1}(y) = \{x \mid h(x) = y\}$. If L is a language over Σ_2, then $h^{-1}(L)$ is the language over Σ_1 consisting of those strings which get mapped by h into a string in L. Formally, $h^{-1}(L) = \bigcup_{y \in L} h^{-1}(y) = \{x \mid h(x) \in L\}$.

Example 0.13

Let h be a homomorphism such that $h(0) = a$ and $h(1) = a$. It follows that $h^{-1}(a) = \{0, 1\}$ and $h^{-1}(a^*) = \{0, 1\}^*$.

As a second example, suppose that h is a homomorphism such that $h(0) = a$ and $h(1) = e$. Then $h^{-1}(e) = 1^*$ and $h^{-1}(a) = 1^* 0 1^*$. Here $1^* 0 1^*$ denotes the language $\{1^i 0 1^j \mid i, j \geq 0\}$, which is consistent with our definitions and the convention which identifies a and $\{a\}$. ☐

EXERCISES

0.2.1. Give all the (a) prefixes, (b) suffixes, and (c) substrings of the string abc.

0.2.2. Prove or disprove: $L^+ = L^* - \{e\}$.

0.2.3. Let h be the homomorphism defined by $h(0) = a$, $h(1) = bb$, and $h(2) = e$. What is $h(L)$, where $L = \{012\}^*$?†

0.2.4. Let h be as in Exercise 0.2.3. What is $h^{-1}(\{ab\}^*)$?

*0.2.5. Prove or disprove the following:
(a) $h^{-1}(h(L)) = L$.
(b) $h(h^{-1}(L)) = L$.

0.2.6. Can L^* or L^+ ever be $\varnothing$? Under what circumstances are L^* and L^+ finite?

†Note that $\{012\}^*$ is not $\{0, 1, 2\}^*$.

*0.2.7.   Give well orders on the following languages:
     (a) $\{a, b\}^*$.
     (b) $a^*b^*c^*$.
     (c) $\{w \mid w \in \{a, b\}^*$ and the number of a's in w equals the number of b's$\}$.

0.2.8.   Which of the following languages have the prefix (suffix) property?
     (a) $\varnothing$.
     (b) $\{e\}$.
     (c) $\{a^n b^n \mid n \geq 1\}$.
     (d) L^*, if L has the prefix property.
     (e) $\{w \mid w \in \{a, b\}^*$ and the number of a's in w equals the number of b's$\}$.

0.3. CONCEPTS FROM LOGIC

In this book we shall present a number of algorithms which are useful in language-processing applications. For some functions several algorithms are known, and it is desirable to present the algorithms in a common framework in which they can be evaluated and compared.

Above all, it is most desirable to know that an algorithm performs the function that it is supposed to perform. For this reason, we shall provide proofs that the various algorithms that we shall present function as advertised. In this section, we shall briefly comment on what is a proof and mention some useful techniques of proof.

0.3.1. Proofs

A formal mathematical system can be characterized by the following basic components:

(1) Basic symbols,
(2) Formation rules,
(3) Axioms, and
(4) Rules of inference.

The set of basic symbols would include the symbols for constants, operators, and so forth. Statements can then be constructed from these basic symbols according to a set of *formation rules*. Certain primitive statements can be defined, and the validity of these statements can be accepted without justification. These statements are known as the *axioms* of the system.

Then certain rules can be specified whereby valid statements can be used to infer new valid statements. Such rules are called *rules of inference*.

The objective may be to prove that a certain statement is true in a certain mathematical system. A proof of that statement is a sequence of statements such that

(1) Each statement is either an axiom or can be created from one or more of the previous statements by means of a rule of inference.

(2) The last statement in the sequence is the statement to be proved.

A statement for which we can find a proof is called a *theorem* of that formal system. Obviously, every axiom of a formal system is a theorem.

In spirit at least, the proof of any mathematical theorem can be formulated in these terms. However, going to a level of detail in which each statement is either an axiom or follows from previous statements by rudimentary rules of inference makes the proofs of all but the most elementary theorems too long. The task of finding proofs of theorems in this fashion is in itself laborious, even for computers.

Consequently, mathematicians invariably employ various shortcuts to reduce the length of a proof. Statements which are previously proved theorems can be inserted into proofs. Also, statements can be omitted when it is (hopefully) clear what is being done. This technique is practiced virtually everywhere, and this book is no exception.

It is known to be impossible to provide a universal method for proving theorems. However, in the next sections we shall mention a few of the more commonly used techniques.

0.3.2.   Proof by Induction

Suppose that we wish to prove that a statement $S(n)$ about an integer n is true for all integers in a set N.

If N is finite, then one method of proof is to show that $S(n)$ is true for each value of n in N. This method of proof is sometimes called proof by *perfect induction* or proof by *exhaustion*.

If N is an infinite subset of the integers, then we may use *simple mathematical induction*. Let n_0 be the smallest value in N. To show that $S(n)$ is true for all n in N, we may equivalently show that

(1) $S(n_0)$ is true. (This is called the *basis* of the induction.)

(2) Assuming that $S(m)$ is true for all $m < n$ in N, show that $S(n)$ is also true. (This is the *inductive step*.)

Example 0.14

Suppose then that $S(n)$ is the statement

$$1 + 3 + 5 + \cdots + 2n - 1 = n^2$$

That is, the sum of odd integers is a perfect square. Suppose we wish to show that $S(n)$ is true for all positive integers. Thus $N = \{1, 2, 3, \ldots\}$.

Basis.   For $n = 1$ we have $1 = 1^2$.

Inductive Step.   Assuming $S(1), \ldots, S(n)$ are true [in particular, that $S(n)$

is true], we have

$$1 + 3 + 5 + \cdots + [2n - 1] + [2(n + 1) - 1] = n^2 + 2n + 1$$
$$= (n + 1)^2$$

so that $S(n + 1)$ must then also be true.

We thus conclude that $S(n)$ is true for all positive integers. $\square$

The reader is referred to Section 0.5.5 for some methods of induction on sets other than integers.

0.3.3. Logical Connectives

Often a statement (theorem) may read "P if and only if Q" or "P is a necessary and sufficient condition for Q," where P and Q are themselves statements. The terms *if, only if, necessary*, and *sufficient* have precise meanings in logic.

A *logical connective* is a symbol that can be used to create a statement out of simpler statements. For example, *and, or, not, implies* are logical connectives, *not* being a unary connective and the others binary connectives. If P and Q are statements, then P *and* Q, P *or* Q, *not* P, and P *implies* Q are also statements.

The symbol $\wedge$ is used to denote *and*, $\vee$ to denote *or*, $\sim$ to denote *not*, and $\longrightarrow$ to denote *implies*.

There are well-defined rules governing the truth or falsehood of a statement containing logical connectives. For example, the statement P *and* Q is true only when both P is true and Q is also true. We can summarize the properties of a logical connective by a table, called a *truth table*, which displays the value of a composite statement in terms of the values of its components. Figure 0.5 shows the truth table for the logical connectives *and, or, not* and *implies*.

P	Q	$P \wedge Q$	$P \vee Q$	$\sim P$	$P \longrightarrow Q$
F	F	F	F	T	T
F	T	F	T	T	T
T	F	F	T	F	F
T	T	T	T	F	T

Fig. 0.5 Truth tables for *and, or, not*, and *implies*.

From the table (Fig. 0.5) we see that $P \longrightarrow Q$ is false only when P is true and Q is false. It may seem a little odd that if P is false, then P *implies* Q

is always true, regardless of the value of Q. But in logic this is customary; from falsehood as a hypothesis, anything follows.

We can now return to consideration of a statement of the form *P if and only if Q*. This statement consists of two parts: *P if Q* and *P only if Q*. It is more common to state *P if Q* as *if Q then P*, which is only another way of saying *Q implies P*.

In fact the following five statements are equivalent:

(1) *P implies Q*.
(2) *If P then Q*.
(3) *P only if Q*.
(4) *Q is a necessary condition for P*.
(5) *P is a sufficient condition for Q*.

To show that the statement *P if and only if Q* is true we must show both that *Q implies P* and that *P implies Q*. Thus, *P if and only if Q* is true exactly when *P* and *Q* are either both true or both false.

There are several alternative methods of showing that the statement *P implies Q* is always true. One method is to show that the statement *not Q implies not P*† is always true. The reader should verify that *not Q implies not P* has exactly the same truth table as *P implies Q*. The statement *not Q implies not P* is called the *contrapositive* of *P implies Q*.

One important technique of proof is *proof by contradiction*, sometimes called the *indirect proof* or *reductio ad absurdum*. Here, to show that *P implies Q* is true, we show that *not Q and P implies falsehood* is true. That is to say, we assume that *Q* is not true, and if assuming that *P* is true we are able to obtain a statement known to be false, then *P implies Q* must be true.

The *converse* of the statement *if P then Q* is *if Q then P*. The statement *P if and only if Q* is often written *if P then Q and conversely*. Note that a statement and its converse do not have the same truth table.

EXERCISES

DEFINITION

Propositional calculus is a good example of a mathematical system. Formally, propositional calculus can be defined as a system $\mathcal{S}$ consisting of

(1) A set of primitive symbols,
(2) Rules for generating well-formed statements,
(3) A set of axioms, and
(4) Rules of inference.

---

†We assume "not" takes precedence over "implies." Thus the proper phrasing of the sentence is (not *P*) implies (not *Q*). In general, "not" takes precedence over "and," which takes precedence over "or," which takes precedence over "implies."

(1) The primitive symbols of $\S$ are (,), $\rightarrow$, $\sim$, and an infinite set of statement letters $a_1, a_2, a_3, \ldots$. The symbol $\rightarrow$ can be thought of as *implies* and $\sim$ as *not*.

(2) A *well-formed statement* is formed by one or more applications of the following rules:

   (a) A statement letter is a statement.

   (b) If A and B are statements, then so are $(\sim A)$ and $(A \rightarrow B)$.

(3) Let A, B, and C be statements. The axioms of $\S$ are

$$A1: \quad (A \rightarrow (B \rightarrow A))$$

$$A2: \quad ((A \rightarrow (B \rightarrow C)) \rightarrow ((A \rightarrow B) \rightarrow (A \rightarrow C)))$$

$$A3: \quad ((\sim B \rightarrow \sim A) \rightarrow ((\sim B \rightarrow A) \rightarrow B))$$

(4) The rule of inference is *modus ponens*, i.e., from the statements $(A \rightarrow B)$ and A we can infer the statement B.

We shall leave out parentheses wherever possible. The statement $a \rightarrow a$ is a theorem of $\S$ and has as proof the sequence of statements

   (i) $(a \rightarrow ((a \rightarrow a) \rightarrow a)) \rightarrow ((a \rightarrow (a \rightarrow a)) \rightarrow (a \rightarrow a))$ from A2 with $A = a$, $B = (a \rightarrow a)$, and $C = a$.

   (ii) $a \rightarrow ((a \rightarrow a) \rightarrow a)$ from A1.

   (iii) $(a \rightarrow (a \rightarrow a)) \rightarrow (a \rightarrow a)$ by *modus ponens* from (i) and (ii).

   (iv) $a \rightarrow (a \rightarrow a)$ from A1.

   (v) $a \rightarrow a$ by *modus ponens* from (iii) and (iv).

*0.3.1.   Prove that $(\sim a \rightarrow a) \rightarrow a$ is a theorem of $\S$.

0.3.2.   A *tautology* is a statement that is true for all possible truth values of the statement variables. Show that every theorem of $\S$ is a tautology. *Hint:* Prove the theorem by induction on the number of steps necessary to obtain the theorem.

**0.3.3.   Prove the converse of Exercise 0.3.2, i.e., that every tautology is a theorem. Thus a simple method to determine whether a statement of propositional calculus is a theorem is to determine whether that statement is a tautology.

0.3.4.   Give the truth table for the statement *if P then if Q then R*.

DEFINITION

   Boolean algebra can be interpreted as a system for manipulating truth-valued variables using logical connectives informally interpreted as *and*, *or*, and *not*. Formally, a *Boolean algebra* is a set B together with operations $\cdot$ (*and*), $+$ (*or*), and $^{-}$ (*not*). The axioms of Boolean algebra are the following: For all a, b, and c in B,

   (1) $a + (b + c) = (a + b) + c$ (associativity)
   $a \cdot (b \cdot c) = (a \cdot b) \cdot c.$

   (2) $a + b = b + a$ (commutativity)
   $a \cdot b = b \cdot a.$

   (3) $a \cdot (b + c) = (a \cdot b) + (a \cdot c)$ (distributivity)
   $a + (b \cdot c) = (a + b) \cdot (a + c).$

In addition, there are two distinguished members of B, 0 and 1 (in the most common Boolean algebra, these are the only members of B, representing falsehood and truth, respectively), with the following laws:

(4) $a + 0 = a$
$a \cdot 1 = a$.
(5) $a + \bar{a} = 1$
$a \cdot \bar{a} = 0$.

The rule of inference is substitution of equals for equals.

*0.3.5.   Show that the following statements are theorems in any Boolean algebra:
(a) $0 = \bar{1}$.
(b) $a + (b \cdot \bar{a}) = a + b$.
(c) $a = a$.
What are the informal interpretations of these theorems?

0.3.6.   Let A be a set. Show that $\mathcal{P}(A)$ is a Boolean algebra if $+$, $\cdot$, and $^-$ are $\cup$, $\cap$, and complementation with respect to the universe A.

**0.3.7.   Let B be a Boolean algebra where $\#B = n$. Show that $n = 2^m$ for some integer m.

0.3.8.   Prove by induction that

$$1 + 2 + \cdots + n = \frac{n(n+1)}{2}$$

0.3.9.   Prove by induction that

$$(1 + 2 + \cdots + n)^2 = 1^3 + 2^3 + \cdots + n^3$$

*0.3.10.   What is wrong with the following?

THEOREM

All marbles have the same color.

Proof. Let A be any set of n marbles, $n \geq 1$. We shall "prove" by induction on n that all marbles in A have the same color.
Basis. If $n = 1$, all marbles in A are clearly of the same color.
Inductive Step. Assume that if A is any set of n marbles, then all marbles in A are the same color. Let A' be a set of $n + 1$ marbles, $n \geq 1$. Remove one marble from A'. We are then left with a set A'' of n marbles, which, by the inductive hypothesis, has marbles all the same color. Remove from A'' a second marble and then add to A'' the marble originally removed. We again have a set of n marbles, which by the inductive hypothesis has marbles the same color. Thus the two marbles removed must have been the same color so that the set A' must contain marbles all the same color. Thus, in any set of n marbles, all marbles are the same color. $\square$

*0.3.11.   Let R be a well order on a set A and $S(a)$ a statement about a in A. Assume that if $S(b)$ is true for all $b \neq a$ such that $b \, R \, a$, then $S(a)$ is true.

Show that then $S(a)$ is true for all a in A. Note that this is a generalization of the principle of simple induction.

0.3.12. Show that there are only four unary logical connectives. Give their truth tables.

0.3.13. Show that there are 16 binary logical connectives.

0.3.14. Two logical statements are *equivalent* if they have the same truth table. Show that
(a) $\sim(P \wedge Q)$ is equivalent to $\sim P \vee \sim Q$.
(b) $\sim(P \vee Q)$ is equivalent to $\sim P \wedge \sim Q$.

0.3.15. Show that $P \longrightarrow Q$ is equivalent to $\sim Q \longrightarrow \sim P$.

0.3.16. Show that $P \longrightarrow Q$ is equivalent to $P \wedge \sim Q \longrightarrow$ false.

*0.3.17. A set of logical connectives is *complete* if for any logical statement we can find an equivalent statement containing only those logical connectives. Show that $\{\wedge, \sim\}$ and $\{\vee, \sim\}$ are complete sets of logical connectives.

BIBLIOGRAPHIC NOTES

Church [1956] and Mendelson [1968] give good treatments of mathematical logic. Halmos [1963] gives a nice introduction to Boolean algebras.

0.4 PROCEDURES AND ALGORITHMS

The concept of algorithm is central to computing. The definition of algorithm can be approached from a variety of directions. In this section we shall discuss the term algorithm informally and hint at how a more formal definition can be obtained.

0.4.1. Procedures

We shall begin with a slightly more general concept, that of a procedure. Broadly speaking, a procedure consists of a finite set of instructions each of which can be mechanically executed in a fixed amount of time with a fixed amount of effort. A procedure can have any number of inputs and outputs.

To be precise, we should define the terms instruction, input, and output. However, we shall not go into the details of such a definition here since any "reasonable" definition is adequate for our needs.

A good example of a procedure is a machine language computer program. A program consists of a finite number of machine instructions, and each instruction usually requires a fixed amount of computation. However, procedures in the form of computer programs may often be very difficult to understand, so a more descriptive notation will be used in this book. The following example is representative of the notation we shall use to describe procedures and algorithms.

Example 0.15

Consider Euclid's algorithm to determine the greatest common divisor of two positive integers p and q.

Procedure 1. Euclidean algorithm.
Input. p and q, positive integers.
Output. g, the greatest common divisor of p and q.
Method. Step 1: Let r be the remainder of p/q.
Step 2: If $r = 0$, set $g = q$ and halt. Otherwise set $p = q$, then $q = r$, and go to step 1. $\square$

Let us see if procedure 1 qualifies as a procedure under our definition. Procedure 1 certainly consists of a finite set of instructions (each step is considered as one instruction) and has input and output. However, can each instruction be mechanically executed with a fixed amount of effort?

Strictly speaking, the answer to this question is no, because if p and q are sufficiently large, the computation of the remainder of p/q may require an amount of effort that is proportional in some way to the size of p and q.

However, we could replace step 1 by a sequence of steps whose net effect is to compute the remainder of p/q, although the amount of effort in each step would be fixed and independent of the size of p and q. (Thus the number of times each step is executed is an increasing function of the size of p and q.) These steps, for example, could implement the customary paper-and-pencil method of doing integer division.

Thus we shall permit a step of a procedure to be a procedure in itself. So under this liberalized notion of procedure, procedure 1 qualifies as a procedure.

In general, it is convenient to assume that integers are basic entities, and we shall do so. Any integer can be stored in one memory cell, and any integer arithmetic operation can be performed in one step. This is a fair assumption only if the integers are less than 2^k, where k is the number of bits in a computer word, as often happens in practice. However, the reader should bear in mind the additional effort necessary to handle integers of arbitrary size when the elementary steps handle only integers of bounded size.

We must now face perhaps the most important consideration—proving that the procedure does what it is supposed to do. For each pair of integers p and q, does procedure 1 in fact compute g to be the greatest common divisor of p and q? The answer is yes, but we shall leave the proof of this particular assertion to the Exercises.

We might note in passing, however, that one useful technique of proof for showing that procedures work as intended is induction on the number of steps taken.

0.4.2. Algorithms

We shall now place an all-important restriction on a procedure to obtain what is known as an algorithm.

DEFINITION

A procedure *halts* on a given input if there is a finite number t such that after executing t (not necessarily different) elementary instructions of the procedure, either there is no instruction to be executed next or a "halt" instruction was last executed. A procedure which halts on all inputs is called an *algorithm*.

Example 0.16

Consider the procedure of Example 0.15. We observe that steps 1 and 2 must be executed alternately. After step 1, step 2 must be executed. After step 2, step 1 may be executed, or there may be no next step; i.e., the procedure halts. We can prove that for every input p and q, the procedure halts after at most $2q$ steps,† and that thus the procedure is an algorithm. The proof turns on observing that the value r computed in step 1 is less than the value of q, and that, hence, successive values of q when step 1 is executed form a monotonically decreasing sequence. Thus, by the qth time step 2 is executed, r, which cannot be negative and is less than the current value of q, must attain the value zero. When $r = 0$, the procedure halts. □

There are several reasons why a procedure may fail to halt on some inputs. It is possible that a procedure can get into an infinite loop under certain conditions. For example, if a procedure contained the instruction
  Step 1: If $x = 0$, then go to Step 1, else halt,
then for $x = 0$ the procedure would never halt. Variations on this situation are countless.

Our interest will be almost exclusively in algorithms. We shall be interested not only in proving that algorithms are correct, but also in evaluating algorithms. The two main criteria for evaluating how well algorithms perform will be

(1) The number of elementary mechanical operations executed as a function of the size of the input (*time complexity*), and
(2) How large an auxiliary memory is required to hold intermediate

---

†In fact, $4 \log_2 q$ is an upper bound on the number of steps executed for $q > 1$. We leave this as an exercise.

results that arise during the execution, again as a function of the size of the input (*space complexity*).

Example 0.17

In Example 0.16 we saw that the number of steps of procedure 1 (Example 0.15) that would be executed with input (p, q) is bounded above by $2q$. The amount of memory used is one cell for each of p, q, and r, assuming that any integer can be stored in a single cell. If we assume that the amount of memory needed to store an integer depends on the length of the binary representation of that integer, the amount of memory needed is proportional to $\log_2 n$, where n is the maximum of inputs p and q.   □

0.4.3. Recursive Functions

A procedure defines a mapping from the set of all allowable inputs to a set of outputs. The mapping defined by a procedure is called a *partial recursive function* or *recursive function*. If the procedure is an algorithm, then the mapping is called a *total recursive function*.

A procedure can also be used to define a language. We could have a procedure to which we can present an arbitrary string x. After some computation, the procedure would output "yes" when string x is in the language. If x is not in the language, then the procedure may halt and say "no" or the procedure may never halt.

This procedure would then define a language L as the set of input strings for which the procedure has output "yes." The behavior of the procedure on a string not in the language is not acceptable from a practical point of view. If the procedure has not halted after some length of time on an input x, we would not know whether x was in the language but the procedure had not finished computing or whether x was not in the language and the procedure would never terminate.

If we had used an algorithm to define a language, then the algorithm would halt on all inputs. Consequently, patience is justified with an algorithm in that we know that if we wait long enough, the algorithm will eventually halt and say either "yes" or "no."

A set which can be defined by a procedure is said to be *recursively enumerable*. A set which can be defined by an algorithm is called *recursive*.

If we use more precise definitions, then we can rigorously show that there are sets which are not recursively enumerable. We can also show that there are recursively enumerable sets which are not recursive.

We can state this in another way. There are mappings which cannot be specified by any procedure. There are also mappings which can be specified by a procedure but which cannot be specified by an algorithm.

We shall see that these concepts have great underlying significance for a theory of programming. In Section 0.4.5 we shall give an example of a procedure for which it can be shown that there is no equivalent algorithm.

0.4.4. Specification of Procedures

In the previous section we informally defined what we meant by procedure and algorithm. It is possible to give a rigorous definition of these terms in a variety of formalisms. In fact there are a large number of formal notations for describing procedures. These notations include

(1) Turing machines [Turing, 1936–1937].
(2) Chomsky type 0 grammars [Chomsky, 1959a and 1963].
(3) Markov algorithms [Markov, 1951].
(4) Lambda calculus [Church, 1941].
(5) Post systems [Post, 1943].
(6) Tag systems [Post, 1965].
(7) Most programming languages [Sammet, 1969].

This list can be extended readily. The important point to be made here is that it is possible to simulate a procedure written in one of these notations by means of a procedure written in any other of these notations. In this sense all these notations are equivalent.

Many years ago the logicians Church and Turing hypothesized that any computational process which could be reasonably called a procedure could be simulated by a Turing machine. This hypothesis is known as the *Church–Turing thesis* and has been generally accepted. Thus the most general class of sets that we would wish to deal with in a practical way would be included in the class of recursively enumerable sets.

Most programming languages, at least in principle, have the capability of specifying any procedure. In Chapter 11 (Volume 2) we shall see what consequences this capability produces when we attempt to optimize programs.

We shall not discuss the details of these formalisms for procedures here, although some of them appear in the exercises. Minsky [1967] gives a very readable introduction to this topic.

In our book we shall use the rather informal notation for describing procedures and algorithms that we have already seen.

0.4.5. Problems

We shall use the word *problem* in a rather specific way in this book.

DEFINITION

A *problem* (or *question*) is a statement (predicate) which is either true or false, depending on the value of some number of unknowns of designated type in the statement. A problem is usually presented as a question, and we say the answer to the problem is "yes" if the statement is true and "no" if the statement is false.

Example 0.18

An example of a problem is "x is less than y, for integers x and y." More colloquially, we can express the statement in question form and delete mention of the type of x and y: "Is x less than y?"   □

DEFINITION

An *instance* of a problem is a set of allowable values for its unknowns.

For example, the instances of the problem of Example 0.18 are ordered pairs of integers.

A mapping from the set of instances of a problem to {yes, no} is called a *solution* to the problem. If this mapping can be specified by an algorithm, then the problem is said to be (recursively) *decidable* or *solvable*. If no algorithm exists to specify this mapping, then the problem is said to be (recursively) *undecidable* or *unsolvable*.

One of the remarkable achievements of twentieth-century mathematics was the discovery of problems that are undecidable. We shall see later that undecidable problems seriously hamper the development of a broadly applicable theory of computation.

Example 0.19

Let us discuss the particular problem "Is procedure P an algorithm?" Its analysis will go a long way toward exhibiting why some problems are undecidable. First, we must assume that all procedures are specified in some formal system such as those mentioned earlier in this section.

It appears that every formal specification language for procedures admits only a countable number of procedures. While we cannot prove this in general, we give one example, the formalism for representing absolute machine language programs, and leave the other mentioned specifications for the Exercises. Any absolute machine language program is a finite sequence of 0's and 1's (which we imagine are grouped 32, 36, 48, or some number to a machine word).

Suppose that we have a string of 0's and 1's representing a machine language program. We can assign an integer to this program by giving its position in some well ordering of all strings of 0's and 1's. One such ordering can be obtained by ordering the strings of 0's and 1's in terms of increasing length and lexicographically ordering strings of equal length by treating each string as a binary number. Since there are only a finite number of strings of any length, every string in {0, 1}* is thus mapped to some integer. The first few pairs in this bijection are

Integer	String
1	e
2	0
3	1
4	00
5	01
6	10
7	11
8	000
9	001

In this fashion we see that for each machine language program we can find a unique integer and that for each integer we can find a certain machine language program.

It seems that no matter what formalism for specifying procedures is taken, we shall always be able to find a one-to-one correspondence between procedures and integers. Thus it makes sense to talk about the ith procedure in any given formalism for specifying procedures. Moreover, the correspondence between procedures and integers is sufficiently simple that one can, given an integer i, write out the ith procedure, or given a procedure, find its corresponding number.

Let us suppose that there is a procedure P_j which is an algorithm and takes as input a specification of a procedure in our formalism and returns the answer "yes" if and only if its input is an algorithm. All known formalisms for procedure specification have the property that procedures can be combined in certain simple ways. In particular, given the hypothetical procedure (algorithm) P_j, we could construct an algorithm P_k to work as follows:

ALGORITHM P_k

Input. Any procedure P which requires one input.
Output.

(1) "No" if (a) P is not an algorithm or (b) P is an algorithm and $P(P) = $ "yes."
(2) "Yes" otherwise.

The notation $P(P)$ means that we are applying procedure P to its own specification as input.
Method.

(1) If $P_j(P) = $ "yes," then go to step (2). Otherwise output "no" and halt.
(2) If the input P is an algorithm and P takes a procedure specification

as input and gives "yes" or "no" as output, P_k applies P to itself (P) as input. (We assume that procedure specifications are such that these questions about input and output forms can be ascertained by inspection. The assumption is true in known cases.)

(3) P_k gives output "no" or "yes" if P gives output "yes" or "no," respectively. □

We see that P_k is an algorithm, on the assumption that P_j is an algorithm. Also P_k requires one input. But what does P_k do when its input is itself? Presumably, P_j determines that P_k is an algorithm [i.e., $P_j(P_k) =$ "yes"]. P_k then simulates itself on itself. But now P_k cannot give an output that is consistent. If P_k determines that this simulation gives "yes" as output, P_k gives "no" as output. But P_k just determined that it gave "yes" when applied to itself. A similar paradox occurs if P_k finds that the simulation gives "no." We must conclude that it is fallacious to assume that the algorithm P_j exists, and thus the question "Is P an algorithm?" is not decidable for any of the known procedure formalisms. □

We should emphasize that a problem is decidable if and only if there is an algorithm which will take as input an arbitrary instance of that problem and give the answer yes or no. Given a specific instance of a problem, we are often able to answer yes or no for that specific instance. This does not necessarily make the problem decidable. We must be able to give a uniform algorithm which will work for all instances of the problem before we can say that the problem is decidable.

As an additional caveat, we should point out that the encoding of the instances of a problem is vitally important. Normally a "standard" encoding (one that can be mapped by means of an algorithm into a Turing machine specification) is assumed. If nonstandard encodings are used, then problems which are normally undecidable can become decidable. In such cases, however, there will be no algorithm to go from the standard encoding to the nonstandard. (See Exercise 0.4.21.)

0.4.6. Post's Correspondence Problem

In this section we shall introduce one of the paradigm undecidable problems, called Post's correspondence problem. Later in the book we shall use this problem to show that other problems are undecidable.

DEFINITION

An instance of *Post's correspondence problem over alphabet* Σ is a finite set of pairs in $\Sigma^+ \times \Sigma^+$ (i.e., a set of pairs of nonempty strings over Σ). The problem is to determine if there exists a finite sequence of (not necessarily distinct) pairs $(x_1, y_1), (x_2, y_2), \ldots, (x_m, y_m)$ such that $x_1 x_2 \cdots x_m =$

$y_1 y_2 \cdots y_m$. We shall call such a sequence a *viable sequence* for this instance of Post's correspondence problem. We shall often use $x_1 x_2 \cdots x_m$ to represent the viable sequence.

Example 0.20

Consider the following instance of Post's correspondence problem over $\{a, b\}$:

$$\{(abbb, b), (a, aab), (ba, b)\}$$

The sequence (a, aab), (a, aab), (ba, b), $(abbb, b)$ is viable, since $(a)(a)(ba)(abbb) = (aab)(aab)(b)(b)$.

The instance $\{(ab, aba), (aba, baa), (baa, aa)\}$ of Post's correspondence problem has no viable sequences, since any such sequence must begin with the pair (ab, aba), and from that point on, the total number of a's in the first components of the pairs in the sequence will always be less than the number of a's in the second components. $\square$

There is a procedure which is in a sense a "solution" to Post's correspondence problem. Namely, one can linearly order all possible sequences of pairs of strings that can be constructed from a given instance of the problem. One can then proceed to test each sequence to see if that sequence is viable. On encountering the first viable sequence, the procedure would halt and report yes. Otherwise the procedure would continue to operate forever.

However, there is no algorithm to solve Post's correspondence problem, for one can show that if there were such an algorithm, then one could solve the halting problem for Turing machines (Exercise 0.4.22)—but the halting problem for Turing machines is undecidable (Exercise 0.4.14).

EXERCISES

0.4.1. A *perfect number* is an integer which is equal to the sum of all its divisors (including 1 but excluding the number itself). For example, $6 = 1 + 2 + 3$ and $28 = 1 + 2 + 4 + 7 + 14$ are the first two perfect numbers. (The next three are 496, 8128, and 33550336.) Construct a procedure which has input i and output the ith perfect number. (At present it is not known whether there are a finite or infinite number of perfect numbers.)

0.4.2. Prove that the Euclidean algorithm of Example 0.15 is correct.

0.4.3. Provide an algorithm to add two n-digit decimal numbers. How much time and space does the algorithm require as a function of n? (See Winograd [1965] for a discussion of the time complexity of addition.)

0.4.4. Provide an algorithm to multiply two n-digit decimal numbers. How much time and space does the algorithm require? (See Winograd [1967] and Cook and Aanderaa [1969] for a discussion of the time complexity of multiplication.)

0.4.5. Give an algorithm to multiply two integer-valued n by n matrices. Assume that integer arithmetic operations can be done in one step. What is the speed of your algorithm? If it is proportional to n^3 steps, see Strassen [1969] for an asymptotically faster one.

0.4.6. Let $L \subseteq \{a, b\}^*$. The *characteristic function* for L is a mapping $f_L : Z \to \{0, 1\}$, where Z is the set of nonnegative integers, such that $f_L(i) = 1$ if the ith string in $\{a, b\}^*$ is in L and $f_L(i) = 0$ otherwise. Show that L is recursively enumerable if and only if f_L is a partial recursive function.

0.4.7. Show that L is a recursive set if and only if both L and $\bar{L}$ are recursively enumerable.

0.4.8. Let P be a procedure which defines a recusively enumerable set $L \subseteq \{a, b\}^*$. From P construct a procedure P' which will generate all and only all the elements of L. That is, the output of P' is to be an infinite string of the form $x_1 \# x_2 \# x_3 \# \cdots$, where $L = \{x_1, x_2, \ldots\}$. *Hint:* Construct P' to apply i steps of procedure P to the jth string in $\{a, b\}^*$ for all (i, j), in a reasonable order.

DEFINITION

A *Turing machine* consists of a finite set of *states* (Q), *tape symbols* (Γ), and a function δ (the *next move function*, i.e., program) that maps a subset of $Q \times \Gamma$ to $Q \times \Gamma \times \{L, R\}$. A subset $\Sigma \subseteq \Gamma$ is designated as the set of *input symbols* and one symbol in $\Gamma - \Sigma$ is designated the *blank*. One state, q_0, is designated the *start state*. The Turing machine operates on a tape, one square of which is pointed to by a *tape head*. All but a finite number of squares hold the blank at any time. A *configuration* of a Turing machine is a pair $(q, \alpha \restriction \beta)$, where q is the state, $\alpha\beta$ is the nonblank portion of the tape, and $\restriction$ is a special symbol, indicating that the tape head is at the square immediately to its right. ($\restriction$ does not occupy a square.)

The *next configuration* after configuration $(q, \alpha \restriction \beta)$ is determined by letting A be the symbol scanned by the tape head (the leftmost symbol of β, or the blank if $\beta = e$) and finding $\delta(q, A)$. Suppose that $\delta(q, A) = (p, A', D)$, where p is a state, A' a tape symbol, and $D = L$ or R. Then the next configuration is $(p, \alpha' \restriction \beta')$, where $\alpha'\beta'$ is formed from $\alpha \restriction \beta$ by replacing the A to the right of $\restriction$ by A' and then moving the symbol in direction D (left if $D = L$, right if $D = R$). It may be necessary to insert a blank at one end in order to move $\restriction$.

The Turing machine can be thought of as a formalism for defining procedures. Its input may be any finite length string w in Σ^*. The procedure is executed by starting with configuration $(q_0, \restriction w)$ and repeatedly computing next configurations. If the Turing machine *halts*, i.e., it has reached a configuration for which no move is defined (recall that δ may not be specified for all pairs in $Q \times \Gamma$), then the output is the nonblank portion of the Turing machine's tape.

*0.4.9. Exhibit a Turing machine that, given an input w in $\{0, 1\}^*$, will write YES on its tape if w is a palindrome (i.e., $w = w^R$) and write NO otherwise, halting in either case.

*0.4.10. Assume that all Turing machines use a finite subset of some countable set of symbols, $a_1 a_2, \ldots$ for their states and tape symbols. Show that there is a one-to-one correspondence between the integers and Turing machines.

**0.4.11. Show that there is no Turing machine which halts on all inputs (i.e., algorithm) and determines, given integer i written in binary on its tape, whether the ith Turing machine halts. (See Exercise 0.4.10.)

*0.4.12. Let $a_1, a_2, \ldots$ be a countable set of symbols. Show that the set of finite-length strings over these symbols is countable.

*0.4.13. Informally describe a Turing machine which takes a pair of integers i and j as input, and halts if and only if the ith Turing machine halts when given the jth string (as in Exercise 0.4.12) as input. Such a Turing machine is called *universal*.

**0.4.14. Show that there exists no Turing machine which always halts, takes input (i, j) a pair of integers, and prints YES on its tape if Turing machine i halts with input j and NO otherwise. *Hint:* Assume such a Turing machine existed, and derive a contradiction as in Example 0.19. The existence of a universal Turing machine is useful in many proofs.

**0.4.15. Show that there is no Turing machine (not necessarily an algorithm) which determines whether an arbitrary Turing machine is an algorithm. Note that this statement is stronger than Exercise 0.4.14, where we essentially showed that no such Turing machine which always halts exists.

*0.4.16. Show that it is undecidable whether a given Turing machine halts when started with blank tape.

0.4.17. Show that the problem of determining whether a statement is a theorem in propositional calculus is decidable. *Hint:* See Exercises 0.3.2 and 0.3.3.

0.4.18. Show that the problem of deciding whether a string is in a particular recursive set is decidable.

0.4.19. Does Post's correspondence problem have a viable sequence in the following instances?
(a) (01, 011), (10, 000), (00, 0).
(b) (1, 11), (11, 101), (101, 011), (011, 1011).
How do you reconcile being able to answer this exercise with the fact that Post's correspondence problem is undecidable?

0.4.20. Show that Post's correspondence problem with strings restricted to be over the alphabet $\{a\}$ is decidable. How do you reconcile this result with the undecidability of Post's correspondence problem?

*0.4.21. Let $P_1, P_2, \ldots$ be an enumeration of procedures in some formalism. Define a new enumeration $P'_1, P'_2, \ldots$ as follows:

(1) Let P'_{2i-1} be the ith of $P_1, P_2, \ldots$ which is not an algorithm.
(2) Let P'_{2i} be the ith of $P_1, P_2, \ldots$ which is an algorithm.

Then there is a simple algorithm to determine, given j, whether P'_j is an algorithm—just see whether j is even or odd. Moreover, each of $P_1, P_2, \ldots$ is P'_j for some j. How do you reconcile the existence of this one-to-one correspondence between integers and procedures with the claims of Example 0.19?

**0.4.22. Show that Post's correspondence problem is undecidable. *Hint:* Given a Turing machine, construct an instance of Post's problem which has a viable sequence if and only if the Turing machine halts when started with blank tape.

*0.4.23. Show that the Euclidean algorithm in Example 0.15 halts after at most $4 \log_2 q$ steps when started with inputs p and q, where $q > 1$.

DEFINITION

A variant of Post's correspondence problem is the *partial correspondence problem* over alphabet Σ. An instance of the partial correspondence problem is to determine, given a finite set of pairs in $\Sigma^+ \times \Sigma^+$, whether there exists for each $m > 0$ a sequence of not necessarily distinct pairs $(x_1, y_1), (x_2, y_2), \ldots, (x_m, y_m)$ such that the first m symbols of the string $x_1 x_2 \cdots x_m$ coincide with the first m symbols of $y_1 y_2 \cdots y_m$.

**0.4.24. Prove that the partial correspondence problem is undecidable.

BIBLIOGRAPHIC NOTES

Davis [1965] is a good anthology of many early papers in the study of procedures and algorithms. Turing's paper [Turing, 1936–1937] in which Turing machines first appear makes particularly interesting reading if one bears in mind that the paper was written before modern electronic computers were conceived.

The study of recursive and partial recursive functions is part of a now well-developed branch of mathematics called recursive function theory. Rogers [1967], Kleene [1952], and Davis [1958] are good references in this subject.

Post's correspondence problem first appeared in Post [1947]. The partial correspondence problem preceding Exercise 0.4.24 is from Knuth [1965].

Computational complexity is the study of algorithms from the point of view of measuring the number of primitive operations (time complexity) or the amount of auxiliary storage (space complexity) required to compute a given function. Borodin [1970] and Hartmanis and Hopcroft [1971] give readable surveys of this topic, and Irland and Fischer [1970] have compiled a bibliography on this subject.

Solutions to many of the *'d exercises in this section can be found in Minsky [1967] and Hopcroft and Ullman [1969].

0.5. CONCEPTS FROM GRAPH THEORY

Graphs and trees provide convenient descriptions of many structures that are useful in performing computations. In this section we shall examine a number of concepts from graph theory which we shall use throughout the remainder of our book.

0.5.1. Directed Graphs

Graphs can be directed or undirected and ordered or unordered. Our primary interest will be in ordered and unordered directed graphs.

DEFINITION

An *unordered directed graph* G is a pair (A, R), where A is a set of elements called *nodes* (or *vertices*) and R is a relation on A. Unless stated otherwise, the term *graph* will mean *directed graph*.

Example 0.21

Let $G = (A, R)$, where $A = \{1, 2, 3, 4\}$ and $R = \{(1, 1), (1, 2), (2, 3), (2, 4), (3, 4), (4, 1), (4, 3)\}$. We can draw a picture of the graph G by numbering four points 1, 2, 3, 4 and drawing an arrow from point a to point b if (a, b) is in R. Figure 0.6 shows a picture of this directed graph. $\square$

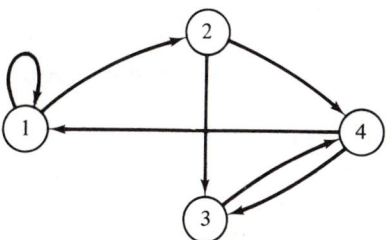

Fig. 0.6 Example of a directed graph.

A pair (a, b) in R is called an *edge* or *arc* of G. This edge is said to *leave* node a and *enter* node b (or *be incident upon* node b). For example, $(1, 2)$ is an edge in the example graph. If (a, b) is an edge, we say that a is a *predecessor* of b and b is a *successor* of a.

Loosely speaking, two graphs are the same if we can draw them to look the same, independently of what names we give to the nodes. Formally, we define equality of unordered directed graphs as follows.

DEFINITION

Let $G_1 = (A_1, R_1)$ and $G_2 = (A_2, R_2)$ be graphs. We say G_1 and G_2 are *equal* (or *the same*) if there is a bijection $f: A_1 \rightarrow A_2$ such that $a\, R_1\, b$ if and only if $f(a) \, R_2 \, f(b)$. That is, there is an edge between nodes a and b in G_1 if and only if there is an edge between their corresponding nodes in G_2.

It is common to have certain information attached to the nodes and/or edges of a graph. We call such information a labeling.

DEFINITION

Let (A, R) be a graph. A *labeling* of the graph is a pair of functions f and g, where f, the *node labeling*, maps A to some set, and g, the *edge labeling*, maps R to some (possibly distinct) set. Let $G_1 = (A_1, R_1)$ and $G_2 = (A_2, R_2)$ be labeled graphs, with labelings (f_1, g_1) and (f_2, g_2), respectively. Then G_1 and G_2 are *equal labeled graphs* if there is a bijection $h : A_1 \rightarrow A_2$ such that

(1) $a \, R_1 \, b$ if and only if $h(a) \, R_2 \, h(b)$ (i.e., G_1 and G_2 are equal as unlabeled graphs).

(2) $f_1(a) = f_2(h(a))$ (i.e., corresponding nodes have the same labels).

(3) $g_1((a, b)) = g_2((h(a), h(b)))$ (i.e., corresponding edges have the same label.)

In many cases, only the nodes or only the edges are labeled. These situations correspond, respectively, to f or g having a single element for its range. In these cases, condition (2) or (3), respectively, is trivially satisfied.

Example 0.22

Let $G_1 = (\{a, b, c\}, \{(a, b), (b, c), (c, a)\})$ and $G_2 = (\{0, 1, 2\}, \{(1, 0), (2, 1), (0, 2)\})$. Let the labeling of G_1 be defined by $f_1(a) = f_1(b) = X$, $f_1(c) = Y$, $g_1((a, b)) = g_1((b, c)) = \alpha$, $g_1((c, a)) = \beta$. Let the labeling of G_2 be $f_2(0) = f_2(2) = X$, $f_2(1) = Y$, $g_2((0, 2)) = g_2((2, 1)) = \alpha$, and $g_2((1, 0)) = \beta$. G_1 and G_2 are shown in Fig. 0.7.

G_1 and G_2 are equal. The correspondence is $h(a) = 0$, $h(b) = 2$, $h(c) = 1$.   □

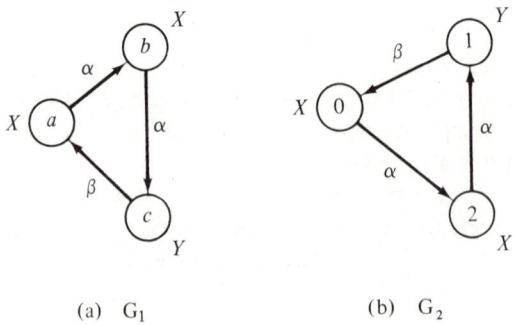

(a) G_1 (b) G_2

Fig. 0.7 Equal labelled graphs.

DEFINITION

A sequence of nodes $(a_0, a_1, \ldots, a_n)$, $n \geq 1$, is a *path of length n* from node a_0 to node a_n if there is an edge which leaves node a_{i-1} and enters node a_i for $1 \leq i \leq n$. For example, $(1, 2, 4, 3)$ is a path in Fig. 0.6. If there is a path from node a_0 to node a_n, we say that a_n is *accessible* from a_0.

A *cycle* (or *circuit*) is a path $(a_0, a_1, \ldots, a_n)$ in which $a_0 = a_n$. In Fig. 0.6, $(1, 1)$ is a cycle of length 1.

A directed graph is *strongly connected* if there is a path from a to b for every pair of distinct nodes a and b.

Finally we introduce the concept of the degree of a node. The *in-degree* of a node a is the number of edges entering a and the *out-degree* of a is the number of edges leaving a.

0.5.2. Directed Acyclic Graphs

DEFINITION

A *dag* (short for directed acyclic graph) is a directed graph that has no cycles. Figure 0.8 shows an example of a dag.

A node having in-degree 0 will be called a *base* node. One having out-degree 0 is called a *leaf*. In Fig. 0.8, nodes 1, 2, 3, and 4 are base nodes and nodes 2, 4, 7, 8, and 9 are leaves.

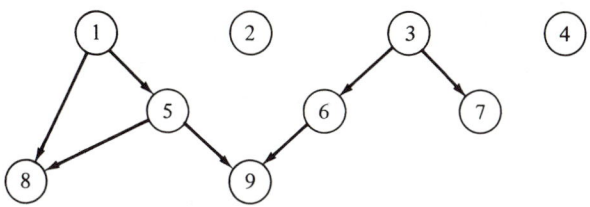

Fig. 0.8 Example of a dag.

If (a, b) is an edge in a dag, a is called a *direct ancestor* of b, and b a *direct descendant* of a.

If there is a path from node a to node b, then a is said to be an *ancestor* of b and b a *descendant* of a. In Fig. 0.8, node 9 is a descendant of node 1; node 1 is an ancestor of node 9.

Note that if R is a partial order on a set A, then (A, R) is a dag. Moreover, if we have a dag (A, R) and let R' be the relation "is a descendant of" on A, then R' is a partial order on A.

0.5.3. Trees

A tree is a special type of dag and has many important applications in compiler theory.

DEFINITION

An (oriented) *tree* T is a directed graph $G = (A, R)$ with a specified node r in A called the *root* such that

(1) r has in-degree 0,
(2) All other nodes of T have in-degree 1, and
(3) Every node in A is accessible from r.

Figure 0.9 provides an example of a tree with six nodes. The root is

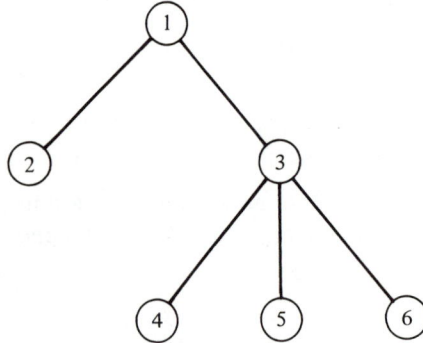

Fig. 0.9   Example of a tree.

numbered 1. We shall follow the convention of drawing trees with the root on top and having all arcs directed downward. Adopting this convention we can omit the arrowheads.

THEOREM 0.3

A tree T has the following properties:

(1) T is acyclic.
(2) For each node in a tree there is a unique path from the root to that node.

Proof. Exercise. □

DEFINITION

A *subtree* of a tree $T = (A, R)$ is any tree $T' = (A', R')$ such that

(1) A' is nonempty and contained in A,
(2) $R' = A' \times A' \cap R$, and
(3) No node of $A - A'$ is a descendant of a node in A'.

For example,

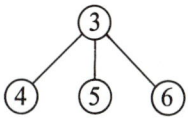

is a subtree of the tree in Fig. 0.9. We say that the root of a subtree *dominates* the subtree.

0.5.4. Ordered Graphs

DEFINITION

An *ordered directed graph* is a pair (A, R) where A is a set of vertices as before and R is a set of linearly ordered lists of edges such that each element of R is of the form $((a, b_1), (a, b_2), \ldots, (a, b_n))$, where a is a distinct member of A. This element would indicate that, for vertex a, there are n arcs leaving a, the first entering vertex b_1, the second entering vertex b_2, and so forth.

Example 0.23

Figure 0.10 shows a picture of an ordered directed graph. The linear ordering on the arcs leaving a vertex is indicated by numbering the arcs leaving a vertex by $1, 2, \ldots, n$, where n is the out-degree of that vertex.

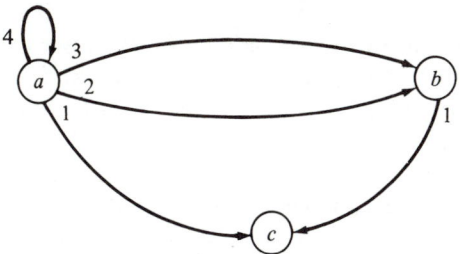

Fig. 0.10 Ordered directed graph.

The formal specification for Fig. 0.10 is (A, R), where $A = \{a, b, c\}$ and $R = \{((a, c), (a, b), (a, b), (a, a)), ((b, c))\}$. $\square$

Notice that Fig. 0.10 is not a directed graph according to our definition, since there are two arcs leaving node a and entering node b. (Recall that in a set there is only one instance of each element.)

As for unordered graphs, we define the notions of labeling and equality of ordered graphs.

Definition

A *labeling* of an ordered graph $G = (A, R)$ is a pair of mappings f and g such that

(1) $f: A \longrightarrow S$ for some set S (f labels the nodes), and
(2) g maps R to sequences of symbols from some set T such that g maps $((a, b_1), \ldots, (a, b_n))$ to a sequence of n symbols of T. (g labels the edges.)

Labeled graphs $G_1 = (A_1, R_1)$ and $G_2 = (A_2, R_2)$ with labelings (f_1, g_1) and (f_2, g_2), respectively, are *equal* if there exists a bijection $h: A_1 \longrightarrow A_2$ such that

(1) R_1 contains $((a, b_1), \ldots, (a, b_n))$ if and only if R_2 contains $((h(a), h(b_1)), \ldots, (h(a), h(b_n)))$,
(2) $f_1(a) = f_2(h(a))$ for all a in A_1, and
(3) $g_1(((a, b_1), \ldots, (a, b_n))) = g_2((h(a), h(b_1)), \ldots, (h(a), h(b_n)))$.

Informally, two labeled ordered graphs are equal if there is a one-to-one correspondence between nodes that preserves the node and edge labels. If the labeling functions all have a range with one element, then the graph is essentially unlabeled, and only condition (1) needs to be shown. Similarly, only the node labeling or only the edge labeling may map to a single element, and condition (2) or (3) will become trivial.

For each ordered graph (A, R), there is an underlying unordered graph (A, R') formed by allowing R' to be the set of (a, b) such that there is a list $((a, b_1), \ldots, (a, b_n))$ in R, and $b = b_i$ for some i, $1 \leq i \leq n$.

An *ordered dag* is an ordered graph whose underlying graph is a dag.

An *ordered tree* is an ordered graph (A, R) whose underlying graph is a tree, and such that if $((a, b_1), \ldots, (a, b_n))$ is in R, then $b_i \neq b_j$, if $i \neq j$.

Unless otherwise stated, we shall assume that the direct descendants of a node of an ordered dag or tree are always linearly ordered from left to right in a diagram.

There is a great distinction between ordered graphs and unordered graphs from the point of view of when two graphs are the same.

For example the two trees T_1 and T_2 in Fig. 0.11 are equivalent if T_1 and

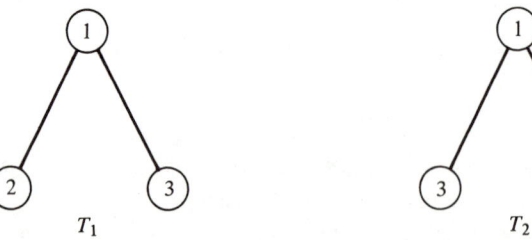

Fig. 0.11   Two trees.

T_2 are unordered. But if T_1 and T_2 are ordered, then T_1 and T_2 are not the same.

0.5.5. Inductive Proofs Involving Dags

Many theorems about dags, and especially trees, can be proved by induction, but it is often not clear on what to base the induction. Theorems which yield to this kind of proof are often of the form that something is true for all, or a certain subset of, the nodes of the tree. Thus we must prove something about nodes of the tree, and we need some parameter of nodes such that the inductive step can be proved.

Two such parameters are the *depth* of a node, the minimum path length (or in the case of a tree, the path length) from a base node (root in the case of a tree) to the given node, and the *height* (or *level*) of a node, the maximum path length from the node to a leaf.

Another approach to inductions on finite ordered trees is to order the nodes in some way and perform the induction on the position of the node in that sequence. Two common orderings are defined below.

DEFINITION

Let T be a finite ordered tree. A *preorder* of the nodes of T is obtained by applying step 1 recursively, beginning at the root of T.

Step 1: Let this application of step 1 be to node a. If a is a leaf, list node a and halt. If a is not a leaf, let its direct descendants be $a_1, a_2, \ldots, a_n$. Then list a and subsequently apply step 1 to $a_1, a_2, \ldots, a_n$ in that order.

A *postorder* of T is formed by changing the last sentence of step 1 to read "Apply step 1 to $a_1, a_2, \ldots, a_n$ in that order and then list a."

Example 0.24

Consider the ordered tree of Fig. 0.12. The preorder of the nodes is 123456789. The postorder is 342789651. □

Sometimes it is possible to perform an induction on the place that a node has in some order, such as pre- or postorder. Examples of these forms of induction appear throughout the book.

0.5.6. Linear Orders from Partial Orders

If we have a partial order R on a set A, often we wish to find a linear order which is a superset of the partial order. This problem of embedding a partial order in a linear order is called *topological sorting*.

Intuitively, topological sorting corresponds to taking a dag, which is in effect a partial order, and squeezing the dag into a single column of nodes

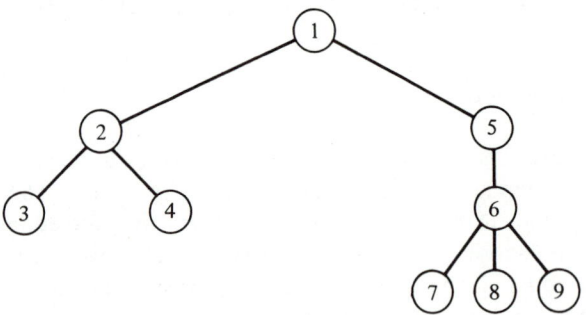

Fig. 0.12   Ordered tree.

such that all edges point downward. The linear order is given by the position of nodes in the column.

For example, under this type of transformation the dag of Fig. 0.8 could look as shown in Fig. 0.13.

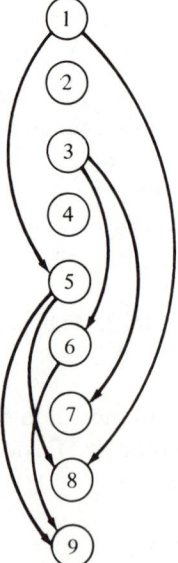

Fig. 0.13   Linear order from the dag of Fig. 0.8.

Formally we say that R' is a *linear order that embeds a partial order R* on a set A if R' is a linear order and $R \subseteq R'$, i.e., $a\,R\,b$ implies that $a\,R'\,b$ for all a, b in A. Given a partial order R, there are many linear orders that embed R (Exercise 0.5.5). The following algorithm finds one such linear order.

ALGORITHM 0.1

Topological sort.

Input. A partial order R on a finite set A.

Output. A linear order R' on A such that $R \subseteq R'$.

Method. Since A is a finite set, we can represent the linear order R' on A as a list $a_1, a_2, \ldots, a_n$ such that $a_i \, R' \, a_j$ if $i < j$, and $A = \{a_1, \ldots, a_n\}$. The following steps construct this sequence of elements:

(1) Let $i = 1$, $A_i = A$, and $R_i = R$.

(2) If A_i is empty, halt, and $a_1, a_2, \ldots, a_{i-1}$ is the desired linear order. Otherwise, let a_i be an element in A_i such that $a \, R_i \, a_i$ is false for all $a \in A_i$.

(3) Let A_{i+1} be $A_i - \{a_i\}$ and R_{i+1} be $R_i \cap (A_{i+1} \times A_{i+1})$. Then let i be $i + 1$ and repeat step (2). □

If we represent a partial order as a dag, then Algorithm 0.1 has a particularly simple interpretation. At each step (A_i, R_i) is a dag and a_i is a base node of (A_i, R_i). The dag (A_{i+1}, R_{i+1}) is formed from (A_i, R_i) by deleting node a_i and all edges leaving a_i.

Example 0.25

Let $A = \{a, b, c, d\}$ and $R = \{(a, b), (a, c), (b, d), (c, d)\}$. Since a is the only node in A such that $a' \, R \, a$ is false for all $a' \in A$, we must choose $a_1 = a$.

Then $A_2 = \{b, c, d\}$ and $R_2 = \{(b, d), (c, d)\}$; we now choose either b or c for a_2. Let us choose $a_2 = b$. Then $A_3 = \{c, d\}$ and $R_3 = \{(c, d)\}$. Continuing, we find $a_3 = c$ and $a_4 = d$.

The complete linear order R' is $\{(a, b), (b, c), (c, d), (a, c), (b, d), (a, d)\}$.
□

THEOREM 0.4

Algorithm 0.1 produces a linear order R' which embeds the given partial order R.

Proof. A simple inductive exercise. □

0.5.7. Representations for Trees

A tree is a two-dimensional structure, but in many situations it is convenient to use only one-dimensional data structures. Consequently we are interested in having one-dimensional representations for trees which have all the information contained in the two-dimensional picture. What we mean by this is that the two-dimensional picture can be recovered from the one-dimensional representation.

Obviously one one-dimensional representation of a tree $T = (A, R)$ would be the sets A and R themselves.

But there are also other representations. For example, we can use nested brackets to indicate the nodes at each depth of a tree. Recall that the *depth* of a node in a tree is the length of the path from the root to that node. For example, in Fig. 0.9, node 1 is at depth 0, node 3 is at depth 1, and node 6 is at depth 2. The *depth* of a tree is the length of the longest path. The tree of Fig. 0.9 has depth 2.

Using brackets to indicate depth, the tree of Fig. 0.9 could be represented as 1(2, 3(4, 5, 6)). We shall call this the left-bracketed representation, since a subtree is represented by the expression appearing inside a balanced pair of parentheses and the node which is the root of that subtree appears immediately to the left of the left parenthesis.

DEFINITION

In general the *left-bracketed representation* of a tree T can be obtained by applying the following recursive rules to T. The string $lrep(T)$ denotes the left-bracketed representation of tree T.

(1) If T has a root numbered a with subtrees $T_1, T_2, \ldots, T_k$ in order, then $lrep(T) = a(lrep(T_1), lrep(T_2), \ldots, lrep(T_k))$.

(2) If T has a root numbered a with no direct descendants, then $lrep(T) = a$.

If we delete the parentheses from a left-bracketed representation of a tree, we are left with a preorder of the nodes.

We can also obtain a *right-bracketed representation* for a tree T, $rrep(T)$, as follows:

(1) If T has a root numbered a with subtrees $T_1, T_2, \ldots, T_k$, then $rrep(T) = (rrep(T_1), rrep(T_2), \ldots, rrep(T_k))a$.

(2) If T has a root numbered a with no direct descendants, then $rrep(T) = a$.

Thus $rrep(T)$ for the tree of Fig. 0.12 would be $((3, 4)2, ((7, 8, 9)6)5)1$. In this representation, the direct ancestor is immediately to the right of the first right parenthesis enclosing that node. Also, note that if we delete the parentheses we are left with a postorder of the nodes.

Another representation of a tree is to list the direct ancestor of nodes $1, 2, \ldots, n$ of a tree in that order. The root would be recognized by letting its ancestor be 0.

Example 0.26

The tree shown in Fig. 0.14 would be represented by 0122441777. Here 0 in position 1 indicates that node 1 has "node 0" as its direct ancestor (i.e., node 1 is the root). The 1 in position 7 indicates that node 7 has direct ancestor 1. □

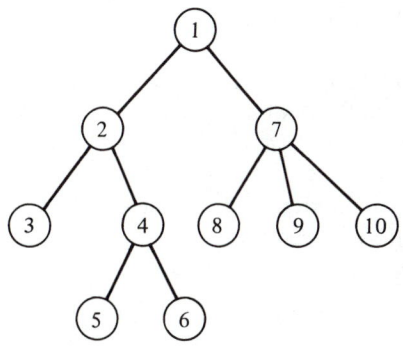

Fig. 0.14 A tree.

0.5.8. Paths Through a Graph

In this section we shall outline a computationally efficient method of computing the transitive closure of a relation R on a set A. If we view the relation as an unordered graph (A, R), then the transitive closure of R is equivalent to the set of pairs of nodes (a, b) such that there is a path from node a to node b.

Another possible interpretation is to view the relation (or the unordered graph) as a (square) Boolean matrix (that is, a matrix of 0's and 1's) called an *adjacency matrix*, in which the entry in row i, column j is 1 if and only if the element corresponding to row i is R-related to the element corresponding to column j. Figure 0.15 shows the Boolean matrix M corresponding to the

	1	2	3	4
1	1	1	0	0
2	0	0	1	1
3	0	0	0	1
4	1	0	1	0

Fig. 0.15 Boolean matrix for Fig. 0.6.

graph of Fig. 0.6. If M is a Boolean matrix, then $M^+ = \sum_{n=1}^{\infty} M^n$ (where M^n represents M Boolean multiplied† by itself n times) represents the transitive

---

†That is, use the usual formula for matrix multiplication with the Boolean operations · and + for multiplication and addition, respectively.

closure of the relation represented by M. Thus the algorithm could also be used as a method of computing M^+.

For Fig. 0.15, M^+ would be a matrix of all 1's.

Actually we shall give a slightly more general algorithm here. We assume that we have an unordered directed graph in which there is a nonnegative cost c_{ij} associated with an edge from node i to node j. (If there is no edge from node i to node j, c_{ij} is infinite.) The algorithm will compute the minimum cost of a path between any pair of nodes. The case in which we wish to compute only the transitive closure of a relation R over $\{a_1, \ldots, a_n\}$ is expressed by letting $c_{ij} = 0$ if $a_i \, R \, a_j$ and $c_{ij} = \infty$ otherwise.

ALGORITHM 0.2

Minimum cost of paths through a graph.

Input. A graph with n nodes numbered $1, 2, \ldots, n$ and a cost function c_{ij} for $1 \leq i, j \leq n$ with $c_{ij} \geq 0$ for all i and j.

Output. An $n \times n$ matrix $M = [m_{ij}]$, with m_{ij} the lowest cost of any path from node i to node j, for all i and j.

Method.

(1) Set $m_{ij} = c_{ij}$ for all i and j such that $1 \leq i, j \leq n$.
(2) Set $k = 1$.
(3) For all i and j, if $m_{ij} > m_{ik} + m_{kj}$, set m_{ij} to $m_{ik} + m_{kj}$.
(4) If $k < n$, increase k by 1 and go to step (3). If $k = n$, halt.   □

The heart of Algorithm 0.2 is step (3), in which we deduce whether the current cost of going from node i to node j can be made smaller by first going from node i to node k and then from node k to node j.

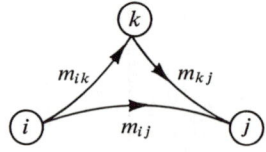

Since step (3) is executed once for all possible values of i, j, and k, Algorithm 0.2 is n^3 in time complexity.

It is not immediately clear that Algorithm 0.2 does produce the minimum cost of any path from node i to j. Thus we should prove that Algorithm 0.2 does what it claims.

THEOREM 0.5

When Algorithm 0.2 terminates, m_{ij} is the smallest value expressible as $c_{v_1 v_2} + \cdots + c_{v_{m-1} v_m}$ such that $v_1 = i$ and $v_m = j$. (This sum is the cost of the path $v_1, v_2, \ldots, v_m$ from node i to node j.)

Proof. To prove the theorem we shall prove the following statement by induction on l, the value of k in step (3) of the algorithm.

Statement (0.5.1). After step (3) is executed with $k = l$, m_{ij} has the smallest value expressible as a sum of the form $c_{v_1 v_2} + \cdots + c_{v_{m-1} v_m}$, where $v_1 = i$, $v_m = j$, and none of $v_2, \ldots, v_{m-1}$ is greater than l.

We shall call this minimum value the correct value of m_{ij} with $k = l$. This value is the cost of a cheapest path from node i to node j which does not pass through a node whose number is higher than l.

Basis. Let us consider the initial condition, which we can represent by letting $l = 0$. [If you like, we can think of step (1) as step (3) with $k = 0$.] When $l = 0$, $m = 2$, so $m_{ij} = c_{ij}$, which is the correct initial value.

Inductive Step. Assume that statement (0.5.1) is true for all $l < l_0$. Let us consider the value of m_{ij} after step (3) has been executed with $k = l_0$.

Suppose that the minimum sum $c_{v_1 v_2} + \cdots + c_{v_{m-1} v_m}$ for m_{ij} with $k = l_0$ is such that no v_p, $2 \leq p \leq m - 1$, is equal to l_0. From the inductive hypothesis $c_{v_1 v_2} + \cdots + c_{v_{m-1} v_m}$ is the correct value of m_{ij} with $k = l_0 - 1$, so $c_{v_1 v_2} + \cdots + c_{v_{m-1} v_m}$ is also the correct value of m_{ij} with $k = l_0$.

Now suppose that the minimum sum $s_{ij} = c_{v_1 v_2} + \cdots + c_{v_{m-1} v_m}$ for m_{ij} with $k = l_0$ is such that $v_p = l_0$ for some $2 \leq p \leq m - 1$. That is, s_{ij} is the cost of the path $v_1, v_2, \ldots, v_m$. We can assume that there is no node v_q on this path, $q \neq p$, such that v_q is l_0. Otherwise the path $v_1, v_2, \ldots, v_m$ contains a cycle, and we can delete at least one term from the sum $c_{v_1 v_2} + \cdots + c_{v_{m-1} v_m}$ without increasing the value of the sum s_{ij}. Thus we can always find a sum for s_{ij} in which $v_p = l_0$ for only one value of p, $2 \leq p \leq m - 1$.

Let us assume that $2 < p < m - 1$. The cases $p = 2$ and $p = m - 1$ are left to the reader. Let us consider the sum $s_{iv_p} = c_{v_1 v_2} + \cdots + c_{v_{p-1} v_p}$ and $s_{v_p j} = c_{v_p v_{p+1}} + \cdots + c_{v_{m-1} v_m}$ (the costs of the paths from node i to node v_p and from node v_p to node j in the sum s_{ij}). From the inductive hypothesis we can assume that s_{iv_p} is the correct value for m_{iv_p} with $k = l_0 - 1$ and that $s_{v_p j}$ is the correct value for $m_{v_p j}$ with $k = l_0 - 1$. Thus when step (3) is executed with $k = l_0$, m_{ij} is correctly given the value $m_{iv_p} + m_{v_p j}$.

We have thus shown that statement (0.5.1) is true for all l. When $l = n$, statement (0.5.1) states that at the end of Algorithm 0.2, m_{ij} has the lowest possible value. $\square$

A common special case of finding minimum cost paths through a graph occurs when we want to determine the set of nodes which are accessible from a given node. Equivalently, given a relation R on set A, with a in A, we want to find the set of b in A such that $a\, R^+ b$, where R^+ is the transitive closure of R. For this purpose we can use the following algorithm of quadratic time complexity.

ALGORITHM 0.3

Finding the set of nodes accessible from a given node of a directed graph.

Input. Graph (A, R), with A a finite set and a in A.

Output. The set of nodes b in A such that $a\ R^*\ b$.

Method. We form a list L and update it repeatedly. We shall also *mark* members of A during the course of the algorithm. Initially, all members of A are unmarked. The nodes marked will be those accessible from a.

(1) Set $L = a$ and mark a.

(2) If L is empty, halt. Otherwise, let b be the first element on list L. Delete b from L.

(3) For all c in A such that $b\ R\ c$ and c is unmarked, add c to the bottom of list L, mark c, and go to step (2). □

We leave a proof that Algorithm 0.3 works correctly to the Exercises.

EXERCISES

0.5.1. What is the maximum number of edges a dag with n nodes can have?

0.5.2. Prove Theorem 0.3.

0.5.3. Give the pre- and postorders for the tree of Fig. 0.14. Give left- and right-bracketed representations for the tree.

*0.5.4. (a) Design an algorithm that will map a left-bracketed representation of a tree into a right-bracketed representation.
(b) Design an algorithm that will map a right-bracketed representation of a tree into a left-bracketed representation.

0.5.5. How many linear orders embed the partial order of the dag of Fig. 0.8?

0.5.6. Complete the proof of Theorem 0.5.

0.5.7. Give upper bounds on the time and space necessary to implement Algorithm 0.1. Assume that one memory cell is needed to store any node name or integer, and that one elementary step is needed for each of a reasonable set of primitive operations, including the arithmetic operations and examination or alteration of a cell in an array indexed by a known integer.

0.5.8. Let $A = \{a, b, c, d\}$ and $R = \{(a, b), (b, c), (a, c), (b, d)\}$. Find a linear order R' such that $R \subseteq R'$. How many such linear orders are there?

DEFINITION

An *undirected graph* G is a triple (A, E, f) where A is a set of nodes, E is a set of edge names and f is a mapping from E to the set of unordered pairs of nodes. If $f(e) = \{a, b\}$, then we mean that edge e connects nodes a and b. A *path* in an undirected graph is a sequence of nodes $a_0, a_1, a_2, \ldots, a_n$ such that there is an edge connecting a_{i-1} and a_i for $1 \leq i \leq n$. An undirected graph is *connected* if there is a path between every pair of distinct nodes.

DEFINITION

An undirected tree can be defined recursively as follows. An *undirected tree* is a set of one or more nodes with one distinguished node r called the root of the tree. The remaining nodes can be partitioned into zero or more sets $T_1, \ldots, T_k$ each of which forms a tree. The trees $T_1, \ldots, T_k$ are called the subtrees of the root and an undirected edge connects r with all of and only the subtree roots.

A *spanning tree* for a connected undirected graph G is a tree which contains all nodes of N.

0.5.9. Provide an algorithm to construct a spanning tree for a connected undirected graph.

0.5.10. Let (A, R) be an unordered graph such that $A = \{1, 2, 3, 4\}$ and $R = \{(1, 2), (2, 3), (4, 1), (4, 3)\}$. Find R^+, the transitive closure of R. Let the adjacency matrix for R be M. Compute M^+ and show that M^+ is the adjacency matrix for (A, R^+).

0.5.11. Show that Algorithm 0.2 takes time proportional to n^3 in basic steps similar to those mentioned in Exercise 0.5.7.

0.5.12. Prove that Algorithm 0.3 marks node b if and only if $a\ R^+\ b$.

0.5.13. Show that Algorithm 0.3 takes time proportional to the maximum of $\#A$ and $\#R$.

0.5.14. The following are three unordered directed graphs. Which two are the same?

$$G_1 = (\{a, b, c\}, \{(a, b), (b, c), (c, a)\})$$
$$G_2 = (\{a, b, c\}, \{(b, a), (a, c), (b, c)\})$$
$$G_3 = (\{a, b, c\}, \{(c, b), (c, a), (b, a)\})$$

0.5.15. The following are three ordered directed graphs with only nodes labeled. Which two are the same?

$$G_1 = (\{a, b, c\}, \{((a, b), (a, c)), ((b, a), (b, c)), ((c, b))\})$$

with labeling $l_1(a) = X$, $l_1(b) = Z$, and $l_1(c) = Y$.

$$G_2 = (\{a, b, c\}, \{((a, c)), ((b, c), (b, a)), ((c, b), (c, a))\})$$

with labeling $l_2(a) = Y$, $l_2(b) = X$, and $l_2(c) = Z$.

$$G_3 = (\{a, b, c\}, \{((a, c), (a, b)), ((b, c)), ((c, a), (c, b))\})$$

with labeling $l_3(a) = Y$, $l_3(b) = X$, and $l_3(c) = Z$.

0.5.16. Complete the proof of Theorem 0.4.

0.5.17. Provide an algorithm to determine whether an undirected graph is connected.

*0.5.18. Provide an algorithm to determine whether two graphs are equal.

*0.5.19. Provide an efficient algorithm to determine whether two nodes of a tree are on the same path. *Hint:* Consider preordering the nodes.

**0.5.20. Provide an efficient algorithm to determine the first common ancestor of two nodes of a tree.

Programming Exercises

0.5.21. Write a program that will construct an adjacency matrix from a linked list representation of a graph.

0.5.22. Write a program that will construct a linked list representation of a graph from an adjacency matrix.

0.5.23. Write programs to implement Algorithms 0.1, 0.2, and 0.3.

BIBLIOGRAPHIC NOTES

Graphs are an ancient and honorable part of mathematics. Harary [1969], Ore [1962], and Berge [1958] discuss the theory of graphs. Knuth [1968] is a good source for techniques for manipulating graphs and trees inside computers.

Algorithm 0.2 is Warshall's algorithm as given in Floyd [1962a]. One interesting result on computing the transitive closure of a relation is found in Munro [1971], where it is shown that the transitive closure of a relation can be computed in the time required to compute the product of two matrices over a Boolean ring. Thus, using Strassen [1969], the time complexity of transitive closure is no greater than $n^{2.81}$, not n^3, as Algorithm 0.2 takes.

1 AN INTRODUCTION TO COMPILING

This book considers the problems involved in mapping one representation of a procedure into another. The most common occurrence of this mapping is during the compilation of a source program, written in a high-level programming language, into object code for a particular digital computer.

We shall discuss algorithm-translating techniques which are applicable to the design of compilers and other language-processing devices. To put these techniques into perspective, in this chapter we shall summarize some of the salient aspects of the compiling process and mention certain other areas in which parsing or translation plays a major role.

Like the previous chapter, those who have a prior familiarity with the material, in this case compilers, will find the discussion quite elementary. These readers can skip this chapter or merely skim it for terminology.

1.1. PROGRAMMING LANGUAGES

In this section we shall briefly discuss the notion of a programming language. We shall then touch on the problems inherent in the specification of a programming language and in the design of a translator for such a language.

1.1.1. Specification of Programming Languages

The basic machine language operations of a digital computer are invariably very primitive compared with the complex functions that occur in mathematics, engineering, and other disciplines. Although any function that can be specified as a procedure can be implemented as a sequence of exceedingly simple machine language instructions, for most applications it is much preferable to use a higher-level language whose primitive instructions approximate the type of operations that occur in the application. For example, if matrix operations are being performed, it is more convenient to write an instruction of the form

$$A = B * C$$

to represent the fact that A is a matrix obtained by multiplying matrices B and C together rather than a long sequence of machine language operations whose intent is the same.

Programming languages can alleviate much of the drudgery of programming in machine language, but they also introduce a number of new problems of their own. Of course, since computers can still "understand" only machine language, a program written in a high-level language must be ultimately translated into machine language. The device performing this translation has become known as a compiler.

Another problem concerned with programming languages is the specification of the language itself. In a minimal specification of a programming language we need to define

(1) The set of symbols which can be used in valid programs,
(2) The set of valid programs, and
(3) The "meaning" of each valid program.

Defining the permissible set of symbols is easy. One should bear in mind, however, that in some languages such as SNOBOL or FORTRAN, the beginning and/or end of a card has significance and thus should be considered a "symbol." Blank is also considered a symbol in some cases. Defining the set of programs which are "valid" is a much more difficult task. In many cases it is very hard just to decide whether a given program should be considered valid.

In the specification of programming languages it has become customary to define the class of permissible programs by a set of grammatical rules which allow some programs of questionable validity to be constructed. For example, many FORTRAN specifications permit a statement of the form

L   GOTO   L

within a "valid" FORTRAN program. However, the specification of a superset of the truly valid programs is often much simpler than the specification of all and only those programs which we would consider valid in the narrowest sense of the word.

The third and most difficult aspect of language specification is defining the meaning of each valid program. Several approaches to this problem have been taken. One method is to define a mapping which associates with each valid program a sentence in a language whose meaning we understand. For example, we could use functional calculus or lambda calculus as the "well-understood" language. Then we can define the meaning of a program in any programming language in terms of an equivalent "program" in functional calculus or lambda calculus. By *equivalent program*, we mean one which defines the same function.

Another method of giving meaning to programs is to define an idealized machine. The meaning of a program can then be specified in terms of its effect on this machine started off in some predetermined initial configuration. In this scheme the abstract machine becomes an interpreter for the language.

A third approach is to ignore deep questions of "meaning" altogether, and this is the appproach we shall take here. For us, the "meaning" of a source program is simply the output of the compiler when applied to the source program.

In this book we shall assume that we have the specification of a compiler as a set of pairs (x, y), where x is a source language program and y is a target language program into which x is to be translated. We shall assume that we know what this set of pairs is beforehand, and that our main concern is the construction of an efficient device which when given x as input will produce y as output. We shall refer to the set of pairs (x, y) as a *translation*. If each x is a string over alphabet Σ and y is a string over Δ, then a translation is merely a mapping from Σ^* to Δ^*.

1.1.2. Syntax and Semantics

It is often more convenient in specifying and implementing translations to treat a translation as the composition of two simpler mappings. The first of these relations, known as the *syntactic mapping*, associates with each input (program in the source language) some structure which is the domain for the second relation, *the semantic mapping*. It is not immediately apparent that there should be any structure which will aid in the translation process, but almost without exception, a labeled tree turns out to be a very useful structure to place on the input. Without delving into the philosophy of why this should be so, much of this book will be devoted to algorithms for the efficient construction of the proper trees for input programs.

As a natural example of how tree structures are built on strings, every English sentence can be broken down into syntactic categories which are related by grammatical rules. For example, the sentence

"The pig is in the pen"

has a grammatical structure which is indicated by the tree of Fig. 1.1, whose nodes are labeled by syntactic categories and whose leaves are labeled by the terminal symbols, which, in this case, are English words.

Likewise, a program written in a programming language can be broken

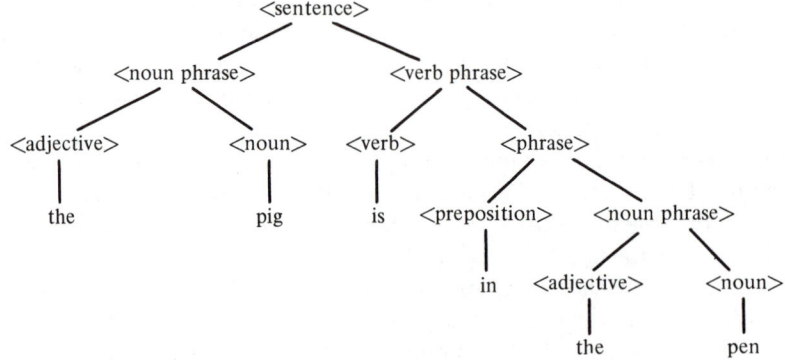

Fig. 1.1   Tree structure for English sentence.

down into syntactic components which are related by syntactic rules governing the language. For example, the string

$$a + b * c$$

may have a syntactic structure given by the tree of Fig. 1.2.† The term *parsing*
or *syntactic analysis* is given to the process of finding the syntactic structure

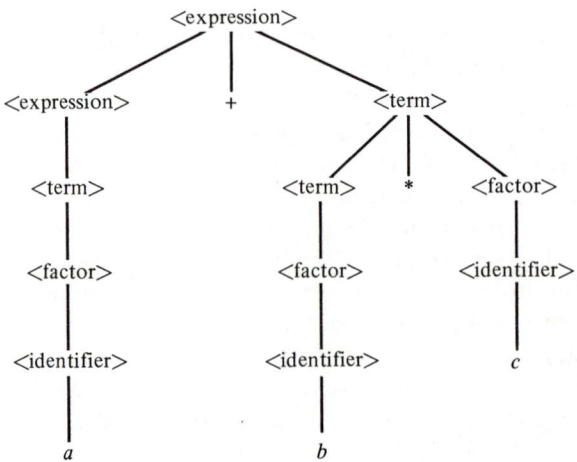

Fig. 1.2   Tree from arithmetic expression.

†The use of three syntactic categories, ⟨expression⟩, ⟨term⟩, and ⟨factor⟩, rather than
just ⟨expression⟩, is forced on us by our desire that the structure of an arithmetic expression be unique. The reader should bear this in mind, lest our subsequent examples of the
syntactic analysis of arithmetic expressions appear unnecessarily complicated.

associated with an input sentence. The syntactic structure of a sentence is useful in helping to understand the relationships among the various symbols of a sentence.

The term *syntax of a language* will refer to a relation which associates with each sentence of a language a syntactic structure. We can then define a valid sentence of a language as a string of symbols which has the overall syntactic structure of ⟨sentence⟩. In the next chapter we shall discuss several methods of rigorously defining the syntax of a language.

The second part of the translation is called the *semantic* mapping, in which the structured input is mapped to an output, normally a machine language program. The term *semantics of a language* will refer to a mapping which associates with the syntactic structure of each input a string in some language (possibly the same language) which we consider the "meaning" of the original sentence. The specification of the semantics of a language is a very difficult matter which has not yet been fully resolved, particularly for natural languages, e.g., English.

Even the specification of the syntax and semantics of a programming language is a nontrivial task. Although there are no universally applicable methods, there are two concepts from language theory which can be used to make up part of the description.

The first of these is the concept of a context-free grammar. Most of the rules for describing syntactic structure can be formalized as a context-free grammar. Moreover, a context-free grammar provides a description which is sufficiently precise to be used as part of the specification of the compiler itself. In Chapter 2 we shall present the relevant concepts from the theory of context-free languages.

The second concept is the syntax-directed translation schema, which can be used to specify mappings from one language to another. We shall study syntax-directed translation schemata in some detail in Chapters 3 and 9.

In this book an attempt has been made to present those aspects of language theory and other formal theories which bear on the design of programming languages and their compilers. In some cases the impact of the theory is only to provide a framework in which to talk about problems that occur in compiling. In other cases the theory will provide uniform and practicable solutions to some of the design problems that occur in compiling.

BIBLIOGRAPHIC NOTES

High-level programming languages evolved in the early 1950's. At that time computers lacked floating-point arithmetic operations, so the first programming languages were representations for floating-point arithmetic. The first major programming language was FORTRAN, which was developed in the mid-1950's.

Several other algebraic languages were also developed at that time, but FORTRAN emerged as the most widely used language. Since that time hundreds of high-level programming languages have been developed. Sammet [1969] gives an account of many of the languages in existence in the mid-1960's.

Much of the theory of programming languages and compilers has lagged behind the practical development. A great stimulus to the theory of formal languages was the use of what is now known as Backus Naur Form (BNF) in the syntactic definition of ALGOL 60 (Naur [1963]). This report, together with the early work of Chomsky [1959a, 1963], stimulated the vigorous development of the theory of formal languages during the 1960's. Much of this book presents results from language theory which have relevance to the design and understanding of language translators.

Most of the early work on language theory was concerned with the syntactic definition of languages. The semantic definition of languages, a much more difficult question, received less attention and even at the time of the writing of this book was not a fully resolved matter. Two good anthologies on the formal specification of semantics are Steel [1966] and Engeler [1971]. The IBM Vienna laboratory definition of PL/I [Lucas and Walk, 1969] is one example of a totally formal approach to the specification of a major programming language.

One of the more interesting developments in programming languages has been the creation of extensible languages—languages whose syntax and semantics can be changed within a program. One of the earliest and most commonly proposed schemes for language extension is the macro definition. See McIlroy [1960], Leavenworth [1966], and Cheatham [1966], for example. Galler and Perlis [1967] have suggested an extension scheme whereby new data types and new operators can be introduced into ALGOL. Later developments in extensible languages are contained in Christensen and Shaw [1969] and Wegbreit [1970]. ALGOL 68 is an example of a major programming language with language extension facilities [Van Wijngaarden, 1969].

1.2. AN OVERVIEW OF COMPILING

We shall discuss techniques and algorithms which are applicable to the design of compilers and other language-processing devices. To put these algorithms into perspective, in this section we shall take a global picture of the compiling process.

1.2.1. The Portions of a Compiler

Many compilers for many languages have certain processes in common. We shall attempt to abstract the essence of some of these processes. In doing so we shall attempt to remove from these processes as many machine-dependent and operating-system-dependent considerations as possible. Although implementation considerations are important (a bad implementation can destroy a good algorithm), we feel that understanding the fundamental nature of a problem is essential and will make the techniques for solution of that problem applicable to other basically similar problems.

A source program in a programming language is nothing more than a string of characters. A compiler ultimately converts this string of characters into a string of bits, the object code. In this process, subprocesses with the following names can often be identified:

(1) Lexical analysis.
(2) Bookkeeping, or symbol table operations.
(3) Parsing or syntax analysis.
(4) Code generation or translation to intermediate code (e.g. assembly language).
(5) Code optimization.
(6) Object code generation (e.g. assembly).

In any given compiler, the order of the processes may be slightly different from that shown, and several of the processes may be combined into a single phase. Moreover, a compiler should not be shattered by any input it receives; it must be capable of responding to any input string. For those input strings which do not represent syntactically valid programs, appropriate diagnostic messages must be given.

We shall describe the first five phases of compilation briefly. These phases do not necessarily occur separately in an actual compiler. However, it is often convenient to conceptually partition a compiler into these phases in order to isolate the problems that are unique to that part of the compilation process.

1.2.2. Lexical Analysis

The lexical analysis phase comes first. The input to the compiler and hence the lexical analyzer is a string of symbols from an alphabet of characters. In the reference version of PL/I for example, the terminal symbol alphabet contains the 60 symbols

$$A \ B \ C \ \cdots \ Z \ \$ \ @ \ \#$$
$$0 \ 1 \ 2 \ \cdots \ 9 \ \_ \ blank$$
$$= + - * / (\ ) , . ; : ' \& | \neg > < ? \%$$

In a program, certain combinations of symbols are often treated as a single entity. Some typical examples of this would include the following:

(1) In languages such as PL/I a string of one or more blanks is normally treated as a single blank.

(2) Certain languages have keywords such as BEGIN, END, GOTO, DO, INTEGER, and so forth which are treated as single entities.

(3) Strings representing numerical constants are treated as single items.

(4) Identifiers used as names for variables, functions, procedures, labels, and the like are another example of a single lexical unit in a programming language.

It is the job of the lexical analyzer to group together certain terminal characters into single syntactic entities, called *tokens*. What constitutes a token is implied by the specification of the programming language. A token is a string of terminal symbols, with which we associate a lexical structure consisting of a pair of the form (token type, data). The first component is a syntactic category such as "constant" or "identifier," and the second component is a pointer to data that have been accumulated about this particular token. For a given language the number of token types will be presumed finite. We shall call the pair (token type, data) a "token" also, when there is no source of confusion.

Thus the lexical analyzer is a translator whose input is the string of symbols representing the source program and whose output is a stream of tokens. This output forms the input to the syntactic analyzer.

Example 1.1

Consider the following assignment statement from a FORTRAN-like language:

$$COST = (PRICE + TAX) * 0.98$$

The lexical analysis phase would find COST, PRICE, and TAX to be tokens of type identifier and 0.98 to be a token of type constant. The characters $=$, $($, $+$, $)$, and $*$ are tokens by themselves. Let us assume that all constants and identifiers are to be mapped into tokens of the type $\langle id \rangle$. We assume that the data component of a token is a pointer, an entry to a table containing the actual name of the identifier together with other data we have collected about that particular identifier. The first component of a token is used by the syntactic analyzer for parsing. The second component is used by the code generation phase to produce appropriate machine code.

Thus the output of the lexical analyzer operating directly on our input string would be the following sequence of tokens:

$$\langle id \rangle_1 = (\langle id \rangle_2 + \langle id \rangle_3) * \langle id \rangle_4$$

Here we have indicated the data pointer of a token by means of a subscript. The symbols $=$, $($, $+$, $)$, and $*$ are to be construed as tokens whose token type is represented by themselves. They have no associated data, and hence we indicate no data pointer for them. □

Lexical analysis is easy if tokens of more than one character are isolated by characters which are tokens themselves. In the example above, $=$, $($, $+$, and $*$ cannot appear as part of an identifier, so COST, PRICE, and TAX can be readily distinguished as tokens.

However, lexical analysis may not be so easy in general. For example, consider the following valid FORTRAN statements:

$$(1) \quad \text{DO} \ 10 \ I = 1.15$$
$$(2) \quad \text{DO} \ 10 \ I = 1, 15$$

In statement (1) DO 10 I is a variable† and 1.15 a constant. In statement (2) DO is a keyword, 10 a constant, and I a variable; 1 and 15 are constants.

If a lexical analyzer were implemented as a coroutine [Gentleman, 1971; McIlroy, 1968] and were to start at the beginning of one of these statements, with a command such as "find the next token," it could not determine if that token was DO or DO 10 I until it had reached the comma or decimal point.

Thus a lexical analyzer may need to look ahead of the token it is actually interested in. A worse example occurs in PL/I, where keywords may also be variables. Upon seeing an input string of the form

$$\text{DECLARE}(X1, X2, \ldots, Xn)$$

the lexical analyzer would have no way of telling whether DECLARE was a function identifier and $X1, X2, \ldots, Xn$ were its arguments or whether DECLARE was a keyword causing the identifiers $X1, X2, \ldots, Xn$ to have the attribute (or attributes) immediately following the right parenthesis. Here the distinction would have to be made on what follows the right parenthesis. But since n can be arbitrarily large,‡ the PL/I lexical analyzer might have to look ahead an arbitrary distance. However, there is another approach to lexical analysis that is less convenient but it avoids the problem of arbitrary lookahead.

We shall define two extreme approaches to lexical analysis. Most techniques in use fall into one or the other of these categories and some are a combination of the two:

(1) A lexical analyzer is said to operate *directly* if, given a string of input text and a pointer into that text, the analyzer will determine the token immediately to the right of the place pointed to and move the pointer to the right of the portion of text forming the token.

(2) A lexical analyzer is said to operate *indirectly* if, given a string of text, a pointer into that text, and a token type, it will determine if input

---

†Recall that in FORTRAN blanks are ignored.

‡The language specification does not impose an upper limit on n. However, a given PL/I compiler will.

characters appearing immediately to the right of the pointer form a token of that type. If so, the pointer is moved to the right of the portion of text forming that token.

Example 1.2

Consider the FORTRAN text

$$DO\ 10\ I = 1, 15$$

with the pointer currently at the left end. An indirect lexical analyzer would respond "yes" if asked for a token of type DO or a token of type $\langle$identifier$\rangle$. In the former case, the pointer would be moved two symbols to the right, and in the latter case, five symbols to the right.

A direct lexical analyzer would examine the text up to the comma and conclude that the next token was of type DO. The pointer would then move two symbols to the right, although many more symbols would be scanned in the process. $\square$

Generally, we shall describe parsing algorithms under the assumption that lexical analysis is direct. The backtrack or "nondeterministic" parsing algorithms can be used with indirect lexical analysis. We shall include a discussion of this type of parsing in Chapters 4 and 6.

1.2.3. Bookkeeping

As tokens are uncovered in lexical analysis, information about certain tokens is collected and stored in one or more tables. What this information is depends on the language. In the FORTRAN example we would want to know that COST, PRICE, and TAX were floating-point variables and 0.98 a floating-point constant.

Assuming that COST, PRICE, and TAX have not been declared in a type statement, this information about these variables can be gleaned from the fact that COST, PRICE, and TAX begin with letters other than I, J, K, L, M, or N.

As another example about collecting information about variables, consider a FORTRAN dimension statement of the form

$$DIMENSION\ A(10,20)$$

On encountering this statement, we would have to store information that A is an identifier which is the name of a two-dimensional array whose size is 10 by 20.

In complex languages such as PL/I, the number of facts which might be stored about a given variable is quite large—on the order of a dozen or so. Let us consider a somewhat simplified example of a table in which information about identifiers is stored. Such a table is often called a *symbol table*. The table will list all identifiers together with the relevant information concerning each identifier.

Suppose that we encounter the statement

$$COST = (PRICE + TAX) * 0.98$$

After this statement, the table might appear as follows:

Entry	Identifier	Information
1	COST	Floating-point variable
2	PRICE	Floating-point variable
3	TAX	Floating-point variable
4	0.98	Floating-point constant

On encountering a future identifier in the input stream, this table would be consulted to see whether that identifier has already appeared. If it has, then the data portion of the token for that identifier is made equal to the entry number of the original occurrence of the variable with that name. For example, if a succeeding statement in the FORTRAN program contained the variable COST, then the token for the second occurrence of COST would be $\langle id \rangle_1$, the same as the token for the first occurrence of COST.

Thus such a table must simultaneously allow for

(1) The rapid addition of new identifiers and new items of information, and

(2) The rapid retrieval of information for a given identifier.

The method of data storage usually used is the hash (or scatter) table, which will be discussed in Chapter 10 (Volume II).

1.2.4. Parsing

As we mentioned earlier, the output of the lexical analyzer is a string of tokens. This string of tokens forms the input to the syntactic analyzer, which examines only the first components of the token (the token types). The information about each token (second component) is used later in the compiling process to generate the machine code.

Parsing, or syntax analysis, as it is sometimes known, is a process in which the string of tokens is examined to determine whether the string obeys certain structural conventions explicit in the syntactic definition of the language.

It is also essential in the code generation process to know what the syntactic structure of a given string is. For example, the syntactic structure of the expression $A + B * C$ must reflect the fact that B and C are first multiplied and that then the result is added to A. No other ordering of the operations will produce the desired calculation.

Parsing is one of the best-understood phases of compilation. From a set of syntactic rules it is possible to automatically construct parsers which will make sure that a source program obeys the syntactic structure defined by these syntactic rules. In Chapters 4–7 we shall study several different parsing techniques and algorithms for generating a parser from a given grammar.

The output from the parser is a tree which represents the syntactic structure inherent in the source program. In many ways this tree structure is closely related to the parsing diagrams we used to make for English sentences in elementary school.

Example 1.3

Suppose that the output of the lexical analyzer is the string of tokens

$$(1.2.1) \qquad \langle \text{id} \rangle_1 = (\langle \text{id} \rangle_2 + \langle \text{id} \rangle_3) * \langle \text{id} \rangle_4$$

This string conveys the information that the following three operations are to be performed in exactly the following way:

(1) $\langle \text{id} \rangle_3$ is to be added to $\langle \text{id} \rangle_2$,
(2) The result of (1) is to be multiplied by $\langle \text{id} \rangle_4$, and
(3) The result of (2) is to be stored in the location reserved for $\langle \text{id} \rangle_1$.

This sequence of steps can be pictorially represented in terms of a labeled tree, as shown in Fig. 1.3. That is, the interior nodes of the tree represent

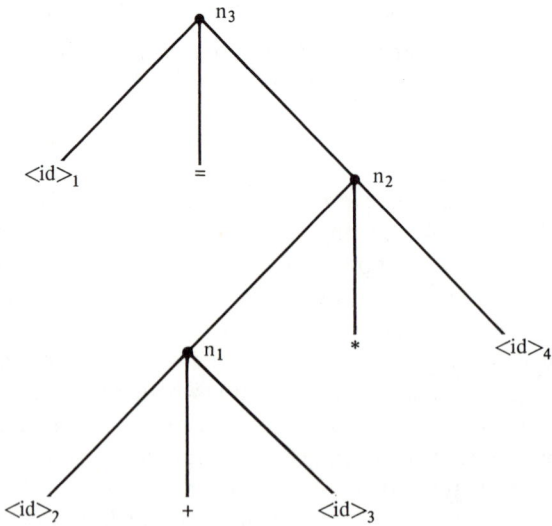

Fig. 1.3 Tree structure.

actions which must be taken. The direct descendants of each node either represent values to which the action is to be applied (if the node is labeled by an identifier or is an interior node) or help to determine what the action should be. (In particular, the $=$, $+$, and $*$ signs do this.) Note that the parentheses in (1.2.1) do not explicitly appear in the tree, although we might want to show them as direct descendants of n_1. The role of the parentheses is only to influence the order of computation. If they did not appear in (1.2.1), then the usual convention that multiplication "takes precedence" over addition would apply, and the first step would be to multiply $\langle id \rangle_3$ and $\langle id \rangle_4$. $\square$

1.2.5. Code Generation

The tree built by the parser is used to generate a translation of the input program. This translation could be a program in machine language, but more often it is in an intermediate language such as assembly language or "three address code." (The latter is a sequence of simple statements; each involves no more than three identifiers, e.g. $A = B$, $A = B + C$, or GOTO A.)

If the compiler is to do extensive code optimization, then code of the three address type is preferred. Since three address code does not pin computations to specific computer registers, it is easier to use registers to advantage when optimizing. If little or no optimization is to be done, then assembly or even machine code is preferred as an intermediate language. We shall give a running example of a translation into an assembly type language to illustrate the salient points of the translation process.

For this discussion let us assume that we have a computer with one working register (the accumulator) and assembly language instructions of the form

Instruction	Effect
LOAD m	c(m) $\longrightarrow$ accumulator
ADD† m	c(accumulator) $+$ c(m) $\longrightarrow$ accumulator
MPY m	c(accumulator) $*$ c(m) $\longrightarrow$ accumulator
STORE m	c(accumulator) $\longrightarrow$ m
LOAD =m	m $\longrightarrow$ accumulator
ADD =m	c(accumulator) $+$ m $\longrightarrow$ accumulator
MPY =m	c(accumulator) $*$ m $\longrightarrow$ accumulator

†Let us assume that ADD and MPY refer to floating-point operations.

Here the notation c(m) $\longrightarrow$ accumulator, for example, means the contents of memory location m are to be placed in the accumulator. The expression =m denotes the numerical value m. With these comments, the effects of the seven instructions should be obvious.

The output of the parser is a tree (or some representation of one) which represents the syntactic structure inherent in the string of tokens coming out of the lexical analyzer. From this tree, and the information stored in the symbol table, it is possible to construct the object code. In practice, tree construction and code generation are often carried out simultaneously, but conceptually it is easier to think of these two processes as occurring serially.

There are several methods for specifying how the intermediate code is to be constructed from the syntax tree. One method which is particularly elegant and effective is the *syntax-directed translation*. Here we associate with each node n a string $C(n)$ of intermediate code. The code for node n is constructed by concatenating the code strings associated with the descendants of n and other fixed strings in a fixed order. Thus translation proceeds from the bottom up (i.e., from the leaves toward the root). The fixed strings and fixed order are determined by the algorithm used. More will be said about this in Chapters 3 and 9.

An important problem which arises is how to select the code $C(n)$ for each node n such that $C(n)$ at the root is the desired code for the entire statement. In general, some interpretation must be placed on $C(n)$ such that the interpretation can be uniformly applied to all situations in which node n can appear.

For arithmetic assignment statements, the desired interpretation is fairly natural and will be explained in the following paragraphs. In general, the interpretation must be specified by the compiler designer if the method of syntax-directed translation is to be used. This task may be easy or hard, and in difficult cases, the detailed structure of the tree may have to be adjusted to aid in the translation process.

For a specific example, we shall describe a syntax-directed translation of simple arithmetic expressions. We notice that in Fig. 1.3, there are three types of interior nodes, depending on whether their middle descendant is labeled $=$, $+$, or $*$. These three types of nodes are shown in Fig. 1.4, where

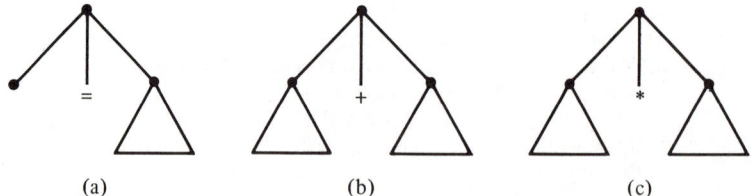

(a)   (b)   (c)

Fig. 1.4   Types of interior nodes.

$\triangle$ represents an arbitrary subtree (possibly a single node). We observe that for any arithmetic assignment statement involving only arithmetic operators $+$ and $*$, we can construct a tree with one node of type (a) (the root) and other interior nodes of types (b) and (c) only.

The code associated with a node n will be subject to the following interpretation:

(1) If n is a node of type (a), then $C(n)$ will be code which computes the value of the expression on the right and stores it in the location reserved for the identifier labeling the left descendant.

(2) If n is a node of type (b) or (c), then $C(n)$ is code which, when preceded by the operation code LOAD, brings to the accumulator the value of the subtree dominated by n.

Thus, in Fig. 1.3, when preceded by LOAD, $C(n_1)$ brings to the accumulator the value of $\langle id \rangle_2 + \langle id \rangle_3$, and $C(n_2)$ brings to the accumulator the value of $(\langle id \rangle_2 + \langle id \rangle_3) * \langle id \rangle_4$. $C(n_3)$ is code, which brings the latter value to the accumulator and stores it in the location of $\langle id \rangle_1$.

We must consider how to build $C(n)$ from the code for n's descendants. In what follows, we assume that assembly language statements are to be generated in one string, with a semicolon or a new line separating the statements. Also, we assume that assigned to each node n of the tree is a *level number* $l(n)$, which denotes the maximum length of a path from that node to a leaf. Thus, $l(n) = 0$ if n is a leaf, and if n has descendants $n_1, \ldots, n_k$, $l(n) = \max_{1 \le i \le k} l(n_i) + 1$. We can compute $l(n)$ bottom up, at the same time that $C(n)$ is computed. The purpose of recording levels is to control the use of temporary stores. We must never store two needed quantities in the same temporary location simultaneously. Figure 1.5 shows the level numbers of each node in the tree of Fig. 1.3.

We shall now define a syntax-directed code generation algorithm to

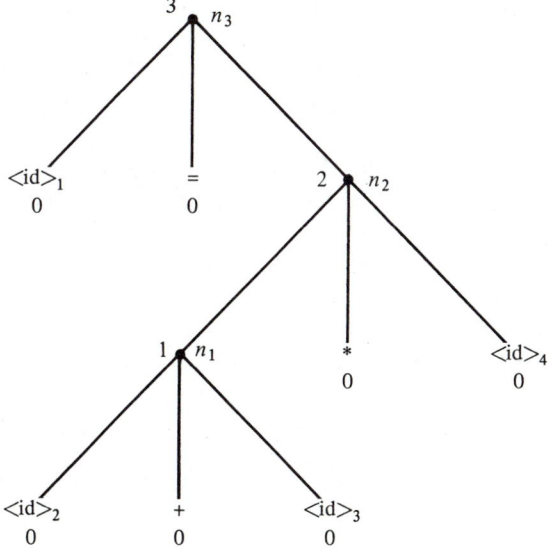

Fig. 1.5 Level numbers.

compute $C(n)$ for all nodes n of a tree consisting of leaves, a root of type (a), and interior nodes of either type (b) or type (c).

ALGORITHM 1.1

Syntax-directed translation of simple assignment statements.

Input. A labeled ordered tree representing an assignment statement involving arithmetic operations $+$ and $*$ only. We assume that the level of each node has been computed.

Output. Assembly language code to perform the assignment.

Method. Do steps (1) and (2) for all nodes of level 0. Then do steps (3), (4), (5) on all nodes of level 1, then level 2, and so forth, until all nodes have been acted upon.

    (1) Suppose that n is a leaf with label $\langle id \rangle_j$.
        (i) Suppose that entry j in the identifier table is a variable. Then $C(n)$ is the name of that variable.
        (ii) Suppose that entry j in the identifier table is a constant k. Then $C(n)$ is '$=k$.'†

    (2) If n is a leaf, with label $=$, $*$, or $+$, then $C(n)$ is the empty string. (In this algorithm, we do not need or wish to produce an output for leaves labeled $=$, $*$, or $+$.)

    (3) If n is a node of type (a) and its descendants are n_1, n_2, and n_3, then $C(n)$ is 'LOAD' $C(n_3)$ '; STORE' $C(n_1)$.

    (4) If n is a node of type (b) and its descendants are n_1, n_2, and n_3, then $C(n)$ is $C(n_3)$ '; STORE \$' $l(n)$ '; LOAD' $C(n_1)$ '; ADD \$' $l(n)$.

This sequence of instructions uses a temporary location whose name is the character \$ followed by the level number of node n. It is straightforward to see that when this sequence is preceded by LOAD, the value finally residing in the accumulator will be the sum of the values of the expressions dominated by n_1 and n_3.

We make two comments on the choice of temporary names. First, these names are chosen to start with \$ so that they cannot be confused with the identifier names in FORTRAN. Second, because of the way $l(n)$ is chosen, we can claim that $C(n)$ contains no reference to a temporary \$i if i is greater than $l(n)$. Thus, in particular, $C(n_1)$ contains no reference to '\$' $l(n)$. We can thus guarantee that the value stored into '\$' $l(n)$ will still be there when it is added to the accumulator.

    (5) If all is as in (4) but node n is of type (c), then $C(n)$ is

$$C(n_3) \text{'; STORE \$' } l(n) \text{ '; LOAD' } C(n_1) \text{ '; MPY \$' } l(n).$$

This code has the desired effect, with the desired result appearing in the accumulator.   □

---

†For emphasis, we surround with quotes those strings which represent themselves, rather than naming a string.

We leave a proof of the correctness for Algorithm 1.1 for the Exercises. It proceeds recursively on the height (i.e., level) of a node.

Example 1.4

Let us apply Algorithm 1.1 to the tree of Fig. 1.3. The tree given in Fig. 1.6 has the code associated with each node explicitly shown on the tree. The nodes labeled $\langle id \rangle_1$ through $\langle id \rangle_4$ are given the associated code COST,

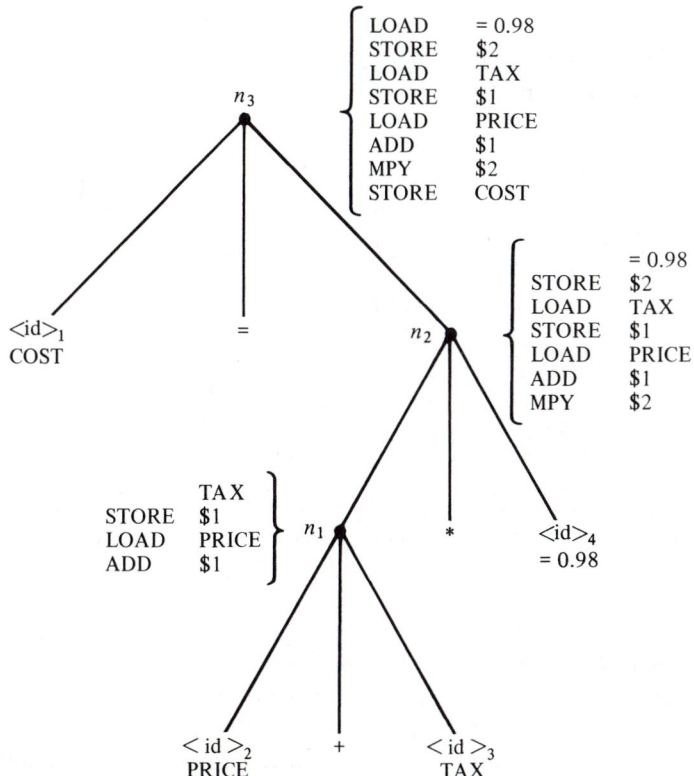

Fig. 1.6 Tree with generated code.

PRICE, TAX, and $=0.98$, respectively. We are now in a position to compute $C(n_1)$. Since $l(n_1) = 1$, the formula of rule (4) gives

$$C(n_1) = \text{'TAX; STORE \$1; LOAD PRICE; ADD \$1'}$$

Thus, when preceded by LOAD, $C(n_1)$ produces the sum of PRICE and TAX in the accumulator, although it does it in an awkward way. The code optimization process can "iron out" some of this awkwardness, or the rules by which the object code is constructed can be elaborated to take care of some special cases.

Next we can evaluate $C(n_2)$ using rule (5), and get

$$C(n_2) = \text{'=0.98; STORE \$2; LOAD' } C(n_1) \text{ '; MPY \$2'}$$

Here, $C(n_1)$ is the string mentioned in the previous paragraph, and $2 is used as temporary, since $l(n_2) = 2$.

We evaluate $C(n_3)$ using rule (3) and get

$$C(n_3) = \text{'LOAD' } C(n_2) \text{ '; STORE COST'}$$

The list of assembly language instructions (with semicolons replaced by new lines) which form the translation of our original "COST $= \cdots$" statement is

(1.2.2)

```
LOAD    =0.98
STORE   $2
LOAD    TAX
STORE   $1
LOAD    PRICE
ADD     $1
MPY     $2
STORE   COST    ☐
```

1.2.6. Code Optimization

In many situations it is desirable to have compilers produce object programs that run efficiently. *Code optimization* is the term generally applied to attempts to make object programs more "efficient," e.g., faster running or more compact.

There is a great spectrum of possibilities for code optimization. At one extreme is true algorithm optimization. Here a compiler might attempt to obtain some idea of the functions that are defined by the procedure specified by the source language program. If a function is recognized, then the compiler might substitute a more efficient procedure to compute a given function and generate machine code for that procedure.

Unfortunately optimization of this nature is exceedingly difficult. It is a sad fact that there is no algorithmic way to find the shortest or fastest-running program equivalent to a given program. In fact it can be shown in an abstract way that there exist algorithms which can be speeded up indefinitely. That is to say, there are some recursive functions for which any given algorithm defining that function can be made to run arbitrarily faster for large enough inputs.

Thus the term optimization is a complete misnomer—in practice we must be content with *code improvement*. Various code improvement techniques can be employed at various phases of the compilation process.

In general, what we can do is perform a sequence of transformations on a given program in hopes of transforming the program to a more efficient one. Such transformations must, of course, preserve the effect of the program on the outside world. These transformations can be applied at various times during the compilation process. For example, we can manipulate the input program itself, the structures produced in the syntax analysis phase, or the code produced as output of the code generation phase. In Chapter 11, we shall discuss code optimization in more detail.

In the remainder of this section we shall discuss some transformations which can be applied to shorten the code (1.2.2):

(1) If we assume that $+$ is a commutative operator, then we can replace a sequence of instructions of the form LOAD α; ADD β by the sequence LOAD β; ADD α, for any α and β. We require, however, that there be no transfer to the statement ADD β from anywhere in the program.

(2) Likewise, if we assume that $*$ is a commutative operator, we can replace LOAD α; MPY β by LOAD β; MPY α.

(3) For any α, a sequence of statements of the form STORE α; LOAD α can be deleted, provided either that α is not subsequently used or that α is stored into before being used again. (We can more often delete the first statement LOAD α alone; to do so, it is required only that no transfers to the statement LOAD α occur elsewhere in the program.)

(4) The sequence LOAD α; STORE β can be deleted if it is followed by another LOAD, provided that there is no transfer to STORE β and that subsequent mention of β is replaced by α until, but not including, such time as another STORE β instruction appears.

Example 1.5

These four transformations have been selected for their applicability to (1.2.2). In general there would be a large set of transformations, and they would be tried in various combinations. In (1.2.2), we notice that rule (1) applies to LOAD PRICE; ADD \$1, and we can, on speculation, temporarily replace these instructions by LOAD \$1; ADD PRICE, obtaining the code

(1.2.3)

LOAD	=0.98
STORE	\$2
LOAD	TAX
STORE	\$1
LOAD	\$1
ADD	PRICE
MPY	\$2
STORE	COST

We now observe that in (1.2.3), the sequence STORE $1; LOAD $1 can be deleted by rule (3). Thus we obtain the code†

(1.2.4)
```
LOAD    =0.98
STORE   $2
LOAD    TAX
ADD     PRICE
MPY     $2
STORE   COST
```

We can now apply rule (4) to the sequence LOAD =0.98; STORE $2. These two instructions are deleted and $2 in the instruction MPY $2 is replaced by MPY =0.98. The final code is

(1.2.5)
```
LOAD    TAX
ADD     PRICE
MPY     =0.98
STORE   COST
```

The code of (1.2.5) is the shortest that can be obtained using our four transformations and is the shortest under any set of reasonable transformations. □

1.2.7. Error Analysis and Recovery

We have so far assumed that the input to the compiler is a well-formed program and that each phase of compiling can be carried out in a way that makes sense. In practice, this will not be the case in many compilations. Programming is still much an art, and there is ample opportunity for various kinds of bugs to creep into most programs. Even if we feel that we have understood the problem for which we are writing a program, and even if we have chosen the proper algorithm to solve the problem, we often cannot be sure that the program we have written faithfully executes the algorithm it should perform.

A compiler has an opportunity to detect errors in a program in at least three of the phases of compilation—lexical analysis, syntactic analysis, and code generation. When an error is encountered, it is a difficult job, bordering on an application of "artificial intelligence," for the compiler to be able to look at an arbitrary faulty program and tell what was probably meant. However, in certain cases, it is easy to make a good guess. For example, if the source statement $A = B * 2C$ is seen, there is a high likelihood that $A = B * 2 * C$ was meant.

---

†A similar simplification could be obtained using rule (4) directly. However, we are trying to give some examples of how different types of transformations can be used.

In general, when the compiler comes to a point in the input stream where it cannot continue producing a valid parse, some compilers attempt to make a "minimal" change in the input in order for the parse to proceed. Some possible changes are

(1) Alteration of a single character. For example, if the parser is given "identifier" INTEJER by the lexical analyzer and it is not proper for an identifier to appear at this point in the program, the parser may guess that the keyword INTEGER was meant.

(2) Insertion of a single token. For example, the parser can replace 2C by $2 * C$. ($2 + C$ would do as well, but in this case, we "know" that $2 * C$ is more likely.)

(3) Deletion of a single token. For example, a comma is often incorrectly inserted after the 10 in a FORTRAN statement such as DO 10 I $= 1, 20$.

(4) Simple permutation of tokens. For example, INTEGER I might be written incorrectly as I INTEGER.

In many programming languages, statements are easily identified. If it becomes hopeless to parse a particular (ill-formed) statement, even after applying changes such as those above, it is often possible to ignore the statement completely and continue parsing as though this ill-formed statement did not appear.

In general, however, there is very little of a mathematical nature known about error recovery algorithms and algorithms to generate "good" diagnostics. In Chapters 4 and 5, we shall discuss certain parsing algorithms, LL, LR, and Earley's algorithm, which have the property that as soon as the input stream is such that there is no possible following sequence which could make a well-formed input, the algorithms announce this fact. This property is useful in error recovery and analysis, but some parsing algorithms discussed do not possess it.

1.2.8. Summary

Our conceptual model of a compiler is summarized in Fig. 1.7. The code optimization phase is shown occurring after the code generation phase, but as we remarked earlier, various attempts at code optimization can be performed throughout the compiler.

An error analysis and recovery procedure can be called from the lexical analysis phase, syntactic analysis phase, or code generation phase, and if the recovery is successful, control is returned to the phase from which the error recovery procedure was called. Errors in which no token appears at some point in the input stream are detected during lexical analysis. Errors in which the input can be broken into tokens but no tree structure can be placed on these tokens are detected during syntactic analysis. Finally, errors in which the input has a syntactic structure, but no meaningful code can be

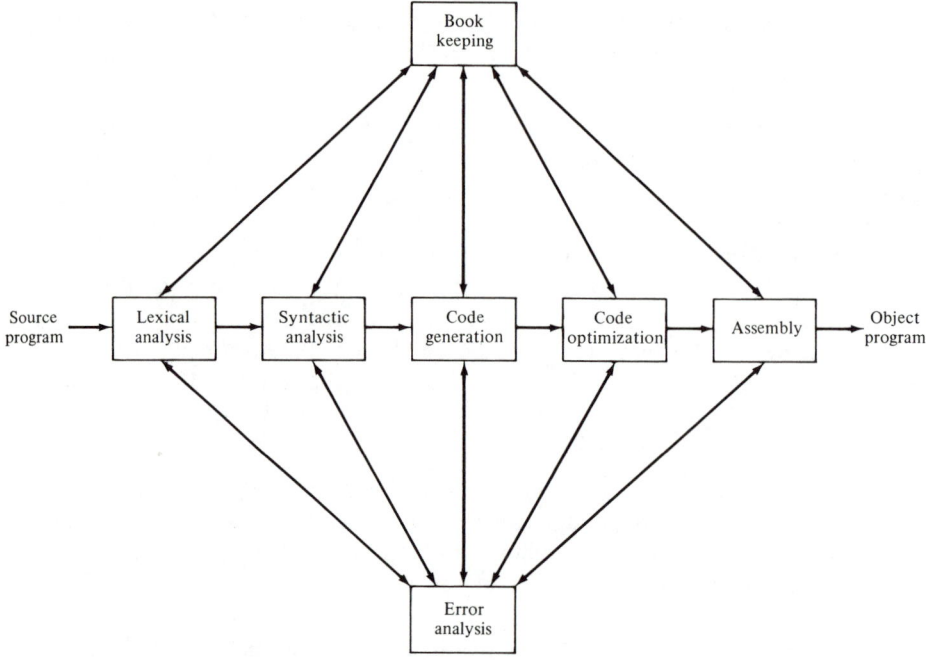

Fig. 1.7   Model of a compiler.

generated from this structure, are detected during code generation. An example of this situation would be a variable used without declaration. The parser ignores the data component of tokens and so could not detect this error.

The symbol tables (bookkeeping) are produced in the lexical analysis process and in some situations also during syntactic analysis when, say, attributes and the identifiers to which they refer are connected in the tree structure being formed. These tables are used in the code generation phase and possibly in the assembly phase of compilation.

A final phase, which we refer to as assembly, is shown in Fig. 1.7. In this phase the intermediate code is processed to produce the final machine language representation of the object program. Some compilers may produce machine language code directly as the result of code generation, so that the assembly phase may not be explicitly present.

The model of a compiler we have portrayed in Fig. 1.7 is a first-order approximation to a real compiler. For example, some compilers are designed to operate using a very small amount of storage and as a consequence may consist of a large number of phases which are called upon successively to gradually change a source program into an object program.

Our goal is not to tabulate all possible ways in which compilers have been built. Rather we are interested in studying the fundamental problems that arise in the design of compilers and other language-processing devices.

EXERCISES

*1.2.1. Describe the syntax and semantics of a FORTRAN assignment statement.

*1.2.2. Can your favorite programming language be used to define any recursively enumerable set? Will a given compiler necessarily compile the resulting program?

1.2.3. Give an example of a FORTRAN program which is syntactically well formed but which does not define an algorithm.

**1.2.4. What is the maximum lookahead needed for the direct lexical analysis of FORTRAN? By lookahead is meant the number of symbols which are scanned by the analyzer but do not form part of the token found.

**1.2.5. What is the maximum lookahead needed for the direct lexical analysis of ALGOL 60? You may assume that superfluous blanks and end of card markers have been deleted.

1.2.6. Parse the statement $X = A * B + C * D$ using a tree with interior nodes of the forms shown in Fig. 1.4. *Hint:* Recall that, conventionally, multiplications are performed before additions in the absence of parentheses.

1.2.7. Parse the statement $X = A * (B + C) * D$, as in Exercise 1.2.6. *Hint:* When several operands are multiplied together, we assume that order of multiplication is unimportant.† Choose any order you like.

1.2.8. Use the rules of code generation developed in Section 1.2.5 to translate the parse trees of Exercises 1.2.6 and 1.2.7 in a syntax-directed way.

*1.2.9. Does the transformation of LOAD α; STORE β; LOAD γ; STORE δ into LOAD γ; STORE δ; LOAD α; STORE β preserve the input–output relation of programs? If not, what restrictions must be placed on identifiers $\alpha, \beta, \gamma, \delta$? We assume that no transfers into the interior of the sequence occur.

1.2.10. Give some transformations on assembly code which preserve the input–output relation of programs.

*1.2.11. Construct a syntax-directed translation for arithmetic assignment statements involving $+$ and $*$ which will, in particular, map the parse of Fig. 1.3 directly into the assembly code (1.2.5).

---

†Strictly speaking, order may be important due to overflow and/or rounding.

*1.2.12. Design a syntax-directed translation scheme which will generate object code for expressions involving both real and integer arithmetic. Assume that the type of each identifier is known, and that the result of operating on a real and an integer is a real.

*1.2.13. Prove that Algorithm 1.1 operates correctly. You must first define when an input assignment statement and output assembly code are equivalent.

Research Problem

There are many research areas and open problems concerned with compiling and translation of algorithms. These will be mentioned in more appropriate chapters. However, we mention one here, because this area will not be treated in any detail in the book.

1.2.14. Develop techniques for proving compilers correct. Some work has been done in this area and in the more general area of proving programs and/or algorithms correct. (See the following Bibliographic Notes.) However, it is clear that more work in the area is needed.

An entirely different approach to the problem of producing reliable compilers is to develop theory applicable to their empirical testing. That is, we assume we "know" our compiling algorithms to be correct. We want to test whether a particular program implements them correctly. In the first approach, above, one would attempt to prove the equivalence of the written program and abstract compiling algorithm. The second approach suggested is to devise a finite set of inputs to the compiler such that if these are compiled correctly, one can say with reasonably certainty (say a 99% confidence level) that the compiler program has no bugs. Apparently, one would have to make some assumption about the frequency and nature of programming errors in the compiler program itself.

BIBLIOGRAPHIC NOTES

The development of compilers and compiling techniques paralleled that of programming languages. The first FORTRAN compiler was designed to produce efficient object code [Backus et al., 1957]. Numerous compilers have been written since, and several new compiling techniques have emerged. The greatest strides have occurred in lexical and syntactic analysis and in some understanding of code generation techniques.

There are a large number of papers in the literature relating to compiler design. We shall not attempt to mention all these sources here. Comprehensive surveys of the history of compilers and compiler development can be found in Rosen [1967], Feldman and Gries [1968], and Cocke and Schwartz [1970]. Several books that describe compiler construction techniques are Randell and Russell [1964], McKeeman et al., [1970], Cocke and Schwartz [1970], and Gries [1971]. Hopgood [1969] gives a brief but readable survey of compiling techniques. An elementary discussion of compilers is given in Lee [1967].

Several compilers have been written which emphasize comprehensive error diagnostics, such as DITRAN [Moulton and Muller, 1967] and IITRAN [Dewar et al., 1969]. Also, a few compilers have been written which attempt to correct each error encountered and to execute the object program no matter how many errors have been encountered. The philosophy here is to continue compilation and execution in spite of errors, in an effort to uncover as many errors as possible. Examples of such compilers are CORC [Conway and Maxwell, 1963, and Freeman, 1964], CUPL [Conway and Maxwell, 1968], and PL/C [Conway et al., 1970].

Spelling mistakes are a frequent source of errors in programs. Freeman [1964] and Morgan [1970] describe some techniques they have found effective in correcting spelling errors in programs.

A general survey of error recovery in compiling can be found in Elspas et al. [1971].

Some work on providing the theoretical foundations for proving that compilers work correctly is reported in McCarthy [1963], McCarthy and Painter [1967], Painter [1970], and Floyd [1967a].

The implementation of a compiler is a task that involves a considerable amount of effort. A large number of programming systems called compiler-compilers have been developed in an attempt to make the implementation of compilers a less onerous task. Brooker and Morris [1963], Cheatham [1965], Cheatham and Standish [1970], Ingerman [1966], Irons [1963b], Feldman [1966], McClure [1965], McKeeman et al. [1970], Reynolds [1965], Schorre [1964], and Warshall and Shapiro [1964] are just a few of the many references on this subject. A compiler-compiler can be simply viewed as a programming language in which a source program is the description of a compiler for some language and the object program is the compiler for that language.

As such, the source program for a compiler-compiler is merely a formalism for describing a compiler. Consequently, the source program must contain explicitly or implicitly, a description of the lexical analyzer, the syntactic analyzer, the code generator, and the various other phases of the compiler to be constructed. The compiler-compiler is an attempt at providing an environment in which these descriptions can be easily written down.

Several compiler-compilers provide some variant of a syntax-directed translation scheme for the specification of a compiler, and some also provide an automatic parsing mechanism. TMG [McClure, 1965] is a prime example of this type of system. Other compiler-compilers, such as TGS [Cheatham, 1965] for example, instead provide an elaborate high-level language in which to describe the various algorithms that go into the making of a compiler. Feldman and Gries [1968] have provided a comprehensive survey of compiler-compilers.

1.3. OTHER APPLICATIONS OF PARSING AND TRANSLATING ALGORITHMS

In this section we shall mention two areas, other than compiling, in which hierarchical structures such as those found in parsing and translating algorithms can play a major role. These are the areas of natural language translation and pattern recognition.

1.3.1. Natural Languages

It would seem that text in a natural language could be translated, either to another natural language or to machine language (if the sentences described a procedure), exactly as programming languages are translated. Problems first appear in the parsing phase, however. Computer languages are precisely defined (with occasional exceptions, of course), and the structure of statements can be easily discerned. The usual model of the structure of statements is a tree, as described in Section 1.2.4.

Natural languages, first of all, are afflicted with both syntactic and semantic ambiguities. To take English as the obvious example of a natural language, the sentence "I have drawn butter" has at least two meanings, depending on whether "drawn" is an adjective or part of the verb of the sentence. Thus it is impossible always to produce a unique parse tree for an English sentence, especially if the sentence is treated outside of the context in which it appears.

A more difficult problem concerning natural languages is that the words, i.e., terminal symbols of the language, relate to other words in the sentence, outside the sentence and possibly the general environment itself. Thus the simple tree structure is not always sufficient to describe all the information about English sentences that one would wish to have around when translation (the analog of code generation for programming languages) occurred.

For a commonly used example, the noun "pen" is really at least two different nouns which we might refer to as "fountain pen" and "pig pen." We might wish to translate English into some language in which "fountain pen" and "pig pen" are distinct words. If we were given the sentence "This pen leaks" to translate, it seems clear that "fountain pen" is correct. However, if the sentence were taken from the report *Preventing Nose Colds in Hogs*," we might want to reconsider our decision.

The point to be made is that the meaning and structure of an English sentence can be determined only by examining its total environment: the surrounding sentences, physical information (i.e., "Put the pen in the glass" refers to "fountain pen" because a pig pen won't fit in a glass), and even the nature of the speaker or writer (i.e., what does "This pen leaks" mean if the speaker is a convict?).

To describe in more detail the information that can be gleaned from natural language sentences, linguists use structure systems that are more complicated than the tree structures sufficient for programming languages. Many of these efforts fall under the heading of context-sensitive grammars and transformational grammars. We shall not cover either theory in detail, although context-sensitive grammars are defined in the next chapter, and a rudimentary form of transformational grammar can be discussed as a generalized form of syntax-directed translation on trees. This notion will be mentioned in Chapter 9. The bibliographic notes for this section include some places to look for more information on natural language parsing.

1.3.2. Structural Description of Patterns

Certain important sets of patterns have natural descriptions that lend themselves to a form of syntactic analysis. For example, Shaw [1970] analyzed cloud chamber photographs by putting a tree structure on relevant lines and curves appearing therein. We shall here describe a particularly appealing way of defining sets of graphs, called "web grammars" [Pfaltz and Rosenfeld, 1969]. While a complete description of web grammars would require knowledge of Section 2.1, we can give a simple example here to illustrate the essential ideas.

Example 1.6

Our example concerns graphs called "d-charts,"† which can be thought of as the flow charts for a programming language whose programs are defined by the following rules:

(1) A simple assignment statement is a program.

(2) If S_1 and S_2 are programs, then so is $S_1; S_2$.

(3) If S_1 and S_2 are programs and A is a predicate, then

$$\textbf{if } A \textbf{ then } S_1 \textbf{ else } S_2 \textbf{ end}$$

is a program.

(4) If S is a program and A a predicate, then

$$\textbf{while } A \textbf{ do } S \textbf{ end}$$

is a program.

We can write flow charts for all such programs, where the nodes (blocks) of the flow chart represent code either to test a predicate or perform a simple assignment statement. All the d-charts can be constructed by beginning with a single node, representing a program, and repeatedly replacing nodes representing programs by one of the three structures shown in Fig. 1.8. These replacement rules correspond to rules (2), (3), and (4) above, respectively.

The rules for connecting these structures to the rest of the graph are the following. Suppose that node n_0 is replaced by the structure of Fig. 1.8(a), (b), or (c).

(1) Edges entering n_0 now enter n_1, n_3, or n_6, respectively.

(2) An edge from n_0 to node n is replaced by an edge from n_2 to n in Fig. 1.8(a), by edges from both n_4 and n_5 to n in Fig. 1.8(b), and by an edge from n_6 to n in Fig. 1.8(c).

Nodes n_3 and n_6 represent predicate tests and may not be further replaced. The other nodes represent programs and may be further replaced.

---

†The d honors E. Dijkstra.

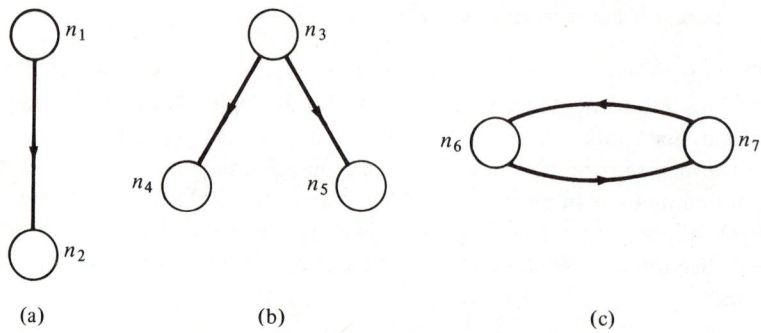

Fig. 1.8 Structures representing subprograms in a d-chart.

Let us build the d-chart which corresponds, in a sense, to a program of the form

> **if** B_1 **then**
>> **while** B_2 **do**
>>> **if** B_3 **then** S_1 **else** S_2 **end end**;
>>
>> S_3
>
> **else if** B_4 **then**
>> S_4;
>> S_5;
>> **while** B_5 **do** S_6 **end**
>
> **else** S_7 **end end**

The entire program is of the form **if** B_1 **then** S_8 **else** S_9 **end**, where S_8 represents everything from the first **while** to S_3 and S_9 represents **if** $B_4 \cdots S_7$ **end**. We can also show this analysis by replacing a single node by the structure of Fig. 1.8(b).

Continuing the analysis, S_8 is of the form S_{10}; S_3, where S_{10} is **while** $B_2 \cdots S_2$ **end end**. Thus we can reflect this analysis by replacing node n_4 of Fig. 1.8(b) by Fig. 1.8(a). The result is shown in Fig. 1.9(a). Then, we see S_{10} is of the form **while** B_2 **do** S_{11} **end**, where S_{11} is **if** $B_3 \cdots S_2$ **end**. We can thus replace the left direct descendant of the root in Fig. 1.9(a) by the structure of Fig. 1.8(c). The result is shown in Fig. 1.9(b).

The result of analyzing the program in this way is shown in Fig. 1.10. Here, we have taken the liberty of drawing contours around each node that is replaced and of making sure that all subsequent replacements remain inside the contour. Thus we can place a natural tree structure on the d-chart by representing nodes of the d-chart as leaves, and contours by interior nodes. Nodes have as direct ancestor the contour most closely including what they represent. The tree structure is shown in Fig. 1.11. Nodes are labeled by the node or contour they represent. ☐

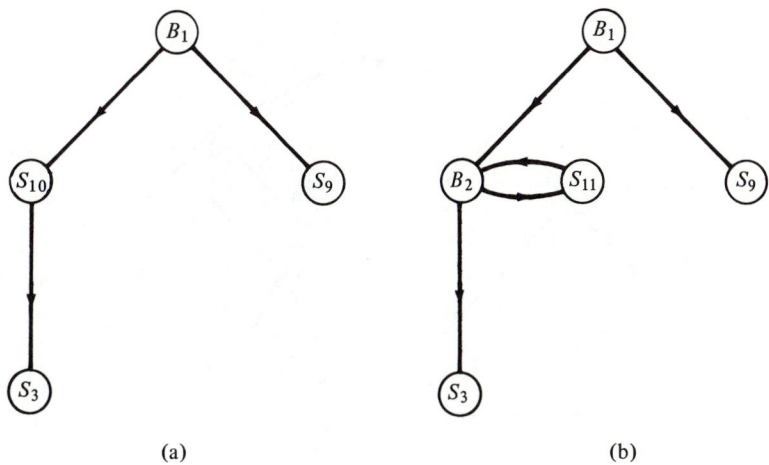

Fig. 1.9 Constructing a d-chart.

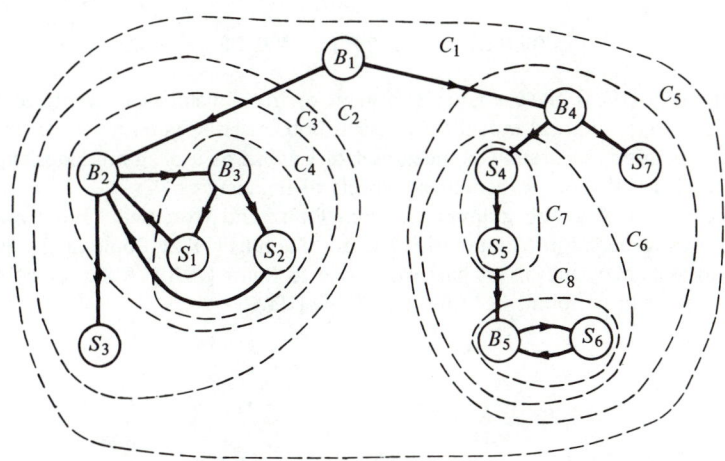

Fig. 1.10 Complete d-chart.

In a sense, the example above is a fraud. The d-chart structure, as reflected in Fig. 1.11, is essentially the same structure that the parsing phase of a compiler would place on the original program. Thus it appears that we are discussing the same kind of syntax analysis as in Section 1.2.3. However, it should be borne in mind that this kind of structural analysis can be done without reference to the program, looking only at the d-chart. Moreover, while we used this example of a web grammar because of its relation to programming languages, there are many purely graph-theoretic notions that

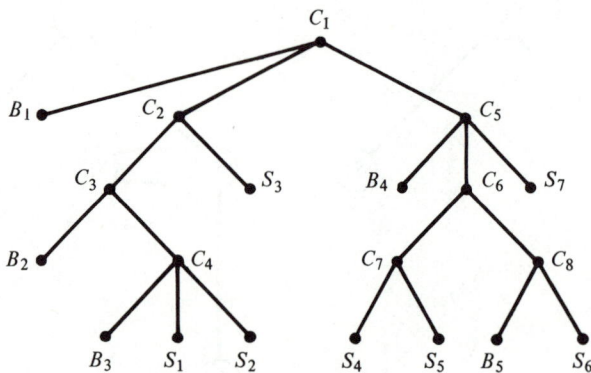

Fig. 1.11 Tree describing d-chart structure.

can be defined using web grammars (suitably generalized from Example 1.8), for example, the class of planar graphs or the class of binary trees.

BIBLIOGRAPHIC NOTES

Chomsky [1965] gives a good treatment of the difficulties in trying to find a satisfactory grammatical model for English. Bobrow [1963] surveys efforts at using English or, more accurately, some subset of English as a programming language. Bar-Hillel [1964] surveys theoretical aspects of linguistics.

The notion of a web grammar is from Pfaltz and Rosenfeld [1969] and the theory was extended in Montanari [1970] and Pavlidis [1972]. Some of the original work in syntactic analysis of patterns is due to Shaw [1970]. A survey of results in this area can be found in Miller and Shaw [1968].

2 ELEMENTS OF LANGUAGE THEORY

In this chapter we shall present those aspects of formal language theory which are relevant to parsing and translation. Initially, we shall concentrate on the syntactic aspects of language. As most of the syntax of modern programming languages can be described by means of a context-free grammar, we shall focus our attention on the theory of context-free languages.

We shall first study an important subclass of the context-free languages, namely the regular sets. Concepts from the theory of regular sets have widespread application and pervade much of the material of this book.

Another important class of languages is the deterministic context-free languages. These are context-free languages that have grammars which are easily parsed, and fortunately, or by intent, modern programming languages can be viewed as deterministic context-free languages with good, although not complete, precision.

These three classes of languages, the context-free, regular, and deterministic context-free, will be defined and some of their principal properties given. Since the theory of languages encompasses an enormous body of material, and since not all of it is relevant to parsing and translation, some important theorems of language theory are here proved in a very sketchy way or relegated to the Exercises. We try to emphasize only those aspects of language theory which are useful in the development of this book.

As in Chapters 0 and 1, we invite the reader who has been introduced to the theory of languages to skip or skim this chapter.

2.1. REPRESENTATIONS FOR LANGUAGES

In this section, we shall discuss from a general point of view the two principal methods of defining languages—the generator and the recognizer.

We shall discuss only the most common kind of generator, the Chomsky grammar. We treat recognizers in somewhat greater generality, and in subsequent sections we shall introduce some of the great variety of recognizers that have been studied.

2.1.1. Motivation

Our definition of a language L is a set of finite-length strings over some finite alphabet Σ. The first important question is how to represent L when L is infinite. Certainly, if L consisted of a finite number of strings, then one obvious way would be to list all the strings in L.

However, for many languages it is not possible (or perhaps not desirable) to put an upper bound on the length of the longest string in that language. Consequently, in many cases it is reasonable to consider languages which contain arbitrarily many strings. Obviously, languages of this nature cannot be specified by an exhaustive enumeration of the sentences of the language, and some other representation must be sought. Invariably, we want our specification of a language to be of finite size, although the language being specified may not be finite.

There are several methods of specification which fulfill this requirement. One method is to use a generative system, called a grammar. Each sentence in the language can be constructed by well-defined methods, using the rules (usually called productions) of the grammar. One advantage of defining a language by means of a grammar is that the operations of parsing and translation are often made simpler by the structure imparted to the sentences of the language by the grammar. We shall treat grammars, particularly the "context-free" grammars, in detail.

A second method for language specification is to use a procedure which when presented with an arbitrary input string will halt and answer "yes" after a finite amount of computation if that string is in the language. In the most general case, we could allow the procedure to either halt and answer "no" or to continue operating forever if the string under consideration were not in the language. In practical situations, however, we must insist that the procedure be an algorithm, so that it will halt for all inputs.

We shall use a somewhat stylized device to represent procedures for defining languages. This device, called a *recognizer*, will be introduced in Section 2.1.4.

2.1.2. Grammars

Grammars are probably the most important class of generators of languages. A grammar is a mathematical system for defining a language, as well as a device for giving the sentences in the language a useful structure. In this section we shall look at a class of grammars called Chomsky grammars, or sometimes phrase structure grammars.

A grammar for a language L uses two finite disjoint sets of symbols. These are the set of nonterminal symbols, which we shall often denote by N,† and the set of terminal symbols, which we shall denote by Σ. The set of terminal symbols is the alphabet over which the language is defined. Nonterminal symbols are used in the generation of words in the language in a way which will become clear later.

The heart of a grammar is a finite set P of formation rules, or productions as we shall call them, which describe how the sentences of the language are to be generated. A production is merely a pair of strings, or, more precisely, an element of $(N \cup \Sigma)^*N(N \cup \Sigma)^* \times (N \cup \Sigma)^*$. That is, the first component is any string containing at least one nonterminal, and the second component is any string.

For example, a pair (AB, CDE) might be a production. If it is determined that some string α can be generated (or "derived") by the grammar, and α has AB, the left side of the production, as a substring, then we can form a new string β by replacing one instance of the substring AB in α by CDE. We then say that β is derived by the grammar. For example, if $FGABH$ can be derived, then $FGCDEH$ can also be derived. The language defined by the grammar is the set of strings which consist only of terminals and which can be derived starting with one particular string consisting of one designated symbol, usually denoted S.

CONVENTION

If (α, β) is a production, we use the descriptive shorthand $\alpha \longrightarrow \beta$ and refer to the production as $\alpha \longrightarrow \beta$ rather than (α, β).

We now give a formal definition of grammar.

DEFINITION

A *grammar* is a 4-tuple $G = (N, \Sigma, P, S)$ where

(1) N is a finite set of *nonterminal symbols* (sometimes called variables or syntactic categories).

(2) Σ is a finite set of *terminal symbols*, disjoint from N.

(3) P is a finite subset of

$$(N \cup \Sigma)^*N(N \cup \Sigma)^* \times (N \cup \Sigma)^*$$

An element (α, β) in P will be written $\alpha \longrightarrow \beta$ and called a *production*.

(4) S is a distinguished symbol in N called the *sentence* (or *start*) symbol.

Example 2.1

An example of a grammar is $G_1 = (\{A, S\}, \{0, 1\}, P, S)$, where P consists of

†According to our convention about alphabet names, this symbol is a capital Greek nu, although the reader will probably want to call it "en," as is more customary anyway.

$$S \longrightarrow 0A1$$

$$0A \longrightarrow 00A1$$

$$A \longrightarrow e$$

The nonterminal symbols are A and S and the terminal symbols are 0 and 1. □

A grammar defines a language in a recursive manner. We define a special kind of string called a *sentential form* of a grammar $G = (N, \Sigma, P, S)$ recursively as follows:

(1) S is a sentential form.
(2) If $\alpha\beta\gamma$ is a sentential form and $\beta \longrightarrow \delta$ is in P, then $\alpha\delta\gamma$ is also a sentential form.

A sentential form of G containing no nonterminal symbols is called a *sentence* generated by G.

The *language generated by a grammar* G, denoted $L(G)$, is the set of sentences generated by G.

We shall now introduce some terminology which we shall find useful. Let $G = (N, \Sigma, P, S)$ be a grammar. We can define a relation $\underset{G}{\Rightarrow}$ (to be read as *directly derives*) on $(N \cup \Sigma)^*$ as follows: If $\alpha\beta\gamma$ is a string in $(N \cup \Sigma)^*$ and $\beta \longrightarrow \delta$ is a production in P, then $\alpha\beta\gamma \underset{G}{\Rightarrow} \alpha\delta\gamma$.

We shall use $\underset{G}{\overset{+}{\Rightarrow}}$ (to be read *derives in a nontrivial way*) to denote the transitive closure of $\underset{G}{\Rightarrow}$, and $\underset{G}{\overset{*}{\Rightarrow}}$ (to be read *derives*) to denote the reflexive and transitive closure of $\underset{G}{\Rightarrow}$. When it is clear which grammar we are talking about, we shall drop the subscript G from $\Rightarrow$, $\overset{+}{\Rightarrow}$, and $\overset{*}{\Rightarrow}$.

We shall also use the notation $\overset{k}{\Rightarrow}$ to denote the k-fold product of the relation $\Rightarrow$. That is to say, $\alpha \overset{k}{\Rightarrow} \beta$ if there is a sequence $\alpha_0, \alpha_1, \ldots, \alpha_k$ of $k + 1$ strings (not necessarily distinct) such that $\alpha = \alpha_0, \alpha_{i-1} \Rightarrow \alpha_i$ for $1 \leq i \leq k$ and $\alpha_k = \beta$. This sequence of strings is called a *derivation of length k* of β from α in G. Thus, $L(G) = \{w \mid w \text{ is in } \Sigma^* \text{ and } S \overset{*}{\Rightarrow} w\}$. Also notice that $\alpha \overset{*}{\Rightarrow} \beta$ if and only if $\alpha \overset{i}{\Rightarrow} \beta$ for some $i \geq 0$, and $\alpha \overset{+}{\Rightarrow} \beta$ if and only if $\alpha \overset{i}{\Rightarrow} \beta$ for some $i \geq 1$.

Example 2.2

Let us consider grammar G_1 of Example 2.1 and the following derivation: $S \Rightarrow 0A1 \Rightarrow 00A11 \Rightarrow 0011$. That is, in the first step, S is replaced by $0A1$ according to the production $S \longrightarrow 0A1$. At the second step, $0A$ is replaced by $00A1$, and at the third, A is replaced by e. We may say that $S \overset{3}{\Rightarrow} 0011$, $S \overset{+}{\Rightarrow} 0011$, $S \overset{*}{\Rightarrow} 0011$, and that 0011 is in $L(G_1)$. It can be shown that

$$L(G_1) = \{0^n 1^n \mid n \geq 1\}$$

and we leave this result for the Exercises. $\square$

CONVENTION

A notational shorthand which is quite useful for representing a set of productions is to use

$$\alpha \longrightarrow \beta_1 \mid \beta_2 \mid \cdots \mid \beta_n$$

to denote the n productions

$$\alpha \longrightarrow \beta_1$$
$$\alpha \longrightarrow \beta_2$$
$$\vdots$$
$$\alpha \longrightarrow \beta_n$$

We shall also use the following conventions to represent various symbols and strings concerned with a grammar:

(1) a, b, c, and d represent terminals, as do the digits $0, 1, \ldots, 9$.

(2) A, B, C, D, and S represent nonterminals; S represents the start symbol.

(3) $U, V, \ldots, Z$ represent either nonterminals or terminals.

(4) $\alpha, \beta, \ldots$ represent strings of nonterminals and terminals.

(5) $u, v, \ldots, z$ represent strings of terminals only.

Subscripts and superscripts do not change these conventions. When a symbol obeys these conventions, we shall often omit mention of the convention. We can thus specify a grammar by merely listing its productions if all terminals and nonterminals obey conventions (1) and (2). Thus grammar G_1 can be specified simply as

$$S \longrightarrow 0A1$$
$$0A \longrightarrow 00A1$$
$$A \longrightarrow e$$

No mention of the nonterminal or terminal sets or the start symbol is necessary.

We now give further examples of grammars.

Example 2.3

Let $G = (\{\langle\text{digit}\rangle\}, \{0, 1, \ldots, 9\}, \{\langle\text{digit}\rangle \rightarrow 0 \mid 1 \mid \cdots \mid 9\}, \langle\text{digit}\rangle)$. Here $\langle\text{digit}\rangle$ is treated as a single nonterminal symbol. $L(G)$ is clearly the set of the ten decimal digits. Notice that $L(G)$ is a finite set.   □

Example 2.4

Let $G_0 = (\{E, T, F\}, \{a, +, *, (,)\}, P, E)$, where P consists of the productions

$$E \longrightarrow E + T \mid T$$
$$T \longrightarrow T * F \mid F$$
$$F \longrightarrow (E) \mid a$$

An example of a derivation in this grammar would be

$$
\begin{aligned}
E &\Longrightarrow E + T \\
&\Longrightarrow T + T \\
&\Longrightarrow F + T \\
&\Longrightarrow a + T \\
&\Longrightarrow a + T * F \\
&\Longrightarrow a + F * F \\
&\Longrightarrow a + a * F \\
&\Longrightarrow a + a * a
\end{aligned}
$$

$L(G_0)$ is the set of arithmetic expressions that can be built up using the symbols a, $+$, $*$, (, and).   □

The grammar in Example 2.4 will be used repeatedly in the book and is always referred to as G_0.

Example 2.5

Let G be defined by

$$
\begin{aligned}
S &\longrightarrow aSBC \mid abC \\
CB &\longrightarrow BC \\
bB &\longrightarrow bb \\
bC &\longrightarrow bc \\
cC &\longrightarrow cc
\end{aligned}
$$

We have the following derivation in G:

$$S \Longrightarrow aSBC$$
$$\Longrightarrow aabCBC$$
$$\Longrightarrow aabBCC$$
$$\Longrightarrow aabbCC$$
$$\Longrightarrow aabbcC$$
$$\Longrightarrow aabbcc$$

The language generated by G is $\{a^n b^n c^n \mid n \geq 1\}$. $\square$

Example 2.6

Let G be the grammar with productions

$$S \longrightarrow CD \qquad Ab \longrightarrow bA$$
$$C \longrightarrow aCA \qquad Ba \longrightarrow aB$$
$$C \longrightarrow bCB \qquad Bb \longrightarrow bB$$
$$AD \longrightarrow aD \qquad C \longrightarrow e$$
$$BD \longrightarrow bD \qquad D \longrightarrow e$$
$$Aa \longrightarrow aA$$

An example of a derivation in G is

$$S \Longrightarrow CD$$
$$\Longrightarrow aCAD$$
$$\Longrightarrow abCBAD$$
$$\Longrightarrow abBAD$$
$$\Longrightarrow abBaD$$
$$\Longrightarrow abaBD$$
$$\Longrightarrow ababD$$
$$\Longrightarrow abab$$

We shall show that $L(G) = \{ww \mid w \in \{a, b\}^*\}$. That is, $L(G)$ consists of strings of a's and b's of even length such that the first half of each string is the same as the second half.

Since $L(G)$ is a set, the easiest way to show that $L(G) = \{ww \mid w \in \{a, b\}^*\}$ is to show that $\{ww \mid w \in \{a, b\}^*\} \subseteq L(G)$ and that $L(G) \subseteq \{ww \mid w \in \{a, b\}^*\}$.

To show that $\{ww \,|\, w \in \{a, b\}^*\} \subseteq L(G)$ we must show that every string of the form ww can be derived from S. By a simple inductive proof we can show that the following derivations are possible in G:

(1) $S \Longrightarrow CD$.

(2) For $n \geq 0$,

$$C \overset{n}{\Longrightarrow} c_1 c_2 \cdots c_n C X_n X_{n-1} \cdots X_1$$
$$\Longrightarrow c_1 c_2 \cdots c_n X_n X_{n-1} \cdots X_1$$

where, for $1 \leq i \leq n$, $c_i = a$ if and only if $X_i = A$, and $c_i = b$ if and only if $X_i = B$.

(3)
$$X_n \cdots X_2 X_1 D \Longrightarrow X_n \cdots X_2 c_1 D$$
$$\overset{n-1}{\Longrightarrow} c_1 X_n \cdots X_2 D$$
$$\Longrightarrow c_1 X_n \cdots X_3 c_2 D$$
$$\overset{n-2}{\Longrightarrow} c_1 c_2 X_n \cdots X_3 D$$
$$\vdots$$
$$\Longrightarrow c_1 c_2 \cdots c_{n-1} X_n D$$
$$\Longrightarrow c_1 c_2 \cdots c_{n-1} c_n D$$
$$\Longrightarrow c_1 c_2 \cdots c_{n-1} c_n$$

The details of such an inductive proof are straightforward and will be omitted here.

In derivation (2), C derives a string of a's and b's followed by a mirror image string of A's and B's. In derivation (3), the A's and B's migrate to the right end of the string, where an A becomes a and B becomes b on contact with D, which acts as a right endmarker. The only way an A or B can be replaced by a terminal is for it to move to the right end of the string. In this fashion the string of A's and B's is reversed and thus matches the string of a's and b's derived from C in derivation (2).

Combining derivations (1), (2), and (3) we have for $n \geq 0$

$$S \overset{+}{\Longrightarrow} c_1 c_2 \cdots c_n c_1 c_2 \cdots c_n$$

where $c_i \in \{a, b\}$ for $1 \leq i \leq n$. Thus $\{ww \,|\, w \in \{a, b\}^*\} \subseteq L(G)$.

We would now like to show that $L(G) \subseteq \{ww \,|\, w \in \{a, b\}^*\}$. To do this we must show that S derives terminal strings only of the form ww. In general, to show that a grammar generates only strings of a certain form is a much more difficult matter than showing that it generates certain strings.

At this point it is convenient to define two homomorphisms g and h such that

$$g(a) = a, \qquad g(b) = b, \qquad g(A) = g(B) = e$$

and

$$h(a) = h(b) = e, \qquad h(A) = A, \qquad h(B) = B$$

For this grammar G we can prove by induction on $m \geq 1$ that if $S \overset{m}{\Rightarrow} \alpha$, then α can be written as a string $c_1 c_2 \cdots c_n U \beta V$ such that

(1) Each c_i is either a or b;
(2) U is either C or e;
(3) β is a string in $\{a, b, A, B\}^n$ such that $g(\beta) = c_1 c_2 \cdots c_i$,

$$h(\beta) = X_n X_{n-1} \cdots X_{i+1},$$

and X_j is A or B as c_j is a or b, $i < j \leq n$; and
(4) V is either D or e.

The details of this induction will be omitted.

We now observe that the sentential forms of G which consist entirely of terminal symbols are all of the form $c_1 c_2 \cdots c_n c_1 c_2 \cdots c_n$, where each

$$c_i \in \{a, b\}.$$

Thus, $L(G) \subseteq \{ww \mid w \in \{a, b\}^*\}$.

We can now conclude that $L(G) = \{ww \mid w \in \{a, b\}^*\}$.　$\square$

2.1.3. Restricted Grammars

Grammars can be classified according to the format of their productions. Let $G = (N, \Sigma, P, S)$ be a grammar.

DEFINITION

G is said to be

(1) *Right-linear* if each production in P is of the form $A \longrightarrow xB$ or $A \longrightarrow x$, where A and B are in N and x is in Σ^*.

(2) *Context-free* if each production in P is of the form $A \longrightarrow \alpha$, where A is in N and α is in $(N \cup \Sigma)^*$.

(3) *Context-sensitive* if each production in P is of the form $\alpha \longrightarrow \beta$, where $|\alpha| \leq |\beta|$.

A grammar with no restrictions as above is called *unrestricted*.

The grammar of Example 2.3 is a right-linear grammar. Another example of a right-linear grammar is the grammar with the productions

$$S \longrightarrow 0S \mid 1S \mid e$$

This grammar generates the language $\{0, 1\}^*$.

The grammar of Example 2.4 is an important example of a context-free grammar. Notice that according to our definition, every right-linear grammar is also a context-free grammar.

The grammar of Example 2.5 is clearly a context-sensitive grammar.

We should emphasize that the definition of context-sensitive grammar does not permit a production of the form $A \rightarrow e$, commonly known as an *e-production*. Thus a context-free grammar having *e*-productions would not be a context-sensitive grammar.

The reason for not permitting *e*-productions in context-sensitive grammars is to ensure that the language generated by a context-sensitive grammar is recursive. That is to say, we want to be able to give an algorithm which, presented with an arbitrary context-sensitive grammar G and input string w, will determine whether or not w is in $L(G)$. (See Exercise 2.1.18.)

Even if we permitted just one *e*-production in a context-sensitive grammar (without imposing additional conditions on the grammar), then the expanded class of grammars would be capable of defining any recursively enumerable set (see Exercise 2.1.20). The grammar in Example 2.6 is unrestricted. Note that it is not right-linear, context-free, or context-sensitive.

CONVENTION

If a language L can be generated by a type x grammar, then L is said to be a type x language, for all the "*type x*" 's that we have defined or shall define.

Thus $L(G)$ of Example 2.3 is a right-linear language, $L(G_0)$ in Example 2.4 is a context-free language, and $L(G)$ of Example 2.5 is a paradigm context-sensitive language. The language generated by the grammar in Example 2.6 is an unrestricted language, although $\{ww \mid w \in \{a, b\}^* \text{ and } w \neq e\}$ also happens to be a context-sensitive language.

The four types of grammars and languages we have defined are often referred to as the *Chomsky hierarchy*.

CONVENTION

We shall hereafter abbreviate context-free grammar and language by CFG and CFL, respectively, Likewise, CSG and CSL stand for context-sensitive grammar and context-sensitive language.

Every right-linear language is a CFL, and there are CFL's, such as $\{0^n 1^n \mid n \geq 1\}$, that are not right-linear. The CFL's which do not contain the empty string likewise form a proper subset of the context-sensitive languages. These in turn are a proper subset of the recursive sets, which are in turn a proper subset of the recursively enumerable sets. The (unrestricted) grammars define exactly the recursively enumerable sets. These matters are left for the Exercises.

Often, the context-sensitive languages are defined to be the languages that we have defined plus all those languages $L \cup \{e\}$, where L is a context-sensitive language as defined here. In that case, we may call the CFL's a proper subset of the CSL's.

We should emphasize the fact that although we may be given a certain type of grammar, the language generated by that grammar might be generated by a less powerful grammar. As a simple example, the context-free grammar

$$S \longrightarrow AS \,|\, e$$
$$A \longrightarrow 0 \,|\, 1$$

generates the language $\{0, 1\}^*$, which, as we have seen, can also be generated by a right-linear grammar.

We should also mention that there are a number of grammatical models that have been recently introduced outside the Chomsky hierarchy. Some of the motivation in introducing new grammatical models is to find a generative device that can better represent all the syntax and/or semantics of programming languages. Some of these models are introduced in the Exercises.

2.1.4. Recognizers

A second common method of providing a finite specification for a language is to define a recognizer for the language. In essence a recognizer is merely a highly stylized procedure for defining a set. A recognizer can be pictured as shown in Fig. 2.1.

There are three parts to a recognizer—an input tape, a finite state control, and an auxiliary memory.

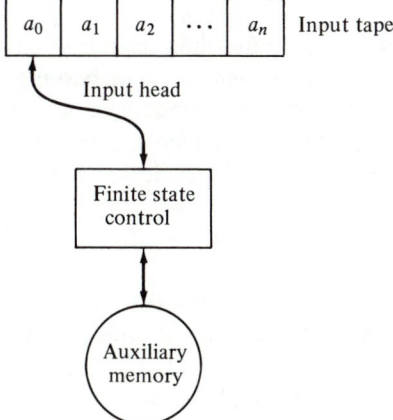

Fig. 2.1   A recognizer.

The *input tape* can be considered to be divided into a linear sequence of tape squares, each tape square containing exactly one input symbol from a finite input alphabet. Both the leftmost and rightmost tape squares may be occupied by unique endmarkers, or there may be a right endmarker and no left endmarker, or there may be no endmarkers on either end of the input tape.

There is an *input head*, which can read one input square at a given instant of time. In a move by a recognizer, the input head can move one square to the left, remain stationary, or move one square to the right. A recognizer which can never move its input head left is called a *one-way* recognizer.

Normally, the input tape is assumed to be a *read-only* tape, meaning that once the input tape is set no symbols can be changed. However, it is possible to define recognizers which utilize a read-write input tape.

The *memory* of a recognizer can be any type of data store. We assume that there is a finite *memory alphabet* and that the memory contains only symbols from this finite memory alphabet in some data organization. We also assume that at any instant of time we can finitely describe the contents and structure of the memory, although as time goes on, the memory may become arbitrarily large. An important example of an auxiliary memory is the pushdown list, which can be abstractly represented as a string of memory symbols, e.g., $Z_1 Z_2 \cdots Z_n$, where each Z_i is assumed to be from some finite memory alphabet Γ, and Z_1 is assumed to be on top.

The behavior of the auxiliary memory for a class of recognizers is characterized by two functions—a store function and a fetch function. It is assumed that the *fetch function* is a mapping from the set of possible memory configurations to a finite set of *information symbols*, which could be the same as the memory alphabet.

For example, the only information that can be accessed from a pushdown list is the topmost symbol. Thus a fetch function f for a pushdown list would be a mapping from Γ^+ to Γ such that $f(Z_1 \cdots Z_n) = Z_1$.

The *store function* is a mapping which describes how memory may be altered. It maps memory and a *control string* to memory. If we assume that a store operation for a pushdown list replaces the topmost symbol on the pushdown list by a finite length string of memory symbols, then the store function g could be represented as $g: \Gamma^+ \times \Gamma^* \longrightarrow \Gamma^*$, such that

$$g(Z_1 Z_2 \cdots Z_n, Y_1 \cdots Y_k) = Y_1 \cdots Y_k Z_2 \cdots Z_n.$$

If we replace the topmost symbol Z_1 on a pushdown list by the empty string, then the symbol Z_2 becomes the topmost symbol and can then be accessed by a fetch operation.

Generally speaking, it is the type of memory which determines the name of a recognizer. For example a recognizer having a pushdown list for a memory would be called a pushdown recognizer (or more usually, pushdown automaton).

The heart of a recognizer is the *finite state control*, which can be thought of as a program which dictates the behavior of the recognizer. The control can be represented as a finite set of states together with a mapping which describes how the states change in accordance with the current input symbol (i.e., the one under the input head) and the current information fetched from the memory. The control also determines in which direction the input head is to be shifted and what information is to be stored in the memory.

A recognizer operates by making a sequence of moves. At the start of a *move*, the current input symbol is read, and the memory is probed by means of the fetch function. The current input symbol and the information fetched from the memory, together with the current state of the control, determine what the move is to be. The move itself consists of

(1) Shifting the input head one square left, one square right, or keeping the input head stationary;

(2) Storing information into the memory; and

(3) Changing the state of the control.

The behavior of a recognizer can be conveniently described in terms of configurations of the recognizer. A *configuration* is a picture of the recognizer describing

(1) The state of the finite control;

(2) The contents of the input tape, together with the location of the input head; and

(3) The contents of the memory.

We should mention here that the finite control of a recognizer can be deterministic or nondeterministic. If the control is *nondeterministic*, then in each configuration there is a finite set of possible moves that the recognizer can make.

The control is said to be *deterministic* if in each configuration there is at most one possible move. Nondeterministic recognizers are a convenient mathematical abstraction, but, unfortunately, they are often difficult to simulate in practice. We shall give several examples and applications of nondeterministic recognizers in the sections that follow.

The *initial configuration* of a recognizer is one in which the finite control is in a specified initial state, the input head is scanning the leftmost symbol on the input tape, and the memory has a specified initial content.

A *final configuration* is one in which the finite control is in one of a specified set of final states and the input head is scanning the right endmarker or, if there is no right endmarker, has moved off the right end of the input tape. Often, the memory must also satisfy certain conditions if the configuration is to be considered final.

We say that a recognizer *accepts an input string w* if, starting from the initial configuration with w on the input tape, the recognizer can make a sequence of moves and end in a final configuration.

We should point out that a nondeterministic recognizer may be able to make many different sequences of moves from an initial configuration. However, if at least one of these sequences ends in a final configuration, then the initial input string will be accepted.

The language defined by a recognizer is the set of input strings it accepts.

For each class of grammars in the Chomsky hierarchy there is a natural class of recognizers that defines the same class of languages. These recognizers are finite automata, pushdown automata, linear bounded automata, and Turing machines. Specifically, the following characterizations of the Chomsky languages exist:

(1) A language L is right-linear if and only if L is defined by a (one-way deterministic) finite automaton.

(2) A language L is context-free if and only if L is defined by a (one-way nondeterministic) pushdown automaton.

(3) A language L is context-sensitive if and only if L is defined by a (two-way nondeterministic) linear bounded automaton.

(4) A language L is recursively enumerable if and only if L is defined by a Turing machine.

The precise definition of these recognizers will be found in the Exercises and later sections. Finite automata and pushdown automata are important in the theory of compiling and will be studied in some detail in this chapter.

EXERCISES

2.1.1. Construct right-linear grammars for

(a) Identifiers which can be of arbitrary length but must start with a letter (as in ALGOL).

(b) Identifiers which can be one to six symbols in length and must start with I, J, K, L, M, or N (as for FORTRAN integer variables).

(c) Real constants as in PL/I or FORTRAN, e.g., -10.8, 3.14159, $2.$, $6.625E-27$.

(d) All strings of 0's and 1's having both an odd number of 0's and an odd number of 1's.

2.1.2. Construct context-free grammars that generate

(a) All strings of 0's and 1's having equal numbers of 0's and 1's.

(b) $\{a_1 a_2 \cdots a_n a_n \cdots a_2 a_1 \mid a_i \in \{0, 1\}, 1 \leq i \leq n\}$.

(c) Well-formed statements in propositional calculus.

(d) $\{0^i 1^j \mid i \neq j \text{ and } i, j \geq 0\}$.

(e) All possible sequences of balanced parentheses.

*2.1.3. Describe the language generated by the productions $S \longrightarrow bSS \mid a$. Observe that it is not always easy to describe what language a grammar generates.

*2.1.4. Construct context-sensitive grammars that generate

  (a) $\{a^{n^2} \mid n \geq 1\}$.
  (b) $\{ww \mid w \in \{a, b\}^+\}$.
  (c) $\{w \mid w \in \{a, b, c\}^+$ and the number of a's in w equals the number of b's which equals the number of c's$\}$.
  (d) $\{a^m b^n a^m b^n \mid m, n \geq 1\}$.

  Hint: Think of the set of productions in a context-sensitive grammar as a program. You can use special nonterminal symbols as a combination "input head" and terminal symbol.

*2.1.5. A "true" context-sensitive grammar G is a grammar (N, Σ, P, S) in which each production in P is of the form

$$\alpha A \beta \longrightarrow \alpha \gamma \beta$$

where α and β are in $(N \cup \Sigma)^*$, $\gamma \in (N \cup \Sigma)^+$, and $A \in N$. Such a production can be interpreted to mean that A can be replaced by γ only in the context α_β. Show that every context-sensitive language can be generated by a "true" context-sensitive grammar.

**2.1.6. What class of languages can be generated by grammars with only *left context*, that is, grammars in which each production is of the form $\alpha A \longrightarrow \alpha \beta$, α in $(N \cup \Sigma)^*$, β in $(N \cup \Sigma)^+$?

2.1.7. Show that every context-free language can be generated by a grammar $G = (N, \Sigma, P, S)$ in which each production is of either the form $A \longrightarrow \alpha$, α in N^*, or $A \longrightarrow w$, w in Σ^*.

2.1.8. Show that every context-sensitive language can be generated by a grammar $G = (N, \Sigma, P, S)$ in which each production is either of the form $\alpha \longrightarrow \beta$, where α and β are in N^+, or $A \longrightarrow w$, where $A \in N$ and $w \in \Sigma^+$.

2.1.9. Prove that $L(G) = \{a^n b^n c^n \mid n \geq 1\}$, where G is the grammar in Example 2.5.

*2.1.10. Can you describe the set of context-free grammars by means of a context-free grammar?

*2.1.11. Show that every recursively enumerable set can be generated by a grammar with at most two nonterminal symbols. Can you generate every recursively enumerable set with a grammar having only one nonterminal symbol?

2.1.12. Show that if $G = (N, \Sigma, P, S)$ is a grammar such that $\#N = n$, and Σ does not contain any of the symbols $A_1, A_2, \ldots$, then there is an equivalent grammar $G' = (N', \Sigma, P', A_1)$ such that

$$N' = \{A_1, A_2, \ldots, A_n\}.$$

2.1.13. Prove that the grammar G_1 of Example 2.1 generates $\{0^n1^n \mid n \geq 1\}$. *Hint:* Observe that each sentential form has at most one nonterminal. Thus productions can be applied in only one place in a string.

DEFINITION

In an unrestricted grammar G there are many ways of deriving a given sentence that are essentially the same, differing only in the order in which productions are applied. If G is context-free, then we can represent these essentially similar derivations by means of a derivation tree. However, if G is context-sensitive or unrestricted, we can define equivalence classes of derivations in the following manner.

Let $G = (N, \Sigma, P, S)$ be an unrestricted grammar. Let D be the set of all derivations of the form $S \overset{+}{\Rightarrow} w$. That is, elements of D are sequences of the form $(\alpha_0, \alpha_1, \ldots, \alpha_n)$ such that $\alpha_0 = S$, $\alpha_n \in \Sigma^*$, and $\alpha_{i-1} \Rightarrow \alpha_i$ $1 \leq i \leq n$.

Define a relation R_0 on D by $(\alpha_0, \alpha_1, \ldots, \alpha_n)$ R_0 $(\beta_0, \beta_1, \ldots, \beta_n)$ if and only if there is some i between 1 and $n - 1$ such that

(1) $\alpha_j = \beta_j$ for all $1 \leq j \leq n$ such that $j \neq i$.

(2) We can write $\alpha_{i-1} = \gamma_1\gamma_2\gamma_3\gamma_4\gamma_5$ and $\alpha_{i+1} = \gamma_1\delta\gamma_3\epsilon\gamma_5$ such that $\gamma_2 \rightarrow \delta$ and $\gamma_4 \rightarrow \epsilon$ are in P, and either $\alpha_i = \gamma_1\delta\gamma_3\gamma_4\gamma_5$ and $\beta_i = \gamma_1\gamma_2\gamma_3\epsilon\gamma_5$, or conversely.

Let R be the least equivalence relation containing R_0. Each equivalence class of R represents the essentially similar derivations of a given sentence.

**2.1.14. What is the maximum size of an equivalence class of R (as a function of n and $|\alpha_n|$) if G is

(a) Right-linear.

(b) Context-free.

(c) Such that every production is of the form $\alpha \rightarrow \beta$ and $|\alpha| < |\beta|$.

*2.1.15. Let G be defined by

$$S \longrightarrow A0B \mid B1A$$
$$A \longrightarrow BB \mid 0$$
$$B \longrightarrow AA \mid 1$$

What is the size of the equivalence class under R which contains the derivation

$$S \Rightarrow A0B \Rightarrow BB0B \Rightarrow 1B0B \Rightarrow 1AA0B \Rightarrow 10A0B$$
$$\Rightarrow 1000B \Rightarrow 10001$$

DEFINITION

A grammar G is said to be *unambiguous* if each w in $L(G)$ appears as the last component of a derivation in one and only one equivalence class under R, as defined above. For example,

$$S \longrightarrow abC \mid aB$$
$$B \longrightarrow bc$$
$$bC \longrightarrow bc$$

is an ambiguous grammar since the sequences

$$(S, abC, abc) \quad \text{and} \quad (S, aB, abc)$$

are in two distinct equivalence classes.

*2.1.16. Show that every right-linear language has an unambiguous right-linear grammar.

*2.1.17. Let $G = (N, \Sigma, P, S)$ be a context-sensitive grammar, and let $N \cup \Sigma$ have m members. Let w be a word in $L(G)$. Show that $S \overset{n}{\underset{G}{\Longrightarrow}} w$, where $n \leq (m + 1)^{|w|}$.

2.1.18. Show that every context-sensitive language is recursive. *Hint:* Use the result of Exercise 2.1.17 to construct an algorithm to determine if w is in $L(G)$ for arbitrary word w and context-sensitive grammar G.

2.1.19. Show that every CFL is recursive. *Hint:* Use Exercise 2.1.18, but be careful about the empty word.

*2.1.20. Show that if $G = (N, \Sigma, P, S)$ is an unrestricted grammar, then there is a context-sensitive grammar $G' = (N', \Sigma \cup \{c\}, P', S')$ such that

$$w \text{ is in } L(G) \text{ if and only if } wc^i \text{ is in } L(G') \text{ for some } i \geq 0$$

Hint: Fill out every noncontext-sensitive production of G with c's. Then add productions to allow the c's to be shifted to the right end of any sentential form.

2.1.21. Show that if $L = L(G)$ for any arbitrary grammar G, then there is a context-sensitive language L_1 and a homomorphism h such that $L = h(L_1)$.

2.1.22. Let $\{A_1, A_2, \ldots\}$ be a countable set of nonterminal symbols, not including the symbols 0 and 1. Show that every context-sensitive language $L \subseteq \{0, 1\}^*$ has a CSG $G = (N, \{0, 1\}, P, A_1)$, where $N = \{A_1, A_2, \ldots, A_i\}$, for some i. We call such a context-sensitive grammar "normalized."

*2.1.23. Show that the set of normalized context-sensitive grammars as defined above is countable.

*2.1.24. Show that there is a recursive set contained in $\{0, 1\}^*$ which is not a context-sensitive language. *Hint:* Order the normalized, context-sensitive grammars so that one may talk about the ith grammar. Likewise, lexicographically order $\{0, 1\}^*$ so that we may talk about the ith string in $\{0, 1\}^*$. Then define $L = \{w_i \mid w_i \text{ is not in } L(G_i)\}$ and show that L is recursive but not context-sensitive.

**2.1.25. Show that a language is defined by a grammar if and only if it is recognized by a Turing machine. (A Turing machine is defined in the Exercises of Section 0.4 on page 34.)

2.1.26. Define a nondeterministic recognizer whose memory is an initially blank Turing machine tape, which is not permitted to grow longer than the input. Show that a language is defined by such a recognizer if and only if it is a CSL. This recognizer is called a *linear bounded automaton* (LBA, for short).

DEFINITION

An *indexed grammar* is a 5-tuple $G = (N, \Sigma, \Delta, P, S)$, where N, Σ, and Δ are finite sets of *nonterminals*, *terminals*, and *intermediates*, respectively. S in N is the *start symbol* and P is a finite set of productions of the forms

$$A \longrightarrow X_1\psi_1 X_2\psi_2 \cdots X_n\psi_n, \qquad n \geq 0$$

and

$$Af \longrightarrow X_1\psi_1 X_2\psi_2 \cdots X_n\psi_n, \qquad n \geq 0$$

where A is in N, the X's in $N \cup \Sigma$, f in Δ, and the ψ's in Δ^*, such that if X_i is in Σ, then $\psi_i = e$. Let α and β be strings in $(N\Delta^* \cup \Sigma)^*$, $A \in N$, $\theta \in \Delta^*$, and let $A \longrightarrow X_1\psi_1 \cdots X_n\psi_n$ be in P. Then we write

$$\alpha A\theta\beta \underset{G}{\Longrightarrow} \alpha X_1\psi_1\theta'_1 X_2\psi_2\theta'_2 \cdots X_n\psi_n\theta'_n\beta$$

where $\theta'_i = \theta$ if $X_i \in N$ and $\theta'_i = e$ if $X_i \in \Sigma$. That is, the string of intermediates following a nonterminal distributes over the nonterminals, but not over the terminals, which can never be followed by an intermediate. If $Af \longrightarrow X_1\psi_1 \cdots X_n\psi_n$ is in P, then

$$\alpha Af\theta\beta \underset{G}{\Longrightarrow} \alpha X_1\psi_1\theta'_1 \cdots X_n\psi_n\theta'_n\beta,$$

as above. Such a step "consumes" the intermediate following A, but otherwise is the same as the first type of step. Let $\overset{*}{\underset{G}{\Longrightarrow}}$ be the reflexive, transitive closure of $\underset{G}{\Longrightarrow}$, and define

$$L(G) = \{w \mid w \text{ in } \Sigma^* \text{ and } S \overset{*}{\underset{G}{\Longrightarrow}} w\}.$$

Example 2.7

Let $G = (\{S, T, A, B, C\}, \{a, b, c\}, \{f, g\}, P, S)$, where P consists of

$$S \longrightarrow Tg$$
$$T \longrightarrow Tf$$
$$T \longrightarrow ABC$$
$$Af \longrightarrow aA$$
$$Bf \longrightarrow bB$$

$$Cf \longrightarrow cC$$
$$Ag \longrightarrow a$$
$$Bg \longrightarrow b$$
$$Cg \longrightarrow c$$

Then $L(G) = \{a^n b^n c^n \mid n \geq 1\}$. For example, $aabbcc$ has the derivation

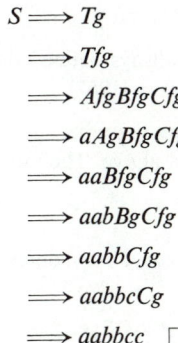

$$S \Longrightarrow Tg$$
$$\Longrightarrow Tfg$$
$$\Longrightarrow AfgBfgCfg$$
$$\Longrightarrow aAgBfgCfg$$
$$\Longrightarrow aaBfgCfg$$
$$\Longrightarrow aabBgCfg$$
$$\Longrightarrow aabbCfg$$
$$\Longrightarrow aabbcCg$$
$$\Longrightarrow aabbcc \quad \square$$

*2.1.27. Give indexed grammars for the following languages:

(a) $\{ww \mid w \in \{a, b\}^*\}$.
(b) $\{a^n b^{n^2} \mid n \geq 1\}$.

**2.1.28. Show that every indexed language is context-sensitive.

2.1.29. Show that every CFL is an indexed language.

2.1.30. Let us postulate a recognizer whose memory is a single integer (written in binary if you will). Suppose that the memory control strings as described in Section 2.1.4 are only X and Y. Which of the following could be memory fetch functions for the above recognizer?

(a) $f(i) = \begin{cases} 0, & \text{if } i \text{ is even} \\ 1, & \text{if } i \text{ is odd.} \end{cases}$

(b) $f(i) = \begin{cases} a, & \text{if } i \text{ is even} \\ b, & \text{if } i \text{ is odd.} \end{cases}$

(c) $f(i) = \begin{cases} 0, & \text{if } i \text{ is even and the input symbol under the input} \\ & \text{head is } a \\ 1, & \text{otherwise.} \end{cases}$

2.1.31. Which of the following could be memory store functions for the recognizer in Exercise 2.1.30?

(a) $g(i, X) = 0$
  $g(i, Y) = i + 1$.

(b) $g(i, X) = 0$
  $g(i, Y) = \begin{cases} i + 1, & \text{if the previous store instruction was } X \\ i + 2, & \text{if the previous store instruction was } Y. \end{cases}$

DEFINITION

A *tag system* consists of two finite alphabets N and Σ and a finite set of *rules* of the form (α, β), where α and β are in $(N \cup \Sigma)^*$. If γ is an arbitrary string in $(N \cup \Sigma)^*$ and (α, β) is a rule, then we write $\alpha\gamma \vdash \gamma\beta$. That is, the prefix α may be removed from the front of any string provided β is then placed at the end of the string. Let $\overset{*}{\vdash}$ be the reflexive, transitive closure of $\vdash$. For any string γ in $(N \cup \Sigma)^*$, L_γ is $\{w | w$ is in Σ^* and $\gamma \overset{*}{\vdash} w\}$.

**2.1.32. Show that L_γ is always defined by some grammar. *Hint:* Use Exercise 2.1.25 or see Minsky [1967].

**2.1.33. Show that for any grammar G, $L(G)$ is defined by a tag system in the manner described above. The hint of Exercise 2.1.32 again applies.

Open Problems

2.1.34. Is the complement of a context-sensitive language always context-sensitive?

The recognizer of Exercise 2.1.26 is called a *linear bounded automaton* (LBA). If we make it deterministic, we have a *deterministic LBA* (DLBA).

2.1.35. Is every context-sensitive language recognized by a DLBA?

2.1.36. Is every indexed language recognized by a DLBA?

By Exercise 2.1.28, a positive answer to Exercise 2.1.35 implies a positive answer to Exercise 2.1.36.

BIBLIOGRAPHIC NOTES

Formal language theory was greatly stimulated by the work of Chomsky in the late 1950's [Chomsky, 1956, 1957, 1959a, 1959b]. Good references to early work on generative systems are Chomsky [1963] and Bar-Hillel [1964].

The Chomsky hierarchy of grammars and languages has been extensively studied. Many of the major results concerning the Chomsky hierarchy are given in the Exercises. Most of these results are proved in detail in Hopcroft and Ullman [1969] or Ginsburg [1966].

Since Chomsky introduced phrase structure grammars, many other models of grammars have also appeared in the literature. Some of these models use specialized forms of productions. Indexed grammars [Aho, 1968], macro grammars [Fischer, 1968], and scattered context grammars [Greibach and Hopcroft, 1969] are examples of such grammars. Other grammatical models impose restrictions on the order in which productions can be applied. Programmed grammars [Rosenkrantz, 1968] are a prime example.

Recognizers for languages have also been extensively studied. Turing machines were defined by A. Turing in 1936. Somewhat later, the concept of a finite state machine appeared in McCulloch and Pitts [1943]. The study of recognizers was stimulated by the work of Moore [1956] and Rabin and Scott [1959].

A significant amount of effort in language theory has been expended in determining the algebraic properties of classes of languages and in determining decidability results for classes of grammars and recognizers. For each of the four classes of grammars in the Chomsky hierarchy there is a class of recognizers which defines precisely those languages generated by that class of grammars. These observations have led to a study of abstract families of languages and recognizers in which classes of languages are defined in terms of algebraic properties. Certain algebraic properties in a class of languages are necessary and sufficient to guarantee the existence of a class of recognizers for those languages. Work in this area was pioneered by Ginsburg and Greibach [1969] and Hopcroft and Ullman [1967]. Book [1970] gives a good survey of language theory circa 1970.

Haines [1970] claims that the left context grammars in Exercise 2.1.6 generate exactly the context-sensitive languages. Exercise 2.1.28 is from Aho [1968].

2.2. REGULAR SETS, THEIR GENERATORS, AND THEIR RECOGNIZERS

The regular sets are a class of languages central to much of language theory. In this section we shall study several methods of specifying languages, all of which define exactly the regular sets. These methods include regular expressions, right-linear grammars, deterministic finite automata, and nondeterministic finite automata.

2.2.1. Regular Sets and Regular Expressions

DEFINITION

Let Σ be a finite alphabet. We define a *regular set over* Σ recursively in the following manner:

(1) $\varnothing$ (the empty set) is a regular set over Σ.
(2) $\{e\}$ is a regular set over Σ.
(3) $\{a\}$ is a regular set over Σ for all a in Σ.
(4) If P and Q are regular sets over Σ, then so are
   (a) $P \cup Q$.
   (b) PQ.
   (c) P^*.
(5) Nothing else is a regular set.

Thus a subset of Σ^* is regular if and only if it is $\varnothing$, $\{e\}$, or $\{a\}$, for some a in Σ, or can be obtained from these by a finite number of applications of the operations union, concatenation, and closure.

We shall define a convenient method for denoting regular sets over a finite alphabet Σ.

DEFINITION

Regular expressions over Σ and the regular sets they *denote* are defined recursively, as follows:

(1) $\emptyset$ is a regular expression denoting the regular set $\emptyset$.
(2) e is a regular expression denoting the regular set $\{e\}$.
(3) a in Σ is a regular expression denoting the regular set $\{a\}$.
(4) If p and q are regular expressions denoting the regular sets P and Q, respectively, then
     (a) $(p + q)$ is a regular expression denoting $P \cup Q$.
     (b) (pq) is a regular expression denoting PQ.
     (c) $(p)^*$ is a regular expression denoting P^*.
(5) Nothing else is a regular expression.

We shall use the shorthand notation p^+ to denote the regular expression pp^*. Also, we shall remove redundant parentheses from regular expressions whenever no ambiguity can arise. In this regard, we assume that * has the highest precedence, then concatenation, and then +. Thus, $0 + 10^*$ means $(0 + (1(0^*)))$.

Example 2.8

Some examples of regular expressions are

(1) 01, denoting $\{01\}$.
(2) 0^*, denoting $\{0\}^*$.
(3) $(0 + 1)^*$, denoting $\{0, 1\}^*$.
(4) $(0 + 1)^* 011$, denoting the set of all strings of 0's and 1's ending in 011.
(5) $(a + b)(a + b + 0 + 1)^*$, denoting the set of all strings in $\{0, 1, a, b\}^*$ beginning with a or b.
(6) $(00 + 11)^*((01 + 10)(00 + 11)^*(01 + 10)(00 + 11)^*)^*$, denoting the set of all strings of 0's and 1's containing both an even number of 0's and an even number of 1's. □

It should be quite clear that for each regular set we can find at least one regular expression denoting that regular set. Also, for each regular expression we can construct the regular set denoted by that regular expression. Unfortunately, for each regular set there is an infinity of regular expressions denoting that set.

We shall say two regular expressions are *equal* (=) if they denote the same set.

Some basic algebraic properties of regular expressions are stated in the following lemma.

LEMMA 2.1

Let α, β, and γ be regular expressions. Then

    (1) $\alpha + \beta = \beta + \alpha$ (2) $\emptyset^* = e$

(3) $\alpha + (\beta + \gamma) = (\alpha + \beta) + \gamma$ (4) $\alpha(\beta\gamma) = (\alpha\beta)\gamma$

(5) $\alpha(\beta + \gamma) = \alpha\beta + \alpha\gamma$ (6) $(\alpha + \beta)\gamma = \alpha\gamma + \beta\gamma$

(7) $\alpha e = e\alpha = \alpha$ (8) $\varnothing\alpha = \alpha\varnothing = \varnothing$

(9) $\alpha^* = \alpha + \alpha^*$ (10) $(\alpha^*)^* = \alpha^*$

(11) $\alpha + \alpha = \alpha$ (12) $\alpha + \varnothing = \alpha$

Proof. (1) Let α and β denote the sets L_1 and L_2, respectively. Then $\alpha + \beta$ denotes $L_1 \cup L_2$ and $\beta + \alpha$ denotes $L_2 \cup L_1$. But $L_1 \cup L_2 = L_2 \cup L_1$ from the definition of union. Hence, $\alpha + \beta = \beta + \alpha$.

The remaining parts are left for the Exercises. ☐

In what follows, we shall not distinguish between a regular expression and the set it denotes unless confusion will arise. For example, under this convention the symbol a will represent the set $\{a\}$.

When dealing with languages it is often convenient to use equations whose indeterminates and coefficients represent sets. Here, we shall consider sets of equations whose coefficients are regular expressions and shall call such equations *regular expression equations.*

For example, consider the regular expression equation

$$(2.2.1) \qquad\qquad X = aX + b$$

where a and b are regular expressions. We can easily verify by direct substitution that $X = a^*b$ is a solution to Eq. (2.2.1). That is to say, when we substitute the set represented by a^*b in both sides of Eq. (2.2.1), then each side of the equation represents the same set.

We can also have sets of equations that define languages. For example, consider the pair of equations

$$(2.2.2) \qquad \begin{aligned} X &= a_1 X + a_2 Y + a_3 \\ Y &= b_1 X + b_2 Y + b_3 \end{aligned}$$

where each a_i and b_i is a regular expression. We shall show how we can solve this pair of simultaneous equations to obtain the solutions

$$X = (a_1 + a_2 b_2{}^* b_1)^*(a_3 + a_2 b_2{}^* b_3)$$
$$Y = (b_2 + b_1 a_1{}^* a_2)^*(b_3 + b_1 a_1{}^* a_3)$$

However, we should first mention that not all regular expression equations have unique solutions. For example, if

$$(2.2.3) \qquad\qquad X = \alpha X + \beta$$

is a regular expression equation and α denotes a set which contains the empty string, then $X = \alpha^*(\beta + \gamma)$ is also a solution to (2.2.3) for all γ. (γ does not even have to be regular. See Exercise 2.2.7.) Thus Eq. (2.2.3) has an infinity of solutions. In situations of this nature we shall use the smallest solution, which we call the minimal fixed point. The minimal fixed point for Eq. (2.2.3) is $X = \alpha^*\beta$.

DEFINITION

A set of regular expression equations is said to be *in standard form* over a set of indeterminates $\Delta = \{X_1, X_2, \ldots, X_n\}$ if for each X_i in Δ there is an equation of the form

$$X_i = \alpha_{i0} + \alpha_{i1}X_1 + \alpha_{i2}X_2 + \cdots + \alpha_{in}X_n$$

with α_{ij} a regular expression over some alphabet disjoint from Δ.

The α's are the coefficients. Note that if $\alpha_{ij} = \varnothing$, a possible regular expression, then effectively there is no term for X_j in the equation for X_i. Also, if $\alpha_{ij} = e$, then effectively the term for X_j in the equation for X_i is just X_j. That is, $\varnothing$ plays the role of coefficient 0, and e the role of coefficient 1 in ordinary linear equations.

ALGORITHM 2.1

Solving a set of regular expression equations in standard form.

Input. A set Q of regular expression equations in standard form over Δ, whose coefficients are regular expressions over alphabet Σ. Let Δ be the set $\{X_1, X_2, \ldots, X_n\}$.

Output. A set of solutions of the form $X_i = \alpha_i$, $1 \leq i \leq n$, where α_i is a regular expression over Σ.

Method. The method is reminiscent of solving linear equations using Gaussian elimination.

Step 1: Let $i = 1$.

Step 2: If $i = n$, go to step 4. Otherwise, using the identities of Lemma 2.1, write the equation for X_i as $X_i = \alpha X_i + \beta$, where α is a regular expression over Σ and β is a regular expression of the form $\beta_0 + \beta_i X_{i+1} + \cdots + \beta_n X_n$ with each β_i a regular expression over Σ. We shall see that this will always be possible. Then in the equations for $X_{i+1}, \ldots, X_n$, we replace X_i on the right by the regular expression $\alpha^*\beta$.

Step 3: Increase i by 1 and return to step 2.

Step 4: After executing step 2 the equation for X_i will have only symbols in Σ and $X_i, \ldots, X_n$ on the right. In particular, the equation for X_n will have only X_n and symbols in Σ on the right. At this point $i = n$ and we now go to step 5.

Step 5: The equation for X_i is of the form $X_i = \alpha X_i + \beta$, where α and β are regular expressions over Σ. Emit the statement $X_i = \alpha^*\beta$ and substitute $\alpha^*\beta$ for X_i in the remaining equations.

Step 6: If $i = 1$, end. Otherwise, decrease i by 1 and return to step 5. $\square$

Example 2.9

Let $\Delta = \{X_1, X_2, X_3\}$, and let the set of equations be

$$(2.2.4) \qquad\qquad X_1 = 0X_2 + 1X_1 + e$$
$$(2.2.5) \qquad\qquad X_2 = 0X_3 + 1X_2$$
$$(2.2.6) \qquad\qquad X_3 = 0X_1 + 1X_3$$

From (2.2.4) we obtain $X_1 = 1X_1 + (0X_2 + e)$. We then replace X_1 by $1^*(0X_2 + e)$ in the remaining equations. Equation (2.2.6) becomes

$$X_3 = 01^*(0X_2 + e) + 1X_3,$$

which can be written, using Lemma 2.1, as

$$(2.2.7) \qquad\qquad X_3 = 01^*0X_2 + 1X_3 + 01^*$$

If we now work on (2.2.5), which was not changed by the previous step, we replace X_2 by 1^*0X_3, in (2.2.7), and obtain

$$(2.2.8) \qquad\qquad X_3 = (01^*01^*0 + 1)X_3 + 01^*$$

We now reach step 5 of Algorithm 2.1. From Eq. (2.2.8) we obtain the solution for X_3:

$$(2.2.9) \qquad\qquad X_3 = (01^*01^*0 + 1)^*01^*$$

We substitute (2.2.9) in (2.2.5), to yield

$$(2.2.10) \qquad\qquad X_2 = 0(01^*01^*0 + 1)^*01^* + 1X_2$$

Since X_3 does not appear in (2.2.4), that equation is not modified. We then solve (2.2.10), obtaining

$$(2.2.11) \qquad\qquad X_2 = 1^*0(01^*01^*0 + 1)^*01^*$$

Substituting (2.2.11) into (2.2.4), we obtain

$$(2.2.12) \qquad\qquad X_1 = 01^*0(01^*01^*0 + 1)^*01^* + 1X_1 + e$$

The solution to (2.2.12) is

$$(2.2.13) \qquad\qquad X_1 = 1^*(01^*0(01^*01^*0 + 1)^*01^* + e)$$

The output of Algorithm 2.1 is the set of Eq. (2.2.9), (2.2.11), and (2.2.13).

$\square$

We must show that the output of Algorithm 2.1 is truly a solution to the equations, in the sense that when the solutions are substituted for the indeterminates, the sets denoted by both sides of each equation are the same. As we have pointed out, the solution to a set of standard form equations is not always unique. However, when a set of equations does not have a unique solution we shall see that Algorithm 2.1 yields the minimal fixed point.

DEFINITION

Let Q be a set of standard form equations over Δ with coefficients over Σ. We say that a mapping f from Δ to languages in Σ^* is a *solution* to Q if upon substituting $f(X)$ for X in each equation, for all X in Δ, the equations become set equalities. We say that $f: \Delta \longrightarrow \mathcal{P}(\Sigma^*)$ is a *minimal fixed point* of Q if f is a solution, and if g is any other solution, $f(X) \subseteq g(X)$ for all X in Δ.

The following two lemmas provide useful information about minimal fixed points.

LEMMA 2.2

Every set Q of standard form equations over Δ has a unique minimal fixed point.

Proof. Let $f(X) = \{w \,|\, \text{for all solutions } g \text{ to } Q, w \text{ is in } g(X)\}$, for all X in Δ. It is straightforward to show that f is a solution and that $f(X) \subseteq g(X)$ for all solutions g. Thus, f is the unique minimal fixed point of Q. $\square$

We shall now characterize the minimal fixed point of a set of equations.

LEMMA 2.3

Let Q be a set of standard form equations over Δ, where $\Delta = \{X_1, \ldots, X_n\}$ and the equation for each X_i is

$$X_i = \alpha_{i0} + \alpha_{i1}X_1 + \alpha_{i2}X_2 + \cdots + \alpha_{in}X_n$$

Then the minimal fixed point of Q is f, where

$$f(X_i) = \{w_1 \cdots w_m \,|\, \text{for some sequence of integers } j_1, \ldots, j_m, m \geq 1,$$
$$w_m \text{ is in } \alpha_{j_m 0}, \text{ and } w_k \text{ is in } \alpha_{j_k j_{k+1}}, 1 \leq k < m, \text{ where } j_1 = i\}.$$

Proof. It is straightforward to show that the following set equations are valid:

$$f(X_i) = \alpha_{i0} \cup \alpha_{i1}f(X_1) \cup \cdots \cup \alpha_{in}f(X_n)$$

for all i. Thus, f is a solution.

To show that f is the minimal fixed point, suppose that g is a solution and that for some i there exists a string w in $f(X_i) - g(X_i)$. Since w is in $f(X_i)$, we can write $w = w_1 \cdots w_m$, where for some sequence of integers $j_1, \ldots, j_m$, we have w_m in $\alpha_{j_m 0}$, w_k in $\alpha_{j_k j_{k+1}}$, for $1 \leq k < m$, and $j_1 = i$.

Since g is a solution, we have $g(X_j) = \alpha_{j0} \cup \alpha_{j1}g(X_1) \cup \cdots \cup \alpha_{jn}g(X_n)$ for all j. In particular, $\alpha_{j0} \subseteq g(X_j)$ and $\alpha_{jk}g(X_k) \subseteq g(X_j)$ for all j and k. Thus, w_m is in $g(X_{j_m})$, $w_{m-1}w_m$ is in $g(X_{j_{m-1}})$, and so forth. Finally, $w = w_1 w_2 \cdots w_m$ is in $g(X_{j_1}) = g(X_i)$. But then we have a contradiction, since we supposed that w was not in $g(X_i)$. Thus we can conclude that $f(X_i) \subseteq g(X_i)$ for all i.

It immediately follows that f is the minimal fixed point of Q. $\quad\square$

LEMMA 2.4

Let Q_1 and Q_2 be the set of equations before and after a single application of step 2 of Algorithm 2.1. Then Q_1 and Q_2 have the same minimal fixed point.

Proof. Suppose that in step 2 the equation

$$A_i = \alpha_{i0} + \alpha_{ii}A_i + \alpha_{i,i+1}A_{i+1} + \cdots + \alpha_{in}A_n$$

is under consideration. (*Note:* The coefficient for A_h is $\varnothing$ for $1 \leq h < i$.) In Q_1 and Q_2 the equations for A_h, $h \leq i$, are the same.

Suppose that

$$(2.2.14) \qquad A_j = \alpha_{j0} + \sum_{k=1}^{n} \alpha_{jk}A_k$$

is the equation for A_j, $j > i$, in Q_1. In Q_2 the equation for A_j becomes

$$(2.2.15) \qquad A_j = \beta_0 + \sum_{k=i+1}^{n} \beta_k A_k$$

where

$$\beta_0 = \alpha_{j0} + \alpha_{ji}\alpha_{ii}^*\alpha_{i0}$$
$$\beta_k = \alpha_{jk} + \alpha_{ji}\alpha_{ii}^*\alpha_{ik} \qquad \text{for } i < k \leq n$$

We can use Lemma 2.3 to express the minimal fixed points of Q_1 and Q_2, which we shall denote by f_1 and f_2, respectively. From the form of Eq. (2.2.15), every string in $f_2(A_j)$ is in $f_1(A_j)$. This follows from the fact that any string w which is in the set denoted by $\alpha_{ji}\alpha_{ii}^*\alpha_{ik}$ can be expressed as $w_1 w_2 \cdots w_m$, where w_1 is in α_{ji}, w_m is in α_{ik}, and $w_2, \ldots, w_{m-1}$ are in α_{ii}. Thus, w is the concatenation of a sequence of strings in the sets denoted by coefficients of Q_1, for which the subscripts satisfy the condition of Lemma 2.3. A similar observation holds for strings in $\alpha_{ji}\alpha_{ii}^*\alpha_{i0}$. Thus it can be shown that $f_2(A_j) \subseteq f_1(A_j)$.

Conversely, suppose w is in $f_1(A_j)$. Then by Lemma 2.3 we may write $w = w_1 \cdots w_m$, for some sequence of nonzero subscripts $l_1, \ldots, l_m$ such that w_m is in $\alpha_{l_m 0}$, w_p is in $\alpha_{l_p l_{p+1}}$, $1 \leq p < m$, and $l_1 = j$. We can group the w_p's uniquely, such that we can write $w = y_1 \cdots y_r$, where $y_p = w_t \cdots w_s$, and

(1) If $l_t \leq i$, then $s = t + 1$.

(2) If $l_t > i$, then s is chosen such that $l_{t+1}, \ldots, l_s$ are all i and $l_{s+1} \neq i$.

It follows that in either case, y_p is in the coefficient of $A_{j_{s+1}}$ in the equation of Q_2 for A_{l_t}, and hence w is in $f_2(A_j)$. We conclude that $f_1(A_j) = f_2(A_j)$ for all j. $\square$

LEMMA 2.5

Let Q_1 and Q_2 be the sets of equations before and after a single application of step 5 in Algorithm 2.1. Then Q_1 and Q_2 have the same minimal fixed points.

Proof. Exercise, similar to Lemma 2.4. $\square$

THEOREM 2.1

Algorithm 2.1 correctly determines the minimal fixed point of a set of standard form equations.

Proof. After step 5 has been applied for all j, the equations are all of the form $A_i = \alpha_i$, where α_i is a regular expression over Σ. The minimal fixed point of such a set is clearly $f(A_i) = \alpha_i$. $\square$

2.2.2. Regular Sets and Right-Linear Grammars

We shall show that a language is defined by a right-linear grammar if and only if it is a regular set. A few observations are needed to show that every regular set has a right-linear grammar. Let Σ be a finite alphabet.

LEMMA 2.6

(i) $\varnothing$, (ii) $\{e\}$, and (iii) $\{a\}$ for all a in Σ are right-linear languages.

Proof.

(i) $G = (\{S\}, \Sigma, \varnothing, S)$ is a right-linear grammar such that $L(G) = \varnothing$.

(ii) $G = (\{S\}, \Sigma, \{S \rightarrow e\}, S)$ is a right-linear grammar for which $L(G) = \{e\}$.

(iii) $G_a = (\{S\}, \Sigma, \{S \rightarrow a\}, S)$ is a right-linear grammar for which $L(G_a) = \{a\}$. $\square$

LEMMA 2.7

If L_1 and L_2 are right-linear languages, then so are (i) $L_1 \cup L_2$, (ii) $L_1 L_2$, and (iii) L_1^*.

Proof. Since L_1 and L_2 are right-linear, we can assume that there exist right-linear grammars $G_1 = (N_1, \Sigma, P_1, S_1)$ and $G_2 = (N_2, \Sigma, P_2, S_2)$ such that $L(G_1) = L_1$ and $L(G_2) = L_2$. We shall also assume that N_1 and N_2 are disjoint. That is, we know we can rename nonterminals arbitrarily, so this assumption is without loss of generality.

(i) Let G_3 be the right-linear grammar

$$(N_1 \cup N_2 \cup \{S_3\}, \Sigma, P_1 \cup P_2 \cup \{S_3 \rightarrow S_1 \mid S_2\}, S_3),$$

where S_3 is a new nonterminal symbol not in N_1 or N_2. It should be clear that $L(G_3) = L(G_1) \cup L(G_2)$ because for each derivation $S_3 \overset{+}{\Rightarrow} w$ there is either a derivation $S_1 \overset{+}{\underset{G_1}{\Rightarrow}} w$ or $S_2 \overset{+}{\underset{G_2}{\Rightarrow}} w$ and conversely. Since G_3 is a right-linear grammar, $L(G_3)$ is a right-linear language.

(ii) Let G_4 be the right-linear grammar $(N_1 \cup N_2, \Sigma, P_4, S_1)$ in which P_4 is defined as follows:

(1) If $A \rightarrow xB$ is in P_1, then $A \rightarrow xB$ is in P_4.
(2) If $A \rightarrow x$ is in P_1, then $A \rightarrow xS_2$ is in P_4.
(3) All productions in P_2 are in P_4.

Note that if $S_1 \overset{+}{\underset{G_1}{\Rightarrow}} w$, then $S_1 \overset{+}{\underset{G_4}{\Rightarrow}} wS_2$, and that if $S_2 \overset{+}{\underset{G_2}{\Rightarrow}} x$, then $S_2 \overset{+}{\underset{G_4}{\Rightarrow}} x$. Thus, $L(G_1)L(G_2) \subseteq L(G_4)$. Now suppose that $S_1 \overset{+}{\underset{G_4}{\Rightarrow}} w$. Since there are no productions of the form $A \rightarrow x$ in P_4 that "came out of" P_1 we can write the derivation in the form $S_1 \overset{+}{\underset{G_4}{\Rightarrow}} xS_2 \overset{+}{\underset{G_4}{\Rightarrow}} xy$, where $w = xy$ and all productions used in the derivation $S_1 \overset{+}{\Rightarrow} xS_2$ arose from rules (1) and (2) of the construction of P_4. Thus we must have the derivations $S_1 \overset{+}{\underset{G_1}{\Rightarrow}} x$ and $S_2 \overset{+}{\underset{G_2}{\Rightarrow}} y$. Hence, $L(G_4) \subseteq L(G_1)L(G_2)$. It thus follows that $L(G_4) = L(G_1)L(G_2)$.

(iii) Let $G_5 = (N_1 \cup \{S_5\}, \Sigma, P_5, S_5)$ such that S_5 is not in N_1 and P_5 is constructed as follows:

(1) If $A \rightarrow xB$ is in P_1, then $A \rightarrow xB$ is in P_5.
(2) If $A \rightarrow x$ is in P_1, then $A \rightarrow xS_5$ and $A \rightarrow x$ are in P_5.
(3) $S_5 \rightarrow S_1 \,|\, e$ are in P_5.

A proof that $S_5 \overset{+}{\underset{G_5}{\Rightarrow}} x_1 S_5 \overset{+}{\underset{G_5}{\Rightarrow}} x_1 x_2 S_5 \overset{+}{\underset{G_5}{\Rightarrow}} \cdots \overset{+}{\underset{G_5}{\Rightarrow}} x_1 x_2 \cdots x_{n-1} S_5 \overset{+}{\underset{G_5}{\Rightarrow}} x_1 x_2 \cdots x_{n-1} x_n$ if and only if $S_1 \overset{+}{\underset{G_1}{\Rightarrow}} x_1, S_1 \overset{+}{\underset{G_1}{\Rightarrow}} x_2, \ldots, S_1 \overset{+}{\underset{G_1}{\Rightarrow}} x_n$ is left for the Exercises.

From the above, we have $L(G_5) = (L(G_1))^*$. $\quad\square$

We can now equate the class of right-linear languages with the class of regular sets.

THEOREM 2.2

A language is a regular set if and only if it is a right-linear language.

Proof.
Only if: This portion follows from Lemmas 2.6 and 2.7 and induction on the number of applications of the definition of regular set necessary to show a particular regular set to be one.

If: Let $G = (N, \Sigma, P, S)$ be a right-linear grammar with $N = \{A_1, \ldots, A_n\}$. We can construct a set of regular expression equations in standard form with the nonterminals in N as indeterminates. The equation for A_i is

$A_i = \alpha_{i0} + \alpha_{i1}A_1 + \cdots + \alpha_{in}A_n$, where

(1) $\alpha_{i0} = w_1 + \cdots + w_k$, where $A_i \to w_1 \mid \cdots \mid w_k$ are all productions with A_i on the left and only terminals on the right. If $k = 0$, take α_{i0} to be $\varnothing$.

(2) α_{ij}, $j > 0$, is $x_1 + \cdots + x_m$, where $A_i \to x_1A_j \mid \cdots \mid x_mA_j$ are all productions with A_i on the left and a right side ending in A_j. Again, if $m = 0$, then $\alpha_{ij} = \varnothing$.

Using Lemma 2.3, it is straightforward to show that $L(G)$ is $f(S)$, where f is the minimal fixed point of the constructed set of equations. This portion of the proof is left for the Exercises. But $f(S)$ is a language with a regular expression, as constructed by Algorithm 2.1. Thus, $L(G)$ is a regular set.   □

Example 2.10

Let G be defined by the productions

$$S \longrightarrow 0A \mid 1S \mid e$$
$$A \longrightarrow 0B \mid 1A$$
$$B \longrightarrow 0S \mid 1B$$

Then the set of equations generated is that of Example 2.9, with S, A, and B, respectively, identified with X_1, X_2, and X_3. In fact, $L(G)$ is the set of strings whose number of 0's is divisible by 3. It is not hard to show that this set is denoted by the regular expression of (2.2.13).   □

2.2.3. Finite Automata

We have seen three ways of defining the class of regular sets:

(1) The class of regular sets is the least class of languages containing $\varnothing$, $\{e\}$, and $\{a\}$ for all symbols a and closed under union, concatenation, and *.

(2) The regular sets are those sets defined by regular expressions.

(3) The regular sets are the languages generated by right-linear grammars.

We shall now consider a fourth way, as the sets defined by finite automata. A finite automaton is one of the simplest recognizers. Its "infinite" memory is null. Ordinarily, the finite automaton consists only of an input tape and a finite control. Here, we shall allow the finite control to be nondeterministic, but restrict the input head to be one way. In fact, we require that the input head shift right on every move.† The two-way finite automaton is considered in the Exercises.

---

†Recall that, by definition, a one-way recognizer does not shift its input head left but may keep it stationary during a move. Allowing a finite automaton to keep its input head stationary does not permit the finite automaton to recognize any language not recognizable by a conventional finite automaton.

We specify a finite automaton by defining its finite set of control states, the allowable input symbols, the initial state, and the set of final states, i.e., the states which indicate acceptance of the input. There is a state transition function which, given the "current" state and "current" input symbol, gives all possible next states. It should be emphasized that the device is nondeterministic in an automaton-theoretic sense. That is, the device goes to all its next states, if you will, replicating itself in such a way that one instance of itself exists for each of its possible next states. The device accepts if any of its parallel existences reaches an accepting state.

The nondeterminism of the finite automaton should not be confused with "randomness," in which the automaton could randomly choose a next state according to fixed probabilities but had a single existence. Such an automaton is called "probabilistic" and will not be studied here.

We now give a formal definition of nondeterministic finite automaton.

DEFINITION

A *nondeterministic finite automaton* is a 5-tuple $M = (Q, \Sigma, \delta, q_0, F)$, where

(1) Q is a finite set of *states*;
(2) Σ is a finite set of permissible *input symbols*;
(3) δ is a mapping from $Q \times \Sigma$ to $\mathcal{P}(Q)$ which dictates the behavior of the finite state control; δ is sometimes called the *state transition function*;
(4) q_0 in Q is the *initial state* of the finite state control; and
(5) $F \subseteq Q$ is the set of *final states*.

A finite automaton operates by making a sequence of moves. A move is determined by the current state of the finite control and the input symbol currently scanned by the input head. A move itself consists of the control changing state and the input head shifting one square to the right.

To determine the future behavior of a finite automaton, all we need to know are

(1) The current state of the finite control and
(2) The string of symbols on the input tape consisting of the symbol under the input head followed by all symbols to the right of this symbol.

These two items of information provide an instantaneous description of the finite automaton, which we shall call a *configuration*.

DEFINITION

If $M = (Q, \Sigma, \delta, q_0, F)$ is a finite automaton, then a pair (q, w) in $Q \times \Sigma^*$ is a *configuration* of M. A configuration of the form (q_0, w) is called an *initial* configuration, and one of the form (q, e), where q is in F, is called a *final* (or *accepting*) configuration.

A *move* by M is represented by a binary relation $\vdash_M$ (or $\vdash$, where M is understood) on configurations. If $\delta(q, a)$ contains q', then $(q, aw) \vdash (q', w)$ for all w in Σ^*.

This says that if M is in state q and the input head is scanning the input symbol a, then M may make a move in which it goes into state q' and shifts the input head one square to the right. Since M is in general nondeterministic, there may be states other than q' which it could also enter on one move.

We say that $C \mathbin{\vert\frac{0}{M}} C'$ if and only if $C = C'$. We say that $C_0 \mathbin{\vert\frac{k}{M}} C_k, k \geq 1$, if and only if there exist configurations $C_1, \ldots, C_{k-1}$ such that $C_i \mathbin{\vert\frac{}{M}} C_{i+1}$, for all i, $0 \leq i < k$. $C \mathbin{\vert\frac{+}{M}} C'$ means that $C \mathbin{\vert\frac{k}{M}} C'$ for some $k \geq 1$, and $C \mathbin{\vert\frac{*}{M}} C'$ means that $C \mathbin{\vert\frac{k}{M}} C'$ for some $k \geq 0$. Thus, $\mathbin{\vert\frac{+}{M}}$ and $\mathbin{\vert\frac{*}{M}}$ are, respectively, the transitive and reflexive-transitive closure of $\mathbin{\vert\frac{}{M}}$. We shall drop the subscript M if no ambiguity arises.

We shall say that an input string w is *accepted* by M if $(q_0, w) \mathbin{\vert\frac{*}{}} (q, e)$ for some q in F. The *language defined by* M, denoted $L(M)$, is the set of input strings accepted by M, that is,

$$\{w \mid w \in \Sigma^* \text{ and } (q_0, w) \mathbin{\vert\frac{*}{}} (q, e) \text{ for some } q \text{ in } F\}.$$

We shall now give two examples of finite automata. The first is a simple "deterministic" automaton; the second shows the use of nondeterminism.

Example 2.11

Let $M = (\{p, q, r\}, \{0, 1\}, \delta, p, \{r\})$ be a finite automaton, where δ is specified as follows:

		Input	
	δ	0	1
State p		$\{q\}$	$\{p\}$
q		$\{r\}$	$\{p\}$
r		$\{r\}$	$\{r\}$

M accepts all strings of 0's and 1's which have two consecutive 0's. That is, state p is the initial state and can be interpreted as "Two consecutive 0's have not yet appeared, and the previous symbol was not a 0." State q means "Two consecutive 0's have not appeared, but the previous symbol was a 0." State r means "Two consecutive 0's have appeared." Note that once state r is entered, M remains in that state.

On input 01001, the only possible sequence of configurations, beginning with the initial configuration $(p, 01001)$, is

$$(p, 01001) \vdash (q, 1001)$$
$$\vdash (p, 001)$$
$$\vdash (q, 01)$$

$$\vdash (r, 1)$$
$$\vdash (r, e)$$

Thus, 01001 is in $L(M)$.   □

Example 2.12

Let us design a nondeterministic finite automaton to accept the set of strings in $\{1, 2, 3\}$ such that the last symbol in the input string also appears previously in the string. That is, 121 is accepted, but 31312 is not. We shall have a state q_0, which represents the idea that no attempt has been made to recognize anything. In this state the automaton (or that existence of it, anyway) is "coasting in neutral." We shall have states q_1, q_2, and q_3, which represent the idea that a "guess" has been made that the last symbol of the string is the subscript of the state. We have one final state, q_f. In addition to remaining in q_0, the automaton can go to state q_a if a is the next input. If (an existence of) the automaton is in q_a, it can go to q_f if it sees another a. The automaton goes no place from q_f, since the question of acceptance must be decided anew as each symbol on its input tape becomes the "last." We specify M formally as

$$M = (\{q_0, q_1, q_2, q_3, q_f\}, \{1, 2, 3\}, \delta, q_0, \{q_f\})$$

where δ is given by the following table:

		Input		
	δ	1	2	3
State	q_0	$\{q_0, q_1\}$	$\{q_0, q_2\}$	$\{q_0, q_3\}$
	q_1	$\{q_1, q_f\}$	$\{q_1\}$	$\{q_1\}$
	q_2	$\{q_2\}$	$\{q_2, q_f\}$	$\{q_2\}$
	q_3	$\{q_3\}$	$\{q_3\}$	$\{q_3, q_f\}$
	q_f	$\varnothing$	$\varnothing$	$\varnothing$

On input 12321, the proliferation of configurations is shown in the tree in Fig. 2.2.

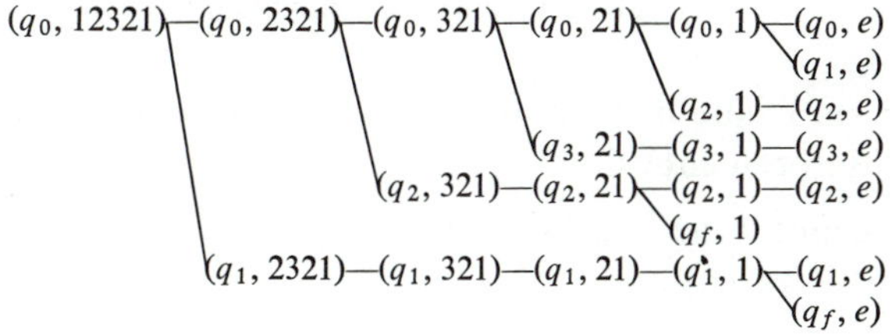

Fig. 2.2 Configurations of M.

Since $(q_0, 12321) \underset{\sim}{\overset{*}{\mid}} (q_f, e)$, the string 12321 is in $L(M)$. Note that certain configurations are repeated in Fig. 2.2, and for this reason a directed acyclic graph might be a more suitable representation for the configurations entered by M. $\square$

It is often convenient to use a pictorial representation of finite automata.

DEFINITION

Let $M = (Q, \Sigma, \delta, q_0, F)$ be a nondeterministic finite automaton. The *transition graph* for M is an unordered labeled graph where the nodes of the graph are labeled by the names of the states and there is an edge (p, q) if there exists an $a \in \Sigma$ such that $\delta(p, a)$ contains q. Further, we *label* the edge (p, q) by the list of a such that $q \in \delta(p, a)$. Thus the transition graphs for the automata of Examples 2.11 and 2.12 are shown in Fig. 2.3. We have

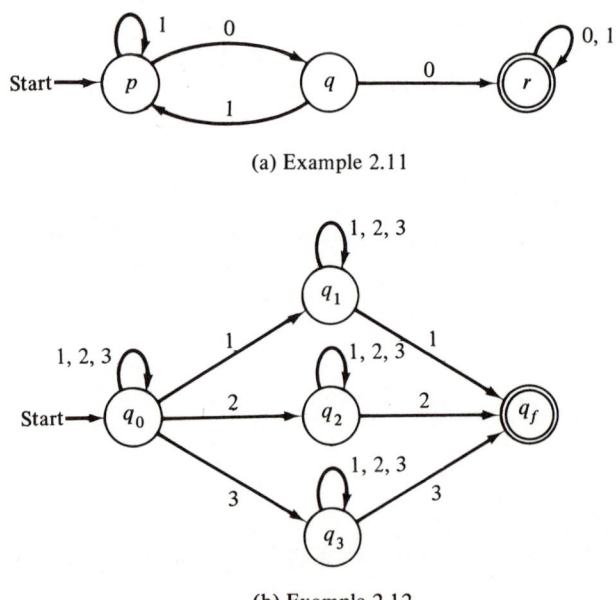

(a) Example 2.11

(b) Example 2.12

Fig. 2.3   Transition graphs.

indicated the start state by pointing to it with an arrow labeled "start," and final states have been circled.

We shall define a deterministic finite automaton as a special case of the nondeterministic variety.

DEFINITION

Let $M = (Q, \Sigma, \delta, q_0, F)$ be a nondeterministic finite automaton. We say that M is *deterministic* if $\delta(q, a)$ has no more than one member for any q in

Q and a in Σ. If $\delta(q, a)$ always has exactly one member, we say that M is *completely specified*.

Thus the automaton of Example 2.11 is a completely specified deterministic finite automaton. We shall hereafter reserve the term *finite automaton* for a completely specified deterministic finite automaton.

One of the most important results from the theory of finite automata is that the classes of languages defined by nondeterministic finite automata and completely specified deterministic finite automata are identical. We shall prove the result now.

CONVENTION

Since we shall be dealing primarily with deterministic finite automata, we shall write "$\delta(q, a) = p$" instead of "$\delta(q, a) = \{p\}$" when the automaton with transition function δ is deterministic. If $\delta(q, a) = \varnothing$, we shall often say that $\delta(q, a)$ is "undefined."

THEOREM 2.3

If $L = L(M)$ for some nondeterministic finite automaton M, then $L = L(M')$ for some finite automaton M'.

Proof. Let $M = (Q, \Sigma, \delta, q_0, F)$. We construct $M' = (Q', \Sigma, \delta', q'_0, F')$, as follows:

(1) $Q' = \mathcal{P}(Q)$. Thus the states of M' are sets of states of M.
(2) $q'_0 = \{q_0\}$.
(3) F' consists of all subsets S of Q such that $S \cap F \neq \varnothing$.
(4) For all $S \subseteq Q, \delta'(S, a) = S'$, where $S' = \{p \,|\, \delta(q, a)$ contains p for some q in $S\}$.

It is left for the Exercises to prove the following statement by induction on i:

(2.2.16) $(S, w)\,|\!\frac{i}{M'}\,(S', e)$ if and only if
$$S' = \{p \,|\, (q, w)\,|\!\frac{i}{M}\,(p, e) \text{ for some } q \text{ in } S\}$$

As a special case of (2.2.16), $(\{q_0\}, w)\,|\!\frac{i}{M'}\,(S', e)$ for some S' in F' if and only if $(q_0, w)\,|\!\frac{i}{M}\,(p, e)$ for some p in F. Thus, $L(M') = L(M)$. $\square$

Example 2.13

Let us construct a finite automaton $M' = (Q, \{1, 2, 3\}, \delta', \{q_0\}, F)$ accepting the language of M in Example 2.12. Since M has 5 states, it seems that M' has 32 states. However, not all of these are accessible from the initial state. That is, we call a state p *accessible* if there is a w such that $(q_0, w)\,|\!\frac{*}{}\,(p, e)$, where q_0 is the initial state. Here, we shall construct only the accessible states.

We begin by observing that $\{q_0\}$ is accessible. $\delta'(\{q_0\}, a) = \{q_0, q_a\}$ for $a = 1, 2$, and 3. Let us consider the state $\{q_0, q_1\}$. We have $\delta'(\{q_0, q_1\}, 1) =$

Input

	1	2	3

State	$A = \{q_0\}$	B	C	D
	$B = \{q_0, q_1\}$	E	F	G
	$C = \{q_0, q_2\}$	F	H	I
	$D = \{q_0, q_3\}$	G	I	J
	$E = \{q_0, q_1, q_f\}$	E	F	G
	$F = \{q_0, q_1, q_2\}$	K	K	L
	$G = \{q_0, q_1, q_3\}$	M	L	M
	$H = \{q_0, q_2, q_f\}$	F	H	I
	$I = \{q_0, q_2, q_3\}$	L	N	N
	$J = \{q_0, q_3, q_f\}$	G	I	J
	$K = \{q_0, q_1, q_2, q_f\}$	K	K	L
	$L = \{q_0, q_1, q_2, q_3\}$	P	P	P
	$M = \{q_0, q_1, q_3, q_f\}$	M	L	M
	$N = \{q_0, q_2, q_3, q_f\}$	L	N	N
	$P = \{q_0, q_1, q_2, q_3, q_f\}$	P	P	P

Fig. 2.4   Transition function of M'.

$\{q_0, q_1, q_f\}$. Proceeding in this way, we find that a set of states of M is accessible if and only if:

(1) It contains q_0, and

(2) If it contains q_f, then it also contains q_1, q_2, or q_3.

The complete set of accessible states, together with the δ' function, is given in Fig. 2.4.

The initial state of M' is A, and the set of final states consists of E, H, J, K, M, N, and P. $\square$

2.2.4.   Finite Automata and Regular Sets

We shall show that a language is a regular set if and only if it is defined by a finite automaton. The method is first to show that a finite automaton language is defined by a right-linear grammar. Then we show that the finite automaton languages include $\varnothing$, $\{e\}$, $\{a\}$ for all symbols a, and are closed under union, concatenation, and *. Thus every regular set is a finite automaton language. The following sequence of lemmas proves these assertions.

LEMMA 2.8

If $L = L(M)$ for finite automaton M, then $L = L(G)$ for some right-linear grammar G.

Proof. Let $M = (Q, \Sigma, \delta, q_0, F)$ (M is deterministic, of course). We let $G' = (Q, \Sigma, P, q_0)$, where P is defined as follows:

(1) If $\delta(q, a) = r$, then P contains the production $q \longrightarrow ar$.

(2) If p is in F, then $p \longrightarrow e$ is a production in P.

We can show that each step of a derivation in G mimics a move by M. We shall prove by induction on i that

(2.2.17)   For q in Q, $q \overset{i+1}{\Rightarrow} w$ if and only if $(q, w) \vdash^{i} (r, e)$ for some r in F

Basis. For $i = 0$, clearly $q \Rightarrow e$ if and only if $(q, e) \vdash^{0} (q, e)$ for q in F.

Inductive Step. Assume that (2.2.17) is true for i and let $w = ax$, where $|x| = i$. Then $q \overset{i+1}{\Rightarrow} w$ if and only if $q \Rightarrow as \overset{i}{\Rightarrow} ax$ for some $s \in Q$. But $q \Rightarrow as$ if and only if $\delta(q, a) = s$. From the inductive hypothesis, $s \overset{i}{\Rightarrow} x$ if and only if $(s, x) \vdash^{i} (r, e)$ for some $r \in F$. Therefore, $q \overset{i+1}{\Rightarrow} w$ if and only if $(q, w) \vdash^{i} (r, e)$ for some $r \in F$. Thus Eq. (2.2.17) is true for all $i \geq 0$.

We now have $q_0 \overset{+}{\Rightarrow} w$ if and only if $(q_0, w) \vdash^{*} (r, e)$ for some $r \in F$. Thus, $L(G) = L(M)$. $\square$

LEMMA 2.9

Let Σ be a finite alphabet. (i) $\varnothing$, (ii) $\{e\}$, and (iii) $\{a\}$ for $a \in \Sigma$ are finite automaton languages.

Proof.

(i) Any finite automaton with an empty set of final states accepts $\varnothing$.

(ii) Let $M = (\{q_0\}, \Sigma, \delta, q_0, \{q_0\})$, where $\delta(q_0, a)$ is undefined for all a in Σ. Then $L(M) = \{e\}$.

(iii) Let $M = (\{q_0, q_1\}, \Sigma, \delta, q_0, \{q_1\})$, where $\delta(q_0, a) = q_1$ and δ is undefined otherwise. Then $L(M) = \{a\}$. $\square$

LEMMA 2.10

Let $L_1 = L(M_1)$ and $L_2 = L(M_2)$ for finite automata M_1 and M_2. Then (i) $L_1 \cup L_2$, (ii) $L_1 L_2$, and (iii) L_1^* are finite automaton languages.

Proof. Let $M_1 = (Q_1, \Sigma, \delta_1, q_1, F_1)$ and $M_2 = (Q_2, \Sigma, \delta_2, q_2, F_2)$. We assume without loss of generality that $Q_1 \cap Q_2 = \varnothing$, since states can be renamed at will.

(i) Let $M = (Q_1 \cup Q_2 \cup \{q_0\}, \Sigma, \delta, q_0, F)$ be a nondeterministic finite automaton, where

(1) q_0 is a new state,

(2) $F = F_1 \cup F_2$ if e is not in L_1 or L_2 and $F = F_1 \cup F_2 \cup \{q_0\}$ if e is in L_1 or L_2, and

(3) (a) $\delta(q_0, a) = \delta(q_1, a) \cup \delta(q_2, a)$ for all a in Σ,
      (b) $\delta(q, a) = \delta_1(q, a)$ for all q in Q_1, a in Σ, and
      (c) $\delta(q, a) = \delta_2(q, a)$ for all q in Q_2, a in Σ.

Thus, M guesses whether to simulate M_1 or M_2. Since M is nondeterministic, it actually does both. It is straightforward to show by induction on $i \geq 1$ that $(q_0, w) \vdash^{i}_{M} (q, e)$ if and only if q is in Q_1 and $(q_1, w) \vdash^{i}_{M_1} (q, e)$ or q is in Q_2

and $(q_2, w) \mid_{\overline{M_2}}^{i} (q, e)$. This result, together with the definition of F, yields $L(M) = L(M_1) \cup L(M_2)$.

(ii) To construct a finite automaton M to recognize $L_1 L_2$ let $M = (Q_1 \cup Q_2, \Sigma, \delta, q_1, F)$, where δ is defined by

    (1) $\delta(q, a) = \delta_1(q, a)$ for all q in $Q_1 - F_1$,

    (2) $\delta(q, a) = \delta_1(q, a) \cup \delta_2(q_2, a)$ for all q in F_1, and

    (3) $\delta(q, a) = \delta_2(q, a)$ for all q in Q_2.

Let

$$F = \begin{cases} F_2, & \text{if } q_2 \notin F_2 \\ F_1 \cup F_2, & \text{if } q_2 \in F_2 \end{cases}$$

That is, M begins by simulating M_1. When M reaches a final state of M_1, it may, nondeterministically, imagine that it is in the initial state of M_2 by rule (2). M will then simulate M_2. Let x be in L_1 and y in L_2. Then $(q_1, xy) \mid_{\overline{M}}^{*} (q, y)$ for some q in F_1. If $x = e$, then $q = q_1$. If $y \neq e$, then, using one rule from (2) and zero or more from (3), $(q, y) \mid_{\overline{M}}^{+} (r, e)$ for some $r \in F_2$. If $y = e$, then q is in F, since $q_2 \in F_2$. Thus, xy is in $L(M)$. Suppose that w is in $L(M)$. Then $(q_1, w) \mid_{\overline{M}}^{*} (q, e)$ for some $q \in F$. There are two cases to consider depending on whether $q \in F_2$ or $q \in F_1$. Suppose that $q \in F_2$. Then we can write $w = xay$ for some a in Σ such that

$$(q_1, xay) \mid_{\overline{M}}^{*} (r, ay) \mid_{\overline{M}} (s, y) \mid_{\overline{M}}^{*} (q, e),$$

where $r \in F_1$, $s \in Q_2$, and $\delta_2(q, a)$ contains s. Then $x \in L_1$ and $ay \in L_2$. Suppose that $q \in F_1$. Then $q_2 \in F_2$ and e is in L_2. Thus, $w \in L_1$. We conclude that $L(M) = L_1 L_2$.

(iii) We construct $M = (Q_1 \cup \{q'\}, \Sigma, \delta, q', F_1 \cup \{q'\})$, where q' is a new state not in Q_1, to accept L_1^* as follows. δ is defined by

    (1) $\delta(q, a) = \delta_1(q, a)$ if q is in $Q_1 - F_1$ and $a \in \Sigma$,

    (2) $\delta(q, a) = \delta_1(q, a) \cup \delta_1(q_1, a)$ if q is in F_1 and $a \in \Sigma$, and

    (3) $\delta(q', a) = \delta_1(q_1, a)$ for all a in Σ.

Thus, whenever M enters a final state of M_1, it has the option of continuing to simulate M_1 or to begin simulating M_1 anew from the initial state. A proof that $L(M) = L_1^*$ is similar to the proof of part (ii). Note that since q' is a final state, $e \in L(M)$. $\square$

THEOREM 2.4

A language is accepted by a finite automaton if and only if it is a regular set.

Proof. Immediate from Theorem 2.2 and Lemmas 2.8, 2.9, and 2.10. $\square$

2.2.5. Summary

The results of Section 2.2 can be summarized in the following theorem.

THEOREM 2.5

The following statements are equivalent:
(1) L is a regular set.
(2) L is a right-linear language.
(3) L is a finite automaton language.
(4) L is a nondeterministic finite automaton language.
(5) L is denoted by a regular expression.   □

EXERCISES

2.2.1. Which of the following are regular sets? Give regular expressions for those which are.
(a) The set of words with an equal number of 0's and 1's.
(b) The set of words in $\{0, 1\}^*$ with an even number of 0's and an odd number of 1's.
(c) The set of words in Σ^* whose length is divisible by 3.
(d) The set of words in $\{0, 1\}^*$ with no substring 101.

2.2.2. Show that the set of regular expressions over Σ is a CFL.

2.2.3. Show that if L is any regular set, then there is an infinity of regular expressions denoting L.

2.2.4. Let L be a regular set. Prove directly from the definition of a regular set that L^R is a regular set. *Hint:* Induction on the number of applications of the definition of regular set used to show L to be regular.

2.2.5. Show the folllowing identities for regular expressions α, β, and γ:
(a) $\alpha(\beta + \gamma) = \alpha\beta + \alpha\gamma.$ (g) $(\alpha + \beta)\gamma = \alpha\gamma + \beta\gamma.$
(b) $\alpha + (\beta + \gamma) = (\alpha + \beta) + \gamma.$ (h) $\varnothing^* = e.$
(c) $\alpha(\beta\gamma) = (\alpha\beta)\gamma.$ (i) $\alpha^* + \alpha = \alpha^*.$
(d) $\alpha e = e\alpha = \alpha.$ (j) $(\alpha^*)^* = \alpha^*.$
(e) $\varnothing\alpha = \alpha\varnothing = \varnothing.$ (k) $(\alpha + \beta)^* = (\alpha^*\beta^*)^*.$
(f) $\alpha + \alpha = \alpha.$ (l) $\alpha + \varnothing = \alpha.$

2.2.6. Solve the following set of regular expression equations:

$$A_1 = (01^* + 1)A_1 + A_2$$
$$A_2 = 11 + 1A_1 + 00A_3$$
$$A_3 = e + A_1 + A_2$$

2.2.7. Consider the single equation

(2.2.18) $X = \alpha X + \beta$

where α and β are regular expressions over Σ and $X \notin \Sigma$. Show that

(a) If e is not in α, then $X = \alpha^*\beta$ is the unique solution to (2.2.18).
(b) If e is in α, then $\alpha^*\beta$ is the minimal fixed point of (2.2.18), but there are an infinity of solutions.

(c) In either case, every solution to (2.2.18) is a set of the form $\alpha^*(\beta \cup L)$ for some (not necessarily regular) language L.

2.2.8. Solve the following general pair of standard form equations:

$$X = \alpha_1 X + \alpha_2 Y + \alpha_3$$
$$Y = \beta_1 X + \beta_2 Y + \beta_3$$

2.2.9. Complete the proof of Lemma 2.4.

2.2.10. Prove Lemma 2.5.

2.2.11. Find right-linear grammars for those sets in Exercise 2.2.1 which are regular sets.

DEFINITION

A grammar $G = (N, \Sigma, P, S)$ is *left-linear* if every production in P is of the form $A \longrightarrow Bw$ or $A \longrightarrow w$.

2.2.12. Show that a language is a regular set if and only if it has a left-linear grammar. *Hint:* Use Exercise 2.2.4.

DEFINITION

A right-linear grammar $G = (N, \Sigma, P, S)$ is called a *regular grammar* when

(1) All productions with the possible exception of $S \longrightarrow e$ are of the form $A \longrightarrow aB$ or $A \longrightarrow a$, where A and B are in N and a is in Σ.

(2) If $S \longrightarrow e$ is in P, then S does not appear on the right of any production.

2.2.13. Show that every regular set has a regular grammar. *Hint:* There are several ways to do this. One way is to apply a sequence of transformations to a right-linear grammar G which will map G into an equivalent regular grammar. Another way is to construct a regular grammar directly from a finite automaton.

2.2.14. Construct a regular grammar for the regular set generated by the right-linear grammar

$$A \longrightarrow B \,|\, C$$
$$B \longrightarrow 0B \,|\, 1B \,|\, 011$$
$$C \longrightarrow 0D \,|\, 1C \,|\, e$$
$$D \longrightarrow 0C \,|\, 1D$$

2.2.15. Provide an algorithm which, given a regular grammar G and a string w, determines whether w is in $L(G)$.

2.2.16. Prove line (2.2.16) in Theorem 2.3.

2.2.17. Complete the proof of Lemma 2.7(iii).

Definition

A production $A \longrightarrow \alpha$ of right-linear grammar $G = (N, \Sigma, P, S)$ is *useless* if there do not exist strings w and x in Σ^* such that

$$S \overset{*}{\Longrightarrow} wA \Longrightarrow w\alpha \overset{*}{\Longrightarrow} wx.$$

2.2.18. Give an algorithm to convert a right-linear grammar to an equivalent one with no useless productions.

*2.2.19. Let $G = (N, \Sigma, P, S)$ be a right-linear grammar. Let $N = \{A_1, \ldots, A_n\}$, and define $\alpha_{ij} = x_1 + x_2 + \cdots + x_m$, where $A_i \longrightarrow x_1 A_j, \ldots, A_i \longrightarrow x_m A_j$ are all the productions of the form $A_i \longrightarrow yA_j$. Also define $\alpha_{i0} = x_1 + \cdots + x_m$, where $A_i \longrightarrow x_1, \ldots, A_i \longrightarrow x_m$ are all productions of the form $A_i \longrightarrow y$. Let Q be the set of standard form equations $A_i = \alpha_{i0} + \alpha_{i1}A_1 + \alpha_{i2}A_2 + \cdots + \alpha_{in}A_n$. Show that the minimal fixed point of Q is $L(G)$. *Hint:* Use Lemma 2.3.

2.2.20. Show that $L(G)$ of Example 2.10 is the set of strings in $\{0, 1\}^*$, whose length is divisible by 3.

2.2.21. Find deterministic and nondeterministic finite automata for those sets of Exercise 2.2.1 which are regular.

2.2.22. Show that the finite automaton of Example 2.11 accepts the language $(0 + 1)^*00(0 + 1)^*$.

2.2.23. Prove that the finite automaton of Example 2.12 accepts the language $\{wa \,|\, a \text{ in } \{1, 2, 3\} \text{ and } w \text{ has an instance of } a\}$.

2.2.24. Complete the proof of Lemma 2.10(iii).

*2.2.25. A two-way finite automaton is a (nondeterministic) finite control with an input head that can move either left or right or remain stationary. Show that a language is accepted by a two-way finite automaton if and only if it is a regular set. *Hint:* Construct a deterministic one-way finite automaton which, after reading input $w \neq e$, has in its finite control a finite table which tells, for each state q of the two-way automaton in what state, if any, it would move off the right end of w, when started in state q at the rightmost symbol of w.

*2.2.26. Show that allowing a one-way finite automaton to keep its input head stationary does not increase the class of languages defined by the device.

**2.2.27. For arbitrary n, show that there is a regular set which can be recognized by an n-state nondeterministic finite automaton but requires 2^n states in any deterministic finite automaton recognizing it.

2.2.28. Show that every language accepted by an n-state two-way finite automaton is accepted by a $2^{n(n+1)}$-state finite automaton.

**2.2.29. How many different languages over $\{0, 1\}$ are defined by two-state
(a) Nondeterministic finite automata?
(b) Deterministic finite automata?
(c) Finite automata?

DEFINITION

A set S of integers forms an *arithmetic progression* if we can write $S = \{c, c + p, c + 2p, \ldots, c + ip, \ldots\}$. For any language L, let $S(L) = \{i \mid \text{for some } w \text{ in } L, |w| = i\}$.

**2.2.30. Show that for every regular language L, $S(L)$ is the union of a finite number of arithmetic progressions.

Open Problem

2.2.31. How close to the bound of Exercise 2.2.28 for converting n-state two-way nondeterministic finite automata to k-state finite automata is it actually possible to come?

BIBLIOGRAPHIC NOTES

Regular expressions were defined by Kleene [1956]. McNaughton and Yamada [1960] and Brzozowski [1962] cover regular expressions in more detail. Salomaa [1966] describes two axiom systems for regular expressions. The equivalence of regular languages and regular sets is given by Chomsky and Miller [1958]. The equivalence of deterministic and nondeterministic finite automata is given by Rabin and Scott [1959]. Exercise 2.2.25 is from there and from Shepherdson [1959].

2.3. PROPERTIES OF REGULAR SETS

In this section we shall derive a number of useful facts about finite automata and regular sets. A particularly important result is that for every regular set there is an essentially unique minimum state finite automaton that defines that set.

2.3.1. Minimization of Finite Automata

Given a finite automaton M, we can find the smallest finite automaton equivalent to M by eliminating all inaccessible states in M and then merging all redundant states in M. The redundant states are determined by partitioning the set of all accessible states into equivalence classes such that each equivalence class contains indistinguishable states and is as large as possible. We then choose one representative from each equivalence class as a state for the reduced automaton. Thus we can reduce the size of M if M contains inaccessible states or two or more indistinguishable states. We shall show that this reduced machine is the smallest finite automaton that recognizes the regular set defined by the original machine M.

DEFINITION

Let $M = (Q, \Sigma, \delta, q_0, F)$ be a finite automaton, and let q_1 and q_2 be distinct states. We say that x in Σ^* *distinguishes* q_1 from q_2 if $(q_1, x) \models^* (q_3, e)$,

$(q_2, x) \vdash^* (q_4, e)$, and exactly one of q_3 and q_4 is in F. We say that q_1 and q_2 are *k-indistinguishable*, written $q_1 \overset{k}{\equiv} q_2$, if and only if there is no x, with $|x| \leq k$, which distinguishes q_1 from q_2. We say that two states q_1 and q_2 are *indistinguishable*, written $q_1 \equiv q_2$, if and only if they are k-indistinguishable for all $k \geq 0$.

A state $q \in Q$ is said to be *inaccessible* if there is no input string x such that $(q_0, x) \vdash^* (q, e)$.

M is said to be *reduced* if no state in Q is inaccessible and no two distinct states of Q are indistinguishable.

Example 2.14

Consider the finite automaton M whose transition graph is shown in Fig. 2.5.

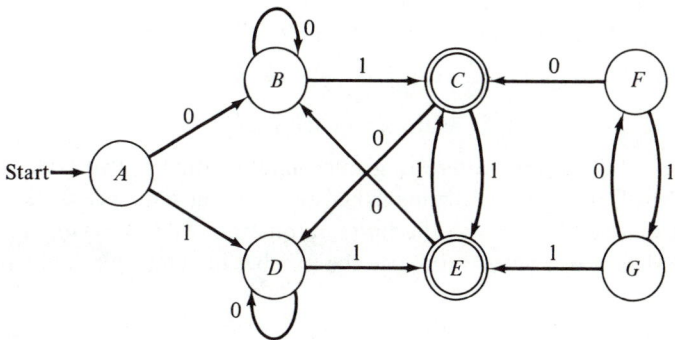

Fig. 2.5　Transition graph of M.

To reduce M we first notice that states F and G are inaccessible from the start state A and thus can be removed. We shall see in the next algorithm that the equivalence classes under $\equiv$ are $\{A\}$, $\{B, D\}$, and $\{C, E\}$. Thus we can represent these sets by the states p, q, and r, respectively, to obtain the finite automaton of Fig. 2.6, which is the reduced automaton for M.　□

Lemma 2.11

Let $M = (Q, \Sigma, \delta, q_0, F)$ be a finite automaton with n states. States q_1 and q_2 are indistinguishable if and only if they are $(n - 2)$-indistinguishable.

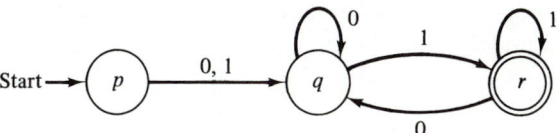

Fig. 2.6　Reduced machine.

Proof. The "only if" portion is trivial. The "if" portion is trivial if F has 0 or n states. Therefore, assume the contrary.

We shall show that the following condition must hold on the k-indistinguishability relations:

$$\overset{n-2}{\equiv} \subseteq \overset{n-3}{\equiv} \subseteq \equiv \subseteq \cdots \subseteq \overset{2}{\equiv} \subseteq \overset{1}{\equiv} \subseteq \overset{0}{\equiv}$$

To see this, we observe that for q_1 and q_2 in Q,

(1) $q_1 \overset{0}{\equiv} q_2$ if and only if both q_1 and q_2 are either in F or not in F.

(2) $q_1 \overset{k}{\equiv} q_2$ if and only if $q_1 \overset{k-1}{\equiv} q_2$ and for all a in Σ, $\delta(q_1, a) \overset{k-1}{\equiv} \delta(q_2, a)$.

The equivalence relation $\overset{0}{\equiv}$ is the coarsest and partitions Q into two equivalence classes, F and $Q - F$. Then if $\overset{k+1}{\equiv} \neq \overset{k}{\equiv}$, $\overset{k+1}{\equiv}$ is a strict refinement of $\overset{k}{\equiv}$, that is, $\overset{k+1}{\equiv}$ contains at least one more equivalence class than $\overset{k}{\equiv}$. Since there are at most $n - 1$ elements in either F or $Q - F$ we can have at most $n - 2$ successive refinements of $\overset{0}{\equiv}$. If for some k, $\overset{k+1}{\equiv} = \overset{k}{\equiv}$, then $\overset{k+1}{\equiv} = \overset{k+2}{\equiv} = \cdots$, by (2). Thus, $\overset{k}{\equiv}$ is the first relation $\overset{k}{\equiv}$ such that $\overset{k+1}{\equiv} = \overset{k}{\equiv}$. $\square$

Lemma 2.11 has the interesting interpretation that if two states can be distinguished, they can be distinguished by an input sequence of length less than the number of states in the finite automaton. The following algorithm gives the details of how to minimize the number of states in a finite automaton.

ALGORITHM 2.2

Construction of the canonical finite automaton.

Input. A finite automaton $M = (Q, \Sigma, \delta, q_0, F)$.

Output. A reduced equivalent finite automaton M'.

Method.

Step 1: Use Algorithm 0.3 on the transition graph of M to find those states which are inaccessible from q_0. Delete all inaccessible states.

Step 2: Construct the equivalence relations $\overset{0}{\equiv}, \overset{1}{\equiv}, \ldots$, as outlined in Lemma 2.11. Continue until $\overset{k+1}{\equiv} = \overset{k}{\equiv}$. Choose $\equiv$ to be $\overset{k}{\equiv}$.

Step 3: Construct the finite automaton $M' = (Q', \Sigma, \delta', q_0', F')$, where

(a) Q' is the set of equivalence classes under $\equiv$. Let $[p]$ be the equivalence class of state p under $\equiv$.

(b) $\delta'([p], a) = [q]$ if $\delta(p, a) = q$.

(c) q_0' is $[q_0]$.

(d) $F' = \{[q] \mid q \in F\}$. $\square$

It is straightforward to show that step 3(b) is consistent; i.e., whatever member of $[p]$ we choose we get the same equivalence class for $\delta([p], a)$. A proof that $L(M') = L(M)$ is also straightforward and left for the Exercises. We prove that no automaton with fewer states than M' accepts $L(M)$.

THEOREM 2.6

M' of Algorithm 2.2 has the smallest number of states of any finite automaton accepting $L(M)$.

Proof. Suppose that M'' had fewer states than M' and that $L(M'') = L(M)$. Each equivalence class under $\equiv$ is nonempty, so each state of M' is accessible. Thus there exist strings w and x such that $(q_0'', w) \vdash_{M''}^* (q, e)$ and $(q_0'', x) \vdash_{M''}^* (q, e)$, where q_0'' is initial state of M'', but w and x take M' to different states. Hence, w and x take M to different states, say p and r, which are distinguishable. That is, there is some y such that exactly one of wy and xy is in $L(M)$. But wy and xy must take M'' to the same state, namely, that state s such that $(q, y) \vdash_{M''}^* (s, e)$. Thus is not possible that exactly one of wy and xy is in $L(M'')$, as supposed. $\square$

Example 2.15

Let us find a reduced finite automaton for the finite automaton M whose transition graph is shown in Fig. 2.7. The equivalence classes for $\overset{k}{\equiv}$, $k \geq 0$, are as follows:

$$\text{For } \overset{0}{\equiv}: \quad \{A, F\}, \{B, C, D, E\}$$

$$\text{For } \overset{1}{\equiv}: \quad \{A, F\}, \{B, E\}, \{C, D\}$$

$$\text{For } \overset{2}{\equiv}: \quad \{A, F\}, \{B, E\}, \{C, D\}.$$

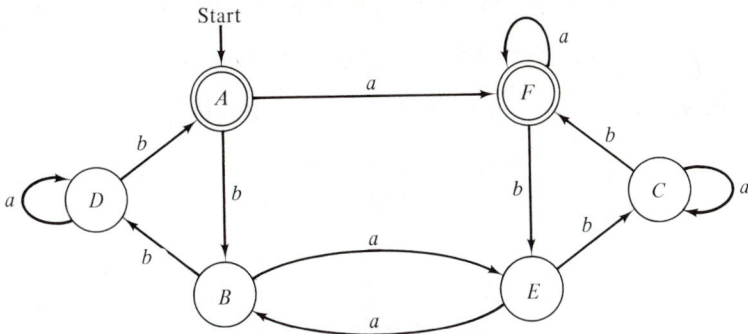

Fig. 2.7 Transition graph of M.

Since $\overset{2}{\equiv} = \overset{1}{\equiv}$ we have $\equiv = \overset{1}{\equiv}$. The reduced machine M' is $(\{[A], [B], [C]\},$ $\{a, b\}, \delta', A, \{[A]\})$, where δ' is defined as

	a	b
$[A]$	$[A]$	$[B]$
$[B]$	$[B]$	$[C]$
$[C]$	$[C]$	$[A]$

Here we have chosen $[A]$ to represent the equivalence class $\{A, F\}$, $[B]$ to represent $\{B, E\}$, and $[C]$ to represent $\{C, D\}$. □

2.3.2. The Pumping Lemma for Regular Sets

We shall now derive a characterization of regular sets that will be useful in proving certain languages not to be regular. The next theorem is referred to as a "pumping" lemma, because it says, in effect, that given any regular set and any sufficiently long sentence in that set, we can find a nonempty substring in that sentence which can be repeated as often as we like (i.e., "pumped") and the new strings so formed will all be in the same regular set. It is often possible to thus derive a contradiction of the hypothesis that the set is regular.

THEOREM 2.7

The pumping lemma for regular sets: Let L be a regular set. There exists a constant p such that if a string w is in L and $|w| \geq p$, then w can be written as xyz, where $0 < |y| \leq p$ and $xy^i z \in L$ for all $i \geq 0$.

Proof. Let $M = (Q, \Sigma, \delta, q_0, F)$ be a finite automaton with n states such that $L(M) = L$. Let $p = n$. If $w \in L$ and $|w| \geq n$, then consider the sequence of configurations entered by M in accepting w. Since there are at least $n + 1$ configurations in the sequence, there must be two with the same state among the first $n + 1$ configurations. Thus we have a sequence of moves such that

$$(q_0, xyz) \overset{*}{\vdash} (q_1, yz) \overset{k}{\vdash} (q_1, z) \overset{*}{\vdash} (q_2, e)$$

for some q_1 and $0 < k \leq n$. Thus, $0 < |y| \leq n$. But then

$$(q_0, xy^i z) \overset{*}{\vdash} (q_1, y^i z)$$
$$\overset{+}{\vdash} (q_1, y^{i-1} z)$$
$$\cdot$$
$$\cdot$$
$$\cdot$$
$$\overset{+}{\vdash} (q_1, yz)$$
$$\overset{+}{\vdash} (q_1, z)$$
$$\overset{*}{\vdash} (q_2, e)$$

must be a valid sequence of moves for all $i > 0$. Since $w = xyz$ is in L, xy^iz is in L for all $i > 1$. The case $i = 0$ is handled similarly. $\square$

Example 2.16

We shall use the pumping lemma to show that $L = \{0^n1^n \,|\, n \geq 1\}$ is not a regular set. Suppose that L is regular. Then for a sufficiently large n, 0^n1^n can be written as xyz such that $y \neq e$ and $xy^iz \in L$ for all $i \geq 0$. If $y \in 0^+$ or $y \in 1^+$, then $xz = xy^0z \notin L$. If $y \in 0^+1^+$, then $xyyz \notin L$. We have a contradiction, so L cannot be regular. $\square$

2.3.3. Closure Properties of Regular Sets

We say that a set A is *closed* under the n-ary operation θ if $\theta(a_1, a_2, \ldots, a_n)$ is in A whenever a_i is in A for $1 \leq i \leq n$. For example, the set of integers is closed under the binary operation addition.

In this section we shall examine certain operations under which the class of regular sets is closed. We can then use these closure properties to help determine whether certain languages are regular. We already know that if L_1 and L_2 are regular sets, then $L_1 \cup L_2, L_1L_2$, and L_1^* are regular.

DEFINITION

A class of sets is a *Boolean algebra of sets* if it is closed under union, intersection, and complementation.

THEOREM 2.8

The class of regular sets included in Σ^* is a Boolean algebra of sets for any alphabet Σ.

Proof. We shall show closure under complementation. We already have closure under union, and closure under intersection follows from the set-theoretic law $\overline{A \cap B} = \overline{A} \cup \overline{B}$ (Exercise 0.1.4). Let $M = (Q, \Delta, \delta, q_0, F)$ be any finite automaton with $\Delta \subseteq \Sigma$. It is easy to show that every regular set $L \subseteq \Sigma^*$ has such a finite automaton. Then the finite automaton $M' = (Q, \Delta, \delta, q_0, Q - F)$ accepts $\Delta^* - L(M)$. Note that the fact that M is completely specified is needed here. Now $\overline{L(M)}$, the complement with respect to Σ^*, can be expressed as $\overline{L(M)} = L(M') \cup \Sigma^*(\Sigma - \Delta)\Sigma^*$. Since $\Sigma^*(\Sigma - \Delta)\Sigma^*$ is regular, the regularity of $\overline{L(M)}$ follows from the closure of regular sets under union. $\square$

THEOREM 2.9

The class of regular sets is closed under reversal.

Proof. Let $M = (Q, \Sigma, \delta, q_0, F)$ be a finite automaton defining the regular set L. To define L^R we "run M backward." That is, let M' be the nondeterministic finite automaton $(Q \cup \{q_0'\}, \Sigma, \delta', q_0', F')$, where F' is $\{q_0\}$ if $e \notin L$ and $F' = \{q_0, q_0'\}$ if $e \in L$.

(1) $\delta'(q_0', a)$ contains q if $\delta(q, a) \in F$.

(2) For all q' in Q and a in Σ, $\delta'(q', a)$ contains q if $\delta(q, a) = q'$.

It is easy to show that $(q_0, w) \mathrel{\overset{+}{\underset{M}{\vdash}}} (q, e)$, where $q \in F$, if and only if $(q_0', w^R) \mathrel{\overset{+}{\underset{M'}{\vdash}}} (q_0, e)$. Thus, $L(M') = (L(M))^R = L^R$. $\quad\square$

The class of regular sets is closed under most common language theoretic operations. More of these closure properties are explored in the Exercises.

2.3.4. Decidable Questions About Regular Sets

We have seen certain specifications for regular sets, such as regular expressions and finite automata. There are certain natural questions concerning these representations that come up. Three questions with which we shall be concerned here are the following:

The *membership problem*: "Given a specification of known type and a string w, is w in the language so specified?"

The *emptiness problem*: "Given a specification of known type, does it specify the empty set?"

The *equivalence problem*: "Given two specifications of the same known type, do they specify the same language?"

The specifications for regular sets that we shall consider are

(1) Regular expressions,
(2) Right-linear grammars, and
(3) Finite automata.

We shall first give algorithms to decide the three problems when the specification is a finite automaton.

ALGORITHM 2.3

Decision of the membership question problem for finite automata.

Input. A finite automaton $M = (Q, \Sigma, \Delta, q_0, F)$ and a word w in Σ^*.

Output. "YES" if $w \in L(M)$, "NO" otherwise.

Method. Let $w = a_1 a_2 \cdots a_n$. Successively find the states $q_1 = \delta(q_0, a_1)$, $q_2 = \delta(q_1, a_2), \ldots, q_n = \delta(q_{n-1}, a_n)$. If q_n is in F, say "YES"; if not, say "NO." $\quad\square$

The correctness of Algorithm 2.3 is too obvious to discuss. However, it is worth discussing the time and space complexity of the algorithm. A natural measure of these complexities is the number of steps and memory cells needed to execute the algorithm on a random access computer in which each memory cell can store an integer of arbitrary size. (Actually there is a bound on the size of integers for real machines, but this bound is so large that we would undoubtedly never come against it for finite automata which we might reasonably consider. Thus the assumption of unbounded integers is a reasonable mathematical simplification here.)

It is easy to see that the time taken is a linear function of the length of w. However, it is not so clear whether or not the "size" of M affects the time taken. We must assume that the actual specification for M is a string of symbols chosen from some finite alphabet. Thus we might suppose that states are named $q_0, q_1, \ldots, q_i, \ldots$, where the integer subscripts are binary numbers. Likewise, the input symbols might be called $a_1, a_2, \ldots$. Assuming a normal kind of computer, one could take the pairs in the relation δ and construct a two-dimensional array that in cell (i, j) gave $\delta(q_i, a_j)$. Thus the total time of the algorithm would be an amount proportional to the length of the specification of M to construct the table, plus an amount proportional to $|w|$ to execute the algorithm.

The space required is primarily the space required by the table, which is seen to be proportional to the length of M's specification. (Recall that δ is really a set of pairs, one for each pair of a state and input symbol.)

We shall now give algorithms to decide the emptiness and equivalence problems when the method of specification is a finite automaton.

ALGORITHM 2.4

Decision of emptiness problem for finite automata.

Input. A finite automaton $M = (Q, \Sigma, \delta, q_0, F)$.

Output. "YES" if $L(M) \neq \varnothing$, "NO" otherwise.

Method. Compute the set of states accessible from q_0. If this set contains a final state, say "YES"; otherwise, say "NO." □

ALGORITHM 2.5

Decision of equivalence problem for finite automata.

Input. Two finite automata $M_1 = (Q_1, \Sigma_1, \delta_1, q_1, F_1)$ and $M_2 = (Q_2, \Sigma_2, \delta_2, q_2, F_2)$ such that $Q_1 \cap Q_2 = \varnothing$.

Output. "YES" if $L(M_1) = L(M_2)$, "NO" otherwise.

Method. Construct the finite automaton

$$M = (Q_1 \cup Q_2, \Sigma_1 \cup \Sigma_2, \delta_1 \cup \delta_2, q_1, F_1 \cup F_2).$$

Using Lemma 2.11 determine whether $q_1 \equiv q_2$. If so, say "YES"; otherwise, say "NO". □

We point out that we could also use Algorithm 2.4 to solve the equivalence problem since $L(M_1) = L(M_2)$ if and only if

$$(L(M_1) \cap \overline{L(M_2)}) \cup (\overline{L(M_1)} \cap L(M_2)) = \varnothing.$$

We now turn to the decidability of the membership, emptiness, and equivalence problems for two other representations of regular sets—the regular expressions and right-linear grammars. It is simple to show that for these representations the three problems are also decidable. A regular expression can be converted, by an algorithm which is implicit in Lemmas 2.9 and 2.10, into a finite automaton. The appropriate one of Algorithms 2.3–2.5 can then be applied. A right-linear grammar can be converted into a regular expression by Algorithm 2.1 and the algorithm implicit in Theorem 2.2. Obviously, these algorithms are too indirect to be practical. Direct, fast-working algorithms will be the subject of several of the Exercises.

We can summarize these results by the following theorem.

THEOREM 2.10

If the method of specification is finite automata, regular expressions, or right-linear grammars, then the membership, emptiness, and equivalence problems are decidable for regular sets. $\square$

It should be emphasized that these three problems are not decidable for every representation of regular sets. In particular, consider the following example.

Example 2.17

We can enumerate the Turing machines. (See the Exercises in Section 0.4.) Let $M_1, M_2, \ldots$ be such an enumeration. We can define the integers to be a representation of the regular sets as follows:

(1) If M_i accepts a regular set, then let integer i represent that regular set.
(2) If M_i does not accept a regular set, then let integer i represent $\{e\}$.

Each integer thus represents a regular set, and each regular set is represented by at least one integer. It is known that for the representation of Turing machines used here the emptiness problem is undecidable (Exercise 0.4.16). Suppose that it were decidable whether integer i represented $\varnothing$. Then it is easy to see that M_i accepts $\varnothing$ if and only if i represents $\varnothing$. Thus the emptiness problem is undecidable for regular sets when regular sets are specified in this manner. $\square$

EXERCISES

2.3.1. Given a finite automaton with n accessible states, what is the smallest number of states the reduced machine can have?

2.3.2. Find the minimum state finite automaton for the language specified by the finite automaton $M = (\{A, B, C, D, E, F\}, \{0, 1\}, \delta, A, \{E, F\})$, where δ is given by

		Input	
	δ	0	1
State	A	B	C
	B	E	F
	C	A	A
	D	F	E
	E	D	F
	F	D	E

2.3.3. Show that for all n there is an n-state finite automaton such that $\overset{n-2}{\equiv} \neq \overset{n-3}{\equiv}$.

2.3.4. Prove that $L(M') = L(M)$ in Algorithm 2.2.

DEFINITION

We say that a relation R on Σ^* is *right-invariant* if $x\,R\,y$ implies $xz\,R\,yz$ for all x, y, z in Σ^*.

2.3.5. Show that L is a regular set if and only if L is the union of some of the equivalence classes of a right-invariant equivalence relation R of finite index. *Hint: Only if:* Let R be the relation $x\,R\,y$ if and only if $(q_0, x) \overset{*}{\vdash} (p, e), (q_0, y) \overset{*}{\vdash} (q, e)$, and $p = q$. (That is, x and y take a finite automaton defining L to the same state.) Show that R is a right-invariant equivalence relation of finite index. *If:* Construct a finite automaton for L using the equivalence classes of R for states.

DEFINITION

We say that E is the *coarsest* right-invariant equivalence relation for a language $L \subseteq \Sigma^*$ if $x\,E\,y$ if and only if for all $z \in \Sigma^*$ we find $xz \in L$ exactly when $yz \in L$.

The following exercise states that every right-invariant equivalence relation defining a language is always contained in E.

2.3.6. Let L be the union of some of the equivalence classes of a right-invariant equivalence relation R on Σ^*. Let E be the coarsest right-invariant equivalence relation for L. Show that $E \supseteq R$.

*2.3.7. Show that the coarsest right invariant equivalence relation for a language is of finite index if and only if that language is a regular set.

2.3.8. Let $M = (Q, \Sigma, \delta, q_0, F)$ be a reduced finite automaton. Define the relation E on Σ^* as follows: $x\,E\,y$ if and only if $(q_0, x) \overset{*}{\vdash} (p, e)$, $(q_0, y) \overset{*}{\vdash} (q, e)$, and $p = q$. Show that E is the coarsest right-invariant equivalence relation for $L(M)$.

DEFINITION

An equivalence relation R on Σ^* is a *congruence relation* if R is both left- and right-invariant (i.e., if $x\,R\,y$, then $wxz\,R\,wyz$ for all w, x, y, z in Σ^*).

2.3.9. Show that L is a regular set if and only if L is the union of some of the equivalence classes of a congruence relation of finite index.

2.3.10. Show that if M_1 and M_2 are two reduced finite automata such that $L(M_1) = L(M_2)$, then the transition graphs of M_1 and M_2 are the same.

*2.3.11. Show that Algorithm 2.2 is of time complexity n^2. (That is, show that there exists a finite automaton M with n states such that Algorithm 2.2 requires n^2 operations to find the reduced automaton for M.) What is the expected time complexity of Algorithm 2.2?

It is possible to find an algorithm for minimizing the states in a finite automaton which always runs in time no greater than $n \log n$, where n is the number of states in the finite automaton to be reduced. The most time-consuming part of Algorithm 2.2 is the determination of the equivalence classes under $\equiv$ in step 2 using the method suggested in Lemma 2.11. However, we can use the following algorithm in step 2 to reduce the time complexity of Algorithm 2.2 to $n \log n$.

This new algorithm refines partitions on the set of states in a manner somewhat different from that suggested by Lemma 2.11. Initially, the states are partitioned into final and nonfinal states.

Then, suppose that we have the partition consisting of the set of blocks $\{\pi_1, \pi_2, \ldots, \pi_{k-1}\}$. A block π_i in this partition and an input symbol a are selected and used to refine this partition. Each block π_j such that $\delta(q, a) \in \pi_i$ for some q in π_j is split into two blocks π'_j and π''_j such that $\pi'_j = \{q \mid q \in \pi_j \text{ and } \delta(q, a) \in \pi_i\}$ and $\pi''_j = \pi_j - \pi'_j$. Thus, in contrast with the method in Lemma 2.11, here blocks are refined when the successor states on a given input have previously been shown inequivalent.

ALGORITHM 2.6

Determining the equivalence classes of a finite automaton.

Input. A finite automaton $M = (Q, \Sigma, \delta, q_0, F)$.

Output. The indistinguishability classes under $\equiv$.

Method.

(1) Define $\delta^{-1}(q, a) = \{p \mid \delta(p, a) = q\}$ for all $q \in Q$ and $a \in \Sigma$. For $a \in \Sigma$, let $\pi_{i,a} = \{q \mid q \in \pi_i \text{ and } \delta^{-1}(q, a) \neq \varnothing\}$.

(2) Let $\pi_1 = F$ and $\pi_2 = Q - F$.

(3) For all $a \in \Sigma$, define the index set

$$I(a) = \begin{cases} \{1\}, & \text{if } \#\pi_{1,a} \leq \#\pi_{2,a} \\ \{2\}, & \text{otherwise} \end{cases}$$

(4) Set $k = 3$.

(5) Select $a \in \Sigma$ and $i \in I(a)$. [If $I(a) = \varnothing$ for all $a \in \Sigma$, halt; the output is the set $\{\pi_1, \pi_2, \ldots, \pi_{k-1}\}$.]

(6) Delete i from $I(a)$.

(7) For all $j < k$ such that there is a state $q \in \pi_j$ and $\delta(q, a) \in \pi_i$ do steps 7(a)–7(d):

    (a) Let $\pi'_j = \{q \,|\, \delta(q, a) \in \pi_i \text{ and } q \in \pi_j\}$ and let $\pi''_j = \pi_j - \pi'_j$.

    (b) Replace π_j by π'_j and let $\pi_k = \pi''_j$. Construct new $\pi_{j,a}$ and $\pi_{k,a}$ for all $a \in \Sigma$.

    (c) For all $a \in \Sigma$, modify $I(a)$ as follows:

$$I(a) = \begin{cases} I(a) \cup \{j\}, & \text{if } j \notin I(a) \text{ and } 0 < \#\pi_{j,a} \leq \#\pi_{k,a} \\ I(a) \cup \{k\}, & \text{otherwise} \end{cases}$$

    (d) Set $k = k + 1$.

(8) Go to step 5. □

2.3.12. Apply Algorithm 2.6 to the finite automata in Example 2.15 and Exercise 2.3.2.

2.3.13. Prove that Algorithm 2.6 correctly determines the indistinguishability classes of a finite automaton.

**2.3.14. Show that Algorithm 2.6 can be implemented in time $n \log n$.

2.3.15. Show that the following are not regular sets:

    (a) $\{0^n 10^n \,|\, n \geq 1\}$.

    (b) $\{ww \,|\, w \text{ is in } \{0, 1\}^*\}$.

    (c) $L(G)$, where G is defined by productions $S \longrightarrow aSbS \,|\, c$.

    (d) $\{a^{n^2} \,|\, n \geq 1\}$.

    (e) $\{a^p \,|\, p \text{ is a prime}\}$.

    (f) $\{w \,|\, w \text{ is in } \{0, 1\}^* \text{ and } w \text{ has an equal number of 0's and 1's}\}$.

2.3.16. Let $f(m)$ be a monotonically increasing function such that for all n there exists m such that $f(m + 1) \geq f(m) + n$. Show that $\{a^{f(m)} \,|\, m \geq 1\}$ is not regular.

DEFINITION

Let L_1 and L_2 be languages. We define the following operations:

(1) $L_1/L_2 = \{w \,|\, \text{for some } x \in L_2, wx \text{ is in } L_1\}$.

(2) $\text{INIT}(L_1) = \{w \,|\, \text{for some } x, wx \text{ is in } L_1\}$.

(3) $\text{FIN}(L_1) = \{w \,|\, \text{for some } x, xw \text{ is in } L_1\}$.

(4) $\text{SUB}(L_1) = \{w \,|\, \text{for some } x \text{ and } y, xwy \text{ is in } L_1\}$.

(5) $\text{MIN}(L_1) = \{w \,|\, w \in L_1 \text{ and for no proper prefix } x \text{ of } w \text{ is } x \in L_1\}$.

(6) $\text{MAX}(L_1) = \{w \,|\, w \in L_1 \text{ and for no } x \neq e \text{ is } wx \in L_1\}$.

Example 2.18

Let $L_1 = \{0^n 1^n 0^m \,|\, n, m \geq 1\}$ and $L_2 = 1^* 0^*$.

    Then $L_1/L_2 = L_1 \cup \{0^i 1^j \,|\, i \geq 1, j \leq i\}$.

    $L_2/L_1 = \varnothing$.

$$\text{INIT}(L_1) = L_1 \cup \{0^i 1^j \,|\, i \geq 1, j \leq i\} \cup 0^*.$$
$$\text{FIN}(L_1) = \{0^i 1^j 0^k \,|\, k \geq 1, j \geq 1, i \leq j\} \cup 1^+ 0^+ \cup 0^*.$$
$$\text{SUB}(L_1) = \{0^i 1^j 0^k \,|\, i \leq j\} \cup 1^* 0^* \cup 0^* 1^*.$$
$$\text{MIN}(L_1) = \{0^n 1^n 0 \,|\, n \geq 1\}.$$
$$\text{MAX}(L_1) = \varnothing. \quad \square$$

*2.3.17. Let L_1 and L_2 be regular. Show that the following are regular:
(a) L_1/L_2.
(b) $\text{INIT}(L_1)$.
(c) $\text{FIN}(L_1)$.
(d) $\text{SUB}(L_1)$.
(e) $\text{MIN}(L_1)$.
(f) $\text{MAX}(L_1)$.

*2.3.18. Let L_1 be a regular set and L_2 an arbitrary language. Show that L_1/L_2 is regular. Does there exist an algorithm to find a finite automaton for L_1/L_2 given one for L_1?

DEFINITION

The *derivative* $D_x \alpha$ of a regular expression α with respect to $x \in \Sigma^*$ can be defined recursively as follows:

(1) $D_e \alpha = \alpha$.
(2) For $a \in \Sigma$
  (a) $D_a \varnothing = \varnothing$.
  (b) $D_a e = \varnothing$.
  (c) $D_a b = \begin{cases} \varnothing, & \text{if } a \neq b \\ e, & \text{if } a = b. \end{cases}$
  (d) $D_a(\alpha + \beta) = D_a \alpha + D_a \beta$.
  (e) $D_a(\alpha\beta) = \begin{cases} (D_a\alpha)\beta, & \text{if } e \notin \alpha \\ (D_a\alpha)\beta + D_a\beta, & \text{if } e \in \alpha. \end{cases}$
  (f) $D_a \alpha^* = (D_a\alpha)\alpha^*$.
(3) For $a \in \Sigma$ and $x \in \Sigma^*$,

$$D_{ax}\alpha = D_x(D_a\alpha)$$

2.3.19. Show that if $\alpha = 10^*1$, then
(a) $D_e \alpha = 10^*1$.
(b) $D_0 \alpha = \varnothing$.
(c) $D_1 \alpha = 0^*1$.

*2.3.20. Show that if α is a regular expression that denotes the regular set R, then $D_x \alpha$ denotes $x\backslash R = \{w \,|\, xw \in R\}$.

**2.3.21. Let L be a regular set. Show that $\{x \,|\, xy \in L$ for some y such that $|x| = |y|\}$ is regular.

A generalization of Exercise 2.3.21 is the following.

**2.3.22. Let L be a regular set and $f(x)$ a polynomial in x with nonnegative integer coefficients. Show that

$$\{w \mid wy \in L \text{ for some } y \text{ such that } |y| = f(|w|)\}$$

is regular.

*2.3.23. Let L be a regular set and h a homomorphism. Show that $h(L)$ and $h^{-1}(L)$ are regular sets.

2.3.24. Prove the correctness of Algorithms 2.4–2.5.

2.3.25. Discuss the time and space complexity of Algorithms 2.4 and 2.5.

2.3.26. Give a formal proof of Theorem 2.9. Note that it is not sufficient to show simply that, say, for every regular expression there is a finite automaton accepting the set denoted thereby. One must show that there is an algorithm to construct the automaton from the regular expression. See Example 2.17 in this connection.

*2.3.27. Give an efficient algorithm to minimize the number of states in an incompletely specified deterministic finite automaton.

2.3.28. Give efficient algorithms to solve the membership, emptiness, and equivalence problems for
(a) Regular expressions.
(b) Right-linear grammars.
(c) Nondeterministic finite automata.

**2.3.29. Show that the membership and equivalence problems are undecidable for the representation of regular sets given in Example 2.17.

*2.3.30. Show that the question "Is $L(M)$ infinite?" is decidable for finite automata. *Hint:* Show that $L(M)$ is infinite, for n-state finite automaton M, if and only if $L(M)$ contains a word w such that $n \leq |w| < 2n$.

*2.3.31. Show that it is decidable, for finite automata M_1 and M_2, whether $L(M_1) \subseteq L(M_2)$.

Open Problem

2.3.32. Find a fast algorithm (say, one which takes time n^k for some constant k on automata of n states) which gives a minimum state nondeterministic finite automaton equivalent to a given one.

Programming Exercises

2.3.33. Write a program that takes as input a finite automaton, right-linear grammar, or regular expression and produces as output an equivalent finite automaton, right-linear grammar, or regular expression. For example, this program can be used to construct a finite automaton from a regular expression.

2.3.34. Construct a program that takes as input a specification of a finite automaton M and produces as output a reduced finite automaton that is equivalent to M.

2.3.35. Write a program that will simulate a nondeterministic finite automaton.

2.3.36. Construct a program that determines whether two specifications of a regular set are equivalent.

BIBLIOGRAPHIC NOTES

The minimization of finite automata was first studied by Huffman [1954] and Moore [1956]. The closure properties of regular sets and decidability results for finite automata are from Rabin and Scott [1959].

The Exercises contain some of the many results concerning finite automata and regular sets. Algorithm 2.6 is from Hopcroft [1971]. Exercise 2.3.22 has been proved by Kosaraju [1970]. The derivative of a regular expression was defined by Brzozowski [1964].

There are many techniques to minimize incompletely specified finite automata (Exercise 2.3.27). Ginsburg [1962] and Prather [1969] consider this problem. Kameda and Weiner [1968] give a partial solution to Exercise 2.3.32.

The books by Gill [1962], Ginsburg [1962], Harrison [1965], Minsky [1967], Booth [1967], Ginzburg [1968], Arbib [1969], and Salomaa [1969a] cover finite automata in detail.

Thompson [1968] outlines a useful programming technique for constructing a recognizer from a regular expression.

2.4.   CONTEXT-FREE LANGUAGES

Of the four classes of grammars in the Chomsky hierarchy, the context-free grammars are the most important in terms of application to programming languages and compiling. A context-free grammar can be used to specify most of the syntactic structure of a programming language. In addition, a context-free grammar can be used as the basis of various schemes for specifying translations.

During the compiling process itself, we can use the syntactic structure imparted to an input program by a context-free grammar to help produce the translation for the input. The syntactic structure of an input sentence can be determined from the sequence of productions used to derive that input string. Thus in a compiler the syntactic analyzer can be viewed as a device which attempts to determine if there is a derivation of the input string according to some context-free grammar. However, given a CFG G and an input string w, it is a nontrivial task to determine whether w is in $L(G)$ and, if so, what is a derivation for w in G. We shall treat this question in detail in Chapters 4–7.

In this section we shall build the foundation on which we shall base our study of parsing. In particular, we shall define derivation trees and study some transformations which can be applied to context-free grammars to make their representation more convenient.

2.4.1. Derivation Trees

In a grammar it is possible to have several derivations that are equivalent, in the sense that all derivations use the same productions at the same places, but in a different order. The definition of when two derivations are equivalent is a complex matter for unrestricted grammars (see the Exercises for Section 2.2), but for context-free grammars we can define a convenient graphical representative of an equivalence class of derivations called a derivation tree.

A derivation tree for a context-free grammar $G = (N, \Sigma, P, S)$ is a labeled ordered tree in which each node is labeled by a symbol from $N \cup \Sigma \cup \{e\}$. If an interior node is labeled A and its direct descendants are labeled $X_1, X_2, \ldots, X_n$, then $A \rightarrow X_1 X_2 \cdots X_n$ is a production in P.

DEFINITION

A labeled ordered tree D is a *derivation tree* (or *parse tree*) for a context-free grammar $G(A) = (N, \Sigma, P, A)$ if

(1) The root of D is labeled A.

(2) If $D_1, \ldots, D_k$ are the subtrees of the direct descendants of the root and the root of D_i is labeled X_i, then $A \rightarrow X_1 \cdots X_k$ is a production in P. D_i must be a derivation tree for $G(X_i) = (N, \Sigma, P, X_i)$ if X_i is a nonterminal, and D_i is a single node labeled X_i if X_i is a terminal.

(3) Alternatively, if D_1 is the only subtree of the root of D and the root of D_1 is labeled e, then $A \rightarrow e$ is a production in P.

Example 2.19

The trees in Fig. 2.8 are derivation trees for the grammar $G = G(S)$ defined by $S \rightarrow aSbS \,|\, bSaS \,|\, e$. □

We note that there is a natural ordering on the nodes of an ordered tree. That is, the direct descendants of a node are ordered "from the left" as defined

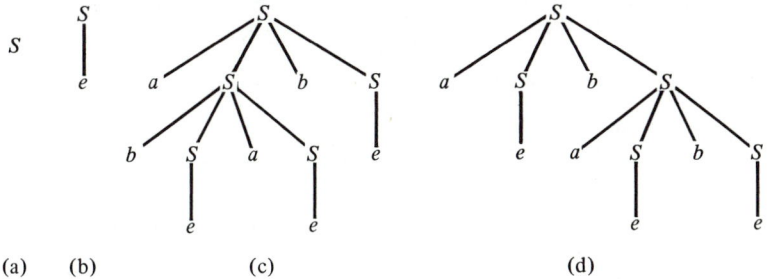

(a)   (b)   (c)   (d)

Fig. 2.8   Derivation trees.

in Section 0.5.4. We extend the from-the-left ordering as follows. Suppose that n is a node and $n_1, \ldots, n_k$ are its direct descendants. Then if $i < j$, n_i and all its descendants are to the left of n_j and all its descendants. It is left for the Exercises to show that this ordering is consistent. All that needs to be shown is that given any two nodes of an ordered tree, they are either on a path or one is to the left of the other.

DEFINITION

The *frontier* of a derivation tree is the string obtained by concatenating the labels of the leaves (in order from the left). For example, the frontiers of the derivation trees in Fig. 2.8 are (a) S, (b) e, (c) $abab$, and (d) *abab*.

We shall now show that a derivation tree is an adequate representation for derivations by showing that for every derivation of a sentential form α in a CFG G there is a derivation tree of G with frontier α, and conversely. To do so we introduce a few more terms. Let D be a derivation tree for a CFG $G = (N, \Sigma, P, S)$.

DEFINITION

A *cut* of D is a set C of nodes of D such that

(1) No two nodes in C are on the same path in D, and
(2) No other node of D can be added to C without violating (1).

Example 2.20

The set of nodes consisting of only the root is a cut. Another cut is the set of leaves. The set of circled nodes in Fig. 2.9 is a cut.   □

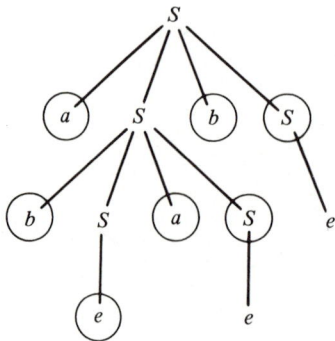

Fig. 2.9 Example of a cut.

DEFINITION

Let us define an *interior frontier* of D as the string obtained by concatenating (in order from the left) the labels of the nodes of a cut of D. For example, $abaSbS$ is an interior frontier of the derivation tree shown in Fig. 2.9.

Lemma 2.12

Let $S = \alpha_0, \alpha_1, \ldots, \alpha_n$ be a derivation of α_n from S in CFG $G = (N, \Sigma, P, S)$. Then there is a derivation tree D for G such that D has frontier α_n and interior frontiers $\alpha_0, \alpha_1, \ldots, \alpha_{n-1}$ (among others).

Proof. We shall construct a sequence of derivation trees D_i, $0 \leq i \leq n$, such that the frontier of D_i is α_i.

Let D_0 be the derivation tree consisting of the single node labeled S.

Suppose that $\alpha_i = \beta_i A \gamma_i$ and this instance of A is rewritten to obtain $\alpha_{i+1} = \beta_i X_1 X_2 \cdots X_k \gamma_i$. Then the derivation tree D_{i+1} is obtained from D_i by adding k direct descendants to the leaf labeled with this instance of A (i.e., the node which contributes the $|\beta_i| + 1$st symbol to the frontier of D_i) and labeling these direct descendants $X_1, X_2, \ldots, X_k$ respectively. It should be evident that the frontier of D_{i+1} is α_{i+1}. The construction of D_{i+1} from D_i is shown in Fig. 2.10.

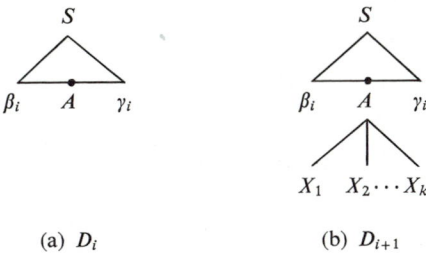

(a) D_i (b) D_{i+1}

Fig. 2.10 Alteration of Trees

D_n will then be the desired derivation tree D. $\square$

We will now obtain the converse of Lemma 2.12. That is, for every derivation tree for G there is at least one derivation in G.

Lemma 2.13

Let D be a derivation tree for a CFG $G = (N, \Sigma, P, S)$ with frontier α. Then $S \overset{*}{\Rightarrow} \alpha$.

Proof. Let $C_0, C_1, C_2, \ldots, C_n$ be any sequence of cuts of D such that

(1) C_0 contains only the root of D.

(2) C_{i+1} is obtained from C_i by replacing one interior node in C_i by its direct descendants, for $0 \leq i < n$.

(3) C_n is the set of leaves of D.

Clearly at least one such sequence exists.

If α_i is the interior frontier associated with C_i, then $\alpha_0, \alpha_1, \ldots, \alpha_n$ is a derivation of α_n from α_0 in G. $\square$

There are two derivations that can be constructed from a derivation tree which will be of particular interest to us.

DEFINITION

In the proof of Lemma 2.13, if C_{i+1} is obtained from C_i by replacing the leftmost nonleaf in C_i by its direct descendants, then the associated derivation $\alpha_0, \alpha_1, \ldots, \alpha_n$ is called a *leftmost* derivation of α_n from α_0 in G. We define a *rightmost* derivation analogously by replacing "leftmost" by "rightmost" above. Notice that the leftmost (or rightmost) derivation associated with a derivation tree is unique.

If $S = \alpha_0, \alpha_1, \ldots, \alpha_n = w$ is a leftmost derivation of the terminal string w, then each α_i, $0 \leq i < n$, is of the form $x_i A_i \beta_i$ with $x_i \in \Sigma^*$, $A_i \in N$, and $\beta_i \in (N \cup \Sigma)^*$. The leftmost nonterminal A_i is rewritten to obtain each succeeding sentential form. The reverse situation holds for rightmost derivations.

Example 2.21

Let G_0 be the CFG

$$E \longrightarrow E + T \,|\, T$$
$$T \longrightarrow T * F \,|\, F$$
$$F \longrightarrow (E) \,|\, a$$

The derivation tree shown in Fig. 2.11 represents ten equivalent derivations

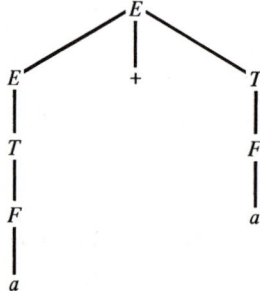

Fig. 2.11   Example of a tree.

of the sentence $a + a$. The leftmost derivation is

$$E \Longrightarrow E + T \Longrightarrow T + T \Longrightarrow F + T \Longrightarrow a + T \Longrightarrow a + F \Longrightarrow a + a$$

and the rightmost derivation is

$$E \Longrightarrow E + T \Longrightarrow E + F \Longrightarrow E + a \Longrightarrow T + a \Longrightarrow F + a \Longrightarrow a + a$$

$\square$

DEFINITION

If $S = \alpha_0, \alpha_1, \ldots, \alpha_n$ is a leftmost derivation in grammar G, then we shall write $S \underset{G\,lm}{\overset{*}{\Rightarrow}} \alpha_n$ or $S \underset{lm}{\overset{*}{\Rightarrow}} \alpha_n$, if G is clear, to indicate the leftmost derivation. We call α_n a *left sentential form*. Likewise, if $S = \alpha_0, \alpha_1, \ldots, \alpha_n$ is a rightmost derivation, we shall write $S \underset{rm}{\overset{*}{\Rightarrow}} \alpha_n$, and call α_n a *right sentential form*. We use $\underset{lm}{\Rightarrow}$ and $\underset{rm}{\Rightarrow}$ to indicate single-step leftmost and rightmost derivations.

We can combine Lemmas 2.12 and 2.13 into the following theorem.

THEOREM 2.11

Let $G = (N, \Sigma, P, S)$ be a CFG. Then $S \overset{*}{\Rightarrow} \alpha$ if and only if there is a derivation tree for G with frontier α.

Proof. Immediate from Lemmas 2.12 and 2.13.   □

Notice that we have been careful not to say that given a derivation $S \overset{*}{\Rightarrow} \alpha$ in a CFG G we can find a unique derivation tree for G with frontier α. The reason for this is that there are context-free grammars which have several distinct derivation trees with the same frontier. The grammar in Example 2.19 is an example of such a grammar. Derivation trees (c) and (d) (Fig. 2.8) in that example have equal frontiers but are not the same trees.

DEFINITION

We say that a CFG G is *ambiguous* if there is at least one sentence w in $L(G)$ for which there is more than one distinct derivation tree with frontier w. This is equivalent to saying that G is ambiguous if there is a sentence w in $L(G)$ with two or more distinct leftmost (or rightmost) derivations (Exercise 2.4.4).

We shall consider ambiguity in more detail in Section 2.6.5.

2.4.2. Transformations on Context-Free Grammars

Given a grammar it is often desirable to modify the grammar so that a certain structure is imposed on the language generated. For example, let us consider $L(G_0)$. This language can be generated by the grammar G with productions

$$E \longrightarrow E + E \,|\, E * E \,|\, (E) \,|\, a$$

But there are two features of G which are not desirable. First of all, G is ambiguous because of the productions $E \rightarrow E + E \,|\, E * E$. This ambiguity can be removed by using the grammar G_1 with productions

$$E \longrightarrow E + T \,|\, E * T \,|\, T$$
$$T \longrightarrow (E) \,|\, a$$

The other drawback to G, which is shared by G_1, is that the operators $+$ and $*$ have the same precedence. That is to say, in the expressions $a + a * a$ and $a * a + a$, the operators would associate from the left as in $(a + a) * a$ and $(a * a) + a$, respectively.

In going to the grammar G_0 we can obtain the conventional precedence of $+$ and $*$.

In general, there is no algorithmic method to impose an arbitrary structure on a given language. However, there are a number of useful transformations which can be used to modify a grammar without disturbing the language generated. In this section and in Sections 2.4.3–2.4.5 we shall consider a number of transformations of this nature.

We shall begin by considering some very obvious but important transformations. In certain situations, a CFG may contain useless symbols and productions. For example, consider the grammar $G = (\{S, A\}, \{a, b\}, P, S)$, where $P = \{S \longrightarrow a, A \longrightarrow b\}$. In G, the nonterminal A and the terminal b cannot appear in any sentential form. Thus these two symbols are irrelevant insofar as $L(G)$ is concerned and can be removed from the specification of G without affecting $L(G)$.

DEFINITION

We say that a symbol $X \in N \cup \Sigma$ is *useless* in a CFG $G = (N, \Sigma, P, S)$ if there does not exist a derivation of the form $S \overset{*}{\Rightarrow} wXy \overset{*}{\Rightarrow} wxy$. Note that w, x, and y are in Σ^*.

To determine whether a nonterminal A is useless, we first provide an algorithm to determine whether a nonterminal can generate any terminal strings; i.e., is $\{w \,|\, A \overset{*}{\Rightarrow} w, w \text{ in } \Sigma^*\} = \varnothing$? The existence of such an algorithm implies that the emptiness problem is solvable for context-free grammars.

ALGORITHM 2.7

Is $L(G)$ nonempty?

Input. CFG $G = (N, \Sigma, P, S)$.

Output. "YES" if $L(G) \neq \varnothing$, "NO" otherwise.

Method. We construct sets $N_0, N_1, \ldots$ recursively as follows:

(1) Let $N_0 = \varnothing$ and set $i = 1$.
(2) Let $N_i = \{A \,|\, A \longrightarrow \alpha \text{ is in } P \text{ and } \alpha \in (N_{i-1} \cup \Sigma)^*\} \cup N_{i-1}$.
(3) If $N_i \neq N_{i-1}$, then set $i = i + 1$ and go to step 2. Otherwise, let $N_e = N_i$.
(4) If S is in N_e, output "YES"; otherwise, output "NO." $\quad\square$

Since $N_e \subseteq N$, Algorithm 2.7 must terminate after at most $n + 1$ iterations of step (2) if N has n members. We shall prove the correctness of Algorithm 2.7. The proof is simple and will serve as a model for several similar proofs.

THEOREM 2.12

Algorithm 2.7 says "YES" if and only if $S \overset{*}{\Rightarrow} w$ for some w in Σ^*.

Proof. We first prove the following statement by induction on i:

(2.4.1) If A is in N_i, then $A \overset{*}{\Longrightarrow} w$ for some w in Σ^*

The basis, $i = 0$, holds vacuously, since $N_0 = \varnothing$. Assume that (2.4.1) is true for i, and let A be in N_{i+1}. If A is also in N_i, the inductive step is trivial. If A is in $N_{i+1} - N_i$, then there is a production $A \to X_1 \cdots X_k$, where each X_j is either in Σ or a nonterminal in N_i. Thus we can find a string w_j such that $X_j \overset{*}{\Rightarrow} w_j$ for each j. If X_j is in Σ, $w_j = X_j$, and otherwise the existence of w_j follows from (2.4.1). It is simple to see that

$$A \Rightarrow X_1 \cdots X_k \overset{*}{\Rightarrow} w_1 X_2 \cdots X_k \overset{*}{\Rightarrow} \cdots \overset{*}{\Rightarrow} w_1 \cdots w_k.$$

The case $k = 0$ (i.e., production $A \to e$) is not ruled out. The inductive step is complete.

The definition of N_i assures us that if $N_i = N_{i-1}$, then $N_i = N_{i+1} = \cdots$. We must show that if $A \overset{*}{\Rightarrow} w$ for some $w \in \Sigma^*$, then A is in N_e. By the above comment, all we need to show is that A is in N_i for some i. We show the following by induction on n:

(2.4.2) If $A \overset{n}{\Longrightarrow} w$, then A is in N_i for some i

The basis, $n = 1$, is trivial; $i = 1$ in this case. Assume that (2.4.2) is true for n, and let $A \overset{n+1}{\Rightarrow} w$. Then we can write $A \Rightarrow X_1 \cdots X_k \overset{n}{\Rightarrow} w$, where $w = w_1 \cdots w_k$ such that $X_j \overset{n_j}{\Rightarrow} w_j$ for each j, where $n_j \leq n$.†

By (2.4.2), if X_j is in N, then X_j is in N_{i_j} for some i_j. If X_j is in Σ, let $i_j = 0$. Let $i = 1 + \max (i_1, \ldots, i_k)$. Then by definition, A is in N_i. The induction is complete. Letting $A = S$ in (2.4.1) and (2.4.2), we have the theorem. $\square$

COROLLARY

It is decidable, for CFG G, if $L(G) = \varnothing$. $\square$

DEFINITION

We say that a symbol X in $N \cup \Sigma$ is *inaccessible* in a CFG $G = (N, \Sigma, P, S)$ if X does not appear in any sentential form.

---

†This is an "obvious" comment that requires a little thought. Think about the derivation tree for the derivation $A \overset{n+1}{\Rightarrow} w$. w_j is the frontier of the subtree with root X_j.

The following algorithm, which is an adaptation of Algorithm 0.3, can be used to remove inaccessible symbols from a CFG.

ALGORITHM 2.8

Removal of inaccessible symbols.

Input. CFG $G = (N, \Sigma, P, S)$.

Output. CFG $G' = (N', \Sigma', P', S)$ such that

(i) $L(G') = L(G)$.
(ii) For all X in $N' \cup \Sigma'$ there exist α and β in $(N' \cup \Sigma')^*$ such that $S \underset{G'}{\overset{*}{\Rightarrow}} \alpha X \beta$.

Method.

(1) Let $V_0 = \{S\}$ and set $i = 1$.
(2) Let $V_i = \{X \mid \text{some } A \rightarrow \alpha X \beta \text{ is in } P \text{ and } A \text{ is in } V_{i-1}\} \cup V_{i-1}$.
(3) If $V_i \neq V_{i-1}$, set $i = i + 1$ and go to step (2). Otherwise, let

$$N' = V_i \cap N$$
$$\Sigma' = V_i \cap \Sigma$$
P' be those productions in P which involve
   only symbols in V_i
$$G' = (N', \Sigma', P', S) \quad \square$$

There is a great deal of similarity between Algorithms 2.7 and 2.8. Note that in Algorithm 2.8, since $V_i \subseteq N \cup \Sigma$, step (2) of the algorithm can be repeated at most a finite number of times. Moreover, a straightforward proof by induction on i shows that $S \underset{G}{\overset{*}{\Rightarrow}} \alpha X \beta$ if and only if X is in V_i for some i.

We are now in a position to remove all useless symbols from a CFG.

ALGORITHM 2.9

Useless symbol removal.

Input. CFG $G = (N, \Sigma, P, S)$, such that $L(G) \neq \varnothing$.

Output. CFG $G' = (N', \Sigma', P', S)$ such that $L(G') = L(G)$ and no symbol in $N' \cup \Sigma'$ is useless.

Method.

(1) Apply Algorithm 2.7 to G to obtain N_e. Let $G_1 = (N \cap N_e, \Sigma, P_1, S)$, where P_1 contains those productions of P involving only symbols in $N_e \cup \Sigma$.
(2) Apply Algorithm 2.8 to G_1 to obtain $G' = (N', \Sigma', P', S)$. $\quad \square$

Step (1) of Algorithm 2.9 removes from G all nonterminals which cannot generate a terminal string. Step (2) then proceeds to remove all symbols which are not accessible. Each symbol X in the resulting grammar must appear in at least one derivation of the form $S \overset{*}{\Rightarrow} wXy \overset{*}{\Rightarrow} wxy$. Note that applying Algorithm 2.8 first and then applying Algorithm 2.7 will not always result in a grammar with no useless symbols.

THEOREM 2.13

G' of Algorithm 2.9 has no useless symbols, and $L(G') = L(G)$.

Proof. We leave it for the Exercises to show that $L(G') = L(G)$. Suppose that $A \in N'$ is useless. From the definition of useless, there are two cases to consider.

Case 1: $S \overset{*}{\underset{G'}{\Rightarrow}} \alpha A \beta$ is false for all α and β. In this case, A would have been removed in step (2) of Algorithm 2.9.

Case 2: $S \overset{*}{\underset{G'}{\Rightarrow}} \alpha A \beta$ for some α and β, but $A \overset{*}{\underset{G'}{\Rightarrow}} w$ is false for all w in Σ'^*. Then A is not removed in step (2), and, moreover, if $A \overset{*}{\underset{G}{\Rightarrow}} \gamma B \delta$, then B is not removed in step (2). Thus, if $A \overset{*}{\underset{G}{\Rightarrow}} w$, it would follow that $A \overset{*}{\underset{G'}{\Rightarrow}} w$. We conclude that $A \overset{*}{\underset{G}{\Rightarrow}} w$ is also false for all w, and A is eliminated in step (1).

The proof that no terminal of G' is useless is handled similarly and is left for the Exercises. $\square$

Example 2.22

Consider the grammar $G = (\{S, A, B\}, \{a, b\}, P, S)$, where P consists of

$$S \longrightarrow a \,|\, A$$
$$A \longrightarrow AB$$
$$B \longrightarrow b$$

Let us apply Algorithm 2.9 to G. In step (1), $N_e = \{S, B\}$ so that $G_1 = (\{S, B\}, \{a, b\}, \{S \rightarrow a, B \rightarrow b\}, S)$. Applying Algorithm 2.8, we have $V_2 = V_1 = \{S, a\}$. Thus, $G' = (\{S\}, \{a\}, \{S \rightarrow a\}, S)$.

If we apply Algorithm 2.8 first to G, we find that all symbols are accessible, so the grammar does not change. Then applying Algorithm 2.7 gives $N_e = \{S, B\}$, so the resulting grammar is G_1 above, not G'. $\square$

It is often convenient to eliminate e-productions, that is, productions of the form $A \rightarrow e$, from a CFG G. However, if e is in $L(G)$, then clearly it is impossible to have no productions of the form $A \rightarrow e$.

DEFINITION

We say that a CFG $G = (N, \Sigma, P, S)$ is *e-free* if either

(1) P has no e-productions, or

(2) There is exactly one e-production $S \longrightarrow e$ and S does not appear on the right side of any production in P.

ALGORITHM 2.10

Conversion to an e-free grammar.

Input. CFG $G = (N, \Sigma, P, S)$.

Output. Equivalent e-free CFG $G' = (N', \Sigma, P', S')$.

Method.

(1) Construct $N_e = \{A \mid A \in N \text{ and } A \overset{+}{\underset{G}{\Rightarrow}} e\}$. The algorithm is similar to that used in Algorithms 2.7 and 2.8 and is left for the Exercises.

(2) Let P' be the set of productions constructed as follows:

(a) If $A \rightarrow \alpha_0 B_1 \alpha_1 B_2 \alpha_2 \cdots B_k \alpha_k$ is in P, $k \geq 0$, and for $1 \leq i \leq k$ each B_i is in N_e but no symbols in any α_j are in N_e, $0 \leq j \leq k$, then add to P' all productions of the form

$$A \longrightarrow \alpha_0 X_1 \alpha_1 X_2 \alpha_2 \cdots X_k \alpha_k$$

where X_i is either B_i or e, without adding $A \rightarrow e$ to P'. (This could occur if all $\alpha_i = e$.)

(b) If S is in N_e, add to P' the productions

$$S' \longrightarrow e \mid S$$

where S' is a new symbol, and let $N' = N \cup \{S'\}$. Otherwise, let $N' = N$ and $S' = S$.

(3) Let $G' = (N', \Sigma, P', S')$. □

Example 2.23

Consider the grammar of Example 2.19 with productions

$$S \longrightarrow aSbS \mid bSaS \mid e$$

Applying Algorithm 2.10 to this grammar, we would obtain the grammar with the following productions:

$$S' \longrightarrow S \mid e$$
$$S \longrightarrow aSbS \mid bSaS \mid aSb \mid abS \mid ab \mid bSa \mid baS \mid ba \quad □$$

THEOREM 2.14

Algorithm 2.10 produces an e-free grammar equivalent to its input grammar.

Proof. By inspection, G' of Algorithm 2.10 is e-free. To prove that

$L(G) = L(G')$, we can prove the following statement by induction on the length of w:

(2.4.3) $$A \underset{G'}{\overset{*}{\Longrightarrow}} w \text{ if and only if } w \neq e \text{ and } A \underset{G}{\overset{*}{\Longrightarrow}} w$$

The proof of (2.4.3) is left for the Exercises. Substituting S for A in (2.4.3), we see that for $w \neq e$, $w \in L(G)$ if and only if $w \in L(G')$. The fact that $e \in L(G)$ if and only if $e \in L(G')$ is evident. Thus, $L(G) = L(G')$. □

Another transformation on grammars which we find useful is the removal of productions of the form $A \longrightarrow B$, which we shall call *single productions*.

ALGORITHM 2.11

Removal of single productions.

Input. An e-free CFG G.

Output. An equivalent e-free CFG G' with no single productions.

Method.

(1) Construct for each A in N the set $N_A = \{B \,|\, A \overset{*}{\Rightarrow} B\}$ as follows:
   (a) Let $N_0 = \{A\}$ and set $i = 1$.
   (b) Let $N_i = \{C \,|\, B \longrightarrow C \text{ is in } P \text{ and } B \in N_{i-1}\} \cup N_{i-1}$.
   (c) If $N_i \neq N_{i-1}$, set $i = i + 1$ and repeat step (b). Otherwise, let $N_A = N_i$.
(2) Construct P' as follows: If $B \longrightarrow \alpha$ is in P and not a single production, place $A \longrightarrow \alpha$ in P' for all A such that $B \in N_A$.
(3) Let $G' = (N, \Sigma, P', S)$. □

Example 2.24

Let us apply Algorithm 2.11 to the grammar G_0 with productions

$$E \longrightarrow E + T \,|\, T$$
$$T \longrightarrow T * F \,|\, F$$
$$F \longrightarrow (E) \,|\, a$$

In step (1), $N_E = \{E, T, F\}$, $N_T = \{T, F\}$, $N_F = \{F\}$. After step (2), P' becomes

$$E \longrightarrow E + T \,|\, T * F \,|\, (E) \,|\, a$$
$$T \longrightarrow T * F \,|\, (E) \,|\, a$$
$$F \longrightarrow (E) \,|\, a \quad □$$

THEOREM 2.15

In Algorithm 2.11, G' has no single productions, and $L(G) = L(G')$.

Proof. By inspection, G' has no single productions. We shall first show that $L(G') \subseteq L(G)$. Let w be in $L(G')$. Then there exists in G' a derivation $S = \alpha_0 \Rightarrow \alpha_1 \Rightarrow \cdots \Rightarrow \alpha_n = w$. If the production applied going from α_i to α_{i+1} is $A \rightarrow \beta$, then there is some B in N (possibly, $A = B$) such that $A \overset{*}{\Rightarrow} B$ and $B \underset{G}{\Rightarrow} \beta$. Thus, $A \overset{*}{\underset{G}{\Rightarrow}} \beta$ and $\alpha_i \overset{*}{\underset{G}{\Rightarrow}} \alpha_{i+1}$. It follows that $S \overset{*}{\underset{G}{\Rightarrow}} w$, and w is in $L(G)$. Thus, $L(G') \subseteq L(G)$.

To show that $L(G') = L(G)$, we must show that $L(G) \subseteq L(G')$. Thus let w be in $L(G)$ and $S = \alpha_0 \underset{\text{lm}}{\Rightarrow} \alpha_1 \underset{\text{lm}}{\Rightarrow} \cdots \underset{\text{lm}}{\Rightarrow} \alpha_n = w$ be a leftmost derivation of w in G. We can find a sequence of subscripts $i_1, i_2, \ldots, i_k$ consisting of exactly those j such that $\alpha_{j-1} \underset{\text{lm}}{\Rightarrow} \alpha_j$ by an application of a production other than a single production. In particular, since the derivation of a terminal string cannot end with a single production, $i_k = n$.

Since the derivation is leftmost, consecutive uses of single productions replace the symbol at the same position in the left sentential forms involved. Thus we see that $S \underset{G'}{\Rightarrow} \alpha_{i_1} \underset{G'}{\Rightarrow} \alpha_{i_2} \underset{G'}{\Rightarrow} \cdots \underset{G'}{\Rightarrow} \alpha_{i_k} = w$. Thus, w is in $L(G')$. We conclude that $L(G') = L(G)$. $\quad\square$

DEFINITION

A CFG $G = (N, \Sigma, P, S)$ is said to be *cycle-free* if there is no derivation of the form $A \overset{+}{\Rightarrow} A$ for any A in N. G is said to be *proper* if it is cycle-free, is e-free, and has no useless symbols.

Grammars which have cycles or e-productions are sometimes more difficult to parse than grammars which are cycle-free and e-free. In addition, in any practical situation useless symbols increase the size of a parser unnecessarily. Throughout this book we shall assume a grammar has no useless symbols. For some of the parsing algorithms to be discussed in this book we shall insist that the grammar at hand be proper. The following theorem shows that this requirement still allows us to consider all context-free languages.

THEOREM 2.16

If L is a CFL, then $L = L(G)$ for some proper CFG G.

Proof. Use Algorithms 2.8–2.11. $\quad\square$

DEFINITION

An *A-production* in a CFG is a production of the form $A \rightarrow \alpha$ for some α. (Do not confuse an "A-production" with an "e-production," which is one of the form $B \rightarrow e$.)

Next we introduce a transformation which can be used to eliminate from a grammar a production of the form $A \rightarrow \alpha B \beta$. To eliminate this production we must add to the grammar a set of new productions formed by replacing the nonterminal B by all right sides of B-productions.

LEMMA 2.14

Let $G = (N, \Sigma, P, S)$ be a CFG and $A \rightarrow \alpha B \beta$ be in P for some $B \in N$ and α and β in $(N \cup \Sigma)^*$. Let $B \rightarrow \gamma_1 | \gamma_2 | \cdots | \gamma_k$ be all the B-productions in P. Let $G' = (N, \Sigma, P', S)$ where

$$P' = P - \{A \rightarrow \alpha B \beta\} \cup \{A \rightarrow \alpha \gamma_1 \beta | \alpha \gamma_2 \beta | \cdots | \alpha \gamma_k \beta\}.$$

Then $L(G) = L(G')$.

Proof. Exercise. $\square$

Example 2.25

Let us replace the production $A \rightarrow aAA$ in the grammar G having the two productions $A \rightarrow aAA | b$. Applying Lemma 2.14, assuming that $\alpha = a$, $B = A$, and $\beta = A$, we would obtain G' having productions

$$A \rightarrow aaAAA | abA | b.$$

Derivation trees corresponding to the derivations of *aabbb* in G and G' are shown in Fig. 2.12(a) and (b). Note that the effect of the transformation is to "merge" the root of the tree in Fig. 2.12(a) with its second direct descendant. $\square$

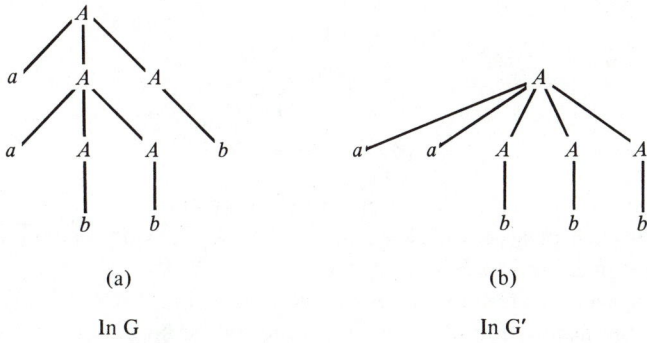

(a)   (b)

In G   In G'

Fig. 2.12 Derivation trees in G and G'.

2.4.3. Chomsky Normal Form

DEFINITION

A CFG $G = (N, \Sigma, P, S)$ is said to be in *Chomsky normal form* (CNF) if each production in P is of one of the forms

(1) $A \rightarrow BC$ with A, B, and C in N, or
(2) $A \rightarrow a$ with $a \in \Sigma$, or

(3) If $e \in L(G)$, then $S \longrightarrow e$ is a production, and S does not appear on the right side of any production.

We shall show that every context-free language has a Chomsky normal form grammar. This result is useful in simplifying the notation needed to represent a context-free language.

ALGORITHM 2.12

Conversion to Chomsky normal form.

Input. A proper CFG $G = (N, \Sigma, P, S)$ with no single productions.

Output. A CFG G' in CNF, with $L(G) = L(G')$.

Method. From G we shall construct an equivalent CNF grammar G' as follows. Let P' be the following set of productions:

(1) Add each production of the form $A \longrightarrow a$ in P to P'.
(2) Add each production of the form $A \longrightarrow BC$ in P to P'.
(3) If $S \longrightarrow e$ is in P, add $S \longrightarrow e$ to P'.
(4) For each production of the form $A \longrightarrow X_1 \cdots X_k$ in P, where $k > 2$, add to P' the following set of productions. We let X'_i stand for X_i if X_i is in N, and let X'_i be a new nonterminal if X_i is in Σ.

$$A \longrightarrow X'_1 \langle X_2 \cdots X_k \rangle$$
$$\langle X_2 \cdots X_k \rangle \longrightarrow X'_2 \langle X_3 \cdots X_k \rangle$$
$$\vdots$$
$$\langle X_{k-2} \cdots X_k \rangle \longrightarrow X'_{k-2} \langle X_{k-1} X_k \rangle$$
$$\langle X_{k-1} X_k \rangle \longrightarrow X'_{k-1} X'_k$$

where each $\langle X_i \cdots X_k \rangle$ is a new nonterminal symbol.

(5) For each production of the form $A \longrightarrow X_1 X_2$, where either X_1 or X_2 or both are in Σ, add to P' the production $A \longrightarrow X'_1 X'_2$.

(6) For each nonterminal of the form a' introduced in steps (4) and (5), add to P' the production $a' \longrightarrow a$. Finally, let N' be N together with all new nonterminals introduced in the construction of P'. Then our desired grammar is $G' = (N', \Sigma, P', S)$. □

THEOREM 2.17

Let L be a CFL. Then $L = L(G)$ for some CFG G in Chomsky normal form.

Proof. By Theorem 2.16, L has a proper grammar. The grammar G' of Algorithm 2.12 is clearly in CNF. It suffices to show that in Algorithm 2.12, $L(G) = L(G')$. This statement follows by an application of Lemma 2.14 to each production of G' with a nonterminal a', and then to each production with a nonterminal of the form $\langle X_i \cdots X_j \rangle$. The resulting grammar will be G. $\square$

Example 2.26

Let G be the proper CFG defined by

$$S \longrightarrow aAB \mid BA$$
$$A \longrightarrow BBB \mid a$$
$$B \longrightarrow AS \mid b$$

We construct P' in Algorithm 2.12 by retaining the productions $S \rightarrow BA$, $A \rightarrow a$, $B \rightarrow AS$, and $B \rightarrow b$. We replace $S \rightarrow aAB$ by $S \rightarrow a'\langle AB \rangle$ and $\langle AB \rangle \rightarrow AB$. $A \rightarrow BBB$ is replaced by $A \rightarrow B\langle BB \rangle$ and $\langle BB \rangle \rightarrow BB$. Finally, we add $a' \rightarrow a$. The resulting grammar is $G' = (N', \{a, b\}, P', S)$, where $N' = \{S, A, B, \langle AB \rangle, \langle BB \rangle, a'\}$ and P' consists of

$$S \longrightarrow a'\langle AB \rangle \mid BA$$
$$A \longrightarrow B\langle BB \rangle \mid a$$
$$B \longrightarrow AS \mid b$$
$$\langle AB \rangle \longrightarrow AB$$
$$\langle BB \rangle \longrightarrow BB$$
$$a' \longrightarrow a \quad \square$$

2.4.4. Greibach Normal Form

We next show that it is possible to find for each CFL a grammar in which every production has a right side beginning with a terminal. Central to the construction is the idea of left recursion and its elimination.

DEFINITION

A nonterminal A in CFG $G = (N, \Sigma, P, S)$ is said to be *recursive* if $A \overset{+}{\Rightarrow} \alpha A \beta$ for some α and β. If $\alpha = e$, then A is said to be *left-recursive*. Similarly, if $\beta = e$, then A is *right-recursive*. A grammar with at least one left- (right-) recursive nonterminal is said to be *left-* (*right-*) *recursive*. A grammar in which all nonterminals, except possibly the start symbol, are recursive is said to be *recursive*.

Certain of the parsing algorithms which we shall discuss do not work with left-recursive grammars. We shall show that every context-free language has at least one non-left-recursive grammar. We begin by showing how to eliminate immediate left recursion from a CFG.

LEMMA 2.15

Let $G = (N, \Sigma, P, S)$ be a CFG in which

$$A \longrightarrow A\alpha_1 \,|\, A\alpha_2 \,|\, \cdots \,|\, A\alpha_m \,|\, \beta_1 \,|\, \beta_2 \,|\, \cdots \,|\, \beta_n$$

are all the A-productions in P and no β_i begins with A. Let

$$G' = (N \cup \{A'\}, \Sigma, P', S),$$

where P' is P with these productions replaced by

$$A \longrightarrow \beta_1 \,|\, \beta_2 \,|\, \cdots \,|\, \beta_n \,|\, \beta_1 A' \,|\, \beta_2 A' \,|\, \cdots \,|\, \beta_n A'$$
$$A' \longrightarrow \alpha_1 \,|\, \alpha_2 \,|\, \cdots \,|\, \alpha_m \,|\, \alpha_1 A' \,|\, \alpha_2 A' \,|\, \cdots \,|\, \alpha_m A'$$

A' is a new nonterminal not in N.† Then $L(G') = L(G)$.

Proof. In G, the strings which can be derived leftmost from A using only A-productions are seen to be exactly those strings in the regular set $(\beta_1 + \beta_2 + \cdots + \beta_n)(\alpha_1 + \alpha_2 + \cdots + \alpha_m)^*$. These are exactly the strings which can be derived rightmost from A using one A-production and some number of A'-productions of G'. (The resulting derivation is no longer leftmost.) All steps of the derivation in G that do not use an A-production can be done directly in G', since the non-A-productions of G and G' are the same. We conclude that w is in $L(G)$ and that $L(G') \subseteq L(G)$.

For the converse, essentially the same argument is used. The derivation in G' is taken to be rightmost, and sequences of one A-production and any number of A'-productions are considered. Thus, $L(G) = L(G')$. □

The effect of the transformation in Lemma 2.15 on derivation trees is shown in Fig. 2.13.

Example 2.27

Let G_0 be our usual grammar with productions

$$E \longrightarrow E + T \,|\, T$$
$$T \longrightarrow T * F \,|\, F$$
$$F \longrightarrow (E) \,|\, a$$

The grammar G' with productions

$$E \longrightarrow T \,|\, TE'$$
$$E' \longrightarrow + T \,|\, + TE'$$
$$T \longrightarrow F \,|\, FT'$$

---

†Note that the $A \longrightarrow \beta_i$'s are in the initial and final sets of A-productions.

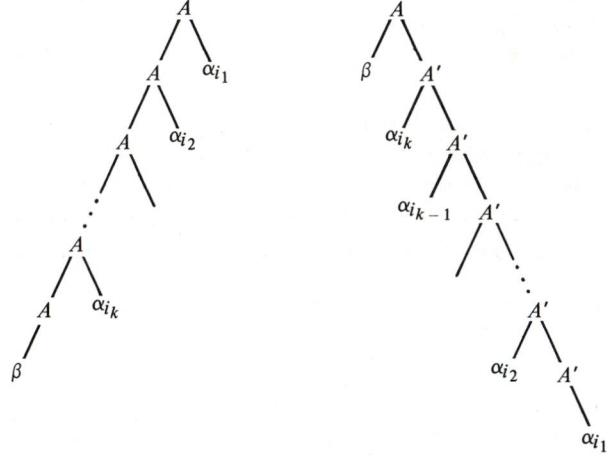

(a) Portion of tree in G (b) Corresponding portion in G'

Fig. 2.13 Portions of trees.

$$T' \longrightarrow *F \,|\, *FT'$$
$$F \longrightarrow (E) \,|\, a$$

is equivalent to G_0 and is the one obtained by applying the construction in Lemma 2.15 with $A = E$ and then $A = T$. $\square$

We are now ready to give an algorithm to eliminate left recursion from a proper CFG. This algorithm is similar in spirit to the algorithm we used to solve regular expression equations.

ALGORITHM 2.13

Elimination of left recursion.

Input. A proper CFG $G = (N, \Sigma, P, S)$.

Output. A CFG G' with no left recursion.

Method.

(1) Let $N = \{A_1, \ldots, A_n\}$. We shall first transform G so that if $A_i \rightarrow \alpha$ is a production, then α begins either with a terminal or some A_j such that $j > i$. For this purpose, set $i = 1$.

(2) Let the A_i-productions be $A_i \rightarrow A_i\alpha_1 \,|\, \cdots \,|\, A_i\alpha_m \,|\, \beta_1 \,|\, \cdots \,|\, \beta_p$, where no β_j begins with A_k if $k \leq i$. (It will always be possible to do this.) Replace these A_i-productions by

$$A_i \longrightarrow \beta_1 \,|\, \cdots \,|\, \beta_p \,|\, \beta_1 A_i' \,|\, \cdots \,|\, \beta_p A_i'$$
$$A_i' \longrightarrow \alpha_1 \,|\, \cdots \,|\, \alpha_m \,|\, \alpha_1 A_i' \,|\, \cdots \,|\, \alpha_m A_i'$$

where A_i' is a new variable. All the A_i-productions now begin with a terminal or A_k for some $k > i$.

(3) If $i = n$, let G' be the resulting grammar, and halt. Otherwise, set $i = i + 1$ and $j = 1$.

(4) Replace each production of the form $A_i \rightarrow A_j\alpha$, by the productions $A_i \rightarrow \beta_1\alpha \mid \cdots \mid \beta_m\alpha$, where $A_j \rightarrow \beta_1 \mid \cdots \mid \beta_m$ are all the A_j-productions. It will now be the case that all A_j-productions begin with a terminal or A_k, for $k > j$, so all A_i-productions will then also have that property.

(5) If $j = i - 1$, go to step (2). Otherwise, set $j = j + 1$ and go to step (4).

$\square$

THEOREM 2.18

Every CFL has a non-left-recursive grammar.

Proof. Let G be a proper grammar for CFL L. If we apply Algorithm 2.13, the only transformations used are those of Lemmas 2.14 and 2.15. Thus the resulting G' generates L.

We must show that G' is free of left recursion. The following two statements are proved by induction on a quantity which we shall subsequently define:

(2.4.4)   After step (2) is executed for i, all A_i-productions begin with a terminal or A_k, for $k > i$

(2.4.5)   After step (4) is executed for i and j, all A_i-productions begin with a terminal or A_k, for $k > j$

We define the *score* of an instance of (2.4.4) to be ni. The *score* of an instance of (2.4.5) is $ni + j$. We prove (2.4.4) and (2.4.5) by induction on the score of an instance of these statements.

Basis (score of n): Here $i = 1$ and $j = 0$. The only instance is (2.4.4) with $i = 1$. None of $\beta_1, \ldots, \beta_n$ in step (2) can begin with A_1, so (2.4.4) is immediate if $i = 1$.

Induction. Assume (2.4.4) and (2.4.5) for scores less than s, and let i and j be such that $0 < j < i \leq n$ and $ni + j = s$. We shall prove this instance of (2.4.5). By inductive hypothesis (2.4.4), all A_j-productions begin with a terminal or A_k, for $k > j$. [This follows because, if $j > 1$, the instance of (2.4.5) with parameters i and $j - 1$ has a score lower than s. The case $j = 1$ follows from (2.4.4).] Statement (2.4.5) with parameters i and j is thus immediate from the form of the new productions.

An inductive proof of (2.4.4) with score s (i.e., $ni = s$, $j = 0$) is left for the Exercises.

It follows from (2.4.4) that none of $A_1, \ldots, A_n$ could be left-recursive. Indeed, if $A_i \overset{+}{\underset{\text{lm}}{\Rightarrow}} A_i\alpha$ for some α, there would have to be A_j and A_k with $k \leq j$ such that $A_i \overset{*}{\underset{\text{lm}}{\Rightarrow}} A_j\beta \overset{*}{\underset{\text{lm}}{\Rightarrow}} A_k\gamma \overset{*}{\underset{\text{lm}}{\Rightarrow}} A_i\alpha$. We must now show that no A_i'

introduced in step (2) can be left-recursive. This follows immediately from the fact that if $A_i' \to A_j'\gamma$ is a production created in step (2), then $j < i$ since A_i' is introduced after A_j'.

Example 2.28

Let G be

$$A \longrightarrow BC \mid a$$
$$B \longrightarrow CA \mid Ab$$
$$C \longrightarrow AB \mid CC \mid a$$

We take $A_1 = A$, $A_2 = B$, and $A_3 = C$. The grammar after each application of step (2) or step (4) of Algorithm 2.13 is shown below. At each step we show only the new productions for nonterminals whose productions change.

Step (2) with $i = 1$: no change.

Step (4) with $i = 2, j = 1$: $B \to CA \mid BCb \mid ab$

Step (2) with $i = 2$: $B \to CA \mid ab \mid CAB' \mid abB'$
$$B' \to CbB' \mid Cb$$

Step (4) with $i = 3, j = 1$: $C \to BCB \mid aB \mid CC \mid a$

Step (4) with $i = 3, j = 2$:
$$C \to CACB \mid abCB \mid CAB'CB \mid abB'CB \mid aB \mid CC \mid a$$

Step (2) with $i = 3$:
$$C \to abCB \mid abB'CB \mid aB \mid a \mid abCBC' \mid abB'CBC' \mid aBC' \mid aC'$$
$$C' \to ACBC' \mid AB'CBC' \mid CC' \mid ACB \mid AB'CB \mid C \quad \square$$

An interesting special case of non-left recursiveness is Greibach normal form.

DEFINITION

A CFG $G = (N, \Sigma, P, S)$ is said to be in *Greibach normal form* (GNF) if G is e-free and each non-e-production in P is of the form $A \to a\alpha$ with $a \in \Sigma$ and $\alpha \in N^*$.

If a grammar is not left-recursive, then we can find a natural partial order on the nonterminals. This partial order can be embedded in a linear order which is useful in putting a grammar into Greibach normal form.

LEMMA 2.16

Let $G = (N, \Sigma, P, S)$ be a non-left-recursive grammar. Then there is a linear order $<$ on N such that if $A \to B\alpha$ is in P, then $A < B$.

Proof. Let R be the relation $A \, R \, B$ if and only if $A \overset{+}{\Rightarrow} B\alpha$ for some α.

By definition of left recursion, R is a partial order. (Transitivity is easy to show.) By Algorithm 0.1, R can be extended to a linear order $<$ with the desired property. $\square$

ALGORITHM 2.14

Conversion to Greibach normal form.

Input. A non-left-recursive proper CFG $G = (N, \Sigma, P, S)$.

Output. A grammar G' in GNF such that $L(G) = L(G')$.

Method.

(1) Construct, by Lemma 2.16, a linear order $<$ on N such that every A-production begins either with a terminal or some nonterminal B such that $A < B$. Let $N = \{A_1, \ldots, A_n\}$, so that $A_1 < A_2 \cdots < A_n$.

(2) Set $i = n - 1$.

(3) If $i = 0$, go to step (5). Otherwise, replace each production of the form $A_i \longrightarrow A_j\alpha$, where $j > i$, by $A_i \longrightarrow \beta_1\alpha \mid \cdots \mid \beta_m\alpha$, where $A_j \longrightarrow \beta_1 \mid \cdots \mid \beta_m$ are all the A_j-productions. It will be true that each of $\beta_1, \ldots, \beta_m$ begins with a terminal.

(4) Set $i = i - 1$ and return to step (3).

(5) At this point all productions (except possibly $S \longrightarrow e$) begin with a terminal. For each production, say $A \longrightarrow aX_1 \cdots X_k$, replace those X_j which are terminals by X'_j, a new nonterminal.

(6) For all X'_j introduced in step (5), add the production $X'_j \longrightarrow X_j$. $\square$

THEOREM 2.19

If L is a CFL, then $L = L(G)$ for some G in GNF.

Proof. A straightforward induction on $n - i$ (that is, backwards, starting at $i = n - 1$ and finishing at $i = 1$) shows that after applying step (3) of Algorithm 2.13 for i all A_i-productions begin with a terminal. The property of the linear order $<$ is crucial here. Step (5) puts the grammar into GNF, and by Lemma 2.14 does not change the language generated. $\square$

Example 2.29

Consider the grammar G with productions

$$E \longrightarrow T \mid TE'$$
$$E' \longrightarrow +T \mid +TE'$$
$$T \longrightarrow F \mid FT'$$
$$T' \longrightarrow *F \mid *FT'$$
$$F \longrightarrow (E) \mid a$$

Take $E' < E < T' < T < F$ as the linear order on nonterminals.

All F-productions begin with a terminal, as they must, since F is highest in the order. The next highest symbol, T, has productions $T \longrightarrow F \mid FT'$, so we substitute for F in both to obtain $T \longrightarrow (E) \mid a \mid (E)T' \mid aT'$. Proceeding to T', we find no change necessary. We then replace the E-productions by $E \longrightarrow (E) \mid a \mid (E)T' \mid aT' \mid (E)E' \mid aE' \mid (E)T'E' \mid aT'E'$. No change for E' is necessary.

Steps (5) and (6) introduce a new nonterminal $)'$ and a production $)' \longrightarrow)$. All instances of $)$ are replaced by $)'$, in the previous productions. Thus the resulting GNF grammar has the productions

$$E \longrightarrow (E)' \mid a \mid (E)'T' \mid aT' \mid (E)' E' \mid aE' \mid (E)' T'E' \mid aT'E'$$
$$E' \longrightarrow +T \mid +TE'$$
$$T \longrightarrow (E)' \mid a \mid (E)'T' \mid aT'$$
$$T' \longrightarrow *F \mid *FT'$$
$$F \longrightarrow (E)' \mid a$$
$$)' \longrightarrow) \quad \square$$

One undesirable aspect of using this technique to put a grammar into GNF is the large number of new productions created. The following technique can be used to find a GNF grammar without introducing too many new productions. However, this new method may introduce more nonterminals.

2.4.5. An Alternative Method of Achieving Greibach Normal Form

There is another way to obtain a grammar in which each production is of the form $A \longrightarrow a\alpha$. This technique requires the grammar to be rewritten only once. Let $G = (N, \Sigma, P, A)$ be a CFG which contains no e-productions (not even $A \longrightarrow e$) and no single productions.

Instead of describing the method in terms of the set of productions we shall use a set of defining equations, of the type introduced in Section 2.2.2, to represent the productions. For example, the set of productions

$$A \longrightarrow AaB \mid BB \mid b$$
$$B \longrightarrow aA \mid BAa \mid Bd \mid c$$

can be represented by the equations

$$(2.4.6) \qquad \begin{aligned} A &= AaB + BB + b \\ B &= aA + BAa + Bd + c \end{aligned}$$

where A and B are now indeterminates representing sets.

DEFINITION

Let Δ and Σ be two disjoint alphabets. A set of *defining equations* over Σ and Δ is a set of equations of the form $A = \alpha_1 + \alpha_2 + \cdots + \alpha_k$, where $A \in \Delta$ and each α_i is a string in $(\Delta \cup \Sigma)^*$. If $k = 0$, the equation is taken to be $A = \varnothing$. There is one equation for each A in Δ. A *solution* to the set of defining equations is a function f from Δ to $\mathcal{P}(\Sigma^*)$ such that if $f(A)$ is substituted everywhere for A, for each $A \in \Delta$, then the equations become set equalities. We say that solution f is a *minimal fixed point* if $f(A) \subseteq g(A)$ for all $A \in \Delta$ and solutions g.

We define a CFG *corresponding* to a set of defining equations by creating the productions $A \rightarrow \alpha_1 \,|\, \alpha_2 \,|\, \cdots \,|\, \alpha_k$ for each equation $A = \alpha_1 + \cdots + \alpha_k$. The nonterminals are the symbols in Δ. Obviously, the correspondence is one-to-one. We shall state some results about defining equations that are generalizations of the results proved for standard form regular expression equations (which are a special case of defining equations). The proofs are left for the Exercises.

LEMMA 2.17

The minimal fixed point of a set of defining equations over Δ and Σ is unique and is given by $f(A) = \{w \,|\, A \overset{*}{\underset{G}{\Rightarrow}} w$ with $w \in \Sigma^*\}$, where G is the corresponding CFG.

Proof. Exercise. $\quad\square$

We shall employ a matrix notation to represent defining equations. Let us assume that $\Delta = \{A_1, A_2, \ldots, A_n\}$. The matrix equation

$$\underline{A} = \underline{A}R + \underline{B}$$

represents n equations. Here $\underline{A}$ is the row vector $[A_1, A_2, \ldots, A_n]$, R is an $n \times n$ matrix whose entries are regular expressions, and $\underline{B}$ is a row vector consisting of n regular expressions.

We take "scalar" multiplication to be concatenation, and scalar addition to be $+$ (i.e., union). Matrix and vector addition and multiplication are defined as in the usual (integer, real, etc.) case. We let the regular expression in row j, column i of R be $\alpha_1 + \cdots + \alpha_k$, if $A_j\alpha_1, \ldots, A_j\alpha_k$ are all terms with leading symbol A_j in the equation for A_i. We let the jth component of $\underline{B}$ be those terms in the equation for A_j which begin with a symbol of Σ. Thus, B_j and R_{ij} are those expressions such that the productions for A_j can be written as

$$A_j = A_1 R_{1j} + A_2 R_{2j} + \cdots + A_i R_{ij} + \cdots + A_n R_{nj} + B_j$$

where B_j is a sum of expressions beginning with terminals.

Thus the defining equations (2.4.6) would be written as

$$(2.4.7) \qquad [A, B] = [A, B]\begin{bmatrix} aB & \varnothing \\ B & Aa + d \end{bmatrix} + [b, aA + c]$$

We shall now find an equivalent set of defining equations for $\underline{A} = \underline{A}R + \underline{B}$ such that the new set of defining equations corresponds to a set of productions all of whose right sides begin with a terminal symbol.

The transformation turns on the following observation.

LEMMA 2.18

Let $\underline{A} = \underline{A}R + \underline{B}$ be a set of defining equations. Then the minimal fixed point is $\underline{A} = \underline{B}R^*$, where $R^* = I + R + R^2 + R^3 + \cdots$. I is an identity matrix (e along the diagonal and $\varnothing$ elsewhere), $R^2 = RR$, $R^3 = RRR$, and so forth.

Proof. Exercise. $\square$

If we let $R^+ = RR^*$, then we can write the minimal fixed point of the equations $\underline{A} = \underline{A}R + \underline{B}$ as $\underline{A} = \underline{B}(R^+ + I) = \underline{B}R^+ + \underline{B}I = \underline{B}R^+ + \underline{B}$. Unfortunately, we cannot find a corresponding grammar for these equations; they are not defining equations, as the elements of R^+ may be infinite sets of terms. However, we can replace R^+ by a new matrix of "unknowns." That is, we can replace R^+ by a matrix Q with q_{ij} as a new symbol in row i, column j.

We can then obtain equations for the q_{ij}'s by observing that $R^+ = RR^+ + R$. Thus, $Q = RQ + R$ is a set of defining equations for the q_{ij}'s. Note that there are n^2 equations if Q and R are $n \times n$ matrices. The following lemma relates the two sets of equations.

LEMMA 2.19

Let $\underline{A} = \underline{A}R + \underline{B}$ be a set of defining equations over Δ and Σ. Let Q be a matrix of the size of R such that each component of Q is a unique new symbol. Then the system of defining equations represented by $\underline{A} = \underline{B}Q + \underline{B}$ and $Q = RQ + R$ has a minimal fixed point which agrees on Δ with that of $\underline{A} = \underline{A}R + \underline{B}$.

Proof. Exercise. $\square$

We now give another algorithm to convert a proper grammar to GNF.

ALGORITHM 2.15

Conversion to Greibach normal form.

Input. A proper grammar $G = (N, \Sigma, P, S)$ such that $S \longrightarrow e$ is not in P.

Output. A grammar $G' = (N', \Sigma, P', S)$ in GNF.

Method.

(1) From G, write the corresponding set of defining equations $\underline{A} = \underline{A}R + \underline{B}$ over N and Σ.

(2) Let Q be an $n \times n$ matrix of new symbols, where $\#\mathrm{N} = n$. Construct the new set of defining equations $\underline{A} = \underline{B}Q + \underline{B}$, $Q = RQ + R$, and let G_1 be the corresponding grammar. Since every term in $\underline{B}$ begins with a terminal, all A-productions of G_1, for $A \in \mathrm{N}$, will begin with terminals.

(3) Since G is proper, e is not a coefficient in R. Thus each q-production of G_1, where q is a component of Q, begins with a symbol in $\mathrm{N} \cup \Sigma$. Replace each leading nonterminal A in these productions by all the right sides of the A-productions. The resulting grammar has only productions whose right sides begin with terminals.

(4) For each terminal a appearing in a production as other than the first symbol on the right side, replace it by new nonterminals of the form a' and add production $a' \to a$. Call the resulting grammar G'. $\square$

THEOREM 2.20

Algorithm 2.15 yields a grammar G' in GNF, and $L(G) = L(G')$.

Proof. That G' is in GNF follows from the properness of G. That is, no component of $\underline{B}$ or R is e. That $L(G') = L(G)$ follows from Lemmas 2.14, 2.17, and 2.19. $\square$

Example 2.30

Let us consider the grammar whose corresponding defining equations are (2.4.7), that is,

$$A \longrightarrow AaB \mid BB \mid b$$
$$B \longrightarrow aA \mid BAa \mid Bd \mid c$$

We rewrite these equations according to step (2) of Algorithm 2.15 as

$$(2.4.8) \qquad [A, B] = [b, aA + c] \begin{bmatrix} W & X \\ Y & Z \end{bmatrix} + [b, aA + c]$$

We then add the equations

$$(2.4.9) \qquad \begin{bmatrix} W & X \\ Y & Z \end{bmatrix} = \begin{bmatrix} aB & \varnothing \\ B & Aa + d \end{bmatrix} \begin{bmatrix} W & X \\ Y & Z \end{bmatrix} + \begin{bmatrix} aB & \varnothing \\ B & Aa + d \end{bmatrix}$$

The grammar corresponding to (2.4.8) and (2.4.9) is

$$A \longrightarrow bW \mid aAY \mid cY \mid b$$
$$B \longrightarrow bX \mid aAZ \mid cZ \mid aA \mid c$$
$$W \longrightarrow aBW \mid a\underline{B}$$
$$X \longrightarrow aBX$$
$$Y \longrightarrow BW \mid AaY \mid dY \mid B$$
$$Z \longrightarrow BX \mid AaZ \mid dZ \mid Aa \mid d$$

Note that X is a useless symbol. In step (3), the productions $Y \rightarrow BW \,|\, AaY \,|\, B$ and $Z \rightarrow BX \,|\, AaZ \,|\, Aa$ are replaced by substituting for the leading A's and B's. We omit this transformation, as well as that of step (4), which should now be familiar to the reader. $\square$

EXERCISES

2.4.1. Let G be defined by

$$S \longrightarrow AB$$
$$A \longrightarrow Aa \,|\, bB$$
$$B \longrightarrow a \,|\, Sb$$

Give derivation trees for the following sentential forms:
(a) *baabaab.*
(b) *bBABb.*
(c) *baSb.*

2.4.2. Give a leftmost and rightmost derivation of the string *baabaab* in the grammar of Exercise 2.4.1.

2.4.3. Give all cuts of the tree of Fig. 2.14.

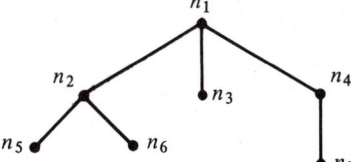

Fig. 2.14 Unlabelled derivation tree.

2.4.4. Show that the following are equivalent statements about a CFG G and sentence w:

(a) w is the frontier of two distinct derivation trees of G.
(b) w has two distinct leftmost derivations in G.
(c) w has two distinct rightmost derivations in G.

**2.4.5. What is the largest number of different derivations that are representable by the same derivation tree of n nodes?

2.4.6. Convert the grammar

$$S \longrightarrow A \,|\, B$$
$$A \longrightarrow aB \,|\, bS \,|\, b$$
$$B \longrightarrow AB \,|\, Ba$$
$$C \longrightarrow AS \,|\, b$$

to an equivalent CFG with no useless symbols.

2.4.7. Prove that Algorithm 2.8 correctly removes inaccessible symbols.

2.4.8. Complete the proof of Theorem 2.13.

2.4.9. Discuss the time and space complexity of Algorithm 2.8. Use a random access computer model.

2.4.10. Give an algorithm to compute for a CFG $G = (N, \Sigma, P, S)$ the set of $A \in N$ such that $A \overset{*}{\Rightarrow} e$. How fast is your algorithm?

2.4.11. Find an e-free grammar equivalent to the following:

$$S \longrightarrow ABC$$
$$A \longrightarrow BB \,|\, e$$
$$B \longrightarrow CC \,|\, a$$
$$C \longrightarrow AA \,|\, b$$

2.4.12. Complete the proof of Theorem 2.14.

2.4.13. Find a proper grammar equivalent to the following:

$$S \longrightarrow A \,|\, B$$
$$A \longrightarrow C \,|\, D$$
$$B \longrightarrow D \,|\, E$$
$$C \longrightarrow S \,|\, a \,|\, e$$
$$D \longrightarrow S \,|\, b$$
$$E \longrightarrow S \,|\, c \,|\, e$$

2.4.14. Prove Theorem 2.16.

2.4.15. Prove Lemma 2.14.

2.4.16. Put the following grammars in Chomsky normal form:
(a) $S \longrightarrow 0S1 \,|\, 01$.
(b) $S \longrightarrow aB \,|\, bA$
  $A \longrightarrow aS \,|\, bAA \,|\, a$
  $B \longrightarrow bS \,|\, aBB \,|\, b$.

2.4.17. If $G = (N, \Sigma, P, S)$ is in CNF, $S \overset{k}{\underset{G}{\Rightarrow}} w$, $|w| = n$, and w is in Σ^*, what is k?

2.4.18. Give a detailed proof of Theorem 2.17.

2.4.19. Put the grammar

$$S \longrightarrow Ba \,|\, Ab$$
$$A \longrightarrow Sa \,|\, AAb \,|\, a$$
$$B \longrightarrow Sb \,|\, BBa \,|\, b$$

into GNF
(a) Using Algorithm 2.14.
(b) Using Algorithm 2.15.

*2.4.20. Give a fast algorithm to test if a CFG G is left-recursive.

2.4.21. Give an algorithm to eliminate right recursion from a CFG.

2.4.22. Complete the proof of Lemma 2.15.

*2.4.23. Prove Lemmas 2.17–2.19.

2.4.24. Complete Example 2.30 to yield a proper grammar in GNF.

2.4.25. Discuss the relative merits of Algorithms 2.14 and 2.15, especially with regard to the size of the resulting grammar.

*2.4.26. Show that every CFL without e has a grammar where all productions are of the forms $A \longrightarrow aBC$, $A \longrightarrow aB$, and $A \longrightarrow a$.

DEFINITION

A CFG is an *operator grammar* if no production has a right side with two adjacent nonterminals.

*2.4.27. Show that every CFL has an operator grammar. *Hint:* Begin with a GNF grammar.

*2.4.28. Show that every CFL is generated by a grammar in which each production is of one of the forms

$$A \longrightarrow aBbC, \qquad A \longrightarrow aBb, \qquad A \longrightarrow aB, \qquad \text{or} \qquad A \longrightarrow a$$

If $e \in L(G)$, then $S \longrightarrow e$ is also in P.

**2.4.29. Consider the grammar with the two productions $S \longrightarrow SS \mid a$. Show that the number of distinct leftmost derivations of a^n is given by $X_n = \sum_{\substack{i+j=n \\ i \neq 0 \\ j \neq 0}} X_i X_j$, where $X_1 = 1$. Show that

$$X_{n+1} = \frac{1}{n+1}\binom{2n}{n}$$

(These are the Catalan numbers.)

*2.4.30. Show that if L is a CFL containing no sentence of length less than 2, then L has a grammar with all productions of the form $A \longrightarrow a\alpha b$.

2.4.31. Show that every CFL has a grammar in which if $X_1 X_2 \cdots X_k$ is the right side of a production, then $X_1, \ldots, X_k$ are all distinct.

DEFINITION

A CFG $G = (N, \Sigma, P, S)$ is *linear* if every production is of the form $A \longrightarrow wBx$ or $A \longrightarrow w$ for w and x in Σ^* and B in N.

2.4.32. Show that every linear language without e has a grammar in which each production is of one of the forms $A \longrightarrow aB$, $A \longrightarrow Ba$, or $A \longrightarrow a$.

*2.4.33. Show that every CFL has a grammar $G = (N, \Sigma, P, S)$ such that if A is in $N - \{S\}$, then $\{w \mid A \overset{*}{\Longrightarrow} w \text{ and } w \text{ is in } \Sigma^*\}$ is infinite.

2.4.34. Show that every CFL has a recursive grammar. *Hint:* Use Lemma 2.14 and Exercise 2.4.33.

*2.4.35. Let us call a CFG $G = (N, \Sigma, P, S)$ *quasi-linear* if for every production $A \longrightarrow X_1 \cdots X_k$ there is at most one X_i which generates an infinite set of terminal strings. Show that every quasi-linear grammar generates a linear language.

DEFINITION

The *graph* of a CFG $G = (N, \Sigma, P, S)$ is a directed unordered graph $(N \cup \Sigma \cup \{e\}, R)$ such that $A \ R \ X$ if and only if $A \longrightarrow \alpha X \beta$ is a production in P for some α and β.

2.4.36. Show that if a grammar has no useless symbols, then all nodes are accessible from S. Is the converse of this statement true?

2.4.37. Let T be the transformation on context-free grammars defined in Lemma 2.14. That is, if G and G' are the grammars in the statement of Lemma 2.14, then T maps G into G'. Show that Algorithms 2.10 and 2.11 can be implemented by means of repeated applications of this transformation T.

Programming Exercises

2.4.38. Construct a program that eliminates all useless symbols from a CFG.

2.4.39. Write a program that maps a CFG into an equivalent proper CFG.

2.4.40. Construct a program that removes all left recursion from a CFG.

2.4.41. Write a program that decides whether a given derivation tree is a valid derivation tree for a CFG.

BIBLIOGRAPHIC NOTES

A derivation tree is also called a variety of other names including generation tree, parsing diagram, parse tree, syntax tree, phrase marker, and *p*-marker. The representation of a derivation in terms of a derivation tree has been a familiar concept in linguistics. The concept of leftmost derivation appeared in Evey [1963].

Many of the algorithms in this chapter have been known since the early 1960's, although many did not appear in the literature until considerably later. Theorem 2.17 (Chomsky normal form) was first presented by Chomsky [1959a]. Theorem 2.18 (Greibach normal form) was presented by Greibach [1965]. The alternative method of achieving GNF (Algorithm 2.15) and the result stated in Exercise 2.4.30 were presented by Rosenkrantz [1967]. Algorithm 2.14 for Greibach normal form has been attributed to M. Paull.

Chomsky [1963], Chomsky and Schutzenberger [1963], and Ginsburg and Rice [1962] have used equations to represent the productions of a context-free grammar.

Operator grammars were first considered by Floyd [1963]. The normal forms given in Exercises 2.4.26–2.4.28 were derived by Greibach [1965].

2.5. PUSHDOWN AUTOMATA

We now introduce the pushdown automaton—a recognizer that is a natural model for syntactic analyzers of context-free languages. The pushdown automaton is a one-way nondeterministic recognizer whose infinite storage consists of one pushdown list, as shown in Fig. 2.15.

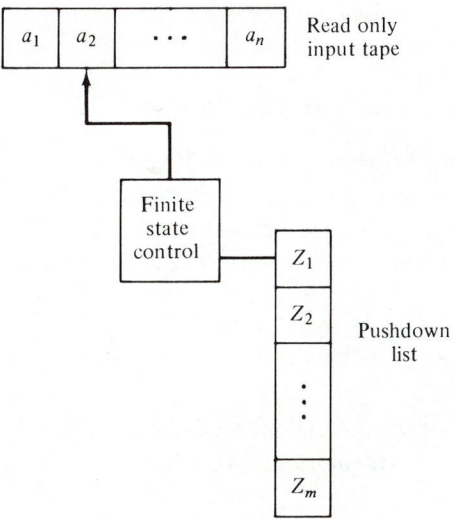

Fig. 2.15 Pushdown automaton.

We shall prove a fundamental result regarding pushdown automata—that a language is context-free if and only if it is accepted by a nondeterministic pushdown automaton. We shall also consider a subclass of context-free languages which are of prime importance when parsability is considered. These, called the deterministic CFL's, are those CFL's which can be recognized by a deterministic pushdown automaton.

2.5.1. The Basic Definition

We shall represent a pushdown list as a string of symbols with the topmost symbol written either on the left or on the right depending on which convention is most convenient for the situation at hand. For the time being we shall assume that the top symbol on the pushdown list is the leftmost symbol of the string representing the pushdown list.

DEFINITION

A *pushdown automaton* (PDA for short) is a 7-tuple

$$P = (Q, \Sigma, \Gamma, \delta, q_0, Z_0, F),$$

where

(1) Q is a finite set of *state* symbols representing the possible states of the finite state control,

(2) Σ is a finite *input alphabet*,

(3) Γ is a finite alphabet of *pushdown list symbols*,

(4) δ is a mapping from $Q \times (\Sigma \cup \{e\}) \times \Gamma$ to the finite subsets of $Q \times \Gamma^*$,

(5) $q_0 \in Q$ is the *initial state* of the finite control,

(6) $Z_0 \in \Gamma$ is the symbol that appears initially on the pushdown list (the *start symbol*), and

(7) $F \subseteq Q$ is the set of *final states*.

A *configuration* of P is a triple (q, w, α) in $Q \times \Sigma^* \times \Gamma^*$, where

(1) q represents the current state of the finite control.

(2) w represents the unused portion of the input. The first symbol of w is under the input head. If $w = e$, then it is assumed that all of the input tape has been read.

(3) α represents the contents of the pushdown list. The leftmost symbol of α is the topmost pushdown symbol. If $\alpha = e$, then the pushdown list is assumed to be empty.

A *move* by P will be represented by the binary relation $\vdash_{\overline{P}}$ (or $\vdash$ whenever P is understood) on configurations. We write

$$(2.5.1) \qquad\qquad (q, aw, Z\alpha) \vdash (q', w, \gamma\alpha)$$

if $\delta(q, a, Z)$ contains (q', γ) for any $q \in Q$, $a \in \Sigma \cup \{e\}$, $w \in \Sigma^*$, $Z \in \Gamma$, and $\alpha \in \Gamma^*$.

If $a \neq e$, Eq. (2.5.1) states that if P is in a configuration such that the finite control is in state q, the current input symbol is a, and the symbol on top of the pushdown list is Z, then P may go into a configuration in which the finite control is now in state q', the input head has been shifted one square to the right, and the topmost symbol on the pushdown list has been replaced by the string γ of pushdown list symbols. If $\gamma = e$, we say that the pushdown list has been *popped*.

If $a = e$, then the move is called an *e-move*. In an *e*-move the current input symbol is not taken into consideration, and the input head is not moved. However, the state of the finite control can be changed, and the contents of the memory can be adjusted. Note that an *e*-move can occur even if all of the input has been read.

No move is possible if the pushdown list is empty.

We can define the relations $\vdash^i$, for $i \geq 0$, $\vdash^*$, and $\vdash^+$ in the customary fashion. Thus, $\vdash^*$ and $\vdash^+$ are, respectively, the reflexive-transitive and transitive closures of $\vdash$.

An *initial configuration* of P is one of the form (q_0, w, Z_0) for some w in Σ^*. That is, the finite state control is in the initial state, the input contains the string to be recognized, and the pushdown list contains only the symbol Z_0. A final configuration is one of the form (q, e, α), where q is in F and α is in Γ^*.

We say that a string w is *accepted* by P if $(q_0, w, Z_0) \vdash^* (q, e, \alpha)$ for some q in F and α in Γ^*. The *language defined by* P, denoted $L(P)$, is the set of strings accepted by P. $L(P)$ will be called a *pushdown automaton language*.

Example 2.31

Let us give a pushdown automaton for the language $L = \{0^n 1^n \mid n \geq 0\}$. Let $P = (\{q_0, q_1, q_2\}, \{0, 1\}, \{Z, 0\}, \delta, q_0, Z, \{q_0\})$, where

$$\delta(q_0, 0, Z) = \{(q_1, 0Z)\}$$
$$\delta(q_1, 0, 0) = \{(q_1, 00)\}$$
$$\delta(q_1, 1, 0) = \{(q_2, e)\}$$
$$\delta(q_2, 1, 0) = \{(q_2, e)\}$$
$$\delta(q_2, e, Z) = \{(q_0, e)\}$$

P operates by copying the initial string of 0's from its input tape onto its pushdown list and then popping one 0 from the pushdown list for each 1 that is seen on the input. Moreover, the state transitions ensure that all 0's must precede the 1's. For example, with the input string 0011, P would make the following sequence of moves:

$$(q_0, 0011, Z) \vdash (q_1, 011, 0Z)$$
$$\vdash (q_1, 11, 00Z)$$
$$\vdash (q_2, 1, 0Z)$$
$$\vdash (q_2, e, Z)$$
$$\vdash (q_0, e, e)$$

In general we can show that

$$(q_0, 0, Z) \vdash (q_1, e, 0Z)$$
$$(q_1, 0^i, 0Z) \vdash^i (q_1, e, 0^{i+1}Z)$$
$$(q_1, 1, 0^{i+1}Z) \vdash (q_2, e, 0^i Z)$$
$$(q_2, 1^i, 0^i Z) \vdash^i (q_2, e, Z)$$
$$(q_2, e, Z) \vdash (q_0, e, e)$$

Stringing all of this together, we have the following sequence of moves by P:

$$(q_0, 0^n1^n, Z) \,|\underline{\smash{2n+1}}\, (q_0, e, e) \qquad \text{for } n \geq 1$$

and

$$(q_0, e, Z) \,|\underline{\smash{0}}\, (q_0, e, Z)$$

Thus, $L \subseteq L(P)$.

Now we need to show that $L \supseteq L(P)$. That is, P will accept only strings of the form 0^n1^n. This is the hard part. It is generally easy to show that a recognizer accepts certain strings. As with grammars, it is invariably much more difficult to show that a recognizer accepts only strings of a certain form.

Here we notice that if P accepts an input string other than e, it must cycle through the sequence of states q_0, q_1, q_2, q_0.

We notice that if $(q_0, w, Z) \,|\underline{\smash{i}}\, (q_1, e, \alpha)$, $i \geq 1$, then $w = 0^i$ and $\alpha = 0^iZ$. Likewise if $(q_2, w, \alpha) \,|\underline{\smash{i}}\, (q_2, e, \beta)$, then $w = 1^i$ and $\alpha = 0^i\beta$. Also, $(q_1, w, \alpha) \vdash (q_2, e, \beta)$ only if $w = 1$ and $\alpha = 0\beta$; $(q_2, w, Z) \,|\underline{\smash{*}}\, (q_0, e, e)$ only if $w = e$. Thus if $(q_0, w, Z) \,|\underline{\smash{i}}\, (q_0, e, \alpha)$, for some $i \geq 0$, either $w = e$ and $i = 0$ or $w = 0^n1^n$, $i = 2n + 1$, and $\alpha = e$. Hence $L \supseteq L(P)$. $\square$

We emphasize that a pushdown automaton, as we have defined it, can make moves even though it has scanned all of its input. However, a pushdown automaton cannot make a move if its pushdown list is empty.

Example 2.32

Let us design a pushdown automaton for the language

$$L = \{ww^R \,|\, w \in \{a, b\}^+\}.$$

Let $P = (\{q_0, q_1, q_2\}, \{a, b\}, \{Z, a, b\}, \delta, q_0, Z, \{q_2\})$, where

(1) $\delta(q_0, a, Z) = \{(q_0, aZ)\}$
(2) $\delta(q_0, b, Z) = \{(q_0, bZ)\}$
(3) $\delta(q_0, a, a) = \{(q_0, aa), (q_1, e)\}$
(4) $\delta(q_0, a, b) = \{(q_0, ab)\}$
(5) $\delta(q_0, b, a) = \{(q_0, ba)\}$
(6) $\delta(q_0, b, b) = \{(q_0, bb), (q_1, e)\}$
(7) $\delta(q_1, a, a) = \{(q_1, e)\}$
(8) $\delta(q_1, b, b) = \{(q_1, e)\}$
(9) $\delta(q_1, e, Z) = \{(q_2, e)\}$

P initially copies some of its input onto its pushdown list, by rules (1), (2), (4), and (5) and the first alternatives of rules (3) and (6). However, P is nondeterministic. Anytime it wishes, as long as its current input matches the top of the pushdown list, it may enter state q_1 and begin matching its pushdown list against the input. The second alternatives of rules (3) and (6) represent this choice, and the matching continues by rules (7) and (8). Note that if P ever fails to find a match, then this instance of P "dies." However, since P is nondeterministic, it makes all possible moves. If any choice causes P to expose the Z on its pushdown list, then by rule (9) that Z is erased and state q_2 entered. Thus P accepts if and only if all matches are made.

For example, with the input string *abba*, P can make the following sequences of moves, among others:

$$(1)\ (q_0, abba, Z) \vdash (q_0, bba, aZ)$$
$$\vdash (q_0, ba, baZ)$$
$$\vdash (q_0, a, bbaZ)$$
$$\vdash (q_0, e, abbaZ)$$

$$(2)\ (q_0, abba, Z) \vdash (q_0, bba, aZ)$$
$$\vdash (q_0, ba, baZ)$$
$$\vdash (q_1, a, aZ)$$
$$\vdash (q_1, e, Z)$$
$$\vdash (q_2, e, e).$$

Since the sequence (2) ends in final state q_2, P accepts the input string *abba*.

Again it is relatively easy to show that if $w = c_1 c_2 \cdots c_n c_n c_{n-1} \cdots c_1$, each c_i in $\{a, b\}$, $1 \leq i \leq n$, then

$$(q_0, w, Z) \overset{n}{\vdash} (q_0, c_n c_{n-1} \cdots c_1, c_n c_{n-1} \cdots c_1 Z)$$
$$\vdash (q_1, c_{n-1} \cdots c_1, c_{n-1} \cdots c_1 Z)$$
$$\overset{n-1}{\vdash} (q_1, e, Z)$$
$$\vdash (q_2, e, e).$$

Thus, $L \subseteq L(P)$.

It is not quite as easy to show that if $(q_0, w, Z) \overset{*}{\vdash} (q_2, e, \alpha)$ for some $\alpha \in \Gamma^*$, then w is of the form xx^R for some x in $(a + b)^+$ and $\alpha = e$. This proof is left for the Exercises. We can then conclude that $L(P) = L$. $\square$

The pushdown automaton of Example 2.32 quite clearly brings out the nondeterministic nature of a PDA. From any configuration of the form $(q_0, aw, a\alpha)$ it is possible for P to make one of two moves—either push another a on the pushdown list or pop the a from the top of the pushdown list.

We should emphasize that although a nondeterministic pushdown automaton may provide a convenient abstract definition for a language, the device must be deterministically simulated to be realized in practice. In Chapter 4 we shall discuss systematic methods for simulating nondeterministic pushdown automata.

2.5.2. Variants of Pushdown Automata

In this section we shall define some variants of PDA's and relate the languages defined to the original PDA languages. First we would like to bring out a fundamental aspect of the behavior of a PDA which should be quite intuitive. This can be stated as "What transpires on top of the pushdown list is independent of what is under the top of the pushdown list."

LEMMA 2.20

Let $P = (Q, \Sigma, \Gamma, \delta, q_0, Z_0, F)$ be a PDA. If $(q, w, A) \mid\overset{n}{\relbar} (q', e, e)$, then $(q, w, A\alpha) \mid\overset{n}{\relbar} (q', e, \alpha)$ for all $A \in \Gamma$ and $\alpha \in \Gamma^*$.

Proof. A proof by induction on n is quite elementary. For $n = 1$, the lemma is certainly true. Assuming that it is true for all $1 \leq n < n'$, let $(q, w, A) \mid\overset{n'}{\relbar} (q', e, e)$. Such a sequence of moves must be of the form

$$(q, w, A) \mid\!\!\!- (q_1, w_1, X_1 \cdots X_k)$$
$$\mid\overset{n_1}{\relbar} (q_2, w_2, X_2 \cdots X_k)$$
$$\cdot$$
$$\cdot$$
$$\cdot$$
$$\mid\overset{n_{k-1}}{\relbar} (q_k, w_k, X_k)$$
$$\mid\overset{n_k}{\relbar} (q', e, e)$$

where $k \geq 1$ and $n_i < n'$ for $1 \leq i \leq k$.[†]
Then the following sequence of moves must also be possible for any $\alpha \in \Gamma^*$:

$$(q, w, A\alpha) \mid\!\!\!- (q_1, w, X_1 \cdots X_k\alpha)$$
$$\mid\overset{n_1}{\relbar} (q_2, w_2, X_2 \cdots X_k\alpha)$$
$$\cdot$$
$$\cdot$$
$$\cdot$$
$$\mid\overset{n_{k-1}}{\relbar} (q_k, w_k, X_k\alpha)$$
$$\mid\overset{n_k}{\relbar} (q', e, \alpha)$$

Except for the first move, we invoke the inductive hypothesis. □

Next, we would like to extend the definition of a PDA slightly to permit the PDA to replace a finite-length string of symbols on top of the pushdown

[†]This is another of those "obvious" statements which may require some thought. Imagine the PDA running through the indicated sequence of configurations. Eventually, the length of the pushdown list becomes $k - 1$ for the first time. Since none of $X_2 \cdots X_k$ has ever been the top symbol, they must still be there, so let n_1 be the number of elapsed moves. Then wait until the length of the list first becomes $k - 2$ and let n_2 be the number of additional moves made. Proceed in this way until the list becomes empty.

list by some other finite-length string in a single move. Recall that our original version of PDA could replace only the topmost symbol on top of the pushdown list on a given move.

DEFINITION

Let an *extended* PDA be a 7-tuple $P = (Q, \Sigma, \Gamma, \delta, q_0, Z_0, F)$, where δ is a mapping from a finite subset of $Q \times (\Sigma \cup \{e\}) \times \Gamma^*$ to the finite subsets of $Q \times \Gamma^*$ and all other symbols have the same meaning as before.

A configuration is as before, and we write $(q, aw, \alpha\gamma) \vdash (q', w, \beta\gamma)$ if $\delta(q, a, \alpha)$ contains (q', β) for q in Q, a in $\Sigma \cup \{e\}$, and α in Γ^*. In this move the string α is replaced by the string β on top of the pushdown list. As before, the language defined by P, denoted $L(P)$, is

$$\{w \,|\, (q_0, w, Z) \vdash^* (q, e, \alpha) \text{ for some } q \text{ in } F \text{ and } \alpha \text{ in } \Gamma^*\}.$$

Notice that unlike a conventional PDA, an extended pushdown automaton is capable of making moves when its pushdown list is empty.

Example 2.33

Let us define an extended PDA P to recognize $L = \{ww^R \,|\, w \in \{a, b\}^*\}$. Let $P = (\{q, p\}, \{a, b\}, \{a, b, S, Z\}, \delta, q, Z, \{p\})$, where

(1) $\delta(q, a, e) = \{(q, a)\}$
(2) $\delta(q, b, e) = \{(q, b)\}$
(3) $\delta(q, e, e) = \{(q, S)\}$
(4) $\delta(q, e, aSa) = \{(q, S)\}$
(5) $\delta(q, e, bSb) = \{(q, S)\}$
(6) $\delta(q, e, SZ) = \{(p, e)\}$

With input *aabbaa*, P can make the following sequence of moves:

$$
\begin{aligned}
(q, aabbaa, Z) &\vdash (q, abbaa, aZ) \\
&\vdash (q, bbaa, aaZ) \\
&\vdash (q, baa, baaZ) \\
&\vdash (q, baa, SbaaZ) \\
&\vdash (q, aa, bSbaaZ) \\
&\vdash (q, aa, SaaZ) \\
&\vdash (q, a, aSaaZ) \\
&\vdash (q, a, SaZ) \\
&\vdash (q, e, aSaZ) \\
&\vdash (q, e, SZ) \\
&\vdash (p, e, e)
\end{aligned}
$$

P operates by first storing a prefix of the input on the pushdown list. Then a centermarker S is placed on top of the pushdown list. P then places the next input symbol on the pushdown list and replaces aSa or bSb by S on the list. P continues in this fashion until all of the input is used. If SZ then remains on the pushdown list, P erases SZ and enters the final state. $\square$

We would now like to show that L is a PDA language if and only if L is an extended PDA language. The "only if" part of this statement is clearly true. The "if" part is the following lemma.

LEMMA 2.21

Let $(Q, \Sigma, \Gamma, \delta, q_0, Z_0, F)$ be an extended PDA. Then there is a PDA P_1 such that $L(P_1) = L(P)$.

Proof. Let

$$m = \max\{|\alpha| \,|\, \delta(q, a, \alpha) \text{ is nonempty for some } q \in Q, a \in \Sigma \cup \{e\}\}.$$

We shall construct a PDA P_1 to simulate P by storing the top m symbols that appear on P's pushdown list in a "buffer" of length m located in the finite state control of P_1. In this way P_1 can tell at the start of each move what the top m symbols of P's pushdown list are. If, in a move, P replaces the top k symbols on the pushdown list by a string of l symbols, then P_1 will replace the first k symbols in the buffer by the string of length l. If $l < k$, then P_1 will make $k - l$ bookkeeping e-moves in which $k - l$ symbols are transferred from the top of the pushdown list to the buffer in the finite control. The buffer will then be full and P_1 ready to simulate another move of P. If $l > k$, symbols are transferred from the buffer to the pushdown list.

Formally, let $P_1 = (Q_1, \Sigma, \Gamma_1, \delta_1, q_1, Z_1, F_1)$, where

(1) $Q_1 = \{[q, \alpha] \,|\, q \in Q, \alpha \in \Gamma_1^*, \text{ and } 0 \leq |\alpha| \leq m\}$.
(2) $\Gamma_1 = \Gamma \cup \{Z_1\}$.
(3) δ_1 is defined as follows:
    (a) Suppose that $\delta(q, a, X_1 \cdots X_k)$ contains $(r, Y_1 \cdots Y_l)$.
        (i) If $l \geq k$, then for all $Z \in \Gamma_1$ and $\alpha \in \Gamma_1^*$ such that $|\alpha| = m - k$,

$$\delta_1([q, X_1 \cdots X_k\alpha], a, Z) \text{ contains } ([r, \beta], \gamma Z)$$

        where $\beta\gamma = Y_1 \cdots Y_l\alpha$ and $|\beta| = m$.
        (ii) If $l < k$, then for all $Z \in \Gamma_1$ and $\alpha \in \Gamma_1^*$ such that $|\alpha| = m - k$,

$$\delta_1([q, X_1 \cdots X_k\alpha], a, Z) \text{ contains } ([r, Y_1 \cdots Y_l\alpha Z], e)$$

    (b) For all $q \in Q, Z \in \Gamma_1$, and $\alpha \in \Gamma_1^*$ such that $|\alpha| < m$,

$$\delta_1([q, \alpha], e, Z) = \{([q, \alpha Z], e)\}$$

These rules cause the buffer in the finite control to fill up (i.e., contain m symbols).

(4) $q_1 = [q_0, Z_0 Z_1^{m-1}]$. The buffer initially contains Z_0 on top and $m-1$ Z_1's below. Z_1's are used as a special marker for the bottom of the pushdown list.

(5) $F_1 = \{[q, \alpha] \mid q \in F, \alpha \in \Gamma_1^*\}$.

It is not difficult to show that

$$(q, aw, X_1 \cdots X_k X_{k+1} \cdots X_n) \vdash_{P} (r, w, Y_1 \cdots Y_l X_{k+1} \cdots X_n)$$

if and only if $([q, \alpha], aw, \beta) \vdash_{P_1}^{+} ([r, \alpha'], w, \beta')$, where

(1) $\alpha\beta = X_1 \cdots X_n Z_1^m$,
(2) $\alpha'\beta' = Y_1 \cdots Y_l X_{k+1} \cdots X_n Z_1^m$,
(3) $|\alpha| = |\alpha'| = m$, and
(4) Between the two configurations of P_1 shown is none whose state has a second component (buffer) of length m. Direct examination of the rules of P_1 is sufficient.

Thus, $(q_0, w, Z_0) \vdash_{P}^{*} (q, e, \alpha)$ for some q in F and α in Γ^* if and only if

$$([q_0, Z_0 Z_1^{m-1}], w, Z_1) \vdash_{P_1}^{*} ([q, \beta], e, \gamma)$$

where $|\beta| = m$ and $\beta\gamma = \alpha Z_1^m$. Thus, $L(P_1) = L(P)$. $\quad\square$

Let us now examine those inputs to a PDA which cause the pushdown list to become empty.

DEFINITION

Let $P = (Q, \Sigma, \Gamma, \delta, q_0, Z_0, F)$ be a PDA, or an extended PDA. We say that a string $w \in \Sigma^*$ is *accepted by P by empty pushdown list* whenever $(q_0, w, Z_0) \vdash^{+} (q, e, e)$ for some $q \in Q$. Let $L_e(P)$ be the set of strings accepted by P by empty pushdown list.

LEMMA 2.22

Let L be $L(P)$ for some PDA $P = (Q, \Sigma, \Gamma, \delta, q_0, Z_0, F)$. We can construct a PDA P' such that $L_e(P') = L$.

Proof. We shall let P' simulate P. Anytime P enters a final state, P' will have a choice to continue simulating P or to enter a special state q_e which causes the pushdown list to be emptied. However, there is one complication. P may make a sequence of moves on an input string w which causes its pushdown list to become empty without the finite control being in a final state. Thus, to prevent P' from accepting w when it should not, we add to P' a special bottom marker for the pushdown list which can be removed only by P' in state q_e. Formally, let P' be $(Q \cup \{q_e, q'\}, \Sigma, \Gamma \cup \{Z'\}, \delta', q', Z', \varnothing)$,†

---

†We shall usually make the set of final states $\varnothing$ if the PDA is to accept by empty pushdown list. Obviously, the set of final states could be anything we wished.

where δ' is defined as follows:

(1) If $\delta(q, a, Z)$ contains (r, γ), then $\delta'(q, a, Z)$ contains (r, γ) for all $q \in Q$, $a \in \Sigma \cup \{e\}$, and $Z \in \Gamma$.

(2) $\delta'(q', e, Z') = \{(q_0, Z_0 Z')\}$. P''s first move is to write $Z_0 Z'$ on the pushdown list and enter the initial state of P. Z' will act as the special marker for the bottom of the pushdown list.

(3) For all $q \in F$ and $Z \in \Gamma \cup \{Z'\}$, $\delta'(q, e, Z)$ contains (q_e, e).

(4) For all $Z \in \Gamma \cup \{Z'\}$, $\delta'(q_e, e, Z) = \{(q_e, e)\}$.

We can clearly see that

$$(q', w, Z') \vdash_{\overline{P'}} (q_0, w, Z_0 Z')$$
$$\vdash_{\overline{P'}}^{n} (q, e, Y_1 \cdots Y_r)$$
$$\vdash_{\overline{P'}} (q_e, e, Y_2 \cdots Y_r)$$
$$\vdash_{\overline{P'}}^{r-1} (q_e, e, e)$$

where $Y_r = Z'$, if and only if

$$(q_0, w, Z_0) \vdash_{\overline{P}}^{n} (q, e, Y_1 \cdots Y_{r-1})$$

for $q \in F$ and $Y_1 \cdots Y_{r-1} \in \Gamma^*$. Hence, $L_e(P') = L(P)$. □

The converse of Lemma 2.22 is also true.

LEMMA 2.23

Let $P = (Q, \Sigma, \Gamma, \delta, q_0, Z_0, \varnothing)$ be a PDA. We can construct a PDA P' such that $L(P') = L_e(P)$.

Proof. P' will simulate P but have a special symbol Z' on the bottom of its pushdown list. As soon as P' can read Z', P' will enter a new final state q_f. A formal construction is left for the Exercises. □

2.5.3. Equivalence of PDA Languages and CFL's

We can now use these results to show that the PDA languages are exactly the context-free languages. In the following lemma we construct the natural (nondeterministic) "top-down" parser for a context-free grammar.

LEMMA 2.24

Let $G = (N, \Sigma, P, S)$ be a CFG. From G we can construct a PDA R such that $L_e(R) = L(G)$.

Proof. We shall construct R to simulate all leftmost derivations in G. Let $R = (\{q\}, \Sigma, N \cup \Sigma, \delta, q, S, \varnothing)$, where δ is defined as follows:

(1) If $A \to \alpha$ is in P, then $\delta(q, e, A)$ contains (q, α).

(2) $\delta(q, a, a) = \{(q, e)\}$ for all a in Σ.

We now want to show that

(2.5.2) $A \overset{m}{\Longrightarrow} w$ if and only if $(q, w, A) \vdash^n (q, e, e)$ for some $m, n \geq 1$

Only if: We shall prove this part by induction on m. Suppose that $A \overset{m}{\Longrightarrow} w$. If $m = 1$ and $w = a_1 \cdots a_k$, $k \geq 0$, then

$$(q, a_1 \cdots a_k, A) \vdash (q, a_1 \cdots a_k, a_1 \cdots a_k)$$
$$\vdash^k (q, e, e)$$

Now suppose that $A \overset{m}{\Longrightarrow} w$ for some $m > 1$. The first step of this derivation must be of the form $A \Longrightarrow X_1 X_2 \cdots X_k$, where $X_i \overset{m_i}{\Longrightarrow} x_i$ for some $m_i < m$, $1 \leq i \leq k$, and where $x_1 x_2 \cdots x_k = w$. Then

$$(q, w, A) \vdash (q, w, X_1 X_2 \cdots X_k)$$

If X_i is in N, then

$$(q, x_i, X_i) \vdash^* (q, e, e)$$

by the inductive hypothesis. If $X_i = x_i$ is in Σ, then

$$(q, x_i, X_i) \vdash (q, e, e)$$

Putting this sequence of moves together we have $(q, w, A) \vdash^+ (q, e, e)$.

If: We shall now show by induction on n that if $(q, w, A) \vdash^n (q, e, e)$, then $A \overset{+}{\Longrightarrow} w$.

For $n = 1$, $w = e$ and $A \rightarrow e$ is in P. Let us assume that this statement is true for all $n' < n$. Then the first move made by R must be of the form

$$(q, w, A) \vdash (q, w, X_1 \cdots X_k)$$

and $(q, x_i, X_i) \vdash^{n_i} (q, e, e)$ for $1 \leq i \leq k$, where $w = x_1 x_2 \cdots x_k$ (Lemma 2.20). Then $A \rightarrow X_1 \cdots X_k$ is a production in P, and $X_i \overset{+}{\Longrightarrow} x_i$ from the inductive hypothesis if $X_i \in$ N. If X_i is in Σ, then $X_i \overset{0}{\Longrightarrow} x_i$. Thus

$$\begin{aligned}
A &\Longrightarrow X_1 \cdots X_k \\
&\overset{*}{\Longrightarrow} x_1 X_2 \cdots X_k \\
&\quad \vdots \\
&\overset{*}{\Longrightarrow} x_1 x_2 \cdots x_{k-1} X_k \\
&\overset{*}{\Longrightarrow} x_1 x_2 \cdots x_{k-1} x_k = w
\end{aligned}$$

is a derivation of w from A in G.

As a special case of (2.5.2), we have the derivation $S \overset{+}{\Longrightarrow} w$ if and only if $(q, w, S) \vdash^+ (q, e, e)$. Thus, $L_e(R) = L(G)$.   □

Example 2.34

Let us construct a PDA P such that $L_e(P) = L(G_0)$, where G_0 is our usual grammar for arithmetic expressions. Let $P = (\{q\}, \Sigma, \Gamma, \delta, q, E, \varnothing)$, where δ is defined as follows:

(1) $\delta(q, e, E) = \{(q, E + T), (q, T)\}$.
(2) $\delta(q, e, T) = \{(q, T{*}F), (q, F)\}$.
(3) $\delta(q, e, F) = \{(q, (E)), (q, a)\}$.
(4) $\delta(q, b, b) = \{(q, e)\}$ for all $b \in \{a, +, *, (,)\}$.

With input $a + a * a$, P can make the following moves among others:

$$
\begin{aligned}
(q, a + a * a, E) &\vdash (q, a + a * a, E + T) \\
&\vdash (q, a + a * a, T + T) \\
&\vdash (q, a + a * a, F + T) \\
&\vdash (q, a + a * a, a + T) \\
&\vdash (q, + a * a, + T) \\
&\vdash (q, a * a, T) \\
&\vdash (q, a * a, T * F) \\
&\vdash (q, a * a, F * F) \\
&\vdash (q, a * a, a * F) \\
&\vdash (q, * a, * F) \\
&\vdash (q, a, F) \\
&\vdash (q, a, a) \\
&\vdash (q, e, e)
\end{aligned}
$$

Notice that in this sequence of moves P has used the rules in a sequence that corresponds to a leftmost derivation of $a + a * a$ from E in G_0.   □

This type of analysis is called "top-down parsing," or "predictive analysis," because we are in effect constructing a derivation tree starting off from the top (at the root) and working down. We shall discuss top-down parsing in greater detail in Chapters 3, 4, and 5.

We can construct an extended PDA that acts as a "bottom-up parser" by simulating rightmost derivations in reverse in a CFG G. Let us consider the sentence $a + a * a$ in $L(G_0)$. The sequence

$$
\begin{aligned}
E &\Longrightarrow E + T \Longrightarrow E + T * F \Longrightarrow E + T * a \Longrightarrow E + F * a \\
&\Longrightarrow E + a * a \Longrightarrow T + a * a \Longrightarrow F + a * a \Longrightarrow a + a * a
\end{aligned}
$$

of right-sentential forms represents a rightmost derivation of $a + a * a$ from E in G_0.

Now suppose that we write this derivation reversed. If we consider that in going from the string $a + a * a$ to the string $F + a * a$ we have applied the production $F \longrightarrow a$ in reverse, then we can say that the string $a + a * a$ has been "left-reduced" to the string $F + a * a$. Moreover, this represents the only leftmost reduction that is possible. Similarly the right sentential form $F + a * a$ can be left-reduced to $T + a * a$ by means of the production $T \longrightarrow F$, and so forth. We can formally define the process of left reduction as follows.

DEFINITION

Let $G = (N, \Sigma, P, S)$ be a CFG, and suppose that

$$S \underset{rm}{\overset{*}{\Longrightarrow}} \alpha A w \underset{rm}{\Longrightarrow} \alpha \beta w \underset{rm}{\overset{*}{\Longrightarrow}} xw$$

is a rightmost derivation. Then we say that the right-sentential form $\alpha \beta w$ can be *left-reduced* under the production $A \longrightarrow \beta$ to the right-sentential form $\alpha A w$. Furthermore, we call the substring β at the explicitly shown position a *handle* of $\alpha \beta w$. Thus a handle of a right-sentential form is any substring which is the right side of some production and which can be replaced by the left side of that production so that the resulting string is also a right-sentential form.

Example 2.35

Consider the grammar with the following productions:

$$S \longrightarrow Ac \,|\, Bd$$
$$A \longrightarrow aAb \,|\, ab$$
$$B \longrightarrow aBbb \,|\, abb$$

This grammar generates the language $\{a^n b^n c \,|\, n \geq 1\} \cup \{a^n b^{2n} d \,|\, n \geq 1\}$.

Consider the right-sentential form $aabbbbd$. The only handle of this string is abb, since $aBbbd$ is a right-sentential form. Note that although ab is the right side of the production $A \longrightarrow ab$, ab is not a handle of $aabbbbd$ since $aAbbbd$ is not a right-sentential form. $\square$

Another way or defining the handle of a right-sentential form is to say that the handle is the frontier of the leftmost complete subtree of depth 1 (i.e., a node all of whose direct descendants are leaves, together with these leaves) of some derivation tree for that right-sentential form.

In the grammar G_0, the derivation tree for $a + a * a$ is shown in Fig. 2.16(a). The leftmost complete subtree has the leftmost node labeled F as root and frontier a.

If we delete the leaves of the leftmost complete subtree, we are left with the derivation tree of Fig. 2.16(b). The frontier of this tree is $F + a * a$, and

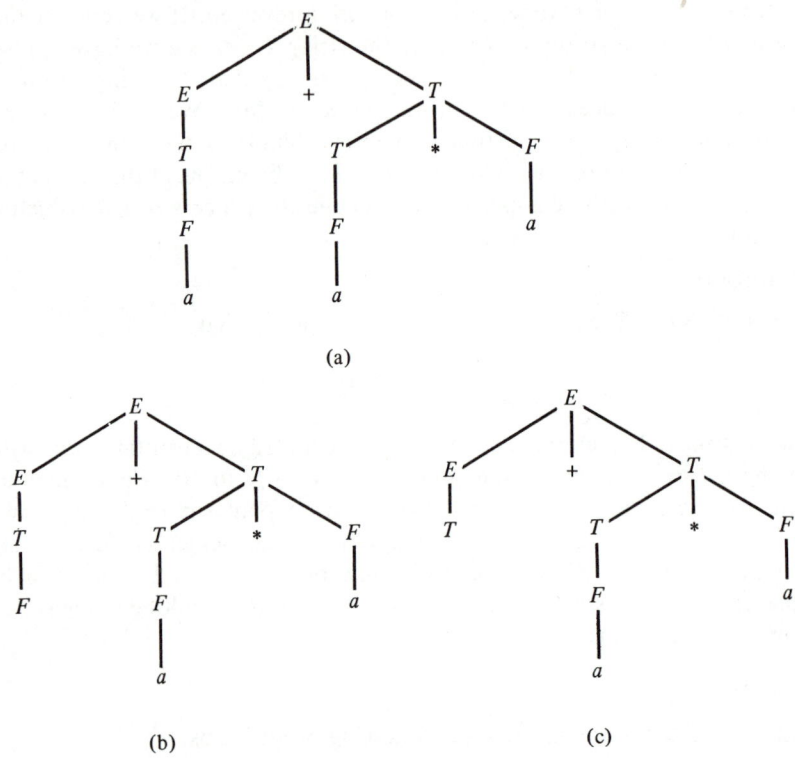

Fig. 2.16   Handle pruning.

this string is precisely the result of left-reducing $a + a * a$. The handle of this tree is the frontier F of the subtree with root labeled T. Again removing the handle we are left with Fig. 2.16(c).

The process of reducing trees in this manner is called *handle pruning*.

From a CFG G we can construct an equivalent extended PDA P which operates by handle pruning. At this point it is convenient to represent a pushdown list as string such that the rightmost symbol of the pushdown list, rather than the leftmost, is at the top. Using this convention, if $P = (Q, \Sigma, \Gamma, \delta, q_0, Z_0, F)$ is a PDA, its configurations are exactly as before. However, the $\vdash$ relation is defined slightly differently. If $\delta(q, a, \alpha)$ contains (p, β), then we write $(q, aw, \gamma\alpha) \vdash (p, w, \gamma\beta)$ for all $w \in \Sigma^*$ and $\gamma \in \Gamma^*$.

Thus a notation such as "$\delta(q, a, YZ)$ contains (p, VWX)" means different things depending on whether the (extended) PDA has the top of its pushdown list at the left or right. If at the left, Y and V are the top symbols before and after the move. If at the right, Z and X are the top symbols. Given a PDA with the top at the left, one can create a PDA doing exactly the same things, but with the pushdown top at the right, by reversing all strings in Γ^*. For example, $(p, VWX) \in \delta(q, a, YZ)$ becomes $(p, XWV) \in \delta(q, a, ZY)$. Of course, one must specify the fact that the top is now at the right. Conversely, a PDA with top at the right can easily be converted to one with the top a the left.

We see that the 7-tuple notation for PDA's can be interpreted as two different PDA's, depending on whether the top is taken at the right or left. We feel that the notational convenience which results from having these two conventions outweighs any initial confusion. As the "default condition," unless it is specified otherwise, ordinary PDA's have their pushdown tops on the left and extended PDA's have their pushdown tops on the right.

LEMMA 2.25

Let (N, Σ, P, S) be a CFG. From G we can construct an extended PDA R such that $L(R) = L(G)$.† R can "reasonably" be said to operate by handle pruning.

Proof. Let $R = (\{q, r\}, \Sigma, N \cup \Sigma \cup \{\$\}, \delta, q, \$, \{r\})$ be an extended PDA‡ in which δ is defined as follows:

(1) $\delta(q, a, e) = \{(q, a)\}$ for all $a \in \Sigma$. These moves cause input symbols to be shifted on top of the pushdown list.

(2) If $A \rightarrow \alpha$ is in P, then $\delta(q, e, \alpha)$ contains (q, A).

(3) $\delta(q, e, \$S) = \{(r, e)\}$.

We shall show that R operates by computing right-sentential forms of G, starting with a string of all terminals (on R's input) and ending with the string S. The inductive hypothesis which will be proved by induction on n is

$$(2.5.3) \qquad S \underset{rm}{\overset{*}{\Longrightarrow}} \alpha A y \underset{rm}{\overset{n}{\Longrightarrow}} xy \text{ implies } (q, xy, \$) \vdash^* (q, y, \$\alpha A)$$

The basis, $n = 0$, is trivial; no moves of R are involved. Let us assume (2.5.3) for values of n smaller than the value we now choose for n. We can write $\alpha A y \underset{rm}{\Longrightarrow} \alpha \beta y \overset{n-1}{\underset{rm}{\Longrightarrow}} xy$. Suppose that $\alpha \beta$ consists solely of terminals. Then $\alpha \beta = x$ and $(q, xy, \$) \vdash^* (q, y, \$\alpha \beta) \vdash (q, y, \$\alpha A)$.

If $\alpha \beta$ is not in Σ^*, then we can write $\alpha \beta = \gamma B z$, where B is the rightmost

---

†Obviously, Lemma 2.25 is implied by Lemmas 2.23 and 2.24. It is the construction that is of interest here.

‡Our convention puts pushdown tops on the right.

nonterminal. By (2.5.3), $S \overset{*}{\underset{rm}{\Rightarrow}} \gamma Bzy \overset{n-1}{\underset{rm}{\Rightarrow}} xy$ implies $(q, xy, \$) \overset{*}{\vdash} (q, zy, \$\gamma B)$.
Also, $(q, zy, \$\gamma B) \overset{*}{\vdash} (q, y, \$\gamma Bz) \vdash (q, y, \$\alpha A)$ is a valid sequence of moves.

We conclude that (2.5.3) is true. Since $(q, e, \$S) \vdash (r, e, e)$, we have $L(G) \subseteq L(R)$.

We must now show the following, in order to conclude that $L(R) \subseteq L(G)$, and hence, $L(G) = L(R)$:

(2.5.4)   If $(q, xy, \$) \overset{n}{\vdash} (q, y, \$\alpha A)$, then $\alpha Ay \overset{*}{\Longrightarrow} xy$

The basis, $n = 0$, holds vacuously. For the inductive step, assume that (2.5.4) is true for all values of $n < m$. When the top symbol of the pushdown list of R is a nonterminal, we know that the last move of R was caused by rule (2) of the definition of δ. Thus we can write

$$(q, xy, \$) \overset{m-1}{\vdash} (q, y, \$\alpha\beta) \vdash (q, y, \$\alpha A),$$

where $A \longrightarrow \beta$ is in P. If $\alpha\beta$ has a nonterminal, then by inductive hypothesis (2.5.4), $\alpha\beta y \overset{*}{\Rightarrow} xy$. Thus, $\alpha Ay \Rightarrow \alpha\beta y \overset{*}{\Rightarrow} xy$, as contended.

As a special case of (2.5.4), $(q, w, \$) \overset{*}{\vdash} (q, e, \$S)$ implies that $S \overset{*}{\Rightarrow} w$. Since R only accepts w if $(q, w, \$) \overset{*}{\vdash} (q, e, \$S) \vdash (r, e, e)$, it follows that $L(R) \subseteq L(G)$. Thus, $L(R) = L(G)$. $\square$

Notice that R stores a right-sentential form of the type αAx with αA on the pushdown list and x remaining on the input tape immediately after a reduction. Then R can proceed to shift symbols of x on the pushdown list until the handle is on top of the pushdown list. Then R can make another reduction. This type of syntactic analysis is called "bottom-up parsing" or "reductions analysis."

Example 2.36

Let us construct a bottom-up analyzer R for G_0. Let R be the extended PDA $(\{q, r\}, \Sigma, \Gamma, \delta, q, \$, \{r\})$, where δ is as follows:

(1) $\delta(q, b, e) = \{(q, b)\}$ for all b in $\{a, +, *, (,)\}$.
(2) $\delta(q, e, E + T) = \{(q, E)\}$
      $\delta(q, e, T) = \{(q, E)\}$
    $\delta(q, e, T * F) = \{(q, T)\}$
      $\delta(q, e, F) = \{(q, T)\}$
     $\delta(q, e, (E)) = \{(q, F)\}$
      $\delta(q, e, a) = \{(q, F)\}$.
(3) $\delta(q, e, \$E) = \{(r, e)\}$.

With input $a + a * a$, R can make the following sequence of moves:

$$(q, a + a * a, \$) \vdash (q, + a * a, \$a)$$
$$\vdash (q, + a * a, \$F)$$
$$\vdash (q, + a * a, \$T)$$
$$\vdash (q, + a * a, \$E)$$
$$\vdash (q, a * a, \$E +)$$
$$\vdash (q, * a, \$E + a)$$
$$\vdash (q, * a, \$E + F)$$
$$\vdash (q, * a, \$E + T)$$
$$\vdash (q, a, \$E + T *)$$
$$\vdash (q, e, \$E + T * a)$$
$$\vdash (q, e, \$E + T * F)$$
$$\vdash (q, e, \$E + T)$$
$$\vdash (q, e, \$E)$$
$$\vdash (r, e, e)$$

Notice that R can make a great number of different sequences of moves with input $a + a * a$. This sequence, however, is the only one that goes from an initial configuration to a final configuration. $\square$

We shall now demonstrate that a language defined by a PDA is a context-free language.

LEMMA 2.26

Let $R = (Q, \Sigma, \Gamma, \delta, q_0, Z_0, F)$ be a PDA. We can construct a CFG such that $L(G) = L_e(R)$.

Proof. We shall construct G so that a leftmost derivation of w in G directly corresponds to a sequence of moves made by R in processing w. We shall use nonterminal symbols of the form $[qZr]$ with q and r in Q and $Z \in \Gamma$. We shall then show that $[qZr] \overset{+}{\Rightarrow} w$ if and only if $(q, w, Z) \overset{+}{\vdash} (r, e, e)$. Formally, let $G = (N, \Sigma, P, S)$, where

(1) $N = \{[qZr] \mid q, r \in Q, Z \in \Gamma\} \cup \{S\}$.
(2) The productions in P are constructed as follows:
   (a) If $\delta(q, a, Z)$ contains $(r, X_1 \cdots X_k)$,† $k \geq 1$, then add to P all productions of the form

$$[qZs_k] \longrightarrow a[rX_1s_1][s_1X_2s_2] \cdots [s_{k-1}X_ks_k]$$

† R has its pushdown list top on the left, since we did not state otherwise.

for every sequence $s_1, s_2, \ldots, s_k$ of states in Q.

(b) If $\delta(q, a, Z)$ contains (r, e), then add the production $[qZr] \rightarrow a$ to P.

(c) Add to P, $S \rightarrow [q_0 Z_0 q]$ for each $q \in Q$.

It is straightforward to show by induction on m and n that for all $q, r \in Q$, and $Z \in \Gamma$, $[qZr] \overset{m}{\Rightarrow} w$ if and only if $(q, w, Z) \vdash^n (r, e, e)$. We leave the proof for the Exercises. Then, $S \Rightarrow [q_0 Z_0 q] \overset{+}{\Rightarrow} w$ if and only if $(q_0, w, Z_0) \vdash^{+} (q, e, e)$ for q in Q. Thus, $L_e(R) = L(G)$.   □

We can summarize these results in the following theorem.

THEOREM 2.21

The following statements are equivalent:

(1) L is $L(G)$ for a CFG G.
(2) L is $L(P)$ for a PDA P.
(3) L is $L_e(P)$ for a PDA P.
(4) L is $L(P)$ for an extended PDA P.

Proof. (3) $\rightarrow$ (1) by Lemma 2.26. (1) $\rightarrow$ (3) by Lemma 2.24. (4) $\rightarrow$ (2) by Lemma 2.21, and (2) $\rightarrow$ (4) is trivial. (2) $\rightarrow$ (3) by Lemma 2.22 and (3) $\rightarrow$ (2) by Lemma 2.23.   □

2.5.4. Deterministic Pushdown Automata

We have seen that for every context-free grammar G we can construct a PDA to recognize $L(G)$. The PDA constructed was nondeterministic, however. For practical applications we are more interested in deterministic pushdown automata—PDA's which can make at most one move in any configuration. In this section we shall study deterministic PDA's and later on we shall see that, unfortunately, deterministic PDA's are not as powerful in their recognitive capability as nondeterministic PDA's. There are context-free languages which cannot be defined by any deterministic PDA.

A language which is defined by a deterministic pushdown automaton will be called a *deterministic CFL*. In Chapter 5 we shall define a subclass of the context-free grammars called *LR(k)* grammars. In Chapter 8 we shall show that every *LR(k)* grammar generates a deterministic CFL and that every deterministic CFL has an LR(1) grammar.

DEFINITION

A PDA $P = (Q, \Sigma, \Gamma, \delta, q_0, Z_0, F)$ is said to be *deterministic* (a DPDA for short) if for each $q \in Q$ and $Z \in \Gamma$ either

(1) $\delta(q, a, Z)$ contains at most one element for each a in Σ and $\delta(q, e, Z) = \varnothing$ or

(2) $\delta(q, a, Z) = \varnothing$ for all $a \in \Sigma$ and $\delta(q, e, Z)$ contains at most one element.

These two restrictions imply that a DPDA has at most one choice of move in any configuration. Thus in practice it is much easier to simulate a deterministic PDA than a nondeterministic PDA. For this reason the deterministic CFL's are an important class of languages for practical applications.

CONVENTION

Since $\delta(q, a, Z)$ contains at most one element for a DPDA, we shall write $\delta(q, a, Z) = (r, \gamma)$ instead of $\delta(q, a, Z) = \{(r, \gamma)\}$.

Example 2.37

Let us construct a DPDA for the language $L = \{wcw^R \mid w \in \{a, b\}^+\}$. Let $P = (\{q_0, q_1, q_2\}, \{a, b, c\}, \{Z, a, b\}, \delta, q_0, Z, \{q_2\})$, where the rules of δ are

$$\delta(q_0, X, Y) = (q_0, XY) \qquad \text{for all } X \in \{a, b\}$$
$$Y \in \{Z, a, b\}$$
$$\delta(q_0, c, Y) = (q_1, Y) \qquad \text{for all } Y \in \{a, b\}$$
$$\delta(q_1, X, X) = (q_1, e) \qquad \text{for all } X \in \{a, b\}$$
$$\delta(q_1, e, Z) = (q_2, e)$$

Until P sees the centermarker c, it stores its input on the pushdown list. When the c is reached, P goes to state q_1 and proceeds to match its subsequent input against the pushdown list. A proof that $L(P) = L$ is left for the Exercises. ☐

The definition of a DPDA can be naturally widened to include the extended PDA's which we would naturally consider deterministic.

DEFINITION

An extended PDA $P = (Q, \Sigma, \Gamma, \delta, q_0, Z_0, F)$ is an (*extended*) *deterministic PDA* if the following conditions hold:
(1) For no $q \in Q$, $a \in \Sigma \cup \{e\}$ and $\gamma \in \Gamma^*$ is $\#\delta(q, a, \gamma) > 1$.
(2) If $\delta(q, a, \alpha) \neq \varnothing$, $\delta(q, a, \beta) \neq \varnothing$, and $\alpha \neq \beta$, then neither of α and β is a suffix of the other.†
(3) If $\delta(q, a, \alpha) \neq \varnothing$, and $\delta(q, e, \beta) \neq \varnothing$, then neither of α and β is a suffix of the other.

We see that in the special case in which the extended PDA is an ordinary PDA, the two definitions agree. Also, if the construction of Lemma 2.21 is

---

†If the extended PDA has its pushdown list top at the left, replace "suffix" by "prefix."

applied to an extended PDA P, the result will be a DPDA if and only if P is an extended DPDA.

When modeling a syntactic analyzer, it is desirable to use a DPDA P that reads all of its input, even when the input is not in $L(P)$. We shall show that it is possible to always find such a DPDA.

We first modify a DPDA so that in any configuration with input remaining there is a next move. The next lemma shows how.

LEMMA 2.27

Let $P = (Q, \Sigma, \Gamma, \delta, q_0, Z_0, F)$ be a DPDA. We can construct an equivalent DPDA $P' = (Q', \Sigma, \Gamma', \delta', q_0', Z_0', F')$ such that

(1) For all $a \in \Sigma, q \in Q'$ and $Z \in \Gamma'$, either
   (a) $\delta'(q, a, Z)$ contains exactly one element and $\delta'(q, e, Z) = \varnothing$ or
   (b) $\delta'(q, a, Z) = \varnothing$ and $\delta'(q, e, Z)$ contains exactly one element.
(2) If $\delta(q, a, Z_0') = (r, \gamma)$ for some a in $\Sigma \cup \{e\}$, then $\gamma = \alpha Z_0'$ for some $\alpha \in \Gamma^*$.

Proof. Z_0' will act as an endmarker on the pushdown list to prevent the pushdown list from becoming completely empty. Let $\Gamma' = \Gamma \cup \{Z_0'\}$, and let $Q' = \{q_0', q_e\} \cup Q$. δ' is defined thus:

(1) $\delta'(q_0', e, Z_0') = (q_0, Z_0 Z_0')$.
(2) For all $q \in Q$, $a \in \Sigma \cup \{e\}$, and $Z \in \Gamma$ such that $\delta(q, a, Z) \neq \varnothing$, $\delta'(q, a, Z) = \delta(q, a, Z)$.
(3) If $\delta(q, e, Z) = \varnothing$ and $\delta(q, a, Z) = \varnothing$ for some $a \in \Sigma$ and $Z \in \Gamma$, let $\delta'(q, a, Z) = (q_e, Z)$.
(4) For all $Z \in \Gamma'$ and $a \in \Sigma$, $\delta'(q_e, a, Z) = (q_e, Z)$.

The first rule allows P' to simulate P by having P' write Z_0 on top of Z_0' on the pushdown list and enter state q_0. The rules in (2) permit P' to simulate P until no next move is possible. In such a situation P' will go into a nonfinal state q_e, by rule (3), and remain there without altering the pushdown list, while consuming any remaining input. A proof that $L(P') = L(P)$ is left for the Exercises. $\square$

It is possible for a DPDA to make an infinite number of e-moves from some configurations without ever using an input symbol. We call these configurations looping.

DEFINITION

Configuration (q, w, α) of DPDA P is *looping* if for all integers i there exists a configuration (p_i, w, β_i) such that $|\beta_i| \geq |\alpha|$ and

$$(q, w, \alpha) \vdash (p_1, w, \beta_1) \vdash (p_2, w, \beta_2) \vdash \cdots.$$

Thus a configuration is looping if P can make an infinite number of

e-moves without creating a shorter pushdown list; that list might grow indefinitely or cycle between several different strings.

Note that there are nonlooping configurations which after popping part of their list using e-moves enter a looping configuration. We shall show that it is impossible to make an infinite number of e-moves from a configuration unless a looping configuration is entered after a finite, calculable number of moves.

If P enters a looping configuration in the middle of the input string, then P will not use any more input, even though P might satisfy Lemma 2.27. Given a DPDA P, we want to modify P to form an equivalent DPDA P' such that P' can never enter a looping configuration.

ALGORITHM 2.16

Detection of looping configurations.

Input. DPDA $P = (Q, \Sigma, \Gamma, \delta, q_0, Z_0, F)$.

Output.

(1) $C_1 = \{(q, A) \mid (q, e, A)$ is a looping configuration and there is no r in F such that $(q, e, A) \stackrel{*}{\vdash} (r, e, \alpha)$ for any $\alpha \in \Gamma^*\}$, and

(2) $C_2 = \{(q, A) \mid (q, e, A)$ is a looping configuration and $(q, e, A) \stackrel{*}{\vdash} (r, e, \alpha)$ for some $r \in F$ and $\alpha \in \Gamma^*\}$.

Method. Let $\#Q = n_1$, $\#\Gamma = n_2$, and let l be the length of the longest string written on the pushdown list by P in a single move. Let $n_3 = n_1(n_2^{n_1 n_2 l} - n_2)/(n_2 - 1)$, where $n_3 = n_1$ if $n_2 = 1$. n_3 is the maximum number of e-moves P can make without looping.

(1) For each $q \in Q$ and $A \in \Gamma$ determine whether $(q, e, A) \stackrel{n_3}{\vdash} (r, e, \alpha)$ for some $r \in Q$ and $\alpha \in \Gamma^+$. Direct simulation of P is used. If so, (q, e, A) is a looping configuration, for then we shall see that there must be a pair (q', A'), with $q' \in Q$ and $A' \in \Gamma$, such that

$$(q, e, A) \stackrel{*}{\vdash} (q', e, A'\beta)$$
$$\stackrel{m}{\vdash} (q', e, A'\gamma\beta)$$
$$\stackrel{m(j-1)}{\vdash} (q', e, A'\gamma^j\beta)$$

where $m > 0$ and $j > 0$. Note that γ can be e.

(2) If (q, e, A) is a looping configuration, determine whether there is an r in F such that $(q, e, A) \stackrel{j}{\vdash} (r, e, \alpha)$ for some $0 \le j \le n_3$. Again, direct simulation is used. If so, add (q, A) to C_2. Otherwise, add (q, A) to C_1. We claim that if P can reach a final configuration from (q, e, A), it must do so in n_3 or fewer moves. $\square$

THEOREM 2.22

Algorithm 2.16 correctly determines C_1 and C_2.

Proof. We first prove that step (1) correctly determines $C_1 \cup C_2$. If (q, A) is in $C_1 \cup C_2$, then, obviously, $(q, e, A) \vdash^{n_3} (r, e, \alpha)$. Conversely, suppose that $(q, e, A) \vdash^{n_3} (r, e, \alpha)$.

Case 1: There exists $\beta \in \Gamma^*$, with $|\beta| > n_1 n_2 l$ and $(q, e, A) \vdash^* (p, e, \beta)$ $\vdash^* (r, e, \alpha)$ for some $p \in Q$. If we consider, for $j = 1, 2, \ldots, n_1 n_2 l + 1$, the configurations which P entered in the sequence of moves $(q, e, A) \vdash^*$ (p, e, β) the last time the pushdown list had length j, then we see that there must exist q' and A' such that at two of those times the state of P was q' and A' was on top of the list. In other words, we can write $(q, e, A) \vdash^* (q', e, A'\delta)$ $\vdash^\pm (q', e, A'\gamma\delta) \vdash^* (p, e, \beta)$. Thus, $(q, e, A) \vdash^* (q', e, A'\delta) \vdash^{mj} (q', e, A'\gamma^j\delta)$ for all $j \geq 0$ by Lemma 2.20. Here, $m > 0$, so an infinity of e-moves can be made from configuration (q, e, A), and (q, A) is in $C_1 \cup C_2$.

Case 2: Suppose that the opposite of case 1 is true, namely that for all β such that $(q, e, A) \vdash^* (p, e, \beta) \vdash^* (r, e, \alpha)$ we have $|\beta| \leq n_1 n_2 l$. Since there are $n_3 + 1$ different β's, n_1 possible states, and $n_2 + n_2^2 + n_2^3 + \cdots + n_2^{n_1 n_2 l}$ $= (n_2^{n_1 n_2 l} - n_2)/(n_2 - 1)$ possible pushdown lists of length at most $n_1 n_2 l$, there must be some repeated configuration. It is immediate that (q, A) is in $C_1 \cup C_2$.

The proof that step (2) correctly apportions $C_1 \cup C_2$ between C_1 and C_2 is left for the Exercises. $\square$

DEFINITION

A DPDA $P = (Q, \Sigma, \Gamma, \delta, q_0, Z_0, F)$ is *continuing* if for all $w \in \Sigma^*$ there exists $p \in Q$ and $\alpha \in \Gamma^*$ such that $(q_0, w, Z_0) \vdash^* (p, e, \alpha)$. Intuitively, a continuing DPDA is one which is capable of reading all of its input string.

LEMMA 2.28

Let $P = (Q, \Sigma, \Gamma, \delta, q_0, Z_0, F)$ be a DPDA. Then there is an equivalent continuing DPDA P'.

Proof. Let us assume by Lemma 2.27 that P always has a next move. Let $P' = (Q \cup \{p, r\}, \Sigma, \Gamma, \delta', q_0, Z_0, F \cup \{p\})$, where p and r are new states. δ' is defined as follows:

(1) For all $q \in Q$, $a \in \Sigma$, and $Z \in \Gamma$, let $\delta'(q, a, Z) = \delta(q, a, Z)$.

(2) For all $q \in Q$ and $Z \in \Gamma$ such that (q, e, Z) is not a looping configuration, let $\delta'(q, e, Z) = \delta(q, e, Z)$.

(3) For all (q, Z) in the set C_1 of Algorithm 2.16, let $\delta'(q, e, Z) = (r, Z)$.

(4) For all (q, Z) in the set C_2 of Algorithm 2.16, let $\delta'(q, e, Z) = (p, Z)$.

(5) For all $a \in \Sigma$ and $Z \in \Gamma$, $\delta'(p, a, Z) = (r, Z)$ and $\delta'(r, a, Z) = (r, Z)$.

Thus, P' simulates P. If P enters a looping configuration, then P' will enter on the next move either state p or r depending on whether the loop of configurations contains or does not contain a final state. Then, under all inputs, P'

enters state r from p and stays in state r without altering the pushdown list. Thus, $L(P') = L(P)$.

It is necessary to show that P' is continuing. Rules (3), (4), and (5) assure us that no violation of the "continuing" condition occurs if P enters a looping configuration. It is necessary to observe only that if P is in a configuration which is not looping, then within a finite number of moves it must either

(1) Make a non-e-move or
(2) Enter a configuration which has a shorter pushdown list.

Moreover, (2) cannot occur indefinitely, because the pushdown list is initially of finite length. Thus either (1) must eventually occur or P enters a looping configuration after some instance of (2). We may conclude that P' is continuing. $\square$

We can now prove an important property of DPDA's, namely that their languages are closed under complementation. We shall see in the next section that this is not true for the class of all CFL's.

THEOREM 2.23

If $L = L(P)$ for DPDA P, then $\bar{L} = L(P')$ for some DPDA P'.

Proof. We may, by Lemma 2.28, assume that P is continuing. We shall construct P' to simulate P and see, between two shifts of its input head, whether or not P has entered an accepting state. Since P' must accept the complement of $L(P)$, P' accepts an input if P has not accepted it and is about to shift its input head (so P could not subsequently accept that input).

Formally, let $P = (Q, \Sigma, \Gamma, \delta, q_0, Z_0, F)$ and $P' = (Q', \Sigma, \Gamma, \delta', q_0', Z_0, F')$, where

(1) $Q' = \{[q, i] \mid q \in Q, i \in \{0, 1, 2\}\}$,
(2) $q_0' = [q_0, 0]$ if $q_0 \notin F$ and $q_0' = [q_0, 1]$ if $q_0 \in F$, and
(3) $F' = \{[q, 2] \mid q \text{ in } Q\}$.

The states $[q, 0]$ are intended to mean that P has not been in a final state since it last made a non-e-move. $[q, 1]$ states indicate that P has entered a final state in that time. $[q, 2]$ states are used only for final states. If P' is in a $[q, 0]$ state and P (in simulation) is about to make a non-e-move, then P' first enters state $[q, 2]$ and then simulates P. Thus, P' accepts if and only if P does not accept. The fact that P is continuing assures us that P' will always get a chance to accept an input if P does not. The formal definition of δ' follows:

(i) If $q \in Q$, $a \in \Sigma$, and $Z \in \Gamma$, then

$$\delta'([q, 1], a, Z) = \delta'([q, 2], a, Z) = ([p, i], \gamma),$$

where $\delta(q, a, Z) = (p, \gamma)$, $i = 0$ if $p \notin F$, and $i = 1$ if $p \in F$.

(ii) If $q \in Q$, $Z \in \Gamma$, and $\delta(q, e, Z) = (p, \gamma)$, then

$$\delta'([q, 1], e, Z) = ([p, 1], \gamma)$$

and $\delta'([q, 0], e, Z) = ([p, i], \gamma)$, where $i = 0$ if $p \notin F$ and $i = 1$ if $p \in F$.
(iii) If $\delta(q, e, Z) = \varnothing$, then $\delta'([q, 0], e, Z) = ([q, 2], Z)$.

Rule (i) handles non-e-moves. The second component of the state is set to 0 or 1 properly. Rule (ii) handles e-moves; again the second component of the state is handled as intended. Rule (iii) allows P' to accept an input exactly when P does not. A formal proof that $L(P') = \overline{L(P)}$ will be omitted. ☐

There are a number of other important properties of deterministic CFL's. We shall defer the discussion of these to the Exercises and the next section.

EXERCISES

2.5.1. Construct PDA's accepting the complements (with respect to $\{a, b\}^*$) of the following languages:
(a) $\{a^n b^n a^n \mid n \geq 1\}$.
(b) $\{ww^R \mid w \in \{a, b\}^*\}$.
(c) $\{a^m b^n a^m b^n \mid m, n \geq 1\}$.
(d) $\{ww \mid w \in \{a, b\}^*\}$.
Hint: Have the nondeterministic PDA "guess" why its input is not in the language and check that its guess is correct.

2.5.2. Prove that the PDA of Example 2.31 accepts $\{ww^R \mid w \in \{a, b\}^+\}$.

2.5.3. Show that every CFL is accepted by a PDA which never increases the length of its pushdown list by more than one on a single move.

2.5.4. Show that every CFL is accepted by a PDA $P = (Q, \Sigma, \Gamma, \delta, q_0, Z_0, F)$ such that if (p, γ) is in $\delta(q, a, Z)$, then either $\gamma = e$, $\gamma = Z$, or $\gamma = YZ$ for some $Y \in \Gamma$. *Hint:* Consider the construction of Lemma 2.21.

2.5.5. Show that every CFL is accepted by a PDA which makes no e-moves. *Hint:* Recall that every CFL has a grammar in Greibach normal form.

2.5.6. Show that every CFL is $L(P)$ for some two-state PDA P.

2.5.7. Complete the proof of Lemma 2.23.

2.5.8. Find bottom-up and top-down recognizers (PDA's) for the following grammars:
(a) $S \longrightarrow aSb \mid e$.
(b) $S \longrightarrow AS \mid b$
$A \longrightarrow SA \mid a$.
(c) $S \longrightarrow SS \mid A$
$A \longrightarrow 0A1 \mid S \mid 01$.

2.5.9. Find a grammar generating $L(P)$, where

$$P = (\{q_0, q_1, q_2\}, \{a, b\}, \{Z_0, A\}, \delta, q_0, Z_0, \{q_2\})$$

and δ is given by

$$\delta(q_0, a, Z_0) = (q_1, AZ_0)$$
$$\delta(q_0, a, A) = (q_1, AA)$$
$$\delta(q_1, a, A) = (q_0, AA)$$
$$\delta(q_1, e, A) = (q_2, A)$$
$$\delta(q_2, b, A) = (q_2, e)$$

Hint: It is not necessary to construct the productions for useless nonterminals.

*2.5.10. Show that if $P = (Q, \Sigma, \Gamma, \delta, q_0, Z_0, F)$ is a PDA, then the set of strings which can appear on the pushdown list is a regular set. That is, show that $\{\alpha \mid (q_0, w, Z_0) \vdash^{*} (q, x, \alpha)$ for some q, w, and $x\}$ is regular.

2.5.11. Complete the proof of Lemma 2.26.

2.5.12. Let P be a PDA for which there is a constant k such that P can never have more than k symbols on its pushdown list at any time. Show that $L(P)$ is a regular set.

2.5.13. Give DPDA's accepting the following languages:

(a) $\{0^i 1^j \mid j \leq i\}$.
(b) $\{w \mid w$ consists of an equal number of a's and b's$\}$.
(c) $L(G_0)$, where G_0 is the usual grammar for rudimentary arithmetic expressions.

2.5.14. Show that the DPDA of Example 2.36 accepts $\{wcw^R \mid w \in \{a, b\}^+\}$.

2.5.15. Show that if the construction of Lemma 2.21 is applied to an extended DPDA, then the result is a DPDA.

2.5.16. Prove that P and P' in Lemma 2.27 accept the same language.

2.5.17. Prove that step (2) of Algorithm 2.16 correctly distinguishes C_1 from C_2.

2.5.18. Complete the proof of Theorem 2.23.

2.5.19. The PDA's we have defined make a move independent of their input unless they move their input head. We could relax this restriction and allow the input symbol scanned to influence the move even when the input head remains stationary. Show that this extension still accepts only the CFL's.

*2.5.20. We could further augment the PDA by allowing it to move two ways on the input. Also, let the device have endmarkers on the input. We call such an automaton a 2PDA, and if it is deterministic, a 2DPDA. Show that the following languages can be recognized by 2DPDA's:

(a) $\{a^n b^n c^n \mid n \geq 1\}$.
(b) $\{ww \mid w \in \{a, b\}^*\}$.
(c) $\{a^{2^n} \mid n \geq 1\}$.

2.5.21. Show that a 2PDA can recognize $\{wxw \mid w$ and x are in $\{0, 1\}^+\}$.

Open Questions

2.5.22. Does there exist a language accepted by a 2PDA that is not accepted by a 2DPDA?

2.5.23. Does there exist a CFL which is not accepted by any 2DPDA?

Programming Exercises

2.5.24. Write a program that simulates a deterministic PDA.

*2.5.25. Devise a programming language that can be used to specify pushdown automata. Construct a compiler for your programming language. A source program in the language is to define a PDA *P*. The object program is to be a recognizer which given an input string *w* simulates the behavior of *P* on *w* in some reasonable sense.

2.5.26. Write a program that takes as input CFG *G* and constructs a nondeterministic top-down (or bottom-up) recognizer for *G*.

BIBLIOGRAPHIC NOTES

The importance of pushdown lists, or stacks, as they are also known, in language processing was recognized by the early 1950's. Oettinger [1961] and Schutzenberger [1963] were the first to formalize the concept of a pushdown automaton. The equivalence of pushdown automaton languages and context-free languages was demonstrated by Chomsky [1962] and Evey [1963].

Two-way pushdown automata have been studied by Hartmanis *et al.* [1965], Gray *et al.* [1967], Aho *et al.* [1968], and Cook [1971].

2.6. PROPERTIES OF CONTEXT-FREE LANGUAGES

In this section we shall examine some of the basic properties of context-free languages. The results mentioned here are actually a small sampling of the great wealth of knowledge about context-free languages. In particular, we shall discuss some operations under which CFL's are closed, some decidability results, and matters of ambiguous context-free grammars and languages.

2.6.1. Ogden's Lemma

We begin by proving a theorem (Ogden's lemma) about context-free grammars from which we can derive a number of results about context-free languages. From this theorem we can derive a "pumping lemma" for context-free languages.

DEFINITION

A *position* in a string of length k is an integer i such that $1 \leq i \leq k$. We say that symbol a occurs at position i of string w if $w = w_1 a w_2$ and $|w_1| = i - 1$. For example, the symbol a occurs at the third position of the string *baacc*.

THEOREM 2.24

For each CFG $G = (N, \Sigma, P, S)$, there is an integer $k \geq 1$ such that if z is in $L(G), |z| \geq k$, and if any k or more distinct positions in z are designated as being "distinguished," then z can be written as $uvwxy$ such that

(1) w contains at least one of the distinguished positions.

(2) Either u and v both contain distinguished positions, or x and y both contain distinguished positions.

(3) vwx has at most k distinguished positions.

(4) There is a nonterminal A such that

$$S \xrightarrow[G]{+} uAy \xrightarrow[G]{+} uvAxy \xrightarrow[G]{+} \cdots \xrightarrow[G]{+} uv^iAx^iy \xrightarrow[G]{+} uv^iwx^iy$$

for all integers i (including $i = 0$, in which case the derivation is $S \xrightarrow[G]{+} uAy \xrightarrow[G]{+} uwy$).

Proof. Let $m = \#N$ and l be the length of the longest right side of a production in P. Choose $k = l^{2m+3}$, and consider a derivation tree T for some sentence z in $L(G)$, where $|z| \geq k$ and at least k positions of z are designated distinguished. Note that T must contain at least one path of length at least $2m + 3$. We can distinguish those leaves of T which, in the frontier z of T, fill the distinguished positions.

Let us call node n of T a *branch node* if n has at least two direct descendants, say n_1 and n_2, such that n_1 and n_2 both have distinguished leaves as descendants.

We construct a path $n_1, n_2, \ldots$ in T as follows:

(1) n_1 is the root of T.

(2) If we have found n_i and only one of n_i's direct descendants has distinguished leaves among its descendants (i.e., n_i is not a branch node), then let n_{i+1} be that direct descendant of n_i.

(3) If n_i is a branch node, choose n_{i+1} to be that direct descendant of n_i with the largest number of distinguished leaves for descendants. If there is a tie, choose the rightmost (this choice is arbitrary).

(4) If n_i is a leaf, terminate the path.

Let $n_1, n_2, \ldots, n_p$ be the path so constructed. A simple induction on i shows that if $n_1, \ldots, n_i$ have r branch nodes among them, then n_{i+1} has at least l^{2m+3-r} distinguished descendants. The basis, $i = 0$, is trivial; $r = 0$, and n_1 has at least $k = l^{2m+3}$ distinguished descendants. For the induction, observe that if n_i is not a branch node, then n_i and n_{i+1} have the same number of distinguished descendants, and that if n_i is a branch node, n_{i+1} has at least $1/l$th as many.

Since n_1 has l^{2m+3} distinguished descendants, the path $n_1, \ldots, n_p$ has at least $2m + 3$ branch nodes. Moreover, n_p is a leaf and so is not a branch node. Thus, $p > 2m + 3$.

Let $b_1, b_2, \ldots, b_{2m+3}$ be the last $2m + 3$ branch nodes in the path $n_1, \ldots, n_p$. We call b_i a *left* branch node if a direct descendant of b_i not on the path has a distinguished descendant to the left of n_p and a *right* branch node otherwise.

We assume that at least $m + 2$ of $b_1, \ldots, b_{2m+3}$ are left branch nodes. The case in which at least $m + 2$ are right branch nodes is handled analogously.

Let $l_1, \ldots, l_{m+2}$ be the last $m + 2$ left branch nodes in the sequence $b_1, \ldots, b_{2m+3}$. Since $\#N = m$, we can find two nodes among $l_2, \ldots, l_{m+2}$, say l_f and l_g, such that $f < g$, and the labels of l_f and l_g are the same, say A. This situation is depicted in Fig. 2.17. The double line represents the path $n_1, \ldots, n_p$; *'s represent distinguished leaves, but there may be others.

If we delete all of l_f's descendants, we have a derivation tree with frontier uAy, where u represents those leaves to the left of l_f and y represents those to the right. Thus, $S \overset{+}{\Rightarrow} uAy$. If we consider the subtree dominated by l_f with the descendants of l_g deleted, we see that $A \overset{+}{\Rightarrow} vAx$, where v and x are the frontiers from the descendant leaves of l_f to the left and right, respectively, of l_g. Finally, let w be the frontier of the subtree dominated by l_g. Then $A \overset{+}{\Rightarrow} w$. We observe that $z = uvwxy$.

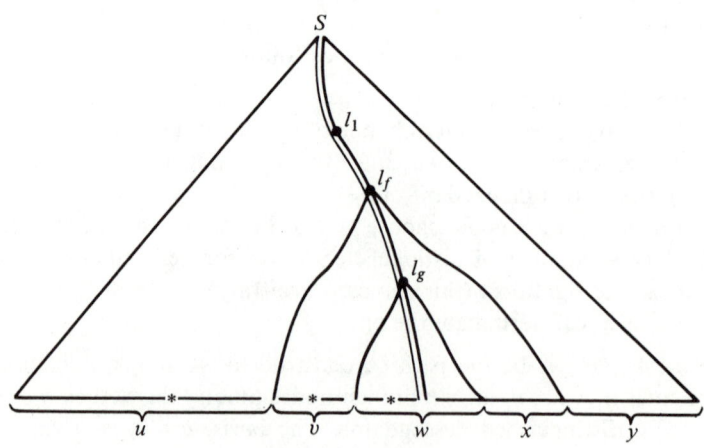

Fig. 2.17 Derivation tree T.

Putting all these derivations together, we have $S \overset{+}{\Rightarrow} uAy \overset{+}{\Rightarrow} uwy$, and for all $i \geq 1$, $S \overset{+}{\Rightarrow} uAy \overset{+}{\Rightarrow} uvAxy \overset{+}{\Rightarrow} uv^2Ax^2y \overset{+}{\Rightarrow} \cdots \overset{+}{\Rightarrow} uv^iAx^iy \overset{+}{\Rightarrow} uv^iwx^iy$. Thus condition (4) is satisfied. Moreover, u has at least one distinguished position, the descendant of some direct descendant of l_1. v likewise has at least one distinguished position, descending from l_f. Thus condition (2) is satisfied. Condition (1) is satisfied, since w has a distinguished position, namely n_p.

To see that condition (3), that vwx has no more than k distinguished positions, is satisfied, we observe that b_1, being the $2m + 3$rd branch node from the end of path $n_1, \ldots, n_p$, has no more than k distinguished positions. Since l_f is a descendant of b_1, our desired result is immediate.

We should also consider the alternative case in which at least $m + 2$ of $b_1, \ldots, b_{2m+3}$ are right branch nodes. However, this case is handled symmetrically, and we shall find condition (2) satisfied because x and y each have distinguished positions. $\square$

An important corollary of Ogden's lemma is what is usually referred to as the pumping lemma for context-free languages.

COROLLARY

Let L be a CFL. Then there exists a constant k such that if $|z| \geq k$ and $z \in L$, then we can write $z = uvwxy$ such that $vx \neq e$, $|vwx| \leq k$, and for all i, uv^iwx^iy is in L.

Proof. In Theorem 2.24, choose any CFG for L and let all positions of each sentence be distinguished. $\square$

It is the corollary to Theorem 2.24 that we most often use when proving certain languages not to be context-free. Theorem 2.24 itself will be used when we talk about inherent ambiguity of CFL's in Section 2.6.5.

Example 2.38

Let us use the pumping lemma to show that $L = \{a^{n^2} | n \geq 1\}$ is not a CFL. If L were a CFL, then we would have an integer k such that if $n^2 \geq k$, then $a^{n^2} = uvwxy$, where v and x are not both e and $|vwx| \leq k$. In particular, let n be k itself. Certainly $k^2 \geq k$. Then uv^2wx^2y is supposedly in L. But since $|vwx| \leq k$, we have $1 \leq |vx| \leq k$, so $k^2 < |uv^2wx^2y| \leq k^2 + k$. But the next perfect square after k^2 is $(k + 1)^2 = k^2 + 2k + 1$. Since $k^2 + k < k^2 + 2k + 1$, we see that $|uv^2wx^2y|$ is not a perfect square. But by the pumping lemma, uv^2wx^2y is in L, which is a contradiction. $\square$

Example 2.39

Let us show that $L = \{a^nb^nc^n | n \geq 1\}$ is not a CFL. If it were, then we would have a constant k as defined in the pumping lemma. Let $z = a^kb^kc^k$.

Then $z = uvwxy$. Since $|vwx| \leq k$, it is not possible that v and x together have occurrences of a's, b's, and c's; vwx will not "stretch" across the k b's. Thus, uwy, which is in L by the pumping lemma, has either k a's or k c's. It does not, however, have k instances of each of the three symbols, because $|uwy| < 3k$. Thus, uwy has more of one symbol than another and is not in L. We thus have a contradiction and can conclude only that L is not context-free. $\square$

2.6.2. Closure Properties of CFL's

Closure properties can often be used to help prove that certain languages are not context-free, as well as being interesting from a theoretical point of view. In this section we shall summarize some of the major closure properties of the context-free languages.

DEFINITION

Let $\mathcal{L}$ be a class of languages and let $L \subseteq \Sigma^*$ be in $\mathcal{L}$. Suppose that for each a in Σ, L_a is a language in $\mathcal{L}$. $\mathcal{L}$ is *closed under substitution* if for all choices of L,

$$L' = \{x_1 x_2 \cdots x_n \,|\, a_1 a_2 \cdots a_n \in L$$
$$x_1 \in L_{a_1}$$
$$x_2 \in L_{a_2}$$
$$\cdot$$
$$\cdot$$
$$\cdot$$
$$x_n \in L_{a_n}\}$$

is in $\mathcal{L}$.

Example 2.40

Let $L = \{0^n 1^n \,|\, n \geq 1\}$, $L_0 = \{a\}$, and $L_1 = \{b^m c^m \,|\, m \geq 1\}$. Then the substitution of L_0 and L_1 into L is

$$L' = \{a^n b^{m_1} c^{m_1} b^{m_2} c^{m_2} \cdots b^{m_n} c^{m_n} \,|\, n \geq 1, m_i \geq 1\} \quad \square$$

THEOREM 2.25

The class of context-free languages is closed under substitution.

Proof. Let $L \subseteq \Sigma^*$ be a CFL where $\Sigma = \{a_1, a_2, \ldots, a_n\}$. Let $L_a \subseteq \Sigma_a^*$ be a CFL for each a in Σ. Call the language that results from the substitution of the L_a's for a in L by the name L'. Let $G = (\mathbf{N}, \Sigma, P, S)$ be a CFG for L and $G_a = (\mathbf{N}_a, \Sigma_a, P_a, a')$ be a CFG for L_a. We assume that $\mathbf{N}$ and all $\mathbf{N}_a$ are mutually disjoint. Let $G' = (\mathbf{N}', \Sigma', P', S)$, where

(1) $N' = \bigcup_{a \in \Sigma} N_a \cup N$.

(2) $\Sigma' = \bigcup_{a \in \Sigma} \Sigma_a$.

(3) Let h be the homomorphism on $N \cup \Sigma$ such that $h(A) = A$ for all A in N and $h(a) = a'$ for a in Σ. Let $P' = \{A \rightarrow h(\alpha) \,|\, A \rightarrow \alpha$ is in $P\} \cup \bigcup_{a \in \Sigma} P_a$.

Thus, P' consists of the productions of the G_a's together with the productions of G with all terminals made (primed) nonterminals. Let $a_1 \cdots a_n$ be in L and x_i in L_{a_i} for $1 \leq i \leq n$. Then $S \overset{*}{\underset{G'}{\Rightarrow}} a'_1 \cdots a'_n \overset{*}{\underset{G'}{\Rightarrow}} x_1 a'_2 \cdots a'_n \overset{*}{\underset{G'}{\Rightarrow}} \cdots \overset{*}{\underset{G'}{\Rightarrow}} x_1 \cdots x_n$. Thus, $L' \subseteq L(G')$.

Suppose that w is in $L(G')$ and consider a derivation tree T of w. Because of the disjointness of N and the N_a's, each leaf with non-e-label has at least one ancestor labeled a' for some a in Σ. If we delete all nodes of T which have an ancestor other than themselves with label a' for $a \in \Sigma$, then we have a derivation tree T' with frontier $a'_1 \cdots a'_n$, where $a_1 \cdots a_n$ is in L. If we let x_i be the frontier of the subtree of T dominated by the ith leaf of T', then $w = x_1 \cdots x_n$ and x_i is in L_{a_i}. Thus, $L(G') = L'$. $\square$

COROLLARY

The context-free languages are closed under (1) union, (2) product, (3) $*$, (4) $+$, and (5) homomorphism.

Proof. Let L_a and L_b be context-free languages.

(1) Substitute L_a for a and L_b for b in the CFL $\{a, b\}$.

(2) Substitute L_a for a and L_b for b in $\{ab\}$.

(3) Substitute L_a for a in a^*.

(4) Substitute L_a for a in a^+.

(5) Let $L_a = \{h(a)\}$ for homomorphism h, and substitute into L to obtain $h(L)$. $\square$

THEOREM 2.26

The class of context-free languages is closed under intersection with regular sets.

Proof. We can show that a PDA P and a finite automaton A running in parallel can be simulated by a PDA P'. The composite PDA P' simulates P directly and changes the state of A each time P makes a non-e-move. P' accepts if and only if both P accepts and A is in a final state. The details of such a proof are left for the Exercises. $\square$

Unlike the regular sets, the context-free languages are not a Boolean algebra of sets.

THEOREM 2.27

The class of context-free languages is not closed under intersection or complement.

Proof. $L_1 = \{a^n b^n c^i \mid n \geq 1, i \geq 1\}$ and $L_2 = \{a^i b^n c^n \mid i \geq 1, n \geq 1\}$ are both context-free languages. However, by Example 2.39, $L_1 \cap L_2 = \{a^n b^n c^n \mid n \geq 1\}$ is not a context-free language. Thus the context-free languages are not closed under intersection.

We can also conclude that the context-free languages are not closed under complement. This follows from the fact that any class of languages closed under union and complement must also be closed under intersection, using De Morgan's law.

The CFL's are closed under union by the corollary to Theorem 2.25.   □

There are many other operations under which the context-free languages are closed. Some of these operations will be discussed in the Exercises. We shall conclude this section by providing a few applications of closure properties in showing that certain sets are not context-free languages.

Example 2.41

$L = \{ww \mid w \in \{a, b\}^+\}$ is not a context-free language. Suppose that L were context-free. Then $L' = L \cap a^+ b^+ a^+ b^+ = \{a^m b^n a^m b^n \mid m, n \geq 1\}$ would also be context-free by Theorem 2.26. But from Exercise 2.6.3(e), we know that L' is not a context-free language.   □

Example 2.42

$L = \{ww \mid w \in \{c, f\}^+\}$ is not a context-free language. Let h be the homomorphism $h(c) = a$ and $h(f) = b$. Then $h(L) = \{ww \mid w \in \{a, b\}^+\}$, which by the previous example is not a context-free language. Since the CFL's are closed under homomorphism (corollary to Theorem 2.25), we conclude that L is not a CFL.   □

Example 2.43

ALGOL is not a context-free language. Consider the following class of ALGOL programs:

$$L = \{\textbf{begin integer } w; \ w := 1; \ \textbf{end} \mid w \text{ is any string in } \{c, f\}^+\}.$$

Let L_A be the set of all valid ALGOL programs. Let R be the regular set denoted by the regular expression

$$\textbf{begin integer } (c + f)^+; \ (c + f)^+ := 1; \ \textbf{end}$$

Then $L = L_A \cap R$. Finally let h be the homomorphism such that $h(c) = c$, $h(f) = f$, and $h(X) = e$ otherwise. Then $h(L) = \{ww \mid w \in \{c, f\}^+\}$.

Consequently, if L_A is context-free, then $h(L_A \cap R)$ must also be context-free. However, we know that $h(L_A \cap R)$ is not context-free so we must conclude that L_A, the set of all valid ALGOL programs, is not a context-free language.   □

Example 2.43 shows that a programming language requiring declaration of identifiers which can be arbitrarily long is not context-free. In a compiler, however, identifiers are usually handled by the lexical analyzer and reduced to single tokens before reaching the syntactic analyzer. Thus the language that is to be recognized by the syntactic analyzer usually can be considered to be a context-free language.

There are other non-context-free aspects of ALGOL and many other languages. For example, each procedure takes the same number of arguments each time it is mentioned. It is thus possible to show that the language which the syntactic analyzer sees is not context-free by mapping programs with three calls of the same procedure to $\{0^n 10^n 10^n \,|\, n \geq 0\}$, which is not a CFL. Normally, however, some process outside of syntactic analysis is used to check that the number of arguments to a procedure is consistent with the definition of the procedure.

2.6.3. Decidability Results

We have already seen that the emptiness problem is decidable for context-free grammars. Algorithm 2.7 will accept any context-free grammar G as input and determine whether or not $L(G)$ is empty.

Let us consider the membership problem for CFG's. We must find an algorithm which given a context-free grammar $G = (N, \Sigma, P, S)$ and a word w in Σ^*, will determine whether or not w is in $L(G)$. Obtaining an efficient algorithm for this problem will provide much of the subject matter of Chapters 4–7. However, from a purely theoretical point of view we can immediately conclude that the membership problem is solvable for CFG's, since we can always transform G into an equivalent proper context-free grammar G' using the transformations of Section 2.4.2. Neglecting the empty word, a proper context-free grammar is a context-sensitive grammar, so we can apply the brute force algorithm for deciding the membership problem for context-sensitive grammars to G'. (See Exercise 2.1.19.)

Let us consider the equivalence problem for context-free grammars. Unfortunately, here we encounter a problem which is not decidable. We shall prove that there is no algorithm which, given any two CFG's G_1 and G_2, can determine whether $L(G_1) = L(G_2)$. In fact, we shall show that even given a CFG G_1 and a right-linear grammar G_2 there is no algorithm to determine whether $L(G_1) = L(G_2)$. As with most undecidable problems, we shall show that if we can solve the equivalence problem for CFG's, then we can solve Post's correspondence problem. We can construct from an instance of Post's correspondence problem two naturally related context-free languages.

DEFINITION

Let $C = (x_1, y_1), \ldots, (x_n, y_n)$ be an instance of Post's problem over alphabet Σ. Let $I = \{1, 2, \ldots, n\}$, assume that $I \cap \Sigma = \varnothing$, and let $\underline{L_C}$

be $\{x_{i_1}x_{i_2} \cdots x_{i_m}i_mi_{m-1} \cdots i_1 \,|\, i_1, \ldots, i_m$ are in $I,\, m \geq 1\}$. Let $\underline{M_C}$ be $\{y_{i_1}y_{i_2} \cdots y_{i_m}i_mi_{m-1} \cdots i_1 \,|\, i_1, \ldots, i_m$ are in $I,\, m \geq 1\}$.

LEMMA 2.29

Let $C = (x_1, y_1), \ldots, (x_n, y_n)$ be an instance of Post's correspondence problem over Σ, where $\Sigma \cap \{1, 2, \ldots, n\} = \varnothing$. Then

(1) We can find extended DPDA's accepting L_C and M_C.

(2) $L_C \cap M_C = \varnothing$ if and only if C has no solution.

Proof.

(1) It is straightforward to construct an extended DPDA (with pushdown top on the right) which stores all symbols in Σ on its pushdown list. When symbols from $\{1, \ldots, n\}$ appear on the input, it pops x_i from the top of its list if integer i appears on the input. If x_i is not at the top of the list, the DPDA halts. The DPDA also checks with its finite control that its input is in $\Sigma^+\{1, \ldots, n\}^+$ and accepts when all symbols from Σ are removed from the pushdown list. Thus, L_C is accepted. We may find an extended DPDA for M_C similarly.

(2) If $L_C \cap M_C$ contains the sentence $wi_m \cdots i_1$, where w is in Σ^+, then w is clearly a viable sequence. If $x_{i_1} \cdots x_{i_m} = y_{i_1} \cdots y_{i_m} = w$, then $wi_m \cdots i_1$ will be in $L_C \cap M_C$. $\square$

Let us return to the equivalence problem for CFG's. We need two additional languages related to an instance of Post's correspondence problem.

DEFINITION

Let $C = (x_1, y_1), \ldots, (x_n, y_n)$ be an instance of Post's correspondence problem over Σ and let $I = \{1, \ldots, n\}$. Assume that $\Sigma \cap I = \varnothing$. Define $\underline{Q_C} = \{w\#w^R \,|\, w$ is in $\Sigma^+I^+\}$, where $\#$ is not in Σ or I. Define $\underline{P_C} = L_C\#M_C^R$.

LEMMA 2.30

Let C be as above. Then

(1) We can find extended DPDA's accepting Q_C and P_C, and

(2) $Q_C \cap P_C = \varnothing$ if and only if C has no solution.

Proof.

(1) A DPDA accepting Q_C can be constructed easily. For P_C, we know by Lemma 2.29 that there exists a DPDA, say M_1, accepting L_C. To find a DPDA M_2 that accepts M_C^R is not much harder; one stores integers and checks them against the portion of input that is in Σ^+. Thus we can construct DPDA M_3 to simulate M_1, check for $\#$, and then simulate M_2.

(2) If $uv\#wx$ is in $Q_C \cap P_C$, where u and x are in Σ^+ and v and w in I^+, then $u = x^R$, and $v = w^R$, because $uv\#wx$ is in Q_C. Because $uv\#wx$ is in P_C, u is a viable sequence. Thus, C has a solution. Conversely, if we have $x_{i_1} \cdots x_{i_m} = y_{i_1} \cdots y_{i_m}$, then $x_{i_1} \cdots x_{i_m}i_m \cdots i_1 \# i_1 \cdots i_mx_{i_m} \cdots x_{i_1}$ is in $Q_C \cap P_C$. $\square$

LEMMA 2.31

Let C be as above. Then

(1) We can find a CFG for $\overline{Q_C} \cup \overline{P_C}$, and

(2) $\overline{Q_C} \cup \overline{P_C} = (\Sigma \cup I)^*$ if and only if C has no solution.

Proof.

(1) From the closure of deterministic CFL's under complement (Theorem 2.23), we can find DPDA's for $\overline{Q_C}$ and $\overline{P_C}$. From the equivalence of CFL's and PDA languages (Lemma 2.26), we can find CFG's for these languages. From closure of CFL's under union, we can find a CFG for $\overline{Q_C} \cup \overline{P_C}$.

(2) Immediate from Lemma 2.30(2) and De Morgan's law.   □

We can now show that it is undecidable whether two CFG's generate the same language. In fact, we can prove something stronger: It is still undecidable even if one of the grammars is right-linear.

THEOREM 2.28

It is undecidable for a CFG G_1 and a right-linear grammar G_2 whether $L(G_1) = L(G_2)$.

Proof. If not, then we could decide Post's problem as follows:

(1) Given an instance C, construct, by Lemma 2.31, a CFG G_1 generating $\overline{Q_C} \cup \overline{P_C}$, and construct a right-linear grammar G_2 generating the regular set $(\Sigma \cup I)^*$, where C is over Σ, C has lists of length n, and $I = \{1, \ldots, n\}$. Again, some renaming of symbols may first be necessary, but the existence or nonexistence of a solution is left intact.

(2) Apply the hypothetical algorithm to determine if $L(G_1) = L(G_2)$. By Lemma 2.31(2), this equality holds if and only if C has no solution.   □

Since there are algorithms to convert a CFG to a PDA and vice versa, Theorem 2.28 also implies that it is undecidable whether two PDA's, or a PDA and a finite automaton, recognize the same language, whether a PDA recognizes the set denoted by a regular expression, and so forth.

2.6.4. Properties of Deterministic CFL's

The deterministic context-free languages are closed under remarkably few of the operations under which the entire class of context-free languages is closed. We already know that the deterministic CFL's are closed under complement. Since $L_1 = \{a^i b^i c^j \mid i, j \geq 1\}$ and $L_2 = \{a^i b^j c^j \mid i, j \geq 1\}$ are both deterministic CFL's and $L_1 \cap L_2 = \{a^n b^n c^n \mid n \geq 1\}$ is a language which is not context-free (Example 2.39), we have the following two nonclosure properties.

THEOREM 2.29

The class of deterministic CFL's is not closed under intersection or union.

Proof. Nonclosure under intersection is immediate from the above. Nonclosure under union follows from De Morgan's law and closure under complement. □

The deterministic CFL's form a proper subset of the CFL's, as we see from the following example.

Example 2.44

We can easily show that the complement of $L = \{a^n b^n c^n \mid n \geq 1\}$ is a CFL. The sentence $w \in \bar{L}$ if and only if one or more of the following hold:

(1) w is not in $a^+ b^+ c^+$.
(2) $w = a^i b^j c^k$, and $i \neq j$.
(3) $w = a^i b^j c^k$, and $j \neq k$.

The set satisfying (1) is regular, and the sets satisfying (2) and (3) are each context-free, as the reader can easily show by constructing nondeterministic PDA's recognizing them. Since the CFL's are closed under union, $\bar{L}$ is a CFL.

But if $\bar{L}$ were a deterministic CFL, then L would be likewise, by Theorem 2.23. But L is not even a CFL. □

The deterministic CFL's have the same positive decidability results as the CFL. That is, given a DPDA P, we can determine whether $L(P) = \varnothing$, and given an input string w, we can easily determine whether w is in $L(P)$.

Moreover, given a deterministic DPDA P and a regular set R, we can determine whether $L(P) = R$, since $L(P) = R$ if and only if we have $(L(P) \cap \bar{R}) \cup (\overline{L(P)} \cap R) = \varnothing$. $(L(P) \cap \bar{R}) \cup (\overline{L(P)} \cap R)$ is easily seen to be a CFL. Other decidability results appear in the Exercises.

2.6.5. Ambiguity

Recall that a context-free grammar $G = (N, \Sigma, P, S)$ is ambiguous if there is a sentence w in $L(G)$ with two or more distinct derivation trees. Equivalently, G is ambiguous if there exists a sentence w with two distinct leftmost (or rightmost) derivations.

When we are using a grammar to help define a programming language we would like that grammar to be unambiguous. Otherwise, a programmer and a compiler may have differing opinions as to the meaning of some sentences.

Example 2.45

Perhaps the most famous example of ambiguity in a programming language is the dangling **else**. Consider the grammar G with productions

$$S \longrightarrow \textbf{if } b \textbf{ then } S \textbf{ else } S \mid \textbf{if } b \textbf{ then } S \mid a$$

G is ambiguous since the sentence

if b then if b then a else a

has two derivation trees as shown in Fig. 2.18. The derivation tree in Fig. 2.18(a) imposes the interpretation

if b then (if b then a) else a

while the tree in Fig. 2.18(b) gives

if b then (if b then a else a) □

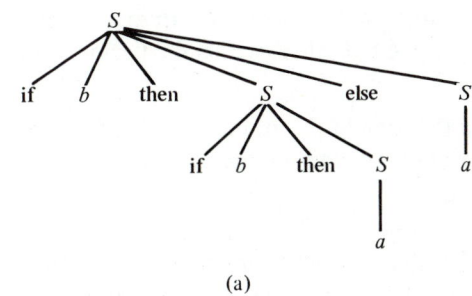

(a)

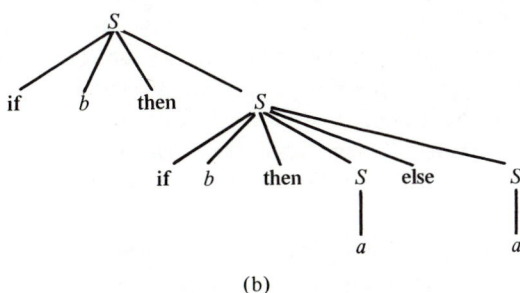

(b)

Fig. 2.18 Two derivation trees.

We might like to have an algorithm to determine whether an arbitrary CFG is unambiguous. Unfortunately, such an algorithm does not exist.

THEOREM 2.30

It is undecidable whether a CFG G is ambiguous.

Proof. Let $C = (x_1, y_1), \ldots, (x_n, y_n)$ be an instance of Post's correspondence problem over Σ. Let G be the CFG $(\{S, A, B\}, \Sigma \cup I, P, S)$, where $I = \{1, 2, \ldots, n\}$, and P contains the productions

$$S \longrightarrow A \mid B$$
$$A \longrightarrow x_i Ai \mid x_i i, \qquad \text{for } 1 \leq i \leq n$$
$$B \longrightarrow y_i Bi \mid y_i i, \qquad \text{for } 1 \leq i \leq n$$

The nonterminals A and B generate the languages L_C and M_C, respectively, defined on p. 199. It is easy to see that no sentence has more than one distinct leftmost derivation from A, or from B. Thus, if there exists a sentence with two leftmost derivations from S, one must begin with $S \underset{lm}{\Longrightarrow} A$, and the other with $S \underset{lm}{\Longrightarrow} B$. But by Lemma 2.29, there is a sentence derived from both A and B if and only if instance C of Post's problem has a solution.

Thus, G is ambiguous if and only if C has a solution. It is then a straightforward matter to show that if there were an algorithm to decide the ambiguity of an arbitrary CFG, then we could decide Post's correspondence problem. □

Ambiguity is a function of the grammar rather than the language. Certain ambiguous grammars may have equivalent unambiguous ones.

Example 2.46

Let us consider the grammar and language of the previous example. The reason that grammar G is ambiguous is that an **else** can be associated with two different **then**'s. For this reason, programming languages which allow both **if–then–else** and **if–then** statements can be ambiguous. This ambiguity can be removed if we arbitrarily decide that an **else** should be attached to the last preceding **then**, as in Fig. 2.18(b).

We can revise the grammar of Example 2.45 to have two nonterminals, S_1 and S_2. We insist that S_2 generate **if–then–else**, while S_1 is free to generate either kind of statement. The rules of the new grammar are

$$S_1 \longrightarrow \textbf{if } b \textbf{ then } S_1 \mid \textbf{if } b \textbf{ then } S_2 \textbf{ else } S_1 \mid a$$
$$S_2 \longrightarrow \textbf{if } b \textbf{ then } S_2 \textbf{ else } S_2 \mid a$$

The fact that only S_2 precedes **else** ensures that between the **then–else** pair generated by any one production must appear either the single symbol a or another **else**. Thus the structure of Fig. 2.18(a) cannot occur. In Chapter 5 we shall develop deterministic parsing methods for various grammars, including the current one, and shall be able at that time to prove our new grammar to be unambiguous. □

Although there is no general algorithm which can be used to determine if a grammar is ambiguous, it is possible to isolate certain constructs in productions which lead to ambiguous grammars. Since ambiguous grammars are often harder to parse than unambiguous ones, we shall mention some of the more common constructs of this nature here so that they can be recognized in practice.

A proper grammar containing the productions $A \to AA \,|\, \alpha$ will be ambiguous because the substring AAA has two parses:

This ambiguity disappears if instead we use the productions

$$A \longrightarrow AB \mid B$$
$$B \longrightarrow \alpha$$

or the productions

$$A \longrightarrow BA \mid B$$
$$B \longrightarrow \alpha$$

Another example of an ambiguous production is $A \to A\alpha A$. The pair of productions $A \to \alpha A \,|\, A\beta$ introduces ambiguity since $A \Rightarrow \alpha A \Rightarrow \alpha A\beta$ and $A \Rightarrow A\beta \Rightarrow \alpha A\beta$ imply two distinct leftmost derivations of $\alpha A\beta$. A slightly more elaborate pair of productions which gives rise to an ambiguous grammar is $A \to \alpha A \,|\, \alpha A \beta A$. Other examples of ambiguous grammars can be found in the Exercises.

We shall call a CFL *inherently ambiguous* if it has no unambiguous CFG. It is not at first obvious that there is such a thing as an inherently ambiguous CFL, but we shall present one in the next example. In fact, it is undecidable whether a given CFG generates an inherently ambiguous language (i.e., whether there exists an equivalent unambiguous CFG). However, there are large subclasses of the CFL's known not to be inherently ambiguous and no inherently ambiguous programming languages have been devised yet. Most important, every deterministic CFL has an unambiguous grammar, as we shall see in Chapter 8.

Example 2.47

Let $L = \{a^i b^j c^l \,|\, i = j \text{ or } j = l\}$. L is an inherently ambiguous CFL. Intuitively, the reason is that the words with $i = j$ must be generated by a set of productions different from those generating the words with $j = l$. At least some of the words with $i = j = l$ must be generated by both mechanisms.

One CFG for L is

$$S \longrightarrow AB \mid DC$$
$$A \longrightarrow aA \mid e$$
$$B \longrightarrow bBc \mid e$$
$$C \longrightarrow cC \mid e$$
$$D \longrightarrow aDb \mid e$$

Clearly the above grammar is ambiguous.

We can use Ogden's lemma to prove that L is inherently ambiguous. Let G be an arbitrary grammar for L, and let k be the constant associated with G in Theorem 2.24. If that constant is less than 3, let $k = 3$. Consider the word $z = a^k b^k c^{k+k!}$, where the a's are all distinguished. We can write $z = uvwxy$. Since w has distinguished positions, u and v consist only of a's. If x consists of two different symbols, then uv^2wx^2y is surely not in L, so x is either in a^*, b^*, or c^*.

If x is in a^*, uv^2wx^2y would be $a^{k+p}b^kc^{k+k!}$, for some p, $1 \leq p \leq k$, which is not in L. If x is in c^*, uv^2wx^2y would be $a^{k+p_1}b^kc^{k+k!+p_2}$, where $1 \leq p_1 \leq k$. This word likewise is not in L.

In the second case, where x is in b^*, we have $uv^2wx^2y = a^{k+p_1}b^{k+p_2}c^{k+k!}$, where $1 \leq p_1 \leq k$. If this word is in L, then either $p_1 = p_2$ or $p_1 \neq p_2$ and $p_2 = k!$ In the latter case, $uv^3wx^3y = a^{k+2p_1}b^{k+2p_2}c^{k+k!}$ is surely not in L. So we conclude that $p_1 = p_2$. Observe that $p_1 = |v|$ and $p_2 = |x|$.

By Theorem 2.24, there is a derivation

$$(2.6.1) \qquad S \overset{+}{\Longrightarrow} uAy \overset{+}{\Longrightarrow} uv^mAx^my \overset{+}{\Longrightarrow} uv^mwx^my \qquad \text{for all } m \geq 0$$

In particular, let $m = k!/p_1$. Since $1 \leq p_1 \leq k$, we know that m is an integer. Then $uv^mwx^my = a^{k+k!}b^{k+k!}c^{k+k!}$.

A symmetric argument starting with the word $a^{k+k!}b^kc^k$ shows that there exist u', v', w', x', y', where only u' has an a, v' is in b^*, and there is a nonterminal B such that

$$
\begin{aligned}
S &\overset{+}{\Longrightarrow} u'By' \overset{+}{\Longrightarrow} u'(v')^{m'}B(x')^{m'}y' \overset{+}{\Longrightarrow} u'(v')^{m'}w(x')^{m'}y \\
(2.6.2) \qquad &= a^{k+k!}b^{k+k!}c^{k+k!}
\end{aligned}
$$

If we can show that the two derivations of $a^{k+k!}b^{k+k!}c^{k+k!}$ have different derivation trees, then we shall have shown that L is inherently ambiguous, since G was chosen without restriction and has been shown ambiguous.

Suppose that the two derivations (2.6.1) and (2.6.2) have the same derivation tree. Since A generates a's and b's and B generates b's and c's, neither A nor B could appear as a label of a descendant of a node labeled by the

other. Thus there exists a sentential form $t_1 A t_2 B t_3$, where the t's are terminal strings. For all i and j, $t_1 v^i w x^i t_2 (v')^j w' (x')^j t_3$ would presumably be in L. But $|v| = |x|$ and $|v'| = |x'|$. Also, x and v' consist exclusively of b's, v consists of a's, and x' consists of c's. Thus choosing i and j equal and sufficiently large will ensure that the above word has more b's than a's or c's. We may thus conclude that G is ambiguous and that L is inherently ambiguous. $\square$

EXERCISES

2.6.1. Let L be a context-free language and R a regular set. Show that the following languages are context-free:
(a) INIT(L).
(b) FIN(L).
(c) SUB(L).
(d) L/R.
(e) $L \cap R$.
The definitions of these operations are found in the Exercises of Section 2.3 on p. 135.

2.6.2. Show that if L is a CFL and h a homomorphism, then $h^{-1}(L)$ is a CFL. *Hint:* Let P be a PDA accepting L. Construct P' to apply h to each of its input symbols in turn, store the result in a buffer (in the finite control), and simulate P on the symbols in the buffer. Be sure that your buffer is of finite length.

2.6.3. Show that the following are not CFL's:
(a) $\{a^i b^i c^j | j \leq i\}$.
(b) $\{a^i b^j c^k | i < j < k\}$.
(c) The set of strings with an equal number of a's, b's, and c's.
(d) $\{a^i b^j a^j b^i | j \leq i\}$.
(e) $\{a^m b^n a^m b^n | m, n \geq 1\}$.
(f) $\{a^i b^j c^k | \text{none of } i, j, \text{ and } k \text{ are equal}\}$.
(g) $\{nHa^n | n \text{ is a decimal integer} \geq 1\}$. (This construct is representative of FORTRAN Hollerith fields.)

**2.6.4. Show that every CFL over a one-symbol alphabet is regular. *Hint:* Use the pumping lemma.

**2.6.5. Show that the following are not always CFL's when L is a CFL:
(a) MAX(L).
(b) MIN(L).
(c) $L^{1/2} = \{x | \text{for some } y, xy \text{ is in } L \text{ and } |x| = |y|\}$.

*2.6.6. Show the following pumping lemma for linear languages. If L is a linear language, there is a constant k such that if $z \in L$ and $|z| \geq k$, then $z = uvwxy$, where $|uvxy| \leq k$, $vx \neq e$ and for all i, $uv^i w x^i y$ is in L.

2.6.7. Show that $\{a^n b^n a^m b^m | n, m \geq 1\}$ is not a linear language.

*2.6.8. A *one-turn* PDA is one which in any sequence of moves first writes

symbols on the pushdown list and then pops symbols from the pushdown list. Once it starts popping symbols from the pushdown list, it can then never write on its pushdown list. Show that a CFL is linear if and only if it can be recognized by a one-turn PDA.

*2.6.9.   Let $G = (N, \Sigma, P, S)$ be a CFG. Show that the following are CFL's:

(a) $\{\alpha \mid S \underset{lm}{\overset{*}{\Rightarrow}} \alpha\}$.

(b) $\{\alpha \mid S \underset{rm}{\overset{*}{\Rightarrow}} \alpha\}$.

(c) $\{\alpha \mid S \overset{*}{\Rightarrow} \alpha\}$.

2.6.10.   Give details of the proof of the corollary to Theorem 2.25.

2.6.11.   Complete the proof of Theorem 2.26.

2.6.12.   Give formal constructions of the DPDA's used in the proofs of Lemmas 2.29(1) and 2.30(1).

*2.6.13.   Show that the language $Q_C \cap P_C$ of Section 2.6.3 is a CFL if and only if it is empty.

2.6.14.   Show that it is undecidable for CFG G whether

(a) $\overline{L(G)}$ is a CFL.

(b) $L(G)$ is regular.

(c) $L(G)$ is a deterministic CFL.

Hint: Use Exercise 2.6.13 and consider a CFG for $\overline{Q_C} \cup \overline{P_C}$.

2.6.15.   Show that it is undecidable whether context-sensitive grammar G generates a CFL.

2.6.16.   Let G_1 and G_2 be CFG's. Show that it is undecidable whether $L(G_1) \cap L(G_2) = \varnothing$.

*2.6.17.   Let G_1 be a CFG and G_2 a right-linear grammar. Show that

(a) It is undecidable whether $L(G_2) \subseteq L(G_1)$.

(b) It is decidable whether $L(G_1) \subseteq L(G_2)$.

*2.6.18.   Let P_1 and P_2 be DPDA's. Show that it is undecidable whether

(a) $L(P_1) \cup L(P_2)$ is a deterministic CFL.

(b) $L(P_1)L(P_2)$ is a deterministic CFL.

(c) $L(P_1) \subseteq L(P_2)$.

(d) $L(P_1)^*$ is a deterministic CFL.

**2.6.19.   Show that it is decidable, for DPDA P, whether $L(P)$ is regular. Contrast Exercise 2.6.14(b).

**2.6.20.   Let L be a deterministic CFL and R a regular set. Show that the following are deterministic CFL's:

(a) LR.   (b) L/R.

(c) $L \cup R$.   (d) MAX(L).

(e) MIN(L).   (f) $L \cap R$.

Hint: For (a, b, e, f), let P be a DPDA for L and M a finite automaton for some regular set R. We must show that there is a DPDA P' which

simulates P but keeps on each cell of its pushdown list the information, "For what states p of M and q of P does there exist w that will take M from state p to a final state and cause P to accept if started in state q with this cell the top of the pushdown list?" We must show that there is but a finite amount of information for each cell and that P' can keep track of it as the pushdown list grows and shrinks. Once we know how to construct P', the four desired DPDA's are relatively easy to construct.

2.6.21. Show that for deterministic CFL L and regular set R, the following may not be deterministic CFL's:
  (a) RL.
  (b) $\{x \mid xR \subseteq L\}$.
  (c) $\{x \mid \text{for some } y \in R, \text{ we have } yx \in L\}$.
  (d) $h(L)$, for homomorphism h.

2.6.22. Show that $h^{-1}(L)$ is a deterministic CFL if L is.

**2.6.23. Show that $\overline{Q_C} \cup \overline{P_C}$ is an inherently ambiguous CFL whenever it is not empty.

**2.6.24. Show that it is undecidable whether a CFG G generates an inherently ambiguous language.

*2.6.25. Show that the grammar of Example 2.46 is unambiguous.

**2.6.26. Show that the language $L_1 \cup L_2$, where $L_1 = \{a^n b^n a^m b^m \mid m, n \geq 1\}$ and $L_2 = \{a^n b^m a^m b^n \mid m, n \geq 1\}$, is inherently ambiguous.

**2.6.27. Show that the CFG with productions $S \longrightarrow aSbSc \mid aSb \mid bSc \mid d$ is ambiguous. Is the language inherently ambiguous?

*2.6.28. Show that it is decidable for a DPDA P whether $L(P)$ has the prefix property. Is the prefix property decidable for an arbitrary CFL?

DEFINITION

A *Dyck language* is a CFL generated by a grammar $G = (\{S\}, \Sigma, P, S)$, where $\Sigma = \{a_1, \ldots, a_k, b_1, \ldots, b_k\}$ for some $k \geq 1$ and P consists of the productions $S \longrightarrow SS \mid a_1 S b_1 \mid a_2 S b_2 \mid \cdots \mid a_k S b_k \mid e$.

**2.6.29. Show that given alphabet Σ, we can find an alphabet Σ', a Dyck language $L_D \subseteq \Sigma'$, and a homorphism h from Σ'^* to Σ^* such that for any CFL $L \subseteq \Sigma^*$ there is a regular set R such that $h(L_D \cap R) = L$.

*2.6.30. Let L be a CFL and $S(L) = \{i \mid \text{for some } w \in L, \text{ we have } |w| = i\}$. Show that $S(L)$ is a finite union of arithmetic progressions.

DEFINITION

An *n-vector* is an n-tuple of nonnegative integers. If $v_1 = (a_1, \ldots, a_n)$ and $v_2 = (b_1, \ldots, b_n)$ are n-vectors and c a nonnegative integer, then $v_1 + v_2 = (a_1 + b_1, \ldots, a_n + b_n)$ and $cv_1 = (ca_1, \ldots, ca_n)$. A set S of n-vectors is *linear* if there are n-vectors $v_0, \ldots, v_k$ such that $S = \{v \mid v = v_0 + c_1 v_1 + \cdots + c_k v_k, \text{ for some nonnegative integers}$

$c_1, \ldots, c_k\}$. A set of n-vectors is *semilinear* if it is the union of a finite number of linear sets.

**2.6.31. Let $\Sigma = a_1, a_2, \ldots, a_n$. Let $\#_b(x)$ be the number of instances of b in the string x. Show that $\{(\#_{a_1}(w), \#_{a_2}(w), \ldots, \#_{a_n}(w)) \mid w \in L\}$ is a semilinear set for each CFL $L \subseteq \Sigma^*$.

DEFINITION

The *index of a derivation* in a CFG G is the maximum number of nonterminals in any sentential form of that derivation. $I(w)$, *the index of a sentence w*, is the smallest index of any derivation of w in G. $I(G)$, *the index of G*, is max $I(w)$ taken over all w in $L(G)$. The index of a CFL L is min $I(G)$ taken over all G such that $L(G) = L$.

**2.6.32. Show that the index of the grammar G with productions

$$S \longrightarrow SS \mid 0S1 \mid e$$

is infinite. Show that the index of $L(G)$ is infinite.

*2.6.33. A CFG $G = (N, \Sigma, P, S)$ is *self-embedding* if $A \xRightarrow{+} uAv$ for some u and v in Σ^+. (Neither u nor v can be e.) Show that a CFL L is not regular if and only if all grammars that generate L are self-embedding.

DEFINITION

Let $\mathcal{L}$ be a class of languages with $L_1 \subseteq \Sigma_1^*$ and $L_2 \subseteq \Sigma_2^*$ in $\mathcal{L}$. Let a and b be new symbols not in $\Sigma_1 \cup \Sigma_2$. $\mathcal{L}$ is closed under

(1) *Marked union* if $aL_1 \cup bL_2$ is in $\mathcal{L}$,
(2) *Marked concatenation* if L_1aL_2 is in L, and
(3) *Marked* $*$ if $(aL_1)^*$ is in $\mathcal{L}$.

2.6.34. Show that the deterministic CFL's are closed under marked union, marked concatenation, and marked $*$.

*2.6.35. Let G be a (not necessarily context-free) grammar (N, Σ, P, S), where each production in P is of the form $xAy \longrightarrow x\gamma y$, x and y are in Σ^*, $A \in N$, and $\gamma \in (N \cup \Sigma)^*$. Show that $L(G)$ is a CFL.

**2.6.36. Let $G_1 = (N_1, \Sigma_1, P_1, S_1)$ and $G_2 = (N_2, \Sigma_2, P_2, S_2)$ be two CFG's. Show it is undecidable whether $\{\alpha \mid S_1 \underset{G_1}{\xRightarrow{*}} \alpha\} = \{\beta \mid S_2 \underset{G_2}{\xRightarrow{*}} \beta\}$ and whether $\{\alpha \mid S_1 \underset{G_1 \, lm}{\xRightarrow{*}} \alpha\} = \{\beta \mid S_2 \underset{G_2 \, lm}{\xRightarrow{*}} \beta\}$.

Open Problem

2.6.37. Is it decidable, for DPDA's P_1 and P_2, whether $L(P_1) = L(P_2)$?

Research Problems

2.6.38. Develop methods for proving certain grammars to be unambiguous. By Theorem 2.30 it is impossible to find a method that will work for an arbitrary unambiguous grammar. However, it would be nice to have techniques that could be applied to large classes of context-free grammars.

2.6.39. A related research area is to find large classes of CFL's which are known to have at least one unambiguous CFG. The reader should be aware that in Chapter 8 we shall prove the deterministic CFL's to be such a class.

2.6.40. Find transformations which can be used to make classes of ambiguous grammars unambiguous.

BIBLIOGRAPHIC NOTES

We shall not attempt to reference here all the numerous papers that have been written on context-free languages. The works by Hopcroft and Ullman [1969], Ginsburg [1966], Gross and Lentin [1970], and Book [1970] contain many of the references on the theoretical developments of context-free languages.

Theorem 2.24, Ogden's lemma, is from Ogden [1968]. Bar-Hillel et al. [1961] give several of the basic theorems about closure properties and decidability results of CFL's. Ginsburg and Greibach [1966] give many of the basic properties of deterministic CFL's.

Cantor [1962], Floyd [1962a], and Chomsky and Schutzenberger [1963] independently discovered that it is undecidable whether a CFG is ambiguous. The existence of inherently ambiguous CFL's was noted by Parikh [1966]. Inherently ambiguous CFL's are treated in detail by Ginsburg [1966] and Hopcroft and Ullman [1969].

The Exercises contain many results that appear in the literature. Exercise 2.6.19 is from Stearns [1967]. The constructions hinted at in Exercise 2.6.20 are given in detail by Hopcroft and Ullman [1969]. Exercise 2.6.29 is proved by Ginsburg [1966]. Exercise 2.6.31 is known as Parikh's theorem and was first given by Parikh [1966]. Exercise 2.6.32 is from Salomaa [1969b]. Exercise 2.6.33 is from Chomsky [1959a]. Exercise 2.6.36 is from Blattner [1972].

3 THEORY OF TRANSLATION

A translation is a set of pairs of strings. A compiler defines a translation in which the pairs are (source program, object program). If we consider a compiler consisting of the three phases lexical analysis, syntactic analysis, and code generation, then each of these phases itself defines a translation. As we mentioned in Chapter 1, lexical analysis can be considered as a translation in which strings representing source programs are mapped into strings of tokens. The syntactic analyzer maps strings of tokens into strings representing trees. The code generator then takes these strings into machine or assembly language.

In this chapter we shall present some elementary methods for defining translations. We shall also present devices which can be used to implement these translations and algorithms which can be used to automatically construct these devices from the specification of a translation.

We shall first explore translations from an abstract point of view and then consider the applicability of the translation models to lexical analysis and syntactic analysis. For the most part, we defer treatment of code generation, which is the principal application of translation theory, to Chapter 9.

In general, when designing a large system, such as a compiler, one should partition the overall system into components whose behavior and properties can be understood and precisely defined. Then it is possible to compare algorithms which can be used to implement the function to be performed by that component and to select the most appropriate algorithm for that component. Once the components have been isolated and specified, it should then also be possible to establish performance standards for each component and tests by which a given component can be evaluated. We must therefore understand the specification and implementation of translations before we can apply engineering design criteria to compilers.

3.1. FORMALISMS FOR TRANSLATIONS

In this section two fundamental methods of defining translations are presented. One of these is the "translation scheme," which is a grammar with a mechanism for producing an output for each sentence generated. The other method is the "transducer," a recognizer which can emit a finite-length string of output symbols on each move. First we shall consider translation schemes based on context-free grammars. We shall then consider finite transducers and pushdown transducers.

3.1.1. Translation and Semantics

In Chapter 2 we considered only the syntactic aspects of languages. There we saw several methods for defining the well-formed sentences of a language. We now wish to investigate techniques for associating with each sentence of a language another string which is to be the output for that sentence. The term "semantics" is sometimes used to denote this association of outputs with sentences when the output string defines the "meaning" of the input sentence.

DEFINITION

Suppose that Σ is an input alphabet and Δ an output alphabet. We define *a translation from a language $L_1 \subseteq \Sigma^*$ to a language $L_2 \subseteq \Delta^*$* as a relation T from Σ^* to Δ^* such that the domain of T is L_1 and the range of T is L_2.

A sentence y such that (x, y) is in T is called an *output* for x. Note that, in general, in a translation a given input can have more than one output. However, any translation describing a programming language should be a function (i.e., there exists at most one output for each input).

There are many examples of translations. Perhaps the most rudimentary type of translation is that which can be specified by a homomorphism.

Example 3.1

Suppose that we wish to change every Greek letter in a sentence in Σ^* into its corresponding English name. We can use the homomorphism h, where

(1) $h(a) = a$ if a is a member of Σ minus the Greek letters and
(2) $h(a)$ is defined in the following table if a is a Greek letter:

Greek Letter		h	Greek Letter		h
A	α	alpha	N	ν	nu
B	β	beta	Ξ	ζ	xi
Γ	γ	gamma	O	o	omicron
Δ	δ	delta	Π	π	pi
E	ϵ	epsilon	P	ρ	rho
Z	ζ	zeta	Σ	σ	sigma
H	η	eta	T	τ	tau
Θ	θ	theta	Υ	υ	upsilon
I	ι	iota	Φ	ϕ	phi
K	κ	kappa	X	χ	chi
Λ	λ	lambda	Ψ	ψ	psi
M	μ	mu	Ω	ω	omega

For example, the sentence $a = \pi r^2$ would have the translation $a =$ pi r^2. □

Another example of a translation, one which is useful in describing a process that often occurs in compilation, is mapping arithmetic expressions in infix notation into equivalent expressions in Polish notation.

DEFINITION

There is a useful way of representing ordinary (or *infix*) arithmetic expressions without using parentheses. This notation is referred to as *Polish notation*.† Let Θ be a set of binary operators (e.g., $\{+, *\}$), and let Σ be a set of operands. The two forms of Polish notation, *prefix* Polish and *postfix* Polish, are defined recursively as follows:

(1) If an infix expression E is a single operand a, in Σ, then both the prefix Polish and postfix Polish representation of E is a.

(2) If $E_1 \theta E_2$ is an infix expression, where θ is an operator, and E_1 and E_2 are infix expressions, the operands of θ, then

    (a) $\theta E_1' E_2'$ is the prefix Polish representation of $E_1 \theta E_2$, where E_1' and E_2' are the prefix Polish representations of E_1 and E_2, respectively, and

    (b) $E_1'' E_2'' \theta$ is the postfix Polish representation of $E_1 \theta E_2$, where E_1'' and E_2'' are the postfix Polish representations of E_1 and E_2, respectively.

(3) If (E) is an infix expression, then

    (a) The prefix Polish representation of (E) is the prefix Polish representation of E, and

    (b) The postfix Polish representation of (E) is the postfix Polish representation of E.

†The term "Polish" is used, as this notation was first described by the Polish mathematician Lukasiewicz, whose name is significantly harder to pronounce than is "Polish."

Example 3.2

Consider the infix expression $(a + b) * c$. This expression is of the form $E_1 * E_2$, where $E_1 = (a + b)$ and $E_2 = c$. Thus the prefix and postfix Polish expressions for E_2 are both c. The prefix expression for E_1 is the same as that for $a + b$, which is $+ab$. Thus the prefix expression for $(a + b) * c$ is $*+abc$.

Similarly, the postfix expression for $a + b$ is $ab +$, so the postfix expression for $(a + b) * c$ is $ab+c *$.   □

It is not at all obvious that a prefix or postfix expression can be uniquely returned to an infix expression. The observations leading to a proof of this fact are found in Exercises 3.1.16 and 3.1.17.

We can use trees to conveniently represent arithmetic expressions. For example, $(a + b) * c$ has the tree representation shown in Fig. 3.1. In the

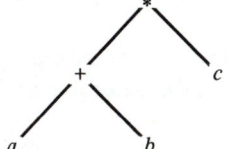

Fig. **3.1** Tree representation for $(a + b) * c$.

tree representation each interior node is labeled by an operator from Θ and each leaf by an operand from Σ. The prefix Polish representation is merely the left-bracketed representation of the tree with all parentheses deleted. Similarly, the postfix Polish representation is the right-bracketed representation of the tree, with parentheses again deleted.

Two important examples of translations are the sets of pairs

$\{(x, y) \mid x$ is an infix expression and y is the prefix (or, alternatively, postfix) Polish representation of $x\}$.

These translations cannot be specified by a homomorphism. We need translation specifiers with more power and shall now turn our attention to formalisms which allow these and other translations to be conveniently specified.

3.1.2. Syntax-Directed Translation Schemata

The problem of finitely specifying an infinite translation is similar to the problem of specifying an infinite language. There are several possible approaches toward the specification of translations. Analogous to a language generator, such as a grammar, we can have a system which generates the pairs in the translation. We can also use a recognizer with two tapes to recognize those pairs in the translation. Or we could define an automaton which takes a string x as input and emits (nondeterministically if necessary) all y such that y is a translation of x. While this list does not exhaust all possibilities, it does cover the models in common use.

Let us call a device which given an input string x, calculates an output string y such that (x, y) is in a given translation T, a *translator* for T. There are several features which are desirable in the definition of a translation. Two of these features are

(1) The definition of the translation should be readable. That is to say, it should be easy to determine what pairs are in the translation.

(2) It should be possible to mechanically construct an efficient translator for that translation directly from the definition.

Features which are desirable in translators are

(1) Efficient operation. For an input string w of length n, the amount of time required to process w should be linearly proportional to n.

(2) Small size.

(3) Correctness. It would be desirable to have a small finite test such that if the translator passed this test, this would be a guarantee that the translator works correctly on all inputs.

One formalism for defining translations is the syntax-directed translation schema. Intuitively, a syntax-directed translation schema is simply a grammar in which translation elements are attached to each production. Whenever a production is used in the derivation of an input sentence, the translation element is used to help compute a portion of the output sentence associated with the portion of the input sentence generated by that production.

Example 3.3

Consider the following translation schema which defines the translation $\{(x, x^R) \mid x \in \{0, 1\}^*\}$. That is, for each input x, the output is x reversed. The rules defining this translation are

Production	Translation Element
(1) $S \longrightarrow 0S$	$S = S0$
(2) $S \longrightarrow 1S$	$S = S1$
(3) $S \longrightarrow e$	$S = e$

An input–output pair in the translation defined by this schema can be obtained by generating a sequence of pairs of strings (α, β) called *translation forms*, where α is an input sentential form and β an output sentential form. We begin with the translation form (S, S). We can then apply the first rule to this form. To do so, we expand the first S using the production $S \to 0S$. Then we replace the output sentential form S by $S0$ in accordance with the translation element $S = S0$. For the time being, we can think of the translation element simply as a production $S \to S0$. Thus we obtain the translation form $(0S, S0)$. We can expand each S in this new translation form by using rule (1) again to obtain $(00S, S00)$. If we then apply rule (2), we obtain $(001S, S100)$. If we then apply rule (3), we obtain $(001, 100)$. No further rules can be applied to this translation form and thus $(001, 100)$ is in the translation defined by this translation schema. $\square$

A translation schema T defines some translation $\tau(T)$. We can build a translator for $\tau(T)$ from the translation schema that works as follows. Given an input string x, the translator finds (if possible) some derivation of x from S using the productions in the translation schema. Suppose that $S = \alpha_0 \Rightarrow \alpha_1 \Rightarrow \alpha_2 \Rightarrow \cdots \Rightarrow \alpha_n = x$ is such a derivation. Then the translator creates a derivation of translation forms

$$(\alpha_0, \beta_0) \Longrightarrow (\alpha_1, \beta_1) \Longrightarrow \cdots \Longrightarrow (\alpha_n, \beta_n)$$

such that $(\alpha_0, \beta_0) = (S, S)$, $(\alpha_n, \beta_n) = (x, y)$, and each β_i is obtained by applying to β_{i-1} the translation element corresponding to the production used in going from α_{i-1} to α_i at the "corresponding" place. The string y is an output for x.

Often the output sentential forms can be created at the time the input is being parsed.

Example 3.4

Consider the following translation scheme which maps arithmetic expressions of $L(G_0)$ to postfix Polish:

Production	Translation Element
$E \to E + T$	$E = ET +$
$E \to T$	$E = T$
$T \to T * F$	$T = TF *$
$T \to F$	$T = F$
$F \to (E)$	$F = E$
$F \to a$	$F = a$

The production $E \to E + T$ is associated with the translation element $E = ET +$. This translation element says that the translation associated with E on the left of the production is the translation associated with E on the right of the production followed by the translation of T followed by $+$.

Let us determine the output for the input $a + a * a$. To do so, let us first find a leftmost derivation of $a + a * a$ from E using the productions of the translation scheme. Then we compute the corresponding sequence of translation forms as shown:

$$
\begin{aligned}
(E, E) &\Longrightarrow (E + T, ET +) \\
&\Longrightarrow (T + T, TT +) \\
&\Longrightarrow (F + T, FT +) \\
&\Longrightarrow (a + T, aT +) \\
&\Longrightarrow (a + T * F, aTF * +) \\
&\Longrightarrow (a + F * F, aFF * +) \\
&\Longrightarrow (a + a * F, aaF * +) \\
&\Longrightarrow (a + a * a, aaa * +)
\end{aligned}
$$

Each output sentential form is computed by replacing the appropriate nonterminal in the previous output sentential form by the right side of translation rule associated with the production used in deriving the corresponding input sentential form.   ☐

The translation schemata in Examples 3.3 and 3.4 are special cases of an important class of translation schemata called syntax-directed translation schemata.

DEFINITION

A *syntax-directed translation schema* (SDTS for short) is a 5-tuple $T = (N, \Sigma, \Delta, R, S)$, where

(1) N is a finite set of *nonterminal symbols*.
(2) Σ is a finite *input alphabet*.
(3) Δ is a finite *output alphabet*.
(4) R is a finite set of *rules* of the form $A \rightarrow \alpha, \beta$, where $\alpha \in (N \cup \Sigma)^*$, $\beta \in (N \cup \Delta)^*$, and the nonterminals in β are a permutation of the nonterminals in α.
(5) S is a distinguished nonterminal in N, the *start symbol*.

Let $A \rightarrow \alpha, \beta$ be a rule. To each nonterminal of α there is *associated* an identical nonterminal of β. If a nonterminal B appears only once in α and β, then the association is obvious. If B appears more than once, we use integer superscripts to indicate the association. This association is an intimate part of the rule. For example, in the rule $A \rightarrow B^{(1)}CB^{(2)}, B^{(2)}B^{(1)}C$, the three positions in $B^{(1)}CB^{(2)}$ are associated with positions 2, 3, and 1, respectively, in $B^{(2)}B^{(1)}C$.

We define a *translation form* of T as follows:

(1) (S, S) is a translation form, and the two S's are said to be *associated*.

(2) If $(\alpha A \beta, \alpha' A \beta')$ is a translation form, in which the two explicit instances of A are associated, and if $A \rightarrow \gamma, \gamma'$ is a rule in R, then $(\alpha \gamma \beta, \alpha' \gamma' \beta')$ is a translation form. The nonterminals of γ and γ' are associated in the translation form exactly as they are associated in the rule. The nonterminals of α and β are associated with those of α' and β' in the new translation form exactly as in the old. The association will again be indicated by superscripts, when needed, and this association is an essential feature of the form.

If the forms $(\alpha A \beta, \alpha' A \beta')$ and $(\alpha \gamma \beta, \alpha' \gamma' \beta')$, together with their associations, are related as above, then we write $(\alpha A \beta, \alpha' A \beta') \underset{T}{\Longrightarrow} (\alpha \gamma \beta, \alpha' \gamma' \beta')$. We use $\underset{T}{\overset{+}{\Longrightarrow}}, \underset{T}{\overset{*}{\Longrightarrow}}$, and $\underset{T}{\overset{k}{\Longrightarrow}}$ to stand for the transitive closure, reflexive-transitive closure, and k-fold product of $\underset{T}{\Longrightarrow}$. As is customary, we shall drop the subscript T whenever possible.

The *translation defined by* T, denoted $\tau(T)$, is the set of pairs

$$\{(x, y) \mid (S, S) \overset{*}{\Longrightarrow} (x, y), \ x \in \Sigma^* \text{ and } y \in \Delta^*\}.$$

Example 3.5

Consider the SDTS $T = (\{S\}, \{a, +\}, \{a, +\}, R, S)$, where R has the rules

$$S \longrightarrow + S^{(1)}S^{(2)}, \qquad S^{(1)} + S^{(2)}$$
$$S \longrightarrow a, \qquad a$$

Consider the following derivation in T:

$$
\begin{aligned}
(S, S) &\Longrightarrow (+ \, S^{(1)}S^{(2)}, \, S^{(1)} + S^{(2)}) \\
&\Longrightarrow (+ + S^{(3)}S^{(4)}S^{(2)}, \, S^{(3)} + S^{(4)} + S^{(2)}) \\
&\Longrightarrow (+ + aS^{(4)}S^{(2)}, \, a + S^{(4)} + S^{(2)}) \\
&\Longrightarrow (+ + aaS, \, a + a + S) \\
&\Longrightarrow (+ + aaa, \, a + a + a)
\end{aligned}
$$

$\tau(T) = \{(x, a(+a)^i) \mid i \geq 0 \text{ and } x \text{ is a prefix polish representation of } a(+a)^i$ with some order of association of the $+$'s$\}$. $\quad \square$

DEFINITION

If $T = (N, \Sigma, \Delta, R, S)$ is an SDTS, then $\tau(T)$ is called a syntax-directed translation (SDT). The grammar $G_i = (N, \Sigma, P, S)$, where

$$P = \{A \rightarrow \alpha \mid A \rightarrow \alpha, \beta \text{ is in } R\},$$

is called the *underlying* (*or input*) *grammar* of the SDTS T. The grammar $G_o = (N, \Delta, P', S)$, where $P' = \{A \longrightarrow \beta \,|\, A \longrightarrow \alpha, \beta$ is in $R\}$ is called the *output grammar* of T.

We can alternatively view a syntax-directed translation as a method of transforming derivation trees in the input grammar G_i into derivation trees in the output grammar G_o. Given an input sentence x, a translation for x can be obtained by constructing a derivation tree for x, then transforming the derivation tree into a tree in the output grammar, and then taking the frontier of the output tree as a translation for x.

ALGORITHM 3.1

Tree transformation via an SDTS.

Input. An SDTS $T = (N, \Sigma, \Delta, R, S)$, with input grammar $G_i = (N, \Sigma, P_i, S)$, output grammar $G_o = (N, \Delta, P_o, S)$, and a derivation tree D in G_i, with frontier in Σ^*.

Output. Some derivation tree D' in G_o such that if x and y are the frontiers of D and D', respectively, then $(x, y) \in \tau(T)$.

Method.

(1) Apply step (2), recursively, starting with the root of D.

(2) Let this step be applied to node n. It will be the case that n is an interior node of D. Let n have direct descendants $n_1, \ldots, n_k$.

    (a) Delete those of $n_1, \ldots, n_k$ which are leaves (i.e., have terminal or e-labels).

    (b) Let the production of G_i represented by n and its direct descendants be $A \longrightarrow \alpha$. That is, A is the label of n and α is formed by concatenating the labels of $n_1, \ldots, n_k$. Choose some rule of the form $A \longrightarrow \alpha, \beta$ in R.† Permute the remaining direct descendants of n, if any, in accordance with the association between the nonterminals of α and β. (The subtrees dominated by these nodes remain in fixed relationship to the direct descendants of n.)

    (c) Insert direct descendant leaves of n so that the labels of its direct descendants form β.

    (d) Apply step (2) to the direct descendants of n which are not leaves, in order from the left.

(3) The resulting tree is D'. $\quad\square$

Example 3.6

Let us consider the SDTS $T = (\{S, A\}, \{0, 1\}, \{a, b\}, R, S)$, where R consists of

---

†Note that β may not be uniquely determined from A and α. If more than one rule is applicable, the choice can be arbitrary.

$$S \longrightarrow 0AS,\ SAa$$
$$A \longrightarrow 0SA,\ ASa$$
$$S \longrightarrow 1,\ b$$
$$A \longrightarrow 1,\ b$$

A derivation tree in the input grammar is shown in Fig. 3.2(a). If we apply step (2) of Algorithm 3.1 to the root of Fig. 3.2(a), we delete the leftmost leaf labeled 0. Then, since $S \rightarrow 0AS$ was the production used at the root and the only translation element for that production is SAa, we must reverse the order of the remaining direct descendants of the root. Then we add a third direct descendant, labeled a, at the rightmost position. The resulting tree is shown in Fig. 3.2(b).

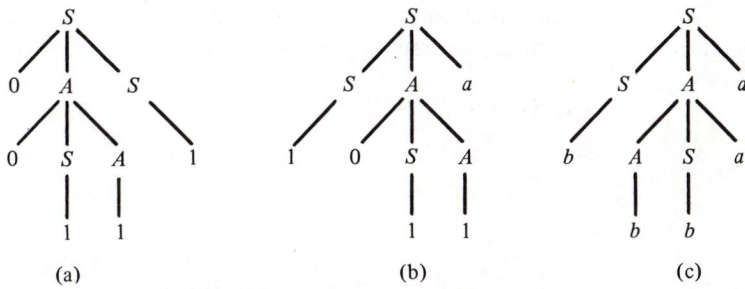

Fig. 3.2 Application of Algorithm 3.1.

We next apply step (2) to the first two direct descendants of the root. Application of step (2) to the second of these descendants results in two more calls of step (2). The resulting tree is shown in Fig. 3.2(c). Notice that $(00111,\ bbbaa)$ is in $\tau(T)$. $\square$

To show the relation between the translation process of Algorithm 3.1 and the SDTS which is input to that algorithm, we prove the following theorem.

THEOREM 3.1

(1) If x and y are the frontiers of D and D', respectively, in Algorithm 3.1, then (x, y) is in $\tau(T)$.

(2) If (x, y) is in $\tau(T)$, then there exists a derivation tree D with frontier x and a sequence of choices for each execution of step (2b) such that the frontier of the resulting tree D' is y.

Proof.

(1) We show the following by induction on the number of interior nodes of a tree E:

(3.1.1)   Let E be a derivation tree in G_i with frontier x and root labeled A, and suppose that step (2) applied to E yields a tree E' with frontier y. Then $(A, A) \overset{*}{\Longrightarrow} (x, y)$

The basis, one interior node, is trivial. All direct descendants are leaves, and there must be a rule $A \longrightarrow x, y$ in R.

For the inductive step, assume that statement (3.1.1) holds for smaller trees, and let the root of E have direct descendants with labels $X_1, \ldots, X_k$. Then $x = x_1 \cdots x_k$, where $X_j \overset{*}{\underset{G_i}{\Longrightarrow}} x_j$, $1 \leq j \leq k$. Let the direct descendants of the root of E' have labels $Y_1 \cdots Y_l$. Then $y = y_1 \cdots y_l$, where $Y_j \overset{*}{\underset{G_o}{\Longrightarrow}} y_j$, $1 \leq j \leq l$. Also, there is a rule $A \longrightarrow X_1 \cdots X_k, Y_1 \cdots Y_l$ in R.

If X_j is a nonterminal, then it is associated with some Y_{p_j}, where $X_j = Y_{p_j}$. By the inductive hypothesis (3.1.1), $(X_j, X_j) \overset{*}{\Longrightarrow} (x_j, y_{p_j})$. Because of the permutation of nodes in step (2b), we know that

$$(A, A) \overset{\cdot}{\Longrightarrow} (X_1 \cdots X_k, Y_1 \cdots Y_l)$$
$$\overset{*}{\Longrightarrow} (x_1 X_2 \cdots X_k, \alpha_1^{(1)} \cdots \alpha_l^{(1)})$$
$$\cdot$$
$$\cdot$$
$$\cdot$$
$$\overset{*}{\Longrightarrow} (x_1 \cdots x_k, \alpha_1^{(k)} \cdots \alpha_l^{(k)}),$$

where $\alpha_j^{(m)}$ is
   (a) y_j if Y_j is in N and is associated with one of $X_1, \ldots, X_m$, and
   (b) Y_j otherwise.
Thus Eq. (3.1.1) follows.
Part (2) of the theorem is a special case of the following statement:

(3.1.2)   If $(A, A) \overset{i}{\Longrightarrow} (x, y)$, then there is a derivation tree D in G_i, with root labeled A, frontier x, and a sequence of choices in step (2b) so that the application of step (2) to D gives a tree with frontier y.

A proof of (3.1.2) by induction on i is left for the Exercises. □

We comment that the order in which step (2) of Algorithm 3.1 is applied to nodes is unimportant. We could choose any order that considered each interior node exactly once. This statement is also left for the Exercises.

DEFINITION

An SDTS $T = (N, \Sigma, \Delta, R, S)$ such that in each rule $A \longrightarrow \alpha, \beta$ in R, associated nonterminals occur in the same order in α and β is called a *simple*

SDTS. The translation defined by a simple SDTS is called a *simple syntax-directed translation* (simple SDT).

The syntax-directed translation schemata of Examples 3.3–3.5 are all simple. That of Example 3.6 is not.

The association of nonterminals in a form of a simple SDTS is straightforward. They must be associated in the order in which they appear.

The simple syntax-directed translations are important because for each simple SDT we can easily construct a translator consisting of a pushdown transducer. This construction will be given in Section 3.1.4. Many, but not all, useful translations can be described as simple SDT's. In Chapter 9 we shall present several generalizations of syntax-directed translation schemata which can be used to define larger classes of translations on context-free languages. We close this section with another example of a simple SDT.

Example 3.7

The following simple SDTS maps the arithmetic expressions in $L(G_o)$ to arithmetic expressions with no redundant parentheses:

$$
\begin{array}{llll}
(1) & E \longrightarrow (E), & E \\
(2) & E \longrightarrow E + E, & E + E \\
(3) & E \longrightarrow T, & T \\
(4) & T \longrightarrow (T), & T \\
(5) & T \longrightarrow A * A, & A * A \\
(6) & T \longrightarrow a, & a \\
(7) & A \longrightarrow (E + E), & (E + E) \\
(8) & A \longrightarrow T, & T
\end{array}
$$

For example, the translation of $((a + (a * a)) * a)$ according to this SDTS is $(a + a * a) * a$.† □

3.1.3. Finite Transducers

We shall now introduce our simplest translator, the finite transducer. A transducer is simply a recognizer which emits an output string during each move made. (The output may be e, however.) The finite transducer is obtained by taking a finite automaton and permitting the machine to emit a string of output symbols on each move (Fig. 3.3). In Section 3.3 we shall use a finite transducer as a model for a lexical analyzer.

---

†Note that the underlying grammar is ambiguous, but that each input word has exactly one output.

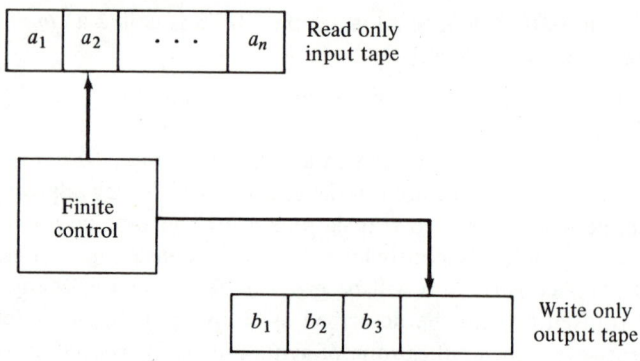

Fig. 3.3 Finite transducer.

For generality we shall consider a nondeterministic finite automaton which is capable of making e-moves, as the basis of a finite transducer.

DEFINITION

A *finite transducer* M is a 6-tuple $(Q, \Sigma, \Delta, \delta, q_0, F)$, where

(1) Q is a finite set of *states*.
(2) Σ is a finite *input alphabet*.
(3) Δ is a finite *output alphabet*.
(4) δ is a mapping from $Q \times (\Sigma \cup \{e\})$ to finite subsets of $Q \times \Delta^*$.
(5) $q_0 \in Q$ is the *initial state*.
(6) $F \subseteq Q$ is the set of *final states*.

We define a *configuration* of M as a triple (q, x, y), where

(1) $q \in Q$ is the current state of the finite control.
(2) $x \in \Sigma^*$ is the input string remaining on the input tape, with the leftmost symbol of x under the input head.
(3) $y \in \Delta^*$ is the output string emitted up to this point.

We define $\vdash_{\overline{M}}$ (or $\vdash$, when M is clear), a binary relation on configurations, to reflect a move by M. Specifically, for all $q \in Q$, $a \in \Sigma \cup \{e\}$, $x \in \Sigma^*$, and $y \in \Delta^*$ such that $\delta(q, a)$ contains (r, z), we write

$$(q, ax, y) \vdash (r, x, yz)$$

We can then define $\vdash^i$, $\vdash^*$, and $\vdash^+$ in the usual fashion.

We say that y is an *output* for x if $(q_0, x, e) \vdash^* (q, e, y)$ for some q in F. The *translation defined by* M, denoted $\tau(M)$, is $\{(x, y) \mid (q_0, x, e) \vdash^* (q, e, y)$ for some q in $F\}$. A translation defined by a finite transducer will be called a *regular translation* or *finite transducer mapping*.

Notice that before an output string y can be considered a translation of an input x, the input string x must take M from an initial state to a final state.

Example 3.8

Let us design a finite transducer which recognizes arithmetic expressions generated by the productions

$$S \longrightarrow a + S \,|\, a - S \,|\, + S \,|\, - S \,|\, a$$

and removes redundant unary operators from these expressions. For example, we would translate $- a + - a - + - a$ into $- a - a + a$. In this language, a represents an identifier, and an arbitrary sequence of unary $+$'s and $-$'s is permitted in front of an identifier. Notice that the input language is a regular set. Let $M = (Q, \Sigma, \Delta, \delta, q_0, F)$, where

(1) $Q = \{q_0, q_1, q_2, q_3, q_4\}$.
(2) $\Sigma = \{a, +, -\}$.
(3) $\Delta = \Sigma$.
(4) δ is defined by the transition graph of Fig. 3.4. A label x/y on an edge directed from the node labeled q_i to the node labeled q_j indicates that $\delta(q_i, x)$ contains (q_j, y).
(5) $F = \{q_1\}$.

M starts in state q_0 and determines whether there are an odd or even

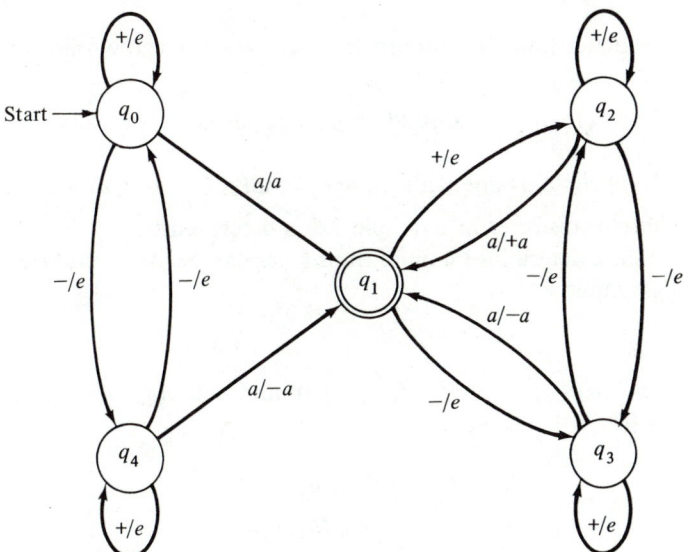

Fig. 3.4 Transition graph.

number of minus signs preceding the first a by alternating between q_0 and q_4 on input $-$. When an a appears, M goes to state q_1, to accept the input, and emits either a or $-a$, depending on whether an even or odd number of $-$'s have appeared. For subsequent a's, M counts whether the number of $-$'s is even or odd using states q_2 and q_3. The only difference between the $q_2 - q_3$ pair and $q_0 - q_4$ is that the former emits $+a$, rather than a alone, if an even number of $-$ signs precede a.

With input $-a + -a - + -a$, M would make the following sequence of moves:

$$(q_0, -a + -a - + -a, e) \vdash (q_4, a + -a - + -a, e)$$
$$\vdash (q_1, + -a - + -a, -a)$$
$$\vdash (q_2, -a - + -a, -a)$$
$$\vdash (q_3, a - + -a, -a)$$
$$\vdash (q_1, - + -a, -a - a)$$
$$\vdash (q_3, + -a, -a - a)$$
$$\vdash (q_3, -a, -a - a)$$
$$\vdash (q_2, a, -a - a)$$
$$\vdash (q_1, e, -a - a + a)$$

Thus, M maps $-a + -a - + -a$ into $-a - a + a$, since q_1 is a final state. $\square$

We say that a finite transducer M is *deterministic* if the following condition holds for all $q \in Q$:

(1) Either $\delta(q, a)$ contains at most one element for each $a \in \Sigma$, and $\delta(q, e)$ is empty, or

(2) $\delta(q, e)$ contains one element, and for all $a \in \Sigma$, $\delta(q, a)$ is empty.

The finite transducer in Example 3.8 is deterministic.

Note that a deterministic finite transducer can define several translations for a single input.

Example 3.9

Let $M = (\{q_0, q_1\}, \{a\}, \{b\}, \delta, q_0, \{q_1\})$ and let $\delta(q_0, a) = \{(q_1, b)\}$ and $\delta(q_1, e) = \{(q_1, b)\}$. Then

$$(q_0, a, e) \vdash (q_1, e, b)$$
$$\vdash^i (q_1, e, b^{i+1})$$

is a valid sequence of moves for all $i \geq 0$. Thus, $\tau(M) = \{(a, b^i) \mid i \geq 1\}$. $\square$

There are several simple modifications of the definition of determinism for finite transducers that will ensure the uniqueness of output. The one we suggest is to require that no e-moves be made in a final state.

A number of closure properties for classes of languages can be obtained by using transducers as operators on languages. For example, if M is a finite transducer and L is included in the domain of $\tau(M)$, then we can define $M(L) = \{y \mid x \in L \text{ and } (x, y) \in \tau(M)\}$.

We can also define an *inverse finite transducer mapping* as follows. Let M be a finite transducer. Then $M^{-1}(L) = \{x \mid y \in L \text{ and } (x, y) \in \tau(M)\}$.

It is not difficult to show that finite transducer mappings and inverse finite transducer mappings preserve both the regular sets and the context-free languages. That is, if L is a regular set (CFL) and M is a finite transducer, then $M(L)$ and $M^{-1}(L)$ are both regular sets (CFL's). Proofs are left for the Exercises. We can use these observations to show that certain languages are not regular or not context-free.

Example 3.10

The language generated by the following grammar G is not regular:

$$S \longrightarrow \text{if } S \text{ then } S \mid a$$

Let

$$L_1 = L(G) \cap (\text{if})^* \; a \; (\text{then } a)^*$$
$$= \{(\text{if})^n \; a \; (\text{then } a)^n \mid n \geq 0\}$$

Consider the finite transducer $M = (Q, \Sigma, \Delta, \delta, q_0, F)$, where

(1) $Q = \{q_i \mid 0 \leq i \leq 6\}$.
(2) $\Sigma = \{a, i, f, t, h, \text{'}e\text{'}, n\}$.
(3) $\Delta = \{0, 1\}$.
(4) δ is defined by the transition graph of Fig. 3.5.
(5) $F = \{q_2\}$.

Here 'e' denotes the letter e, as distinguished from the empty string. Thus $M(L_1) = \{0^k 1^k \mid k \geq 0\}$, which we know is not a regular set. Since the regular sets are closed under intersection and finite transducer mappings, we must conclude that $L(G)$ is not a regular set. $\quad\square$

3.1.4. Pushdown Transducers

We shall now introduce another important class of translators called pushdown transducers. A pushdown transducer is obtained by providing a pushdown automaton with an output. On each move the automaton is permitted to emit a finite-length output string.

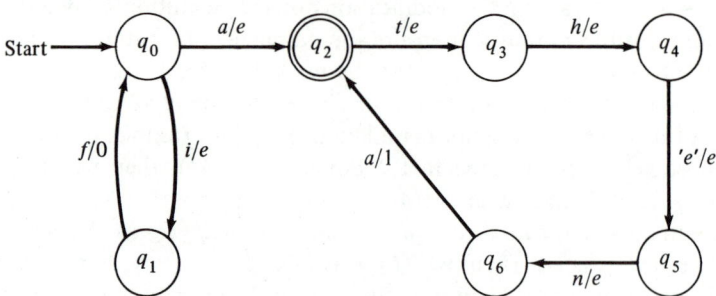

Fig. 3.5   Transition graph of M.

Definition

A *pushdown transducer* (PDT) P is an 8-tuple $(Q, \Sigma, \Gamma, \Delta, \delta, q_0, Z_0, F)$, where all symbols have the same meaning as for a PDA except that Δ is a finite *output alphabet* and δ is now a mapping from $Q \times (\Sigma \cup \{e\}) \times \Gamma$ to finite subsets of $Q \times \Gamma^* \times \Delta^*$.

We define a *configuration* of P as a 4-tuple (q, x, α, y), where q, x, and α are the same as for a PDA and y is the output string emitted to this point. If $\delta(q, a, Z)$ contains (r, α, z), then we write $(q, ax, Z\gamma, y) \vdash (r, x, \alpha\gamma, yz)$ for all $x \in \Sigma^*$, $\gamma \in \Gamma^*$, and $y \in \Delta^*$.

We say that y is an *output* for x if $(q_0, x, Z_0, e) \vdash^* (q, e, \alpha, y)$ for some $q \in F$ and $\alpha \in \Gamma^*$. The *translation defined by* P, denoted $\tau(P)$, is

$$\{(x, y) \mid (q_0, x, Z_0, e) \vdash^* (q, e, \alpha, y) \text{ for some } q \in F \text{ and } \alpha \in \Gamma^*\}.$$

As with PDA's, we can say that y is an output for x *by empty pushdown list* if $(q_0, x, Z_0, e) \vdash^* (q, e, e, y)$ for some q in Q. The *translation defined by* P *by empty pushdown list*, denoted $\tau_e(P)$, is

$$\{(x, y) \mid (q_0, x, Z_0, e) \vdash^* (q, e, e, y) \text{ for some } q \in Q\}.$$

We can also define extended PDT's with their pushdown list top on the right in a way analogous to extended PDA's.

Example 3.11

Let P be the pushdown transducer

$$(\{q\}, \{a, +, *\}, \{+, *, E\}, \{a, +, *\}, \delta, q, E, \{q\}),$$

where δ is defined as follows:

$$\delta(q, a, E) = \{(q, e, a)\}$$
$$\delta(q, +, E) = \{(q, EE +, e)\}$$
$$\delta(q, *, E) = \{(q, EE *, e)\}$$
$$\delta(q, e, +) = \{(q, e, +)\}$$
$$\delta(q, e, *) = \{(q, e, *)\}$$

With input $+ * aaa$, P makes the following sequence of moves:

$$(q, + * aaa, E, e) \vdash (q, * aaa, EE +, e)$$
$$\vdash (q, aaa, EE * E +, e)$$
$$\vdash (q, aa, E * E +, a)$$
$$\vdash (q, a, * E +, aa)$$
$$\vdash (q, a, E +, aa *)$$
$$\vdash (q, e, +, aa * a)$$
$$\vdash (q, e, e, aa * a +)$$

Thus a translation by empty pushdown list of $+ * aaa$ is $aa * a +$. It can be verified that $\tau_e(P)$ is the set

$\{(x, y) \,|\, x$ is a prefix Polish arithmetic expression over $\{+, *, a\}$ and y is the corresponding postfix Polish expression$\}$. $\square$

DEFINITION

If $P = (Q, \Sigma, \Gamma, \Delta, \delta, q_0, Z_0, F)$ is a pushdown transducer, then the pushdown automaton $(Q, \Sigma, \Gamma, \delta', q_0, Z_0, F)$, where $\delta'(q, a, Z)$ contains (r, γ) if and only if $\delta(q, a, Z)$ contains (r, γ, y) for some y, is called the PDA *underlying P*.

We say that the PDT $P = (Q, \Sigma, \Gamma, \Delta, \delta, q_0, Z_0, F)$ is *deterministic* (a DPDT) when

(1) For all $q \in Q$, $a \in \Sigma \cup \{e\}$, and $Z \in \Gamma$, $\delta(q, a, Z)$ contains at most one element, and

(2) If $\delta(q, e, Z) \neq \varnothing$, then $\delta(q, a, Z) = \varnothing$ for all $a \in \Sigma$.†

Clearly, if L is the domain of $\tau(P)$ for some pushdown transducer P, then $L = L(P')$, where P' is the pushdown automaton underlying P.

---

†Note that this definition is slightly stronger than saying that the underlying PDA is deterministic. The latter could be deterministic, but (1) may not hold because the PDT can give two different outputs on two moves which are otherwise identical. Also note that condition (2) implies that if $\delta(q, a, Z) \neq \varnothing$ for some $a \in \Sigma$, then $\delta(q, e, Z) = \varnothing$.

Many of the results proved in Section 2.5 for pushdown automata carry over naturally to pushdown transducers. In particular, the following lemma can be shown in a way analogous to Lemmas 2.22 and 2.23.

LEMMA 3.1

A translation T is $\tau(P_1)$ for a pushdown transducer P_1 if and only if T is $\tau_e(P_2)$ for a pushdown transducer P_2.

Proof. Exercise. $\square$

A pushdown transducer, particularly a deterministic pushdown transducer, is a useful model of the syntactic analysis phase of compiling. In Section 3.4 we shall use the pushdown transducer in this phase of compiling.

Now we shall prove that a translation is a simple SDT if and only if it can be defined by a pushdown transducer. Thus the pushdown transducers characterize the class of simple SDT's in the same manner that pushdown automata characterize the context-free languages.

LEMMA 3.2

Let $T = (N, \Sigma, \Delta, R, S)$ be a simple SDTS. Then there is a pushdown transducer P such that $\tau_e(P) = \tau(T)$.

Proof. Let G_i be the input grammar of T. We construct P to recognize $L(G_i)$ top-down as in Lemma 2.24.

To simulate a rule $A \longrightarrow \alpha, \beta$ of T, P will replace A on top of its pushdown list by α with output symbols of β intermeshed. That is, if $\alpha = x_0 A_1 x_1 \cdots A_n x_n$ and $\beta = y_0 A_1 y_1 \cdots A_n y_n$, then P will place $x_0 y_0 A_1 x_1 y_1 \cdots A_n x_n y_n$ on its pushdown list. We need, however, to distinguish between the symbols of Σ and those of Δ, so that the word $x_i y_i$ can be broken up correctly. If Σ and Δ are disjoint, there is no problem, but to take care of the general case, we define a new alphabet Δ' corresponding to Δ but known to be disjoint from Σ. That is, let Δ' consist of new symbols a' for each $a \in \Delta$. Then $\Sigma \cap \Delta' = \varnothing$. Let h be the homomorphism defined by $h(a) = a'$ for each a in Δ.

Let $P = (\{q\}, \Sigma, N \cup \Sigma \cup \Delta', \Delta, \delta, q, S, \varnothing)$, where δ is defined as follows:

(1) If $A \longrightarrow x_0 B_1 x_1 \cdots B_k x_k, y_0 B_1 y_1 \cdots B_k y_k$ is a rule in R with $k \geq 0$, then $\delta(q, e, A)$ contains $(q, x_0 y_0' B_1 x_1 y_1' \cdots B_k x_k y_k', e)$, where $y_i' = h(y_i)$, $0 \leq i \leq k$.

(2) $\delta(q, a, a) = \{(q, e, e)\}$ for all a in Σ.

(3) $\delta(q, e, a') = \{(q, e, a)\}$ for all a in Δ.

By induction on m and n, we can show that, for A in N and $m, n \geq 1$,

$$(3.1.3) \qquad (A, A) \overset{m}{\Longrightarrow} (x, y) \text{ for some } m \text{ if and only if } (q, x, A, e) \mathrel{\vdash^{n}} (q, e, e, y)$$
$$\text{for some } n$$

Only if: The basis, $m = 1$, holds trivially, as $A \rightarrow x, y$ must be in R. Then $(q, x, A, e) \vdash (q, x, xh(y), e) \vdash^* (q, e, h(y), e) \vdash^* (q, e, e, y)$.

For the inductive step assume (3.1.3) for values smaller than m, and let $(A, A) \Rightarrow (x_0 B_1 x_1 \cdots B_k x_k, y_0 B_1 y_1 \cdots B_k y_k) \overset{m-1}{\Rightarrow} (x, y)$. Because simple SDTS's involve no permutation of the order of nonterminals, we can write $x = x_0 u_1 x_1 \cdots u_k x_k$ and $y = y_0 v_1 y_1 \cdots v_k y_k$, so that $(B_i, B_i) \overset{m_i}{\Rightarrow} (u_i, v_i)$ for $1 \leq i \leq k$, where $m_i < m$ for each i. Thus, by the inductive hypothesis (3.1.3), $(q, u_i, B_i, e) \vdash^* (q, e, e, v_i)$. Putting these sequences of moves together, we have

$$(q, x, A, e) \vdash (q, x, x_0 h(y_0) B_1 \cdots B_k x_k h(y_k), e)$$
$$\vdash^* (q, u_1 x_1 \cdots u_k x_k, h(y_0) B_1 \cdots B_k x_k h(y_k), e)$$
$$\vdash^* (q, u_1 x_1 \cdots u_k x_k, B_1 \cdots B_k x_k h(y_k), y_0)$$
$$\vdash^* (q, x_1 \cdots u_k x_k, x_1 h(y_1) \cdots B_k x_k h(y_k), y_0 v_1)$$
$$\vdash^* \cdots \vdash^* (q, e, e, y)$$

If: Again the basis, $n = 1$, is trivial. It must be that $A \rightarrow e, e$ is in R. For the inductive step, let the first move of P be

$$(q, x, A, e) \vdash (q, x, x_0 h(y_0) B_1 x_1 h(y_1) \cdots B_k x_k h(y_k), e),$$

where the x_i's are in Σ^* and the $h(y_i)$'s denote strings in $(\Delta')^*$, with the y_i's in Δ^*. Then x_0 must be a prefix of x, and the next moves of P remove x_0 from the input and pushdown list and then emit y_0. Let x' be the remaining input. There must be some prefix u_1 of x' that causes the level holding B_1 to be popped from the pushdown list. Let v_1 be emitted up to the time the pushdown list first becomes shorter than $|B_1 \cdots B_k x_k h(y_k)|$. Then $(q, u_1, B_1, e) \vdash^* (q, e, e, v_1)$ by a sequence of fewer than n moves. By inductive hypothesis (3.1.3), $(B_1, B_1) \overset{*}{\Rightarrow} (u_1, v_1)$.

Reasoning in this way, we find that we can write x as $x_0 u_1 x_1 \cdots u_k x_k$ and y as $y_0 v_1 y_1 \cdots v_k y_k$ so that $(B_i, B_i) \overset{*}{\Rightarrow} (u_i, v_i)$ for $1 \leq i \leq k$. Since rule $A \rightarrow x_0 B_1 x_1 \cdots B_k x_k, \; y_0 B_1 y_1 \cdots B_k y_k$ is clearly in R, we have $(A, A) \overset{*}{\Rightarrow} (x, y)$.

As a special case of (3.1.3), we have $(S, S) \overset{*}{\Rightarrow} (x, y)$ if and only if $(q, x, S, e) \vdash^* (q, e, e, y)$, so $\tau_e(P) = \tau(T)$. $\square$

Example 3.12

The simple SDTS T having rules

$$E \longrightarrow + EE, \; EE +$$
$$E \longrightarrow * EE, \; EE *$$
$$E \longrightarrow a, \; a$$

would give rise to the pushdown transducer

$$P = (\{q\}, \{a, +, *\}, \{E, a, +, *, a', +', *'\}, \{a, +, *\}, \delta, q, E, \varnothing),$$

where δ is defined by

(1) $\delta(q, e, E) = \{(q, + EE +', e), (q, * EE *', e), (q, aa', e)\}$
(2) $\delta(q, b, b) = \{(q, e, e)\}$ for all b in $\{a, +, *\}$
(3) $\delta(q, e, b') = \{(q, e, b)\}$ for all b in $\{a, +, *\}$.

This is a nondeterministic pushdown transducer. Example 3.11 gives an equivalent deterministic pushdown transducer. □

LEMMA 3.3

Let $P = (Q, \Sigma, \Gamma, \Delta, \delta, q_0, Z_0, F)$ be a pushdown transducer. Then there is a simple SDTS T such that $\tau(T) = \tau_e(P)$.

Proof. The construction is similar to that of obtaining a CFG from a PDA. Let $T = (N, \Sigma, \Delta, R, S)$, where

(1) $N = \{[pAq] \,|\, p, q \in Q, A \in \Gamma\} \cup \{S\}$.
(2) R is defined as follows:
   (a) If $\delta(p, a, A)$ contains $(r, X_1 X_2 \cdots X_k, y)$, then if $k > 0$, R contains the rules

$$[pAq_k] \longrightarrow a[rX_1q_1][q_1X_2q_2] \cdots [q_{k-1}X_kq_k],$$
$$y[rX_1q_1][q_1X_2q_2] \cdots [q_{k-1}X_kq_k]$$

   for all sequences $q_1, q_2, \ldots, q_k$ of states in Q. If $k = 0$, then the rule is $[pAr] \longrightarrow a, y$.
   (b) For each q in Q, R contains the rule $S \longrightarrow [q_0 Z_0 q], [q_0 Z_0 q]$.

Clearly, T is a simple SDTS. Again, by induction on m and n it is straightforward to show that

(3.1.4) $([pAq], [pAq]) \overset{m}{\Rightarrow} (x, y)$ if and only if $(p, x, A, e) \vdash^n (q, e, e, y)$
for all p and q in Q and $A \in \Gamma$

We leave the proof of (3.1.4) for the Exercises.

Thus we have $(S, S) \Rightarrow ([q_0 Z_0 q], [q_0 Z_0 q]) \overset{+}{\Rightarrow} (x, y)$ if and only if $(q_0, x, Z_0, e) \vdash^+ (q, e, e, y)$. Hence $\tau(T) = \tau_e(P)$. □

Example 3.13

Using the construction in the previous lemma let us build a simple SDTS from the pushdown transducer in Example 3.11. We obtain the SDTS $T = (N, \{a, +, *\}, \{a, +, *\}, R, S)$, where $N = \{[qXq] \,|\, X \in \{+, *, E\}\} \cup S$ and where R has the rules

$$S \longrightarrow [qEq], [qEq]$$
$$[qEq] \longrightarrow a, a$$
$$[qEq] \longrightarrow + [qEq][qEq][q + q], [qEq][qEq][q + q]$$
$$[qEq] \longrightarrow * [qEq][qEq][q * q], [qEq][qEq][q * q]$$
$$[q + q] \longrightarrow e, +$$
$$[q * q] \longrightarrow e, *$$

Notice that using transformations similar to those for removing single and e-productions from a CFG, we can simplify the rules to

$$S \longrightarrow a, a$$
$$S \longrightarrow + SS, SS +$$
$$S \longrightarrow * SS, SS * \quad \square$$

THEOREM 3.2

T is a simple SDT if and only if T is $\tau(P)$ for some pushdown transducer P.

Proof. Immediate from Lemmas 3.1, 3.2, and 3.3. $\square$

In Chapter 9 we shall introduce a machine called the pushdown processor which is capable of defining all syntax-directed translations.

EXERCISES

3.1.1. An operator with one argument is called a *unary* operator, one with two arguments a *binary* operator, and in general an operator with n arguments is called an *n-ary* operator. For example, $-$ can be either a unary operator (as in $-a$) or a binary operator (as in $a - b$). The *degree* of an operator is the number of arguments it takes. Let Θ be a set of operators each of whose degree is known and let Σ be a set of operands. Construct context-free grammars G_1 and G_2 to generate the prefix Polish and postfix Polish expressions over Θ and Σ.

*3.1.2. The "precedence" of infix operators determines the order in which the operators are to be applied. If binary operator θ_1 "takes precedence over" θ_2, then $a \theta_2 b \theta_1 c$ is to be evaluated as $a \theta_2 (b \theta_1 c)$. For example, $*$ takes precedence over $+$, so $a + b * c$ means $a + (b * c)$ rather than $(a + b) * c$. Consider the Boolean operators $\equiv$ (equivalence), $\longrightarrow$ (implication), $\vee$ (or), $\wedge$ (and), and $\neg$ (not). These operators are listed in order of increasing precedence. $\neg$ is a unary operator and the others are binary. As an example, $\neg (a \vee b) \equiv \neg a \wedge \neg b$ has the implied parenthesization $(\neg (a \vee b)) \equiv ((\neg a) \wedge (\neg b))$. Construct a CFG which generates all valid Boolean expressions over these operators and operands a, b, c with no superfluous parentheses.

*3.1.3. Construct a simple SDTS which maps Boolean expressions in infix notation into prefix notation.

*3.1.4. In ALGOL, expressions can be constructed using the following binary operators listed in order of their precedence levels. If more than one operator appears on a level, these operators are applied in left-to-right order. For example $a - b + c$ means $(a - b) + c$.

(1) $\equiv$	(2) $\rightarrow$	(3) $\vee$
(4) $\wedge$	(5) $\neg$	(6) $\leq < = \neq > \geq$
(7) $+ -$	(8) $\times / \div$	(9) $\uparrow$

Construct a simple SDTS which maps infix expressions containing these operators into postfix Polish notation.

3.1.5. Consider the following SDTS. A string of the form $\langle x \rangle$ is a single nonterminal:

$$\langle \text{exp} \rangle \longrightarrow \textbf{sum } \langle \text{exp} \rangle^{(1)} \textbf{ with } \langle \text{var} \rangle \longleftarrow \langle \text{exp} \rangle^{(2)} \textbf{ to } \langle \text{exp} \rangle^{(3)},\dagger$$
$$\textbf{begin } \textbf{local } t;$$
$$t \longleftarrow 0;$$
$$\textbf{for } \langle \text{var} \rangle \longleftarrow \langle \text{exp} \rangle^{(2)} \textbf{ to } \langle \text{exp} \rangle^{(3)} \textbf{ do}$$
$$t \longleftarrow t + \langle \text{exp} \rangle^{(1)}; \quad \textbf{result } t$$
$$\textbf{end}$$

$$\langle \text{var} \rangle \longrightarrow \langle \text{id} \rangle, \langle \text{id} \rangle$$
$$\langle \text{exp} \rangle \longrightarrow \langle \text{id} \rangle, \langle \text{id} \rangle$$
$$\langle \text{id} \rangle \longrightarrow a \langle \text{id} \rangle, a \langle \text{id} \rangle$$
$$\langle \text{id} \rangle \longrightarrow b \langle \text{id} \rangle, b \langle \text{id} \rangle$$
$$\langle \text{id} \rangle \longrightarrow a, a$$
$$\langle \text{id} \rangle \longrightarrow b, b$$

Give the translation for the sentences

(a) **sum** aa **with** $a \longleftarrow b$ **to** bb.

(b) **sum sum** a **with** $aa \longleftarrow aaa$ **to** $aaaa$ **with** $b \longleftarrow bb$ **to** bbb.

*3.1.6. Consider the following translation scheme:

$$\langle \text{statement} \rangle \longrightarrow \textbf{for } \langle \text{var} \rangle \longleftarrow \langle \text{exp} \rangle^{(1)} \textbf{ to } \langle \text{exp} \rangle^{(2)} \textbf{ do } \langle \text{statement} \rangle,$$
$$\textbf{begin } \langle \text{var} \rangle \longleftarrow \langle \text{exp} \rangle^{(1)};$$
$$L: \textbf{ if } \langle \text{var} \rangle \leq \langle \text{exp} \rangle^{(2)} \textbf{ then}$$
$$\textbf{begin } \langle \text{statement} \rangle;$$
$$\langle \text{var} \rangle \longleftarrow \langle \text{var} \rangle + 1;$$
$$\textbf{go to } L$$
$$\textbf{end}$$
$$\textbf{end}$$

†Note that this comma separates the two parts of the rule.

$$\langle \text{var} \rangle \longrightarrow \langle \text{id} \rangle, \langle \text{id} \rangle$$
$$\langle \text{exp} \rangle \longrightarrow \langle \text{id} \rangle, \langle \text{id} \rangle$$
$$\langle \text{statement} \rangle \longrightarrow \langle \text{var} \rangle \leftarrow \langle \text{exp} \rangle, \langle \text{var} \rangle \leftarrow \langle \text{exp} \rangle$$
$$\langle \text{id} \rangle \longrightarrow a\langle \text{id} \rangle, a\langle \text{id} \rangle$$
$$\langle \text{id} \rangle \longrightarrow b\langle \text{id} \rangle, b\langle \text{id} \rangle$$
$$\langle \text{id} \rangle \longrightarrow a, a$$
$$\langle \text{id} \rangle \longrightarrow b, b$$

Why is this not an SDTS? What should the output be for the following input sentence:

$$\textbf{for } a \leftarrow b \textbf{ to } aa \textbf{ do } baa \leftarrow bba$$

Hint: Apply Algorithm 3.1 duplicating the nodes labeled $\langle \text{var} \rangle$ in the output tree.

Exercises 3.1.5 and 3.1.6 provide examples of how a language can be extended using syntax macros. Appendix A.1 contains the details of how such an extension mechanism can be incorporated into a language.

3.1.7. Prove that the domain and range of any syntax-directed translation are context-free languages.

3.1.8. Let $L \subseteq \Sigma^*$ be a CFL and $R \subseteq \Sigma^*$ a regular set. Construct an SDTS T such that

$$\tau(T) = \{(x, y) \,|\, \text{if } x \in L - R, \text{ then } y = 0$$
$$\text{if } x \in L \cap R, \text{ then } y = 1\}$$

*3.1.9. Construct an SDTS T such that

$$\tau(T) = \{(x, y) \,|\, x \in \{a, b\}^* \text{ and } y = c^i, \text{ where}$$
$$i = |\#_a(x) - \#_b(x)|, \text{ where } \#_d(x) \text{ is}$$
$$\text{the number of } d\text{'s in } x\}$$

*3.1.10. Show that if L is a regular set and M is a finite transducer, then $M(L)$ and $M^{-1}(L)$ are regular.

*3.1.11. Show that if L is a CFL and M is a finite transducer, then $M(L)$ and $M^{-1}(L)$ are CFL's.

*3.1.12. Let R be a regular set. Construct a finite transducer M such that $M(L) = L/R$ for any language L. With Exercise 3.1.11, this implies that the regular sets and CFL's are closed under $/R$.

*3.1.13. Let R be a regular set. Construct a finite transducer M such that $M(L) = R/L$ for any language L.

3.1.14. An SDTS $T = (N, \Sigma, \Delta, R, S)$ is *right-linear* if each rule in R is of the form

$$A \longrightarrow xB, yB$$

or

$$A \longrightarrow x, y$$

where A, B are in N, $x \in \Sigma^*$, and $y \in \Delta^*$. Show that if T is right-linear, then $\tau(T)$ is a regular translation.

**3.1.15. Show that if $T \subseteq a^* \times b^*$ is an SDT, then T can be defined by a finite transducer.

3.1.16. Let us consider the class of prefix expressions over operators Θ and operands Σ. If $a_1 \cdots a_n$ is a sequence in $(\Theta \cup \Sigma)^*$, compute s_i, the *score* at position i, $0 \leq i \leq n$, as follows:

(1) $s_0 = 1$.
(2) If a_i is an m-ary operator, let $s_i = s_{i-1} + m - 1$.
(3) If $a_i \in \Sigma$, let $s_i = s_{i-1} - 1$.

Prove that $a_1 \cdots a_n$ is a prefix expression if and only if $s_n = 0$ and $s_i > 0$ for all $i < n$.

*3.1.17. Let $a_1 \cdots a_n$ be a prefix expression in which a_1 is an m-ary operator. Prove that the unique way to write $a_1 \cdots a_n$ as $a_1 w_1 \cdots w_m$, where $w_1, \ldots, w_m$ are prefix expressions, is to choose w_j, $1 \leq j \leq m$, so that it ends with the first a_k such that $s_k = m - j$.

*3.1.18. Show that every prefix expression with binary operators comes from a unique infix expression with no redundant parentheses.

3.1.19. Restate and prove Exercises 3.1.16–3.1.18 for postfix expressions.

3.1.20. Complete the proof of Theorem 3.1.

*3.1.21. Prove that the order in which step (2) of Algorithm 3.1 is applied to nodes does not affect the resulting tree.

3.1.22. Prove Lemma 3.1.

3.1.23. Give pushdown transducers for the simple SDT's defined by the translation schemata of Examples 3.5 and 3.7.

3.1.24. Construct a grammar for SNOBOL4 statements that reflects the associativity and precedence of operators given in Appendix A.2.

3.1.25. Give an SDTS that defines the (empty store) translation of the following PDT:

$$(\{q, p\}, \{a, b\}, \{Z_0, A, B\}, \{a, b\}, \delta, q, Z_0, \varnothing)$$

where δ is given by

$$\delta(q, a, X) = (q, AX, e), \qquad \text{for all } X = Z_0, A, B$$
$$\delta(q, b, X) = (q, BX, e), \qquad \text{for all } X = Z_0, A, B$$
$$\delta(q, e, A) = (p, A, a)$$
$$\delta(p, a, A) = (p, e, b)$$
$$\delta(p, b, B) = (p, e, b)$$
$$\delta(p, e, Z_0) = (p, e, a)$$

3.1.26. Consider two pushdown transducers connected in series, so the output of the first forms the input of the second. Show that with such a tandem connection, the set of possible output strings of the second PDT can be any recursively enumerable set.

3.1.27. Show that T is a regular translation if and only if there is a linear context-free language L such that $T = \{(x, y) \mid xcy^R \in L\}$, where c is a new symbol.

*3.1.28.** Show that it is undecidable for two regular translations T_1 and T_2 whether $T_1 = T_2$.

Open Problems

3.1.29. Is it decidable whether two deterministic finite transducers are equivalent?

3.1.30. Is it decidable whether two deterministic pushdown transducers are equivalent?

Research Problem

3.1.31. It is known to be undecidable whether two nondeterministic finite transducers are equivalent (Exercise 3.1.28). Thus we cannot "minimize" them in the same sense that we minimized finite automata in Section 3.3.1. However, there are some techniques that can serve to make the number of states smaller. Can you find a useful collection of these? The same can be attempted for PDT's.

BIBLIOGRAPHIC NOTES

The concept of syntax-directed translation has occurred to many people. Irons [1961] and Barnett and Futrelle [1962] were among the first to advocate its use. Finite transducers are similar to the generalized sequential machines introduced by Ginsburg [1962]. Our definitions of syntax-directed translation schema and pushdown transducer along with Theorem 3.2 are similar to those of Lewis and Stearns [1968]. Griffiths [1968] shows that the equivalence problem for nondeterministic finite transducers with no e-outputs is also unsolvable.

3.2. PROPERTIES OF SYNTAX-DIRECTED TRANSLATIONS

In this section we shall examine some of the theoretical properties of syntax-directed translations. We shall also characterize those translations which can be defined as simple syntax-directed translations.

3.2.1. Characterizing Languages

DEFINITION

We say that language L *characterizes* a translation T if there exist two homomorphisms h_1 and h_2 such that $T = \{(h_1(w), h_2(w)) \mid w \in L\}$.

Example 3.14

The translation $T = \{(a^n, a^n) \mid n \geq 1\}$ is characterized by 0^+, since $T = \{(h_1(w), h_2(w)) \mid w \in 0^+\}$, where $h_1(0) = h_2(0) = a$. □

We say that a language $L \subseteq (\Sigma \cup \Delta')^*$ *strongly characterizes* a translation $T \subseteq \Sigma^* \times \Delta^*$ if

(1) $\Sigma \cap \Delta' = \varnothing$.
(2) $T = \{(h_1(w), h_2(w)) \mid w \in L\}$, where
   (a) $h_1(a) = a$ for all a in Σ and $h_1(b) = e$ for all b in Δ'.
   (b) $h_2(a) = e$ for all a in Σ and h_2 is a one-to-one correspondence between Δ' and Δ [i.e., $h_2(b) \in \Delta$ for all b in Δ' and $h_2(b) = h_2(b')$ implies that $b = b'$].

Example 3.15

The translation $T = \{(a^n, a^n) \mid n \geq 1\}$ is strongly characterized by $L_1 = \{a^n b^n \mid n \geq 1\}$. It is also strongly characterized by $L_2 = \{w \mid w$ consists of an equal number of a's and b's$\}$. The homomorphisms in each case are $h_1(a) = a$, $h_1(b) = e$ and $h_2(a) = e$, $h_2(b) = a$. T is not strongly characterized by the language 0^+. □

We can use the concept of a characterizing language to investigate the classes of translations defined by finite transducers and pushdown transducers.

LEMMA 3.4

Let $T = (N, \Sigma, \Delta, R, S)$ be an SDTS in which each rule is of the form $A \longrightarrow aB, bB$ or $A \longrightarrow a, b$ for $a \in \Sigma \cup \{e\}$, $b \in \Delta \cup \{e\}$, and $B \in N$. Then $\tau(T)$ is a regular translation.

Proof. Let M be the finite transducer $(N \cup \{f\}, \Sigma, \Delta, \delta, S, \{f\})$, where f is a new symbol. Define $\delta(A, a)$ to contain (B, b) if $A \longrightarrow aB, bB$ is in R, and to contain (f, b) if $A \longrightarrow a, b$ is in R. Then a straightforward induction on n shows that

$$(S, x, e) \vdash^{n} (A, e, y) \text{ if and only if } (S, S) \overset{n}{\Longrightarrow} (xA, yA)$$

It follows that $(S, x, e) \vdash^{*} (f, e, y)$ if and only if $(S, S) \overset{*}{\Rightarrow} (x, y)$. The details are left for the Exercises. Thus, $\tau(T) = \tau(M)$. $\quad\square$

THEOREM 3.3

T is a regular translation if and only if T is strongly characterized by a regular set.

Proof.

If: Suppose that $L \subseteq (\Sigma \cup \Delta')^*$ is a regular set and that h_1 and h_2 are homomorphisms such that $h_1(a) = a$ for $a \in \Sigma$, $h_1(a) = e$ for $a \in \Delta'$, $h_2(a) = e$ for $a \in \Sigma$, and h_2 is a one-to-one correspondence from Δ' to Δ. Let $T = \{(h_1(w), h_2(w)) \mid w \in L\}$, and let $G = (N, \Sigma \cup \Delta', P, S)$ be a regular grammar such that $L(G) = L$. Then consider the SDTS $U = (N, \Sigma, \Delta, R, S)$, where R is defined as follows:

(1) If $A \longrightarrow aB$ is in P, then $A \longrightarrow h_1(a)B, h_2(a)B$ is in R.
(2) If $A \longrightarrow a$ is in P, then $A \longrightarrow h_1(a), h_2(a)$ is in R.

An elementary induction shows that $(A, A) \overset{n}{\underset{U}{\Rightarrow}} (x, y)$ if and only if $A \overset{n}{\underset{G}{\Rightarrow}} w$, $h_1(w) = x$, and $h_2(w) = y$.

Thus we can conclude that $(S, S) \overset{+}{\underset{U}{\Rightarrow}} (x, y)$ if and only if (x, y) is in T. Hence $\tau(U) = T$. By Lemma 3.4, there is a finite transducer M such that $\tau(M) = T$.

Only if: Suppose that $T \subseteq \Sigma^* \times \Delta^*$ is a regular translation, and that $M = (Q, \Sigma, \Delta, \delta, q_0, F)$ is a finite transducer such that $\tau(M) = T$.

Let $\Delta' = \{a' \mid a \in \Delta\}$ be an alphabet of new symbols. Let $G = (Q, \Sigma \cup \Delta', P, q_0)$ be the right-linear grammar in which P has the following productions:

(1) If $\delta(q, a)$ contains (r, y), then $q \longrightarrow ah(y)r$ is in P, where h is a homomorphism such that $h(a) = a'$ for all a in Δ.
(2) If q is in F, then $q \longrightarrow e$ is in P.

Let h_1 and h_2 be the following homomorphisms:

$$h_1(a) = a \qquad \text{for all } a \text{ in } \Sigma$$
$$h_1(b) = e \qquad \text{for all } b \text{ in } \Delta'$$
$$h_2(a) = e \qquad \text{for all } a \text{ in } \Sigma$$
$$h_2(b') = b \qquad \text{for all } b' \text{ in } \Delta'$$

We can now show by induction on m and n that $(q, x, e) \vdash^{m} (r, e, y)$ for some m if and only if $q \overset{n}{\Rightarrow} wr$ for some n, where $h_1(w) = x$ and $h_2(w) = y$. Thus, $(q_0, x, e) \vdash^{+} (q, e, y)$, with q in F, if and only if $q_0 \overset{+}{\Rightarrow} wq \Rightarrow w$, where $h_1(w) = x$ and $h_2(w) = y$. Hence, $T = \{(h_1(w), h_2(w)) \mid w \in L(G)\}$. Thus, $L(G)$ strongly characterizes T. $\square$

COROLLARY

T is a regular translation if and only if T is characterized by a regular set.

Proof. Strong characterization is a special case of characterization. Thus the "only if" portion is immediate. The "if" portion is a simple generalization of the "if" portion of the theorem. $\square$

In much the same fashion we can show an analogous result for simple syntax-directed translations.

THEOREM 3.4

T is a simple syntax-directed translation if and only if it is strongly characterized by a context-free language.

Proof.
If: Let T be strongly characterized by the language generated by $G_1 = (N, \Sigma \cup \Delta', P, S)$, where h_1 and h_2 are the two homomorphisms involved. Construct a simple SDTS $T_1 = (N, \Sigma, \Delta, R, S)$, where R is defined by:
For each production $A \longrightarrow w_0 B_1 w_1 \cdots B_k w_k$ in P, let

$$A \longrightarrow h_1(w_0)B_1 h_1(w_1) \cdots B_k h_1(w_k), \; h_2(w_0)B_1 h_2(w_1) \cdots B_k h_2(w_k)$$

be a rule in R.
A straightforward induction on n shows that

(1) If $A \overset{n}{\underset{G_1}{\Rightarrow}} w$, then $(A, A) \overset{n}{\underset{T_1}{\Rightarrow}} (h_1(w), h_2(w))$.

(2) If $(A, A) \overset{n}{\underset{T_1}{\Rightarrow}} (x, y)$, then there is some w such that $A \overset{n}{\underset{G_1}{\Rightarrow}} w$, $h_1(w) = x$, and $h_2(w) = y$.

Thus, $\tau(T_1) = T$.
Only if: Let $T = \tau(T_2)$, where $T_2 = (N, \Sigma, \Delta, R, S)$, and let $\Delta' = \{a' \mid a \in \Delta\}$ be an alphabet of new symbols. Construct CFG $G_2 = (N, \Sigma \cup \Delta', P, S)$, where P contains production $A \longrightarrow x_0 y_0' B_1 x_1 y_1' \cdots B_k x_k y_k'$ for each rule $A \longrightarrow x_0 B_1 x_1 \cdots B_k x_k, \; y_0 B_1 y_1 \cdots B_k y_k$ in R; y_i' is y_i with each symbol $a \in \Delta$ replaced by a'. Let h_1 and h_2 be the obvious homomorphisms, $h_1(a) = a$ for $a \in \Sigma$, $h_1(a) = e$ for $a \in \Delta'$, $h_2(a) = e$ for $a \in \Sigma$, and $h_2(a') = a$ for $a \in \Delta$. Again it is elementary to prove by induction that

(1) If $A \underset{G_2}{\overset{n}{\Rightarrow}} w$, then $(A, A) \underset{T_2}{\overset{n}{\Rightarrow}} (h_1(w), h_2(w))$.

(2) If $(A, A) \underset{T_2}{\overset{n}{\Rightarrow}} (x, y)$, then for some w, we have $A \underset{G_2}{\overset{n}{\Rightarrow}} w$, $h_1(w) = x$, and $h_2(w) = y$. $\square$

COROLLARY

A translation is a simple SDT if and only if it is characterized by a context-free language. $\square$

We can use Theorem 3.3 and 3.4 to show that certain translations are not regular translations or not simple SDT's. It is easy to show that the domain and range of every simple SDT is a CFL. But there are simple syntax-directed translations whose domain and range are regular sets but which cannot be specified by any finite transducer or even pushdown transducer.

Example 3.16

Consider the simple SDTS T with rules

$$S \longrightarrow 0S, S0$$
$$S \longrightarrow 1S, S1$$
$$S \longrightarrow e, e$$

$\tau(T) = \{(w, w^R) \mid w \in \{0, 1\}^*\}$. We shall show that $\tau(T)$ is not a regular translation.

Suppose that $\tau(T)$ is a regular translation. Then there is some regular language L which strongly characterizes $\tau(T)$. We can assume without loss of generality that $L \subseteq \{0, 1, a, b\}^*$, and that the two homomorphisms involved are $h_1(0) = 0, h_1(1) = 1, h_1(a) = h_1(b) = e$ and $h_2(0) = h_2(1) = e, h_2(a) = 0, h_2(b) = 1$.

If L is regular, it is accepted by a finite automaton

$$M = (Q, \{0, 1, a, b\}, \delta, q_0, F)$$

with s states for some s. There must be some $z \in L$ such that $h_1(z) = 0^s1^s$ and $h_2(z) = 1^s0^s$. This is because $(0^s1^s, 1^s0^s) \in \tau(T)$. All 0's precede all 1's in z, and all b's precede all a's. Thus the first s symbols of z are only 0's and b's. If we consider the states entered by M when reading the first s symbols of z, we see that these cannot all be different; we can write $z = uvw$ such that $(q_0, z) \overset{*}{\vdash} (q, vw) \overset{+}{\vdash} (q, w) \overset{*}{\vdash} (p, e)$, where $|uv| \leq s, |v| \geq 1$, and $p \in F$. Then $uvvw$ is in L. But $h_1(uvvw) = 0^{s+m}1^s$ and $h_2(uvvw) = 1^{s+n}0^s$, where not both m and n are zero. Thus, $(0^{s+m}1^s, 1^{s+n}0^s) \in \tau(T)$, a contradiction. We conclude that $\tau(T)$ is not a regular translation. $\square$

Example 3.17

Consider the SDTS T with the rules

$$S \longrightarrow A^{(1)}cA^{(2)}, A^{(2)}cA^{(1)}$$

$$A \longrightarrow 0A, 0A$$

$$A \longrightarrow 1A, 1A$$

$$A \longrightarrow e, e$$

Here $\tau(T) = \{(ucv, vcu) \mid u, v \in \{0, 1\}^*\}$. We shall show that $\tau(T)$ is not a simple SDT.

Suppose that L is a CFL which strongly characterizes $\tau(T)$. We can suppose that $\Delta' = \{c', 0', 1'\}$, $L \subseteq (\{0, 1, c\} \cup \Delta')^*$, and that h_1 and h_2 are the obvious homomorphisms. For every u and v in $\{0, 1\}^*$, there is a word z_{uv} in L such that $h_1(z_{uv}) = ucv$ and $h_2(z_{uv}) = vcu$. We consider two cases, depending on whether c precedes or follows c' in certain of the z_{uv}'s.

Case 1: For all u there is some v such that c precedes c' in z_{uv}. Let R be the regular set $\{0, 1, 0', 1'\}^*c\{0, 1, 0', 1'\}^*c'\{0, 1, 0', 1'\}^*$. Then $L \cap R$ is a CFL, since the CFL's are closed under intersection with regular sets. Note that $L \cap R$ is the set of sentences in L in which c precedes c'. Let M be the finite transducer which, until it reads c, transmits 0's and 1's, while skipping over primed symbols. After reading c, M does nothing until it reaches c'. Subsequently, M prints 0 for $0'$ and 1 for $1'$, skipping over 0's and 1's. Then $M(L \cap R)$ is a CFL, since the CFL's are closed under finite transductions, and in this case $M(L \cap R) = \{uu \mid u \in \{0, 1\}^*\}$. The latter is not a CFL by Example 2.41.

Case 2: For some u there is no v such that c precedes c' in z_{uv}. Then for every v there is a u such that c' precedes c in z_{uv}. An argument similar to case 1 shows that if L were a CFL, then $\{vv \mid v \in \{0, 1\}^*\}$ would also be a CFL. We leave this argument for the Exercises.

We conclude that $\tau(T)$ is not strongly characterized by any context-free language and hence is not a simple SDT. $\square$

Let $\mathfrak{I}_r$ denote the class of regular translations, $\mathfrak{I}_s$ the simple SDT's, and $\mathfrak{I}$ the SDT's. From these examples we have the following result.

THEOREM 3.5

$$\mathfrak{I}_r \subsetneqq \mathfrak{I}_s \subsetneqq \mathfrak{I}.$$

Proof. $\mathfrak{I}_s \subseteq \mathfrak{I}$ is by definition. $\mathfrak{I}_r \subseteq \mathfrak{I}_s$ is immediate when one realizes that a finite transducer is a special case of a PDT. Proper inclusion follows from Examples 3.16 and 3.17. $\square$

3.2.2. Properties of Simple SDT's

Using the idea of a characterizing language, we can prove analogs for many of the normal form theorems of Section 2.6. We shall mention two of them here and leave some others for the Exercises. The first is an analog of Chomsky normal form.

THEOREM 3.6

Let T be a simple SDT. Then $T = \tau(T_1)$, where $T_1 = (N, \Sigma, \Delta, R, S)$ is a simple SDTS such that each rule in R is of one of the forms

(1) $A \longrightarrow BC, BC$, where A, B, and C are (not necessarily distinct) members of N, or

(2) $A \longrightarrow a, b$, where exactly one of a and b is e and the other is in Σ or Δ, as appropriate.

(3) $S \longrightarrow e, e$ if (e, e) is in T and S does not appear on the right of any rule.

Proof. Apply the construction of Theorem 3.4 to a grammar in CNF. $\square$

The second is an analog of Greibach normal form.

THEOREM 3.7

Let T be a simple SDT. Then $T = \tau(T_1)$, where $T_1 = (N, \Sigma, \Delta, R, S)$ is a simple SDTS such that each rule in R is of the form $A \longrightarrow a\alpha, b\alpha$, where α is in N^*, exactly one of a and b is e, and the other is in Σ or Δ [with the same exception as case (3) of the previous theorem].

Proof. Apply the construction of Theorem 3.4 to a grammar in GNF. $\square$

We comment that in the previous two theorems we cannot make both a be in Σ and b in Δ at the same time. Then the translation would be length preserving, which is not always the case for an arbitrary SDT.

3.2.3. A Hierarchy of SDT's

The main result of this section is that there is no analog of Chomsky normal form for arbitrary syntax-directed translations. With one exception, each time we increase the number of nonterminals which we allow on the right side of rules of an SDTS, we can define a strictly larger class of SDT's. Some other interesting properties of SDT's are proved along the way.

DEFINITION

Let $T = (N, \Sigma, \Delta, R, S)$ be an SDTS. We say that T is of *order* k if for no rule $A \longrightarrow \alpha, \beta$ in R does α (equivalently β) have more than k instances of nonterminals. We also say that $\tau(T)$ is of order k. Let $\mathfrak{I}_k$ be the class of all SDT's of order k.

Obviously, $\mathfrak{I}_1 \subseteq \mathfrak{I}_2 \subseteq \cdots \subseteq \mathfrak{I}_i \subseteq \cdots$. We shall show that each of these inclusions is proper, except that $\mathfrak{I}_3 = \mathfrak{I}_2$. A sequence of preliminary results is needed.

LEMMA 3.5

$\mathfrak{I}_1 \subsetneqq \mathfrak{I}_2$.

Proof. It is elementary to show that the domain of an SDTS of order 1 is a linear CFL. However, by Theorem 3.6, every simple SDT is of order 2, and every CFL is the domain of some simple SDT (say, the identity translation with that language as domain). Since the linear languages are a proper subset of the CFL's (Exercise 2.6.7), the inclusion of $\mathfrak{I}_1$ in $\mathfrak{I}_2$ is proper. $\quad\square$

There are various normal forms for SDTS's. We claim that it is possible to eliminate useless nonterminals from an SDTS as from a CFG. Also, there is a normal form for SDTS's somewhat similar to CNF. All rules can be put in a form where the right side consists wholly of nonterminals or has no nonterminals.

DEFINITION

A nonterminal A in an SDTS $T = (N, \Sigma, \Delta, R, S)$ is *useless* if either

(1) There exist no $x \in \Sigma^*$ and $y \in \Delta^*$ such that $(A, A) \overset{*}{\Rightarrow} (x, y)$, or
(2) For no α_1 and α_2 in $(N \cup \Sigma)^*$ and β_1 and β_2 in $(N \cup \Delta)^*$ does $(S, S) \overset{*}{\Rightarrow} (\alpha_1 A \alpha_2, \beta_1 A \beta_2)$.

LEMMA 3.6

Every SDT of order k is defined by an SDTS of order k with no useless nonterminals.

Proof. Exercise analogous to Theorem 2.13. $\quad\square$

LEMMA 3.7

Every SDT T of order $k \geq 2$ is defined by an SDTS $T_1 = (N, \Sigma, \Delta, R, S)$, where if $A \longrightarrow \alpha, \beta$ is in R, then either

(1) α and β are in N^*, or
(2) α is in Σ^* and β in Δ^*.

Moreover, T_1 has no useless nonterminals.

Proof. Let $T_2 = (N', \Sigma, \Delta, R', S)$ be an SDTS with no useless nonterminals such that $\tau(T_2) = T$. We construct R from R' as follows. Let $A \longrightarrow x_0 B_1 x_1 \cdots B_k x_k, y_0 C_1 y_1 \cdots C_k y_k$ be a rule in R', with $k > 0$. Let π be the permutation on the set of integers 1 to k such that the nonterminal B_i is associated with the nonterminal $C_{\pi(i)}$. Introduce new nonterminals $A', D_1, \ldots, D_k$ and $E_0, \ldots, E_k$, and replace the rule by

$$A \longrightarrow E_0 A', E_0 A'$$
$$E_0 \longrightarrow x_0, y_0$$
$$A' \longrightarrow D_1 \cdots D_k, D'_1 \cdots D'_k \qquad \text{where } D_i = D'_{\pi(i)} \text{ for } 1 \leq i \leq k$$
$$D_i \longrightarrow B_i E_i, B_i E_i, \qquad\qquad \text{for } 1 \leq i \leq k$$
$$E_i \longrightarrow x_i, y_{\pi(i)} \qquad\qquad\qquad \text{for } 1 \leq i \leq k$$

For example, if the rule is $A \longrightarrow x_0 B_1 x_1 B_2 x_2 B_3 x_3, y_0 B_3 y_1 B_1 y_2 B_2 y_3$, then $\pi = (2, 3, 1)$. We would replace this rule by

$$A \longrightarrow E_0 A', E_0 A'$$
$$E_0 \longrightarrow x_0, y_0$$
$$A' \longrightarrow D_1 D_2 D_3, D_3 D_1 D_2$$
$$D_i \longrightarrow B_i E_i, B_i E_i, \qquad \text{for } i = 1, 2, 3$$
$$E_1 \longrightarrow x_1, y_2$$
$$E_2 \longrightarrow x_2, y_3$$
$$E_3 \longrightarrow x_3, y_1$$

Since each D_i and E_i has only one rule, it is easy to see that the effect of all these new rules is exactly the same as the rule they replace. Rules in R' with no nonterminals on the right are placed directly in R. Let N be N' together with the new nonterminals. Then $\tau(T_2) = \tau(T_1)$ and T_2 satisfies the conditions of the lemma. $\square$

LEMMA 3.8

$\mathfrak{I}_2 = \mathfrak{I}_3$.

Proof. It suffices, by Lemma 3.7, to show how a rule of the form $A \rightarrow B_1 B_2 B_3, C_1 C_2 C_3$ can be replaced by two rules with two nonterminals in each component of the right side. Let π be the permutation such that B_i is associated with $C_{\pi(i)}$. There are six possible values for π. In each case, we can introduce a new nonterminal D and replace the rule in question by two rules as shown in Fig. 3.6.

$\pi(1)$	$\pi(2)$	$\pi(3)$	Rules	
1	2	3	$A \longrightarrow B_1 D, B_1 D$	$D \longrightarrow B_2 B_3, B_2 B_3$
1	3	2	$A \longrightarrow B_1 D, B_1 D$	$D \longrightarrow B_2 B_3, B_3 B_2$
2	1	3	$A \longrightarrow DB_3, DB_3$	$D \longrightarrow B_1 B_2, B_2 B_1$
2	3	1	$A \longrightarrow DB_3, B_3 D$	$D \longrightarrow B_1 B_2, B_1 B_2$
3	1	2	$A \longrightarrow B_1 D, DB_1$	$D \longrightarrow B_2 B_3, B_2 B_3$
3	2	1	$A \longrightarrow B_1 D, DB_1$	$D \longrightarrow B_2 B_3, B_3 B_2$

Fig. 3.6 New rules.

It is straightforward to check that the effect of the new rules is the same as the old in each case. $\square$

LEMMA 3.9

Every SDT of order $k \geq 2$ has an SDTS $T = (N, \Sigma, \Delta, R, S)$ satisfying Lemma 3.7, and the following:

(1) There is no rule of the form $A \rightarrow B, B$ in R.

(2) There is no rule of the form $A \rightarrow e, e$ in R (unless $A = S$, and then S does not appear on the right side of any rule).

Proof. Exercise analogous to Theorems 2.14 and 2.15. $\square$

We shall now define a family of translations T_k for $k \geq 4$ such that T_k is of order k but not of order $k - 1$. Subsequent lemmas will prove this.

DEFINITION

Let $k \geq 4$. Define Σ_k, for the remainder of this section only, to be $\{a_1, \ldots, a_k\}$. Define the permutation π_k, for k even, by

$$\pi_k(i) = \begin{cases} \dfrac{k + i + 1}{2}, & \text{if } i \text{ is odd} \\[2mm] \dfrac{i}{2}, & \text{if } i \text{ is even} \end{cases}$$

Thus, π_4 is [3, 1, 4, 2] and π_6 is [4, 1, 5, 2, 6, 3]. Define π_k for k odd by

$$\pi_k(i) = \begin{cases} \dfrac{k + 1}{2}, & \text{if } i = 1 \\[2mm] k - \dfrac{i}{2} + 1, & \text{if } i \text{ is even} \\[2mm] \dfrac{i - 1}{2}, & \text{if } i \text{ is odd and } i \neq 1 \end{cases}$$

Thus, $\pi_5 = [3, 5, 1, 4, 2]$ and $\pi_7 = [4, 7, 1, 6, 2, 5, 3]$.

Let T_k be the one-to-one correspondence which takes

$$a_1^{i_1} a_2^{i_2} \cdots a_k^{i_k} \quad \text{to} \quad a_{\pi(1)}^{i_{\pi(1)}} a_{\pi(2)}^{i_{\pi(2)}} \cdots a_{\pi(k)}^{i_{\pi(k)}}$$

For example, if $a_1, a_2, a_3,$ and a_4 are called $a, b, c,$ and d, then

$$T_4 = \{(a^i b^j c^k d^l, c^k a^i d^l b^j) \mid i, j, k, l \geq 0\}$$

In what follows, we shall assume that k is a fixed integer, $k \geq 4$, and that there is some SDTS $T = (N, \Sigma_k, \Sigma_k, R, S)$ of order $k - 1$ which defines

T_k. We assume without loss of generality that T satisfies Lemma 3.9, and hence Lemmas 3.6 and 3.7. We shall prove, by contradiction, that T cannot exist.

DEFINITION

Let Σ be a subset of Σ_k and $A \in N$. (Recall that we are referring to the hypothetical SDTS T.) We say that Σ is (A, d)-*bounded in the domain* (alt. *range*) if for every (x, y) such that $(A, A) \overset{*}{\underset{T}{\Rightarrow}} (x, y)$, there is some $a \in \Sigma$ such that x (alt. y) has no more than d occurrences of a. If Σ is not (A, d)-bounded in the domain (alt. range) for any d, we say that A *covers* Σ *in the domain* (alt. *range*).

LEMMA 3.10

If A covers Σ in the domain, then it covers Σ in the range, and conversely.

Proof. Suppose that A covers Σ in the domain, but that Σ is (A, d)-bounded in the range. By Lemma 3.6, there exist w_1, w_2, w_3, and w_4 in Σ_k^* such that $(S, S) \overset{*}{\Rightarrow} (w_1 A w_2, w_3 A w_4)$. Let $m = |w_3 w_4|$. Since A covers Σ in the domain, there exist w_5 and w_6 in Σ_k^* such that $(A, A) \overset{*}{\Rightarrow} (w_5, w_6)$, and for all $a \in \Sigma$, w_5 has more than $m + d$ occurrences of a. However, since Σ is (A, d)-bounded in the range, there is some $b \in \Sigma$ such that w_6 has no more than d occurrences of b. But $(w_1 w_5 w_2, w_3 w_6 w_4)$ would be a member of T_k under these circumstances, although $w_1 w_5 w_2$ has more than $m + d$ occurrences of b and $w_3 w_6 w_4$ has no more than $m + d$ occurrences of b.

By contradiction, we see that if Σ is covered by A in the domain, then it is also covered by A in the range. The converse is proved by a symmetric argument.   ☐

As a consequence of Lemma 3.10, we are entitled to say that A *covers* Σ without mentioning domain or range.

LEMMA 3.11

Let A cover Σ_k. Then there is a rule $A \rightarrow B_1 \cdots B_m, C_1 \cdots C_m$ in R, and sets $\Theta_1, \ldots, \Theta_m$, whose union is Σ_k, such that B_i covers Θ_i, for $1 \leq i \leq m$.

Proof. Let d_0 be the largest finite integer such that for some $\Sigma \subseteq \Sigma_k$ and B_i, $1 \leq i \leq m$, Σ is (B_i, d_0)-bounded but not $(B_i, d_0 - 1)$-bounded. Clearly, d_0 exists. Define $d_1 = d_0(k - 1) + 1$. There must exist strings x and y in Σ_k^* such that $(A, A) \overset{*}{\Rightarrow} (x, y)$, and for all $a \in \Sigma_k$, x and y each have at least d_1 occurrences of a, for otherwise Σ_k would be (A, d_1)-bounded.

Let the first step of the derivation $(A, A) \overset{*}{\Rightarrow} (x, y)$ be $(A, A) \Rightarrow (B_1 \cdots B_m, C_1 \cdots C_m)$. Since T is assumed to be of order $k - 1$, we have $m \leq k - 1$. We can write $x = x_1 \cdots x_m$ so that $(B_i, B_i) \overset{*}{\Rightarrow} (x_i, y_i)$ for some y_i.

If a is an arbitrary element of Σ_k, it is not possible that none of x_i has more than d_0 occurrences of a, because then x would have no more than $d_0(k-1)$ $= d_1 - 1$ occurrences of a. Let Θ_i be the subset of Σ_k such that x_i has more than d_0 occurrences of all and only those members of Θ_i. By the foregoing, $\Theta_1 \cup \Theta_2 \cup \cdots \cup \Theta_m = \Sigma_k$. We claim that B_i covers Θ_i for each i. For if not, then Θ_i is (B_i, d)-bounded for some $d > d_0$. By our choice of d_0, this is impossible. $\square$

DEFINITION

Let a_i, a_j, and a_l be distinct members of Σ_k. We say that a_j is *between* a_i and a_l if either

(1) $i < j < l$, or
(2) $\pi_k(i) < \pi_k(j) < \pi_k(l)$.

Thus a symbol is formally between two others if it appears physically between them either in the domain or range of T_k.

LEMMA 3.12

Let A cover Σ_k, and let $A \rightarrow B_1 \cdots B_m$, $C_1 \cdots C_m$ be a rule satisfying Lemma 3.11. If B_i covers $\{a_r\}$ and also covers $\{a_s\}$, and a_t is between a_r and a_s, then B_i covers $\{a_t\}$, and for no $j \neq i$ does B_j cover $\{a_t\}$.

Proof. Let us suppose that $r < t < s$. Suppose that B_j covers $\{a_t\}$, $j \neq i$. There are two cases to consider, depending on whether $j < i$ or $j > i$.

Case 1: $j < i$. Since in the underlying grammar of T, B_i derives a string with a_r in it and B_j derives a string with a_t in it, we have $(A, A) \overset{*}{\Rightarrow} (x, y)$, where x has an instance of a_t preceding an instance of a_r. Then by Lemma 3.6, there exists such a sentence in the domain of T_k, which we know not to be the case.

Case 2: $j > i$. Allow B_i to derive a sentence with a_s in it, and we can similarly find a sentence in the domain of T_k with a_s preceding a_t.

By contradiction, we rule out the possibility that $r < t < s$. The only other possibility, that $\pi_k(r) < \pi_k(t) < \pi_k(s)$, is handled similarly, reasoning about the range of T_k. Thus no B_j, $j \neq i$, covers $\{a_t\}$. If B_j covers Σ, where $a_t \in \Sigma$, then B_j certainly covers $\{a_t\}$. Thus by Lemma 3.11, B_i covers some set containing a_t, and hence covers $\{a_t\}$. $\square$

LEMMA 3.13

If A covers Σ_k, $k \geq 4$, then there is some rule $A \rightarrow B_1 \cdots B_m$, $C_1 \cdots C_m$ and some i, $1 \leq i \leq m$, such that B_i covers Σ_k.

Proof. We shall do the case in which k is even. The case of odd k is similar and will be left for the Exercises. Let $A \rightarrow B_1 \cdots B_m$, $C_1 \cdots C_m$ be a rule satisfying Lemma 3.11. Since $m \leq k - 1$ by hypothesis about T, there must be some B_i which covers two members of Σ_k, say B_i covers $\{a_r, a_s\}$, $r \neq s$. Hence, B_i covers $\{a_r\}$ and $\{a_s\}$, and by Lemma 3.12, if a_t is between a_r and a_s, then B_i covers $\{a_t\}$ and no C_j, $j \neq i$, covers $\{a_t\}$.

If we consider the range of T_k, we see that, should B_i cover $\{a_{k/2}\}$ and $\{a_{k/2+1}\}$, then it covers $\{a\}$ for all $a \in \Sigma_k$, and no other B_j covers any $\{a\}$. It will follow by Lemma 3.11 that B_i covers Σ_k. Reasoning further, if B_i covers $\{a_m\}$ and $\{a_n\}$, where $m \leq k/2$ and $n > k/2$, then consideration of the domain assures us that B_i covers $\{a_{k/2}\}$ and $\{a_{k/2+1}\}$.

Thus, if one of r and s is equal to or less than $k/2$, while the other is greater than $k/2$, the desired result is immediate.

The other cases are that $r \leq k/2$ and $s \leq k/2$ or $r > k/2$, $s > k/2$. But in the range, any distinct r and s, both equal to or less than $k/2$, have some a_t, $t > k/2$, between them. Likewise, if $r > k/2$ and $s > k/2$, we find some a_t, $t \leq k/2$, between them. The lemma thus follows in any case. $\square$

LEMMA 3.14

T_k is in $\mathfrak{I}_k - \mathfrak{I}_{k-1}$, for $k \geq 4$.

Proof. Clearly, T_k is in $\mathfrak{I}_k$. It suffices to show that T, the hypothetical SDTS of order $k - 1$, does not exist. Since S certainly covers Σ_k, by Lemma 3.13 we can find a sequence of nonterminals $A_0, A_1, \ldots, A_{\#N}$ in N, where $A_0 = S$ and for $0 \leq i < \#N$, there is a rule $A_i \rightarrow \alpha_i A_{i+1} \beta_i, \gamma_i A_{i+1} \delta_i$. Moreover, for all i, A_i covers Σ_k. Not all the A's can be distinct, so we can find i and j, with $i < j$ and $A_i = A_j$. By Lemma 3.6, we can find $w_1, \ldots, w_{10}$ so that for all $p \geq 0$,

$$(S, S) \overset{*}{\Longrightarrow} (w_1 A_i w_2, w_3 A_i w_4)$$
$$\overset{*}{\Longrightarrow} (w_1 w_5 A_i w_6 w_2, w_3 w_7 A_i w_8 w_4)$$
$$\vdots$$
$$\overset{*}{\Longrightarrow} (w_1 w_5^p A_i w_6^p w_2, w_3 w_7^p A_i w_8^p w_4)$$
$$\overset{*}{\Longrightarrow} (w_1 w_5^p w_9 w_6^p w_2, w_3 w_7^p w_{10} w_8^p w_4).$$

By Lemma 3.9(1) we can assume that not all of α_i, β_i, γ_i, and δ_i are e, and by Lemma 3.9(2) that not all of w_5, w_6, w_7, and w_8 are e.

For each $a \in \Sigma_k$, it must be that $w_5 w_6$ and $w_7 w_8$ have the same number of occurrences of a, or else there would be a pair in $\tau(T)$ not in T_k. Since A_i covers Σ_k, should w_5, w_6, w_7, and w_8 have any symbol but a_1 or a_k, we could easily choose w_9 to obtain a pair not in T_k. Hence there is an occurrence of a_1 or a_k in w_7 or w_8. Since A_i covers Σ_k again, we could choose w_{10} to yield a pair not in T_k. We conclude that T does not exist, and that T_k is not in $\mathfrak{I}_{k-1}$. $\square$

THEOREM 3.8

With the exception of $k = 2$, $\mathfrak{I}_k$ is properly contained in $\mathfrak{I}_{k+1}$ for $k \geq 1$.

Proof. The case $k = 1$ is Lemma 3.5. The other cases are Lemma 3.14.

□

An interesting practical consequence of Theorem 3.8 is that while it may be attractive to build a compiler writing system that assumes the underlying grammar to be in Chomsky normal form, such a system is not capable of performing any syntax-directed translation of which a more general system is capable. However, it is likely that a practically motivated SDT would at worst be in $\mathfrak{I}_3$ (and hence in $\mathfrak{I}_2$).

EXERCISES

*3.2.1. Let T be a SDT. Show that there is a constant c such that for each x in the domain of T, there exists y such that $(x, y) \in T$ and $|y| \leq c(|x| + 1)$.

*3.2.2   (a) Show that if T_1 is a regular translation and T_2 is an SDT, then
$T_1 \circ T_2 = \{(x, z) \,|\, \text{for some } y, (x, y) \in T_1 \text{ and } (y, z) \in T_2\}$ is an SDT.†
         (b) Show that $T_1 \circ T_2$ is simple if T_2 is.

3.2.3   (a) Show that if T is an SDT, then T^{-1} is an SDT.
         (b) Show that T^{-1} is simple if T is.

*3.2.4   (a) Let T_1 be a regular translation and T_2 an SDT. Show that $T_2 \circ T_1$ is an SDT.
         (b) Show that $T_2 \circ T_1$ is simple if T_2 is.

3.2.5.   Give strong characterizing languages for
         (a) The SDT Example 3.5.
         (b) The SDT of Example 3.7.
         (c) The SDT of Example 3.12

3.2.6.   Give characterizing languages for the SDT's of Exercise 3.2.5 which do not strongly characterize them.

3.2.7.   Complete the proof of Lemma 3.4.

3.2.8.   Complete case 2 of Example 3.17.

3.2.9.   Show that every simple SDT is defined by a simple SDTS with no useless nonterminals.

3.2.10. Let T_1 be a simple SDT and T_2 a regular translation. Is $T_1 \cap T_2$ always a simple SDT?

3.2.11. Prove Lemma 3.6.

---

†Often, this operation on translations, called *composition*, is written with the operands in the opposite order. That is, our definition above would be for $T_2 \circ T_1$, not $T_1 \circ T_2$. We shall not change to the definition given here, for the sake of natural appearance.

3.2.12. Prove Lemma 3.9.

3.2.13. Give an SDTS of order k for T_k.

3.2.14. Let $T = (N, \Sigma, \Sigma, R, S)$, where $N = \{S, A, B, C, D\}$, $\Sigma = \{a, b, c, d\}$, and R has the rules

$$A \longrightarrow aA, aA$$
$$A \longrightarrow e, e$$
$$B \longrightarrow bB, bB$$
$$B \longrightarrow e, e$$
$$C \longrightarrow cC, cC$$
$$C \longrightarrow e, e$$
$$D \longrightarrow dD, dD$$
$$D \longrightarrow e, e$$

and one other rule. Give the minimum order of $\tau(T)$ if that additional rule is
(a) $S \longrightarrow ABCD, ABCD$.
(b) $S \longrightarrow ABCD, BCDA$.
(c) $S \longrightarrow ABCD, DBCA$.
(d) $S \longrightarrow ABCD, BDAC$.

3.2.15. Show that if T is defined by a DPDT, then T is strongly characterized by a deterministic context-free language.

3.2.16. Is the converse of Exercise 3.2.15 true?

3.2.17. Prove the corollaries to Theorems 3.3 and 3.4.

BIBLIOGRAPHIC NOTES

The concept of a characterizing language and the results of Sections 3.2.1 and 3.2.2 are from Aho and Ullman [1969b]. The results of Section 3.2.3 are from Aho and Ullman [1969a].

3.3. LEXICAL ANALYSIS

Lexical analysis is the first phase of the compiling process. In this phase, characters from the source program are read and collected into single logical items called tokens. Lexical analysis is important in compilation for several reasons. Perhaps most significant, replacing identifiers and constants in a program by single tokens makes the representation of a program much more convenient for later processing. Lexical analysis further reduces the length of the representation of the program by removing irrelevant blanks and comments from the representation of the source program. During subsequent stages of compilation, the compiler may make several passes over the internal representation of the program. Consequently, reducing the length of this representation by lexical analysis can reduce the overall compilation time.

In many situations the constructs we choose to isolate as tokens are somewhat arbitrary. For example, if a language allows complex number constants of the form

$$\langle \text{complex constant} \rangle \longrightarrow (\langle \text{real} \rangle, \langle \text{real} \rangle)$$

then two strategies are possible. We can treat $\langle \text{real} \rangle$ as a lexical item and defer recognition of the construct $(\langle \text{real} \rangle, \langle \text{real} \rangle)$ as complex constant until syntactic analysis. Alternatively, utilizing a more complicated lexical analyzer, we might recognize the construct $(\langle \text{real} \rangle, \langle \text{real} \rangle)$ as a complex constant at the lexical level and pass the token identifier to the syntax analyzer. It is also important to note that the variations in the terminal character set local to one computer center can be confined to the lexical level.

Much of the activity that occurs during lexical analysis can be modeled by finite transducers acting in series or parallel. As an example, we might have a series of finite transducers constituting the lexical analyzer. The first transducer in this chain might remove all irrelevant blanks from the source program, the second might suppress all comments, the third might search for constants, and so forth. Another possibility might be to have a collection of finite transducers, one of which would be activated to look for a certain lexical construct.

In this section we shall discuss techniques which can be used in the construction of efficient lexical analyzers. As mentioned in Section 1.2.1, there are essentially two kinds of lexical analyzers—direct and indirect. We shall discuss how to design both from the regular expressions that describe the tokens involved.

3.3.1. An Extended Language for Regular Expressions

The sets of allowable character strings that form the identifiers and other tokens of programming languages are almost invariably regular sets. For example, FORTRAN identifiers are described by "from one to six letters or digits, beginning with a letter." This set is clearly regular and has the regular expression

$$(A + \cdots + Z)(e + (A + \cdots + Z + 0 + \cdots + 9)$$
$$(e + (A + \cdots + Z + 0 + \cdots + 9)(e + (A + \cdots + Z + 0 + \cdots + 9)$$
$$(e + (A + \cdots + Z + 0 + \cdots + 9)(e + A + \cdots + Z + 0 + \cdots + 9)))))$$

Since the above expression is cumbersome, it would be wise to introduce extended regular expressions that would describe this and other regular expressions of practical interest conveniently.

DEFINITION

An *extended regular expression* and the regular set it *denotes* are defined recursively as follows:

(1) If R is a regular expression, then it is an extended regular expression and denotes itself.†

(2) If R is an extended regular expression, then
   (a) R^+ is an extended regular expression and denotes RR^*.
   (b) R^{*n} is an extended regular expression, and denotes

$$\{e\} \cup R \cup RR \cup \cdots \cup R^n.$$

   (c) R^{+n} is an extended regular expression and denotes

$$R \cup RR \cup \cdots \cup R^n.$$

(3) If R_1 and R_2 are extended regular expressions, then $R_1 \cap R_2$ and $R_1 - R_2$ are extended regular expressions and denote $\{x \mid x \in R_1 \text{ and } x \in R_2\}$ and $\{x \mid x \in R_1 \text{ and } x \notin R_2\}$, respectively.

(4) Nothing else is an extended regular expression.

CONVENTION

We shall use $|$ in extended regular expressions in place of the binary $+$ operator (union) to make the distinction between the latter operator and the unary $+$ and $+n$ operators more apparent.

Another useful facility when defining regular sets is the ability to give names to regular sets. We must be careful not to make such definitions circular, or we have essentially a system of defining equations, similar to that in Section 2.6, capable of defining any context-free language. There is, in principle, nothing wrong with using the power of defining equations to make our definitions of tokens (or using a pushdown transducer to recognize tokens). However, as a general rule, the lexical analyzer has simple structure, normally that of a finite automaton. Thus we prefer to use a definition mechanism that can define only regular sets and from which finite transducers can be readily constructed. The inherently context-free portions of a language are analyzed during the parsing phase, which is considerably more complex than the lexical phase.

DEFINITION

A *sequence of regular definitions* over alphabet Σ is a list of definitions $A_1 = R_1, A_2 = R_2, \ldots, A_n = R_n$, where $A_1, \ldots, A_n$ are distinct symbols

†Recall that we do not distinguish between a regular expression and the set it denotes if the distinction is clear.

not in Σ and for $1 \leq i \leq n$, R_i is an extended regular expression over $\Sigma \cup \{A_1, \ldots, A_{i-1}\}$. We define R'_i, for $1 \leq i \leq n$, an extended regular expression over Σ, recursively as follows:

(1) $R'_1 = R_1$.
(2) R'_i is R_i with R'_j substituted for each instance of A_j, $1 \leq j < i$.

The set denoted by A_i is the set denoted by R'_i.

It should be clear that the sets denoted by extended regular expressions and sequences of regular definitions are regular. A proof is requested in the Exercises.

Example 3.18

We can specify the FORTRAN identifiers by the following sequence of regular definitions:

$$\langle \text{letter} \rangle = A \,|\, B \,|\, \cdots \,|\, Z$$
$$\langle \text{digit} \rangle = 0 \,|\, 1 \,|\, \cdots \,|\, 9$$
$$\langle \text{identifier} \rangle = \langle \text{letter} \rangle (\langle \text{letter} \rangle \,|\, \langle \text{digit} \rangle)^{*\,5}$$

If we did not wish to allow the keywords of FORTRAN to be used as identifiers, then we could revise the definition of $\langle \text{identifier} \rangle$ to exclude those strings. Then the last definition should read

$$\langle \text{identifier} \rangle = (\langle \text{letter} \rangle (\langle \text{letter} \rangle \,|\, \langle \text{digit} \rangle)^{*\,5}) - (\text{DO} \,|\, \text{IF} \,|\, \cdots) \quad \square$$

Example 3.19

We can define the usual real constants such as 3.14159, -682, or $6.6\text{E} - 29$, by the following sequence of regular definitions†:

$$\langle \text{digit} \rangle = 0 \,|\, 1 \,|\, \cdots \,|\, 9$$
$$\langle \text{sign} \rangle = + \,|\, - \,|\, e$$
$$\langle \text{integer} \rangle = \langle \text{sign} \rangle \langle \text{digit} \rangle^+$$
$$\langle \text{decimal} \rangle = \langle \text{sign} \rangle (\langle \text{digit} \rangle^* \cdot \langle \text{digit} \rangle^+ \,|\, \langle \text{digit} \rangle^+ \cdot \langle \text{digit} \rangle^*)$$
$$\langle \text{constant} \rangle = \langle \text{integer} \rangle \,|\, \langle \text{decimal} \rangle \,|\, \langle \text{decimal} \rangle \text{E} \langle \text{integer} \rangle \quad \square$$

3.3.2. Indirect Lexical Analysis

In indirect lexical analysis, we are expected to determine, scanning a string of characters, whether a substring forming a particular token appears. If the set of possible strings of characters which can form this token is denoted by a regular set, as it usually can be, then the problem of building an indirect lexical analyzer for this token can be thought of as a problem in the imple-

---

†A specific implementation of a language would usually impose a restriction on the length of a constant.

mentation of a finite transducer. The finite transducer is almost a finite automaton in that it looks at the input without producing any output until it has determined that a token of the given type is present (i.e., reaches a final state). It then signals that this token has appeared, and the output is the string of symbols constituting the token.

Obviously, the final state is itself an indication. However, a lexical analyzer may have to examine one or more symbols beyond the right end of the token. A simple example is that we cannot determine the right end of an ALGOL identifier until we encounter a symbol that is neither a letter nor a digit—symbols normally not considered part of the identifier.

In indirect lexical analysis it is possible to accept an output from the lexical analyzer which says that a certain token might appear, and if we later discover that this token does not appear, then backtracking of the parsing algorithm will ensure that the analyzer for the correct token is eventually set to work on the same string. Using indirect lexical analysis we must be careful that we do not perform any erroneous bookkeeping operations. Normally, we should not enter an identifier in the symbol table until we are sure that it is a valid identifier. (Alternatively, we can provide a mechanism for deleting entries from tables.)

The problem of indirect lexical analysis is thus essentially the problem of constructing a deterministic finite automaton from a regular expression and its implementation in software. The results of Chapter 2 convince us that the construction is possible, although much work is involved. It turns out that it is not hard to go directly from a regular expression to a nondeterministic finite automaton. We can then use Theorem 2.3 to convert to a deterministic one or we can simulate the nondeterministic finite automaton by keeping track of all possible move sequences in parallel. In direct lexical analysis as well, it is convenient to begin the design of a direct lexical analyzer with concise nondeterministic finite automata for each of the tokens.

The nondeterministic finite automaton can be constructed by an algorithm similar to the one by which right-linear grammars were constructed from regular expressions in Section 2.2. It is rather tricky to extend the construction of nondeterministic automata to all the extended regular expressions directly, especially since the $\cap$ and $-$ operations imply constructions on deterministic automata. (It is very difficult to prove that $R_1 \cap R_2$ or $R_1 - R_2$ are regular if R_1 and R_2 are defined by nondeterministic automata without somehow making reference to deterministic automata. On the other hand, proofs of closure under $\cup$, $\cdot$, and $*$ need no reference to deterministic automata.) However, the operators $^+$, $^{+n}$, and $*^n$ are handled naturally.

ALGORITHM 3.2

Construction of a nondeterministic finite automaton from an extended regular expression.

Input. An extended regular expression R over alphabet Σ, with no instance of symbol $\varnothing$ or operator $\cap$ or $-$.

Output. A nondeterministic finite automaton M such that $T(M) = R$.

Method.

(1) Execute step (2) recursively, beginning with expression R. Let M be the automaton constructed by the first call of that step.

(2) Let R_0 be the extended regular expression to which this step is applied. A nondeterministic finite automaton M_0 is constructed. Several cases occur:

(a) R_0 is the symbol e. Let $M_0 = (\{q\}, \Sigma, \varnothing, q, \{q\})$, where q is a new symbol.

(b) R_0 is symbol a in Σ. Let $M_0 = (\{q_1, q_2\}, \Sigma, \delta_0, q_1, \{q_2\})$, where $\delta_0(q_1, a) = \{q_2\}$ and δ_0 is undefined otherwise; q_1 and q_2 are new symbols.

(c) R_0 is $R_1 | R_2$. Then we can apply step (2) to R_1 and R_2 to yield $M_1 = (Q_1, \Sigma, \delta_1, q_1, F_1)$ and $M_2 = (Q_2, \Sigma, \delta_2, q_2, F_2)$, respectively, where Q_1 and Q_2 are disjoint. Construct $M_0 = (Q_1 \cup Q_2 \cup \{q_0\}, \Sigma, \delta_0, q_0, F_0)$, where

    (i) q_0 is a new symbol.

    (ii) δ_0 includes δ_1 and δ_2, and $\delta_0(q_0, a) = \delta_1(q_1, a) \cup \delta_2(q_2, a)$.

    (iii) F_0 is $F_1 \cup F_2$ if neither $q_1 \in F_1$ nor $q_2 \in F_2$, and $F_0 = F_1 \cup F_2 \cup \{q_0\}$ otherwise.

(d) R_0 is $R_1 R_2$. Apply step (2) to R_1 and R_2 to yield M_1 and M_2 as in case (c). Construct $M_0 = (Q_1 \cup Q_2, \Sigma, \delta_0, q_1, F_0)$, where

    (i) δ_0 includes δ_2; for all $q \in Q$, and $a \in \Sigma$, $\delta_0(q, a) = \delta_1(q, a)$ if $q \notin F$, and $\delta_0(q, a) = \delta_1(q, a) \cup \delta_2(q_2, a)$ otherwise.

    (ii) $F_0 = F_2$ if q_2 is not in F_2 and $F_0 = F_1 \cup F_2$ otherwise.

(e) R_0 is R_1^*. Apply step (2) to R_1 to yield $M_1 = (Q_1, \Sigma, \delta_1, q_1, F_1)$. Construct $M_0 = (Q_1 \cup \{q_0\}, \Sigma, \delta_0, q_0, F_1 \cup \{q_0\})$, where q_0 is a new symbol, and δ_0 is defined by

    (i) $\delta_0(q_0, a) = \delta_1(q_1, a)$.

    (ii) If $q \notin F_1$, then $\delta_0(q, a) = \delta_1(q, a)$.

    (iii) If $q \in F$, then $\delta_0(q, a) = \delta_1(q, a) \cup \delta_1(q_1, a)$.

(f) R_0 is R_1^+. Apply step (2) to R_1 to yield M_1 as in (e). Construct $M_0 = (Q_1, \Sigma, \delta_0, q_1, F_1)$, where $\delta_0(q, a) = \delta_1(q, a)$ if $q \notin F_1$ and $\delta_0(q, a) = \delta_1(q, a) \cup \delta_1(q_1, a)$ if $q \in F_1$.

(g) R_0 is R_1^{*n}. Apply step (2) to R_1 to yield M_1 as in (e). Construct $M_0 = (Q_1 \times \{1, \ldots, n\}, \Sigma, \delta_0, [q_1, 1], F_0)$, where

    (i) If $q \notin F_1$ or $i = n$, then $\delta_0([q, i], a) = \{[p, i] \mid \delta_1(q, a)$ contains $p\}$.

    (ii) If $q \in F_1$ and $i < n$, then $\delta_0([q, i], a) =$

$$\{[p, i] \mid \delta_1(q, a) \text{ contains } p\} \cup \{[p, i+1] \mid \delta_1(q_1, a) \text{ contains } p\}.$$

    (iii) $F_0 = \{[q, i] \mid q \in F_1, 1 \leq i \leq n\} \cup \{[q_1, 1]\}$.

(h) R_0 is R_1^{+n}. Do the same as in step (g), but in part (iii) F_0 is defined as $\{[q, i] \mid q \in F_1, 1 \leq i \leq n\}$ instead. $\square$

THEOREM 3.9

Algorithm 3.2 yields a nondeterministic finite automaton M such that $T(M) = R$.

Proof. Inductive exercise. $\square$

We comment that in parts (g) and (h) of Algorithm 3.2 the second component of the state of M_0 can be implemented efficiently in software as a counter, in many cases, even when the automaton is converted to a deterministic version. This is so because in many cases R_1 has the prefix property, and a word in R_1^{+n} can be broken into words in R_1 trivially. For example, R_1 might be $\langle \text{digit} \rangle$ as in Example 3.18, and all members of $\langle \text{digit} \rangle$ are of length 1.

Example 3.20

Let us develop a nondeterministic automaton for the identifiers defined in Example 3.18. To apply step (2) of Algorithm 3.2 to the expression named $\langle \text{identifier} \rangle$, we must apply it to $\langle \text{letter} \rangle$ and $(\langle \text{letter} \rangle \mid \langle \text{digit} \rangle)^{*5}$. The construction for the former actually involves 26 applications of step (2b) and 25 of step (2c). However, the result is seen to be $(\{q_1, q_2\}, \Sigma, \delta_1, q_1, \{q_2\})$, if obvious state identifications are applied,† $\Sigma = \{A, \ldots, Z, 0, \ldots, 9\}$, and $\delta_1(q_1, A) = \delta_1(q_1, B) = \cdots = \delta_1(q_1, Z) = \{q_2\}$.

To obtain an automaton for $(\langle \text{letter} \rangle \mid \langle \text{digit} \rangle)^{*5}$, we need another automaton for $\langle \text{letter} \rangle$, say $(\{q_3, q_4\}, \Sigma, \delta_2, q_3, \{q_4\})$, and the obvious one for $\langle \text{digit} \rangle$, say $(\{q_5, q_6\}, \Sigma, \delta_3, q_5, \{q_6\})$. To take the union of these, we add a new initial state, q_7, and find that q_3 and q_5 cannot be reached therefrom. Moreover, q_4 and q_6 can clearly be identified. The resulting machine is $(\{q_4, q_7\}, \Sigma, \delta_4, q_7, \{q_4\})$, where

$$\delta_4(q_7, A) = \cdots = \delta_4(q_7, Z) = \delta_4(q_7, 0) = \cdots = \delta_4(q_7, 9) = \{q_4\}.$$

To apply case (g), we construct states $[q_4, i]$ and $[q_7, i]$, for $1 \leq i \leq 5$. The final states are $[q_4, i]$, $1 \leq i \leq 5$, and $[q_7, 1]$. The last is also the initial state. We have a machine $(Q_5, \Sigma, \delta_5, [q_7, 1], F_5)$, where F_5 is as above, and $\delta([q_7, 1], \alpha) = \{[q_4, 1]\}$; $\delta([q_4, i], \alpha) = \{[q_4, i + 1]\}$, for all α in Σ and $i =$

---

†That is, two states of a nondeterministic finite automaton can be identified if both are final or both are nonfinal and on each input they transfer to the same set of states. There are other conditions under which two states of a nondeterministic finite automaton can be identified, but this condition is all that is needed here.

1, 2, 3, 4. Thus states $[q_7, 2], \ldots, [q_7, 5]$ are not accessible and do not have to appear in Q_5. Hence, $Q_5 = F_5$.

To obtain the final automaton for $\langle$identifier$\rangle$ we use case (d). The resulting automaton is

$$M = (\{q_1, q_2, [q_4, 1], \ldots, [q_4, 5]\}, \Sigma, \delta, q_1, \{q_2, [q_4, 1], \ldots, [q_4, 5]\}),$$

where δ is defined by

(1) $\delta(q_1, \alpha) = \{q_2\}$ for all letters α.
(2) $\delta(q_2, \alpha) = \{[q_4, 1]\}$ for all α in Σ.
(3) $\delta([q_4, i], \alpha) = \{[q_4, i + 1]\}$ for all α in Σ and $1 \leq i < 5$.

Note that $[q_7, 1]$ is inaccessible and has been removed from M. Also, M is deterministic here, although it need not be in general.

The transition graph for this machine is shown in Fig. 3.7. □

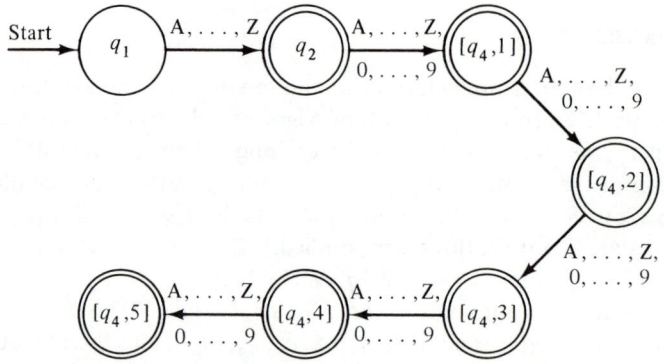

Fig. 3.7 Nondeterministic finite automaton for identifiers.

3.3.3. Direct Lexical Analysis

When the lexical analysis is direct, one must search for one of a large number of tokens. The most efficient way is generally to search for these in parallel, since the search often narrows quite quickly. Thus the model of a direct lexical analyzer is many finite automata operating in parallel, or to be exact, one finite transducer simulating many automata and emitting a signal as to which of the automata has successfully recognized a string.

If we have a set of nondeterministic finite automata to simulate in parallel and their state sets are disjoint, we can merge the state sets and next state functions to create one nondeterministic finite automaton, which may be converted to a deterministic one by Theorem 2.3. (The only nuance is that the initial state of the deterministic automaton is the set of all initial states of the components.) Thus it is more convenient to merge before converting to a deterministic device than the other way round.

The combined deterministic automaton can be considered to be a simple kind of finite transducer. It emits the token name and, perhaps, information that will locate the instance of the token. Each state of the combined automaton represents states from various of the component automata. Apparently, when the combined automaton enters a state which contains a final state of one of the component automata, and no other states, it should stop and emit the name of the token for that component automaton. However, matters are often not that simple.

For example, if an identifier can be any string of characters except for a keyword, it does not make for good practice to define an identifier by the exact regular set, because it is complicated and requires many states. Instead, one uses a simple definition for identifier (Example 3.18 is one such) and leaves it to the combined automaton to make the right decision.

In this case, should the combined automaton enter a state which included a final state for one of the keyword automata and a state of the automaton for identifiers and the next input symbol (perhaps a blank or special sign) indicated the end of the token, the keyword would take priority, and indication that the keyword was found would be emitted.

Example 3.21

Let us consider a somewhat abstract example. Suppose that identifiers are composed of any string of the four symbols D, F, I, and O, followed by a blank (b), except for the keywords DO and IF, which need not be followed by a blank, but may not be followed immediately by any of the letters D, F, I, or O.

The identifiers are recognized by the finite automaton of Fig. 3.8(a), DO by that of Fig. 3.8(b), and IF by Fig. 3.8(c). (All automata here are deterministic, although that need not be true in general, of course.)

The merged automaton is shown in Fig. 3.9. State q_2 indicates that an identifier has been found. However, states $\{q_1, q_8\}$ and $\{q_1, q_5\}$ are ambiguous. They might indicate IF or DO, respectively, or they might just indicate the initial portion of some identifier, such as DOOF. To resolve the conflict, the lexical analyzer must look at an additional character. If a D, O, I, or F follows, we had the prefix of an identifier. If anything else, including a blank, follows (assume that there are more characters than the five mentioned), we enter new states, q_9 or q_{10}, and emit a signal to the effect that DO or IF, respectively, was detected, and that it ends one symbol previously. If we enter q_2, we emit a signal saying that an identifier has been found, ending one symbol previously.

Since it is the output of the device, not the state, that is important, states

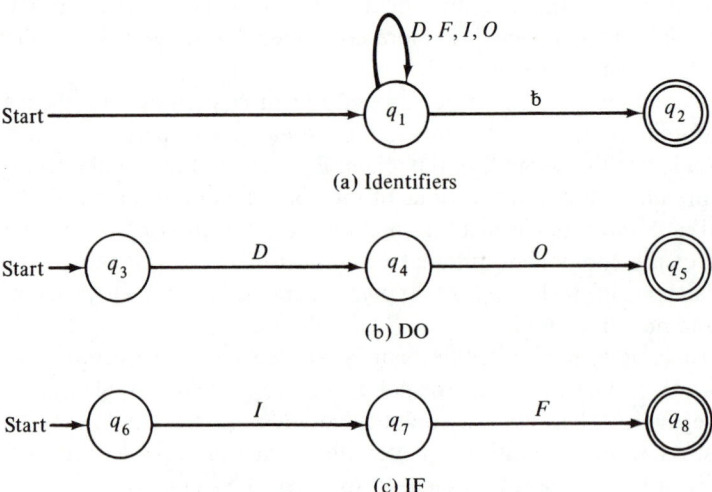

$$D, F, I, O$$

Start $\longrightarrow q_1 \xrightarrow{\text{b}} q_2$

(a) Identifiers

Start $\rightarrow q_3 \xrightarrow{D} q_4 \xrightarrow{O} q_5$

(b) DO

Start $\rightarrow q_6 \xrightarrow{I} q_7 \xrightarrow{F} q_8$

(c) IF

Fig. 3.8 Automata for lexical analysis.

q_2, q_9, and q_{10} can be identified and, in fact, will have no representation at all in the implementation. $\square$

3.3.4. Software Simulation of Finite Transducers

There are several approaches to the simulation of finite automata or transducers. A slow but compact technique is to encode the next move function of the device and execute the encoding interpretively. Since lexical analysis is a major portion of the activity of a translator, this mode of operation is frequently too slow to be acceptable. However, some computers have single instructions that can recognize the kinds of tokens with which we have been dealing. While these instructions cannot simulate an arbitrary finite automaton, they work very well when tokens are either keywords or identifiers.

An alternative approach is to make a piece of program for each state. The function of the program is to determine the next character (a subroutine may be used to locate that character), emit any output required, and transfer to the entry of the program corresponding to the next state.

An important design question is the proper method of determining the next character. If the next state function for the current state were such that most different next characters lead to different next states, there is probably nothing better to do than to transfer indirectly through a table based on the next character. This method is as fast as any, but requires a table whose size is proportional to the number of different characters.

In the typical lexical analyzer, there will be many states such that all but

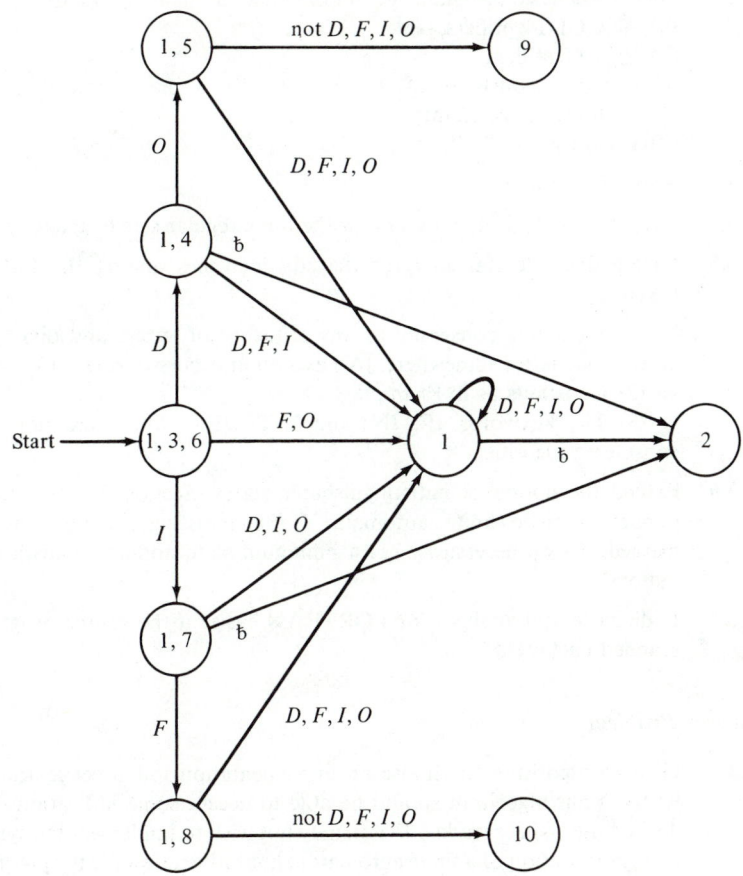

Fig. 3.9 Combined lexical analyzer.†

very few next characters lead to the same state. It may be too expensive of space to allocate a full table for each such state. A reasonable compromise between time and space considerations, for many states, would be to use binary decisions to weed out those few characters that cause a transition to an unusual state.

EXERCISES

3.3.1. Give regular expressions for the following extended regular expressions:
(a) $(a^{+3}b^{+3})^{*2}$.
(b) $(a|b)^* - (ab)^*$.
(c) $(aa|bb)^{*4} \cap a(ab|ba)^+b$.

†Unlike Fig. 3.8(a), Fig. 3.9 does not permit the empty string to be an identifier.

3.3.2. Give a sequence of regular definitions that culminate in the definition of
 (a) ALGOL identifiers.
 (b) PL/I identifiers.
 (c) Complex constants of the form (α, β), where α and β are real FORTRAN constants.
 (d) Comments in PL/I.

3.3.3. Prove Theorem 3.3.

3.3.4. Give indirect lexical analyzers for the three regular sets of Exercise 3.3.2.

3.3.5. Give a direct lexical analyzer that distinguishes among the following tokens:

 (1) Identifiers consisting of any sequence of letters and digits, with at least one letter somewhere. [An exception occurs in rule (3).]
 (2) Constants as in Example 3.19.
 (3) The keywords IF, IN, and INTEGER, which are not to be considered identifiers.

3.3.6. Extend the notion of indistinguishable states (Section 2.3) to apply to nondeterministic finite automata. If all indistinguishable states are merged, do we necessarily get a minimum state nondeterministic automaton?

**3.3.7. Is direct lexical analysis for FORTRAN easier if the source program is scanned backward?

Research Problem

3.3.8. Give an algorithm to choose an implementation for direct lexical analyzers. Your algorithm should be able to accept some indication of the desired time–space trade off. You may not wish to implement the symbol-by-symbol action of a finite automaton, but rather allow for the possibility of other actions. For example, if many of the tokens were arithmetic signs of length 1, and these had to be separated by blanks, as in SNOBOL, it might be wise to separate out these tokens from others as the first move of the lexical analyzer by checking whether the second character was blank.

Programming Exercises

3.3.9. Construct a lexical analyzer for one of the programming languages given in the Appendix. Give consideration to how the lexical analyzer will recover from lexical errors, particularly misspellings.

3.3.10. Devise a programming language based on extended regular expressions. Construct a compiler for this language. The object language program should be an implementation of the lexical analyzer described by the source program.

BIBLIOGRAPHIC NOTES

The AED RWORD (Read a WORD) system was the first major system to use finite state machine techniques in the construction of lexical analyzers. Johnson et al. [1968] provide an overview of this system.

An algorithm that constructs from a regular expression a machine language program that simulates a corresponding nondeterministic finite automaton is given by Thompson [1968]. This algorithm has been used as a pattern-matching mechanism in a powerful text-editing language called QED.

A lexical analyzer should be designed to cope with lexical errors in its input. Some examples of lexical errors are

(1) Substitution of an incorrect symbol for a correct symbol in a token.
(2) Insertion of an extra symbol in a token.
(3) Deletion of a symbol from a token.
(4) Transposition of a pair of adjacent symbols in a token.

Freeman [1964] and Morgan [1970] describe techniques which can be used to detect and recover from errors of this nature. The Bibliographic Notes at the end of Section 1.2 provide additional references to error detection and recovery in compiling.

3.4. PARSING

The second phase of compiling is normally that of parsing or syntax analysis. In this section, formal definitions of two common types of parsing are given, and their capabilities are briefly compared. We shall also discuss what it means for one grammar to "cover" another grammar.

3.4.1. Definition of Parsing

We say that a sentence w in $L(G)$ for some CFG G has been parsed when we know one (or perhaps all) of its derivation trees. In a translator, this tree may be "physically" constructed in the computer memory, but it is more likely that its representation is more subtle. One can deduce the parse tree by watching the steps taken by the syntax analyzer, although the connection would hardly be obvious at first.

Fortunately, most compilers parse by simulating a PDA which is recognizing the input either top-down or bottom-up (see Section 2.5). We shall see that the ability of a PDA to parse top-down is associated with the ability of a PDT to map input strings to their leftmost derivations. Bottom-up parsing is similarly associated with mapping input strings to the reverse of their rightmost derivations. We shall thus treat the parsing problem as that of mapping strings to either leftmost or rightmost derivations. While there are many other parsing strategies, these two definitions serve as the significant benchmarks.

Some other parsing strategies are mentioned in various parts of the book. In the Exercises at the end of Sections 3.4, 4.1, and 5.1 we shall discuss left-corner parsing, a parsing method that is both top-down and bottom-up in nature. In Section 6.2.1 of Chapter 6 we shall discuss generalized top-down and bottom-up parsing.

DEFINITION

Let $G = (N, \Sigma, P, S)$ be a CFG, and suppose that the productions of P are numbered $1, 2, \ldots, p$. Let α be in $(N \cup \Sigma)^*$. Then

(1) A *left parse* of α is a sequence of productions used in a leftmost derivation of α from S.

(2) A *right parse* of α is the reverse of a sequence of productions used in a rightmost derivation of α from S in G.

We can represent these parses by a sequence of numbers from 1 to p.

Example 3.22

Consider the grammar G_0, where the productions are numbered as shown:

$$(1)\ E \longrightarrow E + T$$
$$(2)\ E \longrightarrow T$$
$$(3)\ T \longrightarrow T * F$$
$$(4)\ T \longrightarrow F$$
$$(5)\ F \longrightarrow (E)$$
$$(6)\ F \longrightarrow a$$

The left parse of the sentence $a * (a + a)$ is 23465124646. The right parse of $a * (a + a)$ is 64642641532. ☐

We shall use an extension of the $\Rightarrow$ notation to describe left and right parses.

CONVENTION

Let $G = (N, \Sigma, P, S)$ be a CFG, and assume that the productions are numbered from 1 to p. We write $\alpha \overset{i}{\underset{lm}{\Rightarrow}} \beta$ if $\alpha \Rightarrow \beta$ and the production applied is numbered i. Similarly, we write $\alpha \overset{i}{\underset{rm}{\Rightarrow}} \beta$ if $\alpha \Rightarrow \beta$ and production i is used. We extend these notations by

(1) If $\alpha \overset{\pi_1}{\underset{lm}{\Rightarrow}} \beta$ and $\beta \overset{\pi_2}{\underset{lm}{\Rightarrow}} \gamma$, then $\alpha \overset{\pi_1\pi_2}{\underset{lm}{\Rightarrow}} \gamma$.

(2) If $\alpha \underset{rm}{\overset{\pi_1}{\Rightarrow}} \beta$ and $\beta \underset{rm}{\overset{\pi_2}{\Rightarrow}} \gamma$, then $\alpha \underset{rm}{\overset{\pi_1\pi_2}{\Rightarrow}} \gamma$.

3.4.2. Top-Down Parsing

In this section we wish to examine the nature of the left-parsing problem for CFG's. Let $\pi = i_1 \cdots i_n$ be a left parse of a sentence w in $L(G)$, where G is a CFG. Knowing π, we can construct a parse tree for w in the following "top-down" manner. We begin with the root labeled S. Then i_1 gives the production to be used to expand S. Suppose that i_1 is the number of the production $S \longrightarrow X_1 \cdots X_k$. We then create k descendants of the node labeled S and label these descendants $X_1, X_2, \ldots, X_k$. If $X_1, X_2, \ldots, X_{i-1}$ are terminals, then the first $i - 1$ symbols of w must be $X_1 \cdots X_{i-1}$. Production i_2 must then be of the form $X_i \longrightarrow Y_1 \cdots Y_l$, and we can continue building the parse tree for w by expanding the node labeled X_i. We can proceed in this fashion and construct the entire parse tree for w corresponding to the left parse π.

Now suppose that we are given a CFG $G = (N, \Sigma, P, S)$ in which the productions are numbered from 1 through p and a string $w \in \Sigma^*$ for which we wish to construct a left parse. One way of looking at this problem is that we know the root and frontier of a parse tree and "all" we need to do is fill in the intermediate nodes. Left parsing suggests that we attempt to fill in the parse starting from the root and then working left to right toward the frontier.

It is quite easy to show that there is a simple SDTS which maps strings in $L(G)$ to all their left (or right, if you prefer) parses. We shall define such an SDTS here, although we prefer to examine the PDT which implements the translation, because the latter gives an introduction to the physical execution of its translation.

DEFINITION

Let $G = (N, \Sigma, P, S)$ be a CFG in which the productions have been numbered from 1 to p. Define T_l^G, or T_l, where G is understood, to be the SDTS $(N, \Sigma, \{1, \ldots, p\}, R, S)$, where R consists of rules $A \longrightarrow \alpha, \beta$ such that $A \longrightarrow \alpha$ is production i in P and β is $i\alpha'$, where α' is α with the terminals deleted.

Example 3.23

Let G_0 be the usual grammar with productions numbered as in Example 3.22. Then $T_l = (\{E, T, F\}, \{+, *, (,), a\}, \{1, \ldots, 6\}, R, E)$, where R consists of

$$
\begin{aligned}
E &\longrightarrow E + T, & 1ET \\
E &\longrightarrow T, & 2T \\
T &\longrightarrow T * F, & 3TF \\
T &\longrightarrow F, & 4F \\
F &\longrightarrow (E), & 5E \\
F &\longrightarrow a, & 6
\end{aligned}
$$

The pair of derivation trees in Fig. 3.10 shows the translation defined for $a * (a + a)$. $\square$

The following theorem is left for the Exercises.

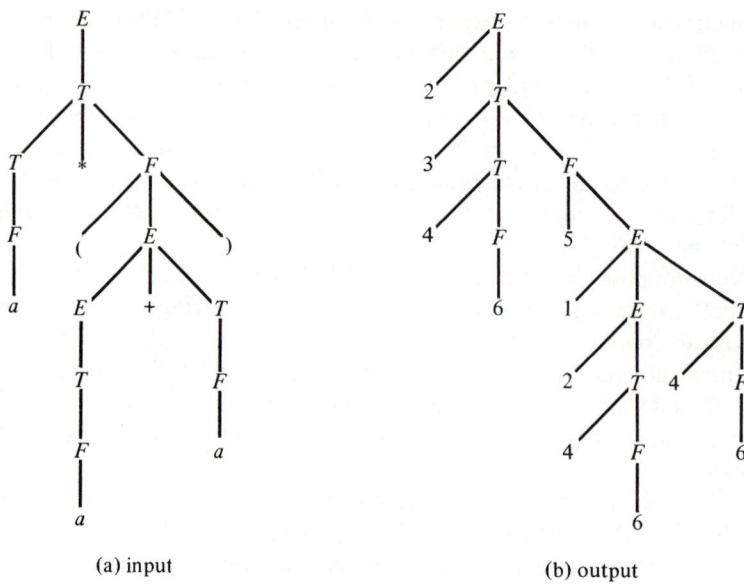

(a) input   (b) output

Fig. 3.10   Translation T_l.

THEOREM 3.10

Let $G = (N, \Sigma, P, S)$ be a CFG. Then $T_l = \{(w, \pi) \mid S \overset{\pi}{\Rightarrow} w\}$.

Proof. We can prove by induction that $(A, A) \overset{*}{\underset{T_l}{\Rightarrow}} (w, \pi)$ if and only if $A \overset{\pi}{\underset{G}{\Rightarrow}} w$. $\square$

Using a construction similar to that in Lemma 3.2, we can construct for any grammar G a nondeterministic pushdown transducer that acts as a left parser for G.

DEFINITION

Let $G = (N, \Sigma, P, S)$ be a CFG in which the productions have been numbered from 1 to p. Let M_l^g (or M_l when G is understood) be the nondeterministic pushdown transducer $(\{q\}, \Sigma, N \cup \Sigma, \{1, 2, \ldots, p\}, \delta, q, S, \varnothing)$, where δ is defined as follows:

(1) $\delta(q, e, A)$ contains (q, α, i) if the ith production in P is $A \to \alpha$.
(2) $\delta(q, a, a) = \{(q, e, e)\}$ for all a in Σ.

We call M_l^g the *left parser* for G.

With input w, M_l simulates a leftmost derivation of w from S in G. Using rules in (1), each time M_l expands a nonterminal on top of the pushdown list according to a production in P, M_l will also emit the number of that production. If there is a terminal symbol on top of the pushdown list, M_l will use a rule in (2) to ensure that this terminal matches the current input symbol. Thus, M_l can produce only a leftmost derivation for w.

THEOREM 3.11

Let $G = (N, \Sigma, P, S)$ be a CFG. Then $\tau_e(M_l) = \{(w, \pi) \mid S \stackrel{\pi}{\Longrightarrow} w\}$.

Proof. Another elementary inductive exercise. The inductive hypothesis this time is that $(q, w, A, e) \stackrel{*}{\vdash} (q, e, e, \pi)$ if and only if $A \stackrel{\pi}{\Longrightarrow} w$. $\square$

Note that M_l^G is almost, but not quite, the PDT that one obtains by Lemma 3.2 from the SDTS T_l^G.

Example 3.24

Let us construct a left parser for G_0. Here

$$M_l = (\{q\}, \Sigma, N \cup \Sigma, \{1, 2, \ldots, 6\}, \delta, q, E, \varnothing),$$

where

$$\delta(q, e, E) = \{(q, E + T, 1), (q, T, 2)\}$$
$$\delta(q, e, T) = \{(q, T * F, 3), (q, F, 4)\}$$
$$\delta(q, e, F) = \{(q, (E), 5), (q, a, 6)\}$$
$$\delta(q, b, b) = \{(q, e, e)\} \qquad \text{for all } b \text{ in } \Sigma$$

With the input string $a + a * a$, $M_l^{G_0}$ can make the following sequence of moves, among others:

$$
\begin{aligned}
(q, a + a * a, E, e) &\vdash (q, a + a * a, E + T, 1) \\
&\vdash (q, a + a * a, T + T, 12) \\
&\vdash (q, a + a * a, F + T, 124) \\
&\vdash (q, a + a * a, a + T, 1246) \\
&\vdash (q, + a * a, + T, 1246) \\
&\vdash (q, a * a, T, 1246) \\
&\vdash (q, a * a, T * F, 12463) \\
&\vdash (q, a * a, F * F, 124634) \\
&\vdash (q, a * a, a * F, 1246346) \\
&\vdash (q, * a, * F, 1246346) \\
&\vdash (q, a, F, 1246346) \\
&\vdash (q, a, a, 12463466) \\
&\vdash (q, e, e, 12463466) \quad \square
\end{aligned}
$$

The left parser is in general a nondeterministic device. To use it in practice, we must simulate it deterministically. There are some grammars, such as those which are not cycle-free, for which a complete simulation is impossible, in this case because there are an infinity of left parses for some words. Moreover, the natural simulation, which we shall discuss in Chapter 4, fails on a larger class of grammars, those which are left-recursive. An essential requirement for doing top-down parsing is that left recursion be eliminated.

There is a natural class of grammars, which we shall call LL (for scanning the input from the left producing a left parse) and discuss in Section 5.1, for which the left parser can be made deterministic by the simple expedient of allowing it to look some finite number of symbols ahead on the input and to base its move on what it sees. The LL grammars are those which can be parsed "in a natural way" by a deterministic left parser.

There is a wider class of grammars for which there is some DPDT which can implement the SDTS T_l. These include all the LL grammars and some others which can be parsed only in an "unnatural" way, i.e., those in which the contents of the pushdown list do not reflect successive steps of a leftmost derivation, as does M_l. Such grammars are of only theoretical interest, insofar as top-down parsing is concerned, but we shall treat them briefly in Section 3.4.4.

3.4.3. Bottom-Up Parsing

Let us now turn our attention to the right-parsing problem. Consider the rightmost derivation of $a + a * a$ from E in G_0:

$$E \Longrightarrow^1 E + T$$
$$\Longrightarrow^3 E + T * F$$
$$\Longrightarrow^6 E + T * a$$
$$\Longrightarrow^4 E + F * a$$
$$\Longrightarrow^6 E + a * a$$
$$\Longrightarrow^2 T + a * a$$
$$\Longrightarrow^4 F + a * a$$
$$\Longrightarrow^6 a + a * a$$

Writing in reverse the sequence of productions used in this derivation gives us the right parse 64264631 for $a + a * a$.

In general, a right parse for a string w in a grammar $G = (N, \Sigma, P, S)$ is a sequence of productions which can be used to reduce w to the sentence symbol S. Viewed in terms of a derivation tree, a right parse for a sentence w represents the sequence of handle prunings in which a derivation tree with frontier w is pruned to a single node labeled S. In effect, this is equivalent to starting with only the frontier of a derivation tree for w and then "filling in" the derivation tree from the leaves to the root. Thus the term "bottom-up" parsing is often associated with the generation of a right parse.

In analogy with the SDTS T_l which maps words in $L(G)$ to their left parses, we can define T_r, an SDTS which maps words to right parses. The translation elements have terminals deleted and the production numbers at the right end. We leave it for the Exercises to show that this SDTS correctly defines the desired translation.

As for top-down parsing, we are really interested in a PDT which implements T_r. We shall define an extended PDT in analogy with the extended PDA.

DEFINITION

An *extended PDT* is an 8-tuple $P = (Q, \Sigma, \Gamma, \Delta, \delta, q_0, Z_0, F)$, where all symbols are as before except δ, which is a map from a finite subset of $Q \times (\Sigma \cup \{e\}) \times \Gamma^*$ to the finite subsets of $Q \times \Gamma^* \times \Delta^*$. Configurations are defined as before, but with the pushdown top normally on the right, and we say that $(q, aw, \beta\alpha, x) \vdash (p, w, \beta\gamma, xy)$ if and only if $\delta(q, a, \alpha)$ contains (p, γ, y).

The extended PDT P is *deterministic*

(1) If for all $q \in Q$, $a \in \Sigma \cup \{e\}$, and $\alpha \in \Gamma^*$, $\#\delta(q, a, \alpha) \leq 1$ and,

(2) If $\delta(q, a, \alpha) \neq \varnothing$ and $\delta(q, b, \beta) \neq \varnothing$, with $b = a$ or $b = e$, then neither of α and β is a suffix of the other.

DEFINITION

Let $G = (N, \Sigma, P, S)$ be a CFG. Let M_r^g be the extended nondeterministic pushdown transducer $(\{q\}, \Sigma, N \cup \Sigma \cup \{\$\}, \{1, \ldots, p\}, \delta, q, \$, \varnothing)$. The pushdown top is on the right, and δ is defined as follows:

(1) $\delta(q, e, \alpha)$ contains (q, A, i) if production i in P is $A \rightarrow \alpha$.

(2) $\delta(q, a, e) = \{(q, a, e)\}$ for all a in Σ.

(3) $\delta(q, e, \$S) = \{(q, e, e)\}$.

This pushdown transducer embodies the elements of what is known as a shift–reduce parsing algorithm. Under rule (2), M_r shifts input symbols onto the top of the pushdown list. Whenever a handle appears on top of the pushdown list, M_r can reduce the handle under rule (1) and emit the number of the production used to reduce the handle. M_r may then shift more input symbols onto the pushdown list, until the next handle appears on top of the pushdown list. The handle can then be reduced and the production number emitted. M_r continues to operate in this fashion until the pushdown list contains only the sentence symbol on top of the end of pushdown list marker. Under rule (3) M_r can then enter a configuration in which the pushdown list is empty.

THEOREM 3.12

Let $G = (N, \Sigma, P, S)$ be a CFG. Then $\tau_e(M_r) = \{(w, \pi^R) \mid S \Rightarrow^{\pi} w\}$.

Proof. The proof is similar to that of Lemma 2.25 and is left for the Exercises. $\square$

Example 3.25

The right parser for G_0 would be

$$M_r^{G_0} = (\{q\}, \Sigma, N \cup \Sigma \cup \{\$\}, \{1, 2, \ldots, 6\}, \delta, q, \$, \varnothing),$$

where

$$\delta(q, e, E + T) = \{(q, E, 1)\}$$
$$\delta(q, e, T) = \{(q, E, 2)\}$$
$$\delta(q, e, T * F) = \{(q, T, 3)\}$$
$$\delta(q, e, F) = \{(q, T, 4)\}$$
$$\delta(q, e, (E)) = \{(q, F, 5)\}$$
$$\delta(q, e, a) = \{(q, F, 6)\}$$
$$\delta(q, b, e) = \{(q, b, e)\} \qquad \text{for all } b \text{ in } \Sigma$$
$$\delta(q, e, \$E) = \{(q, e, e)\}$$

With input $a + a * a$, $M_r^{G_0}$ could make the following sequence of moves, among others:

$$
\begin{aligned}
(q, a + a * a, \$, e) &\vdash (q, +a * a, \$a, e) \\
&\vdash (q, +a * a, \$F, 6) \\
&\vdash (q, + a * a, \$T, 64) \\
&\vdash (q, + a * a, \$E, 642) \\
&\vdash (q, a * a, \$E +, 642) \\
&\vdash (q, * a, \$E + a, 642) \\
&\vdash (q, * a, \$E + F, 6426) \\
&\vdash (q, * a, \$E + T, 64264) \\
&\vdash (q, a, \$E + T *, 64264) \\
&\vdash (q, e, \$E + T * a, 64264) \\
&\vdash (q, e, \$E + T * F, 642646) \\
&\vdash (q, e, \$E + T, 6426463) \\
&\vdash (q, e, \$E, 64264631) \\
&\vdash (q, e, e, 64264631)
\end{aligned}
$$

Thus, M_r would produce the right parse 64264631 for the input string $a + a * a$. $\square$

We shall discuss deterministic simulation of a nondeterministic right parser in Chapter 4. In Section 5.2 we shall discuss an important subclass of CFG's, the LR (for scanning the input from left to right and producing a right parse), for which the PDT can be made to operate deterministically by allowing it to look some finite number of symbols ahead on the input. The LR grammars are thus those which can be parsed naturally bottom-up and deterministically. As in left parsing, there are grammars which may be right-parsed deterministically, but not in the natural way. We shall treat these in the next section.

3.4.4. Comparison of Top-Down and Bottom-Up Parsing

If we consider only nondeterministic parsers, then there is little comparison to be made. By Theorems 3.11 and 3.12, every CFG has both a left and right parser. However, if we consider the important question of whether deterministic parsers exist for a given grammar, things are not so simple.

DEFINITION

A CFG G is *left-parsable* if there exists a DPDT P such that

$$\tau(P) = \{(x\$, \pi) | (x, \pi) \in T_l^G\}.$$

G is *right-parsable* if there exists a DPDT P with

$$\tau(P) = \{(x\$, \pi) | (x, \pi) \in T_r^G\}.$$

In both cases we shall permit the DPDT to use an endmarker to delimit the right end of the input string.

Note that all grammars are left- and right-parsable in an informal sense, but it is determinism that is reflected in the formal definition.

We find that the classes of left- and right-parsable grammars are incommensurate; that is, neither is a subset of the other. This is surprising in view of Section 8.1, where we shall show that the LL grammars, those which can be left-parsed deterministically in a natural way, are a subset of the LR grammars, those which can be right-parsed deterministically in a natural way. The following examples give grammars which are left- (right-) parsable but not right- (left-) parsable.

Example 3.26

Let G_1 be defined by

(1) $S \to BAb$ (2) $S \to CAc$

(3) $A \to BA$ (4) $A \to a$

(5) $B \to a$ (6) $C \to a$

$L(G_1) = aa^+b + aa^+c$. We can show that G_1 is neither LL nor LR, because we do not know whether the first a in any sentence comes from B or C until we have seen the last symbol of the sentence.

However we can "unnaturally" produce a left parse for any input string with a DPDT as follows. Suppose that the input is $a^{n+2}b$, $n \geq 0$. Then the DPDT can produce the left parse $15(35)^n4$ by storing all a's on the pushdown list until the b is seen. No output is generated until the b is encountered. Then the DPDT can emit $15(35)^n4$ by using the a's stored on the pushdown list to count to n. Likewise, if the input is $a^{n+2}c$, we can produce $26(35)^n4$ as output. In either case, the trick is to delay producing any output until b or c is seen.

We shall now attempt to convince the reader that there is no DPDT which can produce a valid right parse for all inputs. Suppose that M were a DPDT which produced the right parses 55^n43^n1 for $a^{n+2}b$ and 65^n43^n2 for $a^{n+2}c$. We shall give an informal proof that M does not exist. The proof draws heavily on ideas in Ginsburg and Greibach [1966] in which it is shown that $\{a^nb^n \mid n \geq 1\} \cup \{a^nb^{2n} \mid n \geq 1\}$ is not a deterministic CFL. The reader is referred there for assistance in constructing a formal proof. We can show each of the following:

(1) Let a^i be input to M. Then the output of M is empty, or else M would emit a 5 or 6, and we could "fool" it by placing c or b, respectively, on the input, causing M to produce an erroneous output.

(2) As a's enter the input of M, they must be stored in some way on the pushdown list. Specifically, we can show that there exist integers j and k, pushdown strings α and β, and state q such that for all integers $p \geq 0$, $(q_0, a^{k+jp}, Z_0, e) \underset{\sim}{\vdash^*} (q, e, \beta^p\alpha, e)$, where q_0 and Z_0 are the initial state and pushdown symbol of M.

(3) If after $k + jp$ a's, one b appears on M's input, M cannot emit symbol 4 before erasing its pushdown tape to α. For if it did, we could "fool" it by previously placing j more a's on the input and finding that M emits the same number of 5's as it did previously.

(4) After reducing its pushdown list to α, M cannot "remember" how many a's were on the input, because the only thing different about M's configurations for different values of p (where $k + jp$ is the number of a's) is now the state. Thus, M does not know how many 3's to emit. $\square$

Example 3.27

Let G_2 be defined by

(1) $S \to Ab$ (2) $S \to Ac$

(3) $A \to AB$ (4) $A \to a$

(5) $B \to a$

$L(G_2) = a^+b + a^+c$. It is easy to show that G_2 is right-parsable. Using an argument similar to that in Example 3.26 it can be shown that G_2 is not left-parsable. $\square$

THEOREM 3.13

The classes of left- and right-parsable grammars are incommensurate.

Proof. By Examples 3.26 and 3.27. $\square$

Despite the above theorem, as a general rule, bottom-up parsing is more appealing than top-down parsing. For a given programming language is often easier to write down a grammar that is right-parsable than one that is left-parsable. Also, as was mentioned, the LL grammars are included in the LR grammars. In the next chapter, we shall also see that the natural simulation of a nondeterministic PDT works for a class of grammars that is, in a sense to be discussed there, more general when the PDT is a right parser than a left parser.

When we look at translation, however, the left parse appears more desirable. We shall show that every simple SDT can be performed by

(1) A PDT which produces left parses of words, followed by
(2) A DPDT which maps the left parses into output strings of the SDT.

Interestingly, there are simple SDT's such that "left parse" cannot be replaced by "right parse" in the above.

If a compiler translated by first constructing the entire parse and then converting the parse to object code, the above claim would be sufficient to prove that there are certain translations which require a left parse at the intermediate stage.

However, many compilers construct the parse tree node by node and compute the translation at each node when that node is constructed. We claim that if a translation cannot be computed directly from the right parse, then it cannot be computed node by node, if the nodes themselves are constructed in a bottom-up way. These ideas will be discussed in more detail in Chapter 9, and we ask the reader to wait until then for the matter of node-by-node translation to be formalized.

DEFINITION

Let $G = (N, \Sigma, P, S)$ be a CFG. We define L_l^G and L_r^G, the *left* and *right* parse languages of G, respectively, by

$$L_l^G = \{\pi \mid S \xrightarrow{\pi} w \text{ for some } w \text{ in } L(G)\}$$

and

$$L_r^G = \{\pi^R \mid S \Longrightarrow^\pi w \text{ for some } w \text{ in } L(G)\}$$

We can extend the $\xrightarrow{\pi}$ and $\Longrightarrow^\pi$ notations to SDT's by saying that

$(\alpha, \beta) \overset{\pi}{\Longrightarrow} (\gamma, \delta)$ if and only if $(\alpha, \beta) \overset{*}{\Longrightarrow} (\gamma, \delta)$ by a sequence of rules such that the leftmost nonterminal of α is replaced at each step and these rules, with translation elements deleted, form the sequence of productions π. We define $\Rightarrow^\pi$ for SDT's analogously.

DEFINITION

An SDTS is *semantically unambiguous* if there are no two distinct rules of the form $A \longrightarrow \alpha, \beta$ and $A \longrightarrow \alpha, \gamma$.

A semantically unambiguous SDTS has exactly one translation element for each production of the underlying grammar.

THEOREM 3.14

Let $T = (N, \Sigma, \Delta, R, S)$ be a semantically unambiguous simple SDTS. Then there exists a DPDT P such that $\tau_e(P) = \{(\pi, y) \,|\, (S, S) \overset{\pi}{\Longrightarrow} (x, y)$ for some $x \in \Sigma^*\}$.

Proof. Assume N and Δ are disjoint. Let $P = (\{q\}, \{1, \ldots, p\}, N \cup \Delta, \Delta, \delta, q, S, \emptyset)$, where $1, \ldots, p$ are the numbers of the productions of the underlying grammar, and δ is defined by

(1) Let $A \longrightarrow \alpha$ be production i, and $A \longrightarrow \alpha, \beta$ the lone rule beginning with $A \longrightarrow \alpha$. Then $\delta(q, i, A) = (q, \beta, e)$.

(2) For all b in Δ, $\delta(q, e, b) = (q, e, b)$.

P is deterministic because rule (1) applies only with a nonterminal on top of the pushdown list, and rule (2) applies only with an output symbol on top. The proof that P works correctly follows from an easy inductive hypothesis: $(q, \pi, A, e) \overset{*}{\vdash} (q, e, e, y)$ if and only if there exists some x in Σ^* such that $(A, A) \overset{\pi}{\Longrightarrow} (x, y)$. We leave the proof for the Exercises. $\square$

To show a simple SDT not to be executable by any DPDT which maps L_r^G, where G is the underlying grammar, to the output of the SDT, we need the following lemma.

LEMMA 3.15

There is no DPDT P such that $\tau(P) = \{(wc, w^R cw) \,|\, w \in \{a, b\}^*\}$.

Proof. Here the symbol c plays the role of a right endmarker. Suppose that with input w, P emitted some non-e-string, say dx, where $d = a$ or b. Let $\bar{d}$ be the other of a and b, and consider the action of P with $w\bar{d}c$ as input. It must emit some string, but that string begins with d. Hence, P does not map $w\bar{d}c$ to $\bar{d}w^R cw\bar{d}$, as demanded. Thus, P may not emit any output until the right endmarker c is reached. At that time, it has some string α_w on its pushdown list and is in state q_w.

Informally, α_w must be essentially w, in which case, by erasing α_w, P can emit w^R. But once P has erased α_w, P cannot then "remember" all of w in order to print it. A formal proof of the lemma draws upon the ideas outlined in Example 3.26. We shall sketch such a proof here.

Consider inputs of the form $w = a^i$. Then there are integers j and k, a state q, and strings α and β such that when the input is $a^{j+nk}c$, P will place $\alpha\beta^n$ on its pushdown list and enter state q. Then P must erase the pushdown list down to α at or before the time it emits w^Rc. But since α is independent of w, it is no longer possible to emit w. $\square$

THEOREM 3.15

There exists a simple SDTS $T = (N, \Sigma, \Delta, R, S)$ such that there is no DPDT P for which $\tau(P) = \{(\pi^R, x) \mid (S, S) \Rightarrow^\pi (w, x) \text{ for some } w\}$.

Proof. Let T be defined by the rules

$$
\begin{aligned}
&(1)\ S \longrightarrow Sa,\ aSa \\
&(2)\ S \longrightarrow Sb,\ bSb \\
&(3)\ S \longrightarrow c,\ c
\end{aligned}
$$

Then $L_r^G = 3(1 + 2)^*$, where G is the underlying grammar. If we let $h(1) = a$ and $h(2) = b$, then the desired $\tau(P)$ is $\{(3\alpha, h(\alpha)^Rch(\alpha)) \mid \alpha \in \{1, 2\}^*\}$. If P existed, with or without a right endmarker, then we could easily construct a DPDT to define the translation $\{(wc, w^Rcw) \mid w \in \{a, b\}^*\}$, in contradiction of Lemma 3.15. $\square$

We conclude that both left parsing and right parsing are of interest, and we shall study both in succeeding chapters. Another type of parsing which embodies features of both top-down and bottom-up parsing is left-corner parsing. Left-corner parsing will be treated in the Exercises.

3.4.5. Grammatical Covering

Let G_1 be a CFG. We can consider a grammar G_2 to be similar from the point of view of the parsing process if $L(G_2) = L(G_1)$ and we can express the left and/or right parse of a sentence generated by G_1 in terms of its parse in G_2. If such is the case, we say that G_2 covers G_1. There are several uses for covering grammars. For example, if a programming language is expressed in terms of a grammar which is "hard" to parse, then it would be desirable to find a covering grammar which is "easier" to parse. Also, certain parsing algorithms which we shall study work only if a grammar is some normal form, e.g., CNF or non-left-recursive. If G_1 is an arbitrary grammar and G_2 a particular normal form of G_1, then it would be desirable if the parses in G_1 can be simply recovered from those in G_2. If this is the case, it is not necessary that we be able to recover parses in G_2 from those in G_1.

For a formal definition of what it means to "recover" parses in one grammar from those in another, we use the notion of a string homomorphism between the parses. Other, stronger mappings could be used, and some of these are discussed in the Exercises.

DEFINITION

Let $G_1 = (N_1, \Sigma, P_1, S_1)$ and $G_2 = (N_2, \Sigma, P_2, S_2)$ be CFG's such that $L(G_1) = L(G_2)$. We say that G_2 *left-covers* G_1 if there is a homomorphism h from P_2 to P_1 such that

(1) If $S_2 \overset{\pi}{\Longrightarrow} w$, then $S_1 \overset{h(\pi)}{\Longrightarrow} w$, and

(2) For all π such that $S_1 \overset{\pi}{\Longrightarrow} w$, there exists π' such that $S_2 \overset{\pi'}{\Longrightarrow} w$ and $h(\pi') = \pi$.

We say G_2 that *right-covers* G_1 if there is a homomorphism h from P_2 to P_1 such that

(1) If $S_2 \Longrightarrow^\pi w$, then $S_1 \Longrightarrow^{h(\pi)} w$, and

(2) For all π such that $S_1 \Longrightarrow^\pi w$, there exists π' such that $S_2 \Longrightarrow^{\pi'} w$ and $h(\pi') = \pi$.

Example 3.28

Let G_1 be the grammar

$$(1) \ S \rightarrow 0S1$$
$$(2) \ S \rightarrow 01$$

and G_2 be the following CNF grammar equivalent to G_1:

$$(1) \ S \rightarrow AB$$
$$(2) \ S \rightarrow AC$$
$$(3) \ B \rightarrow SC$$
$$(4) \ A \rightarrow 0$$
$$(5) \ C \rightarrow 1$$

We see G_2 left-covers G_1 with the homomorphism $h(1) = 1$, $h(2) = 2$, and $h(3) = h(4) = h(5) = e$. For example,

$$S \overset{1432455}{\underset{G_2}{\Longrightarrow}} 0011, \quad h(1432455) = 12, \quad \text{and} \quad S \overset{12}{\underset{G_1}{\Longrightarrow}} 0011$$

G_2 also right-covers G_1, and in this case, the same h can be used. For example,

$$S \underset{G_2}{\Longrightarrow}{}^{1352544} 0011, \quad h(1352544) = 12, \quad \text{and} \quad S \underset{G_1}{\Longrightarrow}{}^{12} 0011$$

G_1 does not left- or right-cover G_2. Since both grammars are unambiguous, the mapping between parses is fixed. Thus a homomorphism g showing that G_1 was a left cover would have to map 1^n2 into $(143)^n24(5)^{n+1}$, which can easily be shown to be impossible. $\square$

Many of the constructions in Section 2.4, which put grammars into normal forms, can be shown to yield grammars which left- or right-cover the original.

Example 3.29

The key step in the Chomsky normal form construction (Algorithm 2.12) is the replacement of a production $A \to X_1 \cdots X_n$, $n > 2$, by $A \to X_1 B_1$, $B_1 \to X_2 B_2, \ldots, B_{n-2} \to X_{n-1} X_n$. The resulting grammar can be shown to left-cover the original if we map production $A \to X_1 B_1$ to $A \to X_1 \cdots X_n$ and each of the productions $B_1 \to X_2 B_2, \ldots, B_{n-2} \to X_{n-1} X_n$ to the empty string. If we wish a right cover instead, we may replace $A \to X_1 \cdots X_n$ by $A \to B_1 X_n$, $B_1 \to B_2 X_{n-1}, \ldots, B_{n-2} \to X_1 X_2$. $\square$

Other covering results are left for the Exercises.

EXERCISES

3.4.1. Give an algorithm to construct a derivation tree from a left or right parse.

3.4.2. Let G be a CFG. Show that L_l^G is a deterministic CFL.

3.4.3. Is L_r^G always a deterministic CFL?

*3.4.4. Construct a determinstic pushdown transducer P such that

$$\tau(P) = \{(\pi, \pi') \mid \pi \text{ is in } L_l^G \text{ and } \pi' \text{ is the right parse}$$
$$\text{for the same derivation tree}\}.$$

*3.4.5. Can you construct a deterministic pushdown transducer P such that $\tau(P) = \{(\pi, \pi') \mid \pi \text{ is in } L_r^G \text{ and } \pi' \text{ is the corresponding left parse}\}$?

3.4.6. Give left and right parses in G_0 for the following words:
(a) $((a))$
(b) $a + (a + a)$
(c) $a * a * a$

3.4.7. Let G be the CFG defined by the following numbered productions
(1) $S \to \textbf{if } B \textbf{ then } S \textbf{ else } S$
(2) $S \to s$
(3) $B \to B \wedge B$
(4) $B \to B \vee B$
(5) $B \to b$
Give SDTS's which define T_l^G and T_r^G.

3.4.8. Give PDT's which define T_l^G and T_r^G, where G is as in Exercise 3.4.7.

3.4.9. Prove Theorem 3.10.

3.4.10. Prove Theorem 3.11.

3.4.11. Give an appropriate definition for T_r^G, and prove that for your SDTS, words in $L(G)$ are mapped to their right parses.

3.4.12. Give an algorithm to convert an extended PDT to an equivalent PDT. Your algorithm should be such that if applied to a deterministic extended PDT, the result is a DPDT. Prove that your algorithm does this.

3.4.13. Prove Theorem 3.12.

*3.4.14. Give deterministic right parsers for the grammars
    (a) (1) $S \longrightarrow S0$
       (2) $S \longrightarrow S1$
       (3) $S \longrightarrow e$

    (b) (1) $S \longrightarrow AB$
       (2) $A \longrightarrow 0A1$
       (3) $A \longrightarrow e$
       (4) $B \longrightarrow B1$
       (5) $B \longrightarrow e$

*3.4.15. Give deterministic left parsers for the grammars
    (a) (1) $S \longrightarrow 0S$
       (2) $S \longrightarrow 1S$
       (3) $S \longrightarrow e$

    (b) (1) $S \longrightarrow 0S1$
       (2) $S \longrightarrow A$
       (3) $A \longrightarrow A1$
       (4) $A \longrightarrow e$

*3.4.16. Which of the grammars in Exercise 3.4.14 have deterministic left parsers? Which in Exercise 3.4.15 have deterministic right parsers?

*3.4.17. Give a detailed proof that the grammars in Examples 3.26 and 3.27 are right- (left-) parsable but not left- (right-) parsable.

3.4.18. Complete the proof of Theorem 3.14.

3.4.19. Complete the proof of Lemma 3.15.

3.4.20. Complete the proof of Theorem 3.15.

DEFINITION

The *left corner* of a non-e-production is the leftmost symbol (terminal or nonterminal) on the right side. A *left-corner parse* of a sentence is the sequence of productions used at the interior nodes of a parse tree in which all nodes have been ordered as follows. If a node n has p direct descendants $n_1, n_2, \ldots, n_p$, then all nodes in the subtree with root n_1 precede n. Node n precedes all its other descendants. The descendants of n_2 precede those of n_3, which precede those of n_4, and so forth.

Roughly speaking, in left-corner parsing the left corner of a production is recognized bottom-up and the remainder of the production is recognized top-down.

Example 3.30

Figure 3.11 shows a parse tree for the sentence *bbaaab* generated by the following grammar:

    (1) $S \longrightarrow AS$ (2) $S \longrightarrow BB$
    (3) $A \longrightarrow bAA$ (4) $A \longrightarrow a$
    (5) $B \longrightarrow b$ (6) $B \longrightarrow e$

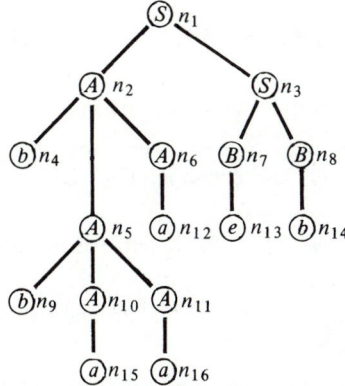

Fig. 3.11 Parse tree.

The ordering of the nodes imposed by the left-corner-parse definition states that node n_2 and its descendants precede n_1, which is then followed by n_3 and its descendants. Node n_4 precedes n_2, which precedes n_5, n_6, and their descendants. Then n_9 precedes n_5, which precedes n_{10}, n_{11}, and their descendants. Continuing in this fashion we obtain the following ordering of nodes:

$$n_4\ n_2\ n_9\ n_5\ n_{15}\ n_{10}\ n_{16}\ n_{11}\ n_{12}\ n_6\ n_1\ n_{13}\ n_7\ n_3\ n_{14}\ n_8$$

The left-corner parse is the sequence of productions applied at the interior nodes in this order. Thus the left-corner parse for *bbaaab* is 334441625. □

Another method of defining the left-corner parse of a sentence of a grammar G is to use the following simple SDTS associated with G.

DEFINITION

Let $G = (N, \Sigma, P, S)$ be a CFG in which the productions are numbered 1 to p. Let T_{lc}^G be the simple SDTS $(N, \Sigma, \{1, 2, \ldots, p\}, R, S)$, where R contains a rule for each production in P determined as follows: If the ith production in P is $A \longrightarrow B\alpha$ or $A \longrightarrow a\alpha$ or $A \longrightarrow e$, then R contains the rule $A \longrightarrow B\alpha, Bi\alpha'$ or $A \longrightarrow a\alpha, i\alpha'$ or $A \longrightarrow e, i$, respectively, where α' is α with all terminal symbols removed. Then, if (w, π) is in $\tau(T_{lc}^G)$, π is a left-corner parse for w.

Example 3.31

T_{lc}^G for the grammar of the previous example is

$$
\begin{array}{ll}
S \longrightarrow AS,\, A1S & S \longrightarrow BB,\, B2B \\
A \longrightarrow bAA,\, 3AA & A \longrightarrow a,\, 4 \\
B \longrightarrow b,\, 5 & B \longrightarrow e,\, 6
\end{array}
$$

We can confirm that ($bbaaab$, 334441625) is in $\tau(T^G_{lc})$. □

3.4.21. Prove that (w, π) is in $\tau(T^G_{lc})$ if and only if π is a left-corner parse for w.

3.4.22. Show that for each CFG there is a (nondeterministic) PDT which maps the sentences of the language to their left-corner parses.

3.4.23. Devise algorithms which will map a left-corner parse into (1) the corresponding left parse and (2) the corresponding right parse and conversely.

3.4.24. Show that if G_3 left- (right-) covers G_2 and G_2 left- (right-) covers G_1, then G_3 left- (right-) covers G_1.

3.4.25. Let G_1 be a cycle-free grammar. Show that G_1 is left- and right-covered by grammars with no single productions.

3.4.26. Show that every cycle-free grammar is left- and right-covered by grammars in CNF.

*3.4.27. Show that not every CFG is covered by an e-free grammar.

3.4.28. Show that Algorithm 2.9, which eliminates useless symbols, produces a grammar which left- and right-covers the original.

**3.4.29. Show that not every proper grammar is left- or right-covered by a grammar in GNF. *Hint:* Consider the grammar $S \longrightarrow S0 \,|\, S1 \,|\, 0 \,|\, 1$.

**3.4.30. Show that Exercise 3.4.29 still holds if the homomorphism in the definition of cover is replaced by a finite transduction.

*3.4.31. Does Exercise 3.4.29 still hold if the homomorphism is replaced by a pushdown transducer mapping?

Research Problem

3.4.32. It would be nice if whenever G_2 left- or right-covered G_1, every SDTS with G_1 as underlying grammar were equivalent to an SDTS with G_2 as underlying grammar. Unfortunately, this is not so. Can you find the conditions relating G_1 and G_2 so that the SDT's with underlying grammar G_1 are a subset of those with underlying grammar G_2?

BIBLIOGRAPHIC NOTES

Additional details concerning grammatical covering can be found in Reynolds and Haskell [1970], Gray [1969] and Gray and Harrison [1969]. In some early articles left-corner parsing was called bottom-up parsing. A more extensive treatment of left-corner parsing is contained in Cheatham [1967].

4 GENERAL PARSING METHODS

This chapter is devoted to parsing algorithms that are applicable to the entire class of context-free languages. Not all these algorithms can be used on all context-free grammars, but each context-free language has at least one grammar for which all these methods are applicable.

The full backtracking algorithms will be discussed first. These algorithms deterministically simulate nondeterministic parsers. As a function of the length of the string to be parsed, these backtracking methods require linear space but may take exponential time.

The algorithms discussed in the second section of this chapter are tabular in nature. These algorithms are the Cocke–Younger–Kasami algorithm and Earley's algorithm. They each take space n^2 and time n^3. Earley's algorithm works for any context-free grammar and requires time n^2 whenever the grammar is unambiguous.

The algorithms in this chapter are included in this book primarily to give more insight into the design of parsers. It should be clearly stated at the outset that backtrack parsing algorithms should be shunned in most practical applications. Even the tabular methods, which are asymptotically much faster than the backtracking algorithms, should be avoided if the language at hand has a grammar for which the more efficient parsing algorithms of Chapters 5 and 6 are applicable. It is almost certain that virtually all programming languages have easily parsable grammars for which these algorithms are applicable.

The methods of this chapter would be used in applications where the grammars encountered do not possess the special properties that are needed by the algorithms of Chapters 5 and 6. For example, if ambiguous grammars are necessary, and all parses are of interest, as in natural language processing, then some of the methods of this chapter might be considered.

4.1. BACKTRACK PARSING

Suppose that we have a nondeterministic pushdown transducer P and an input string w. Suppose further that each sequence of moves that P can make on input w is of bounded length. Then the total number of distinct sequences of moves that P can make is also finite, although possibly an exponential function of the length of w. A crude, but straightforward, way of deterministically simulating P is to linearly order the sequences of moves in some manner and then simulate each sequence of moves in the prescribed order.

If we are interested in all outputs for input w, then we would have to simulate all move sequences. If we are interested in only one output for w, then once we have found the first sequence of moves that terminates in a final configuration, we can stop simulating P. Of course, if no sequence of moves terminates in a final configuration, then all move sequences would have to be tried.

We can think of backtrack parsing in the following terms. Usually, the sequences of moves are arranged in such an order that it is possible to simulate the next move sequence by retracing (backtracking) the last moves made until a configuration is reached in which an untried alternative move is possible. This alternative move would then be taken. In practice, local criteria by which it is possible, without simulating an entire sequence, to determine that the sequence cannot lead to a final configuration, are used to speed up the backtracking process.

In this section we shall describe how we can deterministically simulate a nondeterministic pushdown transducer using backtracking. We shall then discuss two special cases. The first will be top-down backtrack parsing in which we produce a left parse for the input. The second case is bottom-up backtrack parsing in which we produce a right parse.

4.1.1. Simulation of a PDT

Let us consider a PDT P and its underlying PDA M. If we give M an input w, it is convenient to know that while M may nondeterministically try many sequences of moves, each sequence is of bounded length. If so, then these sequences can all be tried in some reasonable order. If there are infinite sequences of moves with input w, it is, in at least one sense, impossible to directly simulate M completely. Thus we make the following definition.

DEFINITION

A PDA $M = (Q, \Sigma, \Gamma, \delta, q_0, Z_0, F)$ is *halting* if for each w in Σ^*, there is a constant k_w such that if $(q_0, w, Z_0) \mathop{\vdash}\limits^{m} (q, x, \gamma)$, then $m \leq k_w$. A PDT is *halting* if its underlying PDA is halting.

It is interesting to observe the conditions on a grammar G under which the left or right parser for G is halting. It is left for the Exercises to show that the left parser is halting if and only if G is not left-recursive; the right parser is halting if and only if G is cycle-free and has no e-productions. We shall show subsequently that these conditions are the ones under which our general top-down and bottom-up backtrack parsing algorithms work, although more general algorithms work on a larger class of grammars.

We should observe that the condition of cycle freedom plus no e-productions is not really very restrictive. Every CFL without e has such a grammar, and, moreover, any context-free grammar can be made cycle-free and e-free by simple transformations (Algorithms 2.10 and 2.11). What is more, if the original grammar is unambiguous, then the modified grammar left and right covers it. Non-left recursion is a more stringent condition in this sense. While every CFL has a non-left-recursive grammar (Theorem 2.18), there may be no non-left-recursive covering grammar. (See Exercise 3.4.29.)

As an example of what is involved in backtrack parsing and, in general, simulating a nondeterministic pushdown transducer, let us consider the grammar G with productions

$$(1) \ \ S \longrightarrow aSbS$$
$$(2) \ \ S \longrightarrow aS$$
$$(3) \ \ S \longrightarrow c$$

The following pushdown transducer T is a left parser for G. The moves of T are given by

$$\delta(q, a, S) = \{(q, SbS, 1), (q, S, 2)\}$$
$$\delta(q, c, S) = \{(q, e, 3)\}$$
$$\delta(q, b, b) = \{(q, e, e)\}$$

Suppose that we wish to parse the input string $aacbc$. Figure 4.1 shows a tree which represents the possible sequences of moves that T can make with this input.

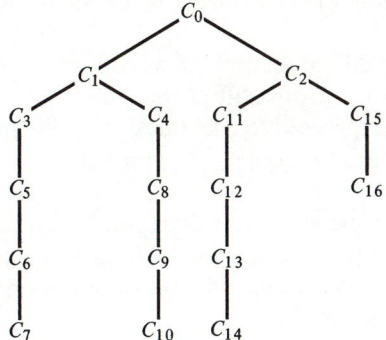

Fig. 4.1 Moves of parser.

C_0 represents the initial configuration $(q, aacbc, S, e)$. The rules of T show that two next configurations are possible from C_0, namely $C_1 = (q, acbc, SbS, 1)$ and $C_2 = (q, acbc, S, 2)$. (The ordering here is arbitrary.) From C_1, T can enter configurations $C_3 = (q, cbc, SbSbS, 11)$ and $C_4 = (q, cbc, SbS, 12)$. From C_2, T can enter configurations $C_{11} = (q, cbc, SbS, 21)$ and $C_{15} = (q, cbc, S, 22)$. The remaining configurations are determined uniquely.

One way to determine all parses for the given input string is to determine all accepting configurations which are accessible from C_0 in the tree of configurations. This can be done by tracing out all possible paths which begin at C_0 and terminate in a configuration from which no next move is possible. We can assign an order in which the paths are tried by ordering the choices of next moves available to T for each combination of state, input symbol, and symbol on top of the pushdown list. For example, let us choose $(q, SbS, 1)$ as the first choice and $(q, S, 2)$ as the second choice of move whenever the rule $\delta(q, a, S)$ is applicable.

Let us now consider how all the accepting configurations of T can be determined by systematically tracing out all possible sequences of moves of T. From C_0 suppose that we make the first choice of next move to obtain C_1. From C_1 we again take the first choice to obtain C_3. Continuing in this fashion we follow the sequence of configurations $C_0, C_1, C_3, C_5, C_6, C_7$. C_7 represents the terminal configuration $(q, e, bS, 1133)$, which is not an accepting configuration. To determine if there is another terminal configuration, we can "backtrack" up the tree until we encounter a configuration from which another choice of next move not yet considered is available. Thus we must be able to restore configuration C_6 from C_7. Going back to C_6 from C_7 can involve moving the input head back on the input, recovering what was previously on the pushdown list, and deleting any output symbols that were emitted in going from C_6 to C_7. Having restored C_6, we must also have available to us the next choice of moves (if any). Since no alternate choices exist in C_6, we continue backtracking to C_5, and then C_3 and C_1.

From C_1 we can then use the second choice of move for $\delta(q, a, S)$ and obtain configuration C_4. We can then continue through configurations C_8 and C_9 to obtain $C_{10} = (q, e, e, 1233)$, which happens to be an accepting configuration.

We can then emit the left parse 1233 as output. If we are interested in obtaining only one parse for the input we can halt at this point. However, if we are interested in all parses, we can proceed to backtrack to configuration C_0 and then try all configurations accessible from C_2. C_{14} represents another accepting configuration, $(q, e, e, 2133)$.

We would then halt after all possible sequences of moves that T could have made have been considered. If the input string had not been syntactically well formed, then all possible move sequences would have to be considered.

After exhausting all choices of moves without finding an accepting configuration we would output the message "error."

The above analysis illustrates the salient features of what is sometimes known as a *nondeterministic algorithm*, one in which choices are allowed at certain steps and all choices must be followed. In effect, we systematically generate all configurations that the data underlying the algorithm can be in until we either encounter a solution or exhaust all possibilities. The notion of a nondeterministic algorithm is thus applicable not only to the simulation of nondeterministic automata, but to many other problems as well. It is interesting to note that something analogous to the halting condition for PDT's always enters into the question of whether a nondeterministic algorithm can be simulated deterministically. Some specific examples of nondeterministic algorithms are found in the Exercises.

In syntax analysis a grammar rather than a pushdown transducer will usually be given. For this reason we shall now discuss top-down and bottom-up parsing directly in terms of the given grammar rather than in terms of the left or right parser for the grammar. However, the manner in which the algorithms work is identical to the serial simulation of the pushdown parser. Instead of cycling through the possible sequences of moves the parser can make, we shall cycle through all possible derivations that are consistent with the input.

4.1.2. Informal Top-Down Parsing

The name top-down parsing comes from the idea that we attempt to produce a parse tree for the input string starting from the top (root) and working down to the leaves. We begin by taking the given grammar and numbering in some order the alternates for every nonterminal. That is, if $A \longrightarrow \alpha_1 | \alpha_2 | \cdots | \alpha_n$ are all the A-productions in the grammar, we assign some ordering to the α_i's (the *alternates* for A).

For example, consider the grammar mentioned in the previous section. The S-productions are

$$S \longrightarrow aSbS \,|\, aS \,|\, c$$

and let us use them in the order given. That is, $aSbS$ will be the first alternate for S, aS the second, and c the third. Let us assume that our input string is *aacbc*. We shall use an input pointer which initially points at the leftmost symbol of the input string.

Briefly stated, a top-down parser attempts to generate a derivation tree for the input as follows. We begin with a tree containing one node labeled S. That node is the initial active node. We then perform the following steps recursively:

(1) If the active node is labeled by a nonterminal, say A, then choose the first alternate, say $X_1 \cdots X_k$, for A and create k direct descendants for A labeled $X_1, X_2, \ldots, X_k$. Make X_1 the active node. If $k = 0$, then make the node immediately to the right of A active.

(2) If the active node is labeled by a terminal, say a, then compare the current input symbol with a. If they match, then make active the node immediately to the right of a and move the input pointer one symbol to the right. If a does not match the current input symbol, go back to the node where the previous production was applied, adjust the input pointer if necessary, and try the next alternate. If no alternate is possible, go back to the next previous node, and so forth.

At all times we attempt to keep the derivation tree consistent with the input string. That is, if $x\alpha$ is the frontier of the tree generated thus far, where α is either e or begins with a nonterminal symbol, then x is a prefix of the input string.

In our example we begin with a derivation tree initially having one node labeled S. We then apply the first S-production, extending the tree in a manner that is consistent with the given input string. Here, we would use $S \rightarrow aSbS$ to extend the tree to Fig. 4.2(a). Since the active node of the tree is a at this instant and the first input symbol is a, we advance the input pointer to the second input symbol and make the S immediately to the right of a the new active node. We then expand this S in Fig. 4.2(a), using the first alternate, to obtain Fig. 4.2(b). Since the new active node is a, which matches

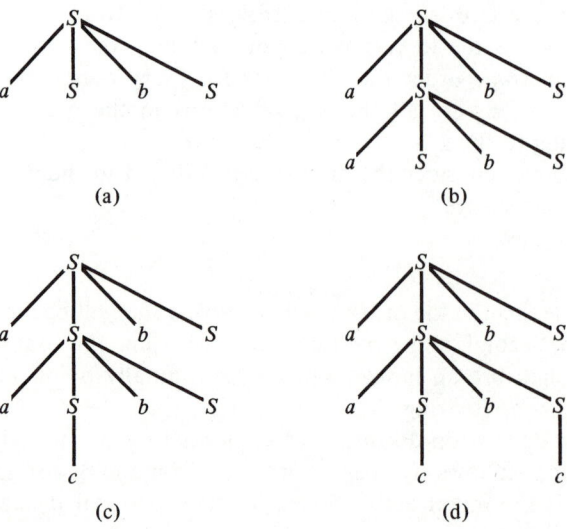

Fig. 4.2 Partial derivation trees.

the second input symbol, we advance the input pointer to the third input symbol.

We then expand the leftmost S in Fig. 4.2(b), but this time we cannot use either the first or second alternate because then the resulting left-sentential form would not be consistent with the input string. Thus we must use the third alternate to obtain Fig. 4.2(c). We can now advance the input pointer from the third to the fourth and then to the fifth input symbol, since the next two active symbols in the left-sentential form represented by Fig. 4.2(c) are c and b.

We can expand the leftmost S in Fig. 4.2(c) using the third alternate for S to obtain Fig. 4.2(d). (The first two alternates are again inconsistent with the input.) The fifth terminal symbol is c, and thus we can advance the input pointer one symbol to the left. (We assume that there is a marker to denote the end of the input string.) However, there are more symbols generated by Fig. 4.2(d), namely bS, than there are in the input string, so we now know that we are on the wrong track in finding a correct parse for the input.

Recalling the pushdown parser of Section 4.1.1, we have at this point gone through the sequence of configurations C_0, C_1, C_3, C_5, C_6, C_7. There is no next move possible from C_7.

We must now find some other left-sentential form. We first see if there is another alternate for the production used to obtain the tree of Fig. 4.2(d) from the previous tree. There is none, since we used $S \rightarrow c$ to obtain Fig. 4.2(d) from Fig. 4.2(c). We then return to the tree of Fig. 4.2(c) and reset the input pointer to position 3 on the input. We determine if there is another alternate for the production used to obtain Fig. 4.2(c) from the previous tree. Again there is none, since we used $S \rightarrow c$ to obtain Fig. 4.2(c) from Fig. 4.2(b). We thus return to Fig. 4.2(b), resetting the input pointer to position 2. We used the first alternate for S to obtain Fig. 4.2(b) from Fig. 4.2(a), so now we try the second alternate and obtain the tree of Fig. 4.3(a).

We can now advance the input pointer to position 3, since the a generated matches the a at position 2 in the input string. Now, we may use only the third alternate to expand the leftmost S in Fig. 4.3(a) to obtain Fig. 4.3(b). The input symbols at positions 3 and 4 are now matched, so we can advance the input pointer to position 5. We can apply only the third alternate for S in Fig. 4.3(b), and we obtain Fig. 4.3(c). The final input symbol is matched with the rightmost symbol of Fig. 4.3(c). We thus know that Fig. 4.3(c) is a valid parse for the input. At this point we can backtrack to continue looking for other parses, or terminate.

Because our grammar is not left-recursive, we shall eventually exhaust all possibilities by backtracking. That is, we would be at the root, and all alternates for S would have been tried. At this point we can halt, and if we have not found a parse, we can report that the input string is not syntactically well formed.

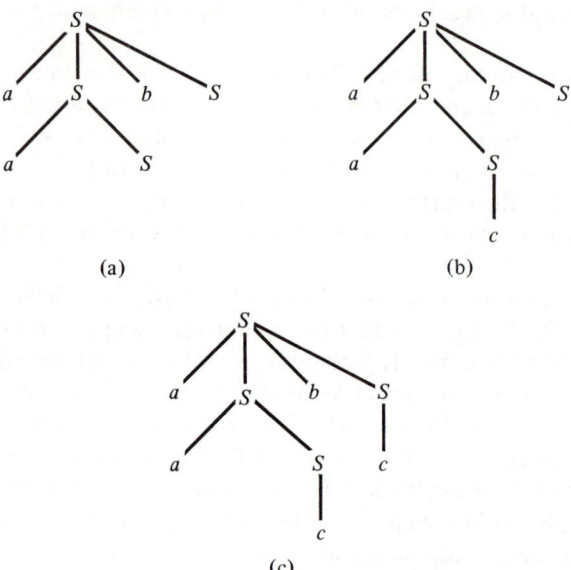

Fig. 4.3   Further attempts at parsing.

There is a major pitfall in this procedure. If the grammar is left-recursive, then this process may never terminate. For example, suppose that $A\alpha$ is the first alternate for A. We would then apply this production forever whenever A is to be expanded.

One might argue that this problem could be avoided by trying the alternate $A\alpha$ for A last. However, the left recursion might be far more subtle, involving several productions. For example, the first A-production might be $A \to SC$. Then if $S \to AB$ is the first production for S, we would have $A \Rightarrow SC \Rightarrow ABC$, and this pattern would repeat. Even if a suitable ordering for the productions of all nonterminals is found, on inputs which are not syntactically well formed, the left-recursive cycles would occur eventually, since all preceding choices would fail.

A second attempt to nullify the effects of left recursion might be to bound the number of nodes in the temporary tree in terms of the length of the input string. If we have a CFG $G = (N, \Sigma, P, S)$ with $\#N = k$ and an input string w of length $n - 1$, we can show that if w is in $L(G)$, then there is at least one derivation tree for w that has no path of length greater than kn. Thus we could confine our search to derivation trees of *depth* (maximum path length) no greater than kn.

However, the number of derivation trees of depth $\leq d$ can be an enormous function of d for some grammars. For example, consider the grammar

G with productions $S \longrightarrow SS \mid e$. The number of derivation trees of depth d for this grammar is given by the recurrence

$$D(1) = 1$$
$$D(d) = (D(d-1))^2 + 1$$

Values of $D(d)$ for d from 1 to 6 are given in Fig. 4.4.

d	$D(d)$
1	1
2	2
3	5
4	26
5	677
6	458330

Fig. 4.4 Values of $D(d)$.

$D(d)$ grows very rapidly, faster than $2^{2^{d-4}}$ for $d \geq 3$. (Also, see Exercise 4.1.4.) This growth is so huge that any grammar in which two productions of this form need to be considered could not possibly be reasonably parsed using this modification of the top-down parsing algorithm.

For these reasons the approach generally taken is to apply the top-down parsing algorithm only to grammars that are free of left recursion.

4.1.3. The Top-Down Parsing Algorithm

We are now ready to describe our top-down backtrack parsing algorithm. The algorithm uses two pushdown lists ($L1$ and $L2$) and a counter containing the current position of the input pointer. To describe the algorithm precisely, we shall use a stylized notation similar to that used to describe configurations of a pushdown transducer.

ALGORITHM 4.1

Top-down backtrack parsing.

Input. A non-left-recursive CFG $G = (N, \Sigma, P, S)$ and an input string $w = a_1 a_2 \cdots a_n$, $n \geq 0$. We assume that the productions in P are numbered $1, 2, \ldots, p$.

Output. One left parse for w if one exists. The output "error" otherwise.

Method.

(1) For each nonterminal A in N, order the alternates for A. Let A_i be the index for the ith alternate of A. For example, if $A \longrightarrow \alpha_1 \mid \alpha_2 \mid \cdots \mid \alpha_k$

are all the A-productions in P and we have ordered the alternates as shown, then A_1 is the index for α_1, A_2 is the index for α_2, and so forth.

(2) A 4-tuple (s, i, α, β) will be used to denote a *configuration* of the algorithm:

- (a) s denotes the state of the algorithm.
- (b) i represents the location of the input pointer. We assume that the $n + 1$st "input symbol" is \$, the right endmarker.
- (c) α represents the first pushdown list ($L1$).
- (d) β represents the second pushdown list ($L2$).

The top of α will be on the right and the top of β will be on the left. $L2$ represents the "current" left-sentential form, the one which our expansion of nonterminals has produced. Referring to our informal description of top-down parsing in Section 4.1.1, the symbol on top of $L2$ is the symbol labeling the active node of the derivation tree being generated. $L1$ represents the current history of the choices of alternates made and the input symbols over which the input head has shifted. The algorithm will be in one of three states q, b, or t; q denotes normal operation, b denotes backtracking, and t is the terminating state.

(3) The initial configuration of the algorithm is $(q, 1, e, S\$)$.

(4) There are six types of steps. These steps will be described in terms of their effect on the configuration of the algorithm. The heart of the algorithm is to compute successive configurations defined by a "goes to" relation, $\vdash$. The notation $(s, i, \alpha, \beta) \vdash (s', i', \alpha', \beta')$ means that if the current configuration is (s, i, α, β), then we are to go next into the configuration $(s', i', \alpha', \beta')$. Unless otherwise stated, i can be any integer from 1 to $n + 1$, α a string in $(\Sigma \cup I)^*$, where I is the set of indices for the alternates, and β a string in $(N \cup \Sigma)^*$. The six types of move are as follows:

(a) *Tree expansion*

$$(q, i, \alpha, A\beta) \vdash (q, i, \alpha A_1, \gamma_1 \beta)$$

where $A \rightarrow \gamma_1$ is a production in P and γ_1 is the first alternate for A. This step corresponds to an expansion of the partial derivation tree using the first alternate for the leftmost nonterminal in the tree.

(b) *Successful match of input symbols and derived symbol*

$$(q, i, \alpha, a\beta) \vdash (q, i + 1, \alpha a, \beta)$$

provided $a_i = a$, $i \leq n$. If the ith input symbol matches the next terminal symbol derived, we move that terminal symbol from the top of $L2$ to the top of $L1$ and increment the input pointer.

(c) *Successful conclusion*

$$(q, n + 1, \alpha, \$) \vdash (t, n + 1, \alpha, e)$$

We have reached the end of the input and have found a left-sentential form which matches the input. We can recover the left parse from α by applying the following homomorphism h to α: $h(a) = e$ for all a in Σ; $h(A_i) = p$, where p is the production number associated with the production $A \longrightarrow \gamma$, and γ is the ith alternate for A.

(d) *Unsuccessful match of input symbol and derived symbol*

$$(q, i, \alpha, a\beta) \vdash (b, i, \alpha, a\beta) \qquad \text{if } a_i \neq a$$

We go into the backtracking mode as soon as the left-sentential form being derived is not consistent with the input.

(e) *Backtracking on input*

$$(b, i, \alpha a, \beta) \vdash (b, i - 1, \alpha, a\beta)$$

for all a in Σ. In the backtracking mode we shift input symbols back from $L1$ to $L2$.

(f) *Try next alternate*

$$(b, i, \alpha A_j, \gamma_j \beta) \vdash$$

- (i) $(q, i, \alpha A_{j+1}, \gamma_{j+1} \beta)$, if γ_{j+1} is the $j + 1$st alternate for A. (Note that γ_j is replaced by γ_{j+1} on the top of $L2$.)
- (ii) No configuration, if $i = 1$, $A = S$, and there are only j alternates for S. (This condition indicates that we have exhausted all possible left-sentential forms consistent with the input w without having found a parse for w.)
- (iii) $(b, i, \alpha, A\beta)$ otherwise. (Here, the alternates for A are exhausted, and we backtrack by removing A_j from $L1$ and replacing γ_j by A on $L2$.)

The execution of the algorithm is as follows.

Step 1: Starting in the initial configuration, compute successive next configurations $C_0 \vdash C_1 \vdash \cdots \vdash C_i \vdash \cdots$ until no further configurations can be computed.

Step 2: If the last computed configuration is $(t, n + 1, \gamma, e)$, emit $h(\gamma)$ and halt. $h(\gamma)$ is the first found left parse. Otherwise, emit the error signal. □

Algorithm 4.1 is essentially the algorithm we described informally earlier, with a few bookkeeping features added to perform the backtracking.

Example 4.1

Let us consider the operation of Algorithm 4.1 using the grammar G with productions

(1) $E \longrightarrow T + E$

(2) $E \longrightarrow T$

(3) $T \longrightarrow F * T$

(4) $T \longrightarrow F$

(5) $F \longrightarrow a$

Let E_1 be $T + E$, E_2 be T, T_1 be $F * T$, and T_2 be F. With the input $a + a$, Algorithm 4.1 computes the following sequence of configurations:

$$(q, 1, e, E\$) \vdash (q, 1, E_1, T + E\$)$$
$$\vdash (q, 1, E_1 T_1, F * T + E\$)$$
$$\vdash (q, 1, E_1 T_1 F_1, a * T + E\$)$$
$$\vdash (q, 2, E_1 T_1 F_1 a, * T + E\$)$$
$$\vdash (b, 2, E_1 T_1 F_1 a, * T + E\$)$$
$$\vdash (b, 1, E_1 T_1 F_1, a * T + E\$)$$
$$\vdash (b, 1, E_1 T_1, F * T + E\$)$$
$$\vdash (q, 1, E_1 T_2, F + E\$)$$
$$\vdash (q, 1, E_1 T_2 F_1, a + E\$)$$
$$\vdash (q, 2, E_1 T_2 F_1 a, + E\$)$$
$$\vdash (q, 3, E_1 T_2 F_1 a +, E\$)$$
$$\vdash (q, 3, E_1 T_2 F_1 a + E_1, T + E\$)$$
$$\vdash (q, 3, E_1 T_2 F_1 a + E_1 T_1, F * T + E\$)$$
$$\vdash (q, 3, E_1 T_2 F_1 a + E_1 T_1 F_1, a * T + E\$)$$
$$\vdash (q, 4, E_1 T_2 F_1 a + E_1 T_1 F_1 a, * T + E\$)$$
$$\vdash (b, 4, E_1 T_2 F_1 a + E_1 T_1 F_1 a, * T + E\$)$$
$$\vdash (b, 3, E_1 T_2 F_1 a + E_1 T_1 F_1, a * T + E\$)$$
$$\vdash (b, 3, E_1 T_2 F_1 a + E_1 T_1, F * T + E\$)$$
$$\vdash (q, 3, E_1 T_2 F_1 a + E_1 T_2, F + E\$)$$
$$\vdash (q, 3, E_1 T_2 F_1 a + E_1 T_2 F_1, a + E\$)$$
$$\vdash (q, 4, E_1 T_2 F_1 a + E_1 T_2 F_1 a, + E\$)$$
$$\vdash (b, 4, E_1 T_2 F_1 a + E_1 T_2 F_1 a, + E\$)$$

$$\vdash (b, 3, E_1 T_2 F_1 a + E_1 T_2 F_1, a + E\$)$$
$$\vdash (b, 3, E_1 T_2 F_1 a + E_1 T_2, F + E\$)$$
$$\vdash (b, 3, E_1 T_2 F_1 a + E_1, T + E\$)$$
$$\vdash (q, 3, E_1 T_2 F_1 a + E_2, T\$)$$
$$\vdash (q, 3, E_1 T_2 F_1 a + E_2 T_1, F * T\$)$$
$$\vdash (q, 3, E_1 T_2 F_1 a + E_2 T_1 F_1, a * T\$)$$
$$\vdash (q, 4, E_1 T_2 F_1 a + E_2 T_1 F_1 a, * T\$)$$
$$\vdash (b, 4, E_1 T_2 F_1 a + E_2 T_1 F_1 a, * T\$)$$
$$\vdash (b, 3, E_1 T_2 F_1 a + E_2 T_1 F_1, a * T\$)$$
$$\vdash (b, 3, E_1 T_2 F_1 a + E_2 T_1, F * T\$)$$
$$\vdash (q, 3, E_1 T_2 F_1 a + E_2 T_2, F\$)$$
$$\vdash (q, 3, E_1 T_2 F_1 a + E_2 T_2 F_1, a\$)$$
$$\vdash (q, 4, E_1 T_2 F_1 a + E_2 T_2 F_1 a, \$)$$
$$\vdash (t, 4, E_1 T_2 F_1 a + E_2 T_2 F_1 a, e)$$

The left parse is $h(E_1 T_2 F_1 a + E_2 T_2 F_1 a) = 145245.$ $\square$

We shall now show that Algorithm 4.1 does indeed produce a left parse for w according to G if one exists.

DEFINITION

A *partial left parse* is the sequence of productions used in a leftmost derivation of a left-sentential form. We say that a partial left parse is *consistent* with the input string w if the associated left-sentential form is consistent with w.

Let $G = (N, \Sigma, P, S)$ be the non-left-recursive grammar of Example 4.1 and let $w = a_1 \cdots a_n$ be the input string. The *sequence* of *consistent partial left parses* for w, $\pi_0, \pi_1, \pi_2, \ldots, \pi_i, \ldots$ is defined as follows:

(1) π_0 is e and represents a derivation of S from S. (π_0 is not strictly a parse.)

(2) π_1 is the production number for $S \to \alpha$, where α is the first alternate for S.

(3) π_i is defined as follows: Suppose that $S \overset{\pi_{i-1}}{\Longrightarrow} xA\gamma$. Let β be the lowest numbered alternate for A, if it exists, such that we can write $x\beta\gamma = xy\delta$, where δ is either e or begins with a nonterminal and xy is a prefix of w. Then $\pi_i = \pi_{i-1} A_k$, where k is the number of alternate β. In this case we call π_i a *continuation* of π_{i-1}. If, on the other hand, no such β exists, or $S \overset{\pi_{i-1}}{\Longrightarrow} x$ for some terminal string x, then let j be the largest integer less than $i - 1$ such that the following conditions hold:

(a) Let $S \overset{\pi_j}{\Longrightarrow} xB\gamma$, and let π_{j+1} be a continuation of π_j, with alternate α_k replacing B in the last step of π_{j+1}. Then there exists an alternate α_m for B which follows α_k in the order of alternates for B.

(b) We can write $x\alpha_m\gamma = xy\delta$, where δ is e or begins with a nonterminal; xy is a prefix of w. Then $\pi_i = \pi_j B_m$, where B_m is the number of production $B \rightarrow \alpha_m$. In this case, we call π_i a *modification* of π_{i-1}.

(c) π_i is undefined if (a) or (b) does not apply.

Example 4.2

For the grammar G of Example 4.1 and the input string $a + a$, the sequence of consistent partial left parses is

$$e$$
$$1$$
$$13$$
$$14$$
$$145$$
$$1451$$
$$14513$$
$$14514$$
$$1452$$
$$14523$$
$$14524$$
$$145245$$
$$2$$
$$23$$
$$24$$

It should be observed that the sequence of consistent partial left parses up to the first correct parse is related to the sequence of strings appearing on $L1$. Neglecting the terminal symbols on $L1$, the two sequences are the same, except that $L1$ will have certain sequences that are not consistent with the input. When such a sequence appears on $L1$, backtracking immediately occurs. □

It should be obvious that the sequence of consistent partial left parses is unique and includes all the consistent partial left parses in a natural lexicographic order.

LEMMA 4.1

Let $G = (N, \Sigma, P, S)$ be a non-left-recursive grammar. Then there exists a constant c such that if $A \overset{i}{\underset{lm}{\Longrightarrow}} wB\alpha$ and $|w| = n$, then $i \leq c^{n+2}$.†

---

†In fact, a stronger result is possible; i is linear in n. However, this result suffices for the time being and will help prove the stronger result.

Proof. Let $\#N = k$, and consider the derivation tree D corresponding to the leftmost derivation $A \overset{i}{\Rightarrow} wB\alpha$. Suppose that there exists a path of length more than $k(n + 2)$ from the root to a leaf. Let n_0 be the node labeled by the explicitly shown B in $wB\alpha$. If the path reaches a leaf to the right of n_0, then the path to n_0 must be at least as long. This follows because in a leftmost derivation the leftmost nonterminal is always rewritten. Thus the direct ancestor of each node to the right of n_0 is an ancestor of n_0. The derivation tree D is shown in Fig. 4.5.

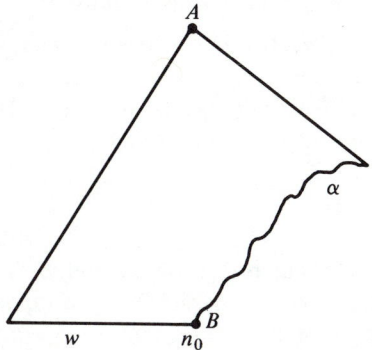

Fig. 4.5 Derivation tree D.

Thus, if there is a path of length greater than $k(n + 2)$ in D, we can find one such path which reaches n_0 or a node to its left. Then we can find $k + 1$ consecutive nodes, say $n_1, \ldots, n_{k+1}$, on the path such that each node yields the same portion of wB. All the direct descendants of n_i, $1 \leq i \leq k$, that lie to the left of n_{i+1} derive e. We must thus be able to find two of $n_1, \ldots, n_{k+1}$ with the same label, and this label is easily shown to be a left-recursive nonterminal.

We may conclude that D has no path of length greater than $k(n + 2)$. Let l be the length of the longest right side of a production. Then D has no more than $l^{k(n+2)}$ interior nodes. We conclude that if $A \overset{i}{\Rightarrow} wB\alpha$, then $i \leq l^{k(n+2)}$. Choosing $c = l^k$ proves the lemma. $\quad\square$

COROLLARY

Let $G = (N, \Sigma, P, S)$ be a non-left-recursive grammar. Then there is a constant c' such that if $S \overset{i}{\underset{lm}{\Rightarrow}} wB\alpha$ and $w \neq e$, then $|\alpha| \leq c'|w|$.

Proof. Referring to Fig. 4.5, we have shown that the path from the root to n_0 is no longer than $k(|w| + 2)$. Thus, $|\alpha| \leq kl(|w| + 2)$. Choose $c' = 3kl$. $\quad\square$

LEMMA 4.2

Let $G = (N, \Sigma, P, S)$ be a CFG with no useless nonterminals and $w = a_1 a_2 \cdots a_n$ an input string in Σ^*. The sequence of consistent left parses for w is finite if and only if G is not left-recursive.

Proof. If G is left-recursive, then clearly the sequence of consistent left parses is infinite for some terminal string. Suppose that G is not left-recursive. Then each consistent left parse is of length at most c^{n+2}, for some c, by Lemma 4.1. There are thus a finite number of consistent left parses. $\square$

DEFINITION

Let $G = (N, \Sigma, P, S)$ be a CFG and γ a sequence of subscripted nonterminals (indices for alternates) and terminals. Let π be a partial left parse consistent with w. We say that γ *describes* π if the following holds:

(1) Let $\pi = p_1 \cdots p_k$, and $S = \alpha_0 \overset{p_1}{\Longrightarrow} \alpha_1 \overset{p_2}{\Longrightarrow} \alpha_2 \cdots \overset{p_k}{\Longrightarrow} \alpha_k$. Let $\alpha_i = x_i\beta_i$, where β_i is e or begins with a nonterminal.

(2) Then $\gamma = A_{i_1}w_1 A_{i_2}w_2 \cdots A_{i_k}w_k$, where A_{i_j} is the index for the production applied going from α_{j-1} to α_j, and w_j is the suffix of x_j such that $x_j = x_{j-1}w_j$.

LEMMA 4.3

Let $G = (N, \Sigma, P, S)$ be a non-left-recursive grammar and $\pi_0, \pi_1, \ldots, \pi_i, \ldots$ be the sequence of consistent partial left parses for w. Suppose that none of $\pi_0, \ldots, \pi_i$ are left parses for w. Let $S \overset{\pi_i}{\Longrightarrow} \alpha$ and $S \overset{\pi_{i+1}}{\Longrightarrow} \beta$. Write α and β, respectively, as $x\alpha_1$ and $y\beta_1$, where α_1 and β_1 are each either e or begin with a nonterminal. Then in Algorithm 4.1,

$$(q, 1, e, S\$) \overset{*}{\vdash} (q, j_1, \gamma_1, \alpha_1 \$) \overset{*}{\vdash} (q, j_2, \gamma_2, \beta_1\$),$$

where $j_1 = |x| + 1$, $j_2 = |y| + 1$, and γ_1 and γ_2 describe π_i and π_{i+1}, respectively.

Proof. The proof is by induction on i. The basis, $i = 0$, is trivial. For the inductive step, we need to consider two cases.

Case 1: π_{i+1} is a continuation of π_i. Let α_1 have first symbol A, with alternates $\beta_1, \ldots, \beta_k$. If $xA\beta_j$ is not consistent with the input, then should Algorithm 4.1 replace A by β_j, rules (d), (e), and (fi) ensure that the alternate β_{j+1} will be the next expansion tried. Since we assumed π_{i+1} to be a continuation of π_i, the desired alternate for A will subsequently be tried. After input symbols are shifted by rule (b), configuration $(q, j_2, \gamma_2, \beta_1\$)$ is reached.

Case 2: Suppose that π_{i+1} is a modification of π_i. Then all untried alternates for A immediately lead to backtracking, and by rules (e) and (fiii), the contents of $L1$ will eventually describe π_j, the partial left parse mentioned in the definition of a modification. Configuration $(q, j_2, \gamma_2, \beta_1\$)$ is then reached as in case 1. $\square$

THEOREM 4.1

Algorithm 4.1 produces a left parse for w if one exists and otherwise emits an error message.

Proof. From Lemma 4.3 we see that the algorithm cycles through all consistent partial left parses until either a left parse is found for the input or all consistent partial left parses are exhausted. From Lemma 4.2 we know that the number of partial left parses is finite, so the algorithm must eventually terminate. $\square$

4.1.4. Time and Space Complexity of the Top-Down Parser

Let us consider a computer in which the space needed to store a configuration of Algorithm 4.1 is proportional to the sum of the lengths of the two lists, a very reasonable assumption. It is also reasonable to assume that the time spent computing configuration C_2 from C_1, if $C_1 \vdash C_2$, is a constant, independent of the configurations involved. Under these assumptions, we shall show that Algorithm 4.1 takes linear space and at most exponential time as functions of input length. The proofs require the following lemma, a strengthening of Lemma 4.1.

LEMMA 4.4

Let $G = (N, \Sigma, P, S)$ be a non-left-recursive grammar. Then there exists a constant c such that if $A \xrightarrow{i} \alpha$ and $|\alpha| \geq 1$, then $i \leq c|\alpha|$.

Proof. By Lemma 4.1, there is a constant c_1 such that if $A \xrightarrow{i} e$, then $i \leq c_1$. Let $\#N = k$ and let l be the length of the longest right side of a production. By Lemma 2.16 we can express N as $\{A_0, A_1, \ldots, A_{k-1}\}$ such that if $A_i \xrightarrow{+} A_j\alpha$, then $j > i$. We shall prove the following statement by induction on the parameter $p = kn - j$:

(4.1.1)   If $A_j \xrightarrow{i} \alpha$ and $|\alpha| = n \geq 1$, then $i \leq klc_1|\alpha| - jlc_1$

Basis. The basis, $p = 0$, holds vacuously, since we assume that $n \geq 1$.

Induction. Assume all instances of (4.1.1) such that $kn - j < p$ are true. Now consider a particular instance with $kn - j = p$. Let the first step in the derivation be $A_j \Rightarrow X_1 \cdots X_r$, for $r \leq l$. Then we can write $\alpha = \alpha_1 \cdots \alpha_r$ such that $X_m \xrightarrow{i_m} \alpha_m$, $1 \leq m \leq r$, and $i = 1 + i_1 + \cdots + i_m$. Let $\alpha_1 = \alpha_2 = \cdots = \alpha_{s-1} = e$, and $\alpha_s \neq e$. Since $\alpha \neq e$, s exists.

Case 1: X_s is a nonterminal, say A_g. Then $A_j \xrightarrow{*} A_g X_{s+1} \cdots X_r$, so $g > j$. Since $k|\alpha_s| - g < p$, we have by (4.1.1), $i_s \leq klc_1|\alpha_s| - glc_1$. Since $|\alpha_m| < |\alpha|$, for $s + 1 \leq m \leq r$, we have by (4.1.1) that $i_m \leq klc_1|\alpha_m|$ whenever $s + 1 \leq m \leq r$ and $\alpha_m \neq e$. Certainly at most $l - 1$ of $\alpha_1, \ldots, \alpha_r$ are e, so the sum of i_m over those m such that $\alpha_m = e$ is at most $(l - 1)c_1$. Thus,

$$
\begin{aligned}
i &= 1 + i_1 + \cdots + i_r \\
&\leq 1 + (l - 1)c_1 + klc_1|\alpha| - glc_1 \\
&\leq klc_1|\alpha| - (g - 1)lc_1 \\
&\leq klc_1|\alpha| - jlc_1.
\end{aligned}
$$

Case 2: X_s is a terminal. It is left for the Exercises to show that in this case $i \leq 1 + klc_1(|\alpha| - 1) \leq klc_1|\alpha| - jlc_1$.

We conclude from (4.1.1) that if $S \overset{i}{\Rightarrow} \alpha$ and $|\alpha| \geq 1$, then $i \leq klc_1|\alpha|$. Let $c = klc_1$ to conclude the lemma. $\square$

COROLLARY 1

Let $G = (N, \Sigma, P, S)$ be a non-left-recursive grammar. Then there exists a constant c' such that if $S \overset{i}{\underset{1m}{\Rightarrow}} wA\alpha$ and $w \neq e$, then $i \leq c'|w|$.

Proof. By the corollary to Lemma 4.1, there is a constant c'' such that $|\alpha| \leq c''|w|$. By Lemma 4.4, $i \leq c|wA\alpha|$. Since $|wA\alpha| \leq (2 + c'')|w|$, the choice $c' = c(2 + c'')$ yields the desired result. $\square$

COROLLARY 2

Let $G = (N, \Sigma, P, S)$ be a non-left-recursive grammar. Then there is a constant k such that if π is a partial left parse consistent with sentence w, and $S \overset{\pi}{\Rightarrow} x\alpha$, where α is either e or begins with a nonterminal, then $|\pi| \leq k(|w| + 1)$.

Proof. If $x \neq e$, then by Corollary 1, we have $|\pi| \leq c'|x|$. Certainly, $|x| \leq |w|$, so $|\pi| \leq c'|w|$. As an exercise, we can show that if $x = e$, then $|\pi| \leq c'$. Thus, $|\pi| \leq c'(|w| + 1)$ in either case. $\square$

THEOREM 4.2

There is a constant c such that Algorithm 4.1, with input w of length $n \geq 1$, uses no more than cn cells, if one cell only is needed for each symbol on the two lists of the configurations.

Proof. Except possibly for the last expansion made, list $L2$ is part of a left-sentential form α such that $S \overset{\pi}{\Rightarrow} \alpha$, where π is a partial left parse consistent with w. By Corollary 2 to Lemma 4.4, $|\pi| \leq k(|w| + 1)$. Since there is a bound on the length of the right side of any production, say l, we know that $|\alpha| \leq kl(|w| + 1) \leq 2kl|w|$. Thus the length of $L2$ is no greater than $2kl|w| + l - 1 \leq 3kl|w|$.

List $L1$ consists of part of the left-sentential form α (most or all of the terminal prefix) and $|\pi|$ indices. It thus follows by Corollary 2 to Lemma 4.4 that the length of $L1$ is at most $2k(l+1)|w|$. The sum of the two lengths is thus proportional to $|w|$. $\quad\square$

THEOREM 4.3

There is a constant c such that Algorithm 4.1, when its input w is of length $n \geq 1$, makes no more than c^n elementary operations, provided the calculation of one step of Algorithm 4.1 takes a constant number of elementary operations.

Proof. By Corollary 2, every partial left parse consistent with w is of length at most $c_1 n$ for some c_1. Thus there are at most c_2^n different partial left parses consistent with w for some constant c_2. Algorithm 4.1 computes at most n configurations between configurations whose contents of $L1$ describe consecutive partial left parses. The total number of configurations computed by Algorithm 4.1 is thus no more than nc_2^n. From the binomial theorem the relation $nc_2^n \leq (c_2 + 1)^n$ is immediate. Choose c to be $(c_2 + 1)m$, where m is the maximum number of elementary operations required to compute one step of Algorithm 4.1. $\quad\square$

Theorem 4.3 is in a sense as strong as possible. That is, there are non-left-recursive grammars which cause Algorithm 4.1 to spend an exponential amount of time, because there are c^n partial left parses consistent with some words of length n.

Example 4.3

Let $G = (\{S\}, \{a, b\}, P, S)$, where P consists of $S \rightarrow aSS \mid e$. Let $X(n)$ be the number of different leftmost parses of a^n, and let $Y(n)$ be the number of partial left parses consistent with a^n. The following recurrence equations define $X(n)$ and $Y(n)$:

(4.1.2)
$$X(0) = 1$$
$$X(n) = \sum_{i=0}^{n-1} X(i)X(n-1-i)$$

(4.1.3)
$$Y(0) = 2$$
$$Y(n) = Y(n-1) + \sum_{i=0}^{n-1} X(i)Y(n-1-i)$$

Line (4.1.2) comes from the fact that every derivation for a sentence a^n with $n \geq 1$ begins with production $S \rightarrow aSS$. The remaining $n-1$ a's can be divided any way between the two S's. In line (4.1.3), the $Y(n-1)$ term corresponds to the possibility that after the first step $S \Rightarrow aSS$, the second S is never rewritten; the summation corresponds to the possibility that the first S derives a^i for some i. The formula $Y(0) = 2$ is from the observation

that the null derivation and the derivation $S \Rightarrow e$ are consistent with string e.
From Exercise 2.4.29 we have

$$X(n) = \frac{1}{n+1}\binom{2n}{n}$$

so $X(n) \geq 2^{n-1}$. Thus

$$Y(n) \geq Y(n-1) + \sum_{i=0}^{n-1} 2^{i-1} Y(n-1-i)$$

from which $Y(n) \geq 2^n$ certainly follows. $\quad\square$

This example points out a major problem with top-down backtrack parsing. The number of steps necessary to parse by Algorithm 4.1 can be enormous. There are several techniques that can be used to speed this algorithm somewhat. We shall mention a few of them here.

(1) We can order productions so that the most likely alternates are tried first. However, this will not help in those cases in which the input is not syntactically well formed, and all possibilities have to be tried.

DEFINITION

For a CFG $G = (N, \Sigma, P, S)$,

$$\text{FIRST}_k(\alpha) = \{x \mid \alpha \overset{*}{\underset{\text{lm}}{\Rightarrow}} x\beta \text{ and } |x| = k \text{ or } \alpha \overset{*}{\Rightarrow} x \text{ and } |x| < k\}.$$

That is, $\text{FIRST}_k(\alpha)$ consists of all terminal prefixes of length k (or less if α derives a terminal string of length less than k) of the terminal strings that can be derived from α.

(2) We can look ahead at the next k input symbols to determine whether a given alternate should be used. For example, we can tabulate, for each alternate α, a lookahead set $\text{FIRST}_k(\alpha)$. If no prefix of the remaining input string is contained in $\text{FIRST}_k(\alpha)$, we can immediately reject α and try the next alternate. This technique is very useful both when the given input is in $L(G)$ and when it is not in $L(G)$. In Chapter 5 we shall see that for certain classes of grammars the use of lookahead can entirely eliminate the need for backtracking.

(3) We can add bookkeeping features which will allow faster backtracking. For example, if we know that the last m-productions applied have no applicable next alternates, when failure occurs we can skip back directly to the position where there is an applicable alternate.

(4) We can restrict the amount of backtracking that can be done. We shall discuss parsing techniques of this nature in Chapter 6.

Another severe problem with backtrack parsing is its poor error-locating capability. If an input string is not syntactically well formed, then a compiler should announce which input symbols are in error. Moreover, once one error has been found, the compiler should recover from that error so that parsing can resume in order to detect any additional errors that might occur.

If the input string is not syntactically well formed, then the backtracking algorithm as formulated will merely announce error, leaving the input pointer at the first input symbol. To obtain more detailed error information, we can incorporate error productions into the grammar. Error productions are used to generate strings containing common syntactic errors and would make syntactically invalid strings well formed. The production numbers in the output corresponding to these error productions can then be used to signal the location of errors in the input string. However, from a practical point of view, the parsing algorithms presented in Chapter 5 have better error-announcing capabilities than backtracking algorithms with error productions.

4.1.5. Bottom-Up Parsing

There is a general approach to parsing that is in a sense opposite to that of top-down parsing. The top-down parsing algorithm can be thought of as building the parse tree by trial and error from the root (top) and proceeding downward to the leaves. Its opposite, bottom-up parsing, starts with the leaves (i.e., the input symbols themselves) and attempts to build the tree upwards toward the root.

We shall describe a formulation of bottom-up parsing that is called shift–reduce parsing. The parsing proceeds using essentially a right parser cycling through all possible rightmost derivations, in reverse, that are consistent with the input. A move consists of scanning the string on top of the pushdown list to see if there is a right side of a production that matches the symbols on top of the list. If so, a reduction is made, replacing these symbols by the left side of the production. If more than one reduction is possible, we order the possible reductions in some arbitrary manner and apply the first.

If no reduction is possible, we shift the next input symbol onto the pushdown list and proceed as before. We shall always attempt to make a reduction before shifting. If we come to the end of the string and no reduction is possible, we backtrack to the last move at which we made a reduction. If another reduction was possible at that point we try that.

Let us consider a grammar with productions $S \rightarrow AB$, $A \rightarrow ab$, and $B \rightarrow aba$. Let the input string be $ababa$. We would shift the first a on the pushdown list. Since no reduction is possible, we would then shift the b on the pushdown list. We then replace ab on top of the pushdown list by A. At this point we have the partial tree of Fig. 4.6(a).

As the A cannot be further reduced, we shift a onto the pushdown list. Again no reduction is possible, so we shift b onto the pushdown list. We can then reduce ab to A. We now have the partial tree of Fig. 4.6(b).

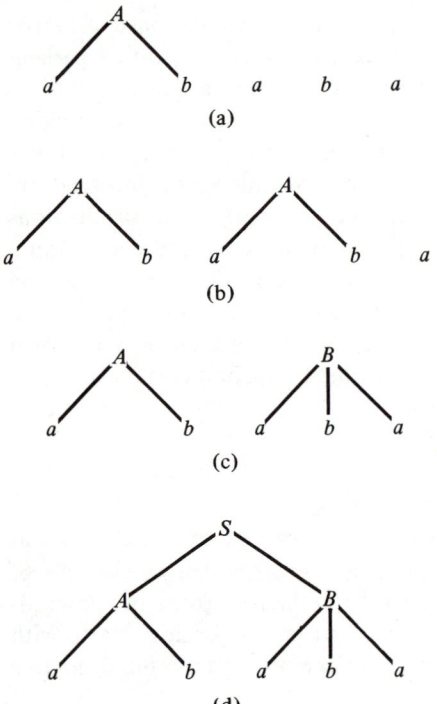

Fig. 4.6 Partial parse trees in bottom-up parse.

We shift a on the pushdown list and find that no reductions are possible. We then backtrack to the last position at which we made a reduction, namely where the pushdown list contained Aab (b is on top here) and we replaced ab by A, i.e., when the partial tree was that of Fig. 4.6(a). Since no other reduction is possible, we now shift instead of reducing. The pushdown list now contains $Aaba$. We can then reduce aba to B, to obtain Fig. 4.6(c). Next, we replace AB by S and thus have a complete tree, shown in Fig. 4.6(d).

This method can be viewed as considering all possible sequences of moves of a nondeterministic right parser for a grammar. However, as with top-down parsing, we must avoid situations in which the number of possible moves is infinite.

One such pitfall occurs when a grammar has cycles, that is, derivations of the form $A \overset{+}{\Rightarrow} A$ for some nonterminal A. The number of partial trees can be infinite in this case, so we shall rule out grammars with cycles. Also, e-productions cause difficulty, since we can make an arbitrary number of reductions in which the empty string is "reduced" to a nonterminal. Bottom-up parsing can be extended to embrace grammars with e-productions, but for simplicity we shall choose to outlaw e-productions here.

ALGORITHM 4.2

Bottom-up backtrack parsing.

Input. CFG $G = (N, \Sigma, P, S)$ with no cycles or e-productions, whose productions are numbered 1 to p, and an input string $w = a_1 a_2 \cdots a_n$, $n \geq 1$.

Output. One right parse for w if one exists. The output "error" otherwise.

Method.

(1) Order the productions arbitrarily.

(2) We shall couch our algorithm in the 4-tuple configurations similar to those used in Algorithm 4.1. In a configuration (s, i, α, β)

    (a) s represents the state of the algorithm.

    (b) i represents the current location of the input pointer. We assume the $n + 1$st input symbol is \$, the right endmarker.

    (c) α represents a pushdown list $L1$ (whose top is on the right).

    (d) β represents a pushdown list $L2$ (whose top is on the left).

As before, the algorithm can be in one of three states q, b, or t. $L1$ will hold a string of terminals and nonterminals that derives the portion of input to the left of the input pointer. $L2$ will hold a history of the shifts and reductions necessary to obtain the contents of $L1$ from the input.

(3) The initial configuration of the algorithm is $(q, 1, \$, e)$.

(4) The algorithm itself is as follows. We begin by trying to apply step 1.

Step 1: Attempt to reduce

$$(q, i, \alpha\beta, \gamma) \vdash (q, i, \alpha A, j\gamma)$$

provided $A \rightarrow \beta$ is the jth production in P and β is the first right side in the linear ordering in (1) that is a suffix of $\alpha\beta$. The production number is written on $L2$. If step 1 applies, return to step 1. Otherwise go to step 2.

Step 2: Shift

$$(q, i, \alpha, \gamma) \vdash (q, i + 1, \alpha a_i, s\gamma)$$

provided $i \neq n + 1$. Go to step 1.

If $i = n + 1$, instead go to step 3.

If step 2 is successful, we write the ith input symbol on top of $L1$, increment the input pointer, and write s on $L2$, to indicate that a shift has been made.

Step 3: Accept

$$(q, n + 1, \$S, \gamma) \vdash (t, n + 1, \$S, \gamma)$$

Emit $h(\gamma)$, where h is the homomorphism

$$h(s) = e$$
$$h(j) = j \qquad \text{for all production numbers}$$

$h(\gamma)$ is a right parse of w in reverse. Then halt.

If step 3 is not applicable, go to step 4.

Step 4: *Enter backtracking mode*

$$(q, n + 1, \alpha, \gamma) \vdash (b, n + 1, \alpha, \gamma)$$

provided $\alpha \neq \$S$. Go to step 5.

Step 5: *Backtracking*

$$\text{(a)} \quad (b, i, \alpha A, j\gamma) \vdash (q, i, \alpha'B, k\gamma)$$

if the jth production in P is $A \longrightarrow \beta$ and the next production in the ordering of (1) whose right side is a suffix of $\alpha\beta$ is $B \longrightarrow \beta'$, numbered k. Note that $\alpha\beta = \alpha'\beta'$. Go to step 1. (Here we have backtracked to the previous reduction, and we try the next alternative reduction.)

$$\text{(b)} \quad (b, n + 1, \alpha A, j\gamma) \vdash (b, n + 1, \alpha\beta, \gamma)$$

if the jth production in P is $A \longrightarrow \beta$ and no other alternative reductions of $\alpha\beta$ remain. Go to step 5. (If no alternative reductions exist, "undo" the reduction and continue backtracking when the input pointer is at $n + 1$.)

$$\text{(c)} \quad (b, i, \alpha A, j\gamma) \vdash (q, i + 1, \alpha\beta a, s\gamma)$$

if $i \neq n + 1$, the jth production in P is $A \longrightarrow \beta$, and no other alternative reductions of $\alpha\beta$ remain. Here $a = a_i$ is shifted onto $L1$, and an s is entered on $L2$. Go to step 1.

Here we have backtracked to the previous reduction. No alternative reductions exist, so we try a shift instead.

$$\text{(d)} \quad (b, i, \alpha a, s\gamma) \vdash (b, i - 1, \alpha, \gamma)$$

if the top entry on $L2$ is the shift symbol. (Here all alternatives at position i have been exhausted, and the shift action must be undone. The input pointer moves left, the terminal symbol a_i is removed from $L1$ and the symbol s is removed from $L2$.) $\square$

Example 4.4

Let us apply this bottom-up parsing algorithm to the grammar G with productions

$$(1) \ E \longrightarrow E + T$$
$$(2) \ E \longrightarrow T$$
$$(3) \ T \longrightarrow T * F$$
$$(4) \ T \longrightarrow F$$
$$(5) \ F \longrightarrow a$$

If $E + T$ appears on top of $L1$, we shall first try reducing, using $E \longrightarrow E + T$ and then using $E \longrightarrow T$. If $T * F$ appears on top of $L1$, we shall first try $T \longrightarrow T * F$ and then $T \longrightarrow F$. With input $a * a$ the bottom-up algorithm would go through the following configurations:

$$
\begin{aligned}
(q, 1, \$, e) &\vdash (q, 2, \$a, s) \\
&\vdash (q, 2, \$F, 5s) \\
&\vdash (q, 2, \$T, 45s) \\
&\vdash (q, 2, \$E, 245s) \\
&\vdash (q, 3, \$E *, s245s) \\
&\vdash (q, 4, \$E * a, ss245s) \\
&\vdash (q, 4, \$E * F, 5ss245s) \\
&\vdash (q, 4, \$E * T, 45ss245s) \\
&\vdash (q, 4, \$E * E, 245ss245s) \\
&\vdash (b, 4, \$E * E, 245ss245s) \\
&\vdash (b, 4, \$E * T, 45ss245s) \\
&\vdash (b, 4, \$E * F, 5ss245s) \\
&\vdash (b, 4, \$E * a, ss245s) \\
&\vdash (b, 3, \$E *, s245s) \\
&\vdash (b, 2, \$E, 245s) \\
&\vdash (q, 3, \$T *, s45s) \\
&\vdash (q, 4, \$T * a, ss45s) \\
&\vdash (q, 4, \$T * F, 5ss45s) \\
&\vdash (q, 4, \$T, 35ss45s) \\
&\vdash (q, 4, \$E, 235ss45s) \\
&\vdash (t, 4, \$E, 235ss45s) \quad \square
\end{aligned}
$$

We can prove the correctness of Algorithm 4.2 in a manner analogous to the way we showed that top-down parsing worked. We shall outline a proof here, leaving most of the details as Exercises.

DEFINITION

Let $G = (N, \Sigma, P, S)$ be a CFG. We say that π is a *partial right parse consistent with* w if there is some α in $(N \cup \Sigma)^*$ and a prefix x of w such that $\alpha \Rightarrow^{\pi R} x$.

LEMMA 4.5

Let G be a cycle-free CFG with no e-productions. Then there is a constant c such that the number of partial right parses consistent with an input of length n is at most c^n.

Proof. Exercise.   □

THEOREM 4.4

Algorithm 4.2 correctly finds a right parse of w if one exists, and signals an error otherwise.

Proof. By Lemma 4.5, the number of partial right parses consistent with the input is finite. It is left as an Exercise to show that unless Algorithm 4.2 finds a parse, it cycles through all partial right parses in a natural order. Namely, each partial right parse can be coded by a sequence of production indices and shift symbols (s). Algorithm 4.2 considers each such sequence that is a partial right parse in a lexicographic order. That lexicographic order is determined by an order of the symbols, placing s last, and ordering the production indices as in step 1 of Algorithm 4.2. Note that not every sequence of such symbols is a consistent partial right parse.   □

Paralleling the analysis for Algorithm 4.1, we can also show that the lengths of the lists in the configurations for Algorithm 4.2 remain linear in the input length.

THEOREM 4.5

Let one cell be needed for each symbol on a list in a configuration of Algorithm 4.2, and let the number of elementary operations needed to compute one step of Algorithm 4.2 be bounded. Then for some constants c_1 and c_2, Algorithm 4.2 requires $c_1 n$ space and c_2^n time, when given input of length $n \geq 1$.

Proof. Exercise.   □

There are a number of modifications we can make to the basic bottom-up parsing algorithm in order to speed up its operations:

(1) We can add "lookahead" so that if we find that the next k symbols to the right of the input pointer could not possibly follow an A in any right-sentential form, then we do not make a reduction according to any A-production.

(2) We can attempt to order the reductions so that the most likely reductions are made first.

(3) We can add information to determine whether certain reductions will lead to success. For example, if the first reduction uses the production $A \rightarrow a_1 \cdots a_k$, where a_1 is the first input symbol and we know that there is no y in Σ^* such that $S \overset{*}{\Rightarrow} Ay$, then this reduction can be immediately ruled out. In general we want to be sure that if $\$\alpha$ is on $L1$, then α is the prefix of a right-sentential form. While this test is complicated in general, certain notions, such as precedence, discussed in Chapter 5, will make it easy to rule out many α's that might appear on $L1$.

(4) We can add features to make backtracking faster. For example, we might store information that will allow us to directly recover the previous configuration at which a reduction was made.

Some of these considerations are explored in Exercises 4.1.12–4.1.14 and 4.1.25. The remarks on error detection and recovery with the backtracking top-down algorithm also apply to the bottom-up algorithm.

EXERCISES

4.1.1. Let G be defined by

$$S \longrightarrow AS \,|\, a$$
$$A \longrightarrow bSA \,|\, b$$

What sequence of steps is taken by Algorithm 4.1 if the order of alternates is as shown, and the input is
(a) *ba*?
(b) *baba*?
What are the sequences if the order of alternates is reversed?

4.1.2. Let G be the grammar

$$S \longrightarrow SA \,|\, A$$
$$A \longrightarrow aA \,|\, b$$

What sequence of steps are taken by Algorithm 4.2 if the order of reductions is longest first, and the input is
(a) *ab*?
(b) *abab*?
What if the order of choice is shortest first?

4.1.3. Show that every cycle-free CFG that does not generate e is right-covered by one for which Algorithm 4.2 works, but may not be left-covered by any for which Algorithm 4.1 works.

*4.1.4. Show that the solution to the recurrence

$$D(1) = 1$$
$$D(d) = (D(d-1)^2) + 1$$

is $D(d) = [k^{2^d}]$, where k is a real number and $[x]$ is the greatest integer $\leq x$. Here, $k = 1.502837 \ldots$.

4.1.5. Complete the proof of Corollary 2 to Lemma 4.4.

4.1.6. Modify Algorithm 4.1 to refrain from using an alternate if it is impossible to derive the next k input symbols, for fixed k, from the resulting left-sentential form.

4.1.7. Modify Algorithm 4.1 to work on an arbitrary grammar by putting bounds on the length to which $L1$ and $L2$ can grow.

**4.1.8. Give a necessary and sufficient condition on the input grammar such that Algorithm 4.1 will never enter the backtrack mode.

4.1.9. Prove Lemma 4.5.

4.1.10. Prove Theorem 4.5.

4.1.11. Modify Algorithm 4.2 to work for an arbitrary CFG by bounding the length of the lists $L1$ and $L2$.

4.1.12. Modify Algorithm 4.2 to run faster by checking that the partial right parse together with the input to the right of the pointer does not contain any sequence of k symbols that could not be part of a right-sentential form.

4.1.13. Modify Algorithms 4.1 and 4.2 to backtrack to any specially designated previous configuration using a finite number of reasonably defined elementary operations.

**4.1.14. Give a necessary and sufficient condition on a grammar such that Algorithm 4.2 will operate with no backtracking. What if the modification of Exercise 4.1.12 is first made?

4.1.15. Find a cycle-free grammar with no e-productions on which Algorithm 4.2 takes an exponential amount of time.

4.1.16. Improve the bound of Lemma 4.4 if the grammar has no e-productions.

4.1.17. Show that if a grammar G with no useless symbols has either a cycle or an e-production, then Algorithm 4.2 will not terminate on any sentence not in $L(G)$.

DEFINITION

We shall outline a programming language in which we can write nondeterministic algorithms. We call the language *NDF* (nondeterministic FORTRAN), because it consists of FORTRAN-like statements plus the statement CHOICE $(n_1, \ldots, n_k)$, where $k \geq 2$ and $n_1, \ldots, n_k$ are statement numbers.

To define the meaning of an NDF program, we postulate the existence of an interpreter capable of executing any finite number of programs in a round robin fashion (i.e., working on the compiled version of each in turn for a fixed number of machine operations). We assume that the meaning of the usual FORTRAN statements is understood. However, if the statement CHOICE $(n_1, \ldots, n_k)$ is executed, the interpreter makes k copies of the program and its entire data region. Control is transferred to statement n_i in the ith copy of the program for $1 \leq i \leq k$. All output appears on a single printer, and all input is received from a single card reader (so that we had better read all input before executing any CHOICE statement).

Example 4.5

The following NDF program prints the legend NOT A PRIME one or more times if the input is not a prime number, and prints nothing if it is a prime:

```
        READ N
        I = 1
C   PICK A VALUE OF I GREATER THAN 1
    1       I = I + 1
        CHOICE (1, 2)
    2       IF (I .EQ. N) STOP
C   FIND IF I IS A DIVISOR OF N AND NOT EQUAL
C   TO N
        IF ((N/I) * I .NE. N) STOP
        WRITE ("NOT A PRIME")
        STOP                              □
```

*4.1.38. Write an NDF program which prints all answers to the "eight queens problem." (Select eight points on an 8×8 grid so that no two lie on any row, column, or diagonal line.)

*4.1.19. Write NDF programs to simulate a left or right parser.

It would be nice if there were an algorithm which determined if a given NDF program could run forever on some input. Unfortunately this is not decidable for FORTRAN, or any other programming language. However, we can make such a determination if we assume that branches (from IF and assigned GOTO statements, not CHOICE statements) are externally controlled by a "demon" who is trying to make the program run forever, rather than by the values of the program variables. We say an NDF program is *halting* if for each input there is no sequence of branches and nondeterministic choices that cause any copy of the program to run beyond some constant number of executed statements, the constant being a function of the number of input cards available for data. (Assume that the program halts if it attempts to read and no data is available.)

*4.1.20. Give an algorithm to determine whether an NDF program is halting under the assumption that no DO loop index is ever decremented.

*4.1.21. Give an algorithm which takes a halting NDF program and constructs from it an equivalent ALGOL program. By "equivalent program," we have to mean that the ALGOL program does input and output in an order which the NDF program might do it, since no order for the NDF program is known. ALGOL, rather than FORTRAN, is preferred here, because recursion is very convenient.

4.1.22. Let $G = (N, \Sigma, P, S)$ be a CFG. From G construct a CFG G' such that $L(G') = \Sigma^*$ and if $S \overset{\pi}{\underset{G}{\Longrightarrow}} w$, then $S \overset{\pi}{\underset{G'}{\Longrightarrow}} w$.

A PDT (with pushdown top on the left) that behaves as a nondeterministic left-corner parser for a grammar can be constructed from the grammar. The parser will use as pushdown symbols nonterminals, terminals, and special symbols of the form $[A, B]$, where A and B are nonterminals.

Nonterminals and terminals appearing on the pushdown list are goals to be recognized top-down. In a symbol $[A, B]$, A is the current goal to be recognized and B is the nonterminal which has just been recognized bottom-up. From a CFG $G = (N, \Sigma, P, S)$ we can construct a PDT $M = (\{q\}, \Sigma, N \times N \cup N \cup \Sigma, \Delta, \delta, q, S, \varnothing)$ which will be a left-corner parser for G. Here $\Delta = \{1, 2, \ldots, p\}$ is the set of production numbers, and δ is defined as follows:

(1) Suppose that $A \longrightarrow \alpha$ is the ith production in P.
  (a) If α is of the form $B\beta$, where $B \in N$, then $\delta(q, e, [C, B])$ contains $(q, \beta[C, A], i)$ for all $C \in N$. Here we assume that we have recognized the left-corner B bottom-up so we establish the symbols in β as goals to be recognized top-down. Once we have recognized β, we shall have recognized an A.
  (b) If α does not begin with a nonterminal, then $\delta(q, e, C)$ contains $(q, \alpha[C, A], i)$ for all nonterminals C. Here, once α is recognized, the nonterminal A will have been recognized.

(2) $\delta(q, e, [A, A])$ contains (q, e, e) for all $A \in N$. Here an instance of the goal A which we have been looking for has been recognized. If this instance of A is not a left corner, we remove $[A, A]$ from the pushdown list signifying that this instance of A was the goal we sought.

(3) $\delta(q, a, a) = \{(q, e, e)\}$ for all $a \in \Sigma$. Here the current goal is a terminal symbol which matches the current input symbol. The goal, being satisfied, is removed.

M defines the translation

$$\{(w, \pi) \mid w \in L(G) \text{ and } \pi \text{ is a left-corner parse for } w\}.$$

Example 4.6

Consider the CFG $G = (N, \Sigma, P, S)$ with the productions

(1) $E \longrightarrow E + T$

(2) $E \longrightarrow T$

(3) $T \longrightarrow F \uparrow T$

(4) $T \longrightarrow F$

(5) $F \longrightarrow (E)$

(6) $F \longrightarrow a$

A nondeterministic left-corner parser for G is the PDT

$$M = (\{q\}, \Sigma, N \times N \cup N \cup \Sigma, \{1, 2, \ldots, 6\}, \delta, q, E, \varnothing)$$

where δ is defined as follows for all $A \in N$:

(1) (a) $\delta(q, e, [A, E])$ contains $(q, + T[A, E], 1)$.

   (b) $\delta(q, e, [A, T])$ contains $(q, [A, E], 2)$.

   (c) $\delta(q, e, [A, F])$ contains $(q, \uparrow T[A, T], 3)$ and $(q, [A, T], 4)$

   (d) $\delta(q, e, A) = \{(q, (E)[A, F], 5), (q, a[A, F], 6)\}$.

(2) $\delta(q, e, [A, A])$ contains (q, e, e).

(3) $\delta(q, a, a) = \{(q, e, e)\}$ for all $a \in \Sigma$.

Let us parse the input string $a \uparrow a + a$ using M. The derivation tree for this string is shown in Fig. 4.7. Since the PDT has only one state, we shall ignore the state. The PDT starts off in configuration

$$(a \uparrow a + a, E, e)$$

The second rule in (1d) is applicable (so is the first), so the PDT can go into configuration

$$(a \uparrow a + a, a[E, F], 6)$$

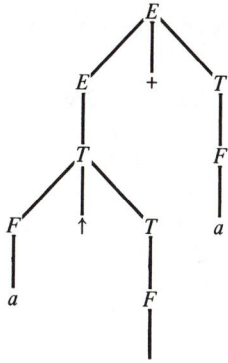

Fig. 4.7   Derivation tree for $a \uparrow a + $ a.

Here, the left-corner a has been generated using production 6. The symbol a is then compared with the current input symbol to yield

$$(\uparrow a + a, [E, F], 6)$$

We can then use the first rule in (1c) to obtain

$$(\uparrow a + a, \uparrow T[E, T], 63)$$

Here we are saying that the left corner of the production $T \longrightarrow F \uparrow T$ will now be recognized once we find $\uparrow$ and T. We can then enter the following configurations:

$$(a + a, T[E, T], 63) \vdash (a + a, a[T, F][E, T], 636)$$
$$\vdash (+ a, [T, F][E, T], 636)$$
$$\vdash (+ a, [T, T][E, T], 6364)$$

At this point T is the current goal and an instance of T which is not a left corner has been found. Thus using rule (2) to erase the goal, we obtain

$$(+ a, [E, T], 6364)$$

Continuing, we can terminate with the following sequence of configurations:

$$(+ a, [E, E], 63642) \vdash (+ a, + T[E, E], 636421)$$
$$\vdash (a, T[E, E], 636421)$$
$$\vdash (a, a[T, F][E, E], 6364216)$$
$$\vdash (e, [T, F][E, E], 6364216)$$
$$\vdash (e, [T, T][E, E], 63642164)$$
$$\vdash (e, [E, E], 63642164)$$
$$\vdash (e, e, 63642164) \quad \square$$

*4.1.23. Show that the construction above yields a nondeterministic left-corner parser for a CFG.

4.1.24. Construct a left-corner backtrack parsing algorithm.

Let $G = (N, \Sigma, P, S)$ be a CFG which contains no production with a right side of length 0 or 1. (Every CFL L such that $w \in L$ implies that $|w| \geq 2$ has such a grammar.) A nondeterministic shift–reduce right parser for G can be constructed such that each entry on the pushdown list is a pair of the form (X, Q), where $X \in N \cup \Sigma \cup \{\$\}$ ($\$$ is an endmarker for the pushdown list) and Q is the set of productions P with an indication of all possible prefixes of the right side of each production which could have been recognized to this point. That is, Q will be P with dots placed between some of the symbols of the right sides. There will be a dot in front of X_i in the production

$A \longrightarrow X_1 X_2 \cdots X_n$ if and only if $X_1 \cdots X_{i-1}$ is a suffix of the list of grammar symbols on the pushdown list.

A shift move can be made if the current input symbol is the continuation of some production. In particular, a shift move can always be made if $A \longrightarrow \alpha$ is in P and the current input symbol is in $\text{FIRST}_1(\alpha)$.

A reduce move can be made if the end of the right side of a production has been reached. Suppose that $A \longrightarrow \alpha$ is such a production. To reduce we remove $|\alpha|$ entries from the top of the pushdown list. If (X, Q) is the entry now on top of the pushdown list, we then write (A, Q') on the list, where Q' is computed from Q by assuming that an A has been recognized. That is, Q' is formed from Q by moving all dots that are immediately to the left of an A to the right of A and adding dots at the left end of the right sides if not already there.

Example 4.7

Consider the grammar $S \longrightarrow Sc|ab$ and the input string abc. Initially, the parser would have $(\$, Q_0)$ on the pushdown list, where Q_0 is $S \longrightarrow \cdot Sc|\cdot ab$. We can then shift the first input symbol and write (a, Q_1) on the pushdown list, where Q_1 is $S \longrightarrow \cdot Sc|\cdot a\cdot b$. Here, we can be beginning the productions $S \longrightarrow Sc|ab$, or we could have seen the first a of production $S \longrightarrow ab$. Shifting the next input symbol b, we would write (b, Q_2) on the pushdown list, where Q_1 is $S \longrightarrow \cdot Sc|\cdot ab\cdot$. We can then reduce using production $S \longrightarrow ab$. The pushdown list would now contain $(\$, Q_0)(S, Q_3)$, where Q_3 is $S \longrightarrow \cdot S\cdot c|\cdot ab$. $\square$

Domolki has suggested implementing this algorithm using a binary matrix M to represent the productions and a binary vector V to store the possible positions in each production. The vector V can be used in place of Q in the algorithm above. Each new vector on the pushdown list can be easily computed from M and the current value of V using simple bit operations.

4.1.25. Use Domolki's algorithm to help determine possible reductions in Algorithm 4.2.

BIBLIOGRAPHIC NOTES

Many of the early compiler-compilers and syntax-directed compilers used nondeterministic parsing algorithms. Variants of top-down backtrack parsing methods were used in Brooker and Morris' compiler-compiler [Rosen, 1967b] and in the META compiler writing systems [Schorre, 1964]. The symbolic programming system COGENT simulated a nondeterministic top-down parser by carrying along all viable move sequences in parallel [Reynolds, 1965]. Top-down backtracking methods have also been used to parse natural languages [Kuno and Oettinger, 1962].

One of the earliest published parsing algorithms is the essentially left-corner parsing algorithm of Irons [1961]. Surveys of early parsing techniques are given by Floyd [1964b], Cheatham and Sattley [1963], and Griffiths and Petrick [1965].

Unger [1968] describes a top-down algorithm in which the initial and final symbols derivable from a nonterminal are used to reduce backtracking. Nondeterministic algorithms are discussed by Floyd [1967b].

One implementation of Domolki's algorithm is described by Hext and Roberts [1970].

The survey article by Cohen and Gotlieb [1970] describes the use of list structure representations for context-free grammars in backtrack and nonbacktrack parsing algorithms.

4.2. TABULAR PARSING METHODS

We shall study two parsing methods that work for all context-free grammars, the Cocke–Younger–Kasami algorithm and Earley's algorithm. Each algorithm requires n^3 time and n^2 space, but the latter requires only n^2 time when the underlying grammar is unambiguous. Moreover, Earley's algorithm can be made to work in linear time and space for most of the grammars which can be parsed in linear time by the methods to be discussed in subsequent chapters.

4.2.1. The Cocke–Younger–Kasami Algorithm

In the last section we observed that the top-down and bottom-up backtracking methods may take an exponential amount of time to parse according to an arbitrary grammar. In this section, we shall give a method guaranteed to do the job in time proportional to the cube of the input length. It is essentially a "dynamic programming" method and is included here because of its simplicity. It is doubtful, however, that it will find practical use, for three reasons:

(1) n^3 time is too much to allow for parsing.

(2) The method uses an amount of space proportional to the square of the input length.

(3) The method of the next section (Earley's algorithm) does at least as well in all respects as this one, and for many grammars does better.

The method works as follows. Let $G = (N, \Sigma, P, S)$ be a Chomsky normal form CFG with no e-production. A simple generalization works for non-CNF grammars as well, but we leave this generalization to the reader. Since a cycle-free CFG can be left- or right-covered by a CFG in Chomsky normal form, the generalization is not too important.

Let $w = a_1 a_2 \cdots a_n$ be the input string which is to be parsed according to G. We assume that each a_i is in Σ for $1 \leq i \leq n$. The essence of the algorithm is the construction of a triangular *parse table* T, whose elements we denote t_{ij} for $1 \leq i \leq n$ and $1 \leq j \leq n - i + 1$. Each t_{ij} will have a value which is a subset of N. Nonterminal A will be in t_{ij} if and only if $A \overset{+}{\Rightarrow} a_i a_{i+1} \cdots a_{i+j-1}$, that is, if A derives the j input symbols beginning at position i. As a special case, the input string w is in $L(G)$ if and only if S is in t_{1n}.

Thus, to determine whether string w is in $L(G)$, we compute the parse table T for w and look to see if S is in entry t_{1n}. Then, if we want one (or all) parses of w, we can use the parse table to construct these parses. Algorithm 4.4 can be used for this purpose.

We shall first give an algorithm to compute the parse table and then the algorithm to construct the parses from the table.

ALGORITHM 4.3

Cocke–Younger–Kasami parsing algorithm.

Input. A Chomsky normal form CFG $G = (N, \Sigma, P, S)$ with no e-production and an input string $w = a_1 a_2 \cdots a_n$ in Σ^+.

Output. The parse table T for w such that t_{ij} contains A if and only if $A \overset{+}{\Rightarrow} a_i a_{i+1} \cdots a_{i+j-1}$.

Method.

(1) Set $t_{i1} = \{A \,|\, A \rightarrow a_i$ is in $P\}$ for each i. After this step, if t_{i1} contains A, then clearly $A \overset{+}{\Rightarrow} a_i$.

(2) Assume that $t_{ij'}$ has been computed for all i, $1 \leq i \leq n$, and all j', $1 \leq j' < j$. Set

$$t_{ij} = \{A \,|\, \text{for some } k, \ 1 \leq k < j, \ A \rightarrow BC \text{ is in } P,$$
$$B \text{ is in } t_{ik}, \text{ and } C \text{ is in } t_{i+k,j-k}\}.\dagger$$

Since $1 \leq k < j$, both k and $j - k$ are less than j. Thus both t_{ik} and $t_{i+k,j-k}$ are computed before t_{ij} is computed. After this step, if t_{ij} contains A, then

$$A \overset{+}{\Longrightarrow} BC \overset{+}{\Longrightarrow} a_i \cdots a_{i+k-1} C \overset{+}{\Longrightarrow} a_i \cdots a_{i+k-1} a_{i+k} \cdots a_{i+j-1}.$$

(3) Repeat step (2) until t_{ij} is known for all $1 \leq i \leq n$, and $1 \leq j \leq n - i + 1$. □

Example 4.8

Consider the CNF grammar G with productions

---

†Note that we are not discussing in detail how this is to be done. Obviously, the computation involved can be done by computer. When we discuss the time complexity of Algorithm 4.3, we shall give details of this step that enable it to be done efficiently.

$$S \longrightarrow AA \,|\, AS \,|\, b$$
$$A \longrightarrow SA \,|\, AS \,|\, a$$

Let *abaab* be the input string. The parse table T that results from Algorithm 4.3 is shown in Fig. 4.8. From step (1), $t_{11} = \{A\}$ since $A \rightarrow a$ is in P and $a_1 = a$. In step (2) we add S to t_{32}, since $S \rightarrow AA$ is in P and A is in both t_{31} and t_{41}. Note that, in general, if the t_{ij}'s are displayed as shown, we can

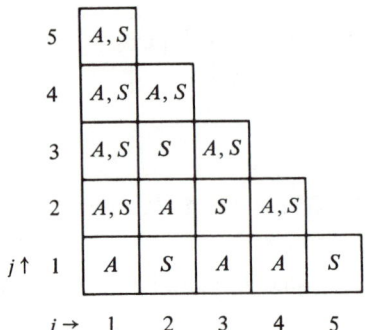

Fig. 4.8 Parse table T.

compute t_{ij}, $i > 1$, by examining the nonterminals in the following pairs of entries:

$$(t_{i1}, t_{i+1,j-1}), (t_{i2}, t_{i+2,j-2}), \ldots, (t_{i,j-1}, t_{i+j-1,1})$$

Then, if B is in t_{ik} and C is in $t_{i+k,j-k}$ for some k such that $1 \leq k < j$ and $A \rightarrow BC$ is in P, we add A to t_{ij}. That is, we move up the ith column and down the diagonal extending to the right of cell t_{ij} simultaneously, observing the nonterminals in the pairs of cells as we go.

Since S is in t_{15}, *abaab* is in $L(G)$. $\square$

THEOREM 4.6

If Algorithm 4.3 is applied to CNF grammar G and input string $a_1 \cdots a_n$, then upon termination, A is in t_{ij} if and only if $A \overset{+}{\Rightarrow} a_i \cdots a_{i+j-1}$.

Proof. The proof is a straightforward induction on j and is left for the Exercises. The most difficult step occurs in the "if" portion, where one must observe that if $j > 1$ and $A \overset{+}{\Rightarrow} a_i \cdots a_{i+j-1}$, then there exist nonterminals B and C and integer k such that $A \rightarrow BC$ is in P, $B \overset{+}{\Rightarrow} a_i \cdots a_{i+k-1}$, and $C \overset{+}{\Rightarrow} a_{i+k} \cdots a_{i+j-1}$. $\square$

Next, we show that Algorithm 4.3 can be executed on a random access computer in n^3 suitably defined elementary operations. For this purpose, we shall assume that we have several integer variables available, one of which is n, the input length. An *elementary operation*, for the purposes of this discussion, is one of the following:

(1) Setting a variable to a constant, to the value held by some variable, or to the sum or difference of the value of two variables or constants;

(2) Testing if two variables are equal,

(3) Examining and/or altering the value of t_{ij}, if i and j are the current values of two integer variables or constants, or

(4) Examining a_i, the ith input symbol, if i is the value of some variable.

We note that operation (3) is a finite operation if the grammar is known in advance. As the grammar becomes more complex, the amount of space necessary to store t_{ij} and the amount of time necessary to examine it both increase, in terms of reasonable steps of a more elementary nature. However, here we are interested only in the variation of time with input length. It is left to the reader to define some more elementary steps to replace (3) and find the functional variation of the computation time with the number of nonterminals and productions of the grammar.

Convention

We take the notation "$f(n)$ is $0(g(n))$" to mean that there exists a constant k such that for all $n \geq 1$, $f(n) \leq kg(n)$. Thus, when we say that Algorithm 4.3 operates in time $0(n^3)$, we mean that there exists a constant k for which it never takes more than kn^3 elementary operations on a word of length n.

Theorem 4.7

Algorithm 4.3 requires $0(n^3)$ elementary operations of the type enumerated above to compute t_{ij} for all i and j.

Proof. To compute t_{i1} for all i merely requires that we set $i = 1$ [operation(1)], then repeatedly set t_{i1} to $\{A \mid A \longrightarrow a_i$ is in $P\}$ [operations (3) and (4)], test if $i = n$ [operation (2)], and if not, increment i by 1 [operation (1)]. The total number of elementary operations performed is $0(n)$.

Next, we must perform the following steps to compute t_{ij}:

(1) Set $j = 1$.

(2) Test if $j = n$. If not, increment j by 1 and perform **line**(j), a procedure to be defined below.

(3) Repeat step (2) until $j = n$.

Exclusive of operations required for **line**(j), this routine involves $2n - 2$ elementary operations. The total number of elementary operations required for Algorithm 4.3 is thus $0(n)$ plus $\sum_{j=2}^{n} l(j)$, where $l(j)$ is the number of elementary operations used in **line**(j). We shall show that $l(j)$ is $0(n^2)$ and thus that the total number of operations is $0(n^3)$.

The procedure **line**(j) computes all entries t_{ij} such that $1 \le i < n - j + 1$. It embodies the procedure outlined in Example 4.8 to compute t_{ij}. It is defined as follows (we assume that all t_{ij} initially have value $\varnothing$):

(1) Let $i = 1$ and $j' = n - j + 1$.
(2) Let $k = 1$.
(3) Let $k' = i + k$ and $j'' = j - k$.
(4) Examine t_{ik} and $t_{k'j''}$. Let

$$t_{ij} = t_{ij} \cup \{A \,|\, A \longrightarrow BC \text{ is in } P, B \text{ in } t_{ik}, \text{ and } C \text{ in } t_{k'j''}\}.$$

(5) Increment k by 1.
(6) If $k = j$, go to step (7). Otherwise, go to step (3).
(7) If $i = j'$, halt. Otherwise do step (8).
(8) Increment i by 1 and go to step (2).

We observe that the above routine consists of an inner loop, (3)–(6), and an outer loop, (2)–(8). The inner loop is executed $j - 1$ times (for values of k from 1 to $j - 1$) each time it is entered. At the end, t_{ij} has the value defined in Algorithm 4.3. It consists of seven elementary operations, and so the inner loop uses $0(j)$ elementary operations each time it is entered.

The outer loop is entered $n - j + 1$ times and consists of $0(j)$ elementary operations each time it is entered. Since $j \le n$, each computation of **line**(j) takes $0(n^2)$ operations.

Since **line**(j) is computed n times, the total number of elementary operations needed to execute Algorithm 4.3 is thus $0(n^3)$. $\quad \square$

We shall now describe how to find a left parse from the parse table. The method is given by Algorithm 4.4.

ALGORITHM 4.4

Left parse from parse table.

Input. A Chomsky normal form CFG $G = (N, \Sigma, P, S)$ in which the productions in P are numbered from 1 to p, an input string $w = a_1 a_2 \cdots a_n$, and the parse table T for w constructed by Algorithm 4.3.

Output. A left parse for w or the signal "error."

Method. We shall describe a recursive routine **gen**(i, j, A) to generate a left parse corresponding to the derivation $A \underset{1m}{\overset{+}{\Longrightarrow}} a_i a_{i+1} \cdots a_{i+j-1}$. The routine **gen**($i, j, A$) is defined as follows:

(1) If $j = 1$ and the mth production in P is $A \longrightarrow a_i$, then emit the production number m.
(2) If $j > 1$, k is the smallest integer, $1 \le k < j$, such that for some B in t_{ik} and C in $t_{i+k,j-k}$, $A \longrightarrow BC$ is a production in P, say the mth. (There

may be several choices for $A \longrightarrow BC$ here. We can arbitrarily choose the one with the smallest m.) Then emit the production number m and execute **gen**(i, k, B), followed by **gen**$(i + k, j - k, C)$.

Algorithm 4.4, then, is to execute **gen**$(1, n, S)$, provided that S is in t_{1n}. If S is not in t_{1n}, emit the message "error." $\square$

We shall extend the notion of an elementary operation to include the writing of a production number associated with a production. We can then show the following result.

THEOREM 4.8

If Algorithm 4.4 is executed with input string $a_1 \cdots a_n$, then it will terminate with some left parse for the input if one exists. The number of elementary steps taken by Algorithm 4.4 is $O(n^2)$.

Proof. An induction on the order in which **gen** is called shows that whenever **gen**(i, j, A) is called, then A is in t_{ij}. It is thus straightforward to show that Algorithm 4.4 produces a left parse.

To show that Algorithm 4.4 operates in time $O(n^2)$, we prove by induction on j that for all j a call of **gen**(i, j, A) takes no more than $c_1 j^2$ steps for some constant c_1. The basis, $j = 1$, is trivial, since step (1) of Algorithm 4.4 applies and uses one elementary operation.

For the induction, a call of **gen**(i, j, A) with $j > 1$ causes step (2) to be executed. The reader can verify that there is a constant c_2 such that step (2) takes no more than $c_2 j$ elementary operations, exclusive of calls. If **gen**(i, k, B) and **gen**$(i + k, j - k, C)$ are called, then by the inductive hypothesis, no more than $c_1 k^2 + c_1 (j - k)^2 + c_2 j$ steps are taken by **gen**(i, j, A). This expression reduces to $c_1 (j^2 + 2k^2 - 2kj) + c_2 j$. Since $1 \leq k < j$ and $j \geq 2$, we know that $2k^2 - 2kj \leq 2 - 2j \leq -j$. Thus, if we chose c_1 to be c_2 in the inductive hypothesis, we would have $c_1 k^2 + c_1 (j - k)^2 + c_2 j \leq c_1 j^2$. Since we are free to make this choice of c_1, we conclude the theorem. $\square$

Example 4.9

Let G be the grammar with the productions

$$(1) \quad S \longrightarrow AA$$
$$(2) \quad S \longrightarrow AS$$
$$(3) \quad S \longrightarrow b$$
$$(4) \quad A \longrightarrow SA$$
$$(5) \quad A \longrightarrow AS$$
$$(6) \quad A \longrightarrow a$$

Let $w = abaab$ be the input string. The parse table for w is given in Example 4.8.

Since S is in T_{15}, w is in $L(G)$. To find a left parse for $abaab$ we call routine **gen**(1, 5, S). We find A in t_{11} and in t_{24} and the production $S \longrightarrow AA$ in the set of productions. Thus we emit 1 (the production number for $S \longrightarrow AA$) and then call **gen**(1, 1, A) and **gen**(2, 4, A). **gen**(1, 1, A) gives the production number 6. Since S is in t_{21} and A is in t_{33} and $A \longrightarrow SA$ is the fourth production, **gen**(2, 4, A) emits 4 and calls **gen**(2, 1, S) followed by **gen**(3, 3, A).   ·

Continuing in this fashion we obtain the left parse 164356263.

Note that G is ambiguous; in fact, $abaab$ has more than one left parse. It is not in general possible to obtain all parses of the input from a parse table in less than exponential time, as there may be an exponential number of left parses for the input.   □

We should mention that Algorithm 4.4 can be made to run faster if, when we construct the parse table and add a new entry, we place pointers to those entries which cause the new entry to appear (see Exercise 4.2.21).

4.2.2. The Parsing Method of Earley

In this section we shall present a parsing method which will parse an input string according to an arbitrary CFG using time $0(n^3)$ and space $0(n^2)$, where n is the length of the input string. Moreover, if the CFG is unambiguous, the time variation is quadratic, and on most grammars for programming languages the algorithm can be modified so that both the time and space variations are linear with respect to input length (Exercise 4.2.18). We shall first give the basic algorithm informally and later show that the computation can be organized in such a manner that the time bounds stated above can be obtained.

The central idea of the algorithm is the following. Let $G = (N, \Sigma, P, S)$ be a CFG and let $w = a_1 a_2 \cdots a_n$ be an input string in Σ^*. An object of the form $[A \longrightarrow X_1 X_2 \cdots X_k \cdot X_{k+1} \cdots X_m, i]$ is called an *item* for w if $A \longrightarrow X_1 \cdots X_m$ is a production in P and $0 \le i \le n$. The dot between X_k and X_{k+1} is a metasymbol not in N or Σ. The integer k can be any number including 0 (in which case the · is the first symbol) or m (in which case it is the last).†

For each integer j, $0 \le j \le n$, we shall construct a list of items I_j such that $[A \longrightarrow \alpha \cdot \beta, i]$ is in I_j for $0 \le i \le j$ if and only if for some γ and δ, we have $S \overset{*}{\Longrightarrow} \gamma A \delta$, $\gamma \overset{*}{\Longrightarrow} a_1 \cdots a_i$, and $\alpha \overset{*}{\Longrightarrow} a_{i+1} \cdots a_j$. Thus the second component of the item and the number of the list on which it appears bracket the portion of the input derived from the string α. The other conditions on the item merely assure us of the possibility that the production $A \longrightarrow \alpha\beta$

---

†If the production is $A \longrightarrow e$, then the item is $[A \longrightarrow \cdot, i]$.

could be used in the way indicated in some input sequence that is consistent with w up to position j.

The sequence of lists $I_0, I_1, \ldots, I_n$ will be called the *parse lists* for the input string w. We note that w is in $L(G)$ if and only if there is some item of the form $[S \rightarrow \alpha \cdot, 0]$ in I_n.

We shall now describe an algorithm which, given any grammar, will generate the parse lists for any input string.

ALGORITHM 4.5

Earley's parsing algorithm.

Input. CFG $G = (N, \Sigma, P, S)$ and an input string $w = a_1 a_2 \cdots a_n$ in Σ^*.

Output. The parse lists $I_0, I_1, \ldots, I_n$.

Method. First, we construct I_0 as follows:

(1) If $S \rightarrow \alpha$ is a production in P, add $[S \rightarrow \cdot \alpha, 0]$ to I_0.

Now perform steps (2) and (3) until no new items can be added to I_0.

(2) If $[B \rightarrow \gamma \cdot, 0]$ is on I_0,† add $[A \rightarrow \alpha B \cdot \beta, 0]$ for all $[A \rightarrow \alpha \cdot B\beta, 0]$ on I_0.

(3) Suppose that $[A \rightarrow \alpha \cdot B\beta, 0]$ is an item in I_0. Add to I_0, for all productions in P of the form $B \rightarrow \gamma$, the item $[B \rightarrow \cdot \gamma, 0]$ (provided this item is not already in I_0).

We now construct I_j, having constructed $I_0, I_1, \ldots, I_{j-1}$.

(4) For each $[B \rightarrow \alpha \cdot a\beta, i]$ in I_{j-1} such that $a = a_j$, add $[B \rightarrow \alpha a \cdot \beta, i]$ to I_j.

Now perform steps (5) and (6) until no new items can be added.

(5) Let $[A \rightarrow \gamma \cdot, i]$ be an item in I_j. Examine I_i for items of the form $[B \rightarrow \alpha \cdot A\beta, k]$. For each one found, we add $[B \rightarrow \alpha A \cdot \beta, k]$ to I_j.

(6) Let $[A \rightarrow \alpha \cdot B\beta, i]$ be an item in I_j. For all $B \rightarrow \gamma$ in P, we add $[B \rightarrow \cdot \gamma, j]$ to I_j.

Note that consideration of an item with a terminal to the right of the dot yields no new items in steps (2), (3), (5) and (6).

The algorithm, then, is to construct I_j for $0 \leq j \leq n$. ☐

Example 4.10

Let us consider the grammar G with the productions

$$
\begin{aligned}
&(1)\ E \longrightarrow T + E \\
&(2)\ E \longrightarrow T \\
&(3)\ T \longrightarrow F * T \\
&(4)\ T \longrightarrow F \\
&(5)\ F \longrightarrow (E) \\
&(6)\ F \longrightarrow a
\end{aligned}
$$

†Note that γ can be e. This is the way rule (2) becomes applicable initially.

and let $(a + a) * a$ be the input string. From step (1) we add new items $[E \rightarrow \cdot T + E, 0]$ and $[E \rightarrow \cdot T, 0]$ to I_0. These items are considered by adding to I_0 the items $[T \rightarrow \cdot F * T, 0]$ and $[T \rightarrow \cdot F, 0]$ from rule (3). Continuing, we then add $[F \rightarrow \cdot (E), 0]$ and $[F \rightarrow \cdot a, 0]$. No more items can be added to I_0.

We now construct I_1. By rule (4) we add $[F \rightarrow (\cdot E), 0]$, since $a_1 = ($. Then rule (6) causes $[E \rightarrow \cdot T + E, 1]$, $[E \rightarrow \cdot T, 1]$, $[T \rightarrow \cdot F * T, 1]$, $[T \rightarrow \cdot F, 1]$, $[F \rightarrow \cdot (E), 1]$, and $[F \rightarrow \cdot a, 1]$ to be added. Now, no more items can be added to I_1.

To construct I_2, we note that $a_2 = a$ and that by rule (4) $[F \rightarrow a \cdot, 1]$ is to be added to I_2. Then by rule (5), we consider this item by going to I_1 and looking for items with F immediately to the right of the dot. We find two, and add $[T \rightarrow F \cdot * T, 1]$ and $[T \rightarrow F \cdot, 1]$ to I_2. Considering the first of these yields nothing, but the second causes us to again examine I_1, this time for items with $\cdot T$ in them. Two more items are added to I_2, $[E \rightarrow T \cdot + E, 1]$ and $[E \rightarrow T \cdot, 1]$. Again the first yields nothing, but the second causes $[F \rightarrow (E \cdot), 0]$ to be added to I_2. Now no more items can be added to I_2, so I_2 is complete.

The values of all the lists are given in Fig. 4.9.

I_0	I_1	I_2
$[E \rightarrow \cdot T + E, 0]$	$[F \rightarrow (\cdot E), 0]$	$[F \rightarrow a \cdot, 1]$
$[E \rightarrow \cdot T, 0]$	$[E \rightarrow \cdot T + E, 1]$	$[T \rightarrow F \cdot * T, 1]$
$[T \rightarrow \cdot F * T, 0]$	$[E \rightarrow \cdot T, 1]$	$[T \rightarrow F \cdot, 1]$
$[T \rightarrow \cdot F, 0]$	$[T \rightarrow \cdot F * T, 1]$	$[E \rightarrow T \cdot + E, 1]$
$[F \rightarrow \cdot (E), 0]$	$[T \rightarrow \cdot F, 1]$	$[E \rightarrow T \cdot, 1]$
$[F \rightarrow \cdot a, 0]$	$[F \rightarrow \cdot (E), 1]$	$[F \rightarrow (E \cdot), 0]$
	$[F \rightarrow \cdot a, 1]$	

I_3	I_4	I_5
$[E \rightarrow T + \cdot E, 1]$	$[F \rightarrow a \cdot, 3]$	$[F \rightarrow (E) \cdot, 0]$
$[E \rightarrow \cdot T + E, 3]$	$[T \rightarrow F \cdot * T, 3]$	$[T \rightarrow F \cdot * T, 0]$
$[E \rightarrow \cdot T, 3]$	$[T \rightarrow F \cdot, 3]$	$[T \rightarrow F \cdot, 0]$
$[T \rightarrow \cdot F * T, 3]$	$[E \rightarrow T \cdot + E, 3]$	$[E \rightarrow T \cdot + E, 0]$
$[T \rightarrow \cdot F, 3]$	$[E \rightarrow T \cdot, 3]$	$[E \rightarrow T \cdot, 0]$
$[F \rightarrow \cdot (E), 3]$	$[E \rightarrow T + E \cdot, 1]$	
$[F \rightarrow \cdot a, 3]$	$[F \rightarrow (E \cdot), 0]$	

I_6	I_7
$[T \rightarrow F * \cdot T, 0]$	$[F \rightarrow a \cdot, 6]$
$[T \rightarrow \cdot F * T, 6]$	$[T \rightarrow F \cdot * T, 6]$
$[T \rightarrow \cdot F, 6]$	$[T \rightarrow F \cdot, 6]$
$[F \rightarrow \cdot (E), 6]$	$[T \rightarrow F * T \cdot, 0]$
$[F \rightarrow \cdot a, 6]$	$[E \rightarrow T \cdot + E, 0]$
	$[E \rightarrow T \cdot, 0]$

Fig. 4.9 Parse lists for Example 4.10.

Since $[E \rightarrow T \cdot, 0]$ is on the last list, the input is in $L(G)$. $\square$

We shall pursue the following course in analyzing Earley's algorithm. First, we shall show that the informal interpretation of the items mentioned before is correct. Then, we shall show that with a reasonable concept of an elementary operation, if G is unambiguous, then the time of execution is quadratic in input length. Finally, we shall show how to construct a parse from the lists and, in fact, how this may be done in quadratic time.

THEOREM 4.9

If parse lists are constructed as in Algorithm 4.5, then $[A \longrightarrow \alpha \cdot \beta, i]$ is on I_j if and only if $\alpha \overset{*}{\Rightarrow} a_{i+1} \cdots a_j$ and, moreover, there are strings γ and δ such that $S \overset{*}{\Rightarrow} \gamma A \delta$ and $\gamma \overset{*}{\Rightarrow} a_1 \cdots a_i$.

Proof.

Only if: We shall do this part by induction on the number of items which have been added to $I_0, I_1, \ldots, I_j$ before $[A \longrightarrow \alpha \cdot \beta, i]$ is added to I_j. For the basis, which we take to be all of I_0, we observe that anything added to I_0 has $\alpha \overset{*}{\Rightarrow} e$, so $S \overset{*}{\Rightarrow} \gamma A \delta$ holds with $\gamma = e$.

For the inductive step, assume that we have constructed I_0 and that the hypothesis holds for all items presently on $I_i, i \leq j$. Suppose that $[A \longrightarrow \alpha \cdot \beta, i]$ is added to I_j because of rule (4). Then $\alpha = \alpha' a_j$ and $[A \longrightarrow \alpha' \cdot a_j \beta, i]$ is on I_{j-1}. By the inductive hypothesis, $\alpha' \overset{*}{\Rightarrow} a_{i+1} \cdots a_{j-1}$ and there exist strings γ' and δ' such that $S \overset{*}{\Rightarrow} \gamma' A \delta'$ and $\gamma' \overset{*}{\Rightarrow} a_1 \cdots a_i$. It then follows that $\alpha = \alpha' a_j \overset{*}{\Rightarrow} a_{i+1} \cdots a_j$, and the inductive hypothesis is satisfied with $\gamma = \gamma'$ and $\delta = \delta'$.

Next, suppose that $[A \longrightarrow \alpha \cdot \beta, i]$ is added by rule (5). Then $\alpha = \alpha' B$ for some B in N, and for some k, $[A \longrightarrow \alpha' \cdot B\beta, i]$ is on I_k. Also, $[B \longrightarrow \eta \cdot, k]$ is on I_j for some η in $(N \cup \Sigma)^*$. By the inductive hypothesis, $\eta \overset{*}{\Rightarrow} a_{k+1} \cdots a_j$ and $\alpha' \overset{*}{\Rightarrow} a_{i+1} \cdots a_k$. Thus, $\alpha = \alpha' B \overset{*}{\Rightarrow} a_{i+1} \cdots a_j$. Also by hypothesis, there exist γ' and δ' such that $S \overset{*}{\Rightarrow} \gamma' A \delta'$ and $\gamma' \overset{*}{\Rightarrow} a_1 \cdots a_i$. Again, the rest of the inductive hypothesis is satisfied with $\gamma = \gamma'$ and $\delta = \delta'$.

The remaining case, in which $[A \longrightarrow \alpha \cdot \beta, i]$ is added by rule (6), has $\alpha = e$ and $i = j$. Its elementary verification is left to the reader, and we conclude the "only if" portion.

If: The "if" portion is the proof of the statement

(4.2.1)   If $S \overset{*}{\Rightarrow} \gamma A \delta$, $\gamma \overset{*}{\Rightarrow} a_1 \cdots a_i$, $A \longrightarrow \alpha\beta$ is in P, and $\alpha \overset{*}{\Rightarrow} a_{i+1} \cdots a_j$, then $[A \longrightarrow \alpha \cdot \beta, i]$ is on list I_j

We must prove all possible instances of (4.2.1). Any instance can be characterized by specifying the strings α, β, γ, and δ, the nonterminal A, and the integers i and j, since S and $a_1 \cdots a_n$ are fixed. We shall denote such an instance by $[\alpha, \beta, \gamma, \delta, A, i, j]$. The conclusion to be drawn from the above instance is that $[A \rightarrow \alpha \cdot \beta, i]$ is on list I_j. Note that γ and δ do not figure explicitly into the conclusion.

The proof will turn on ranking the various instances and proving the result by induction on the rank. The *rank* of the instance $\mathcal{g} = [\alpha, \beta, \gamma, \delta, A, i, j]$ is computed as follows:

Let $\tau_1(\mathcal{g})$ be the length of a shortest derivation $S \overset{*}{\Rightarrow} \gamma A \delta$.

Let $\tau_2(\mathcal{g})$ be the length of a shortest derivation $\gamma \overset{*}{\Rightarrow} a_1 \cdots a_i$.

Let $\tau_3(\mathcal{g})$ be the length of a shortest derivation $\alpha \overset{*}{\Rightarrow} a_{i+1} \cdots a_j$.

The *rank* of $\mathcal{g}$ is defined to be $\tau_1(\mathcal{g}) + 2[j + \tau_2(\mathcal{g}) + \tau_3(\mathcal{g})]$.

We now prove (4.2.1) by induction on the rank of an instance $\mathcal{g} = [\alpha, \beta, \gamma, \delta, A, i, j]$. If the rank is 0, then $\tau_1(\mathcal{g}) = \tau_2(\mathcal{g}) = \tau_3(\mathcal{g}) = j = 0$. We can conclude that $\alpha = \gamma = \delta = e$ and that $A = S$. Then we need to show that $[S \rightarrow \cdot \beta, 0]$ is on list 0. However, this follows immediately from the first rule for that list, as $S \rightarrow \beta$ must be in P.

For the inductive step, let $\mathcal{g}$, as above, be an instance of (4.2.1) of some rank $r > 0$, and assume that (4.2.1) is true for instances of smaller rank. Three cases arise, depending on whether α ends in a terminal, ends in a nonterminal, or is e.

Case 1: $\alpha = \alpha'a$ for some a in Σ. Since $\alpha \overset{*}{\Rightarrow} a_{i+1} \cdots a_j$, we conclude that $a = a_j$. Consider the instance $\mathcal{g}' = [\alpha', a_j\beta, \gamma, \delta, A, i, j - 1]$. Since $A \rightarrow \alpha'a_j\beta$ is in P, $\mathcal{g}'$ is an instance of (4.2.1), and its rank is easily seen to be $r - 2$. We may conclude that $[A \rightarrow \alpha' \cdot a_j\beta, i]$ is on list I_{j-1}. By rule (4), $[A \rightarrow \alpha \cdot \beta, i]$ will be placed on list I_j.

Case 2: $\alpha = \alpha'B$ for some B in N. There is some k, $i \leq k \leq j$, such that $\alpha' \overset{*}{\Rightarrow} a_{i+1} \cdots a_k$ and $B \overset{*}{\Rightarrow} a_{k+1} \cdots a_j$. From the instance of lower rank $\mathcal{g}' = [\alpha', B\beta, \gamma, \delta, A, i, k]$ we conclude that $[A \rightarrow \alpha' \cdot B\beta, i]$ is on list I_k. Let $B \Rightarrow \eta$ be the first step in a minimum length derivation $B \overset{*}{\Rightarrow} a_{k+1} \cdots a_j$. Consider the instance $\mathcal{g}'' = [\eta, e, \gamma\alpha', \beta\delta, B, k, j]$. Since $S \overset{*}{\Rightarrow} \gamma A \delta \Rightarrow \gamma\alpha'B\beta\delta$, we conclude that $\tau_1(\mathcal{g}'') \leq \tau_1(\mathcal{g}) + 1$. Let n_1 be the minimum number of steps in a derivation $\alpha' \overset{*}{\Rightarrow} a_{i+1} \cdots a_k$ and n_2 be the minimum number in a derivation $B \overset{*}{\Rightarrow} a_{k+1} \cdots a_j$. Then $\tau_3(\mathcal{g}) = n_1 + n_2$. Since $B \Rightarrow \eta \overset{*}{\Rightarrow} a_{k+1} \cdots a_j$, we conclude that $\tau_3(\mathcal{g}'') = n_2 - 1$. It is straightforward to see that $\tau_2(\mathcal{g}'') = \tau_2(\mathcal{g}) + n_1$. Hence $\tau_2(\mathcal{g}'') + \tau_3(\mathcal{g}'') = \tau_2(\mathcal{g}) + n_1 + n_2 - 1 = \tau_2(\mathcal{g}) + \tau_3(\mathcal{g}) - 1$. Thus $\tau_1(\mathcal{g}'') + 2[j + \tau_2(\mathcal{g}'') + \tau_3(\mathcal{g}'')]$ is less than r. By the inductive hypothesis for $\mathcal{g}''$ we conclude that $[B \rightarrow \eta \cdot, k]$ is on list I_j, and with $[A \rightarrow \alpha' \cdot B\beta, i]$ on list I_k, conclude by rule (2) or (5) that $[A \rightarrow \alpha \cdot \beta, i]$ is on list I_j.

Case 3: $\alpha = e$. We may conclude that $i = j$ and $\tau_3(\mathcal{g}) = 0$ in this case.

Since $r > 0$, we may conclude that the derivation $S \overset{*}{\Rightarrow} \gamma A \delta$ is of length greater than 0. If it were of length 0, then $\tau_1(\mathscr{I}) = 0$. Then we would have $\gamma = e$, so $\tau_2(\mathscr{I}) = i = 0$. Since $i = j$ and $\tau_3(\mathscr{I}) = 0$ have been shown in general for this case, we would have $r = 0$.

We can thus find some B in N and γ', γ'', δ', and δ'' in $(N \cup \Sigma)^*$ such that $S \overset{*}{\Rightarrow} \gamma' B \delta' \Rightarrow \gamma' \gamma'' A \delta'' \delta'$, where $B \rightarrow \gamma'' A \delta''$ is in P, $\gamma = \gamma' \gamma''$, $\delta = \delta'' \delta'$, and $\gamma' B \delta'$ is the penultimate step in some shortest derivation $S \overset{*}{\Rightarrow} \gamma A \delta$. Consider the instance $\mathscr{I}' = [\gamma'', A\delta'', \gamma', \delta', B, k, j]$, where k is an integer such that $\gamma' \overset{*}{\Rightarrow} a_1 \cdots a_k$ and $\gamma'' \overset{*}{\Rightarrow} a_{k+1} \cdots a_j$. Let the smallest length of the latter derivations be n_1 and n_2, respectively. Then $\tau_2(\mathscr{I}') = n_1$, $\tau_3(\mathscr{I}') = n_2$, and $\tau_2(\mathscr{I}) = n_1 + n_2$. We have already argued that $\tau_3(\mathscr{I}) = 0$, and B, γ', and δ' were selected so that $\tau_1(\mathscr{I}') = \tau_1(\mathscr{I}) - 1$. It follows that the rank of $\mathscr{I}'$ is $r - 1$. We may conclude that $[B \rightarrow \gamma'' \cdot A\delta'', k]$ is on list I_j. By rule (6), or rule (3) for list I_0, we place $[A \rightarrow \cdot \beta, j]$ on list I_j. $\square$

Note that as a special case of Theorem 4.9, $[S \rightarrow \alpha \cdot, 0]$ is on list I_n if and only if $S \rightarrow \alpha$ is in P and $\alpha \overset{*}{\Rightarrow} a_1 \cdots a_n$; i.e., $a_1 \cdots a_n$ is in $L(G)$ if and only if $[S \rightarrow \alpha \cdot, 0]$ is on list I_n for some α.

We shall now examine the running time of Algorithm 4.5. We leave it to the reader to show that in general $0(n^3)$ suitably defined elementary steps are sufficient to parse any word of length n according to a known grammar. We shall concentrate on showing that if the grammar is unambiguous, $0(n^2)$ steps are sufficient.

LEMMA 4.6

Let $G = (N, \Sigma, P, S)$ be an unambiguous grammar and $a_1 \cdots a_n$ a string in Σ^*. Then when executing Algorithm 4.5, we attempt to add an item $[A \rightarrow \alpha \cdot \beta, i]$ to list I_j at most once if $\alpha \neq e$.

Proof. This item can be added only in steps (2), (4), or (5). If added in step (4), the last symbol of α is a terminal, and if in steps (2) or (5), the last symbol is a nonterminal. In the first case, the result is obvious. In the second case, suppose that $[A \rightarrow \alpha' B \cdot \beta, i]$ is added to list I_j when two distinct items, $[B \rightarrow \gamma \cdot, k]$ and $[B \rightarrow \delta \cdot, l]$, are considered. Then it must be that $[A \rightarrow \alpha' \cdot B\beta, i]$ is on both list k and list l. (The case $k = l$ is not ruled out, however.)

Suppose that $k \neq l$. By Theorem 4.9, there exist θ_1, θ_2, θ_3, and θ_4 such that $S \overset{*}{\Rightarrow} \theta_1 A \theta_2 \Rightarrow \theta_1 \alpha' B\beta\theta_2 \overset{*}{\Rightarrow} a_1 \cdots a_j \beta\theta_2$ and $S \overset{*}{\Rightarrow} \theta_3 A \theta_4 \Rightarrow \theta_3 \alpha' B\beta\theta_4 \overset{*}{\Rightarrow} a_1 \cdots a_j \beta\theta_4$. But in the first derivation, $\theta_1 \alpha' \overset{*}{\Rightarrow} a_1 \cdots a_k$, and in the second, $\theta_3 \alpha' \overset{*}{\Rightarrow} a_1 \cdots a_l$. Then there are two distinct derivation trees for some $a_1 \cdots a_n$, with $\alpha' B$ deriving $a_{i+1} \cdots a_j$ in two different ways.

Now, suppose that $k = l$. Then it must be that $\gamma \neq \delta$. It is again easy to find two distinct derivation trees for $a_1 \cdots a_n$. The details are left for the Exercises. $\square$

We now examine the steps of Algorithm 4.5. We shall leave the definition of "elementary operation" for this algorithm to the reader. The crucial step in showing that Algorithm 4.5 is of quadratic time complexity is not how "elementary operation" is defined—any reasonable set of list-processing primitives will do. The crucial step in the argument concerns "bookkeeping" for the costs involved. We here assume that the grammar G is fixed, so that any processes concerning its symbols can be considered elementary. As in the previous section, the matter of time variation with the "size" of the grammar is left for the Exercises.

For I_0, step (1) clearly can be done in a fixed number of elementary operations. Step (3) for I_0 and step (6) for the general case can be done in a finite number of elementary operations each time an item is considered, provided we keep track of those items $[A \longrightarrow \alpha \cdot \beta, j]$ which have been added to I_j. Since grammar G is fixed, this information can be kept in a finite table for each j. If this is done, it is not necessary to scan the entire list I_j to see if items are already on the list.

For steps (2), (4), and (5), addition of items to I_j is facilitated if we can scan some list I_i such that $i < j$ for all those items having a desired symbol to the right of the dot, the desired symbol being a terminal in step (4) and a nonterminal in steps (2) and (5). Thus we need two links from every item on a list.

The first points to the next item on the list. This link allows us to consider each item in turn. The second points to the next item with the same symbol to the right of the dot. It is this link which allows us to scan a list efficiently in steps (2), (4), and (5).

The general strategy will be to consider each item on a list once to add new items. However, immediately upon adding an item of the form $[A \longrightarrow \alpha \cdot B\beta, i]$ to I_j, we consult the finite table for I_j to determine if $[B \longrightarrow \gamma \cdot, j]$ is on I_j for any γ. If so, we also add $[A \longrightarrow \alpha B \cdot \beta, i]$ to I_j.

We observe that there are a fixed number of strings, say k, that can appear as the first half of an item. Thus at most $k(j + 1)$ items appear on I_j. If we can show that Algorithm 4.5 spends a fixed amount of time, say c, for each item on a list, we shall show that the amount of time taken is $0(n^2)$, since

$$c \sum_{j=0}^{n} k(j + 1) = \tfrac{1}{2}ck(n + 1)(n + 2) \leq c'n^2 \qquad \text{for some constant } c'$$

The "bookkeeping trick" is as follows. We charge time to an item, under certain circumstances, both when it is considered and when it is entered onto a list. The maximum amount of time charged in either case is fixed. We also charge a fixed amount of time to the list itself.

We leave it to the reader to show that I_0 can be constructed in a fixed amount of time. We shall consider the items on lists I_j, for $j > 0$. In step (4) of Algorithm 4.5 for I_j, we examine a_j and the previous list. For each entry on I_{j-1} with a_j to the right of the dot, we add an item to I_j. As we can examine only those items on I_{j-1} satisfying that condition, we need charge only a finite amount of time to each item added, and a finite amount of time to I_j for examining a_j and for finding the first item of I_{j-1} with $\cdot\, a_j$ in it.

Now, we consider each item on I_j and charge time to it in order to see if step (5) or step (6) applies. We can accomplish step (6) in a finite amount of time, as we need examine only the table associated with I_j that tells whether all $[A \longrightarrow \cdot\, \alpha, j]$ have been added for the relevant A. This table can be examined in fixed time, and if necessary, a fixed number of items are added to I_j. This time is all charged to the item considered.

If step (5) applies, we must scan some list I_k, $k \leq j$, for all items having $\cdot\, B$ in them for some particular B. Each time one is found, an item is added to list I_j, and the time is charged to the item added, not the one being considered!

To show that the amount of time charged to any item on any list is bounded above by some finite number, we need observe only that by Lemma 4.6, if the grammar is unambiguous, only one attempt will ever be made to add an item to a list. This observation also ensures that in step (5) we do not have to spend time checking to see if an item already appears on a list.

THEOREM 4.10

If the underlying grammar is unambiguous, then Algorithm 4.5 can be executed in $0(n^2)$ reasonably defined elementary operations when the input is of length n.

Proof. A formalization of the above argument and the notion of an elementary operation is left for the Exercises.   □

THEOREM 4.11

In all cases, Algorithm 4.5 can be executed in $0(n^3)$ reasonably defined elementary operations when the input is of length n.

Proof. Exercise.   □

Our last portion of the analysis of Earley's algorithm concerns the method of constructing a parse from the completed lists. For this purpose we give Algorithm 4.6, which generates a right parse from the parse lists. We choose to produce a right parse because the algorithm is slightly simpler. A left parse can also be found with a simple alteration in the algorithm.

Also for the sake of simplicity, we shall assume that the grammar at hand has no cycles. If a cycle does exist in the grammar, then it is possible to have arbitrarily many parses for some input strings. However, Algorithm 4.6 can be modified to accommodate grammars with cycles (Exercise 4.2.23).

It should be pointed out that as for Algorithm 4.4, we can make Algorithm 4.6 simpler by placing pointers with each item added to a list in Algorithm 4.5. Those pointers give the one or two items which lead to its placement on its list.

ALGORITHM 4.6

Construction of a right parse from the parse lists.

Input. A cycle-free CFG $G = (N, \Sigma, P, S)$ with the productions in P numbered from 1 to p, an input string $w = a_1 \cdots a_n$, and the parse lists $I_0, I_1, \ldots, I_n$ for w.

Output. π, a right parse for w, or an "error" message.

Method. If no item of the form $[S \rightarrow \alpha \cdot, 0]$ is on I_n, then w is not in $L(G)$, so emit "error" and halt. Otherwise, initialize the parse π to e and execute the routine $\mathbf{R}([S \rightarrow \alpha \cdot, 0], n)$ where the routine $\mathbf{R}$ is defined as follows:

Routine $\mathbf{R}([A \rightarrow \beta \cdot, i], j)$:

(1) Let π be h followed by the previous value of π, where h is the number of production $A \rightarrow \beta$. (We assume that π is a global variable.)

(2) If $\beta = X_1 X_2 \cdots X_m$, set $k = m$ and $l = j$.

(3) (a) If $X_k \in \Sigma$, subtract 1 from both k and l.

(b) If $X_k \in N$, find an item $[X_k \rightarrow \gamma \cdot, r]$ in I_l for some r such that $[A \rightarrow X_1 X_2 \cdots X_{k-1} \cdot X_k \cdots X_m, i]$ is in I_r. Then execute $\mathbf{R}([X_k \rightarrow \gamma \cdot, r], l)$. Subtract 1 from k and set $l = r$.

(4) Repeat step (3) until $k = 0$. Halt. $\square$

Algorithm 4.6 works by tracing out a rightmost derivation of the input string using the parse lists to determine the productions to use. The routine $\mathbf{R}$ called with arguments $[A \rightarrow \beta \cdot, i]$ and j appends to the left end of the current partial parse the number corresponding to the production $A \rightarrow \beta$. If $\beta = v_0 B_1 v_1 B_2 v_2 \cdots B_s v_s$, where $B_1, \ldots, B_s$ are all the nonterminals in β, then the routine $\mathbf{R}$ determines the first production used to expand each B_t, say $B_t \rightarrow \beta_t$, and the position in the input string w immediately before the first terminal symbol derived from B_t. The following recursive calls of $\mathbf{R}$ are then made in the order shown:

$$\mathbf{R}([B_s \rightarrow \beta_s \cdot, i_s], j_s)$$
$$\mathbf{R}([B_{s-1} \rightarrow \beta_{s-1} \cdot, i_{s-1}], j_{s-1})$$
$$\vdots$$
$$\mathbf{R}([B_1 \rightarrow \beta_1 \cdot, i_1], j_1)$$

where

(1) $j_s = j - |v_s|$ and
(2) $j_q = i_{q+1} - |v_q|$ for $1 \leq q < s$.

Example 4.11

Let us apply Algorithm 4.6 to the parse lists of Example 4.10 in order to produce a right parse for the input string $(a + a) * a$. Initially, we can execute $\mathbf{R}([E \rightarrow T \cdot, 0], 7)$. In step (1), π gets value 2, the number associated with production $E \rightarrow T$. We then set $k = 1$ and $l = 7$ and execute step (3b) of Algorithm 4.6. We find $[T \rightarrow F * T \cdot, 0]$ on I_7 and $[E \rightarrow \cdot T, 0]$ on I_0. Thus we execute $\mathbf{R}([T \rightarrow F * T \cdot, 0], 7)$, which results in production number 3 being appended to the left of π. Thus, $\pi = 32$. Following this call of $\mathbf{R}$, in step (2) we set $k = 3$ and $l = 7$.

Step (3b) is then executed with $k = 3$. We find $[T \rightarrow F \cdot, 6]$ on I_0 and $[T \rightarrow F * \cdot T, 0]$ on I_6, so we call $\mathbf{R}([T \rightarrow F \cdot, 6], 7)$. After completion of this call, we set $k = 2$ and $l = 6$. In Step (3a) we consider $*$ and set $k = 1$ and $l = 5$. We then find $[F \rightarrow (E) \cdot, 0]$ on I_5 and $[T \rightarrow \cdot F * T, 0]$ on I_0, so we call $\mathbf{R}([F \rightarrow (E) \cdot, 0], 5)$.

Continuing in this fashion we obtain the right parse 64642156432.

The calls of routine $\mathbf{R}$ are shown in Fig. 4.10 superimposed on the derivation tree for $(a + a) * a$. □

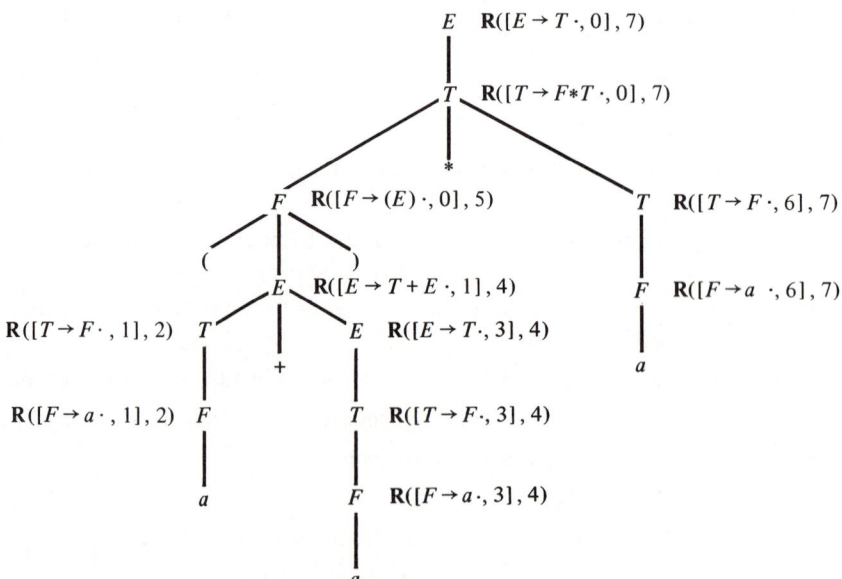

Fig. 4.10　Diagram of execution of Algorithm 4.6.

THEOREM 4.12

Algorithm 4.6 correctly finds a right parse of $a_1 \cdots a_n$ if one exists, and can be made to operate in time $0(n^2)$.

Proof. A straightforward induction on the order of the calls of routine **R** shows that a right parse is produced. We leave this portion of the proof for the Exercises.

In a manner analogous to Theorem 4.10, we can show that a call of $\mathbf{R}([A \longrightarrow \beta \cdot, i], j)$ takes time $0((j - i)^2)$ if we can show that step (3b) takes $0(j - i)$ elementary operations. To do so, we must preprocess the lists in such a way that the time taken to examine all the finite number of items on I_k whose second component is l requires a fixed computation time. That is, for each parse list, we must link the items with a common second component and establish a header pointing to the first entry on that list. This preprocessing can be done in time $0(n^2)$ in an obvious way.

In step (3b), then, we examine the items on list I_l with second component $r = l, l - 1, \ldots, i$ until a desired item of the form $[X_k \longrightarrow \gamma \cdot, r]$ is found. The verification that we have the desired item takes fixed time, since all items with second component i on I_r can be found in finite time. The total amount of time spent in step (3b) is thus proportional to $j - i$.   ☐

EXERCISES

4.2.1. Let G be defined by $S \longrightarrow AS \mid b$, $A \longrightarrow SA \mid a$. Construct the parse tables by Algorithm 4.3 for the following words:
  (a) *bbaab*.
  (b) *ababab*.
  (c) *aabba*.

4.2.2. Use Algorithm 4.4 to obtain left parses for those words of Exercise 4.2.1 which are in $L(G)$.

4.2.3. Construct parse lists for the grammar G of Exercise 4.2.1 and the words of that exercise using Algorithm 4.5.

4.2.4. Use Algorithm 4.6 to construct right parses for those words of Exercise 4.2.1 which are in $L(G)$.

4.2.5. Let G be given by $S \longrightarrow SS \mid a$. Use Algorithm 4.5 to construct a few of the parse lists $I_0, I_1, \ldots$ when the input is $aa \cdots$. How many elementary operations are needed before I_i is computed?

4.2.6. Prove Theorem 4.6.

4.2.7. Prove that Algorithm 4.4 correctly produces a left parse.

4.2.8. Complete the "only if" portion of Theorem 4.9.

4.2.9. Show that Earley's algorithm operates in time $0(n^3)$ on any grammar.

4.2.10. Complete the proof of Lemma 4.6.

4.2.11. Give a reasonable set of elementary operations for Theorems 4.10–4.12.

4.2.12. Prove Theorem 4.10.

4.2.13. Prove Theorem 4.11.

4.2.14. Show that Algorithm 4.6 correctly produces a right parse.

4.2.15. Modify Algorithm 4.3 to work on non-CNF grammars. *Hint:* Each t_{ij} must hold not only those nonterminals A which derive $a_i \cdots a_{i+j-i}$, but also certain substrings of right sides of productions which derive $a_i \cdots a_{i+j-1}$.

*4.2.16. Show that if the underlying grammar is linear, then a modification of Algorithm 4.3 can be made to work in time $0(n^2)$.

*4.2.17. We can modify Algorithm 4.3 to use "lookahead strings" of length $k \geq 0$. Given a grammar G and an input string $w = a_1 a_2 \cdots a_n$, we create a parse table T such that t_{ij} contains A if and only if

(1) $S \overset{*}{\Longrightarrow} \alpha A x$,

(2) $A \overset{+}{\Longrightarrow} a_i \cdots a_{i+j-1}$, and
(3) $a_{i+j} a_{i+j+1} \cdots a_{i+j+k-1} = \text{FIRST}_k(x)$.

Thus, A would be placed in entry t_{ij} provided the k input symbols to the right of input symbol a_{i+j-1} can legitimately appear after A in a sentential form. Algorithm 4.3 uses lookahead strings of length 0. Modify Algorithm 4.3 to use lookahead strings of length $k \geq 1$. What is the time complexity of such an algorithm?

*4.2.18. We can also modify Earley's algorithm to use lookahead. Here we would use items of the form $[A \longrightarrow \alpha \cdot \beta, i, u]$ where u is a lookahead string of length k. We would not enter this item on list I_j unless there is a derivation $S \overset{*}{\Longrightarrow} \gamma A u v$, where $\gamma \overset{*}{\Longrightarrow} a_1 \cdots a_i$, $\alpha \overset{*}{\Longrightarrow} a_{i+1} \cdots a_j$, and $\text{FIRST}_k(\beta u)$ contains $a_{j+1} \cdots a_{j+k}$. Complete the details of modifying Earley's algorithm to incorporate lookahead and then examine the time complexity of the algorithm.

4.2.19. Modify Algorithm 4.4 to produce a right parse.

4.2.20. Modify Algorithm 4.6 to produce a left parse.

4.2.21. Show that it is possible to modify Algorithm 4.4 to produce a parse in linear time if, in constructing the parse table, we add pointers with each A in t_{ij} to the B in t_{ik} and C in $t_{i+k,j-k}$ that caused A to be placed in t_{ij} in step (2) of Algorithm 4.3.

4.2.22. Show that if Algorithm 4.5 is modified to include pointers from an item to the other items which caused it to be placed on a list, then a right (or left) parse can be obtained from the parse lists in linear time.

4.2.23. Modify Algorithm 4.6 to work on arbitrary CFG's (including those with cycles). *Hint:* Include the pointers in the parse lists as in Exercise 4.2.22.

4.2.24. What is the maximum number of items that can appear in a list I_j in Algorithm 4.5?

*4.2.25. A grammar G is said to be of *finite ambiguity* if there is a constant k such that if w is in $L(G)$, then w has no more than k distinct left parses. Show that Earley's algorithm takes time $0(n^2)$ on all grammars of finite ambiguity.

Open Problems

There is little known about the actual time necessary to parse an arbitrary context-free grammar. In fact, no good upper bounds are known for the time it takes to recognize sentences in $L(G)$ for arbitrary CFG G, let alone parse it. We therefore propose the following open problems and research areas.

4.2.26. Does there exist an upper bound lower than $0(n^3)$ on the time needed to recognize an arbitrary CFL on some reasonable model of a random access computer or a multitape Turing machine?

4.2.27. Does there exist an upper bound better than $0(n^2)$ on the time needed to recognize unambiguous CFL's?

Research Problems

4.2.28. Find a CFL which cannot be recognized in time $f(n)$ on a random access computer or Turing machine (the latter would be easier), where $f(n)$ grows faster than n; i.e., $\lim_{n \to \infty} (n/f(n)) = 0$. Can you find a CFL which appears to take more than $0(n^2)$ time for recognition, even if you cannot prove this to be so?

4.2.29. Find large classes of CFG's which can be parsed in linear time by Earley's algorithm. Find large classes of ambiguous CFG's which can be parsed in time $0(n^2)$ by Earley's algorithm. It should be mentioned that all the deterministic CFL's have grammars in the former class.

Programming Exercises

4.2.30. Use Earley's algorithm to construct a parser for one of the grammars in the Appendix.

4.2.31. Construct a program that takes as input any CFG G and produces as output a parser for G that uses Earley's algorithm.

BIBLIOGRAPHIC NOTES

Algorithm 4.3 has been discovered independently by a number of people. Hays [1967] reports a version of it, which he attributes to J. Cocke.

Younger [1967] uses Algorithm 4.3 to show that the time complexity of the membership problem for context-free languages is $0(n^3)$. Kasami [1965] also gives a similar algorithm. Algorithm 4.5 is found in Earley's Ph.D. thesis [1968]. An $0(n^2)$ parsing algorithm for unambiguous CFG's is reported by Kasami and Torii [1969].

5 ONE-PASS NO BACKTRACK PARSING

In Chapter 4 we discussed backtrack techniques that could be used to simulate the nondeterministic left and right parsers for large classes of context-free grammars. However, we saw that in some cases such a simulation could be quite extravagant in terms of time. In this chapter we shall discuss classes of context-free grammars for which we can construct efficient parsers —parsers which make $c_1 n$ operations and use $c_2 n$ space in processing an input of length n, where c_1 and c_2 are small constants.

We shall have to pay a price for this efficiency, as none of the classes of grammars for which we can construct these efficient parsers generate all the context-free languages. However, there is strong evidence that the restricted classes of grammars for which we can construct these efficient parsers are adequate to specify all the syntactic features of programming languages that are normally specified by context-free grammars.

The parsing algorithms to be discussed are characterized by the facts that the input string is scanned once from left to right and that the parsing process is completely deterministic. In effect, we are merely restricting the class of CFG's so that we are always able to construct a deterministic left parser or a deterministic right parser for the grammar under consideration.

The classes of grammars to be discussed in this chapter include

(1) The LL(k) grammars—those for which the left parser can be made to work deterministically if it is allowed to look at k input symbols to the right of its current input position.†

(2) The LR(k) grammars—those for which the right parser can be made

---

†This does not involve an extension of the definition of a DPDT. The k "lookahead symbols" are stored in the finite control.

to work deterministically if it is allowed to look k input symbols beyond its current input position.

(3) The precedence grammars—those for which the right parser can find the handle of a right-sentential form by looking only at certain relations between pairs of adjacent symbols of that sentential form.

5.1. LL(k) GRAMMARS

In this section we shall present the largest "natural" class of left-parsable grammars—the LL(k) grammars.

5.1.1. Definition of LL(k) Grammar

As an introduction, let $G = (N, \Sigma, P, S)$ be an unambiguous grammar and $w = a_1 a_2 \cdots a_n$ a sentence in $L(G)$. Then there exists a unique sequence of left-sentential forms $\alpha_0, \alpha_1, \ldots, \alpha_m$ such that $S = \alpha_0$, $\alpha_i \xRightarrow{p_i} \alpha_{i+1}$ for $0 \le i < m$ and $\alpha_m = w$. The left parse for w is $p_0 p_1 \cdots p_{m-1}$.

Now, suppose that we want to find this left parse by scanning w once from left to right. We might try to do this by constructing $\alpha_0, \alpha_1, \ldots, \alpha_m$, the sequence of left-sentential forms. If $\alpha_i = a_1 \cdots a_j A\beta$, then at this point we could have read the first j input symbols and compared them with the first j symbols of α_i. It would be desirable if α_{i+1} could be determined knowing only $a_1 \cdots a_j$ (the part of the input we have scanned to this point), the next few input symbols ($a_{j+1} a_{j+2} \cdots a_{j+k}$ for some fixed k), and the nonterminal A. If these three quantities uniquely determine which production is to be used to expand A, we can then precisely determine α_{i+1} from α_i and the k input symbols $a_{j+1} a_{j+2} \cdots a_{j+k}$.

A grammar in which each leftmost derivation has this property is said to be an LL(k) grammar. We shall see that for each LL(k) grammar we can construct a deterministic left parser which operates in linear time. A few definitions are needed before we proceed.

DEFINITION

Let $\alpha = x\beta$ be a left-sentential form in some grammar $G = (N, \Sigma, P, S)$ such that x is in Σ^* and β either begins with a nonterminal or is e. We say that x is the *closed portion* of α and that β is the *open portion* of α. The boundary between x and β will be referred to as the *border*.

Example 5.1

Let $\alpha = abacAaB$. The closed portion of α is $abac$; the open portion is AaB. If $\alpha = abc$, then abc is its closed portion and e its open portion. Its border is at the right end. $\square$

The intuitive idea behind LL(k) grammars is that if we are constructing a leftmost derivation $S \underset{lm}{\overset{*}{\Rightarrow}} w$ and we have already constructed $S \underset{lm}{\Rightarrow} \alpha_1 \underset{lm}{\Rightarrow} \alpha_2 \underset{lm}{\Rightarrow} \cdots \underset{lm}{\Rightarrow} \alpha_i$ such that $\alpha_i \underset{lm}{\overset{*}{\Rightarrow}} w$, then we can construct α_{i+1}, the next step of the derivation, by observing only the closed portion of α_i and a "little more," the "little more" being the next k input symbols of w. (Note that the closed portion of α_i is a prefix of w.) It is important to observe that if we do not see all of w when α_{i+1} is constructed, then we do not really know what terminal string is ultimately derived from S. Thus the LL(k) condition implies that α_{i+1} is substantially independent (except for the next k terminal symbols) of what is derived from the open portion of α_i.

Viewed in terms of a derivation tree, we can construct a derivation tree for a sentence wxy in an LL(k) grammar starting from the root and working top-down deterministically. Specifically, if we have constructed the partial derivation tree with frontier $wA\alpha$, then knowing w and the first k symbols of xy we would know which production to use to expand A. The outline of the complete tree is shown in Fig. 5.1.

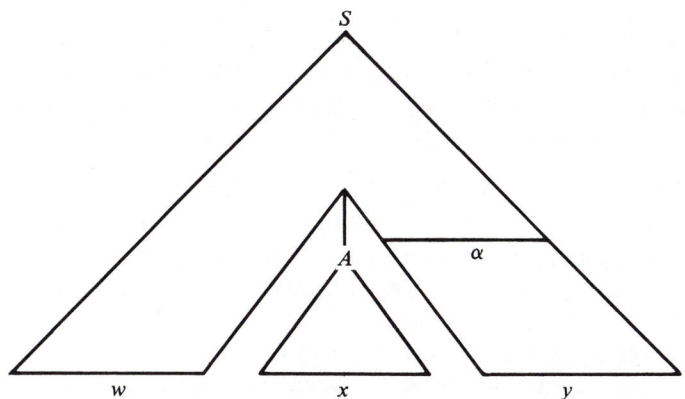

Fig. 5.1 Partial derivation tree for the sentence wxy.

Recall that in Chapter 4 we defined for a CFG $G = (N, \Sigma, P, S)$ the function $\text{FIRST}_k^G(\alpha)$, where k is an integer and α is in $(N \cup \Sigma)^*$, to be $\{w \text{ in } \Sigma^* \mid \text{either } |w| < k \text{ and } \alpha \underset{G}{\overset{*}{\Rightarrow}} w, \text{ or } |w| = k \text{ and } \alpha \underset{G}{\overset{*}{\Rightarrow}} wx \text{ for some } x\}$.

We shall delete the subscript k and/or the superscript G from FIRST whenever no confusion will result.

If α consists solely of terminals, then $\text{FIRST}_k(\alpha)$ is just $\{w\}$, where w is the first k symbols of α if $|\alpha| \geq k$, and $w = \alpha$ if $|\alpha| < k$. We shall write

$\text{FIRST}_k(\alpha) = w$, rather than $\{w\}$, in this case. It is straightforward to determine $\text{FIRST}_k^G(\alpha)$ for particular grammar G. We shall defer an algorithm to Section 5.1.6.

DEFINITION

Let $G = (\text{N}, \Sigma, P, S)$ be a CFG. We say that G is $LL(k)$, for some fixed integer k, if whenever there are two leftmost derivations

(1) $S \underset{\text{lm}}{\overset{*}{\Rightarrow}} wA\alpha \underset{\text{lm}}{\Rightarrow} w\beta\alpha \overset{*}{\Rightarrow} wx$ and

(2) $S \underset{\text{lm}}{\overset{*}{\Rightarrow}} wA\alpha \underset{\text{lm}}{\Rightarrow} w\gamma\alpha \overset{*}{\Rightarrow} wy$

such that $\text{FIRST}_k(x) = \text{FIRST}_k(y)$, it follows that $\beta = \gamma$.

Stated less formally, G is $LL(k)$ if given a string $wA\alpha$ in $(\text{N} \cup \Sigma)^*$ and the first k terminal symbols (if they exist) to be derived from $A\alpha$ there is at most one production which can be applied to A to yield a derivation of any terminal string beginning with w followed by those k terminals.

We say that a grammar is LL if it is $LL(k)$ for some k.

Example 5.2

Let G_1 be the grammar $S \rightarrow aAS\,|\,b$, $A \rightarrow a\,|\,bSA$. Intuitively, G_1 is $LL(1)$ because given C, the leftmost nonterminal in any left-sentential form, and c, the next input symbol, there is at most one production for C capable of deriving a terminal string beginning with c. Going to the definition of an $LL(1)$ grammar, if $S \underset{\text{lm}}{\overset{*}{\Rightarrow}} wS\alpha \underset{\text{lm}}{\Rightarrow} w\beta\alpha \underset{\text{lm}}{\overset{*}{\Rightarrow}} wx$ and $S \underset{\text{lm}}{\overset{*}{\Rightarrow}} wS\alpha \underset{\text{lm}}{\Rightarrow} w\gamma\alpha \underset{\text{lm}}{\overset{*}{\Rightarrow}} wy$ and x and y start with the same symbol, we must have $\beta = \gamma$. Specifically, if x and y start with a, then production $S \rightarrow aAS$ was used and $\beta = \gamma = aAS$. $S \rightarrow b$ is not a possible alternative. Conversely, if x and y start with b, $S \rightarrow b$ must be the production used, and $\beta = \gamma = b$. Note that $x = y = e$ is impossible, since S does not derive e in G_1.

A similar argument prevails when we consider two derivations $S \underset{\text{lm}}{\overset{*}{\Rightarrow}} wA\alpha \underset{\text{lm}}{\Rightarrow} w\beta\alpha \underset{\text{lm}}{\overset{*}{\Rightarrow}} wx$ and $S \underset{\text{lm}}{\overset{*}{\Rightarrow}} wA\alpha \underset{\text{lm}}{\Rightarrow} w\gamma\alpha \underset{\text{lm}}{\overset{*}{\Rightarrow}} wy$. $\square$

The grammar in Example 5.2 is an example of what is known as a simple $LL(1)$ grammar.

DEFINITION

A context-free grammar $G = (\text{N}, \Sigma, P, S)$ with no e-productions such that for all $A \in \text{N}$ each alternate for A begins with a distinct terminal symbol is called a *simple* $LL(1)$ grammar. Thus in a simple $LL(1)$ grammar, given a pair (A, a), where $A \in \text{N}$ and $a \in \Sigma$, there is at most one production of the form $A \rightarrow a\alpha$.

Example 5.3

Let us consider the more complicated case of the grammar G_2 defined by $S \rightarrow e \,|\, abA$, $A \rightarrow Saa \,|\, b$. We shall show that G_2 is LL(2). To do this, we shall show that if $wB\alpha$ is any left-sentential form of G_2 and wx is a sentence in $L(G)$, then there is at most one production $B \rightarrow \beta$ in G_2 such that $\text{FIRST}_2(\beta\alpha)$ contains $\text{FIRST}_2(x)$. Suppose that $S \underset{\text{lm}}{\overset{*}{\Rightarrow}} wS\alpha \underset{\text{lm}}{\Rightarrow} w\beta\alpha \underset{\text{lm}}{\overset{*}{\Rightarrow}} wx$ and $S \underset{\text{lm}}{\overset{*}{\Rightarrow}} wS\alpha \underset{\text{lm}}{\Rightarrow} wy\alpha \underset{\text{lm}}{\overset{*}{\Rightarrow}} wy$, where the first two symbols of x and y agree if they exist. Since G_2 is a linear grammar, α must be in $(a + b)^*$. In fact, we can say more. Either $w = \alpha = e$, or the last production used in the derivation $S \underset{\text{lm}}{\overset{*}{\Rightarrow}} wS\alpha$ was $A \rightarrow Saa$. (There is no other way for S to "appear" in a sentential form.) Thus either $\alpha = e$ or α begins with aa.

Suppose that $S \rightarrow e$ is used going from $wS\alpha$ to $w\beta\alpha$. Then $\beta = e$, and x is either e or begins with aa. Likewise, if $S \rightarrow e$ is used going from $wS\alpha$ to $wy\alpha$, then $\alpha = e$ and $y = e$, or y begins with aa. If $S \rightarrow abA$ is used going from $wS\alpha$ to $w\beta\alpha$, then $\beta = abA$, and x begins with ab. Likewise, if $S \rightarrow abA$ is used going from $wS\alpha$ to $wy\alpha$, then $\gamma = abA$, and y begins with ab. There are thus no possibilities other than $x = y = e$, x and y begin with aa, or both begin with ab. Any other condition on the first two symbols of x and y implies that one or both derivations are impossible. In the first two cases, $S \rightarrow e$ is used in both derivations, and $\beta = \gamma = e$. In the third case, $S \rightarrow abA$ must be used, and $\beta = \gamma = abA$.

It is left for the Exercises to prove that the situation in which A is the symbol to the right of the border of the sentential form in question does not yield a contradiction of the LL(2) condition. The reader should also verify that G_2 is not LL(1). $\square$

Example 5.4

Let us consider the grammar $G_3 = (\{S, A, B\}, \{0, 1, a, b\}, P_3, S)$, where P_3 consists of $S \rightarrow A \,|\, B$, $A \rightarrow aAb \,|\, 0$, $B \rightarrow aBbb \,|\, 1$. $L(G_3)$ is the language $\{a^n 0 b^n \,|\, n \geq 0\} \cup \{a^n 1 b^{2n} \,|\, n \geq 0\}$. G_3 is not LL(k) for any k. Intuitively, if we begin scanning a string of a's which is arbitrarily long, we do not know whether the production $S \rightarrow A$ or $S \rightarrow B$ was first used until a 0 or 1 is seen.

Referring to the definition of LL(k) grammar, we may take $w = \alpha = e$, $\beta = A$, $\gamma = B$, $x = a^k 0 b^k$, and $y = a^k 1 b^{2k}$ in the derivations

$$S \underset{\text{lm}}{\overset{0}{\Longrightarrow}} S \underset{\text{lm}}{\Longrightarrow} A \overset{*}{\Longrightarrow} a^k 0 b^k$$

$$S \underset{\text{lm}}{\overset{0}{\Longrightarrow}} S \underset{\text{lm}}{\Longrightarrow} B \overset{*}{\Longrightarrow} a^k 1 b^{2k}$$

to satisfy conditions (1) and (2) of the definition. Moreover, x and y agree in the first k symbols. However, the conclusion that $\beta = \gamma$ is false. Since k can be arbitrary here, we may conclude that G_3 is not an LL grammar. In fact, in Chapter 8 we shall show that $L(G_3)$ has no LL(k) grammar. $\square$

5.1.2. Predictive Parsing Algorithms

We shall show that we can parse LL(k) grammars very conveniently using what we call a *k-predictive parsing algorithm*. A k-predictive parsing algorithm for a CFG $G = (N, \Sigma, P, S)$ uses an input tape, a pushdown list, and an output tape as shown in Fig. 5.2. The k-predictive parsing algorithm attempts to trace out a leftmost derivation of the string placed on its input tape.

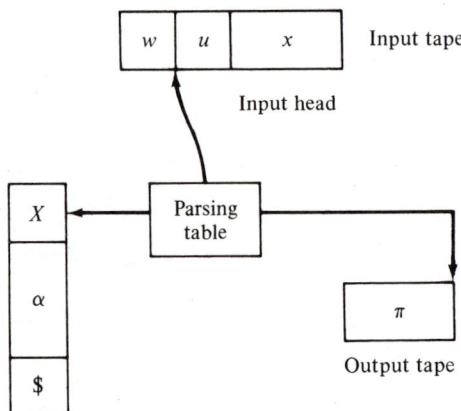

Fig. 5.2   Predictive parsing algorithm.

The input tape contains the input string to be parsed. The input tape is read by an input head capable of reading the next k input symbols (whence the k in k-predictive). The string scanned by the input head will be called the *lookahead string*. In Fig. 5.2 the substring u of the input string wux represents the lookahead string.

The pushdown list contains a string $X\alpha\$$, where $X\alpha$ is a string of pushdown symbols and $\$$ is a special symbol used as a bottom of the pushdown list marker. The symbol X is on top of the pushdown list. We shall use Γ to represent the alphabet of pushdown list symbols (excluding $\$$).

The output tape contains a string π of production indices.

We shall represent the *configuration* of a predictive parsing algorithm by a triple $(x, X\alpha, \pi)$, where

(1) x represents the unused portion of the original input string.
(2) $X\alpha$ represents the string on the pushdown list (with X on top).
(3) π is the string on the output tape.

For example, the configuration in Fig. 5.2 is $(ux, X\alpha\$, \pi)$.

The action of a k-predictive parsing algorithm $\mathcal{C}$ is dictated by a parsing table M, which is a mapping from $(\Gamma \cup \{\$\}) \times \Sigma^{*k}$ to a set containing the following elements:

(1) (β, i), where β is in Γ^* and i is a production number. Presumably, β will be either the right side of production i or a representation of it.

(2) **pop**.

(3) **accept**.

(4) **error**.

The parsing algorithm parses an input by making a sequence of moves, each move being very similar to a move of a pushdown transducer. In a move the lookahead string u and the symbol X on top of the pushdown list are determined. Then the entry $M(X, u)$ in the parsing table is consulted to determine the actual move to be made. As would be expected, we shall describe the moves of the parsing algorithm in terms of a relation $\vdash$ on the set of configurations. Let u be $\text{FIRST}_k(x)$. We write

(1) $(x, X\alpha, \pi) \vdash (x, \beta\alpha, \pi i)$ if $M(X, u) = (\beta, i)$. Here the top symbol X on the pushdown list is replaced by the string $\beta \in \Gamma^*$, and the production number i is appended to the output. The input head is not moved.

(2) $(x, a\alpha, \pi) \vdash (x', \alpha, \pi)$ if $M(a, u) = \textbf{pop}$ and $x = ax'$. When the symbol on top of the pushdown list matches the current input symbol (the first symbol of the lookahead string), the pushdown list is popped and the input head is moved one symbol to the right.

(3) If the parsing algorithm reaches configuration $(e, \$, \pi)$, then parsing ceases, and the output string π is the *parse* of the original input string. We shall assume that $M(\$, e)$ is always **accept**. Configuration $(e, \$, \pi)$ is called *accepting*.

(4) If the parsing algorithm reaches configuration $(x, X\alpha, \pi)$ and $M(X, u) = \textbf{error}$, then parsing ceases, and an error is reported. The configuration $(x, X\alpha, \pi)$ is called an **error** configuration.

If $w \in \Sigma^*$ is the string to be parsed, then the *initial configuration* of the parsing algorithm is $(w, X_0\$, e)$, where X_0 is a designated initial symbol. If $(x, X_0\$, e) \vert^{*} (e, \$, \pi)$, we write $\mathcal{C}(w) = \pi$ and call π the output of $\mathcal{C}$ for input w. If $(w, X_0\$, e)$ does not reach an accepting configuration, we say that $\mathcal{C}(w)$ is undefined. The translation defined by $\mathcal{C}$, denoted $\tau(\mathcal{C})$, is the set of pairs $\{(w, \pi) \mid \mathcal{C}(w) = \pi\}$.

We say that $\mathcal{C}$ is a *valid k-predictive parsing algorithm* for CFG G if

(1) $L(G) = \{w \mid \mathcal{C}(w) \text{ is defined}\}$, and

(2) If $\mathcal{C}(w) = \pi$, then π is a left parse of w.

If a k-predictive parsing algorithm $\mathcal{C}$ uses a parsing table M and $\mathcal{C}$ is a valid parsing algorithm for a CFG G, we say that M is a *valid parsing table* for G.

Example 5.5

Let us construct a 1-predictive parsing algorithm α for G_1, the simple LL(1) grammar of Example 5.2. First, let us number the productions of G_1 as follows:

$$(1) \ S \longrightarrow aAS$$
$$(2) \ S \longrightarrow b$$
$$(3) \ A \longrightarrow a$$
$$(4) \ A \longrightarrow bSA$$

A parsing table for α is shown in Fig. 5.3.

Lookahead string

		a	b	e
Symbol on top of pushdown list	S	$aAS, 1$	$b, 2$	error
	A	$a, 3$	$bSA, 4$	error
	a	pop	error	error
	b	error	pop	error
	$ \$ $	error	error	accept

Fig. 5.3   Parsing table for α.

Using this table, α would parse the input string *abbab* as follows:

$$(abbab, S\$, e) \vdash (abbab, aAS\$, 1)$$
$$\vdash (bbab, AS\$, 1)$$
$$\vdash (bbab, bSAS\$, 14)$$
$$\vdash (bab, SAS\$, 14)$$
$$\vdash (bab, bAS\$, 142)$$
$$\vdash (ab, AS\$, 142)$$
$$\vdash (ab, aS\$, 1423)$$
$$\vdash (b, S\$, 1423)$$
$$\vdash (b, b\$, 14232)$$
$$\vdash (e, \$, 14232)$$

For the first move $M(S, a) = (aAS, 1)$, so S on top of the pushdown list is replaced by aAS, and production number 1 is written on the output tape. For the next move $M(a, a) = $ **pop** so that a is removed from the pushdown list, and the input head is moved one position to the right.

Continuing in this fashion, we obtain the accepting configuration $(e, \$, 14232)$. It should be clear that 14232 is a left parse of *abbab*, and, in fact, $\mathfrak{C}$ is a valid 1-predictive parsing algorithm for G_1. $\square$

A k-predictive parsing algorithm for a CFG G can be simulated by a deterministic pushdown transducer with an endmarker on the input. Since a pushdown transducer can look only at one input symbol, the lookahead string should be stored as part of the state of the finite control. The rest of the simulation should be obvious.

THEOREM 5.1

Let $\mathfrak{C}$ be a k-predictive parsing algorithm for a CFG G. Then there exists a deterministic pushdown transducer T such that $\tau(T) = \{(w\$, \pi) \,|\, \mathfrak{C}(w) = \pi\}$.

Proof. Exercise. $\square$

COROLLARY

Let $\mathfrak{C}$ be a valid k-predictive parsing algorithm for G. Then there is a deterministic left parser for G.

Example 5.6

Let us construct a deterministic left parser P_l for the 1-predictive parsing algorithm in Example 5.5. Since the grammar is simple, we can obtain a smaller DPDT if we move the input head one symbol to the right on each move. The left parser will use $\$$ as both a right endmarker on the input tape and as a bottom of the pushdown list marker.

Let $P_l = (\{q_0, q, \textbf{accept}\}, \{a, b, \$\}, \{S, A, a, b, \$\}, \delta, q_0, \$, \{\textbf{accept}\})$, where δ is defined as follows:

$$\delta(q_0, e, \$) = (q, S\$, e)$$
$$\delta(q, a, S) = (q, AS, 1)$$
$$\delta(q, b, S) = (q, e, 2)$$
$$\delta(q, a, A) = (q, e, 3)$$
$$\delta(q, b, A) = (q, SA, 4)$$
$$\delta(q, \$, \$) = (\textbf{accept}, e, e)$$

It is easy to see that $(w\$, \pi) \in \tau(P_l)$ if and only if $\mathfrak{C}(w) = \pi$. $\square$

5.1.3. Implications of the LL(k) Definition

We shall show that for every LL(k) grammar we can mechanically construct a valid k-predictive parsing algorithm. Since the parsing table is the heart of the predictive parsing algorithm, we shall show how a parsing table can be constructed from the grammar. We begin by examining the implications of the LL(k) definition.

The LL(k) definition states that, given a left-sentential form $wA\alpha$, then w and the next k input symbols following w will uniquely determine which production is to be used to expand A. Thus at first glance it might appear that we have to remember all of w to determine which production is to be used next. However, this is not the case. The following theorem is fundamental to an understanding of LL(k) grammars.

THEOREM 5.2

Let $G = (N, \Sigma, P, S)$ be a CFG. Then G is LL(k) if and only if the following condition holds: If $A \to \beta$ and $A \to \gamma$ are distinct productions in P, then $\text{FIRST}_k(\beta\alpha) \cap \text{FIRST}_k(\gamma\alpha) = \varnothing$ for all $wA\alpha$ such that $S \underset{lm}{\overset{*}{\Rightarrow}} wA\alpha$.

Proof.

Only if: Suppose that there exist w, A, α, β, and γ as above, but $\text{FIRST}_k(\beta\alpha) \cap \text{FIRST}_k(\gamma\alpha)$ contains x. Then by definition of FIRST, we have derivations $S \underset{lm}{\overset{*}{\Rightarrow}} wA\alpha \underset{lm}{\Rightarrow} w\beta\alpha \underset{lm}{\overset{*}{\Rightarrow}} wxy$ and $S \underset{lm}{\overset{*}{\Rightarrow}} wA\alpha \underset{lm}{\Rightarrow} wy\alpha \underset{lm}{\overset{*}{\Rightarrow}} wxz$ for some y and z. (Note that here we need the fact that N has no useless nonterminals, as we assume for all grammars.) If $|x| < k$, then $y = z = e$. Since $\beta \neq \gamma$, G is not LL(k).

If: Suppose that G is not LL(k). Then there exist two derivations $S \underset{lm}{\overset{*}{\Rightarrow}} wA\alpha \underset{lm}{\Rightarrow} w\beta\alpha \underset{lm}{\overset{*}{\Rightarrow}} wx$ and $S \underset{lm}{\overset{*}{\Rightarrow}} wA\alpha \underset{lm}{\Rightarrow} wy\alpha \underset{lm}{\overset{*}{\Rightarrow}} wy$ such that x and y agree up to the first k places, but $\beta \neq \gamma$. Then $A \to \beta$ and $A \to \gamma$ are distinct productions in P, and $\text{FIRST}(\beta\alpha)$ and $\text{FIRST}(\gamma\alpha)$ each contain the string $\text{FIRST}(x)$, which is also $\text{FIRST}(y)$. $\square$

Let us look at some applications of Theorem 5.2 to LL(1) grammars. Suppose that $G = (N, \Sigma, P, S)$ is an e-free CFG, and we wish to determine whether G is LL(1). Theorem 5.2 implies that G is LL(1) if and only if for all A in N each set of A-productions $A \to \alpha_1 | \alpha_2 | \cdots | \alpha_n$ in P is such that $\text{FIRST}_1(\alpha_1), \text{FIRST}_1(\alpha_2), \ldots, \text{FIRST}_1(\alpha_n)$ are all pairwise disjoint. (Note that e-freedom is essential here.)

Example 5.7

The grammar G having the two productions $S \to aS | a$ cannot be LL(1), since $\text{FIRST}_1(aS) = \text{FIRST}_1(a) = a$. Intuitively, in parsing a string beginning with an a, looking only at the first input symbol we would not know whether to use $S \rightarrow aS$ or $S \rightarrow a$ to expand S. On the other hand, G is LL(2). Using the notation in Theorem 5.2, if $S \overset{*}{\underset{\text{lm}}{\Rightarrow}} wA\alpha$, then $A = S$ and $\alpha = e$. The only two productions for S are as given, so that $\beta = aS$ and $\gamma = a$. Since $\text{FIRST}_2(aS) = aa$ and $\text{FIRST}_2(a) = a$, G is LL(2) by Theorem 5.2. $\quad\square$

Let us consider LL(1) grammars with e-productions. At this point it is convenient to introduce the function FOLLOW_k^G.

DEFINITION

Let $G = (N, \Sigma, P, S)$ be a CFG. We define $\text{FOLLOW}_k^G(\beta)$, where k is an integer and β is in $(N \cup \Sigma)^*$, to be the set $\{w \mid S \overset{*}{\Rightarrow} \alpha\beta\gamma$ and w is in $\text{FIRST}_k^G(\gamma)\}$. As is customary, we shall omit k and G whenever they are understood.

Thus, $\text{FOLLOW}_1^G(A)$ includes the set of terminal symbols that can occur immediately to the right of A in any sentential form, and if αA is a sentential form, then e is also in $\text{FOLLOW}_1^G(A)$.

We can extend the functions FIRST and FOLLOW to domains which are sets of strings rather than single strings, in the obvious manner. That is, let $G = (N, \Sigma, P, S)$ be a CFG. If $L \subseteq (N \cup \Sigma)^*$, then

$$\text{FIRST}_k^G(L) = \{w \mid \text{for some } \alpha \text{ in } L, w \text{ is in } \text{FIRST}_k^G(\alpha)\}$$

and $\text{FOLLOW}_k^G(L) = \{w \mid \text{for some } \alpha \text{ in } L, w \text{ is in } \text{FOLLOW}_k^G(\alpha)\}$.

For LL(1) grammars we can make the following important observation.

THEOREM 5.3

A CFG $G = (N, \Sigma, P, S)$ is LL(1) if and only if the following condition holds: For each A in N, if $A \rightarrow \beta$ and $A \rightarrow \gamma$ are distinct productions, then $\text{FIRST}_1(\beta \text{ FOLLOW}_1(A)) \cap \text{FIRST}_1(\gamma \text{ FOLLOW}_1(A)) = \varnothing$.

Proof. Exercise. $\quad\square$

Thus we can show that a grammar G is LL(1) if and only if for each set of A-productions $A \rightarrow \alpha_1 \mid \alpha_2 \mid \cdots \mid \alpha_n$ the following conditions hold:

(1) $\text{FIRST}_1(\alpha_1), \text{FIRST}_1(\alpha_2), \ldots, \text{FIRST}_1(\alpha_n)$ are all pairwise disjoint.

(2) If $\alpha_i \overset{*}{\Rightarrow} e$, then $\text{FIRST}_1(\alpha_j) \cap \text{FOLLOW}_1(A) = \varnothing$ for $1 \le j \le n$, $i \ne j$.

These conditions are merely a restatement of Theorem 5.3. We should caution the reader that, appealing as it may seem, Theorem 5.3 does not generalize directly. That is, let G be a CFG such that statement (5.1.1) holds:

$$(5.1.1) \quad \begin{array}{l} \text{If } A \rightarrow \beta \text{ and } A \rightarrow \gamma \text{ are distinct } A\text{-productions, then} \\[6pt] \text{FIRST}_k(\beta \text{ FOLLOW}_k(A)) \cap \text{FIRST}_k(\gamma \text{ FOLLOW}_k(A)) = \varnothing \end{array}$$

Such a grammar is called a *strong* LL(k) grammar. Every LL(1) grammar is strong. However, the next example shows that when $k > 1$ there are LL(k) grammars that are not strong LL(k) grammars.

Example 5.8

Consider the grammar G, defined by

$$S \longrightarrow aAaa \,|\, bAba$$
$$A \longrightarrow b \,|\, e$$

Using Theorem 5.2, we can verify that G is an LL(2) grammar. Consider the derivation $S \Rightarrow aAaa$. We observe that $\text{FIRST}_2(baa) \cap \text{FIRST}_2(aa) = \varnothing$. Using the notation of Theorem 5.2 here, $\alpha = aa$, $\beta = b$, and $\gamma = e$. Likewise, if $S \Rightarrow bAba$, then $\text{FIRST}_2(bba) \cap \text{FIRST}_2(ba) = \varnothing$. Since all derivations in G are of length 2, we have shown G to be LL(2), by Theorem 5.2. But $\text{FOLLOW}_2(A) = \{aa, ba\}$, so

$$\text{FIRST}_2(b \, \text{FOLLOW}_2(A)) \cap \text{FIRST}_2(\text{FOLLOW}_2(A)) = \{ba\},$$

violating (5.1.1). Hence G is not a strong LL(2) grammar. $\square$

One important consequence of the LL(k) definition is that a left-recursive grammar cannot be LL(k) for any k (Exercise 5.1.1).

Example 5.9

Consider the grammar G with the two productions $S \to Sa \,|\, b$. From Theorem 5.2, consider the derivation $S \overset{i}{\Rightarrow} Sa^i$, $i \geq 0$ with $A = S$, $\alpha = e$, $\beta = Sa$, and $\gamma = b$. Then for $i \geq k$, $\text{FIRST}_k(Saa^i) \cap \text{FIRST}_k(ba^i) = ba^{k-1}$. Thus, G cannot be LL(k) for any k. $\square$

It is also important to observe that every LL(k) grammar is unambiguous (Exercise 5.1.3). Thus, if we are given an ambiguous grammar, we can immediately conclude that it cannot be LL(k) for any k.

In Chapter 8 we shall see that many deterministic context-free languages do not have an LL(k) grammar. For example, $\{a^n0b^n \,|\, n \geq 1\} \cup \{a^n1b^{2n} \,|\, n \geq 1\}$ is such a language. Also, given a CFG G which is not LL(k) for a fixed k, it is undecidable whether G has an equivalent LL(k) grammar. But in spite of these obstacles, there are several situations in which various transformations can be applied to a grammar which is not LL(1) to change the given grammar into an equivalent LL(1) grammar. We shall give two useful examples of such transformations here.

The first is the elimination of left recursion. We shall illustrate the technique with an example.

Example 5.10

Let G be the grammar $S \longrightarrow Sa \,|\, b$, which we saw in Example 5.9 was not

LL. We can replace these two productions by the three productions

$$S \longrightarrow bS'$$
$$S' \longrightarrow aS' | e$$

to obtain an equivalent grammar G'. Using Theorem 5.3, we can readily show G' to be LL(1).   ☐

Another useful transformation is *left factoring*. We again illustrate the technique through an example.

Example 5.11

Consider the LL(2) grammar G with the two productions $S \longrightarrow aS | a$. We can "factor" these two productions by writing them as $S \longrightarrow a(S | e)$. That is, we assume that concatenation distributes over alternation (the vertical bar). We can then replace these productions by

$$S \longrightarrow aA$$
$$A \longrightarrow S | e$$

to obtain an equivalent LL(1) grammar.   ☐

In general, the process of left factoring involves replacing the productions $A \rightarrow \alpha\beta_1 | \cdots | \alpha\beta_n$ by $A \rightarrow \alpha A'$ and $A' \rightarrow \beta_1 | \cdots | \beta_n$.

5.1.4. Parsing LL(1) Grammars

The heart of a k-predictive parsing algorithm is its parsing table M. In this section and the next we show that every LL(k) grammar G can be left-parsed by a k-predictive parsing algorithm by showing how a valid parsing table can be constructed from G. We shall first consider the important special case where G is an LL(1) grammar.

ALGORITHM 5.1

A parsing table for an LL(1) grammar.

Input. An LL(1) CFG $G = (N, \Sigma, P, S)$.

Output. M, a valid parsing table for G.

Method. We shall assume that $ is the bottom of the pushdown list marker. M is defined on $(N \cup \Sigma \cup \{\$\}) \times (\Sigma \cup \{e\})$ as follows:

(1) If $A \rightarrow \alpha$ is the ith production in P, then $M(A, a) = (\alpha, i)$ for all a in $\text{FIRST}_1(\alpha)$, $a \neq e$. If e is also in $\text{FIRST}_1(\alpha)$, then $M(A, b) = (\alpha, i)$ for all b in $\text{FOLLOW}_1(A)$.

(2) $M(a, a) = $ **pop** for all a in Σ.

(3) $M(\$, e) = $ **accept**.

(4) Otherwise $M(X, a) = $ **error**, for X in $N \cup \Sigma \cup \{\$\}$, a in $\Sigma \cup \{e\}$. □

Before we prove that Algorithm 5.1 does produce a valid parsing table for G, let us consider an example of Algorithm 5.1.

Example 5.12

Let us consider producing a parsing table for the grammar G with productions

(1) $E \longrightarrow TE'$ (2) $E' \longrightarrow + TE'$

(3) $E' \longrightarrow e$ (4) $T \longrightarrow FT'$

(5) $T' \longrightarrow * FT'$ (6) $T' \longrightarrow e$

(7) $F \longrightarrow (E)$ (8) $F \longrightarrow a$

Using Theorem 5.3 the reader can verify that G is an LL(1) grammar. In fact, the discerning reader will observe that G has been obtained from G_0 using the transformation eliminating left recursion as in Example 5.10. G_0 is not LL, by the way.

Let us now compute the entries for the E-row using step (1) of Algorithm

	a	$($	$)$	$+$	$*$	e
E	$TE', 1$	$TE', 1$				
E'			$e, 3$	$+TE', 2$		$e, 3$
T	$FT', 4$	$FT', 4$				
T'			$e, 6$	$e, 6$	$*FT', 5$	$e, 6$
F	$a, 8$	$(E), 7$				
a	pop					
$($		pop				
$)$			pop			
$+$				pop		
$*$					pop	
$\$$						accept

Fig. 5.4   Parsing table for G.

5.1. Here, FIRST$_1[TE'] = \{(, a\}$, so $M[E, (] = [TE', 1]$ and $M[E, a] = [TE', 1]$. All other entries in the E-row are **error**. Let us now compute the entries for the E'-row. We note FIRST$_1[+ TE'] = +$, so $M[E', +] = [+ TE', 2]$. Since $E' \rightarrow e$ is a production, we must compute FOLLOW$_1[E'] = \{e,)\}$. Thus, $M[E', e] = M[E',)] = [e, 3]$. All other entries for E' are **error**. Continuing in this fashion, we obtain the parsing table for G shown in Fig. 5.4. Error entries have been left blank.

The 1-predictive parsing algorithm using this table would parse the input string $(a * a)$ in the following sequence of moves:

$$[(a * a), E\$, e] \vdash [(a * a), TE'\$, 1]$$
$$\vdash [(a * a), FT'E'\$, 14]$$
$$\vdash [(a * a), (E)T'E'\$, 147]$$
$$\vdash [a * a), E)T'E'\$, 147]$$
$$\vdash [a * a), TE')T'E'\$, 1471]$$
$$\vdash [a * a), FT'E')T'E'\$, 14714]$$
$$\vdash [a * a), aT'E')T'E'\$, 147148]$$
$$\vdash [* a), T'E')T'E'\$, 147148]$$
$$\vdash [* a), * FT'E')T'E'\$, 1471485]$$
$$\vdash [a), FT'E')T'E'\$, 1471485]$$
$$\vdash [a), aT'E')T'E'\$, 14714858]$$
$$\vdash [), T'E')T'E'\$, 14714858]$$
$$\vdash [), E')T'E'\$, 147148586]$$
$$\vdash [),)T'E'\$, 1471485863]$$
$$\vdash [e, T'E', 1471485863]$$
$$\vdash [e, E'\$, 14714858636]$$
$$\vdash [e, \$, 147148586363] \quad \square$$

THEOREM 5.4

Algorithm 5.1 produces a valid parsing table for an LL(1) grammar G.

Proof. We first note that if G is an LL(1) grammar, then at most one value is defined in step (1) of Algorithm 5.1 for each entry $M(A, a)$ of the parsing matrix. This observation is merely a restatement of Theorem 5.3.

Next, a straightforward induction on the number of moves executed by a 1-predictive parsing algorithm $\mathcal{C}$ using the parsing table M shows that if $(xy, S\$, e) \vdash^* (y, \alpha\$, \pi)$, then $S \overset{\pi}{\Rightarrow} x\alpha$. Another induction on the number of steps in a leftmost derivation can be used to show the converse, namely that if $S \overset{\pi}{\Rightarrow} x\alpha$, where α is the open portion of $x\alpha$, and $\text{FIRST}_1(y)$ is in $\text{FIRST}_1(\alpha)$, then $(xy, S\$, e) \vdash^* (y, \alpha\$, \pi)$. It then follows that $(w, S\$, e) \vdash^* (e, \$, \pi)$ if and only if $S \overset{\pi}{\Rightarrow} w$. Thus $\mathcal{C}$ is a valid parsing algorithm for G, and M a valid parsing table for G. $\square$

5.1.5. Parsing LL(k) Grammars

Let us now consider the construction of a parsing table for an arbitrary LL(k) grammar $G = (\text{N}, \Sigma, P, S)$, where $k \geq 1$. If G is a strong LL(k) grammar, then we can use Algorithm 5.1 with lookahead strings of length up to k symbols. However, the situation is somewhat more complicated when G is not a strong LL(k) grammar. In the LL(1)-predictive parsing algorithm we placed only symbols in $\text{N} \cup \Sigma$ on the pushdown list, and we found that the combination of the nonterminal symbol on top of the pushdown list and the current input symbol was sufficient to uniquely determine the next production to be applied. However, when G is not strong, we find that a non-terminal symbol and the lookahead string are not always sufficient to uniquely determine the next production.

For example, consider the LL(2) grammar

$$S \longrightarrow aAaa \mid bAba$$
$$A \longrightarrow b \mid e$$

of Example 5.8. Given the nonterminal A and the lookahead string ba we do not know whether we should apply production $A \rightarrow b$ or $A \rightarrow e$.

We can, however, resolve uncertainties of this nature by associating with each nonterminal and the portion of a left-sentential form which may appear to its right, a special symbol which we shall call an *LL(k) table* (not to be confused with the parsing table). The LL(k) table, given a lookahead string, will uniquely specify which production is to be applied next in a leftmost derivation in an LL(k) grammar.

DEFINITION

Let Σ be an alphabet. If L_1 and L_2 are subsets of Σ^*, let

$$L_1 \oplus_k L_2 = \{w \mid \text{for some } x \in L_1 \text{ and } y \in L_2, \text{ we have } w = xy$$
$$\text{if } |xy| \leq k \text{ and } w \text{ is the first } k \text{ symbols of } xy \text{ otherwise}\}.$$

Example 5.13

Let $L_1 = \{e, abb\}$ and $L_2 = \{b, bab\}$. Then $L_1 \oplus_2 L_2 = \{b, ba, ab\}$. $\square$

The $\oplus_k$ operator is similar to an infix FIRST operator.

LEMMA 5.1

For any CFG $G = (\text{N}, \Sigma, P, S)$, and for all α and β in $(\text{N} \cup \Sigma)^*$, $\text{FIRST}_k^G(\alpha\beta) = \text{FIRST}_k^G(\alpha) \oplus_k \text{FIRST}_k^G(\beta)$.

Proof. Exercise. □

DEFINITION

Let $G = (N, \Sigma, P, S)$ be a CFG. For each A in N and $L \subseteq \Sigma^{*k}$ we define $T_{A,L}$, the *LL(k) table associated with A and L* to be a function which given a lookahead string u in Σ^{*k} returns either the symbol **error** or an A-production and a finite list of subsets of Σ^{*k}.

Specifically,

(1) $T_{A,L}(u) = $ **error** if there is no production $A \to \alpha$ in P such that $\text{FIRST}_k(\alpha) \oplus_k L$ contains u.

(2) $T_{A,L}(u) = (A \to \alpha, \langle Y_1, Y_2, \ldots, Y_m \rangle)$ if $A \to \alpha$ is the unique production in P such that $\text{FIRST}_k(\alpha) \oplus_k L$ contains u. If

$$\alpha = x_0 B_1 x_1 B_2 x_2 \cdots B_m x_m, \qquad m \geq 0,$$

where each $B_i \in N$ and $x_i \in \Sigma^*$, then $Y_i = \text{FIRST}_k(x_i B_{i+1} x_{i+1} \cdots B_m x_m) \oplus_k L$. We shall call Y_i a *local follow set* for B_i. [If $m = 0$, $T_{A,L}(u) = (A \to \alpha, \varnothing)$.]

(3) $T_{A,L}(u)$ is undefined if there are two or more productions $A \to \alpha_1 | \alpha_2 | \cdots | \alpha_n$ such that $\text{FIRST}_k(\alpha_i) \oplus_k L$ contains u, for $1 \leq i \leq n$, $n \geq 2$. This situation will not occur if G is an LL(k) grammar.

Intuitively, if $T_{A,L}(u) = $ **error**, then there is no possible derivation in G of the form $Ax \overset{+}{\Rightarrow} uv$ for any $x \in L$ and $v \in \Sigma^*$. Whenever $T_{A,L}(u) = (A \to \alpha, \langle Y_1, Y_2, \ldots, Y_m \rangle)$, there is exactly one production, $A \to \alpha$, which can be used in the first step of a derivation $Ax \overset{+}{\Rightarrow} uv$ for any $x \in L$ and $v \in \Sigma^*$. Each set of strings Y_i gives all possible prefixes of length up to k of terminal strings which can follow a string derived from B_i when we use the production $A \to \alpha$, where $\alpha = x_0 B_1 x_1 B_2 x_2 \cdots B_m x_m$, in any derivation of the form $Ax \Rightarrow \alpha x \overset{*}{\Rightarrow} uv$, with x in L.

By Theorem 5.2, $G = (N, \Sigma, P, S)$ is not LL(k) if and only if there exists α in $(N \cup \Sigma)^*$ such that

(1) $S \overset{*}{\underset{\text{lm}}{\Rightarrow}} wA\alpha$, and

(2) $\text{FIRST}_k(\beta\alpha) \cap \text{FIRST}_k(\gamma\alpha) \neq \varnothing$ for some $\beta \neq \gamma$ such that $A \to \beta$ and $A \to \gamma$ are in P.

By Lemma 5.1 we can rephrase condition (2) as

(2′) If $L = \text{FIRST}_k(\alpha)$, then $(\text{FIRST}_k(\beta) \oplus_k L) \cap (\text{FIRST}_k(\gamma) \oplus_k L) \neq \varnothing$.

Therefore, if G is LL(k), and we have the derivation $S \overset{*}{\underset{\text{lm}}{\Rightarrow}} wA\alpha \overset{*}{\underset{\text{lm}}{\Rightarrow}} wx$, then $T_{A,L}(u)$ will uniquely determine which production is to be used to expand A, where u is $\text{FIRST}_k(x)$ and L is $\text{FIRST}_k(\alpha)$.

Example 5.14

Consider the LL(2) grammar

$$S \longrightarrow aAaa \,|\, bAba$$

$$A \longrightarrow b \,|\, e$$

Let us compute the LL(2) table $T_{S, \{e\}}$, which we shall denote T_0. Since $S \longrightarrow aAaa$ is a production, we compute $\text{FIRST}_2(aAaa) \oplus_2 \{e\} = \{aa, ab\}$. Likewise, $S \longrightarrow bAba$ is a production, and $\text{FIRST}_2(bAba) \oplus_2 \{e\} = \{bb\}$. Thus we find $T_0(aa) = (S \longrightarrow aAaa, Y)$. Y is the local follow set for A; $Y = \text{FIRST}_2(aa) \oplus_2 \{e\} = \{aa\}$. The string aa is the string to the right of A in the production $S \longrightarrow aAaa$. Continuing in this fashion, we obtain the table T_0 shown below:

Table T_0

u	Production	Sets
aa	$S \longrightarrow aAaa$	$\{aa\}$
ab	$S \longrightarrow aAaa$	$\{aa\}$
bb	$S \longrightarrow bAba$	$\{ba\}$

For each u in $(a+b)^{*2}$ not shown, $T_0(u) = $ **error**.   □

We shall now provide an algorithm to compute those LL(k) tables for an LL(k) grammar G which are needed to construct a parsing table for G. It should be noted that if G is an LL(1) grammar, this algorithm might produce more than one table per nonterminal. However, the parsers constructed by Algorithms 5.1 and 5.2 will be quite similar. They act the same way on inputs in the language, of course. On other inputs, the parser of Algorithm 5.2 might detect the error while the parser of Algorithm 5.1 proceeds to make a few more moves.

ALGORITHM 5.2

Construction of LL(k) tables.

Input. An LL(k) CFG $G = (N, \Sigma, P, S)$.

Output. $\mathfrak{I}$, the set of LL(k) tables needed to construct a parsing table for G.

Method.

(1) Construct T_0, the LL(k) table associated with S and $\{e\}$.
(2) Initially set $\mathfrak{I} = \{T_0\}$.
(3) For each LL(k) table T in $\mathfrak{I}$ with entry

$$T(u) = (A \longrightarrow x_0 B_1 x_1 B_2 x_2 \cdots B_m x_m, \langle Y_1, Y_2, \ldots, Y_m \rangle),$$

add to $\mathfrak{I}$ the LL(k) table T_{B_i,Y_i}, for $1 \le i \le m$, if T_{B_i,Y_i} is not already in $\mathfrak{I}$.
(4) Repeat step (3) until no new LL(k) tables can be added to $\mathfrak{I}$. $\square$

Example 5.15

Let us construct the relevant set of LL(2) tables for the grammar

$$S \longrightarrow aAaa \mid bAba$$
$$A \longrightarrow b \mid e$$

We begin with $\mathfrak{I} = \{T_{S,\{e\}}\}$. Since $T_{S,\{e\}}(aa) = (S \longrightarrow aAaa, \{aa\})$, we must
add $T_{A,\{aa\}}$ to $\mathfrak{I}$. Likewise, since $T_0(bb) = (S \longrightarrow bAba, \{ba\})$, we must also
add $T_{A,\{ba\}}$ to $\mathfrak{I}$. The nonerror entries for the LL(2) tables $T_{A,\{aa\}}$ and $T_{A,\{ba\}}$
are shown below:

Table $T_{A,\{aa\}}$

u	Production	Sets
ba	$A \longrightarrow b$	—
aa	$A \longrightarrow e$	—

Table $T_{A,\{ba\}}$

u	Production	Sets
ba	$A \longrightarrow e$	—
bb	$A \longrightarrow b$	—

At this point $\mathfrak{I} = \{T_{S,\{e\}}, T_{A,\{aa\}}, T_{A,\{ba\}}\}$ and no new entries can be added to
$\mathfrak{I}$ in Algorithm 5.2 so that the three LL(2) tables in $\mathfrak{I}$ are the relevant LL(2)
table for G. $\square$

From the relevant set of LL(k) tables for an LL(k) grammar G we can
use the following algorithm to construct a valid parsing table for G. The k-
predictive parsing algorithm using this parsing table will actually use the
LL(k) tables themselves as nonterminal symbols on the pushdown list.

ALGORITHM 5.3

A parsing table for an LL(k) grammar $G = (N, \Sigma, P, S)$.

Input. An LL(k) CFG $G = (N, \Sigma, P, S)$ and $\mathfrak{I}$, the set of LL(k) tables
for G.

Output. M, a valid parsing table for G.

Method. M is defined on $(\mathfrak{I} \cup \Sigma \cup \{\$\}) \times \Sigma^{*k}$ as follows:

(1) If $A \longrightarrow x_0 B_1 x_1 B_2 x_2 \cdots B_m x_m$ is the ith production in P and $T_{A,L}$ is

in $\mathfrak{I}$, then for all u such that
$$T_{A,L}(u) = (A \longrightarrow x_0 B_1 x_1 B_2 x_2 \cdots B_m x_m, \langle Y_1, Y_2, \ldots, Y_m \rangle),$$
we have $M(T_{A,L}, u) = (x_0 T_{B_1, Y_1} x_1 T_{B_2, Y_2} x_2 \cdots T_{B_m, Y_m} x_m, i)$.

(2) $M(a, av) = \textbf{pop}$ for all v in $\Sigma^{*(k-1)}$.

(3) $M(\$, e) = \textbf{accept}$.

(4) Otherwise, $M(X, u) = \textbf{error}$.

(5) $T_{S, \{e\}}$ is the initial table. $\square$

Example 5.16

Let us construct the parsing table for the LL(2) grammar

$$(1) \quad S \longrightarrow aAaa$$
$$(2) \quad S \longrightarrow bAba$$
$$(3) \quad A \longrightarrow b$$
$$(4) \quad A \longrightarrow e$$

using the relevant set of LL(2) tables constructed in Example 5.15. The parsing table resulting from Algorithm 5.3 is shown in Fig. 5.5. In Fig. 5.5, $T_0 = T_{S,\{e\}}$, $T_1 = T_{A,\{aa\}}$, and $T_2 = T_{A,\{ba\}}$. Blank entries indicate **error**.

	aa	ab	a	ba	bb	b	e
T_0	$aT_1aa, 1$	$aT_1aa, 1$			$bT_2ba, 2$		
T_1	$e, 4$			$b, 3$			
T_2				$e, 4$	$b, 3$		
a	pop	pop	pop				
b				pop	pop	pop	
$\$$							accept

Fig. 5.5 Parsing table.

The 2-predictive parsing algorithm would make the following sequence of moves with input bba:

$$(bba, T_0\$, e) \vdash (bba, bT_2ba\$, 2)$$
$$\vdash (ba, T_2ba\$, 2)$$
$$\vdash (ba, ba\$, 24)$$
$$\vdash (a, a\$, 24)$$
$$\vdash (e, \$, 24). \quad \square$$

THEOREM 5.5

If $G = (N, \Sigma, P, S)$ is an LL(k) grammar, then the parsing table constructed in Algorithm 5.3 is a valid parsing table for G under a k-predictive parsing algorithm.

Proof. The proof is similar to that of Theorem 5.4. If G is LL(k), then no conflicts occur in the construction of the relevant LL(k) tables for G, since if $A \longrightarrow \beta$ and $A \longrightarrow \gamma$ are in P and $S \overset{*}{\underset{\text{lm}}{\Longrightarrow}} wA\alpha$, then

$$(\text{FIRST}_k(\beta) \oplus_k \text{FIRST}_k(\alpha)) \cap (\text{FIRST}_k(\gamma) \oplus_k \text{FIRST}_k(\alpha)) = \varnothing.$$

In the construction of the relevant LL(k) tables for G, we compute a table $T_{A,L}$ only if for some S, w, and α, we have $S \overset{*}{\underset{\text{lm}}{\Longrightarrow}} wA\alpha$, and $L = \text{FIRST}_k(\alpha)$. That is, L will be a local follow set for A. Thus, if u is in Σ^{*k}, then there is at most one production $A \longrightarrow \beta$ such that u is in $\text{FIRST}_k(\beta) \oplus_k L$.

Let us define the homomorphism h on $\mathfrak{I} \cup \Sigma$ as follows:

$h(a) = a$ for all $a \in \Sigma$

$h(T) = A$ if T is an LL(k) table associated with A and L for some L.

Note that each table in $\mathfrak{I}$ must have at least one entry which is a production index. Thus, A is uniquely determined by T.

We shall now prove that

(5.1.2) $S \overset{\pi}{\Longrightarrow} x\alpha$ if and only if there is some α' in $(\mathfrak{I} \cup \Sigma)^*$ such that $h(\alpha') = \alpha$, and $(xy, T_0\$, e) \overset{*}{\vdash} (y, \alpha'\$, \pi)$ for all y such that $\alpha \overset{*}{\Longrightarrow} y$. T_0 is the LL(k) table associated with S and $\{e\}$.

If: From the manner in which the parsing table is constructed, whenever a production number i is emitted corresponding to the ith production $A \longrightarrow \beta$, the parsing algorithm replaces a table T such that $h(T) = A$ by a string β' such that $h(\beta') = \beta$. The "if" portion of statement (5.1.2) can thus be proved by a straightforward induction on the number of moves made by the parsing algorithm.

Only if: Here we shall show that

(5.1.3)   If $A \overset{\pi}{\Longrightarrow} x$, then the parsing algorithm will make the sequence of moves $(xy, T, e) \overset{*}{\vdash} (y, e, \pi)$ for any LL(k) table T associated with A and L, where $L = \text{FIRST}_k(\alpha)$ for some α such that $S \overset{*}{\underset{\text{lm}}{\Longrightarrow}} wA\alpha$, and y is in L.

The proof will proceed by induction on $|\pi|$. If $A \overset{i}{\Longrightarrow} a_1a_2 \cdots a_n$, then

$$(a_1 a_2 \cdots a_n y, T, e) \vdash (a_1 \cdots a_n y, a_1 \cdots a_n, i)$$

since $T(u) = (A \to a_1 a_2 \cdots a_n, \varnothing)$ for all u in $\text{FIRST}_k(a_1 a_2 \cdots a_n) \oplus_k L$. Then $(a_1 \cdots a_n y, a_1 \cdots a_n, i) \vdash^{\underline{n}} (y, e, i)$. Now suppose that statement (5.1.3) is true for all leftmost derivations of length up to l, and suppose that $A \overset{i}{\Rightarrow} x_0 B_1 x_1 B_2 x_2 \cdots B_m x_m$ and $B_j \overset{\pi_j}{\Rightarrow} y_j$, where $|\pi_j| < l$. Then $(x_0 y_1 x_1 \cdots y_m x_m y, T, e) \vdash^{\underline{*}} (x_0 y_1 x_1 \cdots y_m x_m y, x_0 T_1 x_1 \cdots T_m x_m, i)$, since $T(u) = (A \to x_0 B_1 x_1 \cdots B_m x_m, \langle Y_1 \cdots Y_m \rangle)$ for all u included in $\text{FIRST}_k(x_0 B_1 x_1 \cdots B_m x_m) \oplus_k L$. Each T_j is the LL(k) table associated with B_j and Y_j, $1 \le j \le m$, so that the inductive hypothesis holds for each sequence of moves of the form

$$(y_j x_j \cdots y_m x_m y, T_j, e) \vdash^{\underline{*}} (x_j \cdots y_m x_m y, e, \pi_j)$$

Putting in the popping moves for the x_j's we obtain

$$(x_0 y_1 x_1 y_2 x_2 \cdots y_m x_m y, T, e)$$
$$\vdash (x_0 y_1 x_1 y_2 x_2 \cdots y_m x_m y, x_0 T_1 x_1 T_2 x_2 \cdots T_m x_m, i)$$
$$\vdash^{\underline{*}} (y_1 x_2 y_2 x_2 \cdots y_m x_m y, T_1 x_1 T_2 x_2 \cdots T_m x_m, i)$$
$$\vdash^{\underline{*}} (x_1 y_2 x_2 \cdots y_m x_m y, x_1 T_2 x_2 \cdots T_m x_m, i\pi_1)$$
$$\vdash^{\underline{*}} (y_2 x_2 \cdots y_m x_m y, T_2 x_2 \cdots T_m x_m, i\pi_1)$$
$$\vdots$$
$$\vdash^{\underline{*}} (y, e, i\pi_1 \pi_2 \cdots \pi_m)$$

From statement (5.1.3) we have, as a special case, that if $S \overset{\pi}{\Rightarrow} w$, then $(w, T_0 \$, e) \vdash^{\underline{*}} (e, \$, \pi)$. $\square$

As another example, let us construct the parsing table for the LL(2) grammar G_2 of Example 5.3.

Example 5.17

Consider the LL(2) grammar G_2

(1) $S \longrightarrow e$

(2) $S \longrightarrow abA$

(3) $A \longrightarrow Saa$

(4) $A \longrightarrow b$

Let us first construct the relevant LL(2) tables for G_2. We begin by constructing $T_0 = T_{S,\{e\}}$:

Table T_0

u	Production	Sets
e	$S \longrightarrow e$	—
ab	$S \longrightarrow abA$	$\{e\}$

From T_0 we obtain $T_1 = T_{A,\{e\}}$:

Table T_1

u	Production	Sets
b	$A \longrightarrow b$	—
aa	$A \longrightarrow Saa$	$\{aa\}$
ab	$A \longrightarrow Saa$	$\{aa\}$

From T_1 we obtain $T_2 = T_{S,\{aa\}}$:

Table T_2

u	Production	Sets
aa	$S \longrightarrow e$	—
ab	$S \longrightarrow abA$	$\{aa\}$

From T_2 we obtain $T_3 = T_{A,\{aa\}}$:

Table T_3

u	Production	Sets
aa	$A \longrightarrow Saa$	$\{aa\}$
ab	$A \longrightarrow Saa$	$\{aa\}$
ba	$A \longrightarrow b$	—

From these LL(2) tables we obtain the parsing table shown in Fig. 5.6.

The 2-predictive parsing algorithm using this parsing table would parse the input string *abaa* by the following sequence of moves:

$$
\begin{aligned}
(abaa, T_0\$, e) &\vdash (abaa, abT_1\$, 2) \\
&\vdash (baa, bT_1\$, 2) \\
&\vdash (aa, T_1\$, 2) \\
&\vdash (aa, T_2aa\$, 23) \\
&\vdash (aa, aa\$, 231) \\
&\vdash (a, a\$, 231) \\
&\vdash (e, \$, 231) \quad \square
\end{aligned}
$$

	aa	ab	a	ba	bb	b	e
T_0		$abT_1, 2$					$e, 1$
T_1	$T_2aa, 3$	$T_2aa, 3$				$b, 4$	
T_2	$e, 1$	$abT_3, 2$					
T_3	$T_2aa, 3$	$T_2aa, 3$		$b, 4$			
a	pop	pop	pop				
b				pop	pop	pop	
$							accept

Fig. 5.6 Parsing table for G_2.

We conclude this section by showing that the k-predictive parsing algorithm parses every input string in linear time.

THEOREM 5.6

The number of steps executed by a k-predictive parsing algorithm, using the parsing table resulting from Algorithm 5.3 for an LL(k) context-free grammar $G = (N, \Sigma, P, S)$, with an input of length n, is a linear function of n.

Proof. If G is an LL(k) grammar, G cannot be left-recursive. From Lemma 4.1, the maximum number of steps in a derivation of the form $A \underset{\text{lm}}{\overset{+}{\Rightarrow}} B\alpha$ is less than some constant c. Thus the maximum number of moves that can be made by a k-predictive parsing algorithm α before a **pop** move, which consumes another input symbol, is bounded above by c. Therefore, α can execute at most $O(n)$ moves in processing an input of length n. $\square$

5.1.6. Testing for the LL(k) Condition

Given a grammar G, there are several questions we might naturally ask about G. First, one might ask whether G is LL(k) for a given value of k. Second, is G an LL grammar? That is, does there exist some value of k such that G is LL(k)? Finally, since the left parsers for LL(1) grammars are particularly straightforward to construct, we might ask, if G is not LL(1), whether there is an LL(1) grammar G' such that $L(G') = L(G)$.

Unfortunately we can provide an algorithm to answer only the first question. It can be shown that the second and third questions are undecidable.

In this section we shall provide a test to determine whether a grammar is LL(k) for a specified value of k. If $k = 1$, we can use Theorem 5.3. For arbitrary k, we can use Theorem 5.2. Here we shall give the general case. It is essentially just showing that Algorithm 5.3 succeeds in producing a parsing table only if G is LL(k).

Recall that $G = (N, \Sigma, P, S)$ is not LL(k) if and only if for some α in $(N \cup \Sigma)^*$ the following conditions hold:

(1) $S \overset{*}{\underset{lm}{\Rightarrow}} wA\alpha$,

(2) $L = \text{FIRST}_k(\alpha)$, and

(3) $(\text{FIRST}_k(\beta) \oplus_k L) \cap (\text{FIRST}_k(\gamma) \oplus_k L) \neq \varnothing$,

for some $\beta \neq \gamma$ such that $A \rightarrow \beta$ and $A \rightarrow \gamma$ are productions in P.

ALGORITHM 5.4

Test for LL(k)-ness.

Input. A CFG $G = (N, \Sigma, P, S)$ and an integer k.

Output. "Yes" if G is LL(k). "No," otherwise.

Method.

(1) For a nonterminal A in N such that A has two or more alternates, compute $\sigma(A) = \{L \subseteq \Sigma^{*k} \mid S \overset{*}{\underset{lm}{\Rightarrow}} wA\alpha \text{ and } L = \text{FIRST}_k(\alpha)\}$. (We shall provide an algorithm to do this subsequently.)

(2) If $A \rightarrow \beta$ and $A \rightarrow \gamma$ are distinct A-productions, compute, for each L in $\sigma(A), f(L) = (\text{FIRST}_k(\beta) \oplus_k L) \cap (\text{FIRST}_k(\gamma) \oplus_k L)$. If $f(L) \neq \varnothing$, then halt and return "No." If $f(L) = \varnothing$ for all L in $\sigma(A)$, repeat step (2) for all distinct pairs of A-productions.

(3) Repeat steps (1) and (2) for all nonterminals in N.

(4) Return "yes" if no violation of the LL(k) condition is found. $\quad\square$

To implement Algorithm 5.4, we must be able to compute $\text{FIRST}_k^G(\beta)$ for any β in $(N \cup \Sigma)^*$ and CFG $G = (N, \Sigma, P, S)$. Second, we must be able to find the sets in $\sigma(A) = \{L \subseteq \Sigma^{*k} \mid \text{there exists } \alpha \text{ such that } S \overset{*}{\underset{lm}{\Rightarrow}} wA\alpha, \text{ and } L = \text{FIRST}_k(\alpha)\}$. We shall now provide algorithms to compute both these items.

ALGORITHM 5.5

Computation of $\text{FIRST}_k(\beta)$.

Input. A CFG $G = (N, \Sigma, P, S)$ and a string $\beta = X_1 X_2 \cdots X_n$ in $(N \cup \Sigma)^*$.

Output. $\text{FIRST}_k^G(\beta)$.

Method. We compute $\text{FIRST}_k(X_i)$ for $1 \leq i \leq n$ and observe that by Lemma 5.1

$$\text{FIRST}_k(\beta) = \text{FIRST}_k(X_1) \oplus_k \text{FIRST}_k(X_2) \oplus_k \cdots \oplus_k \text{FIRST}_k(X_n)$$

It will thus suffice to show how to find $\text{FIRST}_k(X)$ when X is in N; if X is in $\Sigma \cup \{e\}$, then obviously $\text{FIRST}_k(X) = \{X\}$.

We define sets $F_i(X)$ for all X in $N \cup \Sigma$ and for increasing values of i, $i \geq 0$, as follows:

(1) $F_i(a) = \{a\}$ for all a in Σ and $i \geq 0$.

(2) $F_0(A) = \{x \in \Sigma^{*k} \mid A \rightarrow x\alpha$ is in P, where either $|x| = k$ or $|x| < k$ and $\alpha = e\}$.

(3) Suppose that $F_0, F_1, \ldots, F_{i-1}$ have been defined for all A in N. Then

$$F_i(A) = \{x \mid A \rightarrow Y_1 \ldots Y_n \text{ is in } P \text{ and } x \text{ is in}$$

$$F_{i-1}(Y_1) \oplus_k F_{i-1}(Y_2) \oplus_k \cdots \oplus_k F_{i-1}(Y_n)\} \cup F_{i-1}(A).$$

(4) As $F_{i-1}(A) \subseteq F_i(A) \subseteq \Sigma^{*k}$ for all A and i, eventually we must reach an i for which $F_{i-1}(A) = F_i(A)$ for all A in N. Let $\text{FIRST}_k(A) = F_i(A)$ for that value of i. $\square$

Example 5.18

Let us construct the sets $F_i(X)$, assuming that k has the value 1, for the grammar G with productions

$$S \longrightarrow BA$$
$$A \longrightarrow + BA \mid e$$
$$B \longrightarrow DC$$
$$C \longrightarrow * DC \mid e$$
$$D \longrightarrow (S) \mid a$$

Initially,

$$F_0(S) = F_0(B) = \varnothing$$
$$F_0(A) = \{+, e\}$$
$$F_0(C) = \{*, e\}$$
$$F_0(D) = \{(, a\}$$

Then $F_1(B) = \{(, a\}$ and $F_1(X) = F_0(X)$ for all other X. Then $F_2(S) = \{(, a\}$ and $F_2(X) = F_1(X)$ for all other X. $F_3(X) = F_2(X)$ for all X, so that

$$\text{FIRST}(S) = \text{FIRST}(B) = \text{FIRST}(D) = \{(, a\}$$
$$\text{FIRST}(A) = \{+, e\}$$
$$\text{FIRST}(C) = \{*, e\} \square$$

THEOREM 5.7

Algorithm 5.5 correctly computes $\text{FIRST}_k(A)$.

Proof. We observe that if for all X in $N \cup \Sigma$, $F_{i-1}(X) = F_i(X)$, then

$F_i(X) = F_j(X)$ for all $j > i$ and all X. Thus we must prove that x is in $\mathrm{FIRST}_k(A)$ if and only if x is in $F_j(A)$ for some j.

If: We show that $F_j(A) \subseteq \mathrm{FIRST}_k(A)$ by induction on j. The basis, $j = 0$, is trivial. Let us consider a fixed value of j and assume that the hypothesis is true for smaller values of j.

If x is in $F_j(A)$, then either it is in $F_{j-1}(A)$, in which case the result is immediate, or we can find $A \rightarrow Y_1 \cdots Y_n$ in P, with x_p in $F_{j-1}(Y_p)$, where $1 \leq p \leq n$, such that $x = \mathrm{FIRST}_k(x_1 \cdots x_n)$. By the inductive hypothesis, x_p is in $\mathrm{FIRST}_k(Y_p)$. Thus there exists, for each p, a derivation $Y_p \overset{*}{\Rightarrow} y_p$, where x_p is $\mathrm{FIRST}_k(y_p)$. Hence, $A \overset{*}{\Rightarrow} y_1 \cdots y_n$. We must now show that $x = \mathrm{FIRST}_k(y_1 \cdots y_n)$, and thus conclude that x is in $\mathrm{FIRST}_k(A)$.

Case 1: $|x_1 \cdots x_n| < k$. Then $y_p = x_p$ for each p, and $x = y_1 \cdots y_n$. Since $y_1 \cdots y_n$ is in $\mathrm{FIRST}_k(A)$ in this case, x is in $\mathrm{FIRST}_k(A)$.

Case 2: For some $s \geq 0$, $|x_1 \cdots x_s| < k$ but $|x_1 \cdots x_{s+1}| \geq k$. Then $y_p = x_p$ for $1 \leq p \leq s$, and x is the first k symbols of $x_1 \cdots x_{s+1}$. Since x_{s+1} is a prefix of y_{s+1}, x is a prefix of $y_1 \cdots y_{s+1}$ and hence of $y_1 \cdots y_n$. Thus, x is $\mathrm{FIRST}_k(A)$.

Only if: Let x be in $\mathrm{FIRST}_k(A)$. Then for some r, $A \overset{r}{\Rightarrow} y$ and $x = \mathrm{FIRST}_k(y)$. We show by induction on r that x is in $F_r(A)$. The basis, $r = 1$, is trivial, since x is in $F_0(A)$. (In fact, the hypothesis could have been tightened somewhat, but there is no point in doing so.)

Fix r, and assume that the hypothesis is true for smaller r. Then

$$A \Rightarrow Y_1 \cdots Y_n \overset{r-1}{\Rightarrow} y,$$

where $y = y_1 \cdots y_n$ and $Y_p \overset{r_p}{\Rightarrow} y_p$ for $1 \leq p \leq n$. Evidently, $r_p < r$. By the inductive hypothesis, x_p is in $F_{r-1}(Y_p)$, where $x_p = \mathrm{FIRST}_k(y_p)$. Thus, $\mathrm{FIRST}_k(x_1 \cdots x_p)$, which is x, is in $F_r(A)$. $\square$

In the next algorithm we shall see a method of computing, for a given grammar $G = (\mathrm{N}, \Sigma, P, S)$, those sets $L \subseteq \Sigma^{*k}$ such that $S \underset{\mathrm{lm}}{\overset{*}{\Rightarrow}} wA\alpha$ and $\mathrm{FIRST}_k(\alpha) = L$ for some w, A, and α.

ALGORITHM 5.6

Computation of $\sigma(A)$.

Input. A CFG $G = (\mathrm{N}, \Sigma, P, S)$.

Output.

$$\sigma(A) = \{L \mid L \subseteq \Sigma^{*k} \text{ such that } S \underset{\mathrm{lm}}{\overset{*}{\Rightarrow}} wA\alpha \text{ and}$$
$$\mathrm{FIRST}_k(\alpha) = L \text{ for some } w \text{ and } \alpha\}.$$

Method. We shall compute, for all A and B in N, sets $\sigma(A, B)$ such that $\sigma(A, B) = \{L \mid L \subseteq \Sigma^{*k}$, and for some x and α, $A \overset{*}{\underset{lm}{\Rightarrow}} xB\alpha$ and $L = $ FIRST$(\alpha)\}$. We construct sets $\sigma_i(A, B)$ for each A and B and for $i = 0, 1, \dots$ as follows:

(1) Let $\sigma_0(A, B) = \{L \subseteq \Sigma^{*k} \mid A \to \beta B\alpha$ is in P and $L = $ FIRST$(\alpha)\}$.

(2) Assume that $\sigma_{i-1}(A, B)$ has been computed for all A and B. Define $\sigma_i(A, B)$ as follows:

    (a) If L is in $\sigma_{i-1}(A, B)$, place L in $\sigma_i(A, B)$.

    (b) If there is a production $A \to X_1 \cdots X_n$ in P, place L in $\sigma_i(A, B)$ if for some j, $1 \leq j \leq n$, there is a set L' in $\sigma_{i-1}(X_j, B)$ and $L = L' \oplus_k$ FIRST$(X_{j+1}) \oplus_k \cdots \oplus_k$ FIRST(X_n).

(3) When for some i, $\sigma_i(A, B) = \sigma_{i-1}(A, B)$ for all A and B, let $\sigma(A, B) = \sigma_i(A, B)$. Since for all i, $\sigma_{i-1}(A, B) \subseteq \sigma_i(A, B) \subseteq \mathcal{P}(\Sigma^{*k})$, such an i must exist.

(4) The desired set is $\sigma(S, A)$.   □

THEOREM 5.8

In Algorithm 5.6, L is in $\sigma(S, A)$ if and only if for some $w \in \Sigma^*$ and $\alpha \in (N \cup \Sigma)^*$, $S \overset{*}{\underset{lm}{\Rightarrow}} wA\alpha$ and $L = $ FIRST$_k(\alpha)$.

Proof. The proof is similar to that of the previous theorem and is left for the Exercises.   □

Example 5.19

Let us test the grammar G with productions

$$S \longrightarrow AS \mid e$$
$$A \longrightarrow aA \mid b$$

for the LL(1) condition.

We begin by computing FIRST$_1(S) = \{e, a, b\}$ and FIRST$_1(A) = \{a, b\}$. We then must compute $\sigma(S) = \sigma(S, S)$ and $\sigma(A) = \sigma(S, A)$. From step (1) of Algorithm 5.4 we have

$$\sigma_0(S, S) = \{\{e\}\} \qquad \sigma_0(S, A) = \{\{e, a, b\}\}$$
$$\sigma_0(A, S) = \varnothing \qquad \sigma_0(A, A) = \{\{e\}\}$$

From step (2) we find no additions to these sets. For example, since $S \to AS$ is a production, and $\sigma_0(A, A)$ contains $\{e\}$ we must add to $\sigma_1(S, A)$ the set $L = \{e\} \oplus_1$ FIRST$(S) = \{e, a, b\}$ by step (2b). But $\sigma_1(S, A)$ already contains $\{e, a, b\}$, because $\sigma_0(S, A)$ contains this set.

Thus, $\sigma(A) = \{\{e, a, b\}\}$ and $\sigma(S) = \{\{e\}\}$. To check that G is LL(1), we have to verify that $(\text{FIRST}(AS) \oplus_1 \{e\}) \cap (\text{FIRST}(e) \oplus_1 \{e\}) = \varnothing$. [This is for the two S-productions and the lone member of $\sigma(S, S)$.] Since

$$\text{FIRST}(AS) = \text{FIRST}(A) \oplus_1 \text{FIRST}(S) = \{a, b\}$$

and $\text{FIRST}(e) = \{e\}$, we indeed verify that $\{a, b\} \cap \{e\} = \varnothing$.

For the two A-productions, we must show that

$$(\text{FIRST}(aA) \oplus_1 \{e, a, b\}) \cap (\text{FIRST}(b) \oplus_1 \{e, a, b\}) = \varnothing.$$

This relation reduces to $\{a\} \cap \{b\} = \varnothing$, which is true. Thus, G is LL(1). $\square$

EXERCISES

5.1.1. Show that if G is left-recursive, then G is not an LL grammar.

5.1.2. Show that if G has two productions $A \longrightarrow a\alpha \,|\, a\beta$, where $\alpha \neq \beta$, then G cannot be LL(1).

5.1.3. Show that every LL grammar is unambiguous.

5.1.4. Show that every grammar obeying statement (5.1.1) on page 343 is LL(k).

5.1.5. Show that the grammar with productions

$$S \longrightarrow aAaB \,|\, bAbB$$
$$A \longrightarrow a \,|\, ab$$
$$B \longrightarrow aB \,|\, a$$

is LL(3) but not LL(2).

5.1.6. Construct the LL(3) tables for the grammar in Exercise 5.1.5.

5.1.7. Construct a deterministic left parser for the grammar in Example 5.17.

5.1.8. Give an algorithm to compute $\text{FOLLOW}_k^G(A)$ for nonterminal A.

*5.1.9. Show that every regular set has an LL(1) grammar.

5.1.10. Show that $G = (N, \Sigma, P, S)$ is an LL(1) grammar if and only if for each set of A-productions $A \longrightarrow \alpha_1 \,|\, \alpha_2 \,|\, \cdots \,|\, \alpha_n$ the following conditions hold:

(1) $\text{FIRST}_1^G(\alpha_i) \cap \text{FIRST}_1^G(\alpha_j) = \varnothing$ for $i \neq j$.

(2) If $\alpha_i \overset{*}{\Longrightarrow} e$, $\text{FIRST}_1^G(\alpha_j) \cap \text{FOLLOW}_1^G(A) = \varnothing$ for $1 \leq j \leq n$, $i \neq j$. Note that at most one α_i can derive e.

**5.1.11. Show that it is undecidable whether there exists an integer k such that a CFG is LL(k). [In contrast, if we are given a fixed value for k, we can determine if G is LL(k) for that particular value of k.]

*5.1.12. Show that it is undecidable whether a CFG generates an LL language.

*5.1.13. The definition of an LL(k) grammar is often stated in the following manner. Let $G = (N, \Sigma, P, S)$ be a CFG. If $S \overset{*}{\Longrightarrow} wAx$, for w and x

in Σ^* and $A \in N$, then for each y in Σ^{*k} there is at most one production $A \longrightarrow \alpha$ such that y is in $\text{FIRST}_k(\alpha x)$. Show that this definition is equivalent to the one given in Section 5.1.1.

5.1.14. Complete the proof of Theorem 5.4.

5.1.15. Prove Lemma 5.1.

5.1.16. Prove Theorem 5.8.

**5.1.17. Show that if L is an LL(k) language, then L has an LL(k) grammar in Chomsky normal form.

5.1.18. Show that an LL(0) language has at most one member.

*5.1.19. Show that the grammar G with productions $S \longrightarrow aaSbb \,|\, a \,|\, e$ is LL(2). Find an equivalent LL(1) grammar for $L(G)$.

**5.1.20. Show that the language $\{a^n 0 b^n \,|\, n \geq 0\} \cup \{a^n 1 b^{2n} \,|\, n \geq 0\}$ is not an LL language.

Exercises 5.1.21–5.1.24 are done in Chapter 8. The reader may wish to try his hand at them now.

**5.1.21. Show that it is decidable for two LL(k) grammars, G_1 and G_2, whether $L(G_1) = L(G_2)$.

**5.1.22. Show that for all $k \geq 0$, there exist languages which are LL($k + 1$) but not LL(k).

**5.1.23. Show that every LL(k) language has an LL($k + 1$) grammar with no e-productions.

**5.1.24. Show that every LL(k) language has an LL($k + 1$) grammar in Greibach normal form.

*5.1.25. Suppose that $A \longrightarrow \alpha\beta \,|\, \alpha\gamma$ are two productions in a grammar G such that α does not derive e and β and γ begin with different symbols. Show that G is not LL(1). Under what conditions will the replacement of these productions by

$$A \longrightarrow \alpha A'$$
$$A' \longrightarrow \beta \,|\, \gamma$$

transform G into an equivalent LL(1) grammar?

5.1.26. Show that if $G = (N, \Sigma, P, S)$ is an LL(k) grammar, then, for all $A \in N$, G_A is LL(k), where G_A is the grammar obtained by removing all useless productions and symbols from the grammar (N, Σ, P, A).

Analogous to the LL grammars there is a class of grammars, called the LC grammars, which can be parsed in a left-corner manner with a deterministic pushdown transducer scanning the input from left to right. Intuitively, a grammar $G = (N, \Sigma, P, S)$ is LC(k) if, knowing the leftmost derivation $S \xLongrightarrow[\text{lm}]{*} wA\delta$, we can uniquely determine that the production to replace A is $A \longrightarrow X_1 \cdots X_p$ once we have seen the portion of the input derived from X_1 (the symbol X_1 is the left corner) and the next k input symbols. In the formal definition, should X_1 be a terminal, we may then look only at the next $k - 1$ symbols. This restriction is made for the sake of simplicity in stating an interesting theorem which will be Exercise 5.1.33. In Fig. 5.7, we would recognize production $A \longrightarrow X_1 \cdots X_p$ after seeing wx and the first k symbols ($k - 1$ if X_1 is in Σ) of y. Note that if G were LL(k), we could recognize the production "sooner," specifically, once we had seen w and $\text{FIRST}_k(xy)$.

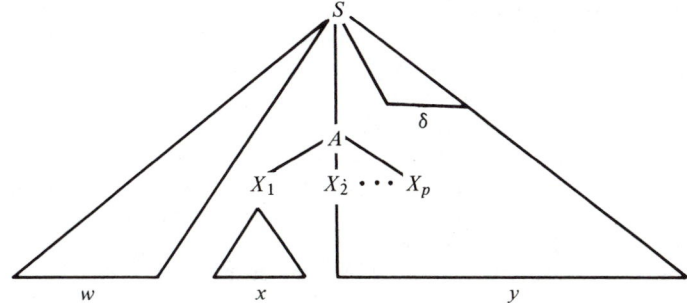

Fig. 5.7 Left-corner parsing.

We shall make use of the following type of derivation in the definition of an LC grammar.

DEFINITION

Let G be a CFG. We say that $S \overset{*}{\underset{lc}{\Longrightarrow}} wA\delta$ if $S \overset{*}{\underset{lm}{\Longrightarrow}} wA\delta$ and the nonterminal A is not the left corner of the production which introduced it into a left-sentential form of the sequence represented by $S \overset{*}{\underset{lm}{\Longrightarrow}} wA\alpha$.

For example, in G_0, $E \overset{*}{\underset{lc}{\Longrightarrow}} E + T$ is false, since the E in $E + T$ arises from the left corner of the production $E \longrightarrow E + T$. On the other hand, $E \overset{*}{\underset{lc}{\Longrightarrow}} a + T$ is true, since T is not the left corner of the production $E \longrightarrow E + T$, which introduced the symbol T in the sequence $E \Longrightarrow E + T \Longrightarrow a + T$.

DEFINITION

CFG $G = (N, \Sigma, P, S)$ is $LC(k)$ if the following conditions are satisfied: Suppose that $S \overset{*}{\underset{lc}{\Longrightarrow}} wA\delta$. Then for each lookahead string u there is at most one production $B \rightarrow \alpha$ such that $A \overset{*}{\Rightarrow} B\gamma$ and

(1) (a) If $\alpha = C\beta$, $C \in N$, then $u \in \text{FIRST}_k(\beta\gamma\delta)$, and
    (b) In addition, if $C = A$, then u is not in $\text{FIRST}_k(\delta)$;
(2) If α does not begin with a nonterminal, then $u \in \text{FIRST}_k(\alpha\gamma\delta)$.

Condition (1a) guarantees that the use of the production $B \longrightarrow C\beta$ can be uniquely determined once we have seen w, the terminal string derived from C (the left corner) and $\text{FIRST}_k(\beta\gamma\delta)$ (the lookahead string).

Condition (1b) ensures that if the nonterminal A is left-recursive (which is possible in an LC grammar), then we can tell after an instance of A has been found whether that instance is the left corner of the production $B \longrightarrow A\gamma$ or the A in the left-sentential form $wA\alpha$.

Condition (2) states that $\text{FIRST}_k(\alpha\gamma\delta)$ uniquely determines that the production $B \longrightarrow \alpha$ is to be used next in a left-corner parse after having seen wB, when α does not begin with a nonterminal symbol. Note that α might be e here.

For each LC(k) grammar G we can construct a deterministic left corner parsing algorithm that parses an input string recognizing the left corner of each production used bottom-up, and the remainder of the production top-down.

Here, we shall outline how such a parser can be constructed for LC(1) grammars. Let $G = (N, \Sigma, P, S)$ be an LC(1) grammar. From G we shall construct a left corner parser $\mathcal{C}$ such that $\tau(\mathcal{C}) = \{(x, \pi) \mid x \in L(G) \text{ and } \pi \text{ is a left-corner parse for } x\}$. $\mathcal{C}$ uses an input tape, a pushdown list and an output tape as does a k-prodictive parser.

The set of pushdown symbols is $\Gamma = N \cup \Sigma \cup (N \times N) \cup \{\$\}$. Initially, the pushdown list contains $S\$$ (with S on top). A single nonterminal or terminal symbol appearing on top of the pushdown list can be interpreted as the current goal to be recognized. When a pushdown symbol is a pair of nonterminals of the form $[A, B]$, we can think of the first component A as the current goal to be recognized and the second component B as a left corner which has just been recognized.

For convenience, we shall construct a *left-corner parsing table T* which is a mapping from $\Gamma \times (\Sigma \cup \{e\})$ to $(\Gamma^* \times (P \cup \{e\})) \cup \{\textbf{pop},$ **accept, error**}. This parsing table is similar to a 1-predictive parsing table for an LL(1) grammar. A configuration of M will be a triple $(w, X\alpha, \pi)$, where w represents the remaining input, $X\alpha$ represents the pushdown list with $X \in \Gamma$ on top, and π is the output to this point. If $T(X, a) = (\beta, i)$, X in $N \cup (N \times N)$, then we write $(aw, X\alpha, \pi) \vdash (aw, \beta\alpha, \pi i)$. If $T(a, a) = \textbf{pop}$, then we write $(aw, a\alpha, \pi) \vdash (w, \alpha, \pi)$. We say that π is a (left-corner) parse of x if $(x, S\$, e) \overset{*}{\vdash} (e, \$, \pi)$.

Let $G = (N, \Sigma, P, S)$ be an LC(1) grammar. T is constructed from G as follows:

(1) Suppose that $B \longrightarrow \alpha$ is the ith production in P.
    (a) If $\alpha = C\beta$, where C is a nonterminal, then $T([A, C], a) = (\beta[A, B], i)$ for all $A \in N$ and $a \in \text{FIRST}_1(\beta\gamma\delta)$ such

that $S \overset{*}{\underset{\text{lc}}{\Rightarrow}} wA\delta$ and $A \overset{*}{\Rightarrow} B\gamma$. Here, $\mathcal{C}$ recognizes left corners bottom-up. Note that A is either S or not the left corner of some production, so at some point in the parsing A will be a goal.

(b) If α does not begin with a nonterminal, then $T(A, a)$ $= (\alpha[A, B], i)$ for all $A \in N$ and $a \in \text{FIRST}_1(\alpha\gamma\delta)$ such that $S \overset{*}{\underset{\text{lc}}{\Rightarrow}} wA\delta$ and $A \overset{*}{\Rightarrow} B\gamma$.

(2) $T([A, A], a) = (e, e)$ for all $A \in N$ and $a \in \text{FIRST}_1(\delta)$ such that $S \overset{*}{\underset{\text{lc}}{\Rightarrow}} wA\delta$.

(3) $T(a, a) = \textbf{pop}$ for all $a \in \Sigma$.

(4) $T(\$, e) = \textbf{accept.}$

(5) $T(X, a) = \textbf{error}$ otherwise.

Example 5.20

Consider the following grammar G with productions

(1) $S \longrightarrow S + A$ (2) $S \longrightarrow A$
(3) $A \longrightarrow A * B$ (4) $A \longrightarrow B$
(5) $B \longrightarrow \langle S \rangle$ (6) $B \longrightarrow a$

G is an LC(1) grammar. G is, in fact, G_0 slightly disguised. A left-corner parsing table for G is shown in Fig. 5.8.

The parser using this left-corner parsing table would make the following sequence of moves on input $\langle a * a \rangle$:

$$(\langle a * a \rangle, S\$, e) \vdash (\langle a * a \rangle, \langle S \rangle [S, B]\$, 5)$$
$$\vdash (a * a \rangle, S \rangle [S, B]\$, 5)$$
$$\vdash (a * a \rangle, a[S, B] \rangle [S, B]\$, 56)$$
$$\vdash (* a \rangle, [S, B] \rangle [S, B]\$, 56)$$
$$\vdash (*a \rangle, [S, A] \rangle [S, B]\$, 564)$$
$$\vdash (*a \rangle, * B[S, A] \rangle [S, B]\$, 5643)$$
$$\vdash (a \rangle, B[S, A] \rangle [S, B]\$, 5643)$$
$$\vdash (a \rangle, a[B, B][S, A] \rangle [S, B]\$, 56436)$$
$$\vdash (\rangle, [B, B][S, A] \rangle [S, B]\$, 56436)$$
$$\vdash (\rangle, [S, A] \rangle [S, B]\$, 56436)$$
$$\vdash (\rangle, [S, S] \rangle [S, B]\$, 564362)$$
$$\vdash (\rangle, \rangle [S, B]\$, 564362)$$
$$\vdash (e, [S, B]\$, 564362)$$
$$\vdash (e, [S, A]\$, 5643624)$$
$$\vdash (e, [S, S]\$, 56436242)$$
$$\vdash (e, \$, 56436242)$$

Pushdown symbol	Input symbol					
	a	$<$	$>$	$+$	$*$	e
S	$a[S,B],6$	$<S>[S,B],5$				
A	$a[A,B],6$	$<S>[A,B],5$				
B	$a[B,B],6$	$<S>[B,B],5$				
$[S,S]$			e,e	$+A[S,S],1$		e,e
$[S,A]$			$[S,S],2$	$[S,S],2$	$*B[S,A],3$	$[S,S],2$
$[S,B]$			$[S,A],4$	$[S,A],4$	$[S,A],4$	$[S,A],4$
$[A,A]$			e,e	e,e	$*B[A,A],3$	e,e
$[A,B]$			$[A,A],4$	$[A,A],4$	$[A,A],4$	$[A,A],4$
$[B,B]$			e,e	e,e	e,e	e,e
a	pop					
$<$		pop				
$>$			pop			
$+$				pop		
$*$					pop	
$\$$						accept

Fig. 5.8   Left-corner parsing table for G.

The reader can easily verify that 56436242 is the correct left corner parse for $\langle a * a \rangle$. $\square$

*5.1.27. Show that the grammar with productions

$$S \longrightarrow A \mid B$$
$$A \longrightarrow aAb \mid 0$$
$$B \longrightarrow aBbb \mid 1$$

is not LC(k) for any k.

*5.1.28. Show that the following grammar is LC(1):

$$E \longrightarrow E + T \mid T$$
$$T \longrightarrow T * F \mid F$$
$$F \longrightarrow P \uparrow F \mid P$$
$$P \longrightarrow (E) \mid a$$

5.1.29. Construct a left-corner parser for the grammar in Exercise 5.1.28.

**5.1.30. Provide an algorithm which will test whether an arbitrary grammar is LC(1).

**5.1.31. Show that every LL(k) grammar is LC (k).

5.1.32. Give an example of an LC(1) grammar which is not LL.

**5.1.33. Show that if Algorithm 2.14 is applied to a grammar G to put it in Greibach normal form, then the resulting grammar is LL(k) if and only if G is LC(k). Hence the class of LC languages is identical to the class of LL languages.

*5.1.34. Provide an algorithm to construct a left-corner parser for an arbitrary LC(k) grammar.

Research Problems

5.1.35. Find transformations which can be used to convert non-LL(k) grammars into equivalent LL(1) grammars.

Programming Exercises

5.1.36. Write a program that takes as input an arbitrary CFG G and constructs a 1-predictive parsing table for G if G is LL(1).

5.1.37. Write a program that takes as input a parsing table and an input string and parses the input string using the given parsing table.

5.1.38. Transform one of the grammars in the Appendix into an LL(1) grammar. Then construct an LL(1) parser for that grammar.

5.1.39. Write a program that tests whether a grammar is LL(1).

Let M be a parsing table for an LL(1) grammar G. Suppose that we are parsing an input string and the parser has reached the configuration $(ax, X\alpha, \pi)$. If $M(X, a) = $ **error,** we would like to announce that an error occurred at this input position and transfer to an error recovery routine which modifies the contents of the pushdown list and input tape so that parsing can proceed normally. Some possible error recovery strategies are

(1) Delete a and try to continue parsing.

(2) Replace a by a symbol b such that $M(X, b) \neq $ **error** and continue parsing.

(3) Insert a symbol b in front of a on the input such that $M(X, b) \neq $ **error** and continue parsing. This third technique should be used with care since an infinite loop is easily possible.

(4) Scan forward on the input until some designated input symbol b is found. Pop symbols from the pushdown list until a symbol X is found such that $X \overset{*}{\Longrightarrow} b\beta$ for some β. Then resume normal parsing.

We also might list for each pair (X, a) such that $M(X, a) = $ **error,** several possible error recovery methods with the most promising method listed first. It is entirely possible that in some situations insertion of a symbol may be the most reasonable course of action, while in other cases deletion or change would be most likely to succeed.

5.1.40. Devise an error recovery algorithm for the LL(1) parser constructed in Exercise 5.1.38.

BIBLIOGRAPHIC NOTES

LL(k) grammars were first defined by Lewis and Stearns [1968]. In an early version of that paper, these grammars were called TD(k) grammars, TD being an acronym for top-down. Simple LL(1) grammars were first investigated by Korenjak and Hopcroft [1966], where they were called s-grammars.

The theory of LL(k) grammars was extensively developed by Rosenkrantz and Stearns [1970], and the answers to Exercises 5.1.21–5.1.24 can be found there. LL(k) grammars and other versions of deterministic top-down grammars have been considered by Knuth [1967], Kurki-Suonio [1969], Wood [1969a, 1970] and Culik [1968].

P. M. Lewis, R. E. Stearns, and D. J. Rosenkrantz have designed compilers for ALGOL and FORTRAN whose syntax analysis phase is based on an LL(1) parser. Details of the ALGOL compiler are given by Lewis and Rosenkrantz [1971]. This reference also contains an LL(1) grammar for ALGOL 60.

LC(k) grammars were first defined by Rosenkrantz and Lewis [1970]. Clues to Exercises 5.1.27–5.1.34 can be found there.

5.2. DETERMINISTIC BOTTOM-UP PARSING

In the previous section, we saw a class of grammars which could be parsed top-down deterministically, while scanning the input from left to right. There is an analogous class of languages that can be parsed deterministically bottom-up, using a left-to-right input scan. These are called LR grammars, and their development closely parallels the development of the LL grammars in the preceding section.

5.2.1. Deterministic Shift–Reduce Parsing

In Chapter 4 we indicated that bottom-up parsing can proceed in a shift–reduce fashion employing two pushdown lists. Shift–reduce parsing consists of shifting input symbols onto a pushdown list until a handle appears on top of the pushdown list. The handle is then reduced. If no errors occur, this process is repeated until all of the input string is scanned and only the sentence symbol appears on the pushdown list. In Chapter 4 we provided a backtrack algorithm that worked in essentially this fashion, normally making some initially incorrect choices for some handles, but ultimately making the correct choices. In this section we shall consider a large class of grammars for which this type of parsing can always be done in a deterministic manner. These are the LR(k) grammars—the largest class of grammars which can be "naturally" parsed bottom-up using a deterministic pushdown transducer. The L stands for left-to-right scanning of the input, the R for producing a right parse, and k for the number of input "lookahead" symbols.

We shall later consider various subclasses of LR(k) grammars, including precedence grammars and bounded-right-context grammars.

Let αx be a right-sentential form in some grammar, and suppose that α is either the empty string or ends with a nonterminal symbol. Then we shall call α the *open portion* of αx and x the *closed portion* of αx. The boundary between α and x is called the *border*. These definitions of open and closed portion of a right-sentential form should not be confused with the previous definitions of open and closed portion, which were for a left-sentential form.

A "shift–reduce" parsing algorithm can be considered a program for an extended deterministic pushdown transducer which parses bottom-up. Given an input string w, the DPDT simulates a rightmost derivation in reverse. Suppose that

$$S = \alpha_0 \underset{\mathrm{rm}}{\Longrightarrow} \alpha_1 \underset{\mathrm{rm}}{\Longrightarrow} \cdots \underset{\mathrm{rm}}{\Longrightarrow} \alpha_m = w$$

is a rightmost derivation of w. Each right-sentential form α_i is stored by the DPDT with the open portion of α_i on the pushdown list and the closed portion as the unexpended input. For example, if $\alpha_i = \alpha A x$, then αA would be on the pushdown list (with A on top) and x would be the as yet unscanned portion of the original input string.

Suppose that $\alpha_{i-1} = \gamma B z$ and that the production $B \to \beta y$ is used in the step $\alpha_{i-1} \underset{\mathrm{rm}}{\Longrightarrow} \alpha_i$, where $\gamma \beta = \alpha A$ and $yz = x$. With αA on the pushdown list, the PDT will shift some number (possibly none) of the leading symbols of x onto the pushdown list until the right end of the handle of α_i is found. In this case, the string y is shifted onto the pushdown list.

Then the PDT must locate the left end of the handle. Once this has been done, the PDT will replace the handle (here βy), which is on top of the pushdown list, by the appropriate nonterminal (here B) and emit the number of the production $B \to \beta y$. The PDT now has γB on its pushdown list, and the unexpended input is z. These strings are the open and closed portions, respectively, of the right-sentential form α_{i-1}.

Note that the handle of $\alpha A x$ can never lie entirely within α, although it could be wholly within x. That is, α_{i-1} could be of the form $\alpha A x_1 B x_2$, and a production of the form $B \to y$, where $x_1 y x_2 = x$ could be applied to obtain α_i. Since x_1 could be arbitrarily long, many shifts may occur before α_i can be reduced to α_{i-1}.

To sum up, there are three decisions which a shift–reduce parsing algorithm must make. The first is to determine before each move whether to shift an input symbol onto the pushdown list or to call for a reduction. This decision is really the determination of where the right end of a handle occurs in a right-sentential form.

The second and third decisions occur after the right end of a handle is located. Once the handle is known to lie on top of the pushdown list, the left end of the handle must be located within the pushdown list. Then, when the handle has been thus isolated, we must find the appropriate nonterminal by which it is to be replaced.

A grammar in which no two distinct productions have the same right side is said to be *uniquely invertible* (UI) or, alternatively, *backwards deterministic*. It is not difficult to show that every context-free language is generated by at least one uniquely invertible context-free grammar.

If a grammar is uniquely invertible, then once we have isolated the handle of a right-sentential form, there is exactly one nonterminal by which it can be replaced. However, many useful grammars are not uniquely invertible, so in general we must have some mechanism for knowing with which nonterminal to replace a handle.

Example 5.21

Let us consider the grammar G with the productions

$$(1)\ \ S \longrightarrow SaSb$$
$$(2)\ \ S \longrightarrow e$$

Consider the rightmost derivation:

$$S \Longrightarrow SaSb \Longrightarrow SaSaSbb \Longrightarrow SaSabb \Longrightarrow Saabb \Longrightarrow aabb$$

Let us parse the sentence *aabb* using a pushdown list and a shift–reduce parsing algorithm. We shall use $ as an endmarker for both the input string and the bottom of the pushdown list.

We shall describe the shift–reduce parsing algorithm in terms of configurations consisting of triples of the form $(\alpha X, x, \pi)$, where

(1) αX represents the contents of the pushdown list, with X on top;
(2) x is the unexpended input; and
(3) π is the output to this point.

We can picture this configuration as the configuration of an extended PDT with the state omitted and the pushdown list preceeding the input. In Section 5.3.1 we shall give a formal description of a shift–reduce parsing algorithm.

Initially, the algorithm will be in configuration ($, *aabb*$, e). The algorithm must then recognize that the handle of the right-sentential form *aabb* is *e*, occurring at the left end, and that this handle is to be reduced to *S*. We defer describing the actual mechanism whereby handle recognition occurs. Thus the algorithm must next enter the configuration ($S, aabb$, 2). It will then shift an input symbol on top of the pushdown list to enter configuration (Sa, abb, 2). Then it will recognize that the handle *e* is on top of the pushdown list and make a reduction to enter configuration (SaS, abb, 22).

Continuing in this fashion, the algorithm would make the following sequence of moves:

$$(\$, aabb\$, e) \vdash (\$S, aabb\$, 2)$$
$$\vdash (\$Sa, abb\$, 2)$$
$$\vdash (\$SaS, abb\$, 22)$$
$$\vdash (\$SaSa, bb\$, 22)$$
$$\vdash (\$SaSaS, bb\$, 222)$$
$$\vdash (\$SaSaSb, b\$, 222)$$
$$\vdash (\$SaS, b\$, 2221)$$
$$\vdash (\$SaSb, \$, 2221)$$
$$\vdash (\$S, \$, 22211)$$
$$\vdash \textbf{accept} \quad \square$$

5.2.2. LR(*k*) Grammars

In this section we shall define a large class of grammars for which we can always construct deterministic right parsers. These grammars are the LR(*k*) grammars.

Informally, we say that a grammar is LR(*k*) if given a rightmost derivation $S = \alpha_0 \underset{rm}{\Rightarrow} \alpha_1 \underset{rm}{\Rightarrow} \alpha_2 \underset{rm}{\Rightarrow} \cdots \underset{rm}{\Rightarrow} \alpha_m = z$, we can isolate the handle of each right-sentential form and determine which nonterminal is to replace the handle by scanning α_i from left to right, but only going at most k symbols past the right end of the handle of α_i.

Suppose that $\alpha_{i-1} = \alpha A w$ and $\alpha_i = \alpha\beta w$, where β is the handle of α_i. Suppose further that $\beta = X_1 X_2 \cdots X_r$. If the grammar is LR(*k*), then we can be sure of the following facts:

(1) Knowing $\alpha X_1 X_2 \cdots X_j$ and the first k symbols of $X_{j+1} \cdots X_r w$, we can be certain that the right end of the handle has not been reached until $j = r$.

(2) Knowing $\alpha\beta$ and at most the first k symbols of w, we can always determine that β is the handle and that β is to be reduced to A.

(3) When $\alpha_{i-1} = S$, we can signal with certainty that the input string is to be accepted.

Note that in going through the sequence $\alpha_m, \alpha_{m-1}, \ldots, \alpha_0$, we begin by looking at only $\text{FIRST}_k(\alpha_m) = \text{FIRST}_k(w)$. At each step our lookahead string will consist only of k or fewer terminal symbols.

We shall now define the term LR(k) grammar. But before we do so, we first introduce the simple concept of an augmented grammar.

DEFINITION

Let $G = (\text{N}, \Sigma, P, S)$ be a CFG. We define the *augmented grammar derived from* G as $G' = (\text{N} \cup \{S'\}, \Sigma, P \cup \{S' \rightarrow S\}, S')$. The augmented grammar G' is merely G with a new starting production $S' \rightarrow S$, where S' is a new start symbol, not in N. We assume that $S' \rightarrow S$ is the zeroth production in G' and that the other productions of G are numbered $1, 2, \ldots, p$. We add the starting production so that when a reduction using the zeroth production is called for, we can interpret this "reduction" as a signal to accept.

We shall now give the precise definition of an LR(k) grammar.

DEFINITION

Let $G = (\text{N}, \Sigma, P, S)$ be a CFG and let $G' = (\text{N}', \Sigma, P', S')$ be its augmented grammar. We say that G is LR(k), $k \geq 0$, if the three conditions

(1) $S' \underset{G'\ \text{rm}}{\overset{*}{\Longrightarrow}} \alpha A w \underset{G'\ \text{rm}}{\Longrightarrow} \alpha \beta w,$

(2) $S' \underset{G'\ \text{rm}}{\overset{*}{\Longrightarrow}} \gamma B x \underset{G'\ \text{rm}}{\Longrightarrow} \alpha \beta y,$ and

(3) $\text{FIRST}_k(w) = \text{FIRST}_k(y)$

imply that $\alpha A y = \gamma B x$. (That is, $\alpha = \gamma$, $A = B$, and $x = y$.)

A grammar is *LR* if it is LR(k) for some k.

Intuitively this definition says that if $\alpha \beta w$ and $\alpha \beta y$ are right-sentential forms of the augmented grammar with $\text{FIRST}_k(w) = \text{FIRST}_k(y)$ and if $A \rightarrow \beta$ is the last production used to derive $\alpha \beta w$ in a rightmost derivation, then $A \rightarrow \beta$ must also be used to reduce $\alpha \beta y$ to $\alpha A y$ in a right parse. Since A can derive β independently of w, the LR(k) condition says that there is sufficient information in $\text{FIRST}_k(w)$ to determine that $\alpha \beta$ was derived from αA. Thus there can never be any confusion about how to reduce any right-sentential form of the augmented grammar. In addition, with an LR(k) grammar we will always know whether we should accept the present input string or continue parsing. If the start symbol does not appear on the right side of any production, we can alternatively define an LR(k) grammar $G = (\text{N}, \Sigma, P, S)$ as one in which the three conditions

(1) $S \overset{*}{\underset{\text{rm}}{\Rightarrow}} \alpha A w \underset{\text{rm}}{\Rightarrow} \alpha \beta w,$

(2) $S \overset{*}{\underset{\text{rm}}{\Rightarrow}} \gamma B x \underset{\text{rm}}{\Rightarrow} \alpha \beta y,$ and

(3) $\text{FIRST}_k(w) = \text{FIRST}_k(y)$

imply that $\alpha A y = \gamma B x$.

The reason we cannot always use this definition is that if the start symbol appears on the right side of some production we may not be able to determine whether we have reached the end of the input string and should accept or whether we should continue parsing.

Example 5.22

Consider the grammar G with the productions

$$S \longrightarrow Sa \,|\, a$$

If we ignore the restriction against the start symbol appearing on the right side of a production, i.e., use the alternative definition, G would be an LR(0) grammar.

However, using the correct definition, G is not LR(0), since the three conditions

(1) $S' \overset{0}{\underset{G'\,\text{rm}}{\Longrightarrow}} S' \underset{G'\,\text{rm}}{\Longrightarrow} S,$

(2) $S' \underset{G'\,\text{rm}}{\Longrightarrow} S \underset{G'\,\text{rm}}{\Longrightarrow} Sa,$ and

(3) $\text{FIRST}_0(e) = \text{FIRST}_0(a) = e$

do not imply that $S'a = S$. Relating this situation to the definition we would have $\alpha = e$, $\beta = S$, $w = e$, $\gamma = e$, $A = S'$, $B = S$, $x = e$, and $y = a$. The problem here is that in the right-sentential form Sa of G' we cannot determine whether S is the handle of Sa (i.e., whether to accept the input derived from S) looking zero symbols past the S. Intuitively, G should not be an LR(0) grammar and it is not, if we use the first definition. Throughout this book, we shall use the first definition of LR(k)-ness. $\square$

In this section we show that for each LR(k) grammar $G = (N, \Sigma, P, S)$ we can construct a deterministic right parser which behaves in the following manner.

First of all, the parser will be constructed from the augmented grammar G'. The parser will behave very much like the shift–reduce parser introduced in Example 5.21, except that the LR(k) parser will put special information symbols, called LR(k) tables, on the pushdown list above each grammar symbol on the pushdown list. These LR(k) tables will determine whether a shift move or a reduce move is to be made and, in the case of a reduce move, which production is to be used.

Perhaps the best way to describe the behavior of an LR(k) parser is via a running example.

Let us consider the grammar G of Example 5.21, which we can verify is an LR(1) grammar. The augmented grammar G' is

$$(0)\ S' \longrightarrow S$$

$$(1)\ S \longrightarrow SaSb$$

$$(2)\ S \longrightarrow e$$

An LR(1) parser for G is displayed in Fig. 5.9.

	Parsing action			Goto		
	a	b	e	S	a	b
T_0	2	X	2	T_1	X	X
T_1	S	X	A	X	T_2	X
T_2	2	2	X	T_3	X	X
T_3	S	S	X	X	T_4	T_5
T_4	2	2	X	T_6	X	X
T_5	1	X	1	X	X	X
T_6	S	S	X	X	T_4	T_7
T_7	1	1	X	X	X	X

Legend
$i\ \equiv$ reduce using production i
$S \equiv$ shift
$A \equiv$ accept
$X \equiv$ error

Fig. 5.9 LR(1) parser for G.

An LR(k) parser for a CFG G is nothing more than a set of rows in a large table, where each row is called an "LR(k) table." One row, here T_0, is distinguished as the initial LR(k) table. Each LR(k) table consists of two functions—a *parsing action function f* and a *goto function g*:

(1) A parsing action function f takes a string u in Σ^{*k} as argument (this string is called the lookahead string), and the value of $f(u)$ is either **shift**, **reduce i**, **error**, or **accept**.

(2) A goto function g takes a symbol X in $N \cup \Sigma$ as argument and has as value either the name of another LR(k) table or **error**.

Admittedly, we have not explained how to construct such a parser at this point. The construction is delayed until Sections 5.2.3 and 5.2.4.

The LR parser behaves as a shift–reduce parsing algorithm, using a pushdown list, an input tape, and an output buffer. At the start, the pushdown list contains the initial LR(k) table T_0 and nothing else. The input tape contains the word to be parsed, and the output buffer is initially empty. If we assume that the input word to be parsed is *aabb*, then the parser would initially be in configuration

$$(T_0, aabb, e)$$

Parsing then proceeds by performing the following algorithm.

ALGORITHM 5.7

LR(k) parsing algorithm.

Input. A set $\mathfrak{I}$ of LR(k) tables for an LR(k) grammar $G = (N, \Sigma, P, S)$, with $T_0 \in \mathfrak{I}$ designated as the initial table, and an input string $z \in \Sigma^*$, which is to be parsed.

Output. If $z \in L(G)$, the right parse of G. Otherwise, an error indication.

Method. Perform steps (1) and (2) until acceptance occurs or an error is encountered. If acceptance occurs, the string in the output buffer is the right parse of z.

(1) The lookahead string u, consisting of the next k input symbols, is determined.

(2) The parsing action function f of the table on top of the pushdown list is applied to the lookahead string u.

    (a) If $f(u) =$ **shift**, then the next input symbol, say a, is removed from the input and shifted onto the pushdown list. The goto function g of the table on top of the pushdown list is applied to a to determine the new table to be placed on top of the pushdown list. We then return to step (1). If there is no next input symbol or $g(a)$ is undefined, halt and declare error.

    (b) If $f(u) =$ **reduce** i and production i is $A \rightarrow \alpha$, then $2|\alpha|$ symbols† are removed from the top of the pushdown list, and production number i is placed in the output buffer. A new table T' is then exposed as the top table of the pushdown list, and the goto function of T' is applied to A to determine the next table to be placed

---

†If $\alpha = X_m \cdots X_r$, at this point the top of the pushdown list will be of the form $T_0 X_1 T_1 X_2 T_2 \cdots X_r T_r$. Removing $2|\alpha|$ symbols removes the handle from the top of the pushdown list along with any intervening LR tables.

on top of the pushdown list. We place A and this new table on top of the pushdown list and return to step (1).

(c) If $f(u) = $ **error**, we halt parsing (and, in practice, transfer to an error recovery routine).

(d) If $f(u) = $ **accept**, we halt and declare the string in the output buffer to be the right parse of the original input string. ☐

Example 5.23

Let us apply Algorithm 5.7 to the initial configuration $(T_0, aabb, e)$ using the LR(1) tables of Fig. 5.9. The lookahead string here is a. The parsing action function of T_0 on a is **reduce** 2, where production 2 is $S \longrightarrow e$. By step (2b), we are to remove $2|e| = 0$ symbols from the pushdown list and emit 2. The table on top of the pushdown list after this process is still T_0. Since the goto part of table T_0 with argument S is T_1, we then place ST_1 on top of the pushdown list to obtain the configuration $(T_0ST_1, aabb, 2)$.

Let us go through this cycle once more. The lookahead string is still a. The parsing action of T_1 on a is **shift**, so we remove a from the input and place a on the pushdown list. The goto function of T_1 on a is T_2, so after this step we have reached the configuration $(T_0ST_1aT_2, abb, 2)$.

Continuing in this fashion, the LR parser would make the following sequence of moves:

$$(T_0, aabb, e) \vdash (T_0ST_1, aabb, 2)$$
$$\vdash (T_0ST_1aT_2, abb, 2)$$
$$\vdash (T_0ST_1aT_2ST_3, abb, 22)$$
$$\vdash (T_0ST_1aT_2ST_3aT_4, bb, 22)$$
$$\vdash (T_0ST_1aT_2ST_3aT_4ST_6, bb, 222)$$
$$\vdash (T_0ST_1aT_2ST_3aT_4ST_6bT_7, b, 222)$$
$$\vdash (T_0ST_1aT_2ST_3, b, 2221)$$
$$\vdash (T_0ST_1aT_2ST_3bT_5, e, 2221)$$
$$\vdash (T_0ST_1, e, 22211)$$

Note that these steps are essentially the same as those of Example 5.21 and that the LR(1) tables explain the way in which choices were made in that example. ☐

In this section we shall develop the necessary algorithms to be able to automatically construct an LR parser of this form for each LR grammar. In fact, we shall see that a grammar G is LR(k) if and only if it has an LR(k) parser. But first, let us return to the basic definition of an LR(k) grammar and examine some of its consequences.

A proof that Algorithm 5.7 correctly parses an LR(k) grammar requires considerable development of the theory of LR(k) grammars. Let us first verify that our intuitive notions of what a deterministically right-parsable grammar ought to be are in fact implied by the LR(k) definition. Suppose that we are given a right-sentential form $\alpha\beta w$ of an augmented LR(k) grammar such that $\alpha A w \underset{rm}{\Rightarrow} \alpha\beta w$. We shall show that by scanning $\alpha\beta$ and FIRST$_k(w)$, there can be no confusion as to

(1) The location of the right end of the handle,
(2) The location of the left end of the handle, or
(3) What reduction to make once the handle has been isolated.

(1) Suppose that there were another right-sentential form $\alpha\beta y$ such that FIRST$_k(y) =$ FIRST$_k(w)$ but that y can be written as $y_1 y_2 y_3$, where $B \rightarrow y_2$ is a production and $\alpha\beta y_1 B y_3$ is a right-sentential form such that $\alpha\beta y_1 B y_3 \underset{rm}{\Rightarrow} \alpha\beta y_1 y_2 y_3$. This case is explicitly ruled out by the LR(k) definition. This becomes evident when we let $x = y_3$ and $\gamma B = \alpha\beta y_1 B$ in that definition. The right end of the handle might occur before the end of β. That is, there may be another right-sentential form $\gamma_1 B v y$ such that $B \rightarrow y_2$ is a production, FIRST$_k(y) =$ FIRST$_k(w)$ and $\gamma_1 B v y \underset{rm}{\Rightarrow} \gamma_1 y_2 v y = \alpha\beta y$. This case is also ruled out if we let $\gamma B = \gamma_1 B$ and $x = v y$ in the LR(k) definition.

(2) Now suppose that we know where the right end of the handle of a right-sentential form is but that there is confusion about its left end. That is, suppose that $\alpha A w$ and $\alpha' A' y$ are right-sentential forms such that FIRST$_k(w) =$ FIRST$_k(y)$ and $\alpha A w \underset{rm}{\Rightarrow} \alpha\beta w$ and $\alpha' A' y \underset{rm}{\Rightarrow} \alpha'\beta' y = \alpha\beta y$. However, the LR($k$) condition stipulates that $\alpha A = \alpha' A'$, so that both $\beta = \beta'$ and $A = A'$. Thus the left end of the handle is uniquely specified.

(3) There can be no confusion of type (3), since $A = A'$ above. Thus the nonterminal which is to replace the handle is always uniquely determined.

Let us now give some examples of LR and non-LR grammars.

Example 5.24

Let G_1 be the right-linear grammar having the productions

$$S \longrightarrow C \mid D$$
$$C \longrightarrow aC \mid b$$
$$D \longrightarrow aD \mid c$$

We shall show G_1 to be LR(1).†

---

† In fact, G_1 is LR(0).

Every (rightmost) derivation in G_1' (the augmented version of G_1) is either of the form

$$S' \Longrightarrow S \Longrightarrow C \overset{i}{\Longrightarrow} a^iC \Longrightarrow a^ib \qquad \text{for } i \geq 0$$

or

$$S' \Longrightarrow S \Longrightarrow D \overset{i}{\Longrightarrow} a^iD \Longrightarrow a^ic \qquad \text{for } i \geq 0$$

Let us refer to the LR(1) definition, and suppose that we have derivation $S' \overset{*}{\underset{rm}{\Rightarrow}} \alpha Aw \underset{rm}{\Rightarrow} \alpha\beta w$ and $S' \overset{*}{\underset{rm}{\Rightarrow}} \gamma Bx \underset{rm}{\Rightarrow} \alpha\beta y$. Then since G_1' is right-linear, we must have $w = x = e$. If $\text{FIRST}_1(w) = \text{FIRST}_1(y)$, then $y = e$ also. We must now show that $\alpha A = \gamma B$; i.e., $\alpha = \gamma$ and $A = B$. Let $B \to \delta$ be the production applied going from γBx to $\alpha\beta y$. There are three cases to consider.

Case 1: $A = S'$ (i.e., the derivation $S' \overset{*}{\underset{rm}{\Rightarrow}} \alpha Aw$ is trivial). Then $\alpha = e$ and $\beta = S$. By the form of derivations in G_1', there is only one way to derive the right-sentential from S, so $\gamma = e$ and $B = S'$, as was to be shown.

Case 2: $A = C$. Then β is either aC or b. In the first case, we must have $B = C$, for only C and S have a production which end in C. If $B = S$, then $\gamma = e$ by the form of derivations in G_1'. Then $\gamma B \neq \alpha\beta$. Thus we may conclude that $B = C$, $\delta = aC$, and $\gamma = \alpha$. In the second case ($\beta = b$), we must have $B = C$, because only C has a production ending in b. The conclusion that $\gamma = \alpha$ and $B = A$ is again immediate.

Case 3: $A = D$. This case is symmetric to case 2.

Note that G_1 is not LL. $\quad\square$

Example 5.25

Let G_2 be the left-linear grammar with productions

$$S \longrightarrow Ab \,|\, Bc$$
$$A \longrightarrow Aa \,|\, e$$
$$B \longrightarrow Ba \,|\, e$$

Note that $L(G_2) = L(G_1)$ for G_1 above. However, G_2 is not LR(k) for any k.

Suppose that G_2 is LR(k). Consider the two rightmost derivations in the augmented grammar G_2':

$$S' \underset{rm}{\Longrightarrow} S \overset{*}{\underset{rm}{\Longrightarrow}} Aa^kb \underset{rm}{\Longrightarrow} a^kb$$

and

$$S' \underset{rm}{\Longrightarrow} S \overset{*}{\underset{rm}{\Longrightarrow}} Ba^kc \underset{rm}{\Longrightarrow} a^kc$$

These two derivations satisfy the hypotheses of the LR(k) definition with $\alpha = e$, $\beta = e$, $w = a^k b$, $\gamma = e$, and $y = a^k c$. Since $A \neq B$, G_2 is not LR(k). Moreover, this violation of the LR(k) condition holds for any k, so that G_2 is not LR. □

The grammar in Example 5.25 is not uniquely invertible, and although we know where the handle is in any right-sentential form, we do not always know whether to reduce the first handle, which is the empty string, to A or B if we allow ourselves to scan only a finite number of terminal symbols beyond the right end of the handle.

Example 5.26

A situation in which the location of a handle cannot be uniquely determined is found in the grammar G_3 with the productions

$$S \longrightarrow AB$$
$$A \longrightarrow a$$
$$B \longrightarrow CD \mid aE$$
$$C \longrightarrow ab$$
$$D \longrightarrow bb$$
$$E \longrightarrow bba$$

G_3 is not LR(1). We can see this by considering the two rightmost derivations in the augmented grammar:

$$S' \Longrightarrow S \Longrightarrow AB \Longrightarrow ACD \Longrightarrow ACbb \Longrightarrow Aabbb$$

and

$$S' \Longrightarrow S \Longrightarrow AB \Longrightarrow AaE \Longrightarrow Aabba$$

In the right-sentential form $Aabw$ we cannot determine whether the right end of the handle occurs between b and w (when $w = bb$) or to the right of Aab (when $w = ba$) if we know only the first symbol of w. Note that G_3 is LR(2), however. □

We can give an informal but appealing definition of an LR(k) grammar in terms of its parse trees. We say that G is LR(k) if when examining a parse tree for G, we know which production is used at any interior node after seeing the frontier to the left of that node, what is derived from that node, and the next k terminal symbols. For example in Fig. 5.10 we can determine with certainty which production is used at node A by examining uv and $\text{FIRST}_k(w)$. In contrast, the LL(k) condition states that the production which is used at A can be determined by examining u and $\text{FIRST}_k(vw)$.

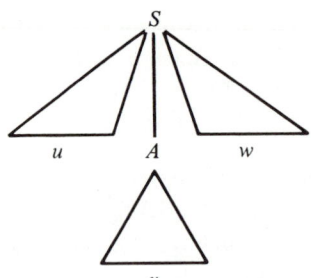

Fig. 5.10   Parse tree.

In Example 5.25 we would argue that G_2 is not LR(k) because after seeing the first k a's, we cannot determine whether production $A \rightarrow e$ or $B \rightarrow e$ is to be used to derive the empty string at the beginning of the input. We cannot tell which production is used until we see the last input symbol, b or c. In Chapter 8 we shall try to make rigorous arguments of this type, but although the notion is intuitively appealing, it is rather difficult to formalize.

5.2.3   Implications of the LR(k) Definition

We shall now develop the theory necessary to construct LR(k) parsers.

DEFINITION

Suppose that $S \underset{rm}{\overset{*}{\Rightarrow}} \alpha A w \underset{rm}{\Rightarrow} \alpha \beta w$ is a rightmost derivation in grammar G. We say that a string γ is a *viable prefix* of G if γ is a prefix of $\alpha \beta$. That is, γ is a string which is a prefix of some right-sentential form but which does not extend past the right end of the handle of that right-sentential form.

The heart of the LR(k) parser is a set of tables. These are analogous to the LL tables for LL grammars, which told us, given a lookahead string, what production might be applied next. For an LR(k) grammar the tables are associated with viable prefixes. The table associated with viable prefix γ will tell us, given a lookahead string consisting of the next k input symbols, whether we have reached the right end of the handle. If so, it tells us what the handle is and which production is to be used to reduce the handle.

Several problems arise. Since γ can be arbitrarily long, it is not clear that any finite set of tables will suffice. The LR(k) condition says that we can uniquely determine the handle of a right-sentential form if we know all of the right-sentential form in front of the handle as well as the next k input symbols. Thus it is not obvious that we can always determine the handle by knowing only a fixed amount of information about the string in front of the handle. Moreover, if $S \underset{rm}{\overset{*}{\Rightarrow}} \alpha A w \underset{rm}{\Rightarrow} \alpha \beta w$ and the question "Can $\alpha \beta w$ be derived rightmost by a sequence of productions ending in production p?" can be answered reasonably, it may not be possible to calculate the tables for αA from those for $\alpha\beta$ in a way that can be "implemented" on a pushdown transducer (or possibly in any other convenient way). Thus we must consider a table that includes enough information to compute the table corresponding to αA from that for $\alpha\beta$ if it is decided that $\alpha Aw \underset{rm}{\Longrightarrow} \alpha\beta w$ for an appropriate w. We thus make the following definitions.

DEFINITION

Let $G = (N, \Sigma, P, S)$ be a CFG. We say that $[A \longrightarrow \beta_1 \cdot \beta_2, u]$ is an LR(k) *item* (*for k and G*, but we usually omit reference to these parameters when they are understood) if $A \longrightarrow \beta_1\beta_2$ is a production in P and u is in Σ^{*k}. We say that LR(k) item $[A \longrightarrow \beta_1 \cdot \beta_2, u]$ is *valid for* $\alpha\beta_1$, a viable prefix of G, if there is a derivation $S \overset{*}{\underset{rm}{\Longrightarrow}} \alpha Aw \underset{rm}{\Longrightarrow} \alpha\beta_1\beta_2 w$ such that $u = \text{FIRST}_k(w)$. Note that β_1 may be e and that every viable prefix has at least one valid LR(k) item.

Example 5.27

Consider grammar G_1 of Example 5.24. Item $[C \longrightarrow a \cdot C, e]$ is valid for aaa, since there is a derivation $S \overset{*}{\underset{rm}{\Longrightarrow}} aaC \underset{rm}{\Longrightarrow} aaaC$. That is, $\alpha = aa$ and $w = e$ in this example. $\quad\square$

Note the similarity of our definition of item here to that found in the description of Earley's algorithm. There is an interesting relation between the two when Earley's algorithm is applied to an LR(k) grammar. See Exercise 5.2.16.

The LR(k) items associated with the viable prefixes of a grammar are the key to understanding how a deterministic right parser for an LR(k) grammar works. In a sense we are primarily interested in LR(k) items of the form $[A \longrightarrow \beta \cdot, u]$, where the dot is at the right end of the production. These items indicate which productions can be used to reduce right-sentential forms. The next definition and the following theorem are at the heart of LR(k) parsing.

DEFINITION

We define the *e-free first* function, $\text{EFF}_k^G(\alpha)$ as follows (we shall delete the k and/or G when clear):

(1) If α does not begin with a nonterminal, then $\text{EFF}_k(\alpha) = \text{FIRST}_k(\alpha)$.
(2) If α begins with a nonterminal, then

$$\text{EFF}_k(\alpha) = \{w \mid \text{there is a derivation } \alpha \underset{rm}{\Rightarrow} \beta \overset{*}{\underset{rm}{\Rightarrow}} wx,$$
$$\text{where } \beta \neq Awx \text{ for any nonterminal } A\}, \text{ and } w = \text{FIRST}_k(wx)$$

Thus, $\text{EFF}_k(\alpha)$ captures all members of $\text{FIRST}_k(\alpha)$ whose derivation does not involve replacing a leading nonterminal by e (equivalently, whose right-most derivation does not use an e-production at the last step, when α begins with a nonterminal).

Example 5.28

Consider the grammar G with the productions

$$S \longrightarrow AB$$
$$A \longrightarrow Ba \,|\, e$$
$$B \longrightarrow Cb \,|\, C$$
$$C \longrightarrow c \,|\, e$$
$$\text{FIRST}_2(S) = \{e, a, b, c, ab, ac, ba, ca, cb\}$$
$$\text{EFF}_2(S) = \{ca, cb\} \quad \square$$

Recall that in Chapter 4 we considered a bottom-up parsing algorithm which would not work on grammars having e-productions. For $\text{LR}(k)$ parsing we can permit e-productions in the grammar, but we must be careful when we reduce the empty string to a nonterminal.

We shall see that using the EFF function we are able to correctly deter-mine when the empty string is the handle to be reduced to a nonterminal. First, however, we introduce a slight revision of the $\text{LR}(k)$ definition. The two derivations involved in that definition really play interchangeable roles, and we can therefore assume without loss of generality that the handle of the second derivation is at least as far right as that of the first.

LEMMA 5.2

If $G = (N, \Sigma, P, S')$ is an augmented grammar which is not $\text{LR}(k)$, then there exist derivations $S' \overset{*}{\underset{\text{rm}}{\Rightarrow}} \alpha A w \underset{\text{rm}}{\Rightarrow} \alpha \beta w$ and $S' \overset{*}{\underset{\text{rm}}{\Rightarrow}} \gamma B x \underset{\text{rm}}{\Rightarrow} \gamma \delta x = \alpha \beta y$, where $\text{FIRST}_k(w) = \text{FIRST}_k(y)$ and $|\gamma \delta| \geq |\alpha \beta|$ but $\gamma B x \neq \alpha A y$.

Proof. We know by the $\text{LR}(k)$ definition that we can find derivations satisfying all conditions, except possibly the condition $|\gamma \delta| \geq |\alpha \beta|$. Thus, assume that $|\gamma \delta| < |\alpha \beta|$. We shall show that there is another counter-example to the $\text{LR}(k)$ condition, where $\gamma \delta$ plays the role of $\alpha \beta$ in that con-dition.

Since we are given that $\gamma \delta x = \alpha \beta y$ and $|\gamma \delta| < |\alpha \beta|$, we find that for some z in Σ^+, we can write $\alpha \beta = \gamma \delta z$. Thus we have the derivations

$$S' \overset{*}{\underset{\text{rm}}{\Longrightarrow}} \gamma B x \underset{\text{rm}}{\Longrightarrow} \gamma \delta x,$$

and

$$S' \overset{*}{\underset{\text{rm}}{\Longrightarrow}} \alpha A w \underset{\text{rm}}{\Longrightarrow} \alpha \beta w = \gamma \delta z w$$

Now z was defined so that $x = zy$. Since $\text{FIRST}_k(w) = \text{FIRST}_k(y)$, it follows that $\text{FIRST}_k(x) = \text{FIRST}_k(zw)$. The $LR(k)$ condition, if it held, would say that $\alpha A w = \gamma B z w$. We would have $\gamma B z = \alpha A$ and $\gamma B z y = \alpha A y$, using operations of "cancellation" and concatenation, which preserve equality. But $zy = x$, so we have shown that $\alpha A y = \gamma B x$, which we originally assumed to be false. If we relate the two derivations above to the $LR(k)$ condition, we see that they satisfy the conditions of the lemma, when the proper substitutions of string names are made, of course. $\quad\square$

$LR(k)$ parsing techniques are based on the following theorem.

THEOREM 5.9

A grammar $G = (N, \Sigma, P, S)$ is $LR(k)$ if and only if the following condition holds for each u in Σ^{*k}. Let $\alpha\beta$ be a viable prefix of a right-sentential form $\alpha\beta w$ of the augmented grammar G'. If $LR(k)$ item $[A \rightarrow \beta \cdot, u]$ is valid for $\alpha\beta$, then there is no other $LR(k)$ item $[A_1 \rightarrow \beta_1 \cdot \beta_2, v]$ which is valid for $\alpha\beta$ with u in $\text{EFF}_k(\beta_2 v)$. (Note that β_2 may be e.)

Proof.

Only if: Suppose that $[A \rightarrow \beta \cdot, u]$ and $[A_1 \rightarrow \beta_1 \cdot \beta_2, v]$ are two distinct items valid for $\alpha\beta$. That is to say, in the augmented grammar

$$S' \underset{rm}{\overset{*}{\Longrightarrow}} \alpha A w \underset{rm}{\Longrightarrow} \alpha\beta w \qquad \text{with } \text{FIRST}_k(w) = u$$

$$S' \underset{rm}{\overset{*}{\Longrightarrow}} \alpha_1 A_1 x \underset{rm}{\Longrightarrow} \alpha_1 \beta_1 \beta_2 x \qquad \text{with } \text{FIRST}_k(x) = v$$

and $\alpha\beta = \alpha_1\beta_1$. Moreover, $\beta_2 x \underset{rm}{\overset{*}{\Longrightarrow}} uy$ for some y in a (possibly zero step) derivation in which a leading nonterminal is never replaced by e.

We claim that G cannot be $LR(k)$. To see this, we shall examine three cases depending on whether (1) $\beta_2 = e$, (2) β_2 is in Σ^+, or (3) β_2 has a nonterminal.

Case 1: If $\beta_2 = e$, then $u = v$, and the two derivations are

$$S' \underset{rm}{\overset{*}{\Longrightarrow}} \alpha A w \underset{rm}{\Longrightarrow} \alpha\beta w$$

and

$$S' \underset{rm}{\overset{*}{\Longrightarrow}} \alpha_1 A_1 x \underset{rm}{\Longrightarrow} \alpha_1 \beta_1 x$$

where $\text{FIRST}_k(w) = \text{FIRST}_k(x) = u = v$. Since the two items are distinct, either $A \neq A_1$ or $\beta \neq \beta_1$. In either case we have a violation of the $LR(k)$ definition.

Case 2: If $\beta_2 = z$ for some z in Σ^+, then

$$S' \underset{rm}{\overset{*}{\Longrightarrow}} \alpha A w \underset{rm}{\Longrightarrow} \alpha \beta w$$

and

$$S' \underset{rm}{\overset{*}{\Longrightarrow}} \alpha_1 A_1 x \underset{rm}{\Longrightarrow} \alpha_1 \beta_1 z x$$

where $\alpha\beta = \alpha_1 \beta_1$ and $\text{FIRST}_k(zx) = u$. But then G is not LR(k), since $\alpha A z x$ cannot be equal to $\alpha_1 A_1 x$ if $z \in \Sigma^+$.

Case 3: Suppose that β_2 contains at least one nonterminal symbol. Then $\beta_2 \underset{rm}{\overset{*}{\Longrightarrow}} u_1 B u_3 \underset{rm}{\Longrightarrow} u_1 u_2 u_3$, where $u_1 u_2 \neq e$, since a leading nonterminal is not to be replaced by e in this derivation. Thus we would have two derivations

$$S' \underset{rm}{\overset{*}{\Longrightarrow}} \alpha A w \underset{rm}{\Longrightarrow} \alpha \beta w$$

and

$$S' \underset{rm}{\overset{*}{\Longrightarrow}} \alpha_1 A_1 x \underset{rm}{\Longrightarrow} \alpha_1 \beta_1 \beta_2 x$$

$$\underset{rm}{\overset{*}{\Longrightarrow}} \alpha_1 \beta_1 u_1 B u_3 x \underset{rm}{\Longrightarrow} \alpha_1 \beta_1 u_1 u_2 u_3 x$$

such that $\alpha_1 \beta_1 = \alpha\beta$ and $u_1 u_2 u_3 x = uy$. The LR(k) definition requires that $\alpha A u_1 u_2 u_3 x = \alpha_1 \beta_1 u_1 B u_3 x$. That is, $\alpha A u_1 u_2 = \alpha_1 \beta_1 u_1 B$. Substituting $\alpha\beta$ for $\alpha_1 \beta_1$, we must have $A u_1 u_2 = \beta u_1 B$. But since $u_1 u_2 \neq e$, this is impossible.

Note that this is the place where the condition that u is in $\text{EFF}_k(\beta_2 v)$ is required. If we had replaced EFF by FIRST in the statement of the theorem, then $u_1 u_2$ could be e and $\alpha A u_1 u_2 u_3 x$ could then be equal to $\alpha_1 \beta_1 u_1 B u_3 x$ (if $u_1 u_2 = e$ and $\beta = e$).

If: Suppose that G is not LR(k). Then there are two derivations in the augmented grammar

(5.2.1)
$$S' \underset{rm}{\overset{*}{\Longrightarrow}} \alpha A w \underset{rm}{\Longrightarrow} \alpha \beta w$$

and

(5.2.2)
$$S' \underset{rm}{\overset{*}{\Longrightarrow}} \gamma B x \underset{rm}{\Longrightarrow} \gamma \delta x = \alpha \beta y$$

such that $\text{FIRST}_k(w) = \text{FIRST}_k(y) = u$, but $\alpha A y \neq \gamma B x$. Moreover, we can choose these derivations such that $\alpha\beta$ is as short as possible.

By Lemma 5.2, we may assume that $|\gamma\delta| \geq |\alpha\beta|$. Let $\alpha_1 A_1 y_1$ be the last right-sentential form in the derivation

$$S' \overset{*}{\underset{rm}{\Longrightarrow}} \gamma Bx$$

such that the length of its open portion is no more than $|\alpha\beta| + 1$. That is, $|\alpha_1 A_1| \leq |\alpha\beta| + 1$. Then we can write (5.2.2) as

$$(5.2.3) \qquad S' \overset{*}{\underset{rm}{\Longrightarrow}} \alpha_1 A_1 y_1 \underset{rm}{\Longrightarrow} \alpha_1 \beta_1 \beta_2 y_1 \overset{*}{\underset{rm}{\Longrightarrow}} \alpha_1 \beta_1 y$$

where $\alpha_1 \beta_1 = \alpha\beta$. By our choice of $\alpha_1 A_1 y_1$, we have $|\alpha_1| \leq |\alpha\beta| \leq |\gamma\delta|$. Moreover, $\beta_2 y_1 \overset{*}{\underset{rm}{\Longrightarrow}} y$ does not use a production $B \rightarrow e$ at the last step from our choice of $\alpha_1 A_1 y_1$. That is to say, if $B \rightarrow e$ were the last production applied, then $\alpha_1 A_1 y_1$ would not be the last right-sentential form in the derivation $S \overset{*}{\underset{rm}{\Longrightarrow}} \gamma Bx$ whose open portion is no longer than $|\alpha\beta| + 1$. Thus, $u = \text{FIRST}_k(y)$ is in $\text{EFF}_k(\beta_2 y_1)$. We may conclude that $[A_1 \rightarrow \beta_1 \cdot \beta_2, v]$ is valid for $\alpha\beta$ where $v = \text{FIRST}_k(y_1)$.

From derivation (5.2.1), $[A \rightarrow \beta \cdot, u]$ is also valid for $\alpha\beta$, so that it remains to show that $A_1 \rightarrow \beta_1 \cdot \beta_2$ is not the same as $A \rightarrow \beta \cdot$.

To show this, suppose that $A_1 \rightarrow \beta_1 \cdot \beta_2$ is $A \rightarrow \beta \cdot$. Then derivation (5.2.3) is of the form

$$S' \overset{*}{\underset{rm}{\Longrightarrow}} \alpha_1 A y \underset{rm}{\Longrightarrow} \alpha_1 \beta y$$

where $\alpha_1 \beta = \alpha\beta$. Thus $\alpha_1 = \alpha$ and $\alpha A y = \alpha Bx$, contrary to the hypothesis that G is not LR(k). $\square$

The construction of a deterministic right parser for an LR(k) grammar requires knowing how to find all valid LR(k) items for each viable prefix of a right-sentential form.

DEFINITION

Let G be a CFG and γ a viable prefix of G. We define $V_k^G(\gamma)$ to be the set of LR(k) items valid for γ with respect to k and G. We again delete k and/or G if understood. We define $\mathcal{S} = \{\mathcal{Q} | \mathcal{Q} = V_k^G(\gamma)$ for some viable prefix γ of $G\}$ as the *collection of the sets of valid LR(k) items* for G. $\mathcal{S}$ contains all sets of LR(k) items which are valid for some viable prefix of G.

We shall next present an algorithm for constructing a set of LR(k) items for any sentential form, followed by an algorithm to construct the collection of the sets of valid items for any grammar G.

ALGORITHM 5.8

Construction of $V_k^G(\gamma)$.

Input. CFG $G = (N, \Sigma, P, S)$ and γ in $(N \cup \Sigma)^*$.

Output. $V_k^G(\gamma)$.

Method. If $\gamma = X_1 X_2 \cdots X_n$, we construct $V_k(\gamma)$ by constructing $V_k(e)$, $V_k(X_1), V_k(X_1 X_2), \ldots, V_k(X_1 X_2 \cdots X_n)$.

(1) We construct $V_k(e)$ as follows:
   (a) If $S \longrightarrow \alpha$ is in P, add $[S \longrightarrow \cdot \alpha, e]$ to $V_k(e)$.
   (b) If $[A \longrightarrow \cdot B\alpha, u]$ is in $V_k(e)$ and $B \longrightarrow \beta$ is in P, then for each x in $\text{FIRST}_k(\alpha u)$ add $[B \longrightarrow \cdot \beta, x]$ to $V_k(e)$, provided it is not already there.
   (c) Repeat step (b) until no more new items can be added to $V_k(e)$.

(2) Suppose that we have constructed $V_k(X_1 X_2 \cdots X_{i-1})$, $i \leq n$. We construct $V_k(X_1 X_2 \cdots X_i)$ as follows:
   (a) If $[A \longrightarrow \alpha \cdot X_i \beta, u]$ is in $V_k(X_1 \cdots X_{i-1})$, add $[A \longrightarrow \alpha X_i \cdot \beta, u]$ to $V_k(X_1 \cdots X_i)$.
   (b) If $[A \longrightarrow \alpha \cdot B\beta, u]$ has been placed in $V_k(X_1 \cdots X_i)$ and $B \longrightarrow \delta$ is in P, then add $[B \longrightarrow \cdot \delta, x]$ to $V_k(X_1 \cdots X_i)$ for each x in $\text{FIRST}_k(\beta u)$, provided it is not already there.
   (c) Repeat step (2b) until no more new items can be added to $V_k(X_1 \cdots X_i)$. $\square$

DEFINITION

The repeated application of step (1b) or (2b) of Algorithm 5.8 to a set of items is called *taking the closure* of that set.

We shall define a function *GOTO* on sets of items for a grammar $G = (N, \Sigma, P, S)$. If α is a set of items such that $\alpha = V_k^G(\gamma)$, where $\gamma \in (N \cup \Sigma)^*$, then $\text{GOTO}(\alpha, X)$ is that α' such that $\alpha' = V_k^G(\gamma X)$, where $X \in (N \cup \Sigma)$. In Algorithm 5.8 step (2) computes

$$V_k(X_1 X_2 \cdots X_i) = \text{GOTO}(V_k(X_1 X_2 \cdots X_{i-1}), X_i).$$

Note that step (2) is really independent of $X_1 \cdots X_{i-1}$, depending only on the set $V_k(X_1 \cdots X_{i-1})$ itself.

Example 5.29

Let us construct $V_1(e)$, $V_1(S)$, and $V_1(Sa)$ for the augmented grammar

$$S' \longrightarrow S$$
$$S \longrightarrow SaSb$$
$$S \longrightarrow e$$

(Note, however, that Algorithm 5.8 does not require that the grammar be augmented.) We first compute $V(e)$ using step 1 of Algorithm 5.8. In step (1a) we add $[S' \longrightarrow \cdot S, e]$ to $V(e)$. In step (1b) we add $[S \longrightarrow \cdot SaSb, e]$ and $[S \longrightarrow \cdot, e]$ to $V(e)$. Since $[S \longrightarrow \cdot SaSb, e]$ is now in $V(e)$, we must also add $[S \longrightarrow \cdot SaSb, x]$ and $[S \longrightarrow \cdot, x]$ to $V(e)$ for all x in $\text{FIRST}(aSb) = a$. Thus, $V(e)$ contains the following items:

$$[S' \longrightarrow \cdot S, e]$$
$$[S \longrightarrow \cdot SaSb, e/a]$$
$$[S \longrightarrow \cdot, e/a]$$

Here we have used the shorthand notation $[A \longrightarrow \alpha \cdot \beta, x_1/x_2/ \cdots /x_n]$ for the set of items $[A \longrightarrow \alpha \cdot \beta, x_1], [A \longrightarrow \alpha \cdot \beta, x_2], \ldots, [A \longrightarrow \alpha \cdot \beta, x_n]$. To obtain $V(S)$, we compute $\text{GOTO}(V(e), S)$. From step (2a) we add the three items $[S' \longrightarrow S \cdot, e]$ and $[S \longrightarrow S \cdot aSb, e/a]$ to $V(S)$. Computing the closure adds no new items to $V(S)$, so $V(S)$ is

$$[S' \longrightarrow S \cdot, e]$$
$$[S \longrightarrow S \cdot aSb, e/a]$$

$V(Sa)$ is computed as $\text{GOTO}(V(S), a)$. $V(Sa)$ contains the following six items:

$$[S \longrightarrow Sa \cdot Sb, e/a]$$
$$[S \longrightarrow \cdot SaSb, a/b]$$
$$[S \longrightarrow \cdot, a/b] \quad \square$$

We now show that Algorithm 5.8 correctly computes $V_k(\gamma)$.

THEOREM 5.10

An LR(k) item is in $V_k(\gamma)$ after step (2) of Algorithm 5.8 if and only if that item is valid for γ.

Proof.

If: It is left to the reader to show that Algorithm 5.8 terminates and correctly computes $V_k(e)$. We shall show that if all and only the valid items for $X_1 \cdots X_{i-1}$ are in $V_k(X_1 X_2 \cdots X_{i-1})$, then all and only the valid items for $X_1 \cdots X_i$ are in $V_k(X_1 \cdots X_i)$.

Suppose that $[A \longrightarrow \beta_1 \cdot \beta_2, u]$ is valid for $X_1 \cdots X_i$. Then there exists a derivation $S \overset{*}{\underset{rm}{\Rightarrow}} \alpha A w \underset{rm}{\Rightarrow} \alpha \beta_1 \beta_2 w$ such that $\alpha \beta_1 = X_1 X_2 \cdots X_i$ and $u = \text{FIRST}_k(w)$. There are two cases to consider.

Suppose $\beta_1 = \beta_1' X_i$. Then $[A \longrightarrow \beta_1' \cdot X_i \beta_2, u]$ is valid for $X_1 \cdots X_{i-1}$

and, by the inductive hypothesis, is in $V_k(X_1 \cdots X_{i-1})$. By step (2a) of Algorithm 5.8, $[A \rightarrow \beta_1' X_i \cdot \beta_2, u]$ is added to $V_k(X_1 \cdots X_i)$.

Suppose that $\beta_1 = e$, in which case $\alpha = X_1 \cdots X_i$. Since $S \overset{*}{\underset{rm}{\Rightarrow}} \alpha A w$ is a rightmost derivation, there is an intermediate step in this derivation in which the last symbol X_i of α is introduced. Thus we can write $S \overset{*}{\underset{rm}{\Rightarrow}} \alpha' B y$ $\underset{rm}{\Rightarrow} \alpha' \gamma X_i \delta y \overset{*}{\underset{rm}{\Rightarrow}} \alpha A w$, where $\alpha' \gamma = X_1 \cdots X_{i-1}$, and every step in the derivation $\alpha' \gamma X_i \delta y \overset{*}{\underset{rm}{\Rightarrow}} \alpha A w$ rewrites a nonterminal to the right of the explicitly shown X_i. Then $[B \rightarrow \gamma \cdot X_i \delta, v]$, where $v = \text{FIRST}_k(y)$, is valid for $X_1 \cdots X_{i-1}$, and by the inductive hypothesis is in $V_k(X_1 \cdots X_{i-1})$. By step (2a) of Algorithm 5.5, $[B \rightarrow \gamma X_i \cdot \delta, v]$ is added to $V_k(X_1 \cdots X_i)$. Since $\delta y \overset{*}{\underset{rm}{\Rightarrow}} A w$, we can find a sequence of nonterminals $D_1, D_2, \ldots, D_m$ and strings $\theta_2, \ldots, \theta_m$ in $(N \cup \Sigma)^*$ such that δ begins with D_1, $A = D_m$, and production $D_i \rightarrow D_{i+1} \theta_{i+1}$ is in P for $1 \le i \le m$. By repeated application of step (2b), $[A \rightarrow \cdot \beta_2, u]$ is added to $V_k(X_1 \cdots X_i)$. The detail necessary to show that u is a valid second component of items containing $A \rightarrow \cdot \beta_2$ is left to the reader.

Only if: Suppose that $[A \rightarrow \beta_1 \cdot \beta_2, u]$ is added to $V_k(X_1 \cdots X_i)$. We show by induction on the number of items previously added to $V_k(X_1 \cdots X_i)$ that this item is valid for $X_1 \cdots X_i$.

The basis, zero items in $V_k(X_1 \cdots X_i)$, is straightforward. In this case $[A \rightarrow \beta_1 \cdot \beta_2, u]$ must be placed in $V_k(X_1 \cdots X_i)$ in step (2a), so $\beta_1 = \beta_1' X_i$ and $[A \rightarrow \beta_1' \cdot X_i \beta_2, u]$ is in $V_k(X_1 \cdots X_{i-1})$. Thus, $S \overset{*}{\underset{rm}{\Rightarrow}} \alpha A w \underset{rm}{\Rightarrow} \alpha \beta_1' X_i \beta_2 w$ and $\alpha \beta_1' = X_1 \cdots X_{i-1}$. Hence, $[A \rightarrow \beta_1 \cdot \beta_2, u]$ is valid for $X_1 \cdots X_i$.

For the inductive step, if $[A \rightarrow \beta_1 \cdot \beta_2, u]$ is placed in $V_k(X_1 \cdots X_i)$ at step (2a), the argument is the same as for the basis. If this item is added in step (2b), then $\beta_1 = e$, and there is an item $[B \rightarrow \gamma \cdot A \delta, v]$ which has been previously added to $V_k(X_1 \cdots X_i)$, with u in $\text{FIRST}_k(\delta v)$. By the inductive hypothesis $[B \rightarrow \gamma \cdot A \delta, v]$ is valid for $X_1 \cdots X_i$, so there is a derivation $S \overset{*}{\underset{rm}{\Rightarrow}} \alpha' B y \underset{rm}{\Rightarrow} \alpha' \gamma A \delta y$, where $\alpha' \gamma = X_1 \cdots X_i$. Then

$$S \overset{*}{\underset{rm}{\Rightarrow}} X_1 \cdots X_i A \delta y \overset{*}{\underset{rm}{\Rightarrow}} X_1 \cdots X_i A z \underset{rm}{\Rightarrow} X_1 \cdots X_i \beta_2 z,$$

where $u = \text{FIRST}_k(z)$. Hence $[A \rightarrow \cdot \beta_2, u]$ is valid for $X_1 \cdots X_i$. $\square$

Algorithm 5.8 provides a method for constructing the set of LR(k) items valid for any viable prefix. In the construction of a right parser for an LR(k) grammar G we are interested in the sets of items which are valid for all viable prefixes of G, namely the collection of the sets of valid items for G. Since a grammar contains a finite number of productions, the number of sets of items is also finite, but often very large. If γ is a viable prefix of a right sentential form γw, then we shall see that $V_k(\gamma)$ contains all the information about γ needed to continue parsing γw.

The following algorithm provides a systematic method for computing the sets of $LR(k)$ items for G.

ALGORITHM 5.9

Collection of sets of valid $LR(k)$ items for G.

Input. CFG $G = (N, \Sigma, P, S)$ and an integer k.

Output. $\mathcal{S} = \{\mathcal{C} \mid \mathcal{C} = V_k(\gamma)$, and γ is a viable prefix of $G\}$.

Method. Initially $\mathcal{S}$ is empty.

(1) Place $V_k(e)$ in $\mathcal{S}$. The set $V_k(e)$ is initially "unmarked."

(2) If a set of items $\mathcal{C}$ in $\mathcal{S}$ is unmarked, mark $\mathcal{C}$ by computing, for each X in $N \cup \Sigma$, $GOTO(\mathcal{C}, X)$. (Algorithm 5.8 can be used here.) If $\mathcal{C}' = GOTO(\mathcal{C}, X)$ is nonempty and is not already in $\mathcal{S}$, then add $\mathcal{C}'$ to $\mathcal{S}$ as an unmarked set of items.

(3) Repeat step (2) until all sets of items in $\mathcal{S}$ are marked. $\square$

DEFINITION

If G is a CFG, then the collection of sets of valid $LR(k)$ items for its augmented grammar will be called the *canonical collection* of sets of $LR(k)$ items for G.

Note that it is never necessary to compute $GOTO(\mathcal{C}, S')$, as this set of items will always be empty.

Example 5.30

Let us compute the canonical collection of sets of $LR(1)$ items for the grammar G whose augmented grammar contains the productions

$$S' \longrightarrow S$$
$$S \longrightarrow SaSb$$
$$S \longrightarrow e$$

We begin by computing $\mathcal{C}_0 = V(e)$. (This was done in Example 5.29.)

$$\mathcal{C}_0: \quad [S' \longrightarrow \cdot S, e]$$
$$[S \longrightarrow \cdot SaSb, e/a]$$
$$[S \longrightarrow \cdot, e/a]$$

We then compute $GOTO(\mathcal{C}_0, X)$ for all $X \in \{S, a, b\}$. Let $GOTO(\mathcal{C}_0, S)$ be $\mathcal{C}_1$.

$$\mathcal{C}_1: \quad [S' \longrightarrow S \cdot, e]$$
$$[S \longrightarrow S \cdot aSb, e/a]$$

GOTO($\mathcal{C}_0$, a) and GOTO($\mathcal{C}_0$, b) are both empty, since neither a nor b are viable prefixes of G. Next we must compute GOTO($\mathcal{C}_1$, X) for $X \in \{S, a, b\}$. GOTO($\mathcal{C}_1$, S) and GOTO($\mathcal{C}_1$, b) are empty and $\mathcal{C}_2 = $ GOTO($\mathcal{C}_1$, a) is

$$\mathcal{C}_2: \quad [S \longrightarrow Sa \cdot Sb, e/a]$$
$$[S \longrightarrow \cdot SaSb, a/b]$$
$$[S \longrightarrow \cdot, a/b]$$

Continuing, we obtain the following sets of items:

$$\mathcal{C}_3: \quad [S \longrightarrow SaS \cdot b, e/a]$$
$$[S \longrightarrow S \cdot aSb, a/b]$$
$$\mathcal{C}_4: \quad [S \longrightarrow Sa \cdot Sb, a/b]$$
$$[S \longrightarrow \cdot SaSb, a/b]$$
$$[S \longrightarrow \cdot, a/b]$$
$$\mathcal{C}_5: \quad [S \longrightarrow SaSb \cdot, e/a]$$
$$\mathcal{C}_6: \quad [S \longrightarrow SaS \cdot b, a/b]$$
$$[S \longrightarrow S \cdot aSb, a/b]$$
$$\mathcal{C}_7: \quad [S \longrightarrow SaSb \cdot, a/b]$$

The GOTO function is summarized in the following table:

		Grammar Symbol		
		S	a	b
Set	$\mathcal{C}_0$	$\mathcal{C}_1$	—	—
of	$\mathcal{C}_1$	—	$\mathcal{C}_2$	—
Items	$\mathcal{C}_2$	$\mathcal{C}_3$	—	—
	$\mathcal{C}_3$	—	$\mathcal{C}_4$	$\mathcal{C}_5$
	$\mathcal{C}_4$	$\mathcal{C}_6$	—	—
	$\mathcal{C}_5$	—	—	—
	$\mathcal{C}_6$	—	$\mathcal{C}_4$	$\mathcal{C}_7$
	$\mathcal{C}_7$	—	—	—

Note that GOTO($\mathcal{C}$, X) will always be empty if all items in $\mathcal{C}$ have the dot at the right end of the production. Here, $\mathcal{C}_5$ and $\mathcal{C}_7$ are examples of such sets of items.

The reader should note the similarity in the GOTO table above and the GOTO function of the LR(1) parser for G in Fig. 5.9. $\square$

THEOREM 5.11

Algorithm 5.9 correctly determines $\mathcal{S}$.

Proof. By Theorem 5.10 it suffices to prove that a set of items $\mathcal{C}$ is placed in $\mathcal{S}$ if and only if there exists a derivation $S \underset{rm}{\overset{*}{\Rightarrow}} \alpha A w \underset{rm}{\Rightarrow} \alpha \beta w$, where γ is a prefix of $\alpha \beta$ and $\mathcal{C} = V_k(\gamma)$. The "only if" portion is a straightforward induction on the order in which the sets of items are placed in $\mathcal{S}$. The "if" portion is a no less straightforward induction on the length of γ. These are both left for the Exercises. $\square$

5.2.4. Testing for the LR(k) Condition

It may be of interest to know that a particular grammar is LR(k) for some given value of k. We can provide an algorithm based on Theorem 5.9 and Algorithm 5.9.

DEFINITION

Let $G = (N, \Sigma, P, S)$ be a CFG and k an integer. A set $\mathcal{C}$ of LR(k) items for G is said to be *consistent* if no two distinct members of $\mathcal{C}$ are of the form $[A \longrightarrow \beta \cdot, u]$ and $[B \longrightarrow \beta_1 \cdot \beta_2, v]$, where u is in $\mathrm{EFF}_k(\beta_2 v)$. β_2 may be e.

ALGORITHM 5.10

Test for LR(k)-ness.

Input. CFG $G = (N, \Sigma, P, S)$ and an integer $k \geq 0$.

Output. "Yes" if G is LR(k); "no" otherwise.

Method.

(1) Using Algorithm 5.9, compute $\mathcal{S}$, the canonical collection of the sets of LR(k) items for G.

(2) Examine each set of LR(k) items in $\mathcal{S}$ and determine whether it is consistent.

(3) If all sets in $\mathcal{S}$ are consistent, output Yes. Otherwise, declare G not to be LR(k) for this particular value of k. $\square$

The correctness of Algorithm 5.10 is merely a restatement of Theorem 5.9.

Example 5.31

Let us test the grammar in Example 5.30 for LR(1)-ness. We have $\mathcal{S} = \{\mathcal{C}_0, \ldots, \mathcal{C}_7\}$. The only sets of LR(1) items which need to be tested are those that contain a dot at the right end of a production. These sets of items are $\mathcal{C}_0$, $\mathcal{C}_1$, $\mathcal{C}_2$, $\mathcal{C}_4$, $\mathcal{C}_5$, and $\mathcal{C}_7$.

Let us consider $\mathcal{C}_0$. In the items $[S' \longrightarrow \cdot S, e]$ and $[S \longrightarrow \cdot SaSb, e/a]$ in $\mathcal{C}_0$, $\mathrm{EFF}(S)$ and $\mathrm{EFF}(Sa)$ are both empty, so no violation of consistency with the items $[S \longrightarrow \cdot, e/a]$ occurs.

Let us consider α_1. Here $\text{EFF}(aSb) = \text{EFF}(aSba) = a$, but a is not a lookahead string of the item $[S' \longrightarrow S \cdot, e]$. Therefore, α_1 is consistent.

The sets of items α_2 and α_4 are consistent because $\text{EFF}(Sbx)$ and $\text{EFF}(SaSbx)$ are both empty for all x. The sets of items α_5 and α_7 are clearly consistent.

Thus all sets in $\mathcal{S}$ are consistent, so we have shown that G is LR(1). $\square$

5.2.5. Deterministic Right Parsers for LR(k) Grammars

In this section we shall informally describe how a deterministic extended pushdown transducer with k symbol lookahead can be constructed from an LR(k) grammar to act as a right parser for that grammar. We can view the pushdown transducer described earlier as a shift–reduce parsing algorithm which decides on the basis of its state, the top pushdown list entry, and the lookahead string whether to make a shift or a reduction and, in the latter use, what reduction to make.

To help make the decisions, the parser will have in every other pushdown list cell an "LR(k) table," which summarizes the parsing information which can be gleaned from a set of items. In particular, if α is a prefix of the pushdown string (top is on the right), then the table attached to the rightmost symbol of α comes from the set of items $V_k(\alpha)$. The essence of the construction of the right parser, then, is finding the LR(k) table associated with a set of items.

DEFINITION

Let G be a CFG and let $\mathcal{S}$ be a collection of sets of LR(k) items for G. $T(\alpha)$, the LR(k) *table associated with* the set of items α in $\mathcal{S}$, is a pair of functions $\langle f, g \rangle$. f is called the *parsing action function* and g the *goto function*.

(1) f maps Σ^{*k} to {**error, shift, accept**} $\cup$ {**reduce** $i|$ i is the number of a production in P, $i \geq 1$}, where

(a) $f(u) = $ **shift** if $[A \longrightarrow \beta_1 \cdot \beta_2, v]$ is in α, $\beta_2 \neq e$, and u is in $\text{EFF}_k(\beta_2 v)$.

(b) $f(u) = $ **reduce** i if $[A \longrightarrow \beta \cdot, u]$ is in α and $A \longrightarrow \beta$ is production i in P, $i \geq 1$.

(c) $f(e) = $ **accept** if $[S' \longrightarrow S \cdot, e]$ is in α.

(d) $f(u) = $ **error** otherwise.

(2) g, the goto function, determines the next applicable table. Some g will be invoked immediately after each shift and reduction. Formally, g maps $N \cup \Sigma$ to the set of tables or the message **error**. $g(X)$ is the table associated with $\text{GOTO}(\alpha, X)$. If $\text{GOTO}(\alpha, X)$ is the empty set, then $g(X) = $ **error**.

We should emphasize that by Theorem 5.9, if G is LR(k) and $\mathcal{S}$ is the canonical collection of sets of LR(k) items for G, then there can be no conflicts between actions specified by rules (1a), (1b), and (1c) above.

We say that the table $T(\mathcal{Q})$ is *associated with* a viable prefix γ of G if $\mathcal{Q} = V_k(\gamma)$.

DEFINITION

The *canonical set of LR(k) tables* for an LR(k) grammar G is the pair $(\mathfrak{I}, T_0)$, where $\mathfrak{I}$ the set of LR(k) tables associated with the canonical collection of sets of LR(k) items for G. T_0 is the LR(k) table associated with $V_k^G(e)$.

We shall usually represent a canonical LR(k) parser as a table, of which each row is an LR(k) table.

The LR(k) parsing algorithm given as Algorithm 5.7 using the canonical set of LR(k) tables will be called the *canonical LR(k) parsing algorithm* or canonical LR(k) parser, for short.

We shall now summarize the process of constructing the canonical set of LR(k) tables from an LR(k) grammar.

ALGORITHM 5.11

Construction of the canonical set of LR(k) tables from an LR(k) grammar.

Input. An LR(k) grammar $G = (N, \Sigma, P, S)$.

Output. The canonical set of LR(k) tables for G.

Method.

(1) Construct the augmented grammar

$$G' = (N \cup \{S'\}, \Sigma, P \cup \{S' \rightarrow S\}, S').$$

$S' \rightarrow S$ is to be the zeroth production.

(2) From G' construct $\mathcal{S}$, the canonical collection of sets of valid LR(k) items for G.

(3) Let $\mathfrak{I}$ be the set of LR(k) tables for G, where $\mathfrak{I} = \{T \mid T = T(\mathcal{Q})$ for some $\mathcal{Q} \in \mathcal{S}\}$. Let $T_0 = T(\mathcal{Q}_0)$, where $\mathcal{Q}_0 = V_k^G(e)$. $\square$

Example 5.32

Let us construct the canonical set of LR(1) tables for the grammar G whose augmented grammar is

$$(0) \quad S' \longrightarrow S$$
$$(1) \quad S \longrightarrow SaSb$$
$$(2) \quad S \longrightarrow e$$

The canonical collection $\mathcal{S}$ of sets of LR(1) items for G is given in Example 5.30. From $\mathcal{S}$ we shall construct the set of LR(k) tables.

Let us construct $T_0 = \langle f_0, g_0 \rangle$, the table associated with $\mathfrak{a}_0$. Since $k = 1$, the possible lookahead strings are a, b, and e. Since $\mathfrak{a}_0$ contains the items $[S \longrightarrow \cdot, e/a]$, $f_0(e) = f_0(a) = $ **reduce** 2. From the remaining items in $\mathfrak{a}_0$ we determine that $f_0(b) = $ **error** [since EFF$(S\alpha)$ is empty]. To compute the GOTO function g_0, we note that GOTO$(\mathfrak{a}_0, S) = \mathfrak{a}_1$ and GOTO$(\mathfrak{a}_0, X)$ is empty otherwise. If T_1 is the name given to $T(\mathfrak{a}_1)$, then $g_0(S) = T_1$ and $g_0(X) = $ **error** for all other X. We have now completed the computation of T_0. We can represent T_0 as follows:

	f_0			g_0		
	a	b	e	S	a	b
T_0	2	X	2	T_1	X	X

Here, 2 represents reduce using production 2, and X represents error.

Let us now compute the entries for $T_1 = \langle f_1, g_1 \rangle$. Since $[S' \longrightarrow S \cdot, e]$ is in $\mathfrak{a}_1$, we have $f_1(e) = $ **accept**. Since $[S \longrightarrow S \cdot aSb, e/a]$ is in $\mathfrak{a}_1$, $f_1(a) = $ **shift**. Note that the lookahead strings in this item have no relevance here. Then, $f_1(b) = $ **error**. Since GOTO$(\mathfrak{a}_1, a) = \mathfrak{a}_2$, we let $g_1(a) = T_2$, where $T_2 = T(\mathfrak{a}_2)$.

Continuing in this fashion we obtain the set of LR(1) tables given in Fig. 5.9 on p. 374. □

In Chapter 7 we shall discuss a number of other methods for producing LR(k) parsers from a grammar. These methods often produce parsers much smaller than the canonical LR(k) parser. However, the canonical LR(k) parser has several outstanding features, and these will be used as a yardstick by which other LR(k) parsers will be evaluated. We will mention several features concerning the behavior of the canonical LR(k) parsing algorithm:

(1) A simple induction on the number of moves made shows that each table on the pushdown list is associated with the string of grammar symbols to its left. Thus as soon as the first k input symbols of the remaining input are such that no possible suffix could yield a sentence in $L(G)$, the parser will report error. At all times the string of grammar symbols on the pushdown list must be a viable prefix of the grammar. Thus an LR(k) parser announces error at the first possible opportunity in a left to right scan of the input string.

(2) Let $T_j = (f_j, g_j)$. If $f_j(u) = $ **shift** and the parser is in configuration

$$(5.2.4) \qquad (T_0 X_1 T_1 X_2 T_2 \cdots X_j T_j, x, \pi)$$

then there is an item $[B \longrightarrow \beta_1 \cdot \beta_2, v]$ which is valid for $X_1 X_2 \cdots X_j$, with u in EFF$(\beta_2 v)$. Thus by Theorem 5.9, if $S' \overset{*}{\underset{rm}{\Longrightarrow}} X_1 X_2 \cdots X_j u y$ for some y in Σ^*, then the right end of the handle of $X_1 \cdots X_j u y$ must occur somewhere to the right of X_j.

(3) If $f_j(u) = $ **reduce** i in configuration (5.2.4) and production i is $A \longrightarrow Y_1 Y_2 \cdots Y_r$, then the string $X_{j-r+1} X_{j-r+2} \cdots X_j$ on the pushdown list in configuration (5.2.4) must be $Y_1 \cdots Y_r$, since the set of items from which table T_j is constructed contains the item $[A \longrightarrow Y_1 Y_2 \cdots Y_r \cdot, u]$. Thus in a reduce move the symbols on top of the pushdown list do not need to be examined. It is only necessary to pop $2r$ symbols from the pushdown list.

(4) If $f_j(u) = $ **accept**, then $u = e$. The pushdown list at this point is $T_0 S T$, where T is the LR(k) table associated with the set of items containing $[S' \longrightarrow S \cdot, e]$.

(5) A DPDT with an endmarker can be constructed to implement the canonical LR(k) parsing algorithm. Once we realize that we can store the lookahead string in the finite control of the DPDT, it should be evident how an extended DPDT can be constructed to implement Algorithm 5.7, the LR(k) parsing algorithm.

We leave the proofs of these observations for the Exercises. They are essentially restatements of the definitions of valid item and LR(k) table. We thus have the following theorem.

THEOREM 5.12

The canonical LR(k) parsing algorithm correctly produces a right parse of its input if there is one, and declares "**error**" otherwise.

Proof. Based on the above observations, it follows immediately by induction on the number of moves made by the parsing algorithm that if α is the string of grammar symbols on its pushdown list and x the unexpended input including the lookahead string, then $\alpha x \Longrightarrow^\pi w$, where w is the original input string and π^R is the current output. As a special case, if it accepts w and emits output π^R, then $S \Longrightarrow^\pi w$. $\square$

A proof of the unambiguity of an LR grammar is a simple application of the LR condition. Given two distinct rightmost derivations $S \underset{rm}{\Longrightarrow} \alpha_1 \underset{rm}{\Longrightarrow} \cdots \underset{rm}{\Longrightarrow} \alpha_n \underset{rm}{\Longrightarrow} w$ and $S \underset{rm}{\Longrightarrow} \beta_1 \underset{rm}{\Longrightarrow} \cdots \underset{rm}{\Longrightarrow} \beta_m \underset{rm}{\Longrightarrow} w$, consider the smallest i such that $\alpha_{n-i} \neq \beta_{m-i}$. A violation of the LR($k$) definition for any k is immediate. We leave details for the Exercises. It follows that the canonical LR(k) parsing algorithm for an LR(k) grammar G produces a right parse for an input w if and only if $w \in L(G)$.

It may not be completely obvious at first that the canonical LR(k) parser operates in linear time, even when the elementary operations are taken to be its own steps. That such is the case is the next theorem.

THEOREM 5.13

The number of steps executed by the canonical LR(k) parsing algorithm in parsing an input of length n is $0(n)$.

Proof. Let us define a C-configuration of the parser as follows:

(1) An initial configuration is a C-configuration.

(2) A configuration immediately after a shift move is a C-configuration.

(3) A configuration immediately after a reduction which makes the stack shorter than in the previous C-configuration is a C-configuration.

In parsing an input of length n the parser can enter at most $2n$ C-configurations. Let the *characteristic* of a C-configuration be the sum of the number of grammar symbols on the pushdown list plus twice the number of remaining input symbols. If C_1 and C_2 are successive C-configurations, then the characteristic of C_1 is at least one more than the characteristic of C_2. Since the characteristic of the initial configuration is $2n$, the parser can enter at most $2n$ C-configurations.

Now it suffices to show that there is a constant c such that the parser can make at most c moves between successive C-configurations. To prove this let us simulate the $LR(k)$ parser by a DPDA which keeps the pushdown list of the algorithm as its own pushdown list. By Theorem 2.22, if the DPDA does not shift an input or reduce the size of its stack in a constant number of moves, then it is in a loop. Hence, the parsing algorithm is also in a loop.

But we have observed that the parsing algorithm detects an error if there is no succeeding input that completes a word in $L(G)$. Thus there is some word in $L(G)$ with arbitrarily long rightmost derivations. The unambiguity of $LR(k)$ grammars is contradicted. We conclude that the parsing algorithm enters no loops and that hence the constant c exists. $\quad\square$

5.2.6. Implementation of LL(*k*) and LR(*k*) Parsers

Both the $LL(k)$ and $LR(k)$ parser implementations seem to require placing large tables on the pushdown list. Actually, we can avoid this situation, as follows:

(1) Make one copy of each possible table in memory. Then, on the pushdown list, replace the tables by pointers to the tables.

(2) Since both the $LL(k)$ tables and $LR(k)$ tables return the names of other tables, we can use pointers to the tables instead of names.

We note that the grammar symbols are actually redundant on the pushdown list and in practice would not be written there.

EXERCISES

5.2.1. Determine which of the following grammars are LR(1):
    (a) G_0.
    (b) $S \longrightarrow AB, A \longrightarrow 0A1\,|\,e, B \longrightarrow 1B\,|\,1$.
    (c) $S \longrightarrow 0S1\,|\,A, A \longrightarrow 1A\,|\,1$.
    (d) $S \longrightarrow S + A\,|\,A, A \longrightarrow (S)\,|\,a(S)\,|\,a$.

The last grammar generates parenthesized expressions with operator $+$ and with identifiers, denoted a, possibly singly subscripted.

5.2.2. Which of the grammars of Exercise 5.2.1 are LR(0)?

5.2.3. Construct the sets of LR(1) tables for those grammars of Exercise 5.2.1 which are LR(1). Do not forget to augment the grammars first.

5.2.4. Give the sequence of moves made by the LR(1) right parser for G_0 with input $(a + a) * (a + (a + a) * a)$.

*5.2.5. Prove or disprove each of the following:
(a) Every right-linear grammar is LL.
(b) Every right-linear grammar is LR.
(c) Every regular grammar is LL.
(d) Every regular grammar is LR.
(e) Every regular set has an LL(1) grammar.
(f) Every regular set has an LR(1) grammar.
(g) Every regular set has an LR(0) grammar.

5.2.6. Show that every LR grammar is unambiguous.

*5.2.7. Let $G = (N, \Sigma, P, S)$, and define $G_R = (N, \Sigma, P_R, S)$, where P_R is P with all right sides reversed. That is, $P_R = \{A \longrightarrow \alpha^R \,|\, A \longrightarrow \alpha$ is in $P\}$. Give an example to show that G_R need not be LR(k) even though G is.

*5.2.8. Let $G = (N, \Sigma, P, S)$ be an arbitrary CFG. Define $R_k^G(i, u)$, for u in Σ^{*k} and production number i, to be $\{\alpha\beta u \,|\, S \overset{*}{\underset{rm}{\Longrightarrow}} \alpha A w \underset{rm}{\Longrightarrow} \alpha\beta w$, where $u = \text{FIRST}_k(w)$ and production i is $A \longrightarrow \beta\}$. Show that $R_k^G(i, u)$ is regular.

5.2.9. Give an alternate parsing algorithm for LR(k) grammars by keeping track of the states of finite automata that recognize $R_k^G(i, u)$ for the various i and u.

*5.2.10. Show that G is LR(k) if and only if for all α, β, u, and v, α in $R_k^G(i, u)$ and $\alpha\beta$ in $R_k^G(j, v)$ implies $\beta = e$ and $i = j$.

*5.2.11. Show that G is LR(k) if and only if G is unambiguous and for all w, x, y, and z in Σ^*, the four conditions $S \overset{*}{\Longrightarrow} wAy$, $A \overset{*}{\Longrightarrow} x$, $S \overset{*}{\Longrightarrow} wxz$, and $\text{FIRST}_k(y) = \text{FIRST}_k(z)$ imply that $S \overset{*}{\Longrightarrow} wAz$.

**5.2.12. Show that it is undecidable whether a CFG is LR(k) for some k.

**5.2.13. Show that it is undecidable whether an LR(k) grammar is an LL grammar.

5.2.14. Show that it is decidable whether an LR(k) grammar is an LL(k) grammar for the same value of k.

*5.2.15. Show that every e-free CFL is generated by some e-free uniquely invertible CFG.

*5.2.16. Let $G = (N, \Sigma, P, S)$ be a CFG grammar, and $w = a_1, \cdots a_n$ a string in Σ^n. Suppose that when applying Earley's algorithm to G, we find item $[A \longrightarrow \alpha \cdot \beta, j]$ (in the sense of Earley's algorithm) on list I_i. Show that there is a derivation $S \underset{rm}{\overset{*}{\Longrightarrow}} \gamma x$ such that item $[A \longrightarrow \alpha \cdot \beta, u]$ (in the LR sense) is valid for γ, $u = \text{FIRST}_k(x)$, and $\gamma \overset{*}{\Longrightarrow} a_1 \cdots a_i$.

*5.2.17. Prove the converse of Exercise 5.2.16.

*5.2.18. Use Exercise 5.2.16 to show that if G is LR(k), then Earley's algorithm with k symbol lookahead (see Exercise 4.2.17) takes linear time and space.

5.2.19. Let X be any symbol. Show that $\text{EFF}_k(X\alpha) = \text{EFF}_k(X) \oplus_k \text{FIRST}_k(\alpha)$.

5.2.20. Use Exercise 5.2.19 to give an efficient algorithm to compute $\text{EFF}(\alpha)$ for any α.

5.2.21. Give formal details to show that cases 1 and 3 of Theorem 5.9 yield violations of the LR(k) condition.

5.2.22. Complete the proof of Theorem 5.11.

5.2.23. Prove the correctness of Algorithm 5.10.

5.2.24. Prove the correctness of Algorithm 5.11 by showing each of the observations following that algorithm.

In Chapter 8 we shall prove various results regarding LR grammars. The reader may wish to try his hand at some of them now (Exercises 5.2.25–5.2.28).

**5.2.25. Show that every LL(k) grammar is an LR(k) grammar.

**5.2.26. Show that every deterministic CFL has an LR(1) grammar.

*5.2.27. Show that there exist grammars which are (deterministically) right-parsable but are not LR.

*5.2.28. Show that there exist languages which are LR but not LL.

**5.2.29. Show that every LC(k) grammar is an LR(k) grammar.

**5.2.30. What is the maximum number of sets of valid items an LR(k) grammar can have as a function of the number of grammar symbols, productions, and the length of the longest production?

*5.2.31. Let us call an item *essential* if it has its dot other than at the left end [i.e., it is added in step (2a) of Algorithm 5.8]. Show that other than for the set of items associated with e, and for reductions of the empty string, the definition of the LR(k) table associated with a set of items could have restricted attention to essential items, with no change in the table constructed.

*5.2.32. Show that the action of an LR(1) table on symbol a is **shift** if and only if a appears immediately to the right of a dot in some item in the set from which the table is constructed.

Programming Exercises

5.2.33. Write a program to test whether an arbitrary grammar is LR(1). Estimate how much time and space your program will require as a function of the size of the input grammar.

5.2.34. Write a program that uses an LR(1) parsing table as in Fig. 5.9 to parse input strings.

5.2.35. Write a program that generates an LR(1) parser for an LR(1) grammar.

5.2.36. Construct an LR(1) parser for a small grammar.

*5.2.37. Write a program that tests whether an arbitrary set of LR(1) tables forms a valid parser for a given CFG.

Suppose that an LR(1) parser is in the configuration $(\alpha T, ax, \pi)$ and that the parsing action associated with T and a is **error**. As in LL parsing, at this point we would like to announce error and transfer to an error recovery routine that modifies the input and/or the pushdown list so that the LR(1) parser can continue. As in the LL case we can delete the input symbol, change it, or insert another input symbol depending on which strategy seems most promising for the situation at hand.

Leinius [1970] describes a more elaborate strategy in which LR(1) tables stored in the pushdown list are consulted.

5.2.38. Write an LR(1) grammar for a small language. Devise an error recovery procedure to be used in conjunction with an LR(1) parser for this grammar. Evaluate the efficacy of your procedure.

BIBLIOGRAPHIC NOTES

LR(k) grammars were first defined by Knuth [1965]. Unfortunately, the method given in this section for producing an LR parser will result in very large parsers for grammars of practical interest. In Chapter 7 we shall investigate techniques developed by De Remer [1969], Korenjak [1969], and Aho and Ullman [1971], which can often be used to construct much smaller LR parsers.

The LR(k) concept has also been extended to context-sensitive grammars by Walters [1970].

The answer to Exercises 5.2.8–5.2.10 are given by Hopcroft and Ullman [1969]. Exercise 5.2.12 is from Knuth [1965].

5.3. PRECEDENCE GRAMMARS

The class of shift–reduce parsable grammars includes the LR(k) grammars and various subsets of the class of LR(k) grammars. In this section we shall precisely define a shift–reduce parsing algorithm and consider the class of precedence grammars, an important class of grammars which can be parsed by an easily implemented shift–reduce parsing algorithm.

5.3.1. Formal Shift–Reduce Parsing Algorithms

DEFINITION

Let $G = (N, \Sigma, P, S)$ be a CFG in which the productions have been numbered from 1 to p. A *shift–reduce parsing algorithm* for G is a pair of functions $\mathfrak{C} = (f, g)$,† where f is called the *shift–reduce function* and g the *reduce function*. These functions are defined as follows:

(1) f maps $V^* \times (\Sigma \cup \{\$\})^*$ to {**shift, reduce, error, accept**}, where $V = N \cup \Sigma \cup \{\$\}$, and $\$$ is a new symbol, the endmarker.

(2) g maps $V^* \times (\Sigma \cup \{\$\})^*$ to $\{1, 2, \ldots, p, \mathbf{error}\}$, under the constraint that if $g(\alpha, w) = i$, then the right side of production i is a suffix of α.

A shift–reduce parsing algorithm uses a left-to-right input scan and a pushdown list. The function f decides on the basis of what is on the pushdown list and what remains on the input tape whether to shift the current input symbol onto the pushdown list or call for a reduction. If a reduction is called for, then the function g is invoked to decide what reduction to make.

We can view the action of a shift–reduce parsing algorithm in terms of configurations which are triples of the form

$$(\$X_1 \cdots X_m, a_1 \cdots a_n \$, p_1 \cdots p_r)$$

where

(1) $\$X_1 \cdots X_m$ represents the pushdown list, with X_m on top. Each X_i is in $N \cup \Sigma$, and $\$$ acts as a bottom of the pushdown list marker.

(2) $a_1 \cdots a_n$ is the remaining portion of the original input. a_1 is the current input symbol, and $\$$ acts as a right endmarker for the input.

(3) $p_1 \cdots p_r$ is the string of production numbers used to reduce the original input to $X_1 \cdots X_m a_1 \cdots a_n$.

We can describe the action of $\mathfrak{C}$ by two relations, $\vdash_{\overline{\mathfrak{C}}}^{s}$ and $\vdash_{\overline{\mathfrak{C}}}^{r}$, on configurations. (The subscript $\mathfrak{C}$ will be dropped whenever possible.)

(1) If $f(\alpha, aw) = \mathbf{shift}$, then $(\alpha, aw, \pi) \vdash^{s} (\alpha a, w, \pi)$ for all α in V^*, w in $(\Sigma \cup \{\$\})^*$, and π in $\{1, \ldots, p\}^*$.

(2) If $f(\alpha\beta, w) = \mathbf{reduce}$, $g(\alpha\beta, w) = i$, and production i is $A \rightarrow \beta$, then $(\alpha\beta, w, \pi) \vdash^{r} (\alpha A, w, \pi i)$.

(3) If $f(\alpha, w) = \mathbf{accept}$, then $(\alpha, w, \pi) \vdash^{s} \mathbf{accept}$.

(4) Otherwise, $(\alpha, w, \pi) \vdash^{s} \mathbf{error}$.

†These functions are not the functions associated with an LR(k) table.

We define $\vdash$ to be the union of $\vdash^{s}$ and $\vdash^{r}$. We then define $\vdash^{+}$ and $\vdash^{*}$ to have their usual meanings.

We define $\mathcal{G}(w)$ for $w \in \Sigma^*$ to be π if $(\$, w\$, e) \vdash^{*} (\$S, \$, \pi) \vdash$ **accept**, and $\mathcal{G}(w) = $ **error** if no such π exists.

We say that the shift–reduce parsing algorithm is *valid* for G if

(1) $L(G) = \{w \mid \mathcal{G}(w) \neq $ **error**$\}$, and
(2) If $\mathcal{G}(w) = \pi$, then π is a right parse of w.

Example 5.33

Let us construct a shift–reduce parsing algorithm $\mathcal{G} = (f, g)$ for the grammar G with productions

$$(1)\ S \longrightarrow SaSb$$
$$(2)\ S \longrightarrow e$$

The shift–reduce function f is specified as follows: For all $\alpha \in V^*$ and $x \in (\Sigma \cup \{\$\})^*$,

(1) $f(\alpha S, cx) = $ **shift** if $c \in \{a, b\}$.
(2) $f(\alpha c, dx) = $ **reduce** if $c \in \{a, b\}$ and $d \in \{a, b\}$.
(3) $f(\$, ax) = $ **reduce**.
(4) $f(\$, bx) = $ **error**.
(5) $f(\alpha X, \$) = $ **error** for $X \in \{S, a\}$.
(6) $f(\alpha b, \$) = $ **reduce**.
(7) $f(\$S, \$) = $ **accept**.
(8) $f(\$, \$) = $ **error**.

The reduce function g is as follows. For all $\alpha \in V^*$ and $x \in (\Sigma \cup \{\$\})^*$,

(1) $g(\$, ax) = 2$
(2) $g(\alpha a, cx) = 2$ for $c \in \{a, b\}$.
(3) $g(\$SaSb, cx) = 1$ for $c \in \{a, \$\}$.
(4) $g(\alpha aSaSb, cx) = 1$ for $c \in \{a, b\}$.
(5) Otherwise, $g(\alpha, x) = $ **error**.

Let us parse the input string *aabb* using $\mathcal{G}$. The parsing algorithm starts off in the initial configuration

$$(\$, aabb\$, e)$$

The first move is determined by $f(\$, aabb\$)$, which we see, from the specification of f, is **reduce**. To determine the reduction we consult $g(\$, aabb\$)$, which we find is 2. Thus the first move is the reduction

$$(\$, aabb\$, e) \vdash^{r} (\$S, aabb\$, 2)$$

The next move is determined by $f(\$S, aabb\$)$, which is **shift**. Thus the next move is

$$(\$S, aabb\$, 2) \vdash^{s} (\$Sa, abb\$, 2)$$

Continuing in this fashion, the shift–reduce parsing algorithm $\mathcal{A}$ would make the following sequence of moves:

$$
\begin{aligned}
(\$, aabb\$, e) &\vdash^{r} (\$S, aabb\$, 2) \\
&\vdash^{s} (\$Sa, abb\$, 2) \\
&\vdash^{r} (\$SaS, abb\$, 22) \\
&\vdash^{s} (\$SaSa, bb\$, 22) \\
&\vdash^{r} (\$SaSaS, bb\$, 222) \\
&\vdash^{s} (\$SaSaSb, b\$, 222) \\
&\vdash^{r} (\$SaS, b\$, 2221) \\
&\vdash^{s} (\$SaSb, \$, 2221) \\
&\vdash^{r} (\$S, \$, 22211) \\
&\vdash^{s} \textbf{accept}
\end{aligned}
$$

Thus, $\mathcal{A}(aabb) = 22211$. Clearly, 22211 is the right parse of *aabb*. □

In practice, we do not want to look at the entire string in the pushdown list and all of the remaining input string to determine what the next move of a parsing algorithm should be. Usually, we want the shift–reduce function to depend only on the top few symbols on the pushdown list and the next few input symbols. Likewise, we would like the reduce function to depend on only one or two symbols below the left end of the handle and on only one or two of the next input symbols.

In the previous example, in fact, we notice that f depends only on the symbol on top of the pushdown list and the next input symbol. The reduce function g depends only on one symbol below the handle and the next input symbol.

The LR(k) parser that we constructed in the previous section can be viewed as a "shift–reduce parsing algorithm" in which the pushdown alphabet is augmented with LR(k) tables. Treating the LR(k) parser as a shift–reduce parsing algorithm, the shift–reduce function depends only on the symbol on top of the pushdown list [the current LR(k) table] and the next k input symbols. The reduce function depends on the table immediately below the handle on the pushdown list and on zero input symbols. However, in our present formalism, we may have to look at the entire contents of the stack in order to determine what the top table is. The algorithms to be discussed subsequently in this chapter will need only information near the top of the stack. We therefore adopt the following convention.

CONVENTION

If f and g are functions of a shift–reduce parsing algorithm and $f(\alpha, w)$ is defined, then we assume that $f(\beta\alpha, wx) = f(\alpha, w)$ for all β and x, unless otherwise stated. The analogous statement applies to g.

5.3.2. Simple Precedence Grammars

The simplest class of shift–reduce algorithms are based on "precedence relations." In a precedence grammar the boundaries of the handle of a right-sentential form can be located by consulting certain (precedence) relations that hold among symbols appearing in right-sentential forms.

Precedence-oriented parsing techniques were among the first techniques to be used in the construction of parsers for programming languages and a number of variants of precedence grammars have appeared in the literature. We shall discuss left-to-right deterministic precedence parsing in which a right parse is to be produced. In this discussion we shall introduce the following types of precedence grammars:

(1) Simple precedence.
(2) Extended precedence.
(3) Weak precedence.
(4) Mixed strategy precedence.
(5) Operator precedence.

The key to precedence parsing is the definition of a precedence relation $\gtrdot$ between grammar symbols such that scanning from left to right a right-sentential form $\alpha\beta w$, of which β is the handle, the precedence relation $\gtrdot$ is first found to hold between the last symbol of β and the first symbol of w.

If we use a shift–reduce parsing algorithm, then the decision to reduce will occur whenever the precedence relation $\gtrdot$ holds between what is on top of the pushdown list and the first remaining input symbol. If the relation $\gtrdot$ does not hold, then a shift may be called for.

Thus the relation $\gtrdot$ is used to locate the right end of a handle in a right-sentential form. Location of the left end of the handle and determination of the exact reduction to be made is done in one of several ways, depending on the type of precedence being used.

The so-called "simple precedence" parsing technique uses three prece-dence relations $\lessdot$, $\doteq$, and $\gtrdot$ to isolate the handle in a right-sentential form $\alpha\beta w$. If β is the handle, then the relation $\lessdot$ or $\doteq$ is to hold between all pairs of symbols in α, $\lessdot$ is to hold between the last symbol of α and the first symbol of β, $\doteq$ is to hold between all pairs of symbols in the handle itself, and the relation $\gtrdot$ is to hold between the last symbol of β and the first symbol of w.

Thus the handle of a right-sentential form of a simple precedence grammar can be located by scanning the sentential form from left to right until the precedence relation $\gtrdot$ is first encountered. The left end of the handle is located by scanning backward until the precedence relation $\lessdot$ holds. The handle is the string between $\lessdot$ and $\gtrdot$. If we assume that the grammar is uniquely invertible, then the handle can be uniquely reduced. This process can be repeated until the input string is either reduced to the sentence symbol or no further reductions are possible.

DEFINITION

The *Wirth–Weber precedence relations* $\lessdot$, $\doteq$, and $\gtrdot$ for a CFG $G = (N, \Sigma, P, S)$ are defined on $N \cup \Sigma$ as follows:

(1) We say that $X \lessdot Y$ if there exists $A \longrightarrow \alpha X B \beta$ in P such that $B \overset{+}{\Rightarrow} Y\gamma$.

(2) We say that $X \doteq Y$ if there exists $A \longrightarrow \alpha X Y \beta$ in P.

(3) $\gtrdot$ is defined on $(N \cup \Sigma) \times \Sigma$, since the symbol immediately to the right of a handle in a right-sentential form is always a terminal. We say that $X \gtrdot a$ if $A \longrightarrow \alpha B Y \beta$ is in P, $B \overset{+}{\Rightarrow} \gamma X$, and $Y \overset{*}{\Rightarrow} a\delta$. Notice that Y will be a in the case $Y \overset{0}{\Rightarrow} a\delta$.

In precedence parsing procedures we shall find it convenient to add a left and right endmarker to the input string. We shall use $ as this endmarker and we assume that $ \lessdot X$ for all X such that $S \overset{+}{\Rightarrow} X\alpha$ and $Y \gtrdot $ for all Y such that $S \overset{+}{\Rightarrow} \alpha Y$.

The calculation of Wirth–Weber precedence relations is not hard. We leave it to the reader to devise an algorithm, or he may use the algorithm to calculate extended precedence relations given in Section 5.3.3.

DEFINITION

A CFG $G = (N, \Sigma, P, S)$ which is proper,† which has no e-productions, and in which at most one Wirth–Weber precedence relation exists between any pair of symbols in $N \cup \Sigma$ is called a *precedence grammar*. A precedence grammar which is uniquely invertible is called a *simple precedence grammar*.

By our usual convention, we define the language generated by a (simple) precedence grammar to be a (*simple*) *precedence language*.

Example 5.34

Let G have the productions

$$S \longrightarrow aSSb \mid c$$

---

†Recall that a CFG G is proper if there is no derivation of the form $A \overset{+}{\Rightarrow} A$, if G has no useless symbols, and if there are no e-productions except possibly $S \longrightarrow e$ in which case S does not appear on the right side of any production.

The precedence relations for G, together with the added precedence relations involving the endmarkers, are shown in the precedence matrix of Fig. 5.11. Each entry gives the precedence relations that hold between the symbol labeling the row and the symbol labeling the column. Blank entries are interpreted as **error**.

	S	a	b	c	$\$$
S	$\doteq$	$\lessdot$	$\doteq$	$\lessdot$	
a	$\doteq$	$\lessdot$		$\lessdot$	
b		$\gtrdot$	$\gtrdot$	$\gtrdot$	$\gtrdot$
c		$\gtrdot$	$\gtrdot$	$\gtrdot$	$\gtrdot$
$\$$		$\lessdot$		$\lessdot$	

Fig. 5.11 Precedence relations.

The following technique is a systematic approach to the construction of the precedence relations. First, $\doteq$ is easy to compute. We scan the right sides of the productions and find that $a \doteq S$, $S \doteq S$, and $S \doteq b$.

To compute $\lessdot$, we scan the right sides of the productions for adjacent pairs XC. Then X is related by $\lessdot$ to any leftmost symbol of a string derived nontrivially from C. (We leave it to the reader to give an algorithm to find all such symbols.) In our example, we consider the pairs aS and SS. In each case, C can be identified with S, and S derives strings beginning with a and c. Thus, $X \lessdot Y$, where X is any of a or S and Y is any of a or c.

To compute $\gtrdot$, we again consider adjacent pairs in the right sides, this time of the form CX. We find those symbols Y that can appear at the end of a string derived in one or more steps from C and those terminals d at the beginning of a string derived in zero or more steps from X. If X is itself a terminal, then $X = d$ is the only possibility. Here, SS and Sb are substrings of this form. Y is b or c, and d is a or c in the first case and b in the second.

It should be emphasized that $\doteq$, $\lessdot$, and $\gtrdot$ do not have the properties normally ascribed to $=$, $<$, and $>$ on the reals, integers, etc. For example, $\doteq$ is not usually an equivalence relation; $\lessdot$ and $\gtrdot$ are not normally transitive, and they may be symmetric or reflexive.

Since there is at most one precedence relation in each entry of Fig. 5.11, G is a precedence grammar. Moreover, all productions in G have unique right sides, so that G is a simple precedence grammar, and $L(G)$ is a simple precedence language.

Let us consider $\$accb\$$, a right-sentential form of G delimited by endmarkers. We have $\$ \lessdot a$, $a \lessdot c$, and $c \gtrdot c$. The handle of $accb$ is the first c, so the precedence relations have isolated this handle. $\square$

We can often represent the relevant information in an $n \times n$ precedence matrix by two vectors of dimension n. We shall discuss such representations of precedence matrices in Section 7.1.

The following theorem shows that the precedence relation $\lessdot$ occurs at the beginning of a handle in a right-sentential form, $\doteq$ holds between adjacent symbols of a handle, and $\gtrdot$ holds at the right end of a handle. This is true for all grammars with no e-productions, but it is only in a precedence grammar that there is at most one precedence relation between any pair of symbols in a viable prefix of a right-sentential form.

First we shall show a consequence of a precedence relation holding between two symbols.

LEMMA 5.3

Let $G = (N, \Sigma, P, S)$ be a proper CFG with no e-productions.

(1) If $X \lessdot A$ or $X \doteq A$ and $A \rightarrow Y\alpha$ is in P, then $X \lessdot Y$.
(2) If $A \lessdot a$, $A \doteq a$, or $A \gtrdot a$ and $A \rightarrow \alpha Y$ is a production, then $Y \gtrdot a$.

Proof. We leave (1) for the Exercises and prove (2). If $A \lessdot a$, then there is a right side $\beta_1 AB\beta_2$ such that $B \overset{+}{\Rightarrow} a\gamma$ for some γ. Since $A \overset{+}{\Rightarrow} \alpha Y$, $Y \gtrdot a$ is immediate. If $A \doteq a$, there is a right side $\beta_1 Aa\beta_2$. As we have $a \overset{*}{\Rightarrow} a$ and $A \overset{+}{\Rightarrow} \alpha Y$, it follows that $Y \gtrdot a$ again. If $A \gtrdot a$, then there is a right side $\beta_1 BX\beta_2$, where $B \overset{+}{\Rightarrow} \gamma A$ and $X \overset{*}{\Rightarrow} a\delta$ for some γ and δ. Since $B \overset{+}{\Rightarrow} \gamma\alpha Y$, we again have the desired conclusion. $\square$

THEOREM 5.14

Let $G = (N, \Sigma, P, S)$ be a proper CFG with no e-productions. If

$$\$S\$ \overset{n}{\underset{\text{rm}}{\Longrightarrow}} X_p X_{p-1} \cdots X_{k+1} A a_1 \cdots a_q$$

$$\underset{\text{rm}}{\Longrightarrow} X_p X_{p-1} \cdots X_{k+1} X_k \cdots X_1 a_1 \cdots a_q$$

then

(1) For $p < i < k$, either $X_{i+1} \lessdot X_i$ or $X_{i+1} \doteq X_i$;
(2) $X_{k+1} \lessdot X_k$;
(3) For $k > i \geq 1$, $X_{i+1} \doteq X_i$; and
(4) $X_1 \gtrdot a_1$.

Proof. The proof will proceed by induction on n. For $n = 0$, we have $\$S\$ \underset{\text{rm}}{\Longrightarrow} \$X_k \cdots X_1\$$. From the definition of the precedence relations we have $\$ \lessdot X_k$, $X_{i+1} \doteq X_i$ for $k > i \geq 1$ and $X_1 \gtrdot \$$. Note that $X_k \cdots X_1$ cannot be the empty string, since G is assumed to be free of e-productions.

For the inductive step suppose that the statement of the theorem is true for n. Now consider a derivation:

$$\$S\$ \underset{\text{rm}}{\overset{n}{\Longrightarrow}} X_p \cdots X_{k+1}Aa_1 \cdots a_q$$

$$\underset{\text{rm}}{\Longrightarrow} X_p \cdots X_{k+1}X_k \cdots X_1a_1 \cdots a_q$$

$$\underset{\text{rm}}{\Longrightarrow} X_p \cdots X_{j+1}Y_r \cdots Y_1X_{j-1} \cdots X_1a_1 \cdots a_q$$

That is, X_j is replaced by $Y_r \cdots Y_1$ at the last step. Thus, $X_{j-1}, \ldots, X_1$ are terminals; the case $j = 1$ is not ruled out.

By the inductive hypothesis, $X_{j+1} \lessdot X_j$ or $X_{j+1} \doteq X_j$. Thus, $X_{j+1} \lessdot Y_r$ by Lemma 5.3(1). Also, X_j is related by one of the three relations to the symbol on its right (which may be a_1). Thus, $Y_1 \gtrdot X_{j-1}$, or $Y_1 \gtrdot a_1$ if $j = 1$. We have $Y_r \doteq Y_{r-1} \doteq \cdots \doteq Y_1$, since $Y_r \cdots Y_1$ is a right side. Finally, $X_{i+1} \lessdot X_i$ or $X_{i+1} \doteq X_i$ follows by the inductive hypothesis, for $p < i < j$. Thus the induction is complete. $\square$

COROLLARY 1

If G is a precedence grammar, then conclusion (1) of Theorem 5.14 can be strengthened by adding "exactly one of $\lessdot$ and $\doteq$." Conclusions (1)–(4) can be strengthened by appending "and no other relations hold."

Proof. Immediate from the definition of a precedence grammar. $\square$

COROLLARY 2

Every simple precedence grammar is unambiguous.

Proof. All we need to do is observe that for any right-sentential form β, other than S, the previous right-sentential form α such that $\alpha \underset{\text{rm}}{\Longrightarrow} \beta$ is unique. From Corollary 1 we know that the handle of β can be uniquely determined by scanning β surrounded by endmarkers from left to right until the first $\gtrdot$ relation is found, and then scanning back until a $\lessdot$ relation is encountered. The handle lies between these points. Because a simple precedence grammar is uniquely invertible, the nonterminal to which the handle is to be reduced is unique. Thus, α can be uniquely found from β. $\square$

We note that since we are dealing only with proper grammars, the fact that this and subsequent parsing algorithms operate in linear time is not difficult to prove. The proofs are left for the Exercises.

We shall now describe how a deterministic right parser can be constructed for a simple precedence grammar.

Algorithm 5.12

Shift–reduce parsing algorithm for a simple precedence grammar.

Input. A simple precedence grammar $G = (N, \Sigma, P, S)$ in which the productions in P are numbered from 1 to p.

Output. $\mathcal{C} = (f, g)$, a shift–reduce parsing algorithm.

Method.

(1) The shift–reduce parsing algorithm will employ $ as a bottom marker for the pushdown list and a right endmarker for the input.

(2) The shift–reduce function f will be independent of the contents of the pushdown list except for the topmost symbol and independent of the remaining input except for the leftmost input symbol. Thus we shall define f only on $(N \cup \Sigma \cup \{\$\}) \times (\Sigma \cup \{\$\})$, except in one case (rule c).

 (a) $f(X, a) = $ **shift** if $X \lessdot a$ or $X \doteq a$.
 (b) $f(X, a) = $ **reduce** if $X \gtrdot a$.
 (c) $f(\$S, \$) = $ **accept.**†
 (d) $f(X, a) = $ **error** otherwise.

(These rules can be implemented by consulting the precedence matrix itself.)

(3) The reduce function g depends only on the string on top of the push-down list up to one symbol below the handle. The remaining input does not affect g. Thus we define g only on $(N \cup \Sigma \cup \{\$\})^*$ as follows:

 (a) $g(X_{k+1}X_kX_{k-1} \cdots X_1, e) = i$ if $X_{k+1} \lessdot X_k$, $X_{j+1} \doteq X_j$ for $k > j \geq 1$, and production i is $A \rightarrow X_kX_{k-1} \cdots X_1$. (Note that the reduce function g is only invoked when $X_1 \gtrdot a$, where a is the current input symbol.)
 (b) $g(\alpha, e) = $ **error**, otherwise. □

Example 5.35

Let us construct a shift–reduce parsing algorithm $\mathcal{C} = (f, g)$ for the grammar G with productions

(1) $S \longrightarrow aSSb$

(2) $S \longrightarrow c$

The precedence relations for G are given in Fig. 5.11 on p. 405. We can use the precedence matrix itself for the shift–reduce function f. The reduce function g is as follows:

(1) $g(XaSSb) = 1$ if $X \in \{S, a, \$\}$.
(2) $g(Xc) = 2$ if $X \in \{S, a, \$\}$.
(3) $g(\alpha) = $ **error**, otherwise.

†Note that this rule may take priority over rules (2a) and (2b) when $X = S$ and $a = \$$.

With input *accb*, α would make the following sequence of moves:

$$(\$, accb\$, e) \vdash^{s} (\$a, ccb\$, e)$$
$$\vdash^{s} (\$ac, cb\$, e)$$
$$\vdash^{r} (\$aS, cb\$, 2)$$
$$\vdash^{s} (\$aSc, b\$, 2)$$
$$\vdash^{r} (\$aSS, b\$, 22)$$
$$\vdash^{s} (\$aSSb, \$, 22)$$
$$\vdash^{r} (\$S, \$, 221)$$

In configuration $(\$ac, cb\$, e)$, for example, we have $f(c, b) = $ **reduce** and $g(ac, e) = 2$. Thus

$$(\$ac, cb\$, e) \vdash (\$aS, cb\$, 2)$$

Let us examine the behavior of α on *acb*, an input not in $L(G)$. With *acb* as input α would make the following moves:

$$(\$, acb\$, e) \vdash^{s} (\$a, cb\$, e)$$
$$\vdash^{s} (\$ac, b\$, e)$$
$$\vdash^{r} (\$aS, b\$, 2)$$
$$\vdash^{s} (\$aSb, \$, 2)$$
$$\vdash \textbf{error}$$

In configuration $(\$aSb, \$, 2)$, $f(b, \$) = $ **reduce**. Since $\$ \lessdot a$ and $a \doteq S \doteq b$, we can make a reduction only if aSb is the right side of some production. However, no such production exists, so $g(aSb, e) = $ **error**.

In practice we might keep a list of "error productions." Whenever an error is encountered by the g function, we could then consult the list of error productions to see if a reduction by an error production can be made. Other precedence-oriented error recovery techniques are discussed in the bibliographical notes at the end of this section. $\square$

THEOREM 5.15

Algorithm 5.12 constructs a valid shift–reduce parsing algorithm for a simple precedence grammar.

Proof. The proof is a straightforward consequence of Theorem 5.14, the unique invertibility property, and the construction in Algorithm 5.12. The details are left for the Exercises. $\square$

It is interesting to consider the classes of languages which can be generated by precedence grammars and simple precedence grammars. We discover that every CFL without e has a precedence grammar but that not every CFL without e has a simple precedence grammar. Moreover, for every CFL without e we can find an e-free uniquely invertible CFG. Thus, insisting that grammars be both precedence and uniquely invertible diminishes their language-generating capability. Every simple precedence grammar is an LR(1) grammar, but the LR(1) language $\{a0^i1^i \,|\, i \geq 1\} \cup \{b0^i1^{2i} \,|\, i \geq 1\}$ has no simple precedence grammar, as we shall see in Section 8.3.

5.3.3. Extended Precedence Grammars

It is possible to extend the definition of the Wirth–Weber precedence relations to pairs of strings rather than pairs of symbols. We shall give a definition of extended precedence relations that relate strings of m symbols to strings of n symbols. Our definition is designed with shift–reduce parsing in mind.

Understanding the motivation of extended precedence requires that we recall the two roles of precedence relations in a shift–reduce parsing algorithm:

(1) Let αX be the m symbols on top of the pushdown list (with X on top) and aw the next n input symbols. If $\alpha X \lessdot aw$ or $\alpha X \doteq aw$, then a is to be shifted on top of the pushdown list. If $\alpha X \gtrdot aw$, then a reduction is to be made.

(2) Suppose that $X_p \cdots X_2 X_1$ is the string on the pushdown list and that $a_1 \cdots a_q$ is the remaining input string when a reduction is called for (i.e., $X_m \cdots X_1 \gtrdot a_1 \cdots a_n$). If the handle is $X_k \cdots X_1$, we then want

$$X_{m+j}X_{m+j-1} \cdots X_{j+1} \doteq X_j X_{j-1} \cdots X_1 a_1 \cdots a_{n-j}$$

for $k > j \geq 1$ and

$$X_{m+k} \cdots X_{k+1} \lessdot X_k \cdots X_1 a_1 \cdots a_{n-k}.\dagger$$

Thus parsing according to a uniquely invertible extended precedence grammar is similar to parsing according to a simple Wirth–Weber precedence grammar, except that the precedence relation between a pair of symbols X and Y is determined by αX and $Y\beta$, where α is the $m - 1$ symbols to the left of X and β is the $n - 1$ symbols to the right of Y.

We keep shifting symbols onto the pushdown list until a $\gtrdot$ relation is encountered between the string on top of the pushdown list and the remaining input. We then scan back into the pushdown list over $\doteq$ relations until

---

$\dagger$We assume that $X_r X_{r-1} \cdots X_1 a_1 \cdots a_{n-r}$ is $X_r X_{r-1} \cdots X_{r-n+1}$ if $r \geq n$.

the first $\lessdot$ relation is encountered. The handle lies between the $\lessdot$ and $\gtrdot$ relations.

This discussion motivates the following definition.

DEFINITION

Let $G = (N, \Sigma, P, S)$ be a proper CFG with no e-production. We define the (m, n) precedence relations $\lessdot$, $\doteq$, and $\gtrdot$ on $(N \cup \Sigma \cup \{\$\})^m \times (N \cup \Sigma \cup \{\$\})^n$ as follows: Let

$$\$^m S\$^n \underset{\text{rm}}{\overset{*}{\Longrightarrow}} X_p X_{p-1} \cdots X_{k+1} A a_1 \cdots a_q$$

$$\underset{\text{rm}}{\Longrightarrow} X_p X_{p-1} \cdots X_{k+1} X_k \cdots X_1 a_1 \cdots a_q$$

be any rightmost derivation. Then,

(1) $\alpha \lessdot \beta$ if α consists of the last m symbols of $X_p X_{p-1} \cdots X_{k+1}$, and either

    (a) β consists of the first n symbols of $X_k \cdots X_1 a_1 \cdots a_q$, or

    (b) X_k is a terminal and β is in $\text{FIRST}_n(X_k \cdots X_1 a_1 \cdots a_q)$.

(2) $\alpha \doteq \beta$ for all $j, k > j \geq 1$, such that α consists of the last m symbols of $X_p X_{p-1} \cdots X_{j+1}$, and either

    (a) β consists of the first n symbols of $X_j X_{j-1} \cdots X_1 a_1 \cdots a_q$, or

    (b) X_j is a terminal and β is in $\text{FIRST}_n(X_j X_{j-1} \cdots X_1 a_1 \cdots a_q)$.

(3) $X_m X_{m-1} \cdots X_1 \gtrdot a_1 \cdots a_n$.

We say that G is an (m, n) *precedence grammar* if G is a proper CFG with no e-production and the relations $\lessdot$, $\doteq$, and $\gtrdot$ are pairwise disjoint. It should be clear from Lemma 5.3 that G is a precedence grammar if and only if G is a $(1, 1)$ precedence grammar. The details concerning endmarkers are easy to handle. Whenever $n = 1$, conditions (1b) and (2b) yield nothing new.

We also comment that the disjointness of the portions of $\lessdot$ and $\doteq$ arising solely from definitions (1b) and (2b) do not really affect our ability to find a shift-reduce parsing algorithm for extended precedence grammars. We could have given a more complicated but less restrictive definition, and leave the development of such a class of grammars for the Exercises.

We shall give an algorithm to compute the extended precedence relations. It is clearly applicable to Wirth–Weber precedence relations also.

ALGORITHM 5.13

Construction of (m, n) precedence relations.

Input. A proper CFG $G = (N, \Sigma, P, S)$ with no e-production.

Output. The (m, n) precedence relations $\lessdot$, $\doteq$, and $\gtrdot$ for G.

Method. We begin by constructing the set $\mathcal{S}$ of all substrings of length $m + n$ that can appear in a string $\alpha \beta u$ such that $\$^m S\$^n \underset{\text{rm}}{\overset{*}{\Longrightarrow}} \alpha A w \underset{\text{rm}}{\Longrightarrow} \alpha \beta w$ and

$u = \text{FIRST}_n(w)$. The following steps do the job:

(1) Let $S = \{\$^m S\$^{n-1}, \$^{m-1} S\$^n\}$. The two strings in S have not been "considered."

(2) If δ is an unconsidered string in S, "consider" it by performing the following two operations.

(a) If δ is not of the form $\alpha A x$, where $|x| \leq n$, do nothing.

(b) If $\delta = \alpha A x$, $|x| \leq n$, and $A \in N$, add to S, if not already there, those strings γ such that there exists $A \rightarrow \beta$ in P and γ is a substring of length $m + n$ of $\alpha \beta x$. Note that since G is proper, we have $|\alpha \beta x| \geq m + n$. New strings added to S are not yet considered.

(3) Repeat step (2) until no string in S remains unconsidered.

From set S, we construct the relations $\lessdot$, $\doteq$, and $\gtrdot$, as follows:

(4) For each string $\alpha A w$ in S such that $|\alpha| = m$ and for each $A \rightarrow \beta$ in P, let $\alpha \lessdot \delta$, where δ is the first n symbols of βw or β begins with a terminal and δ is in $\text{FIRST}_n(\beta w)$.

(5) For each string αA in S such that $|\alpha| = m$ and for each production $A \rightarrow \beta_1 X Y \beta_2$ in P, let $\delta_1 \doteq \delta_2$, where δ_1 is the last m symbols of $\alpha \beta_1 X$ and δ_2 is the first n symbols of $Y \beta_2 \gamma$, or Y is a terminal and $\delta_2 = Y w$ for some w in $\text{FIRST}_{n-1}(\beta_2 \gamma)$.

(6) For each string $\alpha A w$ in S such that $|w| = n$ and for each $A \rightarrow \beta$ in P, let $\delta \gtrdot w$, where δ is the last m symbols of $\alpha \beta$. $\square$

Example 5.36

Consider the grammar G having the productions

$$S \longrightarrow 0S11 \mid 011$$

The $(1, 1)$ precedence relations for G are shown in Fig. 5.12. Since $1 \doteq 1$ and $1 \gtrdot 1$, G is not a $(1, 1)$ precedence grammar.

Let us use Algorithm 5.13 to compute the $(2, 1)$ precedence relations for G. We start by computing S. Initially, $S = \{\$S\$, \$\$S\}$. We consider $\$S\$$ by adding $\$0S, 0S1, S11, 11\$$, (these are all the substrings of $\$0S11\$$ of length 3),

	S	0	1	$
S			$\doteq$	
0	$\doteq$	$\lessdot$	$\doteq$	
1			$\doteq, \gtrdot$	$\gtrdot$
$		$\lessdot$		

Fig. 5.12   (1, 1) precedence relations.

and \$01 and 011 (substrings of \$011\$ of length 3). Consideration of \$\$$S$ adds \$\$0. Consideration of \$0S adds \$00, 00S, and 001. Consideration of 0S1 adds 111, and consideration of 00S adds 000. These are all the members of $\mathcal{S}$.

To construct $\lessdot$, we consider those strings in $\mathcal{S}$ with S at the right. We obtain \$\$ $\lessdot$ 0, \$0 $\lessdot$ 0, and 00 $\lessdot$ 0. To construct $\doteq$, we again consider the strings in $\mathcal{S}$ with S at the right and find \$0 $\doteq$ S, 0S $\doteq$ 1, S1 $\doteq$ 1, \$0 $\doteq$ 1, 01 $\doteq$ 1, 00 $\doteq$ S, and 00 $\doteq$ 1.

To construct $\gtrdot$, we consider strings in $\mathcal{S}$ with S in the middle. We find 11 $\gtrdot$ \$ from \$$S$\$ and 11 $\gtrdot$ 1 from 0S1.

The (2,1) precedence relations for G are shown in Fig. 5.13. Strings of length 2 which are not in the domain of $\doteq$, $\lessdot$, or $\gtrdot$ do not appear.

	S	0	1	\$
\$\$		$\lessdot$		
\$0	$\doteq$	$\lessdot$	$\doteq$	
0S			$\doteq$	
00	$\doteq$	$\lessdot$	$\doteq$	
01			$\doteq$	
S1			$\doteq$	
11			$\gtrdot$	$\gtrdot$

Fig. 5.13 (2, 1) precedence relations.

Since there are no (2, 1) precedence conflicts, G is a (2, 1) precedence grammar. $\square$

THEOREM 5.16

Algorithm 5.13 correctly computes $\lessdot$, $\doteq$, and $\gtrdot$.

Proof. We first show that $\mathcal{S}$ is defined correctly. That is, $\gamma \in \mathcal{S}$ if and only if $|\gamma| = m + n$ and γ is a substring of $\alpha\beta u$, where $\$^m S \$^n \underset{rm}{\overset{*}{\Rightarrow}} \alpha A w \underset{rm}{\Rightarrow} \alpha\beta w$ and $u = \text{FIRST}_n(w)$.

Only if: The proof is by induction on the order in which strings are added to $\mathcal{S}$. The basis, the first two members of $\mathcal{S}$, is immediate. For the induction, suppose that γ is added to $\mathcal{S}$, because $\alpha A x$ is in $\mathcal{S}$ and $A \rightarrow \beta$ is in P; that is, γ is a substring of $\alpha\beta x$. Since $\alpha A x$ is in $\mathcal{S}$, from the inductive hypothesis we have the derivation $\$^m S\$^n \overset{*}{\underset{rm}{\Rightarrow}} \alpha' A' w \underset{rm}{\Rightarrow} \alpha' \beta' uv$, where $u = \text{FIRST}_n(w)$ and $\alpha' \beta' u$ can be written as $\delta_1 \alpha A x \delta_2$ for some δ_1 and δ_2 in $(\text{N} \cup \Sigma \cup \{\$\})^*$. Since G is proper, there is some $y \in (\Sigma \cup \{\$\})^*$ such that $\delta_2 \overset{*}{\underset{rm}{\Rightarrow}} y$. Thus, $\$^m S\$^n \overset{*}{\underset{rm}{\Rightarrow}} \delta_1 \alpha A x y v \underset{rm}{\Rightarrow} \delta_1 \alpha \beta x y v$. Since γ is a substring of $\alpha \beta x$ of length $m + n$, it is certainly a substring of $\alpha \beta z$, where $z = \text{FIRST}_n(xyv)$.

If: An induction on k shows that if $\$^m S\$^n \overset{k}{\underset{rm}{\Rightarrow}} \alpha A w \underset{rm}{\Rightarrow} \alpha \beta w$, then every substring of $\alpha \beta u$ of length $m + n$ is in $\mathcal{S}$, where $u = \text{FIRST}_n(w)$.

That steps (4)–(6) correctly compute $\lessdot$, $\doteq$, and $\gtrdot$ is a straightforward consequence of the definitions of these relations. $\square$

We may show the following theorem, which is the basis of the shift–reduce parser for uniquely invertible (m, n) precedence grammars analogous to that of Algorithm 5.12.

THEOREM 5.17

Let $G = (\text{N}, \Sigma, P, S)$ be an arbitrary proper CFG and let m and n be integers. Let

(5.3.1) $$\$^m S\$^n \overset{*}{\underset{rm}{\Rightarrow}} X_p X_{p-1} \cdots X_{k+1} A a_1 \cdots a_q$$

$$\underset{rm}{\Rightarrow} X_p X_{p-1} \cdots X_{k+1} X_k \cdots X_1 a_1 \cdots a_q$$

(1) For j such that $p - m \geq j > k$, let α be the last m symbols of $X_p X_{p-1} \cdots X_{j+1}$ and let β be the first n symbols of $X_j X_{j-1} \cdots X_1 a_1 \cdots a_q$. If $\beta \in (\Sigma \cup \{\$\})^*$, then either $\alpha \lessdot \beta$ or $\alpha \doteq \beta$.

(2) $X_{m+k} X_{m+k-1} \cdots X_{k+1} \lessdot \beta$, where β consists of the first n symbols of $X_k \cdots X_1 a_1 \cdots a_q$.

(3) For $k > j \geq 1$ let α be the last m symbols in $X_p X_{p-1} \cdots X_{j+1}$ and let β be the first n symbols of $X_j X_{j-1} \cdots X_1 a_1 \cdots a_p$. Then $\alpha \doteq \beta$.

(4) $X_m X_{m-1} \cdots X_1 \gtrdot a_1 \cdots a_n$.

Proof. All but statement (1) are immediate consequences of the definitions. To prove (1), we observe that since $j > k$, β does not consist entirely of $\$$'s. Thus the derivation (5.3.1) can be written as

(5.3.2) $$\$^m S\$^n \overset{i}{\underset{rm}{\Rightarrow}} \gamma B w$$

$$\underset{rm}{\Rightarrow} \gamma \delta_1 \delta_2 w$$

$$\overset{*}{\underset{rm}{\Rightarrow}} X_p X_{p-1} \cdots X_{k+1} A a_1 \cdots a_q$$

$$\underset{rm}{\Rightarrow} X_p X_{p-1} \cdots X_{k+1} X_k \cdots X_1 a_1 \cdots a_q$$

where i is as large as possible such that $B \longrightarrow \delta_1 \delta_2$ is a production in which $\delta_2 \neq e$, B derives both X_{j+1} and X_j, and $\gamma \delta_1 = X_p X_{p-1} \cdots X_{j+1}$.

If the first symbol of δ_2 is a terminal, say $\delta_2 = a\delta_3$, then by rule 2(b) in the definition of $\doteq$, we have $X_{j+m} X_{j+m-1} \cdots X_{j+1} \doteq \beta$, where $\beta = ax$ and x is in $\mathrm{FIRST}_{n-1}(\delta_3 w)$.

If the first symbol of δ_2 is a nonterminal, let $\delta_2 = C\delta_3$. Since X_j is a terminal, by hypothesis, C must be subsequently rewritten after several steps of derivation (5.3.2) as $D\epsilon$, for some D in N and ϵ in $(N \cup \Sigma)^*$. Then, D is replaced by $X_j\theta$ for some θ, and the desired relation follows from rule 2(b) of the definition of $\lessdot$. $\quad\square$

COROLLARY

If G of Theorem 5.17 is an (m, n) precedence grammar, then Theorem 5.17 can be strengthened by adding the condition that no other relation holds between the strings in question to each of (1)–(4) in the statement of the theorem. $\quad\square$

The shift–reduce parsing algorithm for uniquely invertible extended precedence grammars is exactly analogous to Algorithm 5.12 for simple precedence grammars, and we shall only outline it here. The first n unexpended input symbols can be kept on top of the pushdown list. If $X_m \cdots X_1$ appears top, $a_1 \cdots a_n$ is the first n input symbols and $X_m \cdots X_1 \doteq a_1 \cdots a_n$ or $X_m \cdots X_1 \lessdot a_1 \cdots a_n$, then we shift. If $X_m \cdots X_1 \gtrdot a_1 \cdots a_n$, we reduce. Part (1) of Theorem 5.17 assures us that one of the first two cases will occur whenever the handle lies to the right of X_1. By part (4) of Theorem 5.17, the right end of the handle has been reached if and only if the third case applies.

To reduce, we search backwards through $\doteq$ relations for a $\lessdot$ relation, exactly as in Algorithm 5.12. Parts (2) and (3) of Theorem 5.17 imply that the handle will be correctly isolated.

5.3.4. Weak Precedence Grammars

Many naturally occurring grammars are not simple precedence grammars, and in many cases rather awkward grammars result from an attempt to find a simple precedence grammar for the language at hand. We can obtain a larger class of grammars which can be parsed using precedence techniques by relaxing the restriction that the $\lessdot$ and $\doteq$ precedence relations be disjoint.

We still use the $\gtrdot$ relation to locate the right end of the handle. We can then use the right sides of the productions to locate the left end of the handle by finding a production whose right side matches the symbols immediately to the left of the right end of the handle. This is not much more expensive than simple precedence parsing. When parsing with a simple precedence grammar, once we had isolated the handle we still needed to determine which production was to be used in making the reduction, and thus had to examine these symbols anyway.

To make this scheme work, we must be able to determine which production to use in case the right side of one production is a suffix of the right side of another. For example, suppose that $\alpha\beta\gamma w$ is a right-sentential form in which the right end of the handle occurs between γ and w. If $A \rightarrow \gamma$ and $B \rightarrow \beta\gamma$ are two productions, then it is not apparent which production should be used to make the reduction.

We shall restrict ourselves to applying the longest applicable production. The weak precedence grammars are one class of grammars for which this rule is the correct one.

DEFINITION

Let $G = (N, \Sigma, P, S)$ be a proper CFG with no e-productions. We say that G is a *weak precedence grammar* if the following conditions hold:

(1) The relation $\gtrdot$ is disjoint from the union of $\lessdot$ and $\doteq$.

(2) If $A \rightarrow \alpha X\beta$ and $B \rightarrow \beta$ are in P with X in $N \cup \Sigma$, then neither of the relations $X \lessdot B$ and $X \doteq B$ are valid.

Example 5.37

The grammar G with the following productions is an example of a weak precedence grammar[†]:

$$E \longrightarrow E + T \,|\, + T \,|\, T$$
$$T \longrightarrow T * F \,|\, F$$
$$F \longrightarrow (E) \,|\, a$$

The precedence matrix for G is shown in Fig. 5.14.

Note that the only precedence conflicts are between $\lessdot$ and $\doteq$, so condition (1) of the definition of a weak precedence grammar is satisfied. To see that condition (2) is not violated, first consider the three productions $E \rightarrow E + T$, $E \rightarrow + T$, and $E \rightarrow T$.[‡] From the precedence table we see that no precedence relation holds between E and E or between $+$ and E (with $+$ on the left side of the relation, that is). Thus these three productions do not cause a violation of condition (2). The only other productions having one right side a suffix of the other are $T \rightarrow T * F$ and $T \rightarrow F$. Since there is no precedence relation between $*$ and T, condition (2) is again satisfied. Thus G is a weak precedence grammar.

[†] It should be obvious that G is related to our favorite grammar G_0. In fact, $L(G)$ is just $L(G_0)$ with superfluous unary $+$ signs, as in $+ a * (+ a + a)$, included. G_0 is another example of a uniquely invertible weak precedence grammar which is not a simple precedence grammar.

[‡] The fact that these three productions have the same left side is coincidental.

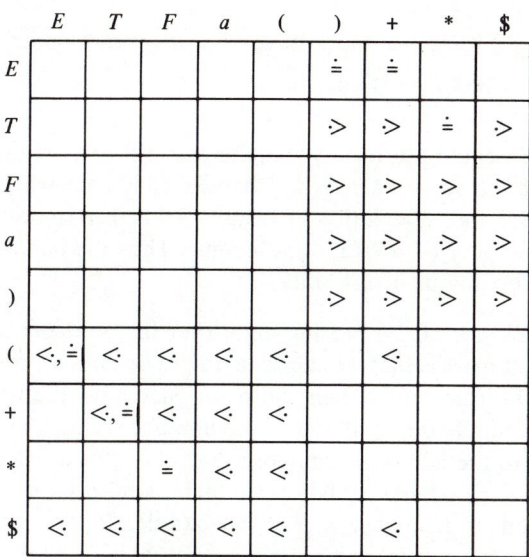

	E	T	F	a	(	)	+	*	$
E						≐	≐		
T						·>	·>	≐	·>
F						·>	·>	·>	·>
a						·>	·>	·>	·>
)						·>	·>	·>	·>
(	<·,≐	<·	<·	<·	<·		<·		
+		<·,≐	<·	<·	<·				
*			≐	<·	<·				
$	<·	<·	<·	<·	<·		<·		

Fig. 5.14   Precedence matrix.

Although G is not a simple precedence grammar, it does generate a simple precedence language. Later we shall see that this is always true. Every uniquely invertible weak precedence grammar generates a simple precedence language. □

Let us now verify that in a right-sentential form of a weak precedence grammar the handle is always the right side of the longest applicable production.

LEMMA 5.4

Let $G = (N, \Sigma, P, S)$ be a weak precedence grammar, and let P contain production $B \rightarrow \beta$. Suppose that $\$S\$ \underset{\text{rm}}{\overset{*}{\Rightarrow}} \gamma Cw \underset{\text{rm}}{\Rightarrow} \delta X \beta w$. If there exists a production $A \rightarrow \alpha X \beta$ for any α, then the last production applied was not $B \rightarrow \beta$.

Proof. Assume on the contrary that $C = B$ and $\gamma = \delta X$. Then $X \lessdot B$ or $X \doteq B$ by Theorem 5.14 applied to derivation $S \underset{\text{rm}}{\overset{*}{\Rightarrow}} \gamma Cw$. This follows because the handle of γCw ends somewhere to the right of C, and thus C is one of the X's of Theorem 5.14. But we then have an immediate violation of the weak precedence condition. □

LEMMA 5.5

Let G be as in Lemma 5.4, and suppose that G is uniquely invertible. If there is no production of the form $A \rightarrow \alpha X \beta$, then in the derivation

$\$S\$ \overset{*}{\underset{\text{rm}}{\Rightarrow}} \gamma Cw \underset{\text{rm}}{\Rightarrow} \delta X\beta w$, we must have $C = B$ and $\gamma = \delta X$ (i.e., the last production used was $B \rightarrow \beta$).

Proof. Obviously, C was replaced at the last step. The left end of the handle of $\delta X\beta w$ could not be anywhere to the left of X by the nonexistence of any production $A \rightarrow \alpha X\beta$. If the handle ends somewhere right of the first symbol of β, then a violation of Lemma 5.4 is seen to occur with $B \rightarrow \beta$ playing the role of $A \rightarrow \alpha X\beta$ in that lemma. Thus the handle is β, and the result follows by unique invertibility. $\quad\square$

Thus the essence of the parsing algorithm for uniquely invertible weak precedence grammars is that we can scan a right-sentential form (surrounded by endmarkers) from left to right until we encounter the first $>$ relation. This relation delimits the right end of the handle. We then examine symbols one at a time to the left of $>$. Suppose that $B \rightarrow \beta$ is a production and we see $X\beta$ to the left of the $>$ relation. If there is no production of the form $A \rightarrow \alpha X\beta$, then by Lemma 5.5, β is the handle. If there is a production $A \rightarrow \alpha X\beta$, then we can infer by Lemma 5.4 that $B \rightarrow \beta$ is not applicable. Thus the decision whether to reduce β can be made examining only one symbol to the left of β.

We can thus construct a shift–reduce parsing algorithm for each uniquely invertible weak precedence grammar.

ALGORITHM 5.14

Shift–reduce parsing algorithm for weak precedence grammars.

Input. A uniquely invertible weak precedence grammar $G = (N, \Sigma, P, S)$ in which the productions are numbered from 1 to p.

Output. $\mathcal{C} = (f, g)$, a shift–reduce parsing algorithm for G.

Method. The construction is similar to Algorithm 5.12. The shift–reduce function f is defined directly from the precedence relations:

(1) $f(X, a) = $ **shift** if $X \lessdot a$ or $X \doteq a$.
(2) $f(X, a) = $ **reduce** if $X > a$.
(3) $f(\$S, \$) = $ **accept**.
(3) $f(X, a) = $ **error** otherwise.

The reduce function g is defined to reduce using the longest applicable production:

(4) $g(X\beta) = i$ if $B \rightarrow \beta$ is the ith production in P and there is no production in P of the form $A \rightarrow \alpha X\beta$ for any A and α.
(5) $g(\alpha) = $ **error** otherwise. $\quad\square$

THEOREM 5.18

Algorithm 5.14 constructs a valid shift–reduce parsing algorithm for G.

Proof. The proof is a straightforward consequence of Lemmas 5.4 and 5.5, the definition of a uniquely invertible weak precedence grammar, and the construction of $\mathcal{C}$ itself.   □

There are several transformations which can be used to eliminate precedence conflicts from grammars. Here we shall present some useful transformations of this nature which can often be used to map a nonprecedence grammar into an equivalent (1, 1) precedence grammar or a weak precedence grammar.

Suppose that in a grammar we have a precedence conflict of the form $X \doteq Y$ and $X \gtrdot Y$. Since $X \doteq Y$ there exist one or more productions in which the substring XY appears on the right side. If in these productions we replace X by a new nonterminal A, we will eliminate the precedence relation $X \doteq Y$ and thus resolve this precedence conflict. We can then add the production $A \rightarrow X$ to the grammar to preserve equivalence. If X alone is not the right side of any other production, then unique invertibility will be preserved.

Example 5.38

Consider the grammar G having the productions

$$S \longrightarrow 0S11 \mid 011$$

We saw in Example 5.36 that G is not a simple precedence grammar because $1 \doteq 1$ and $1 \gtrdot 1$. However, if we substitute the new nonterminal A for the first 1 in each right side and add the production $A \rightarrow 1$, we obtain the simple precedence grammar G' with productions

$$S \longrightarrow 0SA1 \mid 0A1$$
$$A \longrightarrow 1$$

The precedence relations for G' are shown in Fig. 5.15.   □

	S	A	0	1	$\$$
S		$\doteq$		$\lessdot$	
A				$\doteq$	
0	$\doteq$	$\doteq$	$\lessdot$	$\lessdot$	
1				$\gtrdot$	$\gtrdot$
$\$$			$\lessdot$		

Fig. 5.15 Precedence relations for G'.

Similar transformations can be used to eliminate some precedence conflicts of the form $X \lessdot Y$, $X \gtrdot Y$ (and also of the form $X \lessdot Y$, $X \doteq Y$ if simple precedence is desired).

When these techniques destroy unique invertibility, it may be possible to resolve precedence conflicts by eliminating productions as in Lemma 2.14.

Example 5.39

Consider the grammar G with productions

$$E \longrightarrow E + T \mid T$$
$$T \longrightarrow T * F \mid F$$
$$F \longrightarrow a \mid (E) \mid a(L)$$
$$L \longrightarrow L, E \mid E$$

In this grammar L represents a list of expressions, and variables can be subscripted by an arbitrary sequence of expressions.

G is not a weak precedence grammar since $E \doteq)$ and $E \gtrdot)$. We could eliminate this precedence conflict by replacing E in $F \longrightarrow (E)$ by E' and adding the production $E' \longrightarrow E$. But then we would have two productions with E as the right side. However, if we instead eliminate the production $F \longrightarrow a(L)$ from G by substituting for L as in Lemma 2.14, we obtain the equivalent grammar G with the productions

$$E \longrightarrow E + T \mid T$$
$$T \longrightarrow T * F \mid F$$
$$F \longrightarrow a \mid (E) \mid a(L, E) \mid a(E)$$
$$L \longrightarrow L, E \mid E$$

Since L no longer appears to the left of), we do not have $E \gtrdot)$ in this grammar. We can easily verify that G' is a weak precedence grammar.   □

We can use a slight generalization of these techniques to show that every uniquely invertible weak precedence grammar can be transformed into a simple precedence grammar. Thus the uniquely invertible weak precedence grammars are no more powerful than the simple precedence grammars in their language-generating capability, although, as we saw in Example 5.37, there are uniquely invertible weak precedence grammars which are not simple precedence grammars.

THEOREM 5.19

A language is defined by a uniquely invertible weak precedence grammar if and only if it is a simple precedence language.

Proof.

If: Let $G = (N, \Sigma, P, S)$ be a simple precedence grammar. Then clearly, condition (1) of the definition of weak precedence grammar is satisfied. Suppose that condition (2) were not satisfied. That is, there exist $A \longrightarrow \alpha XY\beta$ and $B \longrightarrow Y\beta$ in P, and either $X \lessdot B$ or $X \doteq B$. Then $X \lessdot Y$, by Lemma 5.3. But $X \doteq Y$ because of the production $A \longrightarrow \alpha XY\beta$. This situation is impossible because G is a precedence grammar.

Only if: Let $G = (N, \Sigma, P, S)$ be a uniquely invertible weak precedence grammar. We construct a simple precedence grammar $G' = (N', \Sigma, P', S)$ such that $L(G') = L(G)$. The construction of G' is given as follows:

(1) Let N' be N plus new symbols of the form $[\alpha]$ for each $\alpha \neq e$ such that $A \longrightarrow \beta\alpha$ is in P for some A and β.

(2) Let P' consist of the following productions:
    (a) $[X] \longrightarrow X$ for each $[X]$ in N' such that X is in $N \cup \Sigma$.
    (b) $[X\alpha] \longrightarrow X[\alpha]$ for each $[X\alpha]$ in N', where X is in $N \cup \Sigma$ and $\alpha \neq e$.
    (c) $A \longrightarrow [\alpha]$ for each $A \longrightarrow \alpha$ in P.

We shall show that $\lessdot$, $\doteq$, and $\gtrdot$ for the grammar G' are mutually disjoint. No conflicts can involve the endmarker. Thus let X and Y be in $N' \cup \Sigma$. We observe that

(1) If $X \lessdot Y$, then X is in $N \cup \Sigma$;
(2) If $X \doteq Y$, then X is in $N \cup \Sigma$, and Y is in $N' - N$, since right sides of length greater than one only appear in rule (2b); and
(3) If $X \gtrdot Y$, then X is in $N' \cup \Sigma$ and Y is in Σ.

Part 1: $\doteq \cap \gtrdot = \varnothing$. If $X \doteq Y$, then Y is in $N' - N$. If $X \gtrdot Y$, then Y is in Σ. Clearly, $\doteq \cap \gtrdot = \varnothing$.

Part 2: $\lessdot \cap \gtrdot = \varnothing$. Suppose that $X \lessdot Y$ and $X \gtrdot Y$. Then X is in $N \cup \Sigma$ and Y is in Σ. Since $X \lessdot Y$ in G', there is a production of the form $[X\alpha_1] \longrightarrow X[\alpha_1]$ in P' such that $[\alpha_1] \underset{G'}{\overset{+}{\Rightarrow}} Y\alpha_2$ for some α_2 in $(N' \cup \Sigma)^*$. But $X\alpha_1$ must be the suffix of some production $A \longrightarrow \alpha_3 X\alpha_1$ in P. Now $\alpha_1 \underset{G}{\overset{*}{\Rightarrow}} Y\alpha_2'$ for some α_2' in $(N \cup \Sigma)^*$. Thus in G we have $X \doteq Y$ or $X \lessdot Y$.

Now consider $X \gtrdot Y$ in G'. There must be a production $[B\beta_1] \longrightarrow B[\beta_1]$ in P' such that $B \underset{G'}{\overset{+}{\Rightarrow}} \beta_2 X$ and $[\beta_1] \underset{G'}{\overset{+}{\Rightarrow}} Y\beta_3$ for some β_2 in $(N \cup \Sigma)^*$ and β_3 in $(N' \cup \Sigma)^*$. In G, $B\beta_1$ is the suffix of some production $C \longrightarrow \gamma B\beta_1$ in P. Moreover, $B \underset{G}{\overset{+}{\Rightarrow}} \beta_2 X$ and $\beta_1 \underset{G}{\overset{*}{\Rightarrow}} Y\beta_3'$ for some β_3' in $(N \cup \Sigma)^*$. Thus $X \gtrdot Y$ in G.

We have shown that if in G' we have $X \lessdot Y$ and $X \gtrdot Y$, then in G, either $X \lessdot Y$ and $X \gtrdot Y$ or $X \doteq Y$ and $X \gtrdot Y$. Either situation contradicts the assumption that G is a weak precedence grammar. Thus, $< \cap > = \varnothing$ in G'.

Part 3: $< \cap \doteq = \varnothing$. We may assume that $X < [Y\alpha]$ and $X \doteq [Y\alpha]$, for some X in $N \cup \Sigma$, and $[Y\alpha]$ in $N' - N$. This implies that there are productions $[XA\beta] \rightarrow X[A\beta]$ and $B \rightarrow [Y\alpha]$ in P' such that $[A\beta] \overset{+}{\underset{G'}{\Rightarrow}} By\beta \underset{G'}{\Rightarrow} [Y\alpha]y\beta$ for some y in $(N' \cup \Sigma)^*$, A and B in N.

This, in turn, implies that there are productions $C \rightarrow \delta XA\beta$ and $B \rightarrow Y\alpha$ in P such that $A \overset{*}{\underset{G}{\Rightarrow}} By'$ for some y' in $(N \cup \Sigma)^*$. Thus in G we have $X < B$ or $X \doteq B$. (The latter occurs if and only if $B = A$.)

Now consider $X \doteq [Y\alpha]$. Then there is a production $[XY\alpha] \rightarrow X[Y\alpha]$ in P', and thus there is a production $D \rightarrow \epsilon XY\alpha$ in P.

Therefore if $X < [Y\alpha]$ and $X \doteq [Y\alpha]$ in G', then there are two productions in P of the form $B \rightarrow Y\alpha$ and $D \rightarrow \epsilon XY\alpha$, and $X < B$ or $X \doteq B$ in G, violating condition (2) of the definition of weak precedence grammar.

The form of the productions in P' allows us to conclude immediately that G' is uniquely invertible if G is. Thus we have that $L(G')$ is a simple precedence language. A proof that $L(G') = L(G)$ is quite straightforward and is left for the Exercises.   □

COROLLARY

Every uniquely invertible weak precedence grammar is unambiguous.

Proof. If there were two distinct rightmost derivations in G of Theorem 5.19, we could construct distinct rightmost derivations in G' in a straightforward manner.   □

The construction in the proof of Theorem 5.19 is more appropriate for a theoretical proof than a practical tool. In practice we could use a far less exhaustive approach. We shall give a simple algorithm to convert a uniquely invertible weak precedence grammar to a simple precedence grammar. We leave it for the Exercises to show that the algorithm works.

ALGORITHM 5.15

Conversion from uniquely invertible weak precedence to simple precedence.

Input. A uniquely invertible weak precedence grammar $G = (N, \Sigma, P, S)$.

Output. A simple precedence grammar G' with $L(G') = L(G)$.

Method.

(1) Suppose that there exists a particular X and Y in the vocabulary of G such that $X \doteq Y$ and $X < Y$. Remove from P each production of the form $A \rightarrow \alpha XY\beta$, and replace it by $A \rightarrow \alpha X[Y\beta]$, where $[Y\beta]$ is a new nonterminal.

(2) For each $[Y\beta]$ introduced in step (1), replace any productions of the form $B \longrightarrow Y\beta$ by $B \longrightarrow [Y\beta]$, and add the production $[Y\beta] \longrightarrow Y\beta$ to P.

(3) Return to step (1) as often as it is applicable. When it is no longer applicable, let the resulting grammar be G', and halt. $\square$

Example 5.40

Let G be as in Example 5.37. We can apply Algorithm 5.15 to obtain the grammar G' having productions

$$E \longrightarrow E + [T] \mid + [T] \mid [T]$$
$$T \longrightarrow T * F \mid F$$
$$F \longrightarrow ([E)] \mid a$$
$$[T] \longrightarrow T$$
$$[E)] \longrightarrow E)$$

The two applications of step (1) are to the pairs $X = ($, $Y = E$ and $X = +$, $Y = T$. The precedence relations for G' are given in Fig. 5.16. $\square$

	E	T	F	[T]	[E)]	a	(	)	+	*	$
E								$\doteq$	$\doteq$		
T								$\gtrdot$	$\gtrdot$	$\doteq$	$\gtrdot$
F								$\gtrdot$	$\gtrdot$	$\gtrdot$	$\gtrdot$
[T]								$\gtrdot$	$\gtrdot$		$\gtrdot$
[E)]								$\gtrdot$	$\gtrdot$	$\gtrdot$	$\gtrdot$
a								$\gtrdot$	$\gtrdot$	$\gtrdot$	$\gtrdot$
)								$\gtrdot$	$\gtrdot$	$\gtrdot$	$\gtrdot$
(	$\lessdot$	$\lessdot$	$\lessdot$	$\lessdot$	$\doteq$	$\lessdot$	$\lessdot$		$\lessdot$		
+		$\lessdot$	$\lessdot$	$\doteq$		$\lessdot$	$\lessdot$				
*			$\doteq$			$\lessdot$	$\lessdot$				
$	$\lessdot$	$\lessdot$	$\lessdot$	$\lessdot$		$\lessdot$	$\lessdot$		$\lessdot$		

Fig. 5.16 Simple precedence matrix.

EXERCISES

5.3.1. Which of the following grammars are simple precedence grammars?
(a) G_0.
(b) $S \longrightarrow$ **if** E **then** S **else** $S \,|\, a$
$E \longrightarrow E$ **or** $b \,|\, b$.
(c) $S \longrightarrow AS \,|\, A$
$A \longrightarrow (S) \,|\, ( )$.
(d) $S \longrightarrow SA \,|\, A$
$A \longrightarrow (S) \,|\, ( )$.

5.3.2. Which of the grammars of Exercise 5.3.1 are weak precedence grammars?

5.3.3. Which of the grammars of Exercise 5.3.1 are $(2, 1)$ precedence grammars?

5.3.4. Give examples of precedence grammars for which
(a) $\doteq$ is neither reflexive, symmetric, nor transitive.
(b) $\lessdot$ is neither irreflexive nor transitive.
(c) $\gtrdot$ is neither irreflexive nor transitive.

*5.3.5. Show that every regular set has a simple precedence grammar. *Hint:* Make sure your grammar is uniquely invertible.

*5.3.6. Show that every uniquely invertible (m, n) precedence grammar is an LR grammar.

*5.3.7. Show that every weak precedence grammar is an LR grammar.

5.3.8. Prove that Algorithm 5.12 correctly produces a right parse.

5.3.9. Prove that G is a precedence grammar if and only if G is a $(1, 1)$ precedence grammar.

5.3.10. Prove Lemma 5.3(1).

5.3.11. Prove that Algorithm 5.14 correctly produces a right parse.

5.3.12. Give a right parsing algorithm for uniquely invertible (m, n) precedence grammars.

5.3.13. Prove the corollary to Theorem 5.17.

*5.3.14. Show that the construction of Algorithm 5.15 yields a simple precedence grammar equivalent to the original.

5.3.15. For those grammars of Exercise 5.3.1 which are weak precedence grammars, give equivalent simple precedence grammars.

*5.3.16. Show that the language $L = \{a0^n1^n \,|\, n \geq 1\} \cup \{b0^n1^{2n} \,|\, n \geq 1\}$ is not a simple precedence language. *Hint:* Think of the action of the right parser of Algorithm 5.12 on strings of the form $a0^n1^n$ and $b0^n1^n$, if L had a simple precedence grammar.

*5.3.17. Give a $(2, 1)$ precedence grammar for the language of Exercise 5.3.16.

*5.3.18. Give a simple precedence grammar for the language $\{0^n a 1^n \mid n \geq 1\}$ $\cup \{0^n b 1^{2n} \mid n \geq 1\}$.

*5.3.19. Show that every context-free grammar with no e-productions can be transformed into a $(1, 1)$ precedence grammar.

5.3.20. For CFG $G = (N, \Sigma, P, S)$, define the relations λ, μ, and ρ as follows:
(1) $A \lambda X$ if $A \longrightarrow X \alpha$ is in P for some α.
(2) $X \mu Y$ if $A \longrightarrow \alpha X Y \beta$ is in P for some α and β. Also, $\$\mu S$ and $S \mu \$$.
(3) $X \rho A$ if $A \longrightarrow \alpha X$ is in P for some α.
Show the following relations between the Wirth–Weber precedence relations and the above relations ($+$ denotes the transitive closure; $*$ denotes reflexive and transitive closure):
(a) $\lessdot = \mu \lambda^+$.
(b) $\doteq \cup \{(\$, S), (S, \$)\} = \mu$.
(c) $\gtrdot = \rho^+ \mu \lambda^* \cap ((N \cup \Sigma) \times \Sigma)$.

**5.3.21. Show that it is undecidable whether a given grammar is an extended precedence grammar [i.e., whether it is (m, n) precedence for some m and n].

*5.3.22. Show that if G is a weak precedence grammar, then G is an extended precedence grammar (for some m and n).

5.3.23. Show that a is in $\text{FOLLOW}_1(A)$ if and only if $A \lessdot a$, $A \doteq a$, or $A \gtrdot a$.

5.3.24. Generalize Lemma 5.3 to extended precedence grammars.

5.3.25. Suppose that we relax the extended precedence conditions to permit $\alpha \lessdot w$ and $\alpha \doteq w$ if they are generated only by rules (1b) and (2b). Give a shift–reduce algorithm to parse any grammar meeting the relaxed definition.

Research Problem

5.3.26. Find transformations which can be used to convert grammars into simple or weak precedence grammars.

Open Problem

5.3.27. Is every simple precedence language generated by a simple precedence grammar in which the start symbol does not appear on the right side of any production? It would be nice if so, as otherwise, we might attempt to reduce when $\$S$ is on the pushdown list and $\$$ on the input.

Programming Exercises

5.3.28. Write a program to construct the Wirth–Weber precedence relations for a context-free grammar G. Use your program on the grammar for PL360 in the Appendix.

5.3.29. Write a program that takes a context-free grammar G as input and constructs a shift–reduce parsing algorithm for G, if G is a simple precedence grammar. Use your program to construct a parser for PL360.

5.3.30. Write a program that will test whether a grammar is a uniquely invertible weak precedence grammar.

5.3.31. Write a program to construct a shift–reduce parsing algorithm for a uniquely invertible weak precedence grammar.

BIBLIOGRAPHIC NOTES

The origins of shift–reduce parsing appear in Floyd [1961]. Our treatment here follows Aho et al. [1972]. Simple precedence grammars were defined by Wirth and Weber [1966] and independently by Pair [1964]. The simple precedence concept has been used in compilers for several languages, including Euler [Wirth and Weber, 1966], ALGOL W [Bauer et al., 1968], and PL360 [Wirth, 1968]. Fischer [1969] proved that every CFL without e is generated by a (not necessarily UI) (1, 1) precedence grammar (Exercise 5.3.19).

Extended precedence was suggested by Wirth and Weber. Gray [1969] points out that several of the early definitions of extended precedence were incorrect. Because of its large memory requirements, (m, n) extended precedence with $m + n > 3$ seems to have little practical utility. McKeeman [1966] studies methods of reducing the table size for an extended precedence parser. Graham [1970] gives the interesting theorem that every deterministic language has a UI (2, 1) precedence grammar.

Weak precedence grammars were defined by Ichbiah and Morse [1970]. Theorem 5.19 is from Aho et al. [1972].

Several error recovery schemes are possible for shift–reduce parsers. In shift–reduce parsing an error can be announced both in the shift–reduce phase and in the reduce phase. If an error is reported by the shift–reduce function, then we can make deletions, changes, and insertions as in both LL and LR parsing. When a reduce error occurs, it is possible to maintain a list of error productions which can then be applied to the top of the pushdown list.

Error recovery techniques for simple precedence grammars are discussed by Wirth [1968] and Leinius [1970]. To enhance the error detection capability of a simple precedence parser, Leinius also suggests checking after a reduction is made that a permissible precedence relation holds between symbols X and A, where A is the new nonterminal on top of the pushdown list and X the symbol immediately below.

5.4. OTHER CLASSES OF SHIFT–REDUCE PARSABLE GRAMMARS

We shall mention several other subclasses of the LR grammars having shift–reduce parsing algorithms. These are the bounded-right-context grammars, mixed strategy precedence grammars, and operator precedence grammars. We shall also consider the Floyd–Evans production language, which is essentially a programming language for deterministic parsing algorithms.

5.4.1. Bounded-Right-Context Grammars

We would like to enlarge the class of weak precedence grammars that we have considered by relaxing the requirement of unique invertibility. We cannot remove the requirement of unique invertibility altogether, since an economical parsing algorithm is not known for all precedence grammars. However, we can parse many grammars using the weak precedence concept to locate the right end of a handle and then using local context, if the grammar is not uniquely invertible, to locate the left end of the handle and to determine which nonterminal is to replace the handle.

A large class of grammars which can be parsed in this fashion are the (m, n)-bounded-right-context (BRC) grammars. Informally, $G = (N, \Sigma, P, S)$ is an (m, n)-BRC grammar if whenever there is a rightmost derivation

$$S' \overset{*}{\underset{\text{rm}}{\Rightarrow}} \alpha A w \underset{\text{rm}}{\Rightarrow} \alpha \beta w,$$

in the augmented grammar $G' = (N \cup \{S'\}, \Sigma, P \cup \{S' \rightarrow S\}, S')$, then the handle β and the production $A \rightarrow \beta$ which is used to reduce the handle in $\alpha \beta w$ can be uniquely determined by

(1) Scanning $\alpha \beta w$ from left to right until the handle is encountered.

(2) Basing the decision of whether δ is the handle of $\alpha \beta w$, where $\gamma \delta$ is a prefix of $\alpha \beta$, only on δ, the m symbols to the left of δ and n symbols to the right of δ.

(3) Choosing for the handle the leftmost substring which includes, or is to the right of, the rightmost nonterminal of $\alpha \beta w$, from among possible candidates suggested in (2).

For notational convenience we shall append m \$'s to the left and n \$'s to the right of every right-sentential form. With the added \$'s we can be sure that there will always be at least m symbols to the left of and n symbols to the right of the handle in a padded right-sentential form.

DEFINITION

$G = (N, \Sigma, P, S)$ is an (m, n)-*bounded right-context* (BRC) grammar if the four conditions:

(1) $\$^m S' \$^n \overset{*}{\underset{G' \text{ rm}}{\Rightarrow}} \alpha A w \underset{G' \text{ rm}}{\Rightarrow} \alpha \beta w$ and

(2) $\$^m S' \$^n \overset{*}{\underset{G' \text{ rm}}{\Rightarrow}} \gamma B x \underset{G' \text{ rm}}{\Rightarrow} \gamma \delta x = \alpha' \beta y$ are rightmost derivations in the augmented grammar $G' = (N \cup \{S'\}, \Sigma, P \cup \{S' \rightarrow S\}, S')$.

(3) $|x| \leq |y|$

(4) the last m symbols of α and α' coincide, and the first n symbols of w and y coincide

imply that $\alpha' A y = \gamma B x$; that is, $\alpha' = \gamma$, $A = B$, and $y = x$.

A grammar is *BRC* if it is (m, n)-BRC for some m and n.

If we think of derivation (2) as the "real" derivation and of (1) as a possible cause of confusion, then condition (3) ensures that we shall not encounter a substring that looks like a handle (β surrounded by the last m symbols of α and the first n of w) to the left of the real handle δ. Thus we can choose as the handle the leftmost substring that "looks" like a handle. Condition (4) assures that we only use m symbols of left context and n symbols of right context to decide whether something is a handle or not.

As with LR(k) grammars, the use of the augmented grammar in the definition is required only when S appears on the right side of some production. For example, the grammar G with the two productions

$$S \longrightarrow Sa \,|\, a$$

would be $(1, 0)$-BRC without the proviso of an augmented grammar. As in Example 5.22 (p. 373), we cannot determine whether to accept S in the right-sentential form Sa without looking ahead one symbol. Thus we do not want G to be considered $(1, 0)$-BRC.

We shall prove later than every (m, k)-BRC grammar is LR(k). However, not every LR(0) grammar is (m, n)-BRC for any m and n, intuitively because the LR definition allows us to use the entire portion of a right-sentential form to the left of the handle to make our parsing decisions, while the BRC condition limits the portion to the left of the handle which we may use to m symbols. Both definitions limit the use of the portion to the right of the handle, of course.

Example 5.41

The grammar G_1 with productions

$$S \longrightarrow aAc$$
$$A \longrightarrow Abb \,|\, b$$

is a $(1, 0)$-BRC grammar. The right-sentential forms (other than S' and S) are $aAb^{2n}c$ for all $n \geq 0$ and $ab^{2n+1}c$ for $n \geq 0$. The possible handles are aAc, Abb, and b, and in each right-sentential form the handle can be uniquely determined by scanning the sentential form from left to right until aAc or Abb is encountered or b is encountered with an a to its left. Note that neither b in Abb could possibly be a handle by itself, because A or b appears to its left.

On the other hand, the grammar G_2 with productions

$$S \longrightarrow aAc$$
$$A \longrightarrow bAb \,|\, b$$

generates the same language but is not even an LR grammar. $\square$

Example 5.42

The grammar G with productions

$$S \longrightarrow aA \mid bB$$
$$A \longrightarrow 0A \mid 1$$
$$B \longrightarrow 0B \mid 1$$

is an LR(0) grammar, but fails to be BRC, since the handle in either of the right-sentential forms $a0^n1$ and $b0^n1$ is 1, but knowing only a fixed number of symbols immediately to the left of 1 is not sufficient to determine whether $A \rightarrow 1$ or $B \rightarrow 1$ is to be used to reduce the handle.

Formally, we have derivations

$$\$^m S'\$^n \xrightarrow[\text{rm}]{*} \$^m a0^m A\$^n \xrightarrow[\text{rm}]{} \$^m a0^m 1\$^n$$

and

$$\$^m S'\$^n \xrightarrow[\text{rm}]{*} \$^m b0^m B\$^n \xrightarrow[\text{rm}]{} \$^m b0^m 1\$^n$$

Referring to the BRC definition, we note that $\alpha = \$^m a0^m$, $\alpha' = \gamma = \$^m b0^m$, $\beta = \delta = 1$, and $y = w = x = \$^n$. Then α and α' end in the same m symbols, 0^m; w and y begin with the same n, $\$^n$; and $|x| \leq |y|$, but $\alpha' Ay \neq \gamma Bx$. ($A$ and B are themselves in the BRC definition.)

The grammar with productions

$$S \longrightarrow aA \mid bA$$
$$A \longrightarrow 0A \mid 1$$

generates the same language and is (0, 0)-BRC. $\square$

Condition (3) in the definition of BRC may at first seem odd. However, it is this condition that guarantees that if, in a right-sentential form $\alpha'\beta y$, β is the leftmost substring which is the right side of some production $A \rightarrow \beta$ and the left and right context of β in $\alpha'\beta y$ is correct, then the string $\alpha'Ay$ which results after the reduction will be a right-sentential form.

The BRC grammars are related to some of the classes of grammars we have previously considered in this chapter. As mentioned, they are a subset of the LR grammars. The BRC grammars are extended precedence grammars, and every uniquely invertible (m, n) precedence grammar is a BRC grammar. The (1, 1)-BRC grammars include all uniquely invertible weak precedence grammars. We shall prove this relation first.

THEOREM 5.20

If $G = (N, \Sigma, P, S)$ is a uniquely invertible weak precedence grammar, then it is a (1, 1)-BRC grammar.

Proof. Suppose that we have a violation of the $(1, 1)$-BRC condition, i.e., a pair of derivations

$$\$S'\$ \xRightarrow[\text{rm}]{*} \alpha A w \xRightarrow[\text{rm}]{} \alpha \beta w$$

and

$$\$S'\$ \xRightarrow[\text{rm}]{*} \gamma B x \xRightarrow[\text{rm}]{} \gamma \delta x = \alpha'\beta y$$

where α and α' end in the same symbol; w and y begin with the same symbol; and $|x| \le |y|$, but $\gamma B x \ne \alpha' A y$. Since G is weak precedence, by Theorem 5.14 applied to $\gamma \delta x$, we encounter the $\gtrdot$ relation first between δ and x. Applying Theorem 5.14 to $\alpha \beta w$, we encounter $\gtrdot$ between β and w, and since w and y begin with the same symbol, we encounter $\gtrdot$ between β and y. Thus, $|\alpha'\beta| \ge |\gamma \delta|$. Since we are given $|x| \le |y|$, we must have $\alpha'\beta = \gamma \delta$ and $x = y$.

If we can show that $\beta = \delta$, we shall have $\alpha' = \gamma$. But by unique invertibility, $A = B$. We would then contradict the hypothesis that $\gamma B x \ne \alpha' A y$.

If $\beta \ne \delta$, then one is a suffix of the other. We consider cases to show $\beta = \delta$.

Case 1: $\beta = \epsilon X \delta$ for some ϵ and X. X is the last symbol of γ, and therefore we have $X \lessdot B$ or $X \doteq B$ by Theorem 5.14 applied to right-sentential form $\gamma B x$. This violates the weak precedence condition.

Case 2: $\delta = \epsilon X \beta$ for some ϵ and X. This case is symmetric to the above.

We conclude that $\beta = \delta$ and that G is $(1, 1)$-BRC. $\square$

THEOREM 5.21

Every (m, k)-BRC grammar is an LR(k) grammar.

Proof. Let $G = (N, \Sigma, P, S)$ be (m, k)-BRC but not LR(k). Then by Lemma 5.2, we have two derivations in the augmented grammar G'

$$S' \xRightarrow[\text{rm}]{*} \alpha A w \xRightarrow[\text{rm}]{} \alpha \beta w$$

and

$$S' \xRightarrow[\text{rm}]{*} \gamma B x \xRightarrow[\text{rm}]{} \gamma \delta x = \alpha \beta y$$

where $|\gamma \delta| \ge |\alpha \beta|$ and $\mathrm{FIRST}_k(y) = \mathrm{FIRST}_k(w)$, but $\gamma B x \ne \alpha A y$. If we surround all strings by \$'s and let $\alpha' = \alpha$, we have an immediate violation of the (m, k)-BRC condition. $\square$

COROLLARY

Every BRC grammar is unambiguous. $\square$

We shall now give a shift–reduce parsing algorithm for BRC grammars and discuss its efficient implementation. Suppose that we are using a shift–reduce parsing algorithm to parse a BRC grammar G and that the parsing algorithm is in configuration (α, w, π). Then we can define sets $\mathcal{3C}$ and $\mathcal{N}$, which will tell us whether the handle in the right-sentential form αw appears on top of the stack (i.e., is a suffix of α) or whether the right end of the handle is somewhere in w (and we need to shift). If the handle is on top of the stack, these sets will also tell us what the handle is and what production is to be used to reduce the handle.

DEFINITION

Let G be an (m, n)-BRC grammar. $\mathcal{3C}^G_{m,n}(A)$, for $A \in N$, is the set of triples (α, β, x) such that $|\alpha| = m, |x| = n$, and there exists a derivation $\$^m S' \$^n \underset{\text{rm}}{\overset{*}{\Rightarrow}} \gamma \alpha A x y \underset{\text{rm}}{\Rightarrow} \gamma \alpha \beta x y$ in the augmented grammar.
$\mathcal{N}^G_{m,n}$ is the set of pairs (α, x) such that

(1) Either $|\alpha| = m + l$, where l is the length of the longest right side in P or $|\alpha| < m + l$ and α begins with $\$^m$.

(2) $|x| = n$.

(3) There is a derivation $\$^m S' \$^n \underset{\text{rm}}{\overset{*}{\Rightarrow}} \beta A y \underset{\text{rm}}{\Rightarrow} \beta \gamma y$, where αx is a substring of $\beta \gamma y$ positioned so that α lies within $\beta \gamma$ and does not include the last symbol of $\beta \gamma$.

We delete G, m, and n from $\mathcal{3C}(A)$ and $\mathcal{N}$ when they are obvious.

The intention is that the appearance of substring $\alpha \beta x$ in scanning a right-sentential form from left to right should indicate that the handle is β and that it is to be reduced to A whenever (α, β, x) is in $\mathcal{3C}(A)$. The appearance of αx, when (α, x) is in $\mathcal{N}$, indicates that we do not have the handle yet, but it is possible that the handle exists to the right of α. The following lemma assures us that this is, in fact, the case.

LEMMA 5.6

$G = (N, \Sigma, P, S)$ is (m, n)-BRC if and only if

(1) Let $A \rightarrow \beta$ and $B \rightarrow \delta$ be distinct productions. Then if (α, β, x) is in $\mathcal{3C}_{m,n}(A)$ and (γ, δ, x) is in $\mathcal{3C}_{m,n}(B)$, then $\alpha \beta$ is not a suffix of $\gamma \delta$, or vice versa;

(2) For all $A \in N$, if (α, β, x) is in $\mathcal{3C}_{m,n}(A)$, then $(\theta \alpha \beta, x)$ is not in $\mathcal{N}_{m,n}$ for any θ.

Proof.

If: Suppose that G is not (m, n)-BRC. Then we can find derivations in the augmented grammar G

$$\$^m S' \$^n \underset{\text{rm}}{\overset{*}{\Rightarrow}} \alpha A w \underset{\text{rm}}{\Rightarrow} \alpha \beta w$$

and

$$\$^m S' \$^n \xrightarrow[\text{rm}]{*} \gamma Bx \xrightarrow[\text{rm}]{} \gamma \delta x = \alpha' \beta y$$

where α and α' coincide in the last m places, w and y coincide in the first n places, and $|x| \le |y|$, but $\gamma Bx \ne \alpha' Ay$. Let ϵ be the last m places of α and z the first n places of w. Then (ϵ, β, z) is in $\mathfrak{K}(A)$. If $x \ne y$, and $|x| \le |y|$, we must have $(\theta \epsilon \beta, z)$ in $\mathfrak{N}$ for some θ and thus condition (2) is violated. If $x = y$, then (η, δ, z) is in $\mathfrak{K}(B)$, where η is the last m symbols of γ. If $A \to \beta$ and $B \to \delta$ are the same, then with $x = y$ we conclude $\gamma Bx = \alpha' Ay$, contrary to hypothesis. But since one of $\eta \delta$ or $\epsilon \beta$ is a suffix of the other, we have a violation of (1) if $A \to \beta$ and $B \to \delta$ are distinct.

Only if: Given a violation of (1) or (2), a violation of the (m, n)-BRC condition is easy to construct. We leave this part for the Exercises. □

We can now give a shift–reduce parsing algorithm for BRC grammars. Since it involves knowing the sets $\mathfrak{K}(A)$ and $\mathfrak{N}$, we shall first discuss how to compute them.

ALGORITHM 5.16

Construction of $\mathfrak{K}_{m,n}(A)$ and $\mathfrak{N}_{m,n}$.

Input. A proper grammar $G = (N, \Sigma, P, S)$.

Output. The sets $\mathfrak{K}_{m,n}(A)$ for $A \in N$ and $\mathfrak{N}$.

Method.

(1) Let l be the length of the longest right side of a production. Compute $\mathcal{S}$, the set of strings γ such that
   (a) $|\gamma| = m + n + l$, or $|\gamma| < m + n + l$ and γ begins with $\$^m$;
   (b) γ is a substring of $\alpha \beta u$, where $\alpha \beta w$ is a right-sentential form with handle β and $u = \text{FIRST}_n(w)$; and
   (c) γ contains at least one nonterminal.
We can use a method similar to the first part of Algorithm 5.13 here.

(2) For $A \in N$, let $\mathfrak{K}(A)$ be the set of (α, β, x) such that there is a string $\gamma \alpha Axy$ in $\mathcal{S}$, $A \to \beta$ is in P, $|\alpha| = m$, and $|x| = n$.

(3) Let $\mathfrak{N}$ be the set of (α, x) such that there exists γBy in $\mathcal{S}$, $B \to \delta$ in P, αx is a substring of $\gamma \delta y$, and α is within $\gamma \delta$, exclusive of the last symbol of $\gamma \delta$. Of course, we also require that $|x| = n$ and that $|\alpha| = m + l$, where l is the longest right side of a production or α begins with $\$^m$ and $|\alpha| < m + l$. □

THEOREM 5.22

Algorithm 5.6 correctly computes $\mathfrak{K}(A)$ and $\mathfrak{N}$.

Proof. Exercise. □

ALGORITHM 5.17

Shift–reduce parsing algorithm for BRC grammars.

Input. An (m, n)-BRC grammar $G = (N, \Sigma, P, S)$, with augmented grammar $G' = (N', \Sigma, P, S')$.

Output. $\mathcal{Q} = (f, g)$, a shift–reduce parsing algorithm for G.

Method.

(1) Let $f(\alpha, w) = $ **shift** if (α, w) is in $\mathfrak{N}_{m,n}$.
(2) $f(\alpha, w) = $ **reduce** if $\alpha = \alpha_1\alpha_2$, and (α_1, α_2, w) is in $\mathfrak{K}_{m,n}(A)$ for some A, unless $A = S'$, $\alpha_1 = \$$, and $\alpha_2 = S$.
(3) $f(\$^m S, \$^n) = $ **accept**.
(4) $f(\alpha, w) = $ **error** otherwise.
(5) $g(\alpha, w) = i$ if we can write $\alpha = \alpha_1\alpha_2$, (α_1, α_2, w) is in $\mathfrak{K}(A)$, and the ith production is $A \rightarrow \alpha_2$.
(6) $g(\alpha, w) = $ **error** otherwise. $\quad\square$

THEOREM 5.23

The shift–reduce parsing algorithm constructed by Algorithm 5.17 is valid for G.

Proof. By Lemma 5.6, there is never any ambiguity in defining f and g. By definition of $\mathfrak{K}(A)$, whenever a reduction is made, the string reduced, α_2, is the handle of some string $\beta\alpha_1\alpha_2wz$. If it is the handle of some other string $\beta'\alpha_1\alpha_2wz'$, a violation of the BRC condition is immediate. The only difficult point is ensuring that condition (3), $|x| \leq |y|$, of the BRC definition is satisfied. It is not hard to show that the derivations of $\beta\alpha_1\alpha_2wz$ and $\beta'\alpha_1\alpha_2wz'$ can be made the first and second derivations in the BRC definition in one order or the other, so condition (3) will hold. $\quad\square$

The shift–reduce algorithm of Algorithm 5.17 has f and g functions which clearly depend only on bounded portions of the argument strings, although one must look at substrings of varying lengths at different times. Let us discuss the implementation of f and g together as a decision tree. First, given α on the pushdown list and x on the input, one might branch on the first n symbols of x. For each such sequence of n symbols, one might then scan α backwards, at each step making the decision whether to proceed further on α or announce an error, a shift, or a reduction. If a reduction is called for, we have enough information to tell exactly which production is used, thus incorporating the g function into the decision tree as well. It is also possible to generalize Domolki's algorithm (See the Exercises of Section 4.1.) to make the decisions.

Example 5.43

Let us consider the grammar G given by

$$(0)\ S' \longrightarrow S$$
$$(1)\ S \longrightarrow 0A$$
$$(2)\ S \longrightarrow 1S$$
$$(3)\ A \longrightarrow 0A$$
$$(4)\ A \longrightarrow 1$$

G is $(1, 0)$-BRC. To compute $\mathcal{K}(A)$, $\mathcal{K}(S)$, and $\mathcal{N}$, we need the set of strings of length 3 or less that can appear in the viable prefix of a right-sentential form and have a nonterminal. These are $\$S'$, $\$S$, $\$0A$, $\$1S$, $00A$, $11S$, $10A$, and substrings thereof.

We calculate

$$\mathcal{K}_{1,0}(S') = \{(\$, S, e)\}$$
$$\mathcal{K}_{1,0}(S) = \{(\$, 0A, e), (\$, 1S, e), (1, 0A, e), (1, 1S, e)\}$$
$$\mathcal{K}_{1,0}(A) = \{(0, 0A, e), (0, 1, e)\}$$

$\mathcal{N}$ consists of the pairs (α, e), where α is $\$$, $\$0$, $\$00$, 000, $\$1$, $\$11$, $\$10$, 111, 100, or 110. The functions f and g are given in Fig. 5.17. By "ending of α" we mean the shortest suffix of α necessary to determine $f(\alpha, e)$ and to determine $g(\alpha, e)$ if necessary.

Ending of α	$f(\alpha, e)$	$g(\alpha, e)$
$\$0A$	reduce	1
$10A$	reduce	1
$00A$	reduce	3
$\$1S$	reduce	2
$11S$	reduce	2
01	reduce	4
00	shift	
$\$0$	shift	
$\$10$	shift	
110	shift	
$\$1$	shift	
$\$11$	shift	
111	shift	
$\$$	shift	
$\$S$	accept	

Fig. 5.17 Shift–reduce functions.

A decision tree implementing f and g is shown in Fig. 5.18 on p. 436. We omit nodes with labels A and S below level 1. They would all have the outcome error, of course. □

5.4.2. Mixed Strategy Precedence Grammars

Unfortunately, the shift–reduce algorithm of Algorithm 5.17 is rather expensive to implement because of the storage requirements for the f and g functions. We can define a less costly shift–reduce parsable class of grammars by using precedence to locate the right end of the handle and then using local context to both isolate the left end of the handle and determine which nonterminal is to replace the handle.

Example 5.44

Consider the (non-UI) weak precedence grammar G with productions

$$S \longrightarrow aA \,|\, bB$$
$$A \longrightarrow CA1 \,|\, C1$$
$$B \longrightarrow DBE1 \,|\, DE1$$
$$C \longrightarrow 0$$
$$D \longrightarrow 0$$
$$E \longrightarrow 1$$

G generates the language $\{a0^n1^n \,|\, n \geq 1\} \cup \{b0^n1^{2n} \,|\, n \geq 1\}$, which we shall show in Chapter 8 not to be a simple precedence language. Precedence relations for G are given in Fig. 5.19 (p. 437). Note that G is not uniquely invertible, because 0 appears as the right side in two productions, $C \rightarrow 0$ and $D \rightarrow 0$. However, $\mathfrak{IC}_{1,0}(C) = \{(a, 0, e), (C, 0, e)\}$ and $\mathfrak{IC}_{1,0}(D) = \{(b, 0, e), (D, 0, e)\}$ Thus, if we have isolated 0 as the handle of a right-sentential form, then the symbol immediately to the left of 0 will determine whether to reduce the 0 to C or to D. Specifically, we reduce 0 to C if that symbol is a or C and we reduce 0 to D if that symbol is b or D. □

This example suggests the following definition.

Definition

Let $G = (N, \Sigma, P, S)$ be a proper CFG with no e-productions. We say that G is a $(p, q; m, n)$ *mixed strategy precedence (MSP) grammar* if

(1) The extended (p, q) precedence relation $\gtrdot$ is disjoint from the union of the (p, q) precedence relations $\lessdot$ and $\doteq$.

(2) If $A \rightarrow \alpha\beta$ and $B \rightarrow \beta$ are distinct productions in P, then the following three conditions can never be all true simultaneously:

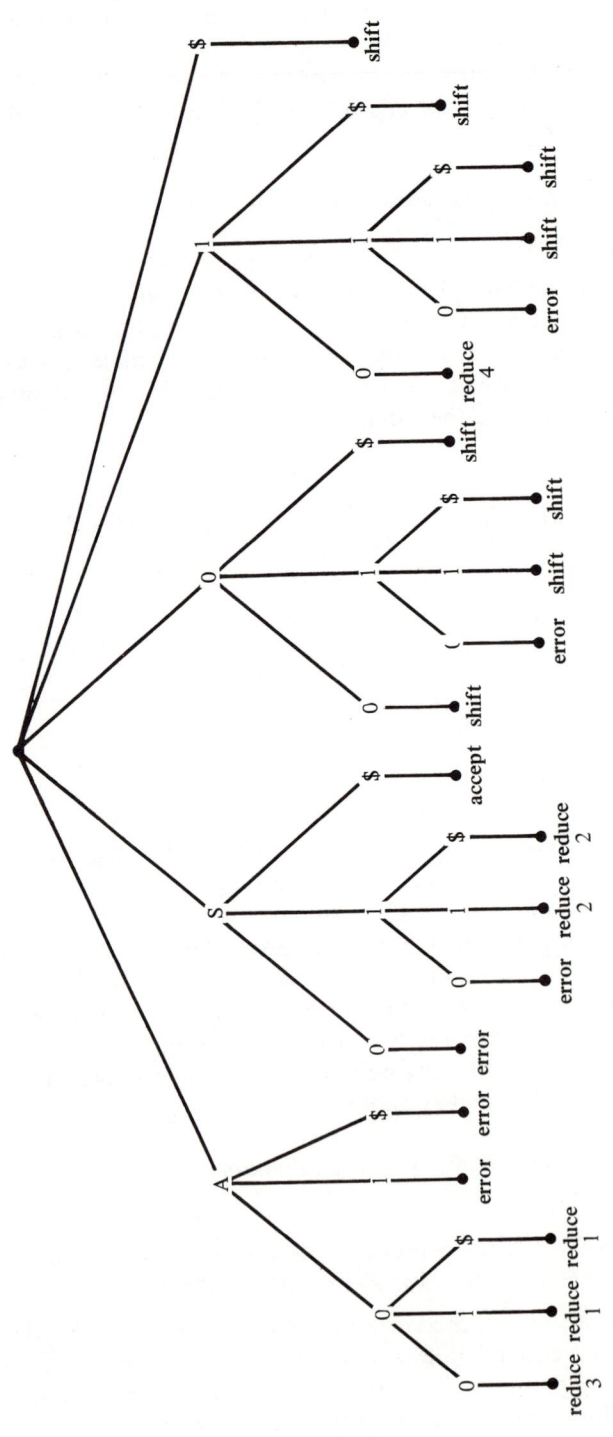

Fig. 5.18 Decision tree.

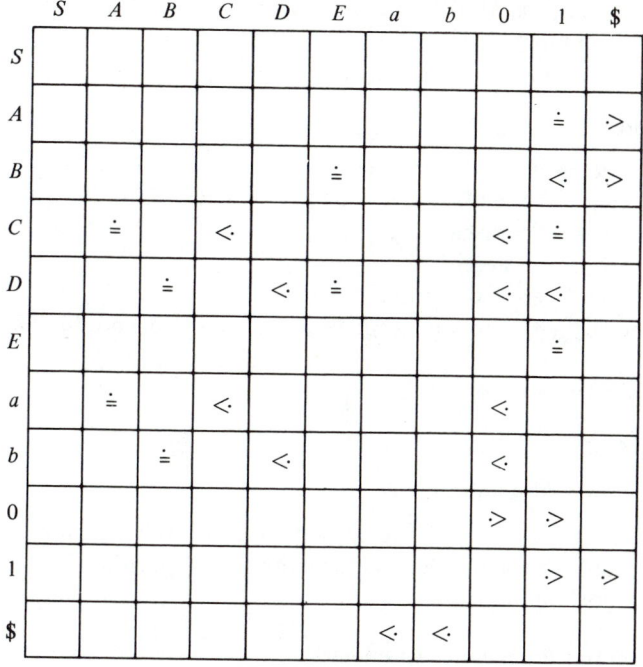

	S	A	B	C	D	E	a	b	0	1	$
S											
A									≐	⋗	
B						≐			⋖	⋗	
C		≐		⋖					⋖	≐	
D			≐	⋖	≐				⋖	⋖	
E										≐	
a		≐		⋖					⋖		
b			≐	⋖					⋖		
0									⋗	⋗	
1									⋗	⋗	
$							⋖	⋖			

Fig. 5.19 Precedence relations for G.

(a) $\mathcal{K}_{m,n}(A)$ contains $(\gamma, \alpha\beta, x)$.
(b) $\mathcal{K}_{m,n}(B)$ contains (δ, β, x).
(c) δ is the last m symbols of $\gamma\alpha$.

A $(1, 1; 1, 0)$-MSP grammar will be called a *simple* MSP grammar. For example, the grammar of Example 5.44 is simple MSP. In fact, every uniquely invertible weak precedence grammar is a simple MSP grammar.

Let $l(A) = \{X \mid X \lessdot A \text{ or } X \doteq A\}$. For a simple MSP grammar, condition (2) above reduces to the following:

(2a) If $A \to \beta'X\beta$ and $B \to \beta$ are productions, then X is not in $l(B)$.
(2b) If $A \to \beta$ and $B \to \beta$ are productions, $A \neq B$, then $l(A)$ and $l(B)$ are disjoint.

Condition (1) above and condition (2a) are recognizable as the weak precedence conditions. Thus a simple MSP grammar can be thought of as a (possibly non-UI) weak precedence grammar in which one symbol of left context is sufficient to distinguish between productions with the same right side [condition (2b)].

ALGORITHM 5.18

Parsing algorithm for MSP grammars.

Input. A $(p, q; m, n)$-MSP grammar $G = (N, \Sigma, P, S)$ in which the productions are numbered.

Output. $\mathcal{a} = (f, g)$, a shift–reduce parsing algorithm for G.

Method.

(1) Let $|\alpha| = p$ and $|x| = q$. Then
    (a) $f(\alpha, x) = $ **shift** if $\alpha \lessdot x$ or $\alpha \doteq x$, and
    (b) $f(\alpha, x) = $ **reduce** if $\alpha \gtrdot x$.
(2) $f(\$^p S, \$^q) = $ **accept**.
(3) $f(\gamma, w) = $ **error** otherwise.
(4) Let $\mathcal{H}_{m,n}(A)$ contain (α, β, x) and $A \rightarrow \beta$ be production i. Then $g(\alpha\beta, x) = i$.
(5) $g(\gamma, w) = $ **error** otherwise. $\square$

THEOREM 5.24

Algorithm 5.18 is valid for G.

Proof. Exercise. It suffices to show that every MSP grammar is a BRC grammar, and then show that the functions of Algorithm 5.18 agree with those of Algorithm 5.17. $\square$

5.4.3. Operator Precedence Grammars

An efficient parsing procedure can be given for a class of grammars called operator precedence grammars. Operator precedence parsing is simple to implement and has been used in many compilers.

DEFINITION

An *operator grammar* is a proper CFG with no e-productions in which no production has a right side with two adjacent nonterminals.

For an operator grammar we can define precedence relations on the set of terminal symbols and $\$$, while ignoring nonterminals. Let $G = (N, \Sigma, P, S)$ be an operator grammar and let $\$$ be a new symbol. We define three *operator precedence relations* on $\Sigma \cup \{\$\}$ as follows:

(1) $a \doteq b$ if $A \rightarrow \alpha a \gamma b \beta$ is in P with γ in $N \cup \{e\}$.

(2) $a \lessdot b$ if $A \rightarrow \alpha a B \beta$ is in P and $B \overset{+}{\Rightarrow} \gamma b \delta$, where γ is in $N \cup \{e\}$.

(3) $a \gtrdot b$ if $A \rightarrow \alpha B b \beta$ is in P and $B \overset{+}{\Rightarrow} \delta a \gamma$, where γ is in $N \cup \{e\}$.

(4) $\$ \lessdot a$ if $S \overset{+}{\Rightarrow} \gamma a \alpha$ with γ in $N \cup \{e\}$.

(5) $a \gtrdot \$$ if $S \overset{+}{\Rightarrow} \alpha a \gamma$ with γ in $N \cup \{e\}$.

G is an *operator precedence grammar* if G is an operator grammar and at most one operator precedence relation holds between any pair of terminal symbols.

Example 5.45

The grammar G_0 is a classic example of an operator precedence grammar:

(1) $E \rightarrow E + T$ (2) $E \rightarrow T$
(3) $T \rightarrow T * F$ (4) $T \rightarrow F$
(5) $F \rightarrow (E)$ (6) $F \rightarrow a$

The operator precedence relations are given in Fig. 5.20. □

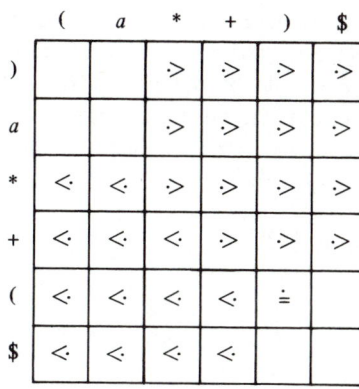

	(	a	*	+	)	$
)			$\gtrdot$	$\gtrdot$	$\gtrdot$	$\gtrdot$
a			$\gtrdot$	$\gtrdot$	$\gtrdot$	$\gtrdot$
*	$\lessdot$	$\lessdot$	$\gtrdot$	$\gtrdot$	$\gtrdot$	$\gtrdot$
+	$\lessdot$	$\lessdot$	$\lessdot$	$\gtrdot$	$\gtrdot$	$\gtrdot$
(	$\lessdot$	$\lessdot$	$\lessdot$	$\lessdot$	$\doteq$	
$	$\lessdot$	$\lessdot$	$\lessdot$	$\lessdot$		

Fig. 5.20 Operator precedence relations for G_0.

We can produce skeletal parses for operator precedence grammars very efficiently. The parsing principle is the same as for simple precedence analysis. It is easy to verify the following theorem.

THEOREM 5.25

Let $G = (N, \Sigma, P, S)$ be an operator grammar, and let us suppose that $\$S\$ \overset{*}{\underset{rm}{\Rightarrow}} \alpha A w \underset{rm}{\Rightarrow} \alpha \beta w$. Then

(1) The operator precedence relation $\lessdot$ or $\doteq$ holds between consecutive terminals (and $) of α;

(2) The operator precedence relation $\lessdot$ holds between the rightmost terminal symbol of α and the leftmost terminal symbol of β;

(3) The relation $\doteq$ holds between the consecutive terminal symbols of β;

(4) The relation $\gtrdot$ holds between the rightmost terminal symbol of β and the first symbol of w.

Proof. Exercise. □

COROLLARY

If G is an operator precedence grammar, then we can add to (1)–(4) of Theorem 5.25 that "no other relations hold."

Proof. By definition of operator precedence grammar. □

Thus we can readily isolate the terminal symbols appearing in a handle using a shift–reduce parsing algorithm. However, nonterminal symbols cause some problems, as no precedence relations are defined on nonterminal symbols. Nevertheless, the fact that we have an operator grammar allows us to produce a "skeletal" right parse.

Example 5.46

Let us parse the string $(a + a) * a$ according to the operator precedence relations of Fig. 5.20 obtained from G_0. However, we shall not worry about nonterminals and merely keep their place with the symbol E. That way we do not have to worry about whether F should be reduced to T, or T to F (although in this particular case, we could handle such matters by going outside the methods of operator precedence parsing). We are effectively parsing according to the grammar G:

$$(1) \ E \longrightarrow E + E$$
$$(3) \ E \longrightarrow E * E$$
$$(5) \ E \longrightarrow (E)$$
$$(6) \ E \longrightarrow a$$

derived from G_0 by replacing all nonterminals by E and deleting single productions. (Note that we cannot have a production with no terminals on the right side in an operator grammar unless it is a single production.)

Obviously, G is ambiguous, but the operator precedence relations will assure us that a unique parse is found. The shift–reduce algorithm which we shall use on grammar G is given by the functions f and g below. Note that strings which form arguments for f and g are expected to consist only of the terminals of G_0 and the symbols $\$$ and E. Below, γ is either E or the empty string; b and c are terminals or $\$$.

$$(1) \qquad f(b\gamma, c) = \begin{cases} \textbf{shift} & \text{if } b \lessdot c \text{ or } b \doteq c \\ \textbf{reduce} & \text{if } b \gtrdot c \\ \textbf{accept} & \text{if } b = \$, \ \gamma = E, \text{ and } c = \$ \\ \textbf{error} & \text{otherwise} \end{cases}$$

$$(2) \qquad \begin{aligned} g(b\gamma a, x) &= 6 & \text{if } b \lessdot a \\ g(bE * E, x) &= 3 & \text{if } b \lessdot * \\ g(bE + E, x) &= 1 & \text{if } b \lessdot + \\ g(b\gamma(E), x) &= 5 & \text{if } b \lessdot (\\ g(\alpha, x) &= \textbf{error} & \text{otherwise} \end{aligned}$$

Thus $\mathcal{Q}$ would make the following sequence of moves with $(a + a) * a$ as input:

$$
\begin{aligned}
[\$, (a + a) * a\$, e] &\vdash^s [\$(, a + a) * a\$, e] \\
&\vdash^s [\$(a, + a) * a\$, e] \\
&\vdash^r [\$(E, + a) * a\$, 6] \\
&\vdash^s [\$(E +, a) * a\$, 6] \\
&\vdash^s [\$(E + a,) * a\$, 6] \\
&\vdash^r [\$(E + E,) * a\$, 66] \\
&\vdash^r [\$(E,) * aS, 661] \\
&\vdash^s [\$(E), * a\$, 661] \\
&\vdash^r [\$E, * a\$, 6615] \\
&\vdash^s [\$E *, a\$, 6615] \\
&\vdash^s [\$E * a, \$, 6615] \\
&\vdash^r [\$E * E, \$, 66156] \\
&\vdash^r [\$E, \$, 661563] \\
&\vdash \textbf{accept}
\end{aligned}
$$

We can verify that 661563 is indeed a skeletal right parse for $(a + a) * a$ according to G. We can view this skeletal parse as a tree representation of $(a + a) * a$, as shown in Fig. 5.21. □

We should observe that it is possible to fill in the skeletal parse tree of Fig. 5.21 to build the corresponding tree of G_0. But in a practical sense, this is not often necessary. The purpose of building the tree is for translation, and the natural translation of E, T and F in G_0 is a computer program which computes the expression derived from that nonterminal. Thus when production $E \rightarrow T$ or $T \rightarrow F$ is applied, the translation of the right is very likely to be the same as the translation of the left.

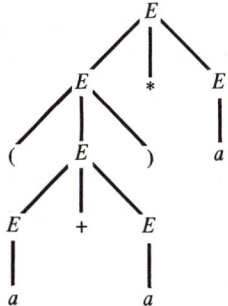

Fig. 5.21 Skeletal parse tree.

Example 5.46 is a special case of a technique that works for many grammars, especially those that define languages which are sets of arithmetic expressions. Involved is the construction of a new grammar with all nonterminals of the old grammar replaced by one nonterminal and single productions deleted. If we began with an operator precedence grammar, we can always find one parse of each input by a shift–reduce algorithm. Quite often the new grammar and its parser are sufficient for the purposes of translation, and in such situations the operator precedence parsing technique is a particularly simple and efficient one.

DEFINITION

Let $G = (N, \Sigma, P, S)$ be an operator grammar. Define $G_s = (\{S\}, \Sigma, P', S)$, the *skeletal grammar* for G, to consist of all productions $S \rightarrow X_1 \cdots X_m$ such that there is a production $A \rightarrow Y_1 \cdots Y_m$ in P, and for $1 \leq i \leq m$,

(1) $X_i = Y_i$ if $Y_i \in \Sigma$.
(2) $X_i = S$ if $Y_i \in N$.

However, we do not allow $S \rightarrow S$ in P'.

We should warn the reader that $L(G) \subseteq L(G_s)$ and in general $L(G_s)$ may contain strings not in $L(G)$. We can now give a shift–reduce algorithm for operator precedence grammars.

ALGORITHM 5.19

Operator precedence parser.

Input. An operator precedence grammar $G = (N, \Sigma, P, S)$.

Output. Shift–reduce parsing functions f and g for G_s.

Method. Let β be S or e.

(1) $f(a\beta, b) = \textbf{shift}$ if $a \lessdot b$ or $a \doteq b$.
(2) $f(a\beta, b) = \textbf{reduce}$ if $a \gtrdot b$.
(3) $f(\$S, \$) = \textbf{accept}$.
(4) $f(\alpha, w) = \textbf{error}$ otherwise.
(5) $g(a\beta b\gamma, w) = i$ if
   (a) β is S or e;
   (b) $a \lessdot b$;
   (c) The $\doteq$ relation holds between consecutive terminal symbols of γ, if any; and
   (d) Production i of G_s is $S \rightarrow \beta b\gamma$.
(6) $g(\alpha, w) = \textbf{error}$ otherwise. $\square$

Example 5.46 is an example of Algorithm 5.19 applied to G_0. To show the correctness of Algorithm 5.19, two lemmas are needed.

LEMMA 5.7

If α is a right-sentential form of an operator grammar, then α does not have two adjacent nonterminals.

Proof. Elementary induction on the length of the derivation of α. ☐

LEMMA 5.8

If α is a right-sentential form of an operator grammar, then the symbol appearing immediately to the left of the handle cannot be a nonterminal.

Proof. If it were, then the right-sentential form to which α is reduced would have two adjacent nonterminals. ☐

THEOREM 5.26

Algorithm 5.19 parses all sentences in $L(G)$.

Proof. By the corollary to Theorem 5.25, the first $>$ and the previous $<$ correctly isolate a handle. Lemma 5.7 justifies the restriction that β be only S or e (rather than any string in S^*). Lemma 5.8 justifies inclusion of β in the handle in rule (5). ☐

5.4.4. Floyd–Evans Production Language

What we shall next discuss is not another parsing algorithm, but rather a language in which deterministic (nonbacktracking) top-down and bottom-up parsing algorithms can be described. This language is called the Floyd–Evans production language, and a number of compilers have been implemented using this syntactic metalanguage. The name is somewhat of a misnomer, since the statements of the language need not refer to any particular productions in a grammar. A program written in Floyd–Evans productions is a specification of a parsing algorithm with a finite state control influencing decisions.†

A production language parser is a list of production language statements. Each statement has a label, and the labels can be considered to be the states of the finite control. We assume that no two statements have the same label. The statements act on an input string and a pushdown list and cause a right parse to be constructed. We can give an instantaneous description of the parser as a configuration of the form

$$(q, \$X_m \cdots X_1, a_1 \cdots a_n\$, \pi)$$

where

(1) q is the label of the currently active statement;

---

†We might add that this is not the ultimate generalization of shift–reduce algorithms. The LR(k) parsing algorithm uses a finite control and also keeps extra information on its pushdown list. In fact, a DPDT might really be considered the most general kind of shift–reduce algorithm. However, as we saw in Section 3.4 the DPDT is not really constrained to parse by making reductions according to the grammar for which its output is a presumed parse, as is the LR(k) algorithm and the algorithms of Sections 5.3 and 5.4.

(2) $X_m \cdots X_1$ is the contents of the pushdown list with X_1 on top ($\$$ is used as a bottom of pushdown list marker);

(3) $a_1 \cdots a_n$ is the remaining input string ($\$$ is also used as a right end-marker for the input tape);

(4) π represents the output of the parser to this point, presumably the right parse of the input according to some CFG.

A *production language statement* is of the form

$$\langle label \rangle : \alpha \,|\, a \longrightarrow \beta \,|\, \langle action \rangle * \langle next\ label \rangle$$

where the metasymbols $\longrightarrow$ and $*$ are optional.

Suppose that the parser is in configuration

$$(L1, \gamma\alpha, ax, \pi)$$

and statement $L1$ is

$$L1: \quad \alpha \,|\, a \longrightarrow \beta \,|\, \textbf{emit}\ s * L2$$

$L1$ says that if the string on top of the pushdown list is α and the current input symbol is a, then replace α by β, emit the string s, move the input head one symbol to the right (indicated by the presence of $*$), and go next to statement $L2$. Thus the parser would enter the configuration $(L2, \gamma\beta, x, \pi s)$. The symbol a may be e, in which case the current input symbol is not relevant, although if the $*$ is present, an input symbol will be shifted anyway.

If statement $L1$ did not apply, because the top of the pushdown list did not match α or the current input symbol was not a, then the statement immediately following $L1$ on the list of statements must be applied next.

Both labels on a statement are optional (although we assume that each statement has a name for use in configurations). If the symbol $\longrightarrow$ is missing, then the pushdown list is not to be changed, and there would be no point in having $\beta \neq e$. If the symbol $*$ is missing, then the input head is not to be moved. If the $\langle next\ label \rangle$ is missing, the next statement on the list is always taken.

Other possible actions are **accept** and **error**. A blank in the action field indicates that no action is to be taken other than the pattern matching and possible reduction.

Initially, the parser is in configuration $(L, \$, w\$, e)$, where w is the input string to be parsed and L is a designated statement. The statements are then serially checked until an applicable statement is found. The various actions specified by this statement are performed, and then control is transferred to the statement specified by the next label.

The parser continues until an error or accept action is encountered. The output is valid only when the accept is executed.

We shall discuss production language in the context of shift–reduce parsing, but the reader should bear in mind that top-down parsing algorithms can also be implemented in production language. There, the presumption is that we can write $\alpha = \alpha_1 \alpha_2 \alpha_3$ and $\beta = \alpha_1 A \alpha_3$ or $\beta = \alpha_1 A \alpha_3 a$ if the $*$ is present. Moreover, $A \longrightarrow \alpha_2$ is a production of the grammar we are attempting to parse, and the output s is just the number of production $A \longrightarrow \alpha_2$.

Floyd–Evans productions can be modified to take "semantic routines" as actions. Then, instead of emitting a parse, the parser would perform a syntax-directed translation, computing the translation of A in terms of the translations of the various components of α_2. Feldman [1966] describes such a system.

Example 5.47

We shall construct a production language parser for the grammar G_0 with the productions

(1) $E \rightarrow E + T$ (2) $E \rightarrow T$
(3) $T \rightarrow T * F$ (4) $T \rightarrow F$
(5) $F \rightarrow (E)$ (6) $F \rightarrow a$

The symbol $\#$ is used as a match for any symbol. It is presumed to represent the same symbol on both sides of the arrow. $L11$ is the initial statement.

$L0:$	$(\mid \# \longrightarrow (\#$	$\mid$		$*L0$
$L1:$	$a \mid \# \longrightarrow F\#$	$\mid$	**emit 6**	$*$
$L2:$	$T * F\# \mid \longrightarrow T\#$	$\mid$	**emit 3**	$L4$
$L3:$	$F\# \mid \longrightarrow T\#$	$\mid$	**emit 4**	
$L4:$	$T * \mid \# \longrightarrow T * \#$	$\mid$		$*L0$
$L5:$	$E + T\# \mid \longrightarrow E\#$	$\mid$	**emit 1**	$L7$
$L6:$	$T\# \mid \longrightarrow E\#$	$\mid$	**emit 2**	
$L7:$	$E + \mid \# \longrightarrow E + \# \mid$	$\mid$		$*L0$
$L8:$	$(E) \mid \# \longrightarrow F\#$	$\mid$	**emit 5**	$*L2$
$L9:$	$\$E\$ \mid \longrightarrow$	$\mid$	**accept**	
$L10:$	$\$ \mid \longrightarrow$	$\mid$	**error**	
$L11:$	$\mid \# \longrightarrow \#$	$\mid$		$*L0$

The parser would go through the following configurations under input $(a + a) * a$:

$$[L11, \$, (a + a) * a\$, e] \vdash [L0, \$(, a + a) * a\$, e]$$
$$\vdash [L0, \$(a, + a) * a\$, e]$$
$$\vdash [L1, \$(a, + a) * a\$, e]$$
$$\vdash [L2, \$(F +, a) * a\$, 6]$$
$$\vdash [L3, \$(F +, a) * a\$, 6]$$
$$\vdash [L4, \$(T +, a) * a\$, 64]$$
$$\vdash [L5, \$(T +, a) * a\$, 64]$$
$$\vdash [L6, \$(T +, a) * a\$, 64]$$
$$\vdash [L7, \$(E +, a) * a\$, 642]$$
$$\vdash [L0, \$(E + a,) * a\$, 642]$$
$$\vdash [L1, \$(E + a,) * a\$, 642]$$
$$\vdash [L2, \$(E + F), * a\$, 6426]$$
$$\vdash [L3, \$(E + F), * a\$, 6426]$$
$$\vdash [L4, \$(E + T), * a\$, 64264]$$
$$\vdash [L5, \$(E + T), * a\$, 64264]$$
$$\vdash [L7, \$(E), * a\$, 642641]$$
$$\vdash [L8, \$(E), * a\$, 642641]$$
$$\vdash [L2, \$F *, a\$, 6426415]$$
$$\vdash [L3, \$F *, a\$, 6426415]$$
$$\vdash [L4, \$T *, a\$, 64264154]$$
$$\vdash [L0, \$T * a, \$, 64264154]$$
$$\vdash [L1, \$T * a, \$, 64264154]$$
$$\vdash [L2, \$T * F\$, e, 642641546]$$
$$\vdash [L4, \$T\$, e, 6426415463]$$
$$\vdash [L5, \$T\$, e, 6426415463]$$
$$\vdash [L6, \$T\$, e, 6426415463]$$
$$\vdash [L7, \$E\$, e, 64264154632]$$
$$\vdash [L8, \$E\$, e, 64264154632]$$
$$\vdash [L9, \$E\$, e, 64264154632]$$
$$\vdash \textbf{accept} \quad \square$$

It should be observed that a Floyd–Evans parser can be simulated by a DPDT. Thus each Floyd–Evans parser recognizes a deterministic CFL. However, the language recognized may not be the language of the grammar for which the Floyd–Evans parser is constructing a parse. This phenomenon occurs because the flow of control in the statements may cause certain reductions to be overlooked.

Example 5.48

Let G consist of the productions

$$(1)\ S \longrightarrow aS$$
$$(2)\ S \longrightarrow bS$$
$$(3)\ S \longrightarrow a$$

$L(G) = (a + b)^*a$. The following sequence of statements parses words in b^*a according to G, but accepts no other words:

$L0$:	$\|\# \longrightarrow \#\ \|$			*	
$L1$:	$a\| \longrightarrow S\ \|$		**emit 3**		$L4$
$L2$:	$b\|$	$\|$			$L0$
$L3$:	$\$\|$	$\|$	**error**		
$L4$:	$aS\| \longrightarrow S\ \|$		**emit 1**		$L4$
$L5$:	$bS\| \longrightarrow S\ \|$		**emit 2**		$L4$
$L6$:	$\$S\|\$ \longrightarrow \$S\$\|$		**accept**	*	
$L7$:	$\|$	$\|$	**error**		

With input ba, the parser makes the following moves:

$$[L0,\ \$,\ ba\$,\ e] \vdash [L1,\ \$b,\ a\$,\ e]$$
$$\vdash [L2,\ \$b,\ a\$,\ e]$$
$$\vdash [L0,\ \$b,\ a\$,\ e]$$
$$\vdash [L1,\ \$ba,\ \$,\ e]$$
$$\vdash [L4,\ \$bS,\ \$,\ 3]$$
$$\vdash [L5,\ \$bS,\ \$,\ 3]$$
$$\vdash [L4,\ \$S,\ \$,\ 32]$$
$$\vdash [L5,\ \$S,\ \$,\ 32]$$
$$\vdash [L6,\ \$S,\ \$,\ 32]$$

The input is accepted at statement $L6$. However, with input aa, the following sequence of moves is made:

$$[L0, \$, aa\$, e] \vdash [L1, \$a, a\$, e]$$
$$\vdash [L4, \$S, a\$, 3]$$
$$\vdash [L5, \$S, a\$, 3]$$
$$\vdash [L6, \$S, a\$, 3]$$
$$\vdash [L7, \$S, a\$, 3]$$

An error is declared at $L7$, even though aa is in $L(G)$.

There is nothing mysterious going on in Example 5.48. Production language programs are not tied to the grammar that they are parsing in the way that the other parsing algorithms of this chapter are tied to their grammars. □

In Chapter 7 we shall provide an algorithm for mechanically generating a Floyd–Evans production language parser for a uniquely invertible weak precedence grammar.

5.4.5. Chapter Summary

The diagram in Fig. 5.22 gives the hierarchy of grammars encountered in this chapter.

All containments in Fig. 5.22 can be shown to be proper. Those inclusions which have not been proved in this chapter are left for the Exercises. The inclusion of LL grammars in the LR grammars is proved in Chapter 8.

Insofar as the classes of languages that are generated by these classes of grammars are concerned, we can demonstrate the following results:

(1) The class of languages generated by each of the following classes of grammars is precisely the class of deterministic context-free languages:

(a) LR.   (b) LR(1).
(c) BRC.   (d) (1, 1)-BRC.
(e) MSP.   (f) Simple MSP.
(g) Uniquely invertible (2, 1)   (h) Floyd–Evans parsable.
    precedence.

(2) The class of LL languages is a proper subset of the deterministic CFL's.

(3) The uniquely invertible weak precedence grammars generate exactly the simple precedence languages, which are

(a) A proper subset of the deterministic CFL's and

(b) Incommensurate with the LL languages.

(4) The class of languages generated by operator precedence grammars is the same as that generated by the uniquely invertible operator precedence grammars. This class of languages is properly contained in the class of simple precedence languages.

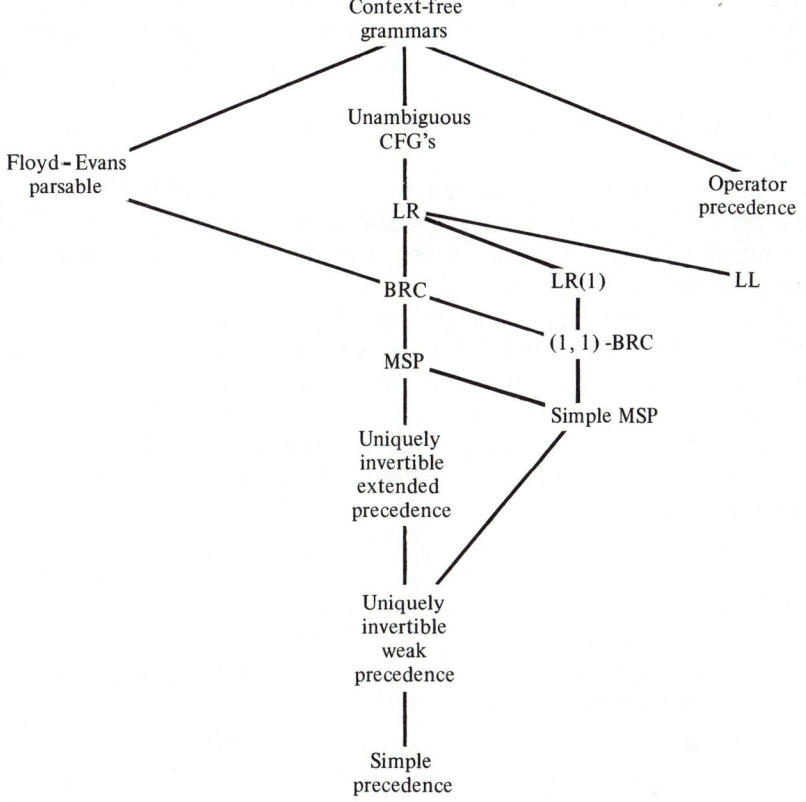

Fig. 5.22   Hierarchy of grammars.

Many of these results on languages will be found in Chapter 8.

The reader may well ask which class of grammars is best suited for describing programming languages and which parsing technique is best. There is no clear-cut answer to such a question. The simplest class of grammars may often require manipulating a given grammar in order to make it fall into that class. Often the grammar becomes unnatural and unsuitable for use in a syntax-directed translation scheme.

The LL(1) grammars are particularly attractive for practical use. For each LL(1) grammar we can find a parser which is small, fast, and produces a left parse, which is advantageous for translation purposes. However, there are some disadvantages. An LL(1) grammar for a given language can be unnatural and difficult to construct. Moreover, not every deterministic CFL has an LL grammar, let alone an LL(1) grammar, as we shall see in Chapter 8.

Operator precedence techniques have been used in several compilers, are easy to implement and work quite efficiently. The $(1, 1)$-precedence grammars are also easy to parse, but obtaining a $(1, 1)$-precedence grammar for a language often requires the addition of many single productions of the form $A \longrightarrow X$ to make the precedence relations disjoint. Also, there are many deterministic CFL's for which no uniquely invertible simple or weak precedence grammar exists.

The LR(1) technique presented in this chapter closely follows Knuth's original work. The resulting parsers can be extremely large. However, the techniques to be presented in Chapter 7 produce LR(1) parsers whose size and operating speed are competitive with precedence parsers for a wide variety of programming languages. See Lalonde et al. [1971] for some empirical results. Since the LR(1) grammars embrace a large class of grammars, LR(1) parsing techniques are also attractive.

Finally we should point out that it is often possible to improve the performance of any given parsing technique in a specific application. In Chapter 7 we shall discuss some methods which can be used to reduce the size and increase the speed of parsers.

EXERCISES

5.4.1. Give a shift reduce parsing algorithm based on the $(1, 0)$-BRC technique for G_1 of Example 5.41.

5.4.2. Which of the following grammars are $(1, 1)$-BRC?
    (a) $S \longrightarrow aA \,|\, B$
        $A \longrightarrow 0A1 \,|\, a$
        $B \longrightarrow 0B1 \,|\, b.$
    (b) $S \longrightarrow aA \,|\, bB$
        $A \longrightarrow 0A1 \,|\, 01$
        $B \longrightarrow 0B1 \,|\, 01.$
    (c) $E \longrightarrow E + T \,|\, E - T \,|\, T$
        $T \longrightarrow T * F \,|\, T/F \,|\, F$
        $F \longrightarrow (E) \,|\, -E \,|\, a.$

DEFINITION

A proper CFG $G = (N, \Sigma, P, S)$ is an (m, n)-*bounded context* (BC) grammar if the three conditions

(1) $\$^m S' \$^n \overset{*}{\Longrightarrow} \alpha_1 A_1 \gamma_1 \Longrightarrow \alpha_1 \beta_1 \gamma_1$ in the augmented grammar,

(2) $\$^m S' \$^n \overset{*}{\Longrightarrow} \alpha_2 A_2 \gamma_2 \Longrightarrow \alpha_2 \beta_2 \gamma_2 = \alpha_3 \beta_1 \gamma_3$ in the augmented grammar, and

(3) The last m symbols of α_1 and α_3 agree and the first n symbols of γ_1 and γ_3 agree

imply that $\alpha_3 A_1 \gamma_3 = \alpha_2 A_2 \gamma_2.$

5.4.3. Show that every (m, n)-BC grammar is an (m, n)-BRC grammar.

5.4.4. Give a shift–reduce parsing algorithm for BC grammars.

5.4.5. Give an example of a BRC grammar that is not BC.

5.4.6. Show that every uniquely invertible extended precedence grammar is BRC.

5.4.7. Show that every BRC grammar is extended precedence (not necessarily uniquely invertible, of course).

5.4.8. For those grammars of Exercise 5.4.2 which are $(1, 1)$-BRC, give shift–reduce parsing algorithms and implement them with decision trees.

5.4.9. Prove the "only if" portion of Lemma 5.6.

5.4.10. Prove Theorem 5.22.

5.4.11. Which of the following grammars are simple MSP grammars?
(a) G_0.
(b) $S \longrightarrow A \,|\, B$
$A \longrightarrow 0A1 \,|\, 01$
$B \longrightarrow 2B1 \,|\, 1$.
(c) $S \longrightarrow A \,|\, B$
$A \longrightarrow 0A1 \,|\, 01$
$B \longrightarrow 0B1 \,|\, 1$.
(d) $S \longrightarrow A \,|\, B$
$A \longrightarrow 0A1 \,|\, 01$
$B \longrightarrow 01B1 \,|\, 01$.

5.4.12. Show that every uniquely invertible weak precedence grammar is a simple MSP grammar.

5.4.13. Is every $(m, n; m, n)$-MSP grammar an (m, n)-BRC grammar?

5.4.14. Prove Theorem 5.24.

5.4.15. Are the following grammars operator precedence?
(a) The grammar of Exercise 5.4.2(b).
(b) $S \longrightarrow$ **if** B **then** S **else** S
$S \longrightarrow$ **if** B **then** S
$S \longrightarrow s$
$B \longrightarrow B$ **or** b
$B \longrightarrow b$.
(c) $S \longrightarrow$ **if** B **then** S_1 **else** S
$S \longrightarrow$ **if** B **then** S
$S_1 \longrightarrow$ **if** B **then** S_1 **else** S_1
$S \longrightarrow s$
$S_1 \longrightarrow s$
$B \longrightarrow B$ **or** b
$B \longrightarrow b$.
The intention in (b) and (c) is that the terminal symbols are **if, then, else, or,** b, and s.

5.4.16. Give the skeletal grammars for the grammars of Exercise 5.4.15.

5.4.17. Give shift–reduce parsing functions for those grammars of Exercise 5.4.15 which are operator precedence.

5.4.18. Prove Theorem 5.25.

5.4.19. Show that the skeletal grammar G_s is uniquely invertible for every operator grammar G.

*5.4.20. Show that every operator precedence language has an operator precedence grammar with no single productions.

*5.4.21. Show that every operator precedence language has a uniquely invertible operator precedence grammar.

5.4.22. Give production language parsers for the grammars of Exercise 5.4.2.

5.4.23. Show that every BRC grammar has a Floyd–Evans production language parser.

5.4.24. Show that every LL(k) grammar has a production language parser (generating left parses).

**5.4.25. Show that it is undecidable whether a grammar is
(a) BRC.
(b) BC.
(c) MSP.

5.4.26. Prove that a grammar $G = (N, \Sigma, P, S)$ is simple MSP if and only if it is a weak precedence grammar and if $A \longrightarrow \alpha$ and $B \longrightarrow \alpha$ are in P, $A \neq B$, then $l(A) \cap l(B) = \varnothing$.

*5.4.27. Suppose we relax the condition on an operator grammar that it be proper and have no e-productions. Show that under this new definition, L is an operator precedence language if and only if $L - \{e\}$ is an operator precedence language under our definition.

5.4.28. Extend Domolki's algorithm as presented in the Exercises of Section 4.1 to carry along information on the pushdown list so that it can be used to parse BRC grammars.

DEFINITION

We can generalize the idea of operator precedence to utilize for our parsing a set of symbols including all the terminals and, perhaps, some of the nonterminals as well. Let $G = (N, \Sigma, P, S)$ be a proper CFG with no e-production and T a subset of $N \cup \Sigma$, with $\Sigma \subseteq T$. Let V denote $N \cup \Sigma$. We say that G is a *T-canonical grammar* if

(1) For each right side of a production, say $\alpha X Y \beta$, if X is not in T, then Y is in Σ, and

(2) If A is in T and $A \overset{*}{\Rightarrow} \alpha$, then α has a symbol of T.

Thus a Σ-canonical grammar is the same as an operator grammar. If G is a T-canonical grammar, we say that T is a *token set* for G.

If G is a T-canonical grammar, we define *T-canonical precedence relations*, $\lessdot$, $\doteq$, and $\gtrdot$ on $T \cup \{\$\}$, as follows:

(1) If there is a production $A \longrightarrow \alpha X \beta Y \gamma$, X and Y are in T, and β is either e or in $(V - T)$, then $X \doteq Y$.

(2) If $A \longrightarrow \alpha X B \beta$ is in P and $B \overset{+}{\Rightarrow} \gamma Y \delta$, where X and Y are in T and γ is either e or in $V - T$, then $X \lessdot Y$.

(3) Let $A \longrightarrow \alpha_1 B \alpha_2 Z \alpha_3$ be in P, where α_2 is either e or a symbol of $V - T$. Suppose that $Z \overset{*}{\Rightarrow} \beta_1 a \beta_2$, where β_1 is either e or in $V - T$, and a is in Σ. (Note that this derivation must be zero steps if $\alpha_2 \neq e$, by the T-canonical grammar definition.) Suppose also that there is a derivation

$$B \Rightarrow \gamma_1 C_1 \delta_1 \Rightarrow \gamma_1 \gamma_2 C_2 \delta_2 \delta_1 \Rightarrow \cdots \Rightarrow \gamma_1 \cdots \gamma_{k-1} C_{k-1} \delta_{k-1} \cdots \delta_1$$
$$\Rightarrow \gamma_1 \cdots \gamma_k X \delta_k \cdots \delta_1,$$

where the C's are replaced at each step, the δ's are all in $\{e\} \cup V - T$, and X is in T. Then we say that $X \gtrdot a$.

(4) If $S \overset{+}{\Rightarrow} \alpha X \beta$ and α is in $\{e\} \cup V - T$, then $\$ \lessdot X$. If β is in $\{e\} \cup V - T$, then $X \gtrdot \$$.

Note that if $T = \Sigma$, we have defined the operator precedence relations, and if $T = V$, we have the Wirth–Weber relations.

Example 5.49

Consider G_0, with token set $\Delta = \{F, a, (,), +, *\}$. We find $(\doteq)$, since (E) is a right side, and E is not a token. We have $+ \lessdot *$, since there is a right side $E + T$, and a derivation $T \overset{+}{\Rightarrow} T * F$, and T is not a token. Also, $+ \gtrdot +$, since there is a right side $E + T$ and a derivation $E \Rightarrow E + T$, and T is not a token. The Δ-canonical relations for G_0 are shown in Fig. 5.23. $\square$

	a	$+$	$*$	$($	$)$	F	$\$$
a		$\gtrdot$	$\gtrdot$		$\gtrdot$		$\gtrdot$
$+$	$\lessdot$	$\gtrdot$	$\lessdot$	$\lessdot$	$\gtrdot$	$\lessdot$	$\gtrdot$
$*$	$\lessdot$			$\lessdot$		$\doteq$	
$($	$\lessdot$	$\lessdot$	$\lessdot$	$\lessdot$	$\doteq$	$\lessdot$	
$)$		$\gtrdot$	$\gtrdot$		$\gtrdot$		$\gtrdot$
F		$\gtrdot$	$\gtrdot$		$\gtrdot$		$\gtrdot$
$\$$	$\lessdot$	$\lessdot$	$\lessdot$	$\lessdot$		$\lessdot$	

Fig. 5.23 Δ-canonical precedence relations.

5.4.29. Find all token sets for G_0.

5.4.30. Show that Σ is a token set for $G = (N, \Sigma, P, S)$ if and only if G is an operator precedence grammar. Show that $N \cup \Sigma$ is a token set if and only if G is a precedence grammar.

DEFINITION

Let $G = (N, \Sigma, P, S)$ be a T-canonical grammar. The T-skeletal grammar for G is formed by replacing all instances of symbols in $V - T$ by a new symbol S_0 and deleting the production $S_0 \longrightarrow S_0$ if it appears.

Example 5.50

Let Δ be as in Example 5.49. The Δ-skeletal grammar for G_0 is

$$S_0 \longrightarrow S_0 + S_0 \mid S_0 * F \mid F$$
$$F \longrightarrow (S_0) \mid a \qquad\qquad \square$$

5.4.31. Give a shift–reduce parsing algorithm for T-canonical precedence grammars whose T-skeletal grammar is uniquely invertible. Parses in the skeletal grammar are produced, of course.

Research Problem

5.4.32. Develop transformations which can be used to make grammars BRC, simple precedence, or operator precedence.

Programming Exercises

5.4.33. Write a program that tests whether a given grammar is an operator precedence grammar.

5.4.34. Write a program that constructs an operator precedence parser for an operator precedence grammar.

5.4.35. Find an operator precedence grammar for one of the languages in the Appendix and then construct an operator precedence parser for that language.

5.4.36. Write a program that constructs a bounded-right-context parser for a grammar G if G is (1, 1)-BRC.

5.4.37. Write a program that constructs a simple mixed strategy precedence parser for a grammar G if G is simple MSP.

5.4.38. Define a programming language centered around the Floyd–Evans production language. Construct a compiler for this programming language.

BIBLIOGRAPHIC NOTES

Various precedence-oriented parsing techniques were employed in the earliest compilers. The formalization of operator precedence is due to Floyd [1963]. Bounded context and bounded-right-context parsing methods were also defined in the early 1960's. Most of the early development of bounded context parsing and variants of it is reported by Eickel et al. [1963], Floyd [1963, 1964a, 1964b], Graham [1964], Irons [1964], and Paul [1962].

The definition of bounded-right-context grammar here is equivalent to that given by Floyd [1964a]. An algorithm for constructing parsers for certain classes of BRC grammars is given by Loeckx [1970]. An extension of Domolki's algorithm to BRC grammars is given by Wise [1971].

Mixed strategy precedence was introduced by McKeeman and used by McKeeman et al. [1970] as the basis of the XPL compiler writing system.

Production language was first introduced by Floyd [1961] and later modified by Evans [1964]. Feldman [1966] used it as the basis of a compiler writing system called Formal Semantic Language (FSL) by permitting general semantic routines in the ⟨action⟩ field of each production language statement.

T-canonical precedence was defined by Gray and Harrison [1969]. Example 5.47 is from Hopgood [1969].

6 LIMITED BACKTRACK PARSING ALGORITHMS

In this chapter we shall discuss several parsing algorithms which, like the general top-down and bottom-up algorithms in Section 4.1, may involve backtracking. However, in the algorithms of this chapter the amount of backtracking that can occur is limited. As a consequence, the parsing algorithms to be presented here are more economical than those in Chapter 4. Nevertheless, these algorithms should not be used in situations where a deterministic nonbacktracking algorithm will suffice.

In the first section we shall discuss two high-level languages in which top-down parsing algorithms with restricted backtracking capabilities can be written. These languages, called TDPL and GTDPL, are capable of specifying recognizers for all deterministic context-free languages with an endmarker and, because of the restricted backtracking, even some non-context-free languages, but (probably) not all context-free languages. We shall then discuss a method of constructing, for a large class of CFG's, precedence-oriented bottom-up parsing algorithms, which allow a limited amount of backtracking.

6.1. LIMITED BACKTRACK TOP-DOWN PARSING

In this section we shall define two formalisms for limited backtrack parsing algorithms that create parse trees top-down, exhaustively trying all alternates for each nonterminal, until one alternate has been found which derives a prefix of the remaining input. Once such an alternate is found, no other alternates will be tried. Of course, the "wrong" prefix may have been found, and in this case the algorithm will not backtrack but will fail. Fortunately, this aspect of the algorithm is rarely a serious problem in practical situations, provided we order the alternates so that the longest is tried first.

We shall show relationships between the two formalisms, discuss their implementation, and then treat them briefly as mechanisms which define classes of languages. We shall discover that the classes of languages defined are different from the class of CFL's.

6.1.1. TDPL

Consider the general top-down parsing algorithm of Section 4.1. Suppose we decide to generate a string from a nonterminal A and that $\alpha_1, \alpha_2, \ldots, \alpha_n$ are the alternates for A. Suppose further that in a correct parse of the input, A derives some prefix x of the remaining input, starting with the derivation $A \underset{\text{lm}}{\Rightarrow} \alpha_m$, $1 \leq m \leq n$, but that $A \underset{\text{lm}}{\Rightarrow} \alpha_j$, for $j < m$, does not lead to a correct parse.

The top-down parsing algorithm in Chapter 4 would try the alternates $\alpha_1, \alpha_2, \ldots, \alpha_m$ in order. After each α_j failed, $j < m$, the input pointer would be reset, and a new attempt would be made, using α_{j+1}. This new attempt would be made regardless of whether α_j derived a terminal string which was a prefix of the remaining input.

Here we shall consider a parsing technique in which nonterminals are treated as string-matching procedures. To illustrate this technique suppose that $a_1 \cdots a_n$ is the input string and that we have generated a partial left parse successfully matching the first $i - 1$ input symbols. If nonterminal A is to be expanded next, then the nonterminal A can be "called" as a procedure, with input position i as an argument. If A derives a terminal string that is a prefix of $a_i a_{i+1} \cdots a_n$, then A is said to *succeed* starting at input position i. Otherwise, A *fails* at position i.

These procedures call themselves recursively. If A were called in this manner, A itself would call the nonterminals of its first alternate, α_1. If α_1 failed, then A would replace the input pointer to where it was when A was first called, and then A would call α_2, and so forth. If α_j succeeds in matching $a_i a_{i+1} \cdots a_k$, then A returns to the procedure that called it and advances the input pointer to position $k + 1$.

The difference between the current algorithm and Algorithm 4.1 is that should the latter fail to find a complete parse in which α_j derives $a_i \cdots a_k$, then it will backtrack and try derivations beginning with productions $A \to \alpha_{j+1}$, $A \to \alpha_{j+2}$, and so forth, possibly deriving a different prefix of $a_i \cdots a_n$ from A. Our algorithm will not do so. Once it has found that α_j derives a prefix of the input and that the subsequent derivation fails to match the input, our parsing algorithm returns to the procedure that called A, reporting failure. The algorithm will act as if A can derive no prefix whatsoever of $a_i \cdots a_n$. Thus our algorithm may miss some parses and may not even recognize the same language as its underlying CFG defines. We shall therefore not tie our algorithm to a particular CFG, but will treat it as a formalism for language definition and syntactic analysis in its own right.

Let us consider a concrete example. If

$$S \longrightarrow Ac$$
$$A \longrightarrow a \,|\, ab$$

are productions and the alternates are taken in the order shown, then the limited backtrack algorithm will not recognize the sentence abc. The nonterminal S called at input position 1 will call A at input position 1. Using the first alternate, A reports success and moves the input pointer to position 2. However, c does not match the second input symbol, so S reports failure starting at input position 1. Since A reported success the first time it was called, it will not be called to try the second alternate. Note that we can avoid this difficulty by writing the alternates for A as

$$A \longrightarrow ab \,|\, a$$

We shall now describe the "top-down parsing language," TDPL, which can be used to describe parsing procedures of this nature. A *statement* (or *rule*) of TDPL is a string of one of the following forms:

$$A \longrightarrow BC/D$$

or

$$A \longrightarrow a$$

where A, B, C, and D are nonterminal symbols and a is a terminal symbol, the empty string, or a special symbol f (for failure).

DEFINITION

A TDPL *program P* is a 4-tuple (N, Σ, R, S), where

(1) N and Σ are finite disjoint sets of *nonterminals* and *terminals*,

(2) R is a sequence of TDPL statements such that for each A in N there is at most one statement with A to the left of the arrow, and

(3) S in N is the *start symbol*.

A TDPL program can be likened to a grammar in a special normal form. A statement of the form $A \longrightarrow BC/D$ is representative of the two productions $A \longrightarrow BC$ and $A \longrightarrow D$, where the former is always to be tried first. A statement of the form $A \longrightarrow a$ represents a production of that form when $a \in \Sigma$ or $a = e$. If $a = f$, then the nonterminal A has a special meaning, which will be described later.

Alternatively, we can describe a TDPL program as a set of procedures (the nonterminals) which are called recursively with certain inputs. The outcome of a call will either be **failure** (no prefix of the input is matched or recognized) or **success** (some prefix of the input is matched).

The following sequence of procedure calls results from a call of a statement of the form $A \rightarrow BC/D$, with input w:

(1) First, A calls B with input w. If $w = xx'$ and B matches x, then B reports **success**. A then calls C with input x'.

    (a) If $x' = yz$ and C matches y, then C reports **success**. A then returns **success** and reports that it has matched the prefix xy of w.

    (b) If C does not match any prefix of x', then C reports **failure**. A then calls D with input w. Note that the success of B is undone in this case.

(2) If, when A calls B with input w, B cannot match any prefix of w, then B reports **failure**. A then calls D with input w.

(3) If D has been called with input $w = uv$ and D matches u, a prefix of w, then D reports **success**. A then returns **success** and reports that it has matched the prefix u of w.

(4) If D has been called with input w and D cannot match any prefix of w, then D reports **failure**. A then reports **failure**.

Note that D gets called unless both B and C succeed. We shall later explore a parsing system in which D is called only if B fails. Note also that if both B and C succeed, then the alternate D can never be called. This feature distinguishes TDPL from the general top-down parsing algorithm of Chapter 4.

The special statements $A \rightarrow a$, $A \rightarrow e$, and $A \rightarrow f$ are handled as follows:

(1) If $A \rightarrow a$ is the rule for A with $a \in \Sigma$ and A is called on an input beginning with a, then A succeeds and matches this a. Otherwise, A fails.

(2) If $A \rightarrow e$ is the rule for A, then A succeeds whenever it is called and always matches the empty string.

(3) If $A \rightarrow f$ is the rule, A fails whenever it is called.

We shall now formalize the notion of a nonterminal "acting on an input string."

DEFINITION

Let $P = (\mathrm{N}, T, R, S)$ be a TDPL program. We define a set of relations $\underset{P}{\overset{n}{\Rightarrow}}$ from nonterminals to pairs of the form $(x \restriction y, r)$, where x and y are in Σ^* and r is either s (for **success**) or f (for **failure**). The metasymbol $\restriction$ is used to indicate the position of the current input symbol. We shall drop the subscript P wherever possible.

(1) If $A \rightarrow e$ is in R, then $A \overset{1}{\Rightarrow} (\restriction w, s)$ for all $w \in \Sigma^*$.

(2) If $A \rightarrow f$ is in R, then $A \overset{1}{\Rightarrow} (\restriction w, f)$ for all $w \in \Sigma^*$.

(3) If $A \rightarrow a$ is in R, with $a \in \Sigma$, then

    (a) $A \overset{1}{\Rightarrow} (a \restriction x, s)$ for all $x \in \Sigma^*$.

    (b) $A \overset{1}{\Rightarrow} (\restriction y, f)$ for all those $y \in \Sigma^*$ (including e) which do not begin with the symbol a.

(4) Let $A \rightarrow BC/D$ be in R.

    (a) $A \overset{m+n+1}{\Longrightarrow} (xy \restriction z, s)$ if

      (i) $B \overset{m}{\Rightarrow} (x \restriction yz, s)$ and

      (ii) $C \overset{n}{\Rightarrow} (y \restriction z, s)$.

    (b) $A \overset{i}{\Rightarrow} (u \restriction v, s)$, with $i = m + n + p + 1$, if

      (i) $B \overset{m}{\Rightarrow} (x \restriction y, s)$,

      (ii) $C \overset{n}{\Rightarrow} (\restriction y, f)$, and

      (iii) $D \overset{p}{\Rightarrow} (u \restriction v, s)$, where $uv = xy$.

    (c) $A \overset{i}{\Rightarrow} (\restriction xy, f)$, with $i = m + n + p + 1$, if

      (i) $B \overset{m}{\Rightarrow} (x \restriction y, s)$,

      (ii) $C \overset{n}{\Rightarrow} (\restriction y, f)$, and

      (iii) $D \overset{p}{\Rightarrow} (\restriction xy, f)$.

    (d) $A \overset{m+n+1}{\Longrightarrow} (x \restriction y, s)$, if

      (i) $B \overset{m}{\Rightarrow} (\restriction xy, f)$, and

      (ii) $D \overset{n}{\Rightarrow} (x \restriction y, s)$.

    (e) $A \overset{m+n+1}{\Longrightarrow} (\restriction x, f)$, if

      (i) $B \overset{m}{\Rightarrow} (\restriction x, f)$, and

      (ii) $D \overset{n}{\Rightarrow} (\restriction x, f)$.

(5) The relations $\overset{n}{\Rightarrow}$ do not hold except when required by (1)–(4).

Case (4a) takes care of the case in which B and C both succeed. In (4b) and (4c), B succeeds but C fails. In (4d) and (4e), B fails. In the last four cases, D is called and alternately succeeds and fails. Note that the integer above the arrow indicates the number of "calls" which were made before the outcome is reached. Observe also that if $A \overset{}{\Rightarrow} (x \restriction y, f)$, then $x = e$. That is, failure always resets the input pointer to where it was at the beginning of the call.

We define $A \overset{+}{\underset{P}{\Rightarrow}} (x \restriction y, r)$ if and only if $A \overset{n}{\Rightarrow} (x \restriction y, r)$ for some $n \geq 1$. The *language defined by* P, denoted $L(P)$, is $\{w \mid S \overset{+}{\Rightarrow} (w \restriction, s)$ and $w \in \Sigma^*\}$.

Example 6.1

Let P be the TDPL program $(\{S, A, B, C\}, \{a, b\}, R, S)$, where R is the sequence of statements

$$S \longrightarrow AB/C$$
$$A \longrightarrow a$$
$$B \longrightarrow CB/A$$
$$C \longrightarrow b$$

Let us investigate the action of P on the input string aba using the relations defined above. To begin, since $S \longrightarrow AB/C$ is the rule for S, S calls A with input aba. A recognizes the first input symbol and returns success. Using part (3) of the previous definition we can write $A \overset{1}{\Rightarrow} (a \upharpoonright ba, s)$. Then, S calls B with input ba. Since $B \longrightarrow CB/A$ is the rule for B, we must examine the behavior of C on ba. We find that C matches b and returns success. Using (3) we write $C \overset{1}{\Rightarrow} (b \upharpoonright a, s)$.

Then B calls itself recursively with input a. However, C fails on a and so $C \overset{1}{\Rightarrow} (\upharpoonright a, f)$. B then calls A with input a. Since A matches a, $A \overset{1}{\Rightarrow} (a \upharpoonright, s)$. Since A succeeds, the second call of B succeeds. Using rule (4d) we write $B \overset{3}{\Rightarrow} (a \upharpoonright, s)$.

Returning to the first call of B on input ba, both C and B have succeeded, so this call of B succeeds and we can write $B \overset{5}{\Rightarrow} (ba \upharpoonright, s)$ using rule (4a).

Now returning to the call of S, both A and B have succeeded. Thus, S matches aba and returns **success**. Using rule (4a) we can write $S \overset{7}{\Rightarrow} (aba \upharpoonright, s)$. Thus, aba is in $L(P)$.

It is not difficult to show that $L(P) = ab^*a + b$. $\square$

An important property of a TDPL is that the outcome of any program on a given input is unique. We prove this in the following lemma.

LEMMA 6.1

Suppose that $P = (N, \Sigma, R, S)$ is a TDPL program such that for some $A \in N$, $A \overset{n_1}{\Rightarrow} (x_1 \upharpoonright y_1, r_1)$ and $A \overset{n_2}{\Rightarrow} (x_2 \upharpoonright y_2, r_2)$, where $x_1 y_1 = x_2 y_2 = w \in \Sigma^*$. Then we must have $x_1 = x_2$, $y_1 = y_2$, and $r_1 = r_2$.

Proof. The proof is a simple induction on the minimum of n_1 and n_2, which we can take without loss of generality to be n_1.

Basis. $n_1 = 1$. Then the rule for A is $A \longrightarrow a$, $a \longrightarrow e$, or $A \longrightarrow f$. The conclusion is immediate.

Induction. Assume the conclusion for $n < n_1$, and let $n_1 > 1$. Let the rule for A be $A \to BC/D$. Suppose that for $i = 1$ and 2, $A \overset{n_i}{\Rightarrow} (x_i \restriction y_i, r_i)$ was formed by rule (4) from $B \overset{m_i}{\Rightarrow} (u_i \restriction v_i, t_i)$ and (possibly) $C \overset{k_i}{\Rightarrow} (u'_i \restriction v'_i, t'_i)$ and/or $D \overset{l_i}{\Rightarrow} (u''_i \restriction v''_i, t''_i)$. Then $m_1 < n_1$, so the inductive hypothesis applies to give $u_1 = u_2$, $v_1 = v_2$, and $t_1 = t_2$. Now two cases, depending on the value of t_1, have to be considered.

Case 1: $t_1 = t_2 = f$. Then since $l_1 < n_1$, we have $u''_1 = u''_2$, $v''_1 = v''_2$, and $t''_1 = t''_2$. Since $x_i = u''_i$, $y_i = v''_i$, and $r_i = t_i$ for $i = 1$ and 2 in this case, the desired result follows.

Case 2: $t_1 = t_2 = s$. Then $u'_i v'_i = v_i$ for $i = 1$ and 2. Since $k_1 < n_1$, we may conclude that $u'_1 = u'_2$, $v'_1 = v'_2$, and $t'_1 = t'_2$. If $t'_1 = s$, then $x_i = u_i u'_i$, $y_i = v'_i$, and $r_i = s$ for $i = 1$ and 2. We reach the desired conclusion. If $t'_1 = f$, the argument proceeds with u''_i and v''_i as in case 1. $\square$

It should also be noted that a TDPL program need not have a response to every input. For example, any program having the rule $S \to SS/S$, where S is the start symbol, will not recognize any sentence (that is, the $\overset{+}{\Rightarrow}$ relation is empty).

The notation we have used for a TDPL to this point was designed for ease of presentation. In practical situations it is desirable to use more general rules. For this purpose, we now introduce *extended* TDPL rules and define their meaning in terms of the basic rules:

(1) We take the rule $A \to BC$ to stand for the pair of rules $A \to BC/D$ and $D \to f$, where D is a new symbol.

(2) We take the rule $A \to B/C$ to stand for the pair of rules $A \to BD/C$ and $D \to e$.

(3) We take the rule $A \to B$ to stand for the rules $A \to BC$ and $C \to e$.

(4) We take the rule $A \to A_1 A_2 \cdots A_n$, $n > 2$, to stand for the set of rules $A \to A_1 B_1$, $B_1 \to A_2 B_2$, ..., $B_{n-3} \to A_{n-2} B_{n-2}$, $B_{n-2} \to A_{n-1} A_n$.

(5) We take the rule $A \to \alpha_1/\alpha_2/ \cdots /\alpha_n$, where the α's are strings of nonterminals, to stand for the set of rules $A \to B_1/C_1$, $C_1 \to B_2/C_2$, ..., $C_{n-3} \to B_{n-2}/C_{n-2}$, $C_{n-2} \to B_{n-1}/B_n$, and $B_1 \to \alpha_1$, $B_2 \to \alpha_2$, ..., $B_n \to \alpha_n$. If $n = 2$, these rules reduce to $A \to B_1/B_2$, $B_1 \to \alpha_1$, and $B_2 \to \alpha_2$. For $1 \leq i \leq n$ if $|\alpha_i| = 1$, we can let B_i be α_i and eliminate the rule $B_i \to \alpha_i$.

(6) We take rule $A \to \alpha_1/\alpha_2/ \cdots /\alpha_n$, where the α's are strings of nonterminals and terminals, to stand for the set of rules $A \to \alpha'_1/\alpha'_2/ \cdots /\alpha'_n$, and $X_a \to a$ for each terminal a, where α'_i is α_i with each terminal a replaced by X_a.

Henceforth we shall allow extended rules of this type in TDPL programs. The definitions above provide a mechanical way of constructing an equivalent TDPL program that meets the original definition.

These extended rules have natural meanings. For example, if A has the rule $A \to Y_1 Y_2 \cdots Y_n$, then A succeeds if and only if Y_1 succeeds at the input position where A is called, Y_2 succeeds where Y_1 left off, Y_3 succeeds where Y_2 left off, and so forth.

Likewise, if A has the rule $A \longrightarrow \alpha_1/\alpha_2/ \cdots /\alpha_n$, then A succeeds if and only if α_1 succeeds where A is called, or if α_1 fails, and α_2 succeeds where A is called, and so forth.

Example 6.2

Consider the extended TDPL program $P = (\{E, F, T\}, \{a, (,), +, *\}, R, S)$, where R consists of

$$E \longrightarrow T + E/T$$
$$T \longrightarrow F * T/F$$
$$F \longrightarrow (E)/a$$

The reader should convince himself that $L(P) = L(G_0)$, where G_0 is our standard grammar for arithmetic expressions.

To convert P to standard form, we first apply rule (6), introducing non-terminals X_a, $X_($, $X_)$, X_+, and X_*. The rules become

$$E \longrightarrow TX_+E/T$$
$$T \longrightarrow FX_*T/F$$
$$F \longrightarrow X_(EX_)/X_a$$
$$X_a \longrightarrow a$$
$$X_(\longrightarrow ($$
$$X_) \longrightarrow)$$
$$X_+ \longrightarrow +$$
$$X_* \longrightarrow *$$

By rule (5), the first rule is replaced by $E \longrightarrow B_1/T$ and $B_1 \longrightarrow TX_+E$. By rule (4), $B_1 \longrightarrow TX_+E$ is replaced by $B_1 \longrightarrow TB_2$ and $B_2 \longrightarrow X_+E$. Then, these are replaced by $B_1 \longrightarrow TB_2/D$, $B_2 \longrightarrow X_+E/D$, and $D \longrightarrow f$. Rule $E \longrightarrow B_1/T$ is replaced by $E \longrightarrow B_1C/T$ and $C \longrightarrow e$. The entire set of rules constructed is

$X_a \longrightarrow a$	$D \longrightarrow f$	$B_4 \longrightarrow X_*T/D$
$X_(\longrightarrow ($	$E \longrightarrow B_1C/T$	$F \longrightarrow B_5C/X_a$
$X_) \longrightarrow)$	$B_1 \longrightarrow TB_2/D$	$B_5 \longrightarrow X_(B_6/D$
$X_+ \longrightarrow +$	$B_2 \longrightarrow X_+E/D$	$B_6 \longrightarrow EX_)/D$
$X_* \longrightarrow *$	$T \longrightarrow B_3C/F$	
$C \longrightarrow e$	$B_3 \longrightarrow FB_4/D$	

We have simplified the rules by identifying each nonterminal X that has rule $X \rightarrow e$ with C and each nonterminal Y that has rule $Y \rightarrow f$ with D. $\square$

Whenever a TDPL program recognizes a sentence w, we can build a "parse tree" for that sentence top-down by tracing through the sequence of TDPL statements executed in recognizing w. The interior nodes of this parse tree correspond to nonterminals which are called during the execution of the program and which report success.

ALGORITHM 6.1

Derivation tree from the execution of a TDPL program.

Input. A TDPL program $P = (N, \Sigma, R, S)$ and a sentence w in Σ^* such that $S \overset{n}{\Rightarrow} (w \upharpoonright, s)$.

Output. A derivation tree for w.

Method. The heart of the algorithm is a recursive routine **buildtree** which takes as argument a statement of the form $A \overset{m}{\Rightarrow} (x \upharpoonright y, s)$ and builds a tree whose root is labeled A and whose frontier is x. Routine **buildtree** is initially called with the statement $S \overset{n}{\Rightarrow} (w \upharpoonright, s)$ as argument.

Routine **buildtree**: Let $A \overset{m}{\Rightarrow} (x \upharpoonright y, s)$ be input to the routine.

(1) If the rule for A is $A \rightarrow a$ or $A \rightarrow e$, then create a node with label A and one direct descendant, labeled a or e, respectively. Halt.

(2) If the rule for A is $A \rightarrow BC/D$ and we can write $x = x_1 x_2$ such that $B \overset{m_1}{\Rightarrow} (x_1 \upharpoonright x_2 y, s)$ and $C \overset{m_2}{\Rightarrow} (x_2 \upharpoonright y, s)$, create a node labeled A. Execute routine **buildtree** with argument $B \overset{m_1}{\Rightarrow} (x_1 \upharpoonright x_2 y, s)$, and then with argument $C \overset{m_2}{\Rightarrow} (x_2 \upharpoonright y, s)$. Attach the resulting trees to the node labeled A, so that the roots of the trees resulting from the first and second calls are the left and right direct descendants of the node. Halt.

(3) If the rule for A is $A \rightarrow BC/D$ but (2) does not hold, then it must be that $D \overset{m_3}{\Rightarrow} (x \upharpoonright y, s)$. Call routine **buildtree** with this argument and make the root of the resulting tree the lone direct descendant of a created node labeled A. Halt. $\square$

Note that routine **buildtree** calls itself recursively only with smaller values of m, so Algorithm 6.1 must terminate.

Example 6.3

Let us use Algorithm 6.1 to construct a parse tree generated by the TDPL program P of Example 6.1 for the input sentence *aba*.

We initially call routine **buildtree** with the statement $S \overset{7}{\Rightarrow} (aba \upharpoonright, s)$ as argument. The rule $S \rightarrow AB/C$ succeeds because A and B each succeed, recognizing a and ba, respectively. We then call routine **buildtree** twice, first with argument $A \xRightarrow{1} (a \restriction, s)$ and then with argument $B \xRightarrow{5} (ba \restriction, s)$. Thus the tree begins as shown in Fig. 6.1(a). A succeeds directly on a, so the node labeled A is given one descendant labeled a. B succeeds because its rule is $B \rightarrow CB/A$ and C and B succeed on b and a, respectively. Thus the tree grows to that in Fig. 6.1(b).

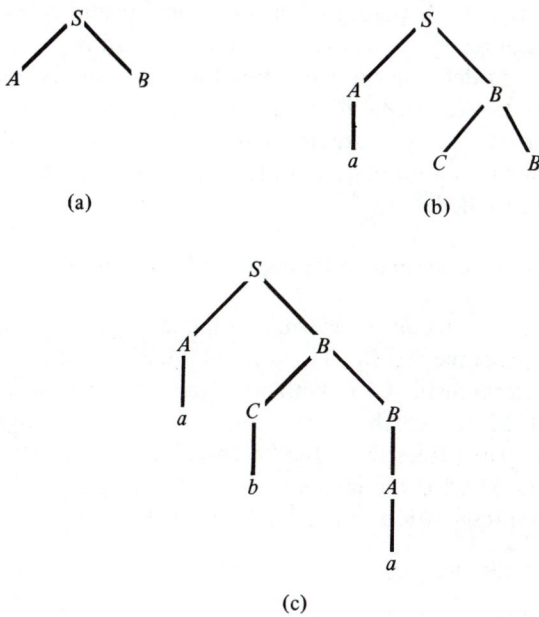

(a)   (b)

(c)

Fig. 6.1   Construction from parse tree in TDPL.

C succeeds directly on b, so the node labeled C gets one descendant labeled b. B succeeds on a because A succeeds, so B gets a descendant labeled A, and that node gets a descendant labeled a. The entire tree is shown in Fig. 6.1(c). □

We note that if the set of TDPL rules is treated as a parsing program, then whenever a nonterminal succeeds, a translation (which may later have to be "canceled") can be produced for the portion of input that it recognizes, in terms of the translations of its "descendants" in the sense of the parse tree just described. This method of translation is similar to the syntax-directed translation for context-free grammars, and we shall have more to say about this in Chapter 9.

It is impossible to "prove" Algorithm 6.1 correct, since, as we mentioned, it itself serves as the constructive definition of a parse tree for a TDPL program. However, it is straightforward to show that the frontier of the parse tree is the input. One shows by induction on the number of calls of routine **buildtree** that when called with argument $A \stackrel{m}{\Rightarrow} (x \restriction y, s)$ the result is a tree with frontier x.

Some of the successful outcomes will be "canceled." That is, if we have $A \stackrel{m}{\Rightarrow} (xy \restriction z, s)$ and the rule for A is $A \longrightarrow BC/D$, we may find that $B \stackrel{+}{\Rightarrow} (x \restriction yz, s)$ but that $C \stackrel{*}{\Rightarrow} (\restriction yz, f)$. Then the relationship $B \stackrel{+}{\Rightarrow} (x \restriction yz, s)$ and all the successful recognitions that served to build up $B \stackrel{+}{\Rightarrow} (x \restriction yz, s)$ are not really involved in defining the parse tree for the input (except in a negative way). These successful recognitions are not reflected in the parse tree, nor is routine **buildtree** called with argument $B \stackrel{m_1}{\Rightarrow} (x \restriction yz, s)$. But all those successful recognitions which ultimately contribute to the successful recognition of the input are included.

6.1.2. TDPL and Deterministic Context-Free Languages

It can be quite difficult to determine what language is defined by a TDPL program. To get some feel for the power of TDPL programs, we shall prove that every deterministic CFL with an endmarker has a TDPL program recognizing it. Moreover, the parse trees for that TDPL program are closely related to the parse trees from the "natural" CFG constructed by Lemma 2.26 from a DPDA for the language. The following lemma will be used to simplify the representation of a DPDA in this section.

LEMMA 6.2

If $L = L_e(M_1)$ for DPDA M_1, then $L = L_e(M)$ for some DPDA M which never increases the length of its pushdown list by more than 1 on any single move.

Proof. A proof was requested in Exercise 2.5.3. Informally, replace a move which rewrites Z as $X_1 \cdots X_k$, $k > 2$, by moves which replace Z by $Y_k X_k$, Y_k by $Y_{k-1} X_{k-1}, \ldots, Y_4$ by $Y_3 X_3$, and Y_3 by $X_1 X_2$. The Y's are new pushdown symbols and the pushdown top is on the left. $\square$

LEMMA 6.3

If L is a deterministic CFL and $\$$ is a new symbol, then $L\$ = L_e(M)$ for some DPDA M.

Proof. The proof is a simple extension of Lemma 2.22. Let $L = L(M_1)$. Then M simulates M_1, keeping the next input symbol in its finite control. M erases its pushdown list if M_1 enters a final state and $\$$ is the next input symbol. No other moves are possible or needed, so M is deterministic. $\square$

THEOREM 6.1

Let $M = (Q, \Sigma, \Gamma, \delta, \bar{q}_0, Z_0, F)$ be a DPDA with $L_e(M) = L$. Then there exists a TDPL program P such that $L = L(P)$.

Proof. Assume that M satisfies Lemma 6.2. We construct $P = (N, \Sigma, R, S)$, an extended TDPL program, such that $L(P) = L_e(M)$. N consists of

(1) The symbol S;
(2) Symbols of the form $[qZp]$, where q and p are in Q, and $Z \in \Gamma$; and
(3) Symbols of the form $[qZp]_a$, where q, Z, and p are as in (2), and $a \in \Sigma$.

The intention is that a call of the nonterminal $[qZp]$ will succeed and recognize string w if and only if $(q, w, Z) \mid\overset{*}{-} (p, e, e)$, and $[qZp]$ will fail under all other conditions, including the case where $(q, w, Z) \mid\overset{*}{-} (p', e, e)$ for some $p' \neq p$. A call of the nonterminal $[qZp]_a$ recognizes a string w if and only if $(q, aw, Z) \mid\overset{*}{-} (p, e, e)$. The rules of P are defined as follows:

(1) The rule for S is $S \rightarrow [q_0 Z_0 q_0]/[q_0 Z_0 q_1]/ \cdots /[q_0 Z_0 q_k]$, where $q_0, q_1, \ldots, q_k$ are all the states in Q.

(2) If $\delta(q, e, Z) = (p, e)$, then the rule for $[qZp]$ is $[qZp] \rightarrow e$, and for all $p' \neq p$, $[qZp'] \rightarrow f$ is a rule.

(3) If $\delta(q, e, Z) = (p, X)$, then the rule for $[qZr]$ is $[qZr] \rightarrow [pXr]$ for all r in Q.

(4) If $\delta(q, e, Z) = (p, XY)$, then for each r in Q, the rule for $[qZr]$ is $[qZr] \rightarrow [pXq_0][q_0 Yr]/[pXq_1][q_1 Yr]/ \cdots /[pXq_k][q_k Yr]$, where $q_0, q_1, \ldots, q_k$ are all the states in Q.

(5) If $\delta(q, e, Z)$ is empty, let $a_1, \ldots, a_l$ be the symbols in Σ for which $\delta(q, a, Z) \neq \varnothing$. Then for $r \in Q$, the rule for nonterminal $[qZr]$ is $[qZr] \rightarrow a_1[qZr]_{a_1}/a_2[qZr]_{a_2}/ \cdots /a_l[qZr]_{a_l}$. If $l = 0$, the rule is $[qZr] \rightarrow f$.

(6) If $\delta(q, a, Z) = (p, e)$ for $a \in \Sigma$, then we have rule $[qZp]_a \rightarrow e$, and for $p' \neq p$, we have rule $[qZp']_a \rightarrow f$.

(7) If $\delta(q, a, Z) = (p, X)$, then for each $r \in Q$, we have a rule of the form $[qZr]_a \rightarrow [pXr]$.

(8) If $\delta(q, a, Z) = (p, XY)$, then for each $r \in Q$, we have the rule $[qZr]_a \rightarrow [pXq_0][q_0 Yr]/[pXq_1][q_1 Yr]/ \cdots /[pXq_k][q_k Yr]$.

We observe that because M is deterministic, these definitions are consistent; no member of N has more than one rule. We shall now show the following:

(6.1.1) $[qZp] \overset{+}{\Rightarrow} (w \upharpoonright x, s)$, for any x, if and only if $(q, wx, Z) \mid\overset{+}{-} (p, x, e)$

(6.1.2)   If $(q, wx, Z) \mid\overset{+}{-} (p, x, e)$, then for all $p' \neq p$, $[qZp'] \overset{+}{\Rightarrow} (\upharpoonright wx, f)$

We shall prove (6.1.2) and the "if" portion of (6.1.1) simultaneously by induction on the number of moves made by M going from configuration (q, wx, Z) to (p, x, e). If one move is made, then $\delta(q, a, Z) = (p, e)$, where a is e or the first symbol of wx. By rule (2) or rules (5) and (6), $[qZp] \rightarrow (a \upharpoonright y, s)$, where $ay = wx$, and $[qZp'] \rightarrow (\upharpoonright wx, f)$ for all $p' \neq p$. Thus the basis is proved.

Suppose that the result is true for numbers of moves fewer than the number required to go from configuration (q, wx, Z) to (p, x, e). Let $w = aw'$ for some $a \in \Sigma \cup \{e\}$. There are two cases to consider.

Case 1: The first move is $(q, wx, Z) \vdash (q', w'x, X)$ for some X in Γ. By the inductive hypothesis, $[q'Xp] \overset{+}{\Rightarrow} (w' \upharpoonright x, s)$ and $[qZp'] \overset{+}{\Rightarrow} (\upharpoonright w'x, f)$ for $p' \neq p$. Thus by rule (3) and rules (5) and (7), we have $[qXp] \Rightarrow (w \upharpoonright x, s)$ and $[qXp'] \overset{+}{\Rightarrow} (\upharpoonright wx, f)$ for all $p' \neq p$. The extended rules of P should be first translated into rules of the original type to prove these contentions rigorously.

Case 2: For some X and Y in Γ, we have, assuming that $w' = yw''$, $(q, wx, Z) \vdash (q', w'x, XY) \vdash^{+} (q'', w''x, Y) \vdash^{+} (p, x, e)$, where the pushdown list always has at least two symbols between configurations $(q', w'x, XY)$ and $(q'', w''x, Y)$. By the inductive hypothesis, $[q'Xq''] \overset{+}{\Rightarrow} (y \upharpoonright w''x, s)$ and $[q''Yp] \overset{+}{\Rightarrow} (w'' \upharpoonright x, s)$. Also, if $p' \neq q''$, then $[q'Xp'] \overset{+}{\Rightarrow} (\upharpoonright w'x, f)$. Suppose first that $a = e$. If we examine rule (4) and use the definition of the extended TDPL statements, we see that every sequence of the form $[q'Xp'][p'Yp]$ fails for $p' \neq q''$. However, $[q'Xq''][q''Yp]$ succeeds and so $[qZp] \overset{+}{\Rightarrow} (w \upharpoonright x, s)$ as desired.

We further note that if $p' \neq p$, then $[q''Yp'] \overset{+}{\Rightarrow} (\upharpoonright w''x, f)$, so that all terms $[q'Xp''][p''Yp']$ fail. (If $p'' \neq q''$, then $[q'Xp'']$ fails, and if $p'' = q''$, then $[p''Yp']$ fails.) Thus, $[qZp'] \overset{+}{\Rightarrow} (\upharpoonright wx, f)$ for $p' \neq p$. The case in which $a \in \Sigma$ is handled similarly, using rules (5) and (8).

We must now show the "only if" portion of (6.1.1). If $[qZp] \overset{+}{\Rightarrow} (w \upharpoonright x, s)$ then $[qZp] \overset{n}{\Rightarrow} (w \upharpoonright x, s)$ for some n.† We prove the result by induction on n. If $n = 1$, then rule (2) must have been used, and the result is elementary. Suppose that it true for $n < n_0$, and let $[qZp] \overset{n_0}{\Rightarrow} (w \upharpoonright x, s)$.

Case 1: The rule for $[qZp]$ is $[qZp] \rightarrow [q'Xp]$. Then $\delta(q, e, Z) = (p, X)$, and $[q'Xp] \overset{n_1}{\Rightarrow} (w \upharpoonright x, s)$, where $n_1 < n_0$. By the inductive hypothesis, $(q', wx, X) \vdash^{+} (p, x, e)$. Thus, $(q, wx, Z) \vdash^{+} (p, x, e)$.

Case 2: The rule for $[qZp]$ is $[qZp] \rightarrow [q'Xq_0][q_0Yp] / \cdots /[q'Xq_k][q_kYp]$. Then we can write $w = w'w''$ such that for some p', $[q'Xp'] \overset{n_1}{\Rightarrow} (w' \upharpoonright w''x, s)$ and $[p'Yp] \overset{n_2}{\Rightarrow} (w'' \upharpoonright x, s)$, where n_1 and n_2 are less than n_0. By hypothesis, $(q', w'w''x, XY) \vdash^{+} (p', w''x, Y) \vdash^{+} (p, x, e)$. By rule (4), $\delta(q, e, Z) = (q', XY)$. Thus, $(q, wx, Z) \vdash^{+} (p, x, e)$.

---

†The step counting must be performed by converting the extended rules to the original form.

Case 3: The rule for $[qZp]$ is defined by rule (5). That is, $\delta(q, e, Z) = \varnothing$. Then it is not possible that $w = e$, so let $w = aw'$. If the rule for nonterminal $[qZp]_a$ is $[qZp]_a \rightarrow e$, we know that $\delta(q, a, Z) = (p, e)$, so $w' = e$, $w = a$, and $(q, w, Z) \vdash (p, e, e)$. The situations in which the rule for $[qZp]_a$ is defined by (7) or (8) are handled analogously to cases 1 and 2, respectively. We omit these considerations.

To complete the proof of the theorem, we note that $S \xRightarrow{+} (w \upharpoonright, s)$ if and only if for some p, $[q_0 Z_0 p] \xRightarrow{+} (w \upharpoonright, s)$. By (6.1.1), $[q_0 Z_0 p] \xRightarrow{+} (w \upharpoonright, s)$ if and only if $(q_0, w, Z_0) \vdash (p, e, e)$. Thus, $L(P) = L_e(M)$. $\square$

COROLLARY

If L is a deterministic CFL and $\$$ a new symbol, then $L\$$ is a TDPL language.

Proof. From Lemma 6.3. $\square$

6.1.3. A Generalization of TDPL

We note that if we have a statement $A \rightarrow BC/D$ in TDPL, then D is called if either B or C fails. There is no way to cause the flow of control to differ in the cases in which B fails or in which B succeeds and C fails. To overcome this defect we shall define another parsing language, which we call GTDPL (generalized TDPL). A program in GTDPL consists of a sequence of statements of one of the forms

(1) $A \rightarrow B[C, D]$
(2) $A \rightarrow a$
(3) $A \rightarrow e$
(4) $A \rightarrow f$

The intuitive meaning of the statement $A \rightarrow B[C, D]$ is that if A is called, it calls B. If B succeeds, C is called. If B fails, D is called at the point on the input where A was called. The outcome of A is the outcome of C or D, whichever gets called. Note that this arrangement differs from that of the TDPL statement $A \rightarrow BC/D$, where D gets called if B succeeds but C fails.

Statements of types (2), (3), and (4) have the same meaning as in TDPL. We formalize the meaning of GTDPL programs as follows.

DEFINITION

A *GTDPL program* is a 4-tuple $P = (N, \Sigma, R, S)$, where N, Σ, and S are as for a TDPL program and R is a list of rules of the forms $A \rightarrow B[C, D]$, $A \rightarrow a$, or $A \rightarrow f$. Here, A, B, C, and D are in N, a is in $\Sigma \cup \{e\}$, and f is the failure metasymbol, as in the TDPL program. There is at most one rule with any particular A to the left of the arrow.

We define relations $\xRightarrow{n}$ as for the TDPL program:

(1) If A has rule $A \rightarrow a$, for a in $\Sigma \cup \{e\}$, then $A \overset{1}{\Rightarrow} (a \restriction w, s)$ for all $w \in \Sigma^*$, and $A \overset{1}{\Rightarrow} (\restriction w, f)$ for all $w \in \Sigma^*$ which do not have prefix a.

(2) If A has rule $A \rightarrow f$, then $A \overset{1}{\Rightarrow} (\restriction w, f)$ for all $w \in \Sigma^*$.

(3) If A has rule $A \rightarrow B[C, D]$, then the following hold:

    (a) If $B \overset{m}{\Rightarrow} (w \restriction xy, s)$ and $C \overset{n}{\Rightarrow} (x \restriction y, s)$, then $A \overset{m+n+1}{\Longrightarrow} (wx \restriction y, s)$.

    (b) If $B \overset{m}{\Rightarrow} (w \restriction x, s)$ and $C \overset{n}{\Rightarrow} (\restriction x, f)$, then $A \overset{m+n+1}{\Longrightarrow} (\restriction wx, f)$.

    (c) If $B \overset{m}{\Rightarrow} (\restriction wx, f)$ and $D \overset{n}{\Rightarrow} (w \restriction x, s)$, then $A \overset{m+n+1}{\Longrightarrow} (w \restriction x, s)$.

    (d) If $B \overset{m}{\Rightarrow} (\restriction w, f)$ and $D \overset{n}{\Rightarrow} (\restriction w, f)$, then $A \overset{m+n+1}{\Longrightarrow} (\restriction w, f)$.

We say that $A \overset{+}{\Rightarrow} (x \restriction y, r)$ if $A \overset{n}{\Rightarrow} (x \restriction y, r)$ for some $n \geq 1$. The *language defined by* P, denoted $L(P)$, is the set $\{w \mid S \overset{+}{\Rightarrow} (w \restriction, s)\}$.

Example 6.4

Let P be a GTDPL program with rules

$$S \longrightarrow A[C, E]$$
$$C \longrightarrow S[B, E]$$
$$A \longrightarrow a$$
$$B \longrightarrow b$$
$$E \longrightarrow e$$

We claim that P recognizes $\{a^n b^n \mid n \geq 0\}$. We can show by simultaneous induction on n that $S \overset{+}{\Rightarrow} (a^n b^n \restriction x, s)$ and $C \overset{+}{\Rightarrow} (a^n b^{n+1} \restriction x, s)$ for all x and n. For example, with input $aabb$, we make the following sequence of observations:

$$A \overset{1}{\Longrightarrow} (\restriction bb, f)$$

$$E \overset{1}{\Longrightarrow} (\restriction bb, s)$$

$$S \overset{3}{\Longrightarrow} (\restriction bb, s)$$

$$B \overset{1}{\Longrightarrow} (b \restriction b, s)$$

$$C \overset{5}{\Longrightarrow} (b \restriction b, s)$$

$$A \overset{1}{\Longrightarrow} (a \restriction bb, s)$$

$$S \overset{7}{\Longrightarrow} (ab \restriction b, s)$$

$$B \overset{1}{\Longrightarrow} (b \restriction, s)$$

$$C \overset{9}{\Longrightarrow} (abb \uparrow, s)$$

$$A \overset{1}{\Longrightarrow} (a \uparrow abb, s)$$

$$S \overset{11}{\Longrightarrow} (aabb \uparrow, s) \quad \square$$

The next example is a GTDPL program that defines a non-context-free language.

Example 6.5

We construct a GTDPL program to recognize the non-CFL $\{0^n 1^n 2^n \mid n \geq 1\}$. By Example 6.4, we know how to write rules that check whether the string at a certain point begins with $0^n 1^n$ or $1^n 2^n$. Our strategy will be to first check that the input has a prefix of the form $0^m 1^m 2$ for $m \geq 0$. If not, we shall arrange it so that acceptance cannot occur. If so, we shall arrange an intermediate failure outcome that causes the input to be reconsidered from the beginning. We shall then check that the input is of the form $0^i 1^j 2^j$. Thus both tests will be met if and only if the input is of the form $0^n 1^n 2^n$ for $n \geq 1$.

We shall need nonterminals that recognize a single terminal or cause immediate success or failure; let us list them first:

$$(1) \quad X \longrightarrow 0$$

$$(2) \quad Y \longrightarrow 1$$

$$(3) \quad Z \longrightarrow 2$$

$$(4) \quad E \longrightarrow e$$

$$(5) \quad F \longrightarrow f$$

We can utilize the program of Example 6.4 to recognize $0^m 1^m 2$ by a nonterminal S_1. The rules associated with S_1 are

$$(6) \quad S_1 \longrightarrow A[Z, Z]$$

$$(7) \quad A \longrightarrow X[B, E]$$

$$(8) \quad B \longrightarrow A[Y, E]$$

Rules (7), (8), (1), (2), and (4) correspond to those of Example 6.4 exactly. Rule (6) assures that S_1 will recognize what A recognizes $(0^m 1^m)$, followed by 2. Note that A always succeeds, so the rule for S_1 could be $S_1 \rightarrow A[Z, W]$ for any W.

Next, we must write rules that recognize 0^* followed by $1^j 2^j$ for some j. The following rules suffice:

$$(9) \ S_2 \longrightarrow X[S_2, C]$$
$$(10) \ C \longrightarrow Y[D, E]$$
$$(11) \ D \longrightarrow C[Z, E]$$

Rules (10), (11), (2), (3), and (4) correspond to Example 6.4, and C recognizes $1^j 2^j$. The rule for S_2 works as follows. As long as there is a prefix of 0's on the input, S_2 recognizes one of them and calls itself further along the input. When X fails, i.e., the input pointer has shifted over the 0's, C is called and recognizes a prefix of the form $1^j 2^j$. Note that C always succeeds, so S_2 always succeeds.

We must now put the subprograms for S_1 and S_2 together. We first create a nontern. nal S_3, which never consumes any input, but succeeds or fails as S_1 fails or succeeds. The rule for S_3 is

$$(12) \ S_3 \longrightarrow S_1[F, E]$$

Note that if S_1 succeeds, S_3 will call F, which must fail and retract the input pointer to the place where S_1 was called. If S_1 fails, S_3 calls E, which succeeds. Thus, S_3 uses no input in any case. Now we can let S be the start symbol, with rule

$$(13) \ S \longrightarrow S_3[F, S_2]$$

If S_1 succeeds, then S_3 fails and S_2 is called at the beginning of the input. Thus, S succeeds whenever S_1 and S_2 succeed on the same input. If S_1 fails, then S_3 succeeds, so S fails. If S_1 succeeds but S_2 fails, then S also fails. Thus the program recognizes $\{0^n 1^n 2^n \,|\, n \geq 1\}$, which is the intersection of the sets recognized by S_1 and S_2. Hence there are languages which are not context-free which can be defined by GTDPL programs. The same is true for TDPL programs, incidentally. (See Exercise 6.1.1.) □

We shall now investigate some properties of GTDPL programs. The following lemma is analogous to Lemma 6.1.

LEMMA 6.4

Let $P = (N, \Sigma, R, S)$ be any GTDPL program. If $A \overset{+}{\Rightarrow} (x \upharpoonright y, r_1)$ and $A \overset{+}{\Rightarrow} (u \upharpoonright v, r_2)$, where $xy = uv$, then $x = u$, $y = v$, and $r_1 = r_2$.

Proof. Exercise. □

We now establish two theorems about GTDPL programs. First, the class of TDPL definable languages is contained in the class of GTDPL definable languages. Second, every language defined by a GTDPL program can be recognized in linear time on a reasonable random access machine.

THEOREM 6.2

Every TDPL definable language is a GTDPL definable language.

Proof. Let $L = L(P)$ for a TDPL program $P = (N, \Sigma, R, S)$. We define the GTDPL program $P' = (N', \Sigma, R', S)$, where R' is defined as follows:

(1) If $A \to e$ is in R, add $A \to e$ to R'.
(2) If $A \to a$ is in R, add $A \to a$ to R'.
(3) If $A \to f$ is in R, add $A \to f$ to R'.
(4) Create nonterminals E and F and add rules $E \to e$ and $F \to f$ to R'. (Note that other nonterminals with the same rules can be identified with these.)
(5) If $A \to BC/D$ is in R, add

$$A \longrightarrow A'[E, D]$$
$$A' \longrightarrow B[C, F]$$

to R', where A' is a new nonterminal.

Let N' be N together with all new nonterminals introduced in the construction of R'.

It is elementary to observe that if B and C succeed, then A' succeeds, and that otherwise A' fails. Thus, A succeeds if and only if A' succeeds (i.e., B and C succeed), or A' fails (i.e., B fails or B succeeds and C fails) and D succeeds. It is also easy to check that B, C, and D are called at the same points on the input by R' that they are called by R. Since R' simulates each rule of R directly, we conclude that $S \underset{P}{\overset{+}{\Rightarrow}} (w \upharpoonright, s)$ if and only if $S \underset{P'}{\overset{+}{\Rightarrow}} (w \upharpoonright, s)$, and $L(P) = L(P')$. $\quad\square$

Seemingly, the GTDPL programs do more in the way of recognition than TDPL programs. For example, a GTDPL program can readily be written to simulate a statement of the form

$$A \longrightarrow BC/(D_1, D_2)$$

in which D_1 is to be called if B fails and D_2 is to be called if B succeeds and C fails. It is open, however, whether the containment of Theorem 6.2 is proper.

As with TDPL, we can embellish GTDPL with extended statements (see Exercise 6.1.12). For example, every extended TDPL statement can be regarded as an extended form of GTDPL statement.

6.1.4. Time Complexity of GTDPL Languages

The main result of this section is that we can simulate the successful recognition of an input sentence by a GTDPL program (and hence a TDPL program) in linear time on a machine that resembles a random access computer. The algorithm recalls both the Cocke–Younger–Kasami algorithm and Earley's algorithm of Section 4.2, and works backward on the input string.

ALGORITHM 6.2

Recognition of GTDPL languages in linear time.

Input. A GTDPL program $P = (N, \Sigma, R, S)$, with $N = \{A_1, A_2, \ldots, A_k\}$, and $S = A_1$, and an input string $w = a_1 a_2 \cdots a_n$ in Σ^*. We assume that $a_{n+1} = \$$, a right endmarker.

Output. A $k \times (n + 1)$ matrix $[t_{ij}]$. Each entry is either undefined, an integer m such that $0 \leq m \leq n$, or the failure symbol f. If $t_{ij} = m$, then $A_i \overset{+}{\Rightarrow} (a_j a_{j+1} \cdots a_{j+m-1} \upharpoonright a_{j+m} \cdots a_n, s)$. If $t_{ij} = f$, $A_i \overset{+}{\Rightarrow} (\upharpoonright a_j \cdots a_n, f)$. Otherwise, t_{ij} is undefined.

Method. We compute the matrix of t_{ij}'s as follows. Initially, all entries are undefined.

(1) Do steps (2)–(4) for $j = n + 1, n, \ldots, 1$.

(2) For each i, $1 \leq i \leq k$, if $A_i \rightarrow f$ is in R, set $t_{ij} = f$. If $A_i \rightarrow e$ is in R, set $t_{ij} = 0$. If $A \rightarrow a_j$ is in R, set $t_{ij} = 1$, and if $A \rightarrow b$ is in R, $b \neq a_j$, set $t_{ij} = f$. (We take a_{n+1} to be a symbol not in Σ, so $A \rightarrow a_{n+1}$ is never in R.)

(3) Do step (4) repeatedly for $i = 1, 2, \ldots, k$, until no changes to the t_{ij}'s occur in a step.

(4) Let the rule for A_i be of the form $A_i \rightarrow A_p[A_q, A_r]$, and suppose that t_{ij} is not yet defined.

    (a) If $t_{pj} = f$ and $t_{rj} = x$, then set $t_{pj} = x$, where x is an integer or f.

    (b) If $t_{pj} = m_1$ and $t_{q(j+m_1)} = m_2 \neq f$, set $t_{ij} = m_1 + m_2$.

    (c) If $t_{pj} = m_1$ and $t_{q(j+m_1)} = f$, set $t_{ij} = f$.

In all other cases do nothing to t_{ij}. $\square$

THEOREM 6.3

Algorithm 6.2 correctly determines the t_{ij}'s.

Proof. We claim that after execution of Algorithm 6.2 on the input string $w = a_1 \cdots a_n$, $t_{ij} = f$ if and only if $A_i \overset{+}{\Rightarrow} (\upharpoonright a_j \cdots a_n, f)$ and $t_{ij} = m$ if and only if $A_i \overset{+}{\Rightarrow} (a_j \cdots a_{j+m-1} \upharpoonright a_{j+m} \cdots a_n, s)$. A straightforward induction on the order in which the t_{ij}'s are computed shows that whenever t_{ij} is given a value, that value is as stated above. Conversely, an induction on l shows that if $A_i \overset{l}{\Rightarrow} (\upharpoonright a_j \cdots a_n, f)$ or $A_i \overset{l}{\Rightarrow} (a_j \cdots a_{j+m-1} \upharpoonright a_{j+m} \cdots a_n, s)$, then t_{ij} is given the value f or m, respectively. Entry t_{ij} is left undefined if A_i called at position j does not halt. The details are left for the Exercises. $\square$

Note that $a_1 \cdots a_n$ is in $L(P)$ if and only if $t_{11} = n$.

THEOREM 6.4

For each GTDPL program there is a constant c such that Algorithm 6.2 takes no more than cn elementary steps on an input string of length $n \geq 1$, where elementary steps are of the type used for Algorithm 4.3.

Proof. The crux of the proof is to observe that in step (3) we cycle through all the nonterminals at most k times for any given j.   □

Last we observe that from the matrix in Algorithm 6.2 it is possible to build a tree-like parse structure for accepted inputs, similar to the structure that was built in Algorithm 6.1 for TDPL programs. Additionally, Algorithm 6.2 can be modified to recognize and "parse" according to a TDPL (rather than GTDPL) program.

Example 6.6

Let $P = (N, \Sigma, R_1, E)$, where

$$N = \{E, E_+, T, T_*, F, F', X, Y, P, M, A, L, R\},$$

$\Sigma = \{a, (,), +, *\}$, and R_1 consists of

$$(1) \quad E \longrightarrow T[E_+, X]$$
$$(2) \quad E_+ \longrightarrow P[E, Y]$$
$$(3) \quad T \longrightarrow F[T_*, X]$$
$$(4) \quad T_* \longrightarrow M[T, Y]$$
$$(5) \quad F \longrightarrow L[F', A]$$
$$(6) \quad F' \longrightarrow E[R, X]$$
$$(7) \quad X \longrightarrow f$$
$$(8) \quad Y \longrightarrow e$$
$$(9) \quad P \longrightarrow +$$
$$(10) \quad M \longrightarrow *$$
$$(11) \quad A \longrightarrow a$$
$$(12) \quad L \longrightarrow ($$
$$(13) \quad R \longrightarrow)$$

This GTDPL program is intended to recognize arithmetic expressions over $+$ and $*$, i.e., $L(G_0)$. E recognizes an expression consisting of a sequence of terms (T's) separated by $+$'s. The nonterminal E_+ is intended to recognize an expression with the first term deleted. Thus rule (2) says that E_+ recognizes a $+$ sign (P) followed by any expression, and if there is no $+$ sign, the empty string (Y) serves. Then we can interpret statement (1) as saying that an expression is a term followed by something recognized by E_+, consisting of either the empty string or an alternating sequence of $+$'s and terms beginning with $+$ and ending in a term. A similar relation applies to statements (3) and (4).

Statements (5) and (6) say that a factor (F) is either (followed by an expression followed by) or, if no (is present, a single symbol a.

Now, suppose that $(a + a) * a$ is the input to Algorithm 6.2. The matrix $[t_{ij}]$ constructed by Algorithm 6.2 is shown in Fig. 6.2.

Let us compute the entries in the eighth column of the matrix. The entries for P, M, A, L, and R have value f, since they look for input symbols in Σ and the eighth input symbol is the right endmarker. X always yields value f, and Y always yields value 0. Applying step (3) of Algorithm 6.2, we find that in the first cycle through step (4) the values for E_+, T_*, and F can be filled in and are 0, 0, and f, respectively. On the second cycle, T is given the value f. The values for E and F' can be computed on the third cycle.

	(	a	+	a	)	*	a	$
E	7	3	f	1	f	f	1	f
E_+	0	0	2	0	0	0	0	0
T	7	1	f	1	f	f	1	f
T_*	0	0	0	0	0	2	0	0
F	5	1	f	1	f	f	1	f
F'	f	4	f	2	f	f	f	f
X	f	f	f	f	f	f	f	f
Y	0	0	0	0	0	0	0	0
P	f	f	1	f	f	f	f	f
M	f	f	f	f	f	1	f	f
A	f	1	f	1	f	f	1	f
L	1	f	f	f	f	f	f	f
R	f	f	f	f	1	f	f	f

Fig. 6.2 Recognition table from Algorithm 6.2.

An example of a less trivial computation occurs in column 3. The bottom seven rows are easily filled in by statement (2). Then, by statement (3), since the P entry in column 3 is 1, we examine the E entry in column 4 ($= 3 + 1$) and find that this is also 1. Thus the E_+ entry in column 3 is 2 ($= 1 + 1$). □

6.1.5. Implementation of GTDPL Programs

In practice, implementation of GTDPL-like parsing systems do not take the tabular form of Algorithm 6.2. Instead, a trial-and-error method is normally used. In this section we shall construct an automaton that "implements" the recognition portion of a GTDPL program. We shall leave it to the reader to show how this automaton could be extended to a transducer which would indicate the successful sequence of routine calls from which a "parse" or translation can be constructed.

The automaton consists of an input tape with an input pointer, which may be reset; a three-state finite control; and a pushdown list consisting of symbols from a finite alphabet and pointers to the input. The device operates in a way that exactly implements our intuitive idea of routines (nonterminals) calling one another, with the retraction of the input pointer required on each failure. The retraction is to the point at which the input pointer dwelt when the call of the failing routine occurred.

DEFINITION

A *parsing machine* is a 6-tuple $M = (Q, \Sigma, \Gamma, \delta, \textbf{begin}, Z_0)$, where

(1) $Q = \{\textbf{success}, \textbf{failure}, \textbf{begin}\}$.

(2) Σ is a finite set of *input symbols*.

(3) Γ is a finite set of *pushdown symbols*.

(4) δ is a mapping from $Q \times (\Sigma \cup \{e\}) \times \Gamma$ to $Q \times \Gamma^{*2}$, which is restricted as follows:

    (a) If q is **success** or **failure**, then $\delta(q, a, Z)$ is undefined if $a \in \Sigma$, and $\delta(q, e, Z)$ is of the form $(\textbf{begin}, Y)$ for some $Y \in \Gamma$.

    (b) If $\delta(\textbf{begin}, a, Z)$ is defined for some $a \in \Sigma$, then $\delta(\textbf{begin}, b, Z)$ is undefined for all $b \neq a$ in $\Sigma \cup \{e\}$.

    (c) For a in Σ, $\delta(\textbf{begin}, a, Z)$ can only be $(\textbf{success}, e)$ if it is defined.

    (d) $\delta(\textbf{begin}, e, Z)$ can only be of the forms $(\textbf{begin}, YZ)$, for some Y in Γ, or of the form (q, e), for $q = \textbf{success}$ or **failure**.

(5) **begin** is the initial state.

(6) Z_0 in Γ is the initial pushdown symbol.

M resembles a pushdown automaton, but there are several major differences. We can think of the elements of Γ as routines that either call or transfer to each other. The pushdown list is used to record recursive calls and the position of the input head each time a call was made. The state **begin** normally causes a call of another routine, reflected in that if $\delta(\textbf{begin}, e, Z) = (\textbf{begin}, YZ)$, where Y is in Γ and Z is on top of the list, then Y will be placed above Z on a new level of the pushdown list. The states **success** and **failure** cause transfers to, rather than calls of, another routine. If, for example, $\delta(\textbf{success}, e, Z) = (\textbf{begin}, Y)$, then Y merely replaces Z on top of the list. We formally define the operation of M as follows.

A *configuration* of M is a triple $(q, w \upharpoonright x, \gamma)$, where

(1) q is one of **success, failure**, or **begin**;

(2) w and x are in Σ^*; $\upharpoonright$ is a metasymbol, the *input head*;

(3) γ is a pushdown list of the form $(Z_1, i_1) \cdots (Z_m, i_m)$, where $Z_j \in \Gamma$ and i_j is an integer, for $1 \leq j \leq m$. The top is at the left. The Z's are "routine" calls; the i's are input pointers.

We define the $\vdash_{\overline{M}}$ relation, or $\vdash$ when M is understood, on configurations as follows:

(1) Let $\delta(\textbf{begin}, e, Z) = (\textbf{begin}, YZ)$ for Y in Γ. Then

$$(\textbf{begin}, w \upharpoonright x, (Z, i)\gamma) \vdash (\textbf{begin}, w \upharpoonright x, (Y, j)(Z, i)\gamma),$$

where $j = |w|$. Here, Y is "called," and the position of the input head when Y is called is recorded, along with the entry on the pushdown list for Y.

(2) Let $\delta(q, e, Z) = (\textbf{begin}, Y)$, where $Y \in \Gamma$, and $q = \textbf{success}$ or $\textbf{failure}$. Then $(q, w \upharpoonright x, (Z, i)\gamma) \vdash (\textbf{begin}, w \upharpoonright x, (Y, i)\gamma)$. Here Z "transfers" to Y. The input position associated with Y is the same as that associated with Z.

(3) Let $\delta(\textbf{begin}, a, Z) = (q, e)$ for a in $\Sigma \cup \{e\}$. If $q = \textbf{success}$, then $(\textbf{begin}, w \upharpoonright ax, (Z, i)\gamma) \vdash (\textbf{success}, wa \upharpoonright x, \gamma)$. If a is not a prefix of x or $q = \textbf{failure}$, then $(\textbf{begin}, w \upharpoonright x, (Z, i)\gamma) \vdash (\textbf{failure}, u \upharpoonright v, \gamma)$, where $uv = wx$ and $|u| = i$. In the latter case the input pointer is retracted to the location given by the pointer on top of the pushdown list.

Note that if $\delta(\textbf{begin}, a, Z) = (\textbf{success}, e)$, then the next state of the parsing machine is $\textbf{success}$ if the unexpended input string begins with a and $\textbf{failure}$ otherwise.

Let $\vdash^{+}$ be the transitive closure of $\vdash$. The *language defined by* M, denoted $L(M)$, is $\{w \mid w \text{ is in } \Sigma^* \text{ and } (\textbf{begin}, \upharpoonright w, (Z_0, 0)) \vdash^{+} (\textbf{success}, w \upharpoonright, e)\}$.

Example 6.7

Let $M = (Q, \{a, b\}, \{Z_0, Y, A, B, E\}, \delta, \textbf{begin}, Z_0)$, where δ is given by

(1) $\delta(\textbf{begin}, e, Z_0) = (\textbf{begin}, YZ_0)$
(2) $\delta(\textbf{success}, e, Z_0) = (\textbf{begin}, Z_0)$
(3) $\delta(\textbf{failure}, e, Z_0) = (\textbf{begin}, E)$
(4) $\delta(\textbf{begin}, e, Y) = (\textbf{begin}, AY)$
(5) $\delta(\textbf{success}, e, Y) = (\textbf{begin}, Y)$
(6) $\delta(\textbf{failure}, e, Y) = (\textbf{begin}, B)$
(7) $\delta(\textbf{begin}, a, A) = (\textbf{success}, e)$
(8) $\delta(\textbf{begin}, b, B) = (\textbf{success}, e)$
(9) $\delta(\textbf{begin}, e, E) = (\textbf{success}, e)$

M recognizes e or any string of a's and b's ending in b, but does so in a peculiar way. A and B recognize a and b, respectively. When Y begins, it looks for an a, and if Y finds it, Y "transfers" to itself. Thus the pushdown list remains intact, and a's are consumed on the input. If b or the end of the input is reached, Y in state $\textbf{failure}$ causes the top of the pushdown list to be erased. That is, Y is replaced by B, and, whether B succeeds or fails, that B is eventually erased.

Z_0 calls Y and transfers to itself in the same way that Y calls A. Thus any string of a's and b's ending in b will eventually cause Z_0 to be erased and state **success** entered. The action of M on input $abaa$ is given by the following sequence of configurations:

$$(\textbf{begin}, \upharpoonright abaa, (Z_0, 0)) \vdash (\textbf{begin}, \upharpoonright abaa, (Y, 0)(Z_0, 0))$$
$$\vdash (\textbf{begin}, \upharpoonright abaa, (A, 0)(Y, 0)(Z_0, 0))$$
$$\vdash (\textbf{success}, a \upharpoonright baa, (Y, 0)(Z_0, 0))$$
$$\vdash (\textbf{begin}, a \upharpoonright baa, (Y, 0)(Z_0, 0))$$
$$\vdash (\textbf{begin}, a \upharpoonright baa, (A, 1)(Y, 0)(Z_0, 0))$$
$$\vdash (\textbf{failure}, a \upharpoonright baa, (Y, 0)(Z_0, 0))$$
$$\vdash (\textbf{begin}, a \upharpoonright baa, (B, 0)(Z_0, 0))$$
$$\vdash (\textbf{success}, ab \upharpoonright aa, (Z_0, 0))$$
$$\vdash (\textbf{begin}, ab \upharpoonright aa, (Z_0, 0))$$
$$\vdash (\textbf{begin}, ab \upharpoonright aa, (Y, 2)(Z_0, 0))$$
$$\vdash (\textbf{begin}, ab \upharpoonright aa, (A, 2)(Y, 2)(Z_0, 0))$$
$$\vdash (\textbf{success}, aba \upharpoonright a, (Y, 2)(Z_0, 0))$$
$$\vdash (\textbf{begin}, aba \upharpoonright a, (Y, 2)(Z_0, 0))$$
$$\vdash (\textbf{begin}, aba \upharpoonright a, (A, 3)(Y, 2)(Z_0, 0))$$
$$\vdash (\textbf{success}, abaa \upharpoonright, (Y, 2)(Z_0, 0))$$
$$\vdash (\textbf{begin}, abaa \upharpoonright, (Y, 2)(Z_0, 0))$$
$$\vdash (\textbf{begin}, abaa \upharpoonright, (A, 4)(Y, 2)(Z_0, 0))$$
$$\vdash (\textbf{failure}, abaa \upharpoonright, (Y, 2)(Z_0, 0))$$
$$\vdash (\textbf{begin}, abaa \upharpoonright, (B, 2)(Z_0, 0))$$
$$\vdash (\textbf{failure}, ab \upharpoonright aa, (Z_0, 0))$$
$$\vdash (\textbf{begin}, ab \upharpoonright aa, (E, 0))$$
$$\vdash (\textbf{success}, ab \upharpoonright aa, e)$$

Note that $abaa$ is not accepted because the end of the input was not reached at the last step. However, ab alone would be accepted. It is important also to note that in the fourth from last configuration B is not "called" but replaces Y. Thus the number 2, rather than 4, appears on top of the list, and when B fails, the input head backtracks. $\square$

We shall now prove that a language is defined by a parsing machine if and only if it is defined by a GTDPL program.

LEMMA 6.5

If $L = L(M)$ for some parsing machine $M = (Q, \Sigma, \Gamma, \delta, \textbf{begin}, Z_0)$, then $L = L(P)$ for some GTDPL program P.

Proof. Let $P = (N, \Sigma, R, Z_0)$, where $N = \Gamma \cup \{X\}$ with X a new symbol. Define R as follows:

(1) X has no rule.

(2) If $\delta(\text{begin}, a, Z) = (q, e)$, let $Z \rightarrow a$ be the rule for Z if $q = $ **success**, and $Z \rightarrow f$ be the rule if $q = $ **failure**.

(3) For the other Z's in Γ define Y_1, Y_2, and Y_3 as follows:

    (a) If $\delta(\text{begin}, e, Z) = (\text{begin}, YZ)$, let $Y_1 = Y$.

    (b) If $\delta(q, e, Z) = (\text{begin}, Y)$, let $Y_2 = Y$ if q is **success** and let $Y_3 = Y$ if q is **failure**.

    (c) If Y_i is not defined by (a) or (b), take Y_i to be X for each Y_i not otherwise defined.

Then the rule for Z is $Z \rightarrow Y_1[Y_2, Y_3]$.

We shall show that the following statements hold for all Z in Γ:

(6.1.3) $Z \overset{n}{\Longrightarrow} (w \upharpoonright x, s)$ if and only if

$$(\text{begin}, \upharpoonright wx, (Z, 0)) \underset{}{\overset{m}{\vdash}} (\text{success}, w \upharpoonright x, e)$$

(6.1.4) $Z \overset{n}{\Longrightarrow} (\upharpoonright w, f)$ if and only if $(\text{begin}, \upharpoonright w, (Z, 0)) \underset{}{\overset{m}{\vdash}} (\text{failure}, \upharpoonright w, e)$

We prove both simultaneously by induction on the length of a derivation in P or computation of M.

Only if: The bases for (6.1.3) and (6.1.4) are both trivial applications of the definition of the $\vdash$ relation.

For the inductive step of (6.1.3), assume that $Z \overset{n}{\Longrightarrow} (w \upharpoonright x, s)$ and that (6.1.3) and (6.1.4) are true for smaller n. Since we may take $n > 1$, let the rule for Z be $Z \rightarrow Y_1[Y_2, Y_3]$.

Case 1: $w = w_1 w_2$, $Y_1 \overset{n_1}{\Longrightarrow} (w_1 \upharpoonright w_2 x, s)$ and $Y_2 \overset{n_2}{\Longrightarrow} (w_2 \upharpoonright x, s)$. Then n_1 and n_2 are less than n, and we have, by the inductive hypothesis (6.1.3),

(6.1.5) $(\text{begin}, \upharpoonright wx, (Y_1, 0)) \underset{}{\overset{+}{\vdash}} (\text{success}, w_1 \upharpoonright w_2 x, e)$

and

(6.1.6) $(\text{begin}, \upharpoonright w_2 x, (Y_2, 0)) \underset{}{\overset{+}{\vdash}} (\text{success}, w_2 \upharpoonright x, e)$

We must now observe that if we insert some string, w_1 in particular, to the left of the input head of M, then M will undergo essentially the same action. Thus from (6.1.6) we obtain

(6.1.7) $(\text{begin}, w_1 \upharpoonright w_2 x, (Y_2, 0)) \underset{}{\overset{+}{\vdash}} (\text{success}, w \upharpoonright x, e)$

This inference requires an inductive proof in its own right, but is left for the Exercises.

From the definition of R we know that $\delta(\textbf{begin}, e, Z) = (\textbf{begin}, Y_1 Z)$ and $\delta(\textbf{success}, e, Z) = (\textbf{begin}, Y_2)$. Thus

$$(6.1.8) \qquad (\textbf{begin}, \upharpoonright wx, (Z, 0)) \vdash (\textbf{begin}, \upharpoonright wx, (Y_1, 0)(Z, 0))$$

and

$$(6.1.9) \qquad (\textbf{success}, w_1 \upharpoonright w_2 x, (Z, 0)) \vdash (\textbf{begin}, w_1 \upharpoonright w_2 x, (Y_2, 0)).$$

Putting (6.1.9), (6.1.5), (6.1.8), and (6.1.7) together, we have

$$(\textbf{begin}, \upharpoonright wx, (Z, 0)) \mathrel{\vdash^{+}} (\textbf{success}, w \upharpoonright x, e),$$

as desired.

Case 2: $Y_1 \overset{n_1}{\Rightarrow} (\upharpoonright wx, f)$ and $Y_3 \overset{n_2}{\Rightarrow} (w \upharpoonright x, s)$. The proof in this case is similar to case 1 and is left for the reader.

We now turn to the induction for (6.1.4). We assume that $Z \overset{n}{\Rightarrow} (\upharpoonright w, f)$.

Case 1: $Y_1 \overset{n_1}{\Rightarrow} (w_1 \upharpoonright w_2, s)$ and $Y_2 \overset{n_2}{\Rightarrow} (\upharpoonright w_2, f)$, where $w_1 w_2 = w$. Then $n_1, n_2 < n$, and by (6.1.3) and (6.1.4), we have

$$(6.1.10) \qquad (\textbf{begin}, \upharpoonright w, (Y_1, 0)) \mathrel{\vdash^{+}} (\textbf{success}, w_1 \upharpoonright w_2, e)$$
$$(6.1.11) \qquad (\textbf{begin}, \upharpoonright w_2, (Y_2, 0)) \mathrel{\vdash^{+}} (\textbf{failure}, \upharpoonright w_2, e)$$

If we insert w_1 to the left of $\upharpoonright$ in (6.1.11), we have

$$(6.1.12) \qquad (\textbf{begin}, w_1 \upharpoonright w_2, (Y_2, 0)) \mathrel{\vdash^{+}} (\textbf{failure}, \upharpoonright w_1 w_2, e)$$

The truth of this implication is left for the Exercises. One has to observe that when $(Y_2, 0)$ is erased, the input head must be set all the way to the left. Otherwise, the presence of w_1 on the input cannot affect matters, because numbers written on the pushdown list above $(Y_1, 0)$ will have $|w_1|$ added to them [when constructing the sequence of steps represented by (6.1.12) from (6.1.11)], and thus there is no way to get the input head to move into w_1 without erasing $(Y_1, 0)$.

By definition of Y_1 and Y_2, we have

$$(6.1.13) \qquad (\textbf{begin}, \upharpoonright w, (Z, 0)) \vdash (\textbf{begin}, \upharpoonright w, (Y_1, 0)(Z, 0))$$

and

$$(6.1.14) \qquad (\textbf{success}, w_1 \upharpoonright w_2, (Z, 0)) \vdash (\textbf{begin}, w_1 \upharpoonright w_2, (Y_2, 0))$$

Putting (6.1.13), (6.1.10), (6.1.14), and (6.1.12) together, we have $(\textbf{begin}, \upharpoonright w, (Z, 0)) \mathrel{\vdash^{+}} (\textbf{failure}, \upharpoonright w, e)$.

Case 2: $Y_1 \overset{n_1}{\Rightarrow} (\uparrow w, f)$ and $Y_3 \overset{n_2}{\Rightarrow} (\uparrow w, f)$. This case is similar and left to the reader.

If: The "if" portion of the proof is similar to the foregoing, and we leave the details for the Exercises.

As a special case of (6.1.3), $Z_0 \overset{+}{\Rightarrow} (w \uparrow, s)$ if and only if $(\textbf{begin}, \uparrow w, (Z_0, 0))$ $\vdash^{+}$ $(\textbf{success}, w \uparrow, e)$, so $L(M) = L(P)$. $\square$

LEMMA 6.6

If $L = L(P)$ for some GTDPL program P, then $L = L(M)$ for a parsing machine M.

Proof. Let $P = (N, \Sigma, R, S)$ and define $M = (Q, \Sigma, N, \delta, \textbf{begin}, S)$. Define δ as follows:

(1) If R contains rule $A \rightarrow B[C, D]$, let $\delta(\textbf{begin}, e, A) = (\textbf{begin}, BA)$, $\delta(\textbf{success}, e, A) = (\textbf{begin}, C)$ and $\delta(\textbf{failure}, e, A) = (\textbf{begin}, D)$.

(2) (a) If $A \rightarrow a$ is in R, where a is in $\Sigma \cup \{e\}$, let $\delta(\textbf{begin}, a, A) = (\textbf{success}, e)$.

(b) If $A \rightarrow f$ is in R, let $\delta(\textbf{begin}, e, A) = (\textbf{failure}, e)$.

A proof that $L(M) = L(G)$ is straightforward and left for the Exercises. $\square$

THEOREM 6.5

A language L is $L(M)$ for some parsing machine M if and only if it is $L(P)$ for some GTDPL program P.

Proof. Immediate from Lemmas 6.5 and 6.6. $\square$

EXERCISES

6.1.1.   Construct TDPL programs to recognize the following languages:
   (a) $L(G_0)$.
   (b) The set of strings with an equal number of a's and b's.
   (c) $\{wcw^R \,|\, w \in (a + b)^*\}$.
   *(d) $\{a^{2^n} \,|\, n \geq 1\}$. *Hint:* Consider $S \rightarrow aSa/aa$.
   (e) Some infinite subset of FORTRAN.

6.1.2.   Construct GTDPL programs to recognize the following languages:
   (a) The languages in Exercise 6.1.1.
   (b) The language generated by (with start symbol E)

$$E \longrightarrow E + T \,|\, T$$
$$T \longrightarrow T * F \,|\, F$$
$$F \longrightarrow (E) \,|\, I$$
$$I \longrightarrow a \,|\, a(L)$$
$$L \longrightarrow a \,|\, a, L$$

   **(c) $\{a^{n^2} \,|\, n \geq 1\}$.

*6.1.3. Show that for every LL(1) language there is a GTDPL program which recognizes the language with no backtracking; i.e., the parsing machine constructed by Lemma 6.6 never moves the input pointer to the left between successive configurations.

*6.1.4. Show that it is undecidable whether a TDPL program $P = (N, \Sigma, R, S)$ recognizes
(a) $\varnothing$.
(b) Σ^*.

6.1.5. Show that every TDPL or GTDPL program is equivalent to one in which every nonterminal has a rule. *Hint:* Show that if A has no rule, you can give it rule $A \rightarrow AA/A$ (or the equivalent in GTDPL) with no change in the language recognized.

*6.1.6. Give a TDPL program equivalent to the following extended program. What is the language defined? From a practical point of view, what defects does this program have?

$$S \longrightarrow A/B/C$$
$$A \longrightarrow a$$
$$B \longrightarrow SCA$$
$$C \longrightarrow b$$

6.1.7. Give a formal proof of Lemma 6.3.

6.1.8. Prove Lemma 6.4.

6.1.9. Give a formal proof that P of Example 6.5 defines $\{0^n1^n2^n \mid n \geq 1\}$.

6.1.10. Complete the proof of Theorem 6.2.

6.1.11. Use Algorithm 6.2 to show that the string $((a)) + a$ is in $L(P)$, where P is given in Example 6.6.

6.1.12. GTDPL statements can be extended in much the same manner we extended TDPL statements. For example, we can permit GTDPL statements of the form

$$A \longrightarrow X_1 g_1 X_2 g_2 \cdots X_k g_k$$

where each X_i is a terminal or nonterminal and each g_i is either e or a pair of the form $[\alpha_i, \beta_i]$, where α_i and β_i are strings of symbols. A reports success if and only if each $X_i g_i$ succeeds where success is defined recursively, as follows. The string $X_i[\alpha_i, \beta_i]$ succeeds if and only if

(1) X_i succeeds and α_i succeeds or
(2) X_i fails and β_i succeeds.

(a) Show how this extended statement can be replaced by an equivalent set of conventional GTDPL statements.
(b) Show that every extended TDPL statement can be replaced by an equivalent set of (extended) GTDPL statements.

6.1.13. Show that there are TDPL (and GTDPL) programs in which the number of statements executed by the parsing machine of Lemma 6.6 is an exponential function of the length of the input string.

6.1.14. Construct a GTDPL program to simulate the meaning of the rule $A \rightarrow BC/(D_1, D_2)$ mentioned on p. 473.

6.1.15. Find a GTDPL program which defines the language $L(M)$, where M is the parsing machine given in Example 6.7.

6.1.16. Find parsing machines to recognize the languages of Exercise 6.1.2.

DEFINITION

A TDPL or GTDPL program $P = (N, \Sigma, R, S)$ has a *partial acceptance failure* on w if $w = uv$ such that $v \neq e$ and $S \stackrel{+}{\Rightarrow} (u \upharpoonright v, s)$. We say that P is *well formed* if for every w in Σ^*, either $S \stackrel{+}{\Rightarrow} (\upharpoonright w, f)$ or $S \stackrel{+}{\Rightarrow} (w, \upharpoonright, s)$.

*6.1.17. Show that if L is a TDPL language (alt. GTDPL language) and \$ is a new symbol, then $L\$$ is defined by a TDPL program (alt. GTDPL program) with no partial acceptance failures.

*6.1.18. Let L_1 be defined by a TDPL (alt. GTDPL) program and L_2 by a well-formed TDPL (alt. GTDPL) program. Show that

(a) $L_1 \cup L_2$,

(b) $\bar{L}_2$,

(c) $L_1 \cap L_2$, and

(d) $L_1 - L_2$

are TDPL (alt. GTDPL) languages.

*6.1.19. Show that every GTDPL program with no partial acceptance failure is equivalent to a well-formed GTDPL program. *Hint:* It suffices to look for and eliminate "left recursion." That is, if we have a normal form GTDPL program, create a CFL by replacing rules $A \rightarrow B[C, D]$ by productions $A \rightarrow BC$ and $A \rightarrow D$. Let $A \rightarrow a$ or $A \rightarrow e$ be productions of the CFL also. The "left recursion" referred to is in the CFL constructed.

**6.1.20. Show that it is undecidable for a well-formed TDPL program $P = (N, \Sigma, R, S)$ whether $L(P) = \varnothing$. *Note:* The natural embedding of Post's correspondence problem proves Exercise 6.1.4(a), but does not always yield a well-formed program.

6.1.21. Complete the proof of Lemma 6.5.

6.1.22. Prove Lemma 6.6.

Open Problems

6.1.23. Does there exist a context-free language which is not a GTDPL language?

6.1.24. Are the TDPL languages closed under complementation?

6.1.25. Is every TDPL program equivalent to a well-formed TDPL program?

6.1.26. Is every GTDPL program equivalent to a TDPL program? Here we conjecture that $\{a^{n^2} | n \geq 1\}$ is a GTDPL language but not a TDPL language.

Programming Exercises

6.1.27. Design an interpreter for parsing machines. Write a program that takes an extended GTDPL program as input and constructs from it an equivalent parsing machine which the interpreter can then simulate.

6.1.28. Design a programming language centered around GTDPL (or TDPL) which can be used to specify translators. A source program would be the specification of a translator and the object program would be the actual translator. Construct a compiler for this language.

BIBLIOGRAPHIC NOTES

TDPL is an abstraction of the parsing language used by McClure [1965] in his compiler-compiler TMG.† The parsing machine in Section 6.1.5 is similar to the one used by Knuth [1967]. Most of the theoretical results concerning TDPL and GTDPL reported in this section were developed by Birman and Ullman [1970]. The solutions to many of the exercises can be found there.

GTDPL is a model of the META family of compiler-compilers [Schorre, 1964] and others.

6.2. LIMITED BACKTRACK BOTTOM-UP PARSING

We shall discuss possibilities of parsing deterministically and bottom-up in ways that allow more freedom than the shift–reduce methods of Chapter 5. In particular, we allow limited backtracking on the input, and the parse produced need not be a right parse. The principal method to be discussed is that of Colmerauer's precedence-based algorithm.

6.2.1. Noncanonical Parsing

There are several techniques which might be used to deterministically parse grammars which are not LR. One technique would be to permit arbitrarily long lookahead by allowing the input pointer to migrate forward along the input to resolve some ambiguity. When a decision has been reached, the input pointer finds its way back to the proper place for a reduction.

---

†TMG comes from the word "transmogrify," whose meaning is "to change in appearance or form, especially, strangely or grotesquely."

Example 6.8

Consider the grammar G with productions

$$S \longrightarrow Aa \mid Bb$$
$$A \longrightarrow 0A1 \mid 01$$
$$B \longrightarrow 0B11 \mid 011$$

G generates the language $\{0^n 1^n a \mid n \geq 1\} \cup \{0^n 1^{2n} b \mid n \geq 1\}$, which is not a deterministic context-free language. However, we can clearly parse G by first moving the input pointer to the end of an input string to see whether the last symbol is a or b and then returning to the beginning of the string and parsing as though the string were $0^n 1^n$ or $0^n 1^{2n}$, as appropriate. $\square$

Another parsing technique would be to reduce phrases which may not be handles.

DEFINITION

If $G = (\mathrm{N}, \Sigma, P, S)$ is a CFG, then β is a *phrase* of a sentential form $\alpha \beta \gamma$ if there is a derivation $S \overset{*}{\Rightarrow} \alpha A \gamma \Rightarrow \alpha \beta \gamma$. If $X_i \cdots X_k$ and $X_j \cdots X_l$ are phrases of a sentential form $X_1 \cdots X_n$, we say that phrase $X_i \cdots X_k$ is *to the left* of phrase $X_j \cdots X_l$ if $i < j$ or if $i = j$ and $k < l$. Thus, if a grammar is unambiguous, the handle is the leftmost phrase of a right-sentential form.

Example 6.9

Consider the grammar G having productions

$$S \longrightarrow 0ABb \mid 0aBc$$
$$A \longrightarrow a$$
$$B \longrightarrow B1 \mid 1$$

$L(G)$ is the regular set $0a1^+(b + c)$, but G is not LR. However, we can parse G bottom-up if we defer the decision of whether a is a phrase in a sentential form until we have scanned the last input symbol. That is, an input string of the form $0a1^n$ can be reduced to $0aB$ independently of whether it is followed by b or c. In the former case, $0aBb$ is first reduced to $0ABb$ and then to S. In the latter case, $0aBc$ is reduced directly to S. Of course, we shall not produce either a left or right parse. $\square$

Let $G = (\mathrm{N}, \Sigma, P, S)$ be a CFG in which the productions are numbered from 1 to p and let

(6.2.1) $$S = \alpha_0 \Longrightarrow \alpha_1 \Longrightarrow \alpha_2 \Longrightarrow \cdots \Longrightarrow \alpha_n = w$$

be a derivation of w from S. For $0 \leq i < n$, let $\alpha_i = \beta_i A_i \delta_i$, suppose that $A_i \longrightarrow \gamma_i$ is production p_i and suppose that this production is used to derive $\alpha_{i+1} = \beta_i \gamma_i \delta_i$ by replacing the explicitly shown A_i. We can represent this step of the derivation by the pair of integers (p_i, l_i), where $l_i = |\beta_i|$. Thus we can represent the derivation (6.2.1) by the string of n pairs

$$(6.2.2) \qquad (p_0, l_0)(p_1, l_1) \cdots (p_{n-1}, l_{n-1})$$

If the derivation is leftmost or rightmost, then the second components in (6.2.2), those giving the position of the nonterminal to be expanded in the next step of the derivation, are redundant.

DEFINITION

We shall call a string of pairs of the form (6.2.2) a *(generalized) top-down parse* for w. Clearly, a left parse is a special case of a top-down parse. Likewise, we shall call the reverse of this string, that is,

$$(p_{n-1}, l_{n-1})(p_{n-2}, l_{n-2}) \cdots (p_1, l_1)(p_0, l_0)$$

a *(generalized) bottom-up parse* of w. Thus a right parse is a special case of a bottom-up parse.

If we relax the restriction of scanning the input string only from left to right, but instead permit backtracking on the input, then we can deterministically parse grammars which cannot be so parsed using only the left-to-right scan.

6.2.2. Two-Stack Parsers

To model some backtracking algorithms, we introduce an automaton with two pushdown lists, the second of which also serves the function of an input tape. The deterministic version of this device is a cousin of the two-stack parser used in Algorithms 4.1 and 4.2 for general top-down and bottom-up parsing. We shall, however, put some restrictions on the device which will make it behave as a bottom-up precedence parser.

DEFINITION

A *two-stack (bottom-up) parser* for grammar $G = (N, \Sigma, P, S)$ is a finite set of rules of the form $(\alpha, \beta) \longrightarrow (\gamma, \delta)$, where α, β, γ, and δ are strings of symbols in $N \cup \Sigma \cup \{\$\}$; $\$$ is a new symbol, an endmarker. Each rule of the parser $(\alpha, \beta) \longrightarrow (\gamma, \delta)$ must be of one of two forms: either

(1) $\beta = X\delta$ for some $X \in N \cup \Sigma$, and $\gamma = \alpha X$, or
(2) $\alpha = \gamma\epsilon$ for some ϵ in $(N \cup \Sigma)^*$, $\delta = A\beta$, and $A \longrightarrow \epsilon$ is a production in P.

In general, a rule $(\alpha, \beta) \longrightarrow (\gamma, \delta)$ implies that if the string α is on top of the first pushdown list and if the string β is on top of the second, then we can replace α by γ on the first pushdown list and β by γ on the second. Rules of type (1) correspond to a shift in a shift–reduce parsing algorithm. Those of type (2) are related to reduce moves; the essential difference is that the symbol A, which is the left side of the production involved, winds up on the top of the second pushdown list rather than the first. This arrangement corresponds to limited backtracking. It is possible to move symbols from the first pushdown list to the second (which acts as the input tape), but only at the time of a reduction. Of course, rules of type (1) allow symbols to move from the second list to the first at any time.

A *configuration* of a two-stack parser T is a triple (α, β, π), where $\alpha \in \$(N \cup \Sigma)^*$, $\beta \in (N \cup \Sigma)^*\$$, and π is a string of pairs consisting of an integer and a production number. Thus, π could be part of a parse of some string in $L(G)$. We say that $(\alpha, \beta, \pi) \vdash_{\overline{T}} (\alpha', \beta', \pi')$ if

(1) $\alpha = \alpha_1\alpha_2$, $\beta = \beta_2\beta_1$, $(\alpha_2, \beta_2) \rightarrow (\gamma, \delta)$ is a rule of T;

(2) $\alpha' = \alpha_1\gamma$, $\beta' = \delta\beta_1$; and

(3) If $(\alpha_2, \beta_2) \rightarrow (\gamma, \delta)$ is a type 1 rule, then $\pi' = \pi$; if a type 2 rule and production i is the applicable production, then $\pi' = \pi(i, j)$, where j is equal to $|\alpha'| - 1$.†

Note that the first stack has its top at the right and that the second has its at the left.

We define $\vdash_{\overline{T}}^{i}$, $\vdash_{\overline{T}}^{+}$, and $\vdash_{\overline{T}}^{*}$ from $\vdash_{\overline{T}}$ in the usual manner. The subscript T will be dropped whenever possible.

The *translation defined by* T, denoted $\tau(T)$, is $\{(w, \pi) \mid (\$, w\$, e) \vdash^{*} (\$, S\$, \pi)\}$. We say that T is *valid* for G if for every $w \in L(G)$, there exists a bottom-up parse π of w such that $(w, \pi) \in \tau(T)$. It is elementary to show that if $(w, \pi) \in \tau(T)$, then π is a bottom-up parse of w.

T is *deterministic* if whenever $(\alpha_1, \beta_1) \rightarrow (\gamma_1, \delta_1)$ and $(\alpha_2, \beta_2) \rightarrow (\gamma_2, \delta_2)$ are rules such that α_1 is a suffix of α_2 or vice versa and β_1 is a prefix of β_2 or vice versa, then $\gamma_1 = \gamma_2$ and $\delta_1 = \delta_2$. Thus for each configuration C, there is at most one C' such that $C \vdash C'$.

Example 6.10

Consider the grammar G with productions

(1) $S \longrightarrow aSA$

(2) $S \longrightarrow bSA$

(3) $S \longrightarrow b$

(4) $A \longrightarrow a$

---

†The -1 term is present since α' includes a left endmarker.

This grammar generates the nondeterministic CFL $\{wba^n \mid w \in (a + b)^*$ and $n = |w|\}$.

We can design a (nondeterministic) two-stack transducer which can parse sentences according to G by first putting all of an input string on the first pushdown list and then parsing in essence from right to left.

The rules of T are the following:

(1) $(e, X) \longrightarrow (X, e)$ for all $X \in \{a, b, S, A\}$. (Any symbol may be shifted from the second pushdown list to the first.)

(2) $(a, e) \longrightarrow (e, A)$. (An a may be reduced to A.)

(3) $(b, e) \longrightarrow (e, S)$. (A b may be reduced to S.)

(4) $(aSA, e) \longrightarrow (e, S)$.

(5) $(bSA, e) \longrightarrow (e, S)$.

[The last two rules allow reductions by productions (1) and (2).]

Note that T is nondeterministic and that many parses of each input can be achieved. One bottom-up parse of *abbaa* is traced out in the following sequence of configurations:

$$(\$, abbaa\$, e) \vdash (\$a, bbaa\$, e)$$
$$\vdash (\$ab, baa\$, e)$$
$$\vdash (\$abb, aa\$, e)$$
$$\vdash (\$ab, Saa\$, (3, 2))$$
$$\vdash (\$abS, aa\$, (3, 2))$$
$$\vdash (\$abSa, a\$, (3, 2))$$
$$\vdash (\$abSaa, \$, (3, 2))$$
$$\vdash (\$abSa, A\$, (3, 2)(4, 4))$$
$$\vdash (\$abS, AA\$, (3, 2)(4, 4)(4, 3))$$
$$\vdash (\$abSA, A\$, (3, 2)(4, 4)(4, 3))$$
$$\vdash (\$a, SA\$, (3, 2)(4, 4)(4, 3)(2, 1))$$
$$\vdash (\$aS, A\$, (3, 2)(4, 4)(4, 3)(2, 1))$$
$$\vdash (\$aSA, \$, (3, 2)(4, 4)(4, 3)(2, 1))$$
$$\vdash (\$, S\$, (3, 2)(4, 4)(4, 3)(2, 1)(1, 0))$$

The string $(3, 2)(4, 4)(4, 3)(2, 1)(1, 0)$ is a bottom-up parse of *abbaa*, corresponding to the derivation

$$S \Rightarrow aSA \Rightarrow abSAA \Rightarrow abSaA \Rightarrow abSaa \Rightarrow abbaa. \quad \square$$

The two-stack parser has an anomaly in common with the general shift–reduce parsing algorithms; if a grammar is ambiguous, it may still be possible to find a deterministic two-stack parser for it by ignoring some of the possible parses. Later developments will rule out this problem.

Example 6.11

Let G be defined by the productions

$$S \longrightarrow A \mid B$$
$$A \longrightarrow aA \mid a$$
$$B \longrightarrow Ba \mid a$$

G is an ambiguous grammar for a^+. By ignoring B and its productions, the following set of rules form a deterministic two-stack parser for G:

$$(e, a) \longrightarrow (a, e)$$
$$(a, \$) \longrightarrow (e, A\$)$$
$$(a, A) \longrightarrow (aA, e)$$
$$(aA, \$) \longrightarrow (e, A\$)$$
$$(\$, A) \longrightarrow (\$A, e)$$
$$(\$A, \$) \longrightarrow (\$, S\$) \quad \square$$

6.2.3. Colmerauer Precedence Relations

The two-stack parser can be made to act in a manner somewhat similar to a precedence parser by assuming the existence of three disjoint relations, $\lessdot, \doteq,$ and $\gtrdot$, on the symbols of a grammar, letting $\gtrdot$ indicate a reduction, and $\lessdot$ and $\doteq$ indicate shifts. When reductions are made, $\lessdot$ will indicate the left end of a phrase (not necessarily a handle). It should be emphasized that, at least temporarily, we are not assuming that the relations $\lessdot, \doteq,$ and $\gtrdot$ bear any connection with the productions of a grammar. Thus, for example, we could have $X \doteq Y$ even though X and Y never appear together on the right side of a production.

DEFINITION

Let $G = (N, \Sigma, P, S)$ be a CFG, and let $\lessdot, \doteq,$ and $\gtrdot$ be three disjoint relations on $N \cup \Sigma \cup \{\$\}$, where $\$$ is a new symbol, the endmarker. The two-stack parser *induced* by the relations $\lessdot, \doteq,$ and $\gtrdot$ is defined by the following set of rules:

(1) $(X, Y) \rightarrow (XY, e)$ if and only if $X \lessdot Y$ or $X \doteq Y$.

(2) $(XZ_1 \cdots Z_k, Y) \rightarrow (X, AY)$ if and only if $Z_k \gtrdot Y$, $Z_i \doteq Z_{i+1}$ for $1 \leq i < k$, $X \lessdot Z_1$, and $A \rightarrow Z_1 \cdots Z_k$ is a production.

We observe that if G is uniquely invertible, then the induced two-stack parser is deterministic, and conversely.

Example 6.12

Let G be the grammar with productions

$$(1) \quad S \longrightarrow aSA$$
$$(2) \quad S \longrightarrow bSA$$
$$(3) \quad S \longrightarrow b$$
$$(4) \quad A \longrightarrow a$$

as in Example 6.10.

Let $<, \doteq,$ and $>$ be defined by Fig. 6.3.

	a	b	S	A	$\$$
$\$$	$\lessdot$	$\lessdot$			
a	$\lessdot$	$\lessdot$	$\doteq$	$\gtrdot$	$\gtrdot$
b	$\lessdot$	$\lessdot$	$\doteq$	$\gtrdot$	$\gtrdot$
S				$\doteq$	
A				$\gtrdot$	$\gtrdot$

Fig. 6.3 "Precedence" relations.

These relations induce the two-stack transducer with rules defined as follows:

$$(X, Y) \longrightarrow (XY, e) \qquad \text{for all } X \in \{\$, a, b\}, Y \in \{a, b\}$$
$$(Xa, Y) \longrightarrow (X, AY) \qquad \text{for all } X \in \{\$, a, b\}, Y \in \{\$, A\}$$
$$(Xb, Y) \longrightarrow (X, SY) \qquad \text{for all } X \in \{\$, a, b\}, Y \in \{\$, A\}$$
$$(X, S) \longrightarrow (XS, e) \qquad \text{for all } X \in \{a, b\}$$
$$(S, A) \longrightarrow (SA, e)$$
$$(XaSA, Y) \longrightarrow (X, SY) \qquad \text{for } X \in \{\$, a, b\} \text{ and } Y \in \{A, \$\}$$
$$(XbSA, Y) \longrightarrow (X, SY) \qquad \text{for } X \in \{\$, a, b\} \text{ and } Y \in \{A, \$\}$$

T accepts a string wba^n such that $|w| = n$ by the following sequence of moves:

$$(\$, wba^n\$, e) \vdash^{2n+1} (\$wba^n, \$, e)$$
$$\vdash^n (\$wb, A^n\$, (4, 2n) \cdots (4, n+1))$$
$$\vdash (\$w, SA^n\$, (4, 2n) \cdots (4, n+1)(3, n))$$
$$\vdash^{3n} (\$, S\$, (4, 2n) \cdots (4, n+1)(3, n)(i_n, n-1) \cdots (i_1, 0))$$

where i_j is 1 or 2, $1 \leq j \leq n$. Note the last $3n$ moves alternately shift S and A, and then reduce either aSA or bSA to S.

It is easy to check that T is deterministic, so no other sequences of moves are possible with words in $L(G)$. Since all reductions of T are according to productions of G, it follows that T is a two-stack parser for G.   □

On certain grammars, we can define "precedence" relations such that the induced two-stack parser is both deterministic and valid. We shall make such a definition here, and in the next section we shall give a simple test by which we can determine whether a grammar has such a parser.

DEFINITION

Let $G = (N, \Sigma, P, S)$ be a CFG. We say that G is a *Colmerauer grammar* if

(1) G is unambiguous,
(2) G is proper, and
(3) There exist disjoint relations $\lessdot$, $\doteq$, and $\gtrdot$ on $N \cup \Sigma \cup \{\$\}$ which induce a deterministic two-stack parser which is valid for G.

We call the three relations above *Colmerauer precedence relations*. Note that condition (3) implies that a Colmerauer grammar must be uniquely invertible.

Example 6.13

The relations of Fig. 6.3 are Colmerauer precedence relations, and G of Examples 6.10 and 6.12 is therefore a Colmerauer grammar.   □

Example 6.14

Every simple precedence grammar is a Colmerauer grammar. Let $\lessdot$, $\doteq$, and $\gtrdot$ be the Wirth–Weber precedence relations for the grammar $G = (N, \Sigma, P, S)$. If G is simple precedence, it is by definition proper and unambiguous. The induced two-stack parser acts almost as the shift–reduce precedence parser.

However, when a reduction of right-sentential form $\alpha\beta w$ to $\alpha A w$ is made, we wind up with $\$\alpha$ on the first stack and $Aw\$$ on the second, whereas in the precedence parsing algorithm, we would have $\$\alpha A$ on the pushdown list and $w\$$ on the input. If X is the last symbol of $\$\alpha$, then either $X \lessdot A$ or $X \doteq A$, by Theorem 5.14. Thus the next move of the two-stack parser must shift the A to the first stack. The two-stack parser then acts as the simple precedence parser until the next reduction.

Note that if the Colmerauer precedence relations are the Wirth–Weber ones, then the induced two-stack parser yields rightmost parses. In general, however, we cannot always expect this to be the case.   □

6.2.4. Test for Colmerauer Precedence

We shall give a necessary and sufficient condition for an unambiguous, proper grammar to be a Colmerauer grammar. The condition involves three relations which we shall define below. We should recall, however, that it is undecidable whether a CFG is unambiguous and that, as we saw in Example 6.12, there are ambiguous grammars which have deterministic two-stack parsers. Thus we cannot always determine whether an arbitrary CFG is a Colmerauer grammar unless we know a priori that the grammar is unambiguous.

DEFINITION

Let $G = (N, \Sigma, P, S)$ be a CFG. We define three new relations λ (for left), μ (for mutual or adjacent), and ρ (for right) on $N \cup \Sigma$ as follows: For all X and Y in $N \cup \Sigma$, A in N,

(1) $A\lambda Y$ if $A \longrightarrow Y\alpha$ is a production,
(2) $X\mu Y$ if $A \longrightarrow \alpha XY\beta$ is a production, and
(3) $X\rho A$ if $A \longrightarrow \alpha X$ is a production.

As is customary, for each relation R we shall use R^+ to denote $\bigcup\limits_{i=1}^{\infty} R^i$ and R^* to denote $\bigcup\limits_{i=0}^{\infty} R^i$. Recall that R^+ and R^* can be conveniently computed using Algorithm 0.2.

Note that the Wirth–Weber precedence relations $\lessdot, \doteq$, and $\gtrdot$ on $N \cup \Sigma$ can be defined in terms of λ, μ, and ρ as follows:

(1) $\lessdot = \mu\lambda^+$.
(2) $\doteq = \mu$.
(3) $\gtrdot = \rho^+\mu\lambda^* \cap (N \cup \Sigma) \times \Sigma$.

The remainder of this section is devoted to proving that an unambiguous, proper CFG has Colmerauer precedence relations if and only if

(1) $\rho^+\mu \cap \mu\lambda^* = \varnothing$, and
(2) $\mu \cap \rho^*\mu\lambda^+ = \varnothing$.

Example 6.15

Consider the previous grammar

$$S \longrightarrow aSA \,|\, bSA \,|\, b$$

$$A \longrightarrow a$$

Here

$$\lambda = \{(S, a), (S, b), (A, a)\}$$
$$\mu = \{(a, S), (S, A), (b, S)\}$$
$$\rho = \{(A, S), (b, S), (a, A)\}$$
$$\rho^+\mu = \{(A, A), (b, A), (a, A)\}$$
$$\mu\lambda^* = \{(a, S), (S, A), (b, S), (a, a), (a, b), (S, a), (b, a), (b, b)\}$$
$$\rho^*\mu\lambda^+ = \{(a, a), (a, b), (b, a), (b, b), (S, a), (A, a)\}$$

Since $\rho^+\mu \cap \mu\lambda^* = \varnothing$ and $\rho^*\mu\lambda^+ \cap \mu = \varnothing$, G has Colmerauer precedence relations, a set of which we saw in Fig. 4.3. □

We shall now show that if a grammar G contains symbols X and Y such that $X\mu Y$ and $X\rho^*\mu\lambda^+ Y$, then G cannot be a Colmerauer grammar. Here, X and Y need not be distinct.

LEMMA 6.7

Let $G = (N, \Sigma, P, S)$ be a Colmerauer grammar with Colmerauer precedence relations $\lessdot$, $\doteq$, and $\gtrdot$. If $X\mu Y$, then $X \doteq Y$.

Proof. Since G is proper, there exists a derivation in which a production $A \longrightarrow \alpha XY\beta$ is used. When parsing a word w in $L(G)$ whose derivation involves that production, at some time $\alpha XY\beta$ must appear at the top of stack 1 and be reduced. This can happen only if $X \doteq Y$. □

LEMMA 6.8

Let $G = (N, \Sigma, P, S)$ be a CFG such that for some X and Y in $N \cup \Sigma$, $X \rho^*\mu\lambda^+ Y$ and $X \mu Y$. Then G is not a Colmerauer grammar.

Proof. Suppose that G is. Let G have Colmerauer relations $\lessdot$, $\doteq$, and $\gtrdot$, and let T be the induced two-stack parser. Since G is assumed to be proper, there exist x and y in Σ^* such that $X \overset{*}{\Rightarrow} x$ and $Y \overset{*}{\Rightarrow} y$. Since $X \mu Y$, there is a production $A \longrightarrow \alpha XY\beta$ and strings w_1, w_2, w_3, and w_4 in Σ^* such that $S \overset{*}{\Rightarrow} w_1 A w_4 \Rightarrow w_1 \alpha XY\beta w_4 \overset{*}{\Rightarrow} w_1 w_2 XY w_3 w_4 \overset{*}{\Rightarrow} w_1 w_2 xy w_3 w_4$. Since $X \rho^*\mu\lambda^+ Y$, there exists a production $B \longrightarrow \gamma ZC\delta$ such that $Z \overset{*}{\Rightarrow} \gamma'X$, $C \overset{+}{\Rightarrow} Y\delta'$, and for some z_1, z_2, z_3, and z_4, we have $S \overset{*}{\Rightarrow} z_1 B z_4 \Rightarrow z_1 \gamma ZC\delta z_4 \overset{*}{\Rightarrow} z_1 \gamma\gamma' XY\delta'\delta z_4 \overset{*}{\Rightarrow} z_1 z_2 XY z_3 z_4 \overset{*}{\Rightarrow} z_1 z_2 xyz_3 z_4$.

By Lemma 6.7, we may assume that $X \doteq Y$. Let us watch the processing by T of the two strings $u = w_1 w_2 xyw_3 w_4$ and $v = z_1 z_2 xyz_3 z_4$. In particular, let us concentrate on the strings to which x and y are reduced in each case, and whether these strings appear on stack 1, stack 2, or spread between them. Let $\theta_1, \theta_2, \ldots$ be the sequence of strings to which xy is reduced in u and $\Psi_1, \Psi_2, \ldots$ that sequence in v. We know that there is some j such that $\theta_j = XY$, because since G is assumed to be unambiguous, X and Y must be reduced together in the reduction of u. If $\Psi_i = \theta_i$ for $1 \leq i \leq j$, then when this Y is reduced in the processing of v, the X to its left will also be reduced, since $X \doteq Y$. This situation cannot be correct, since $C \stackrel{+}{\Rightarrow} Y\delta'$ for some δ' in the derivation of v.†

Therefore, suppose that for some smallest i, $1 < i \leq j$, either $\theta_i \neq \Psi_i$ or Ψ_i does not exist (because the next reduction of a symbol of Ψ_i also involves a symbol outside of Ψ_i). We know that if $i > 2$, then the break point between the stacks when θ_{i-1} and Ψ_{i-1} were constructed by a reduction was at the same position in θ_{i-1} as in Ψ_{i-1}. Therefore, if the break point migrated out of θ_{i-1} before θ_i was created, it did so for Ψ_{i-1}, and it left in the same direction in each case. Taking into account the case $i = 2$, in which $\theta_1 = \Psi_1 = xy$, we know that immediately before the creation of θ_i and Ψ_i, the break point between the stacks is either

(1) Within θ_i and Ψ_i, and at the same position in both cases; i.e., θ_{i-1} and Ψ_{i-1} straddle the two stacks; or

(2) To the right of both θ_{i-1} and Ψ_{i-1}; i.e., both are on stack 1.

Note that it is impossible for the break point to be left of θ_{i-1} and Ψ_{i-1} and still have these altered on the next move. Also, the number of moves between the creation of θ_{i-1} and θ_i may not be the same as the number between Ψ_{i-1} and Ψ_i. We do not worry about the time that the break point spends outside these substrings; changes of these strings occur only when the break point migrates back into them.

It follows that since $\theta_i \neq \Psi_i$, the first reduction which involves a symbol of Ψ_{i-1} must involve at least one symbol outside of Ψ_{i-1}; i.e., Ψ_i really does not exist, for we know that the reduction of θ_{i-1} to θ_i involves only symbols of θ_{i-1}, by definition of the θ's. If the next reduction involving Ψ_{i-1} were wholly within Ψ_{i-1}, the result would, by (1) and (2) above, have to be that Ψ_{i-1} was reduced to θ_i.

Let us now consider several cases, depending on whether, in θ_{i-1}, x has been reduced to X and/or y has been reduced to Y.

Case 1: Both have been reduced. This is impossible because we chose $i \leq j$.

Case 2: y has not been reduced to Y, but x has been reduced to X. Now the reduction of Ψ_{i-1} involves symbols of Ψ_{i-1} and symbols outside of Ψ_{i-1}. Therefore, the breakpoint is written θ_{i-1} and Ψ_{i-1}, and a prefix of both is reduced. The parser on input u thus reduces X before Y. Since we have assumed that T is valid, we must conclude that there are two distinct parse

---

†Note that we are using symbols such as X and Y to represent specific instances of that symbol in the derivations, i.e., particular nodes of the derivation tree. We trust that the intended meaning will be clear.

trees for u, and thus that G is ambiguous. Since G is unambiguous, we discard this case.

Case 3: x has not been reduced to X, but y has been reduced to Y. Then $\theta_{i-1} = \theta Y$ for some θ. We must consider the position of the stack break point in two subcases:

(a) If the break point is within θ_{i-1}, and hence Ψ_{i-1}, the only way that Ψ_i could be different from θ_i occurs when the reduction of θ_{i-1} reduces a prefix of θ_{i-1}, and the symbol to the left of θ_{i-1} is $\lessdot$ related to the leftmost symbol of θ_{i-1}. However, for Ψ_{i-1}, the $\doteq$ relation holds, so a different reduction occurs. But then, some symbols of Ψ_{i-1} that have yet to be reduced to X are reduced along with some symbols outside of Ψ_{i-1}. We rule out this possibility using the argument of case 2.

(b) If the break point is to the right of θ_{i-1}, then its prefix θ can never reach the top of stack 1 without Y being reduced, for the only way to decrease the length of stack 1 is to perform reductions of its top symbols. But then, in the processing of u, by the time x is reduced to X, the Y has been reduced. However, we know that the X and Y must be reduced together in the unique derivation tree for u. We are forced to conclude in this case, too, that either T is not valid or G is ambiguous.

Case 4: Neither x nor y have been reduced to X or Y. Here, one of the arguments of cases 2 and 3 must apply.

We have thus ruled out all possibilities and conclude that $\mu \cap \rho^* \mu \lambda^+$ must be empty for a Colmerauer grammar. $\square$

We now show that if there are symbols X and Y in a CFG G such that $X \rho^+ \mu Y$ and $X \mu \lambda^* Y$, then G cannot be a Colmerauer grammar.

LEMMA 6.9

Let $G = (N, \Sigma, P, S)$ be a CFG such that for some X and Y in $N \cup \Sigma$, $X\rho^+\mu Y$ and $X\mu\lambda^*Y$. Then G is not a Colmerauer grammar.

Proof. The proof is left for the Exercises, and is similar, unfortunately, to Lemma 6.8. Since $X \rho^*\mu Y$, we can find $A \longrightarrow \alpha ZY\beta$ in P such that $Z \overset{*}{\Rightarrow} \alpha'X$. Since $X \mu\lambda^+ Y$, we can find $B \longrightarrow \gamma XC\delta$ in P such that $C \overset{+}{\Rightarrow} Y\delta'$. By the properness of G, we can find words u and v in $L(G)$ such that each derivation of u involves the production $A \longrightarrow \alpha ZY\beta$ and the derivation of $\alpha'X$ from that Z; each derivation of v involves $B \longrightarrow \gamma XC\delta$ and the derivation of $Y\delta'$ from C. In each case, X derives x and Y derives y for some x and y in Σ^*.

As in Lemma 6.8, we watch what happens to xy in u and v. In v, we find that Y must be reduced before X, while in u, either X and Y are reduced at the same time (if $Z \overset{*}{\Rightarrow} \alpha'X$ is a trivial derivation) or X is reduced before

Y (if $Z \overset{+}{\Rightarrow} \alpha'X$). Using arguments similar to those of the previous lemma, we can prove that as soon as the strings to which xy is reduced in u and v differ, one derivation or the other has gone astray. $\square$

Thus the conditions $\mu \cap \rho^*\mu\lambda^+ = \varnothing$ and $\rho^*\mu \cap \mu\lambda^+ = \varnothing$ are necessary in a Colmerauer grammar. We shall now proceed to show that, along with unambiguity, properness, and unique invertibility, they are sufficient.

LEMMA 6.10

Let $G = (N, \Sigma, P, S)$ be any proper grammar. Then if $\alpha XY\beta$ is any sentential form of G, we have $X \, \rho^*\mu\lambda^* \, Y$.

Proof. Elementary induction on the length of a derivation of $\alpha XY\beta$. $\square$

LEMMA 6.11

Let $G = (N, \Sigma, P, S)$ be unambiguous and proper, with $\mu \cap \rho^*\mu\lambda^+ = \varnothing$ and $\rho^+\mu \cap \mu\lambda^* = \varnothing$. If $\alpha YX_1 \cdots X_k Z\beta$ is a sentential form of G, then the conditions $X_1 \, \mu \, X_2, \ldots, X_{k-1} \, \mu \, X_k$, $Y \, \rho^*\mu\lambda^+ \, X_1$, and $X_k \, \rho^+\mu\lambda^* \, Z$ imply that $X_1 \cdots X_k$ is a phrase of $\alpha YX_1 \cdots X_k Z\beta$.

Proof. If not, then there is some other phrase of $\alpha YX_1 \cdots X_k Z\beta$ which includes X_1.

Case 1: Assume that $X_2, \ldots, X_k$ are all included in this other phrase. Then either Y or Z is also included, since the phrase is not $X_1 \cdots X_k$. Assuming that Y is included, then $Y\mu X_1$. But we know that $Y \, \rho^*\mu\lambda^+ \, X_1$, so that $\mu \cap \rho^*\mu\lambda^+ \neq \varnothing$. If Z is included, then $X_k\mu Z$. But we also have $X_k \, \rho^+\mu\lambda^* \, Z$. If λ^* represents at least one instance of λ, i.e., $X_k \, \rho^+\mu\lambda^+ \, Z$, then $\mu \cap \rho^*\mu\lambda^+ \neq \varnothing$. If λ^* represents zero instances of λ, then $X_k\rho^+\mu Z$. Since $X_k \, \mu \, Z$, we have $X_k \, \mu\lambda^* \, Z$, so $\rho^+\mu \cap \mu\lambda^* \neq \varnothing$.

Case 2: X_i is in the phrase, but X_{i+1} is not for some i such that $1 \leq i < k$. Let the phrase be reduced to A. Then by Lemma 6.10 applied to the sentential form to which we may reduce $\alpha YX_1 \cdots X_k Z\beta$, we have $A \, \rho^*\mu\lambda^* \, X_{i+1}$, and hence $X_i \, \rho^+\mu\lambda^* \, X_{i+1}$. But we already have $X_i \, \mu \, X_{i+1}$, so either $\mu \cap \rho^*\mu\lambda^+ \neq \varnothing$ or $\rho^+\mu \cap \mu\lambda^* \neq \varnothing$, depending on whether zero or more instances of λ are represented by λ^* in $\rho^+\mu\lambda^*$. $\square$

LEMMA 6.12

Let $G = (N, \Sigma, P, S)$ be a CFG which is unambiguous, proper, and uniquely invertible and for which $\mu \cap \rho^*\mu\lambda^+ = \varnothing$ and $\rho^+\mu \cap \mu\lambda^* = \varnothing$. Then G is a Colmerauer grammar.

Proof. We define Colmerauer precedence relations as follows:

(1) $X \doteq Y$ if and only if $X\mu Y$.

(2) $X \lessdot Y$ if and only if $X\mu\lambda^{+}Y$ or $X = \$, Y \neq \$$.

(3) $X \gtrdot Y$ if and only if $X \neq \$$ and $Y = \$$, or $X \rho^{+}\mu\lambda^{*} Y$ but $X \mu\lambda^{+} Y$ is false.

It is easy to show that these relations are disjoint. If $\doteq \cap \lessdot \neq \varnothing$ or $\doteq \cap \gtrdot \neq \varnothing$, then $\mu \cap \rho^{*}\mu\lambda^{+} \neq \varnothing$ or $\mu \cap \rho^{+}\mu = \varnothing$, in which case $\mu\lambda^{*} \cap \rho^{+}\mu \neq \varnothing$. If $\lessdot \cap \gtrdot \neq \varnothing$, then $X \mu\lambda^{+} Y$. Also, $X \mu\lambda^{+} Y$ is false, an obvious impossibility.

Suppose that T, the induced two-stack parser, has rule $(YX_1 \cdots X_k, Z)$ $\rightarrow (Y, AZ)$. Then $Y \lessdot X_1$, so $Y = \$$ or $Y \mu\lambda^{+} X_1$. Also, $X_i \doteq X_{i+1}$ for $1 \leq i < k$, so $X_i \mu X_{i+1}$. Finally, $X_k \gtrdot Z$, so $Z = \$$ or $X_k \rho^{+}\mu\lambda^{*} Z$. Ignoring the case $Y = \$$ or $Z = \$$ for the moment, Lemma 6.11 assures us that if the string on the two stacks is a sentential form of G, then $X_1 \cdots X_k$ is a phrase thereof. The cases $Y = \$$ or $Z = \$$ are easily treated, and we can conclude that every reduction performed by T on a sentential form yields a sentential form.

It thus suffices to show that when started with w in $L(G)$, T will continue to perform reductions until it reduces to S.

By Lemma 6.10, if X and Y are adjacent symbols of any sentential form, then $X \rho^{*}\mu\lambda^{*} Y$. Thus either $X \mu Y$, $X \rho^{+}\mu Y$, $X \mu\lambda^{+} Y$, or $X \rho^{+}\mu\lambda^{+} Y$. In each case, X and Y are related by one of the Colmerauer precedence relations.

A straightforward induction on the number of moves made by T shows that if X and Y are adjacent symbols on stack 1, then $X \lessdot Y$ or $X \doteq Y$. The argument is, essentially, that the only way X and Y could become adjacent is for Y to be shifted onto stack 1 when X is the top symbol. The rules of T imply that $X \lessdot Y$ or $X \doteq Y$.

Since $\$$ remains on stack 2, there is always some pair of adjacent symbols on stack 2 related by $\gtrdot$. Thus, unless configuration $(\$, S\$, \pi)$ is reached by T, it will always shift until the tops of stack 1 and 2 are related by $\gtrdot$. At that time, since the $\lessdot$ relation never holds between adjacent symbols on stack 1, a reduction is possible and T proceeds. $\square$

THEOREM 6.6

A grammar is Colmerauer if and only if it is unambiguous, proper, uniquely invertible, and $\mu \cap \rho^{*}\mu\lambda^{+} = \rho^{+}\mu \cap \mu\lambda^{*} = \varnothing$.

Proof. Immediate from Lemmas 6.8, 6.9, and 6.12. $\square$

Example 6.16

We saw in Example 6.15 that the grammar $S \rightarrow aSA \,|\, bSA \,|\, b$, $A \rightarrow a$ satisfies the desired conditions. Lemma 6.12 suggests that we define Colmerauer precedence relations for this grammar according to Fig. 6.4. $\square$

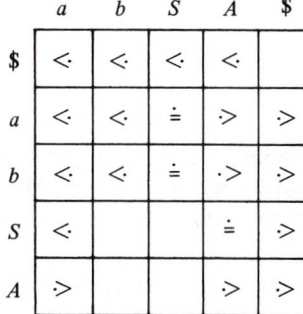

Fig. 6.4 Colmerauer precedence relations.

EXERCISES

6.2.1. Which of the following are top-down parses in G_0? What word is derived if it is?

(a) $(1, 0)$ $(3, 2)$ $(5, 4)$ $(2, 0)$ $(4, 2)$ $(2, 5)$ $(4, 0)$ $(4, 5)$ $(6, 5)$ $(6, 2)$ $(6, 0)$.

(b) $(2, 0)$ $(4, 0)$ $(5, 0)$ $(6, 1)$.

6.2.2. Give a two-stack parser valid for G_0.

6.2.3. Which of the following are Colmerauer grammars?

(a) G_0

(b) $S \longrightarrow aA \,|\, bB$
$A \longrightarrow 0A1 \,|\, 01$
$B \longrightarrow 0B11 \,|\, 011$.

(c) $S \longrightarrow aAB \,|\, b$
$A \longrightarrow bSB \,|\, a$
$B \longrightarrow a$.

*6.2.4. Show that if G is proper, uniquely invertible, $\mu \cap \rho^* \mu \lambda^+ = \varnothing$, and $\rho^+ \mu \cap \mu \lambda^* = \varnothing$, then G is unambiguous. Can you use this result to strengthen Theorem 6.6?

6.2.5. Show that every uniquely invertible regular grammar is a Colmerauer grammar.

6.2.6. Show that every uniquely invertible grammar in GNF such that $\rho^+ \mu \cap \mu = \varnothing$ is a Colmerauer grammar.

6.2.7. Show that the two-stack parser of Example 6.12 is valid.

6.2.8. Show, using Theorem 6.6, that every simple precedence grammar is a Colmerauer grammar.

6.2.9. Prove Lemma 6.9.

6.2.10. Prove Lemma 6.10.

6.2.11. Let G be a Colmerauer grammar with Colmerauer precedence relations $\lessdot$, $\doteq$, and $\gtrdot$ such that the induced two-stack parser not only parses every word in $L(G)$, but correctly parses every sentential form of G. Show that

(a) $\mu \subseteq \doteq \dagger$.
(b) $\mu \lambda^+ \subseteq \lessdot$.
(c) $\rho^+ \mu \subseteq \gtrdot$.
(d) $\rho^+ \mu \lambda^+ \subseteq \lessdot \cup \gtrdot$.

*6.2.12. Let G be a Colmerauer grammar, and let v be any subset of $\rho^+ \mu \lambda^+ - \rho^+ \mu - \mu \lambda^+$. Show that the relations $\doteq = \mu$, $\mathbf{M} = \rho^* \mu \lambda^+ - v$, and $\gtrdot = \rho^+ \mu \cup v$ are Colmerauer percedence relations capable of parsing any sentential form of G.

6.2.13. Show that every two-stack parser operates in time $0(n)$ on strings of length n.

*6.2.14. Show that if L has a Colmerauer grammar, then L^R has a Colmerauer grammar.

*6.2.15. Is every $(1, 1)$-BRC grammar a Colmerauer grammar?

*6.2.16. Show that there exists a Colmerauer language L such that neither L nor L^R is a deterministic CFL. Note that the language $\{wba^n \,|\, |w| = n\}$, which we have been using as an example, is not deterministic but that its reverse is.

*6.2.17. We say that a two-stack parser T *recognizes* the domain of $\tau(T)$ regardless of whether a parse emitted has any relation to the input. Show that every recursively enumerable language is recognized by some deterministic two-stack parser. *Hint:* It helps to make the underlying grammar ambiguous.

Open Problem

6.2.18. Characterize the class of CFG's, unambiguous or not, which have valid deterministic two-stack parsers induced by disjoint "precedence" relations.

BIBLIOGRAPHIC NOTES

Colmerauer grammars and Theorem 6.6 were first given by Colmerauer [1970]. These ideas were related to the token set concept by Gray and Harrison [1969]. Cohen and Culik [1971] consider an LR(k)-based scheme which effectively incorporates backtrack.

†This is a special case of Lemma 6.7 and is included only for completeness.

APPENDIX

The Appendix contains the syntactic descriptions of four programming languages:

(1) A simple base language for an extensible language.
(2) SNOBOL4, a string-manipulating language.
(3) PL360, a high-level machine language for the IBM 360 computers.
(4) PAL, a language combining lambda calculus with assignment statements.

These languages were chosen for their diversity. In addition, the syntactic descriptions of these languages are small enough to be used in some of the programming exercises throughout this book without consuming an excessive amount of time (both human and computer). At the same time the languages are quite sophisticated and will provide a flavor of the problems incurred in implementing the more traditional programming languages such as ALGOL, FORTRAN, and PL/I. Syntactic descriptions of the latter languages can be found in the following references:

(1) ALGOL 60 in Naur [1963].
(2) ALGOL 68 in Van Wijngaarden [1969].
(3) FORTRAN in [ANS X3.9, 1966] (Also see ANSI-X3J3.)
(4) PL/I in the IBM Vienna Laboratory Technical Report TR 25.096.

A.1. SYNTAX FOR AN EXTENSIBLE BASE LANGUAGE

The following language was proposed by Leavenworth† as a base language which can be extended by the use of syntax macros. We shall give the syntax

†B. M. Leavenworth, "Syntax Macros and Extended Translation" *Comm. ACM* 9, No. 11 (November 1966), 790–793. Copyright © 1966, Association for Computing Machinery, Inc. The syntax of the base language is reprinted here by permission of the Association for Computing Machinery.

of this language in two parts. The first part consists of the high-level productions which define the base language. This base language can be used as a block-structured algebraic language by itself.

The second part of the description is the set of productions which defines the extension mechanism. The extension mechanism allows new forms of statements and functions to be declared by means of a syntax macro definition statement using production 37. This production states that an instance of a ⟨statement⟩ can be a ⟨syntax macro definition⟩, which, by productions 39 and 40, can be either a ⟨statement macro definition⟩ or a ⟨function macro definition⟩.

In productions 41 and 42 we see that each of these macro definitions involves a ⟨macro structure⟩ and a ⟨definition⟩. The ⟨macro structure⟩ portion defines the form of the new syntactic construct, and the ⟨definition⟩ portion gives the translation that is to be associated with the new syntactic construct. Both the ⟨macro structure⟩ and ⟨definition⟩ can be any string of nonterminal and terminal symbols except that each nonterminal in the ⟨definition⟩ portion must appear in the ⟨macro structure⟩. (This is similar to a rule in an SDTS except that here there is no restriction on how many times one nonterminal can be used in the translation element.)

We have not given the explicit rules for ⟨macro structure⟩ and ⟨definition⟩. In fact, the specification that each nonterminal in the ⟨definition⟩ portion appear in the ⟨macro structure⟩ portion of a syntax macro definition cannot be specified by context-free productions.

Production 37 indicates that we can use any instance of a ⟨macro structure⟩ defined in a statement macro definition wherever ⟨sentence⟩ appears in a sentential form. Likewise, production 43 allows us to use any instance of a ⟨macro structure⟩ defined in a function macro definition anywhere ⟨primary⟩ appears in a sentential form.

For example, we can define a sum statement by the derivation

$$⟨\text{statement}⟩ \Longrightarrow ⟨\text{syntax macro definition}⟩$$
$$\Longrightarrow ⟨\text{statement macro definition}⟩$$
$$\Longrightarrow \textbf{smacro } ⟨\text{macro structure}⟩ \textbf{ define } ⟨\text{definition}⟩ \textbf{ endmacro}$$

A possible ⟨macro structure⟩ is the following:

$$\textbf{sum } ⟨\text{expression}⟩^{(1)} \textbf{ with } ⟨\text{variable}⟩ \leftarrow ⟨\text{expression}⟩^{(2)} \textbf{ to } ⟨\text{expression}⟩^{(3)}$$

We can define a translation for this macro structure by expanding ⟨definition⟩ as

$$\textbf{begin local } t; \textbf{ local } s; \textbf{ local } r;$$
$$t \leftarrow 0;$$
$$⟨\text{variable}⟩ \leftarrow ⟨\text{expression}⟩^{(2)};$$

r: **if** $\langle$variable$\rangle > \langle$expression$\rangle^{(3)}$ **then goto** s;

$\qquad t \longleftarrow t + \langle$expression$\rangle^{(1)}$;

$\qquad \langle$variable$\rangle \leftarrow \langle$variable$\rangle + 1$;

$\qquad$ **goto** r;

$\quad s$: **result** t

end

Then if we write the statement

$$\textbf{sum } a \textbf{ with } b \longleftarrow c \textbf{ to } d$$

this would first be translated into

begin local t; **local** s; **local** r;

$\qquad t \longleftarrow 0$;

$\qquad b \longleftarrow c$;

r: **if** $b > d$ **then goto** s;

$\qquad t \longleftarrow t + a$;

$\qquad b \longleftarrow b + 1$;

$\qquad$ **goto** r;

$\quad s$: **result** t

end

before being parsed according to the high-level productions.

Finally, the nonterminals $\langle$identifier$\rangle$, $\langle$label$\rangle$, and $\langle$constant$\rangle$ are lexical items which we shall leave unspecified. The reader is invited to insert his favorite definitions of these items or to treat them as terminal symbols.

High-Level Productions

1 $\langle$program$\rangle \rightarrow$
$\qquad \langle$block$\rangle$
2 $\langle$block$\rangle \rightarrow$
$\qquad$ **begin** $\langle$opt local ids$\rangle$ $\langle$statement list$\rangle$ **end**
3 $\langle$opt local ids$\rangle \rightarrow$
$\qquad \langle$opt local ids$\rangle$ **local** $\langle$identifier$\rangle$; $|e$
5 $\langle$statement list$\rangle \rightarrow$
$\qquad \langle$statement$\rangle|\langle$statement list$\rangle$; $\langle$statement$\rangle$
7 $\langle$statement$\rangle \rightarrow$
$\qquad \langle$variable$\rangle \leftarrow \langle$expression$\rangle|$**goto** $\langle$identifier$\rangle|$
$\qquad$ **if** $\langle$expression$\rangle$ **then** $\langle$statement$\rangle|\langle$block$\rangle|$**result** $\langle$expression$\rangle|$
$\qquad \langle$label$\rangle$: $\langle$statement$\rangle$

13 $\langle$expression$\rangle \rightarrow$
   $\langle$arithmetic expression$\rangle \langle$relation op$\rangle \langle$arithmetic expression$\rangle$|
   $\langle$arithmetic expression$\rangle$
15 $\langle$arithmetic expression$\rangle \rightarrow$
   $\langle$arithmetic expression$\rangle \langle$add op$\rangle \langle$term$\rangle$|$\langle$term$\rangle$
17 $\langle$term$\rangle \rightarrow$
   $\langle$term$\rangle \langle$mult op$\rangle \langle$primary$\rangle$|$\langle$primary$\rangle$
19 $\langle$primary$\rangle \rightarrow$
   $\langle$variable$\rangle$|$\langle$constant$\rangle$|($\langle$expression$\rangle$)|$\langle$block$\rangle$
23 $\langle$variable$\rangle \rightarrow$
   $\langle$identifier$\rangle$|$\langle$identifier$\rangle$($\langle$expression list$\rangle$)
25 $\langle$expression list$\rangle \rightarrow$
   $\langle$expression list$\rangle$, $\langle$expression$\rangle$|$\langle$expression$\rangle$
27 $\langle$relation op$\rangle \rightarrow$
   $< | \leq | = | \neq | > | \geq$
33 $\langle$add op$\rangle \rightarrow$
   $+ | -$
35 $\langle$mult op$\rangle \rightarrow$
   $* | /$

Extension Mechanism

37 $\langle$statement$\rangle \rightarrow$
   $\langle$syntax macro definition$\rangle$|$\langle$macro structure$\rangle$
39 $\langle$syntax macro definition$\rangle \rightarrow$
   $\langle$statement macro definition$\rangle$|$\langle$function macro definition$\rangle$
41 $\langle$statement macro definition$\rangle \rightarrow$
   smacro $\langle$macro structure$\rangle$ **define** $\langle$definition$\rangle$ **endmacro**
42 $\langle$function macro definition$\rangle \rightarrow$
   fmacro $\langle$macro structure$\rangle$ **define** $\langle$definition$\rangle$ **endmacro**
43 $\langle$primary$\rangle \rightarrow$
   $\langle$macro structure$\rangle$

Notes

1. $\langle$macro structure$\rangle$ and $\langle$definition$\rangle$ can be any string of nonterminal or terminal symbols. However, any nonterminal used in $\langle$definition$\rangle$ must also appear in the corresponding $\langle$macro structure$\rangle$.

2. $\langle$constant$\rangle$, $\langle$identifier$\rangle$, and $\langle$label$\rangle$ are lexical variables which have not been defined here.

A.2. SYNTAX OF SNOBOL4 STATEMENTS

Here we shall define the syntactic structure of SNOBOL4 statements as described by Griswold et al.† The syntactic description is in two parts. The first part contains the context-free productions describing the syntax in terms of lexical variables which are described in the second part using regular definitions of Chapter 3. The division between the syntactic and lexical parts is arbitrary here, and the syntactic description does not reflect the relative precedence or associativity of the operators. All operators associate from left-to-right except $\neg$, !, and $**$. The precedence of the operators is as follows:

1. &	2. |	3. $\langle$blanks$\rangle$
4. @	5. $+$ $-$	6. #
7. /	8. $*$	9. %
10. ! $**$	11. $.	12. $\neg$?

High-Level Productions

1 $\langle$statement$\rangle$ $\longrightarrow$
    $\langle$assignment statement$\rangle$ | $\langle$matching statement$\rangle$ |
    $\langle$replacement statement$\rangle$ | $\langle$degenerate statement$\rangle$ | $\langle$end statement$\rangle$
6 $\langle$assignment statement$\rangle$ $\longrightarrow$
    $\langle$optional label$\rangle$ $\langle$subject field$\rangle$ $\langle$equal$\rangle$ $\langle$object field$\rangle$ $\langle$goto field$\rangle$
    $\langle$eos$\rangle$
7 $\langle$matching statement$\rangle$ $\longrightarrow$
    $\langle$optional label$\rangle$ $\langle$subject field$\rangle$ $\langle$pattern field$\rangle$ $\langle$goto field$\rangle$ $\langle$eos$\rangle$
8 $\langle$replacement statement$\rangle$ $\longrightarrow$
    $\langle$optional label$\rangle$ $\langle$subject field$\rangle$ $\langle$pattern field$\rangle$ $\langle$equal$\rangle$ $\langle$object
    field$\rangle$ $\langle$goto field$\rangle$ $\langle$eos$\rangle$
9 $\langle$degenerate statement$\rangle$ $\longrightarrow$
    $\langle$optional label$\rangle$ $\langle$subject field$\rangle$ $\langle$goto field$\rangle$ $\langle$eos$\rangle$ |
    $\langle$optional label$\rangle$ $\langle$goto field$\rangle$ $\langle$eos$\rangle$
11 $\langle$end statement$\rangle$ $\longrightarrow$
    END $\langle$eos$\rangle$ | END $\langle$blanks$\rangle$ $\langle$label$\rangle$ $\langle$eos$\rangle$ |
    END $\langle$blanks$\rangle$ END $\langle$eos$\rangle$
14 $\langle$optional label$\rangle$ $\longrightarrow$
    $\langle$label$\rangle$ | e
16 $\langle$subject field$\rangle$ $\longrightarrow$
    $\langle$blanks$\rangle$ $\langle$element$\rangle$

†R. E. Griswold, J. F. Poage, and I. P. Polonsky, *The SNOBOL4 Programming Language* (2nd ed.) (Englewood Cliffs, N.J.: Prentice-Hall, Inc., 1971) pp. 198–199.

17 ⟨equal⟩ →
  ⟨blanks⟩ =
18 ⟨object field⟩ →
  ⟨blanks⟩ ⟨expression⟩
19 ⟨goto field⟩ →
  ⟨blanks⟩ : ⟨optional blanks⟩ ⟨basic goto⟩ | e
21 ⟨basic goto⟩ →
  ⟨goto⟩ | S ⟨goto⟩ ⟨optional blanks⟩ ⟨optional F goto⟩ |
  F ⟨goto⟩ ⟨optional blanks⟩ ⟨optional S goto⟩
24 ⟨goto⟩ →
  (⟨expression⟩) | < ⟨expression⟩ >
26 ⟨optional S goto⟩ →
  S ⟨goto⟩ | e
28 ⟨optional F goto⟩ →
  F ⟨goto⟩ | e
30 ⟨eos⟩ →
  ⟨optional blanks⟩ ; | ⟨optional blanks⟩ ⟨eol⟩
32 ⟨pattern field⟩ →
  ⟨blanks⟩ ⟨expression⟩
33 ⟨element⟩ →
  ⟨optional unaries⟩ ⟨basic element⟩
34 ⟨optional unaries⟩ →
  ⟨operator⟩ ⟨optional unaries⟩ | e
36 ⟨basic element⟩ →
  ⟨identifier⟩ | ⟨literal⟩ | ⟨function call⟩ | ⟨reference⟩ | (⟨expression⟩)
41 ⟨function call⟩ →
  ⟨identifier⟩ (⟨arg list⟩)
42 ⟨reference⟩ →
  ⟨identifier⟩ < ⟨arg list⟩ >
43 ⟨arg list⟩ →
  ⟨arg list⟩ , ⟨expression⟩ | ⟨expression⟩
45 ⟨expression⟩ →
  ⟨optional blanks⟩ ⟨element⟩ ⟨optional blanks⟩ |
  ⟨optional blanks⟩ ⟨operation⟩ ⟨optional blanks⟩ |
  ⟨optional blanks⟩
48 ⟨optional blanks⟩ →
  ⟨blanks⟩ | e
50 ⟨operation⟩ →
  ⟨element⟩ ⟨binary⟩ ⟨element⟩ | ⟨element⟩ ⟨binary⟩ ⟨expression⟩

Regular Definitions for Lexical Syntax

  ⟨digit⟩ =
    0 | 1 | 2 | 3 | 4 | 5 | 6 | 7 | 8 | 9

$\langle$letter$\rangle =$
    $A \mid B \mid C \mid \cdots \mid Z$
$\langle$alphanumeric$\rangle =$
    $\langle$letter$\rangle \mid \langle$digit$\rangle$
$\langle$identifier$\rangle =$
    $\langle$letter$\rangle$ ($\langle$alphanumeric$\rangle \mid \cdot \mid \_$)*
$\langle$blanks$\rangle =$
    $\langle$blank character$\rangle^+$
$\langle$integer$\rangle =$
    $\langle$digit$\rangle^+$
$\langle$real$\rangle =$
    $\langle$integer$\rangle . \langle$integer$\rangle \mid \langle$integer$\rangle .$
$\langle$operator$\rangle =$
    $\neg \mid ? \mid \$ \mid . \mid ! \mid \% \mid * \mid / \mid \# \mid + \mid - \mid @ \mid \| \mid \&$
$\langle$binary$\rangle =$
    $\langle$blanks$\rangle \mid \langle$blanks$\rangle \langle$operator$\rangle \langle$blanks$\rangle \mid \langle$blanks$\rangle ** \langle$blanks$\rangle$
$\langle$sliteral$\rangle =$
    ' ($\langle$EBCDIC character$\rangle - $ ')* '†

$\langle$dliteral$\rangle =$
    " ($\langle$EBCDIC character$\rangle - $ ")* "
$\langle$literal$\rangle =$
    $\langle$sliteral$\rangle \mid \langle$dliteral$\rangle \mid \langle$integer$\rangle \mid \langle$real$\rangle$
$\langle$label$\rangle =$
    $\langle$alphanumeric$\rangle$ ($\langle$EBCDIC character$\rangle - $ ($\langle$blank character$\rangle \mid ;$))*
    $- $ END

Lexical Variables

$\langle$blank character$\rangle$
$\langle$EBCDIC character$\rangle$
$\langle$eol$\rangle$‡

A.3. SYNTAX FOR PL360

This section contains the syntactic description of PL360, a high-level machine language devised by Nicklaus Wirth for the IBM 360 computers. The syntactic description is the precedence grammar given by Wirth [1968].§

†The minus sign is a metasymbol here and on the following lines.
‡end of line.
§Niklaus Wirth, "PL360, a Programming Language for the 360 Computers" J. ACM 15, No. 1 (January, 1968), 37–74. Copyright © 1968, Association for Computing Machinery, Inc. The syntax is reprinted by permission of the Association for Computing Machinery.

High-Level Productions

1 ⟨register⟩ →
 ⟨identifier⟩
2 ⟨cell identifier⟩ →
 ⟨identifier⟩
3 ⟨procedure identifier⟩ →
 ⟨identifier⟩
4 ⟨function identifier⟩ →
 ⟨identifier⟩
5 ⟨cell⟩ →
 ⟨cell identifier⟩|⟨cell1⟩)|⟨cell2⟩)
8 ⟨cell1⟩ →
 ⟨cell2⟩⟨arith op⟩⟨number⟩|⟨cell3⟩⟨number⟩
10 ⟨cell2⟩ →
 ⟨cell3⟩⟨register⟩
11 ⟨cell3⟩ →
 ⟨cell identifier⟩(
12 ⟨unary op⟩ →
 abs|neg|neg abs
15 ⟨arith op⟩ →
 $+|-|*|/|++|--$
21 ⟨logical op⟩ →
 and|or|xor
24 ⟨shift op⟩ →
 shla|shra|shll|shrl
28 ⟨register assignment⟩ →
 ⟨register⟩ := ⟨cell⟩|
 ⟨register⟩ := ⟨number⟩|
 ⟨register⟩ := ⟨string⟩|
 ⟨register⟩ := ⟨register⟩|
 ⟨register⟩ := ⟨unary op⟩⟨cell⟩|
 ⟨register⟩ := ⟨unary op⟩⟨number⟩|
 ⟨register⟩ := ⟨unary op⟩⟨register⟩|
 ⟨register⟩ := @⟨cell⟩|
 ⟨register assignment⟩⟨arith op⟩⟨cell⟩|
 ⟨register assignment⟩⟨arith op⟩⟨number⟩|
 ⟨register assignment⟩⟨arith op⟩⟨register⟩|
 ⟨register assignment⟩⟨logical op⟩⟨cell⟩|
 ⟨register assignment⟩⟨logical op⟩⟨number⟩|
 ⟨register assignment⟩⟨logical op⟩⟨register⟩|
 ⟨register assignment⟩⟨shift op⟩⟨number⟩|
 ⟨register assignment⟩⟨shift op⟩⟨register⟩

44 $\langle$func1$\rangle \rightarrow$
     $\langle$func2$\rangle \langle$number$\rangle$|
     $\langle$func2$\rangle \langle$register$\rangle$|
     $\langle$func2$\rangle \langle$cell$\rangle$|
     $\langle$func2$\rangle \langle$string$\rangle$
48 $\langle$func2$\rangle \rightarrow$
     $\langle$function identifier$\rangle$)|$\langle$func1$\rangle$,
50 $\langle$case sequence$\rangle \rightarrow$
     case $\langle$register$\rangle$ **of begin**|$\langle$case sequence$\rangle \langle$statement$\rangle$;
52 $\langle$simple statement$\rangle \rightarrow$
     $\langle$cell$\rangle$:= $\langle$register$\rangle$|$\langle$register assignment$\rangle$|**null**|**goto** $\langle$identifier$\rangle$|
     $\langle$procedure identifier$\rangle$|$\langle$function identifier$\rangle$|$\langle$func1$\rangle$(|
     $\langle$case sequence$\rangle$ **end**|$\langle$blockbody$\rangle$ end
61 $\langle$relation$\rangle \rightarrow$
     $<$|$=$|$>$|$<=$|$>=$|$\neg=$
67 $\langle$not$\rangle \rightarrow$
     $\neg$
68 $\langle$condition$\rangle \rightarrow$
     $\langle$register$\rangle \langle$relation$\rangle \langle$cell$\rangle$|
     $\langle$register$\rangle \langle$relation$\rangle \langle$number$\rangle$|
     $\langle$register$\rangle \langle$relation$\rangle \langle$register$\rangle$|
     $\langle$register$\rangle \langle$relation$\rangle \langle$string$\rangle$|
     overflow|$\langle$relation$\rangle$|
     $\langle$cell$\rangle$|$\langle$not$\rangle \langle$cell$\rangle$
76 $\langle$compound condition$\rangle \rightarrow$
     $\langle$condition$\rangle$|$\langle$comp aor$\rangle \langle$condition$\rangle$
78 $\langle$comp aor$\rangle \rightarrow$
     $\langle$compound condition$\rangle$ **and**|$\langle$compound condition$\rangle$ **or**
80 $\langle$cond then$\rangle \rightarrow$
     $\langle$compound condition$\rangle$ **then**
81 $\langle$true part$\rangle \rightarrow$
     $\langle$simple statement$\rangle$ **else**
82 $\langle$while$\rangle \rightarrow$
     while
83 $\langle$cond do$\rangle \rightarrow$
     $\langle$compound condition$\rangle$ **do**
84 $\langle$assignment step$\rangle \rightarrow$
     $\langle$register assignment$\rangle$ **step** $\langle$number$\rangle$
85 $\langle$limit$\rangle \rightarrow$
     until $\langle$register$\rangle$|**until** $\langle$cell$\rangle$|**until** $\langle$number$\rangle$
88 $\langle$do$\rangle \rightarrow$
     do
89 $\langle$statement*$\rangle \rightarrow$

⟨simple statement⟩ |
if ⟨cond then⟩ ⟨statement*⟩ |
if ⟨cond then⟩ ⟨true part⟩ ⟨statement*⟩ |
⟨while⟩ ⟨cond do⟩ ⟨statement*⟩ |
for ⟨assignment step⟩ ⟨limit⟩ ⟨do⟩ ⟨statement*⟩

94 ⟨statement⟩ →
⟨statement*⟩

95 ⟨simple type⟩ →
short integer | integer | logical | real | long real | byte | character

102 ⟨type⟩ →
⟨simple type⟩ | **array** ⟨number⟩ ⟨simple type⟩

104 ⟨decl1⟩ →
⟨type⟩ ⟨identifier⟩ | ⟨decl2⟩ ⟨identifier⟩

106 ⟨decl2⟩ →
⟨decl7⟩ ,

107 ⟨decl3⟩ →
⟨decl1⟩ =

108 ⟨decl4⟩ →
⟨decl3⟩ (| ⟨decl5⟩ ,

110 ⟨decl5⟩ →
⟨decl4⟩ ⟨number⟩ | ⟨decl4⟩ ⟨string⟩

112 ⟨decl6⟩ →
⟨decl3⟩

113 ⟨decl7⟩ →
⟨decl1⟩ |
⟨decl6⟩ ⟨number⟩ |
⟨decl6⟩ ⟨string⟩ |
⟨decl5⟩)

117 ⟨function declaration1⟩ →
function | ⟨function declaration7⟩

119 ⟨function declaration2⟩ →
⟨function declaration1⟩ ⟨identifier⟩

120 ⟨function declaration3⟩ →
⟨function declaration2⟩ (

121 ⟨function declaration4⟩ →
⟨function declaration3⟩ ⟨number⟩

122 ⟨function declaration5⟩ →
⟨function declaration4⟩ ,

123 ⟨function declaration6⟩ →
⟨function declaration5⟩ ⟨number⟩

124 ⟨function declaration7⟩ →
⟨function declaration6⟩)

125 ⟨synonymous dc1⟩ →

$\langle$type$\rangle$ $\langle$identifier$\rangle$ **syn** |
$\langle$simple type$\rangle$ **register** $\langle$identifier$\rangle$ **syn** |
$\langle$synonymous dc3$\rangle$ $\langle$identifier$\rangle$ **syn**

128 $\langle$synonymous dc2$\rangle$ $\longrightarrow$
$\langle$synonymous dc1$\rangle$ $\langle$cell$\rangle$ |
$\langle$synonymous dc1$\rangle$ $\langle$number$\rangle$ |
$\langle$synonymous dc1$\rangle$ $\langle$register$\rangle$

131 $\langle$synonymous dc3$\rangle$ $\longrightarrow$
$\langle$synonymous dc2$\rangle$,

132 $\langle$segment head$\rangle$ $\longrightarrow$
segment

133 $\langle$procedure heading1$\rangle$ $\longrightarrow$
procedure | $\langle$segment head$\rangle$ **procedure**

135 $\langle$procedure heading2$\rangle$ $\longrightarrow$
$\langle$procedure heading1$\rangle$ $\langle$identifier$\rangle$

136 $\langle$procedure heading3$\rangle$ $\longrightarrow$
$\langle$procedure heading2$\rangle$ (

137 $\langle$procedure heading4$\rangle$ $\longrightarrow$
$\langle$procedure heading3$\rangle$ $\langle$register$\rangle$

138 $\langle$procedure heading5$\rangle$ $\longrightarrow$
$\langle$procedure heading4$\rangle$)

139 $\langle$procedure heading6$\rangle$ $\longrightarrow$
$\langle$procedure heading5$\rangle$;

140 $\langle$declaration$\rangle$ $\longrightarrow$
$\langle$decl7$\rangle$ | $\langle$function declaration7$\rangle$ | $\langle$synonymous dc2$\rangle$ |
$\langle$procedure heading6$\rangle$ $\langle$statement*$\rangle$ | $\langle$segment head$\rangle$ **base** $\langle$register$\rangle$

145 $\langle$label definition$\rangle$ $\longrightarrow$
$\langle$identifier$\rangle$:

146 $\langle$blockhead$\rangle$ $\longrightarrow$
begin | $\langle$blockhead$\rangle$ $\langle$declaration$\rangle$;

148 $\langle$blockbody$\rangle$ $\longrightarrow$
$\langle$blockhead$\rangle$ |
$\langle$blockbody$\rangle$ $\langle$statement$\rangle$; |
$\langle$blockbody$\rangle$ $\langle$label definition$\rangle$

151 $\langle$program$\rangle$ $\longrightarrow$
. $\langle$statement$\rangle$.

Lexical Variables

$\langle$identifier$\rangle$
$\langle$string$\rangle$
$\langle$number$\rangle$

A.4. A SYNTAX-DIRECTED TRANSLATION SCHEME FOR PAL

Here we provide a simple syntax-directed translation scheme for PAL, a programming language devised by J. Wozencraft and A. Evans† embodying lambda calculus and assignment statements. PAL is an acronym for Pedagogic Algorithmic Language.

The simple SDTS presented here maps programs in a slightly modified version of PAL into a postfix Polish notation. This SDTS is taken from DeRemer [1969].‡ The SDTS is presented in two parts. The first part is the underlying context-free grammar, a simple LR(1) grammar. The second part defines the semantic rule associated with each production of the underlying grammar.

We also provide a regular definition description of the lexical variables $<$relational functor$>$, $<$variable$>$ and $<$constant$>$ used in the SDTS.

High-Level Productions

1 $\langle$program$\rangle \rightarrow$
   $\langle$definition list$\rangle \,|\, \langle$expression$\rangle$
3 $\langle$definition list$\rangle \rightarrow$
   def $\langle$definition$\rangle \langle$definition list$\rangle \,|\,$ **def** $\langle$definition$\rangle$
5 $\langle$expression$\rangle \rightarrow$
   let $\langle$definition$\rangle$ **in** $\langle$expression$\rangle \,|$
   fn $\langle$bv part$\rangle . \langle$expression$\rangle \,|$
   $\langle$where expression$\rangle$
8 $\langle$where expression$\rangle \rightarrow$
   $\langle$valof expression$\rangle$ **where** $\langle$rec definition$\rangle \,|\, \langle$valof expression$\rangle$
10 $\langle$valof expression$\rangle \rightarrow$
   valof $\langle$command$\rangle \,|\, \langle$command$\rangle$
12 $\langle$command$\rangle \rightarrow$
   $\langle$labeled command$\rangle ; \langle$command$\rangle \,|\, \langle$labeled command$\rangle$
14 $\langle$labeled command$\rangle \rightarrow$
   $\langle$variable$\rangle : \langle$labeled command$\rangle \,|\, \langle$conditional command$\rangle$
16 $\langle$conditional command$\rangle \rightarrow$
   test $\langle$boolean$\rangle$ **ifso** $\langle$labeled command$\rangle$ **ifnot** $\langle$labeled command$\rangle \,|$
   test $\langle$boolean$\rangle$ **ifnot** $\langle$labeled command$\rangle$ **ifso** $\langle$labeled command$\rangle \,|$

†A complete description of PAL is given in: John M. Wozencraft and Arthur Evans, Jr., *Notes on Programming Linguistics*, Department of Electrical Engineering, Massachusetts Institute of Technology, Cambridge, Mass., July 1969. The syntax is reprinted by permission of the authors.

‡F. L. DeRemer, *Practical Translators for LR(k) Languages*, Ph.D. Thesis, M.I.T., Cambridge, Mass., 1969, by permission of the author.

```
        if ⟨boolean⟩ do ⟨labeled command⟩|
        unless ⟨boolean⟩ do ⟨labeled command⟩|
        while ⟨boolean⟩ do ⟨labeled command⟩|
        until ⟨boolean⟩ do ⟨labeled command⟩|
        ⟨basic command⟩
23 ⟨basic command⟩ →
        ⟨tuple⟩ := ⟨tuple⟩|goto ⟨combination⟩|
        res ⟨tuple⟩|⟨tuple⟩
27 ⟨tuple⟩ →
        ⟨T1⟩|⟨T1⟩ , ⟨tuple⟩
29 ⟨T1⟩ →
        ⟨T1⟩ aug ⟨conditional expression⟩|⟨conditional expression⟩
31 ⟨conditional expression⟩ →
        ⟨boolean⟩ → ⟨conditional expression⟩|⟨conditional expression⟩|
        ⟨T2⟩
33 ⟨T2⟩ →
        $ ⟨combination⟩|⟨boolean⟩
35 ⟨boolean⟩ →
        ⟨boolean⟩ or ⟨conjunction⟩|⟨conjunction⟩
37 ⟨conjunction⟩ →
        ⟨conjunction⟩ & ⟨negation⟩|⟨negation⟩
39 ⟨negation⟩ →
        not ⟨relation⟩|⟨relation⟩
41 ⟨relation⟩ →
        ⟨arithmetic expression⟩ ⟨relational functor⟩
            ⟨arithmetic expression⟩|
        ⟨arithmetic expression⟩
43 ⟨arithmetic expression⟩ →
        ⟨arithmetic expression⟩ + ⟨term⟩|
        ⟨arithmetic expression⟩ − ⟨term⟩|
        + ⟨term⟩|− ⟨term⟩| ⟨term⟩
48 ⟨term⟩ →
        ⟨term⟩ ∗ ⟨factor⟩|⟨term⟩ / ⟨factor⟩|⟨factor⟩
51 ⟨factor⟩ →
        ⟨primary⟩ ∗∗ ⟨factor⟩|⟨primary⟩
53 ⟨primary⟩ →
        ⟨primary⟩ % ⟨variable⟩ ⟨combination⟩|⟨combination⟩
55 ⟨combination⟩ →
        ⟨combination⟩⟨rand⟩|⟨rand⟩
57 ⟨rand⟩ →
        ⟨variable⟩|⟨constant⟩|(⟨expression⟩)|[⟨expression⟩]
61 ⟨definition⟩ →
```

⟨inwhich definition⟩ **within** ⟨definition⟩|
⟨inwhich definition⟩

63 ⟨inwhich definition⟩ ⟶
⟨inwhich definition⟩ **inwhich** ⟨simultaneous definition⟩|
⟨simultaneous definition⟩

65 ⟨simultaneous definition⟩ ⟶
⟨rec definition⟩ **and** ⟨simultaneous definition⟩|
⟨rec definition⟩

67 ⟨rec definition⟩ ⟶
rec ⟨basic definition⟩|⟨basic definition⟩

69 ⟨basic definition⟩ ⟶
⟨variable list⟩ = ⟨expression⟩|
⟨variable⟩ ⟨bv part⟩ = ⟨expression⟩|
(⟨definition⟩)|[⟨definition⟩]

73 ⟨bv part⟩ ⟶
⟨bv part⟩ ⟨basic bv⟩|⟨basic bv⟩

75 ⟨basic bv⟩ ⟶
⟨variable⟩|(⟨variable list⟩)|( )

78 ⟨variable list⟩ ⟶
⟨variable⟩ , ⟨variable list⟩|⟨variable⟩

Rules Corresponding to the High-Level Productions

1 ⟨program⟩ =
⟨definition list⟩|⟨expression⟩

3 ⟨definition list⟩ =
⟨definition⟩ ⟨definition list⟩ **def**|⟨definition⟩ **lastdef**

5 ⟨expression⟩ =
⟨definition⟩ ⟨expression⟩ **let**|
⟨bv part⟩ ⟨expression⟩ **lambda**|
⟨where expression⟩

8 ⟨where expression⟩ =
⟨valof expression⟩ ⟨rec definition⟩ **where**|
⟨valof expression⟩

10 ⟨valof expression⟩ =
⟨command⟩ **valof**|⟨command⟩

12 ⟨command⟩ =
⟨labeled command⟩ ⟨command⟩ ;|⟨labeled command⟩

14 ⟨labeled command⟩ =
⟨variable⟩ ⟨labeled command⟩ :|⟨conditional command⟩

16 ⟨conditional command⟩ =
⟨boolean⟩ ⟨labeled command⟩ ⟨labeled command⟩ **test-true**|
⟨boolean⟩ ⟨labeled command⟩ ⟨labeled command⟩ **test-false**|

$\langle$boolean$\rangle$ $\langle$labeled command$\rangle$ **if** |
$\langle$boolean$\rangle$ $\langle$labeled command$\rangle$ **unless** |
$\langle$boolean$\rangle$ $\langle$labeled command$\rangle$ **while** |
$\langle$boolean$\rangle$ $\langle$labeled command$\rangle$ **until** |
$\langle$basic command$\rangle$
23 $\langle$basic command$\rangle$ =
$\langle$tuple$\rangle$ $\langle$tuple$\rangle$:= | $\langle$combination$\rangle$ **goto** |
$\langle$tuple$\rangle$ **res** | $\langle$tuple$\rangle$
27 $\langle$tuple$\rangle$ =
$\langle$T1$\rangle$ | $\langle$T1$\rangle$ $\langle$tuple$\rangle$,
29 $\langle$T1$\rangle$ =
$\langle$T1$\rangle$ $\langle$conditional expression$\rangle$ **aug** | $\langle$conditional expression$\rangle$
31 $\langle$conditional expression$\rangle$ =
$\langle$boolean$\rangle$ $\langle$conditional expression$\rangle$
$\langle$conditional expression$\rangle$ **test-true** |
$\langle$T2$\rangle$
33 $\langle$T2$\rangle$ =
$\langle$combination$\rangle$ \$ | $\langle$boolean$\rangle$
35 $\langle$boolean$\rangle$ =
$\langle$boolean$\rangle$ $\langle$conjuction$\rangle$ **or** | $\langle$conjunction$\rangle$
37 $\langle$conjunction$\rangle$ =
$\langle$conjunction$\rangle$ $\langle$negation$\rangle$ **&** | $\langle$negation$\rangle$
39 $\langle$negation$\rangle$ =
$\langle$relation$\rangle$ **not** | $\langle$relation$\rangle$
41 $\langle$relation$\rangle$ =
$\langle$arithmetic expression$\rangle$ $\langle$arithmetic expression$\rangle$
$\langle$relational functor$\rangle$ |
$\langle$arithmetic expression$\rangle$
43 $\langle$arithmetic expression$\rangle$ =
$\langle$arithmetic expression$\rangle$ $\langle$term$\rangle$ + |
$\langle$arithmetic expression$\rangle$ $\langle$term$\rangle$ − |
$\langle$term$\rangle$ **pos** | $\langle$term$\rangle$ **neg** | $\langle$term$\rangle$
48 $\langle$term$\rangle$ =
$\langle$term$\rangle$ $\langle$factor$\rangle$ * | $\langle$term$\rangle$ $\langle$factor$\rangle$ / | $\langle$factor$\rangle$
51 $\langle$factor$\rangle$ =
$\langle$primary$\rangle$ $\langle$factor$\rangle$ **exp** | $\langle$primary$\rangle$
53 $\langle$primary$\rangle$ =
$\langle$primary$\rangle$ $\langle$variable$\rangle$ $\langle$combination$\rangle$ % | $\langle$combination$\rangle$
55 $\langle$combination$\rangle$ =
$\langle$combination$\rangle$ $\langle$rand$\rangle$ **gamma** | $\langle$rand$\rangle$
57 $\langle$rand$\rangle$ =
$\langle$variable$\rangle$ | $\langle$constant$\rangle$ | $\langle$expression$\rangle$ | $\langle$expression$\rangle$
61 $\langle$definition$\rangle$ =

⟨inwhich definition⟩ ⟨definition⟩ **within** |
⟨inwhich definition⟩
63 ⟨inwhich definition⟩ =
⟨inwhich definition⟩ ⟨simultaneous definition⟩ **inwhich** |
⟨simultaneous definition⟩
65 ⟨simultaneous definition⟩ =
⟨rec definition⟩ ⟨simultaneous definition⟩ **and** |
⟨rec definition⟩
67 ⟨rec definition⟩ =
⟨basic definition⟩ **rec** | ⟨basic definition⟩
69 ⟨basic definition⟩ =
⟨variable list⟩ ⟨expression⟩ = |
⟨variable⟩ ⟨bv part⟩ ⟨expression⟩ **ff** |
⟨definition⟩ | ⟨definition⟩
73 ⟨bv part⟩ =
⟨bv part⟩ ⟨basic bv⟩ | ⟨basic bv⟩
75 ⟨basic bv⟩ =
⟨variable⟩ | ⟨variable list⟩ | ( )
78 ⟨variable list⟩ =
⟨variable⟩ ⟨variable list⟩ **vl** | ⟨variable⟩

Regular Definitions

⟨uppercase letter⟩ =
A | B | C | · · · | Z
⟨lowercase letter⟩ =
a | b | c | · · · | z
⟨digit⟩ =
0 | 1 | 2 | · · · | 9
⟨letter⟩ =
⟨uppercase letter⟩ | ⟨lowercase letter⟩
⟨alphanumeric⟩ =
⟨letter⟩ | ⟨digit⟩
⟨truthvalue⟩ =
true | **false**
⟨variable head⟩ =
⟨digit⟩$^+$ (⟨letter⟩ | __) |
⟨lowercase letter⟩$^+$ (⟨uppercase letter⟩ | ⟨digit⟩ | __) |
⟨uppercase letter⟩ | __
⟨variable⟩ =
⟨lowercase letter⟩ | ⟨variable head⟩ (⟨alphanumeric⟩ | __)*
⟨integer⟩ =
⟨digit⟩$^+$

⟨real⟩ =
    ⟨digit⟩⁺ . ⟨digit⟩⁺
⟨quotation element⟩ =
    ⟨any character other than * or '⟩|
    $* n | * t | * b | * s | ** | *' | * k | * r$
⟨quotation⟩ =
    ' ⟨quotation element⟩* '
⟨constant⟩ =
    ⟨integer⟩|⟨real⟩|⟨quotation⟩|⟨truthvalue⟩|e
⟨relational functor⟩ =
    gr | ge | eq | ne | ls | le

BIBLIOGRAPHY

Aho, A. V. [1968]. Indexed grammars—an extension of context-free grammars. *J. ACM* 15:4, 647–671.

Aho, A. V., and J. D. Ullman [1969a]. Syntax directed translations and the pushdown assembler. *J. Computer and System Sciences* 3:1, 37–56.

Aho, A. V., and J. D. Ullman [1969b]. Properties of syntax directed translations. *J. Computer and System Sciences* 3:3, 319–334.

Aho, A. V., and J. D. Ullman [1971]. The care and feeding of LR(*k*) grammars. *Proc. of 3rd ACM Conf. on Theory of Computing*, 159–170.

Aho, A. V., P. J. Denning, and J. D. Ullman [1972]. Weak and mixed strategy precedence parsing. *J. ACM* 19:2, 225–243.

Aho, A. V., J. E. Hopcroft, and J. D. Ullman [1968]. Time and tape complexity of pushdown automaton languages. *Information and Control* 13:3, 186–206.

Ans X3.9 [1966]. *American National Standards FORTRAN.* American National Standards Institute, New York.

Ansi Subcommittee X3J3 [1971]. Clarification of FORTRAN Standards-Second Report. *Comm.* ACM 14:10, 628–642.

Arbib, M. A. [1970]. *Theories of Abstract Automata.* Prentice-Hall, Inc., Englewood Cliffs, N.J.

Backus, J. W., et al. [1957]. The FORTRAN automatic coding system. *Proc. Western Joint Computer Conference* 11, 188–198.

Bar-Hillel, Y. [1964]. *Language and Information.* Addison-Wesley, Reading, Mass.

Bar-Hillel Y., M. Perles, and E. Shamir [1961]. On formal properties of simple phrase structure grammars. *Z. Phonetik, Sprachwissenschaft und Kommunikationsforschung* 14, 143–172. Also in Bar-Hillel [1964], pp. 116–150.

Barnett, M. P., and R. P. Futrelle [1962]. Syntactic analysis by digital computer. *Comm. ACM* 5:10, 515–526.

BAUER, H., S. BECKER, and S. L. GRAHAM [1968]. *ALGOL W Implementation.* CS98, Computer Science Department, Stanford Univ., Stanford, Calif.

BERGE, C. [1958]. *The Theory of Graphs and Its Applications.* Wiley, New York.

BIRMAN, A., and J. D. ULLMAN [1970]. Parsing algorithms with backtrack. *IEEE Conf. Record of 11th Annual Symposium on Switching and Automata Theory,* pp. 153–174.

BLATTNER, M. [1972]. *The Unsolvability of the Equality Problem for Sentential Forms of Context-free Languages,* Unpublished memorandum, UCLA, Los Angeles, Calif.

BOBROW, D. G. [1963]. Syntactic analysis of English by computer—a survey. *Proc. AFIPS Fall Joint Computer Conference,* **24**. Spartan, New York, pp. 365–387.

BOOK, R. V. [1970]. Problems in formal language theory. *Proc. Fourth Annual Princeton Conference on Information Sciences and Systems,* pp. 253–256.

BOOTH, T. L. [1967]. *Sequential Machines and Automata Theory.* Wiley, New York.

BORODIN, A. [1970]. Computational complexity—a survey. *Proc. Fourth Annual Princeton Conference on Information Sciences and Systems,* pp. 257–262.

BRAFFORT, P., and D. HIRSCHBERG (eds.) [1963]. *Computer Programming and Formal Systems.* North-Holland, Amsterdam.

BROOKER, R. A., and D. MORRIS [1963]. The compiler-compiler. *Annual Review in Automatic Programming,* **3**. Pergamon, Elmsford, N.Y., pp. 229–275.

BRZOZOWSKI, J. A. [1962]. A survey of regular expressions and their applications. *IRE Trans. on Electronic Computers* 11:3, 324–335.

BRZOZOWSKI, J. A. [1964]. Derivatives of regular expressions. *J. ACM* 11:4, 481–494.

CANTOR, D. G. [1962]. On the ambiguity problem of Backus systems. *J. ACM* 9:4, 477–479.

CHEATHAM, T. E. [1965]. The TGS-II translator-generator system. *Proc. IFIP Congress 65.* Spartan, New York, pp. 529–593.

CHEATHAM, T. E. [1966]. The introduction of definitional facilities into higher level programming languages. *Proc. AFIPS Fall Joint Computer Conference,* **30**. Spartan, New York, pp. 623–637.

CHEATHAM, T. E. [1967]. *The Theory and Construction of Compilers* (2nd ed.). Computer Associates, Inc., Wakefield, Mass.

CHEATHAM, T. E., and K. SATTLEY [1964]. Syntax directed compiling. *Proc. AFIPS Spring Joint Computer Conference,* **25**. Spartan, New York, pp. 31–57.

CHEATHAM, T. E., and T. STANDISH [1970]. Optimization aspects of compiler-compilers. *ACM SIGPLAN Notices* 5:10, 10–17.

CHOMSKY, N. [1956]. Three models for the description of language. *IEEE Trans. on Information Theory,* 2:3, 113–124.

CHOMSKY, N. [1957]. *Syntactic Structures*. Mouton and Co., The Hague.

CHOMSKY, N. [1959a]. On certain formal properties of grammars. *Information and Control* 2:2, 137–167.

CHOMSKY, N. [1959b]. A note on phrase structure grammars. *Information and Control* 2:4, 393–395.

CHOMSKY, N. [1962]. Context-free grammars and pushdown storage. *Quarterly Progress Report, No.* **65**, Research Laboratory of Electronics, Massachusetts Institute of Technology, Cambridge, Mass.

CHOMSKY, N. [1963]. Formal properties of grammars. In *Handbook of Mathematical Psychology*, **2** (R. D. Luce, R. R. Bush, and E. Galanter, eds.). Wiley, New York.

CHOMSKY, N. [1965]. *Aspects of the Theory of Syntax*. M.I.T. Press, Cambridge, Mass.

CHOMSKY, N., and G. A. MILLER [1958]. Finite state languages. *Information and Control* 1:2, 91–112.

CHOMSKY, N., and M. P. SCHUTZENBERGER [1963]. The algebraic theory of context-free languages. In Braffort and Hirschberg [1963], pp. 118–161.

CHRISTENSEN, C., and J. C. SHAW (eds.) [1969]. Proc. of the extensible languages symposium. *ACM SIGPLAN Notices* 4:8.

CHURCH, A. [1941]. *The Calculi of Lambda Conversion*. Annals of Mathematics Studies **6**. Princeton University Press, Princeton, N.J.

CHURCH, A. [1965]. *Introduction to Mathematical Logic*. Princeton University Press, Princeton, N.J.

COCKE, J., and J. T. SCHWARTZ [1970]. *Programming Languages and Their Compilers*. Courant Institute of Mathematical Sciences, New York University, New York.

COHEN, R. S., and K. CULIK II. [1971]. LR-Regular Grammars—an Extension of LR(k) Grammars. *IEEE Conf. Record of 12th Annual Symposium on Switching and Automata Theory*, pp. 153–165.

COHEN, D. J., and C. C. GOTLIEB [1970]. A list structure form of grammars for syntactic analysis. *Computing Surveys* 2:1, 65–82.

COLMERAUER, A. [1970]. Total precedence relations. *J. ACM* 17:1, 14–30.

CONWAY, M. E. [1963]. Design of a separable transition-diagram compiler. *Comm. ACM* 6:7, 396–408.

CONWAY, R. W., and W. L. MAXWELL [1963]. CORC: the Cornell computing language. *Comm. ACM* 6:6, 317–321.

CONWAY, R. W., and W. L. MAXWELL [1968]. *CUPL—An Approach to Introductory Computing Instruction*. TR No. 68-4, Dept. of Computer Science, Cornell Univ., Ithaca, N.Y.

CONWAY, R. W. et al. [1970]. *PL/C. A High Performance Subset of PL/I*. TR70-55, Dept. of Computer Science, Cornell Univ., Ithaca, N.Y.

COOK, S. A. [1971]. Linear time simulation of deterministic two-way pushdown automata. *Proc. IFIP Congress* **71**, TA-2. North-Holland Publishing Co., Netherlands, pp. 174–179.

COOK, S. A., and S. D. AANDERAA [1969]. On the minimum computation time of functions. *Trans. American Math. Soc.* **142**, 291–314.

CULIK, K. II [1968]. Contribution to deterministic top-down analysis of context-free languages. *Kybernetika* 4:5, 422–431.

DAVIS, M. [1958]. *Computability and Unsolvability*. McGraw-Hill, New York.

DAVIS, M. (ed.) [1965]. *The Undecidable. Basic papers in undecidable propositions, unsolvable problems and computable functions.* Raven Press, New York.

DeREMER, F. L. [1969]. *Practical translators for LR(k) languages.* Ph.D. Thesis, Massachusetts Institute of Technology, Cambridge, Mass.

DeREMER, F. L. [1971]. Simple LR(k) grammars. *Comm. ACM* 14:7, 453–460.

DEWAR, R. B. K., R. R. HOCHSPRUNG, and W. S. WORLEY [1969]. The IITRAN programming language. *Comm. ACM* 12:10, 569–575.

EARLEY, J. [1968]. An efficient context-free parsing algorithm. Ph.D. Thesis, Carnegie-Mellon Univ., Pittsburgh, Pa. Also see *Comm. ACM* 13:2, (February, 1970) 94–102.

EICKEL, J., M. PAUL, F. L. BAUER, and K. SAMELSON [1963]. A syntax-controlled generator of formal language processors. *Comm. ACM* 6:8, 451–455.

ELSPAS, B., M. W. GREEN, and K. N. LEVITT [1971]. Software reliability. *Computer* **1**, 21–27.

ENGELER, E. (ed.) [1971]. *Symposium on Semantics of Algorithmic Languages.* Lecture Notes in Mathematics, Springer, Berlin.

EVANS, A., Jr. [1964]. An ALGOL 60 compiler. *Annual Review in Automatic Programming*, **4**. Pergamon, Elmsford, N.Y., pp. 87–124.

EVEY, R. J. [1963]. Applications of pushdown-store machines. *Proc. AFIPS Fall Joint Computer Conference*, **24**, Spartan, New York, pp. 215–227.

FELDMAN, J. A. [1966]. A formal semantics for computer languages and its application in a compiler-compiler. *Comm. ACM* 9:1, 3–9.

FELDMAN, J., and D. GRIES [1968]. Translator writing systems. *Comm. ACM* 11:2, 77–113.

FISCHER, M. J. [1968]. Grammars with macro-like productions. *IEEE Conf. Record of 9th Annual Symposium on Switching and Automata Theory*, pp. 131–142.

FISCHER, M. J. [1969]. Some properties of precedence languages. *Proc. ACM Symposium on Theory of Computing*, pp. 181–190.

FLOYD, R. W. [1961]. A descriptive language for symbol manipulation. *J. ACM* 8:4, 579–584.

FLOYD, R. W. [1962a]. Algorithm 97: shortest path. *Comm. ACM* 5:6, 345.

FLOYD, R. W. [1962b]. On ambiguity in phrase structure languages. *Comm. ACM* 5:10, 526–534.

FLOYD, R. W. [1963]. Syntactic analysis and operator precedence. *J. ACM* 10:3, 316–333.

FLOYD, R. W. [1964a]. Bounded context syntactic analysis. *Comm. ACM* 7:2, 62–67.

FLOYD, R. W. [1964b]. The syntax of programming languages—a survey. *IEEE Trans. on Electronic Computers* 13:4, 346–353.

FLOYD, R. W. [1967a]. Assigning meanings to programs. In Schwartz [1967], pp. 19–32.

FLOYD, R. W. [1967b]. Nondeterministic algorithms. *J. ACM* 14:4, 636–644.

FREEMAN, D. N. [1964]. Error correction in CORC, the Cornell computing language. *Proc. AFIPS Fall Joint Computer Conference*, **26**. Spartan, New York, pp. 15–34.

GALLER, B. A., and A. J. PERLIS [1967]. A proposal for definitions in ALGOL. *Comm. ACM* 10:4, 204–219.

GARWICK, J. V. [1964]. GARGOYLE, a language for compiler writing. *Comm. ACM* 7:1, 16–20.

GENTLEMAN, W. M. [1971]. A portable coroutine system. *Proc. IFIP Congress* **71**, TA-3, North Holland Publishing Co., Netherlands, pp. 94–98.

GILL, A. [1962]. *Introduction to the Theory of Finite State Machines*. McGraw-Hill, New York.

GINSBURG, S. [1962]. *An Introduction to Mathematical Machine Theory*. Addison-Wesley, Reading, Mass.

GINSBURG, S. [1966]. *The Mathematical Theory of Context-Free Languages*. McGraw-Hill, New York.

GINSBURG, S., and S. GREIBACH [1966]. Deterministic context-free languages. *Information and Control* 9:6, 620–648.

GINSBURG, S., and S. GREIBACH [1969]. Abstract families of languages. *Memoir Amer. Math. Soc. No.* **87**.

GINSBURG, S., and H. G. RICE [1962]. Two families of languages related to ALGOL. *J. ACM* 9:3, 350–371.

GINZBURG, A. [1968]. *Algebraic Theory of Automata*. Academic Press, New York.

GRAHAM, R. M. [1964]. Bounded context translation. *Proc. AFIPS Spring Joint Computer Conference*, **25**, Spartan, New York, pp. 17–29.

GRAHAM, S. L. [1970]. Extended precedence languages, bounded right context languages and deterministic languages. *IEEE Conf. Record of 11th Annual Symposium on Switching and Automata Theory*, pp. 175–180.

GRAU, A. A., U. HILL, and H. LANGMAACK [1967]. *Translation of ALGOL 60*. Springer, Berlin.

GRAY, J. N. [1969]. *Precedence parsers for programming languages*. Ph.D. Thesis, Univ. of California, Berkeley.

GRAY, J. N., and M. A. HARRISON [1969]. Single pass precedence analysis. *IEEE Conf. Record of 10th Annual Symposium on Switching and Automata Theory*, pp. 106–117.

GRAY, J. N., M. A. HARRISON, and O. IBARRA [1967]. Two way pushdown automata. *Information and Control* 11:1, 30–70.

GREIBACH, S. A. [1965]. A new normal form theorem for context-free phrase structure grammars. *J. ACM* 12:1, 42–52.

GREIBACH, S., and J. HOPCROFT [1969]. Scattered context grammars. *J. Computer and System Sciences* 3:3, 233–247.

GRIES, D. [1971]. *Compiler Construction for Digital Computers*. Wiley, New York.

GRIFFITHS, T. V. [1968]. The unsolvability of the equivalence problem for Λ-free nondeterministic generalized machines. *J. ACM* 15:3, 409–413.

GRIFFITHS, T. V., and S. R. PETRICK [1965]. On the relative efficiencies of context-free grammar recognizers. *Comm. ACM* 8:5, 289–300.

GRISWOLD. R. E., J. F. POAGE, and I. P. POLONSKY [1971]. *The SNOBOL 4 Programming Language* (2nd ed.) Prentice-Hall, Inc., Englewood Cliffs, N. J.

GROSS, M., and A. LENTIN [1970]. *Introduction to Formal Grammars*. Springer, Berlin.

HAINES, L. H. [1970]. *Representation Theorems for Context-Sensitive Languages*. Department of Electrical Engineering and Computer Sciences, Univ. of California, Berkeley.

HALMOS, P. R. [1960]. *Naive Set Theory*. Van Nostrand Reinhold, New York.

HALMOS, P. R. [1963]. *Lectures on Boolean Algebras*. Van Nostrand Reinhold, New York.

HARARY, F. [1969]. *Graph Theory*. Addison-Wesley, Reading, Mass.

HARRISON, M. A. [1965]. *Introduction to Switching and Automata Theory*. McGraw-Hill, New York.

HARTMANIS, J., and J. E. HOPCROFT [1970]. An overview of the theory of computational complexity. *J. ACM* 18:3, 444–475.

HARTMANIS, J., P. M. LEWIS II, and R. E. STEARNS [1965]. Classifications of computations by time and memory requirements. *Proc. IFIP Congress.* 65. Spartan, New York, pp. 31–35.

HAYS, D. G. [1967]. *Introduction to Computational Linguistics*. American Elsevier, New York.

HEXT, J. B., and P. S. ROBERTS [1970]. Syntax analysis by Domolki's algorithm. *Computer J.* 13:3, 263–271.

HOPCROFT, J. E. [1971]. *An n log n Algorithm for Minimizing States in a Finite Automaton*. CS71–190, Computer Science Department, Stanford Univ., Stanford, Calif. Also in, *Theory of Machines and Computations* (Z. Kohavi and A. Paz, eds.) Academic Press, New York, 1972, pp. 189–196.

HOPCROFT, J. E., and J. D. ULLMAN [1967]. An approach to a unified theory of automata. *Bell System Tech. J.* 46:8, 1763–1829.

HOPCROFT, J. E., and J. D. ULLMAN [1969]. *Formal Languages and Their Relation to Automata.* Addison-Wesley, Reading, Mass.

HOPGOOD, F. R. A. [1969]. *Compiling Techniques.* American Elsevier, New York.

HUFFMAN, D. A. [1954]. The synthesis of sequential switching circuits. *J. of the Franklin Institute* **257**, 3–4, 161, 190, and 275–303.

ICHBIAH, J. D., and S. P. MORSE [1970]. A technique for generating almost optimal Floyd–Evans productions for precedence grammars. *Comm. ACM* 13:8, 501–508.

INGERMAN, P. Z. [1966]. *A Syntax Oriented Translator.* Academic Press, New York.

IRLAND, M. I., and P. C. FISCHER [1970]. *A Bibliography on Computational Complexity.* CSRR 2028, Dept. of Applied Analysis and Computer Science, Univ. of Waterloo, Waterloo, Ontario.

IRONS, E. T. [1961]. A syntax directed compiler for ALGOL 60. *Comm. ACM* 4:1, 51–55.

IRONS, E. T. [1963a]. An error correcting parse algorithm. *Comm. ACM* 6:11, 669–673.

IRONS, E. T. [1963b]. The structure and use of the syntax directed compiler. *Annual Review in Automatic Programming*, **3**. Pergamon, Elmsford, N.Y., pp. 207–227.

IRONS, E. T. [1964]. Structural connections in formal languages. *Comm. ACM* 7:2, 62–67.

JOHNSON, W. L., J. H. PORTER, S. I. ACKLEY, and D. T. ROSS [1968]. Automatic generation of efficient lexical processors using finite state techniques. *Comm. ACM* 11:12, 805–813.

KAMEDA, T., and P. WEINER [1968]. On the reduction of nondeterministic automata. *Proc. Second Annual Princeton Conference on Information Sciences and Systems*, pp. 348–352.

KASAMI, T. [1965]. *An efficient recognition and syntax analysis algorithm for context-free languages. Sci. Rep. AFCRL-65-758*, Air Force Cambridge Research Laboratory, Bedford, mass.

KASAMI, T., and K. TORII [1969]. A syntax analysis procedure for unambiguous context-free grammars. *J. ACM* 16:3, 423–431.

KLEENE, S. C. [1952]. *Introduction to Metamathematics.* Van Nostrand Reinhold, New York.

KLEENE, S. C. [1956]. Representation of events in nerve nets. In Shannon and McCarthy [1956], pp. 3–40.

KNUTH, D. E. [1965]. On the translation of languages from left to right. *Information and Control* 8:6, 607–639.

KNUTH, D. E. [1967]. Top-down syntax analysis. *Lecture Notes*. International Summer School on Computer Programming, Copenhagen, Denmark.

KNUTH, D. E. [1968]. *The Art of Computer Programming*. Vol. 1: Fundamental Algorithms. Addison-Wesley, Reading, Mass.

KORENJAK, A. J. [1969]. A practical method for constructing LR(k) processors. *Comm. ACM* 12:11, 613–623.

KORENJAK, A. J., and J. E. HOPCROFT [1966]. Simple deterministic languages. *IEEE Conf. Record of 7th Annual Symposium on Switching and Automata Theory*, pp. 36–46.

KOSARAJU, S. R. [1970]. Finite state automata with markers. *Proc. Fourth Annual Princeton Conference on Information Sciences and Systems*, p. 380.

KUNO, S., and A. G. OETTINGER [1962]. Multiple-path syntactic analyzer. *Information Processing*, **62** (IFIP Cong.) (Popplewell, ed.). North-Holland, Amsterdam, pp. 306–311.

KURKI-SUONIO, R. [1969]. Note on top down languages. *BIT* **9**, 225–238.

LAFRANCE, J. [1970]. Optimization of error recovery in syntax directed parsing algorithms. *ACM SIGPLAN Notices* 5:12, 2–17.

LALONDE, W. R., E. S. LEE and J. J. HORNING [1971]. An LALR(k) parser generator, *Proc. IFIP Congress* **71**, TA-3. North Holland Publishing Co., Netherlands, pp. 153–157.

LEAVENWORTH, B. M. [1966]. Syntax macros and extended translation. *Comm. ACM* 9:11, 790–793.

LEE, J. A. N. [1967]. *Anatomy of a Compiler*. Reinhold, New York.

LEINIUS, R. P. [1970]. *Error detection and recovery for syntax directed compiler systems*. Ph.D. Thesis, Univ. of Wisconsin, Madison.

LEWIS, P. M. II, and D. J. ROSENKRANTZ [1971]. An ALGOL compiler designed using automata theory. *Proc. Polytechnic Institute of Brooklyn Symposium on Computers and Automata*.

LEWIS, P. M. II, and R. E. STEARNS [1968]. Syntax directed transduction. *J. ACM* 15:3, 464–488.

LOECKX, J. [1970]. An algorithm for the construction of bounded-context parsers. *Comm. ACM* 13:5, 297–307.

LUCAS, P., and K. WALK [1969]. On the formal description of *PL/I*. *Annual Review in Automatic Programming* 6:3. Pergamon, pp. 105–182.

MARKOV, A. A. [1951]. The theory of algorithms (Russian), Trudi Mathematicheskova Instituta imeni V. A. Steklova **38** pp. 176–189. (English translation, 1961, National Science Foundation, Washington, D.C.)

MCCARTHY, J. [1963]. A basis for the mathematical theory of computation. In Braffort and Hirschberg [1963], pp. 33–71.

McCarthy, J., and J. A. Painter [1967]. Correctness of a compiler for arithmetic expressions. In Schwartz [1967], pp. 33–41.

McClure, R. M. [1965]. TMG—a syntax directed compiler. *Proc. ACM National Conference*, **20**, pp. 262–274.

McCullough W. S., and E. Pitts [1943]. A logical calculus of the ideas immanent in nervous activity. *Bulletin of Mathematical Biophysics*, **5**, 115–133.

McIlroy, M. D. [1960]. Macro instruction extensions of compiler languages. *Comm. ACM* 3:4, 414–220.

McIlroy, M. D. [1968]. *Coroutines.* Unpublished memorandum.

McKeeman, W. M. [1966]. *An Approach to Computer Language Design.* CS48, Computer Science Department, Stanford Univ., Stanford, Calif.

McKeeman, W. M., J. J. Horning, and D. B. Wortman [1970]. *A Compiler Generator.* Prentice-Hall, Inc., Englewood Cliffs, N.J.

McNaughton, R., and H. Yamada [1960]. Regular expressions and state graphs for automata. *IRE Trans. on Electronic Computers* 9:1, 39–47. Reprinted in Moore [1964], pp. 157–174.

Mendelson, E. [1968]. *Introduction to Mathematical Logic.* Van Nostrand Reinhold, New York.

Miller, W. F., and A. C. Shaw [1968]. Linguistic methods in picture processing—a survey. *Proc. AFIPS Fall Joint Computer Conference*, **33**. The Thompson Book Co., Washington, D.C., pp. 279–290.

Minsky, M. [1967]. *Computation: Finite and Infinite Machines.* Prentice-Hall, Inc., Englewoods Cliffs, N.J.

Montanari, U. G. [1970]. Separable graphs, planar graphs and web grammars. *Information and Control* 16:3, 243–267.

Moore, E. F. [1956]. Gedanken experiments on sequential machines. In Shannon and McCarthy [1956], pp. 129–153.

Moore, E. F. [1964]. *Sequential Machines: Selected Papers.* Addison-Wesley, Reading, Mass.

Morgan, H. L. [1970]. Spelling correction in systems programs. *Comm. ACM* 13:2, 90–93.

Moulton, P. G., and M. E. Muller [1967]. A compiler emphasizing diagnostics. *Comm. ACM* 10:1, 45–52.

Munro, I. [1971]. *Efficient Determination of the Transitive Closure of a Directed Graph.* Information Processing Letters 1:2, 56–58.

Naur, P. (ed.) [1963]. Revised report on the algorithmic language ALGOL 60. *Comm. ACM* 6:1, 1–17.

Oettinger, A. [1961]. Automatic syntactic analysis and the pushdown store. In *Structure of Language and its Mathematical Concepts, Proc. 12th Symposium on Applied Mathematics.* American Mathematical Society, Providence, R. I., pp. 104–129.

OGDEN, W. [1968]. A helpful result for proving inherent ambiguity. *Mathematical Systems Theory* 2:3, 191–194.

ORE, O. [1962]. *Theory of Graphs.* Amer. Math. Soc. Colloquium Publications, **38**.

PAINTER, J. A. [1970]. Effectiveness of an optimizing compiler for arithmetic expressions. *ACM SIGPLAN Notices*, 5:7, 101–126.

PAIR, C. [1964]. Trees, pushdown stores and compilation. *RFTI—Chiffres* 7:3, 199–216.

PARIKH, R. J. [1966]. On context-free languages. *J. ACM* 13:4, 570–581.

PAUL, M. [1962]. A general processor for certain formal languages. *Proc. ICC Symposium Symb. Lang. Data Processing.* Gordon & Breach, New York, pp. 65–74.

PAULL, M. C., and S. H. UNGER [1968]. Structural equivalence of context-free grammars. *J. Computer and System Sciences* 2:1, 427–463.

PAVLIDIS, T. [1972]. Linear and context-free graph grammars. *J. ACM* 19:1, 11–23.

PFALTZ, J. L., and A. ROSENFELD [1969]. Web grammars. *Proc. International Joint Conf. on Artificial Intelligence*, Washington, D.C., pp. 609–619.

POST, E. L. [1943]. Formal reductions of the general combinatorial decision problem, *American Journal of Mathematics* **65**, 197–215.

POST E. L. [1947]. Recursive unsolvability of a problem of Thue. *J. of Symbolic Logic* 12, 1–11. Reprinted in Davis [1965], pp. 292–303.

POST, E. L. [1965]. Absolutely unsolvable problems and relatively undecidable propositions. In Davis [1965], pp, 340–433.

PRATHER, R. E. [1969]. Minimal solutions of Paull–Unger problems. *Mathematical Systems Theory* 3:1, 76–85.

RABIN, M. O. [1967]. Mathematical theory of automata. In Schwartz [1967], pp. 173–175.

RABIN, M. O., and D. SCOTT [1959]. Finite automata and their decision problems. *IBM J. of Research and Development* 3, 114–125. Reprinted in Moore [1964], pp. 63–91.

RANDELL, B., and L. J. RUSSELL [1964]. *ALGOL 60 Implementation.* Academic Press, New York.

REYNOLDS, J. C. [1965]. An introduction to the COGENT programming system. *Proc. ACM National Conference*, 422.

REYNOLDS, J. C., and R. HASKELL [1970]. *Grammatical coverings.* Unpublished memorandum.

ROGERS, H., JR. [1967]. *Theory of Recursive Functions and Effective Computability.* McGraw-Hill, New York.

ROSEN, S. (ed.) [1967a]. *Programming Systems and Languages*. McGraw-Hill, New York.

ROSEN, S. [1967b]. A compiler-building system developed by Brooker and Morris. In Rosen [1967a], pp. 306–331.

ROSENKRANTZ, D. J. [1967]. Matrix equations and normal forms for context-free grammars. *J. ACM* 14: 3, 501–507.

ROSENKRANTZ, D. J. [1968]. Programmed grammars and classes of formal languages. *J. ACM* 16: 1, 107–131.

ROSENKRANTZ, D. J., and P. M. LEWIS II [1970]. Deterministic left corner parsing. *IEEE Conf. Record 11th Annual Symposium on Switching and Automata Theory*, pp. 139–152.

ROSENKRANTZ, D. J., and R. E. STEARNS [1970]. Properties of deterministic top-down grammars. *Information and Control* 17: 3, 226–256.

SALOMAA, A. [1966]. Two complete axiom systems for the algebra of regular events. *J. ACM* 13: 1, 158–169.

SALOMAA, A. [1969a]. *Theory of Automata*. Pergamon, Elmsford, N.Y.

SALOMAA, A. [1969b]. On the index of a context-free grammar and language. *Information and Control* 14: 5, 474–477.

SAMMET, J. E. [1969]. *Programming Languages: History and Fundamentals*. Prentice-Hall, Englewood Cliffs, N.J.

SCHORRE, D. V. [1964]. META II, a syntax oriented compiler writing language. *Proc. ACM National Conference* 19, pp. D1.3-1–D1.3-11.

SCHUTZENBERGER, M. P. [1963]. On context-free languages and pushdown automata. *Information and Control* 6: 3, 246–264.

SCHWARTZ, J. T. (ed.) [1967]. Mathematical aspects of computer science. *Proc. Symposia in Applied Mathematics*, 19. American Mathematical Society, Providence, R. I.

SHANNON, C. E., and J. MCCARTHY (eds.) [1956]. *Automata Studies*. Princeton University Press, Princeton, N.J.

SHAW, A. C. [1970]. Parsing of graph-representable pictures. *J. ACM* 17: 3, 453–481.

SHEPHERDSON, J. C. [1959]. The reduction of two-way automata to one-way automata. *IBM J. Res.* 3, 198–200. Reprinted in Moore [1964], pp. 92–97.

STEARNS, R. E. [1967]. A regularity test for pushdown machines. *Information and Control* 11: 3, 323–340.

STEEL, T. B. (ed.) [1966]. *Formal Language Description Languages for Computer Programming*. North-Holland, Amsterdam.

STRASSEN, V. [1969]. Gaussian elimination is not optimal. *Numerische Mathematik* 13, 354–356.

SUPPES, P. [1960]. *Axiomatic Set Theory*. Van Nostrand Reinhold, New York.

THOMPSON, K. [1968]. Regular expression search algorithm. *Comm. ACM* 11:6, 419–422.

TURING, A. M. [1936–1937]. On computable numbers, with an application to the *Entscheidungsproblem*. *Proc. of the London Mathematical Society*, ser. 2, **42**, 230–265. Corrections. *Ibid.* **43** (1937), 544–546.

UNGER, S. H. [1968]. A global parser for context-free phrase structure grammars. *Comm. ACM* 11:4, 240–246, and 11:6, 427.

VAN WIJNGARRDEN, A. (ed.) [1969]. Report on the algorithmic language ALGOL 68. *Numerische Mathematik* **14**, 79–218.

WALTERS, D. A. [1970]. Deterministic context-sensitive languages. *Information and Control* 17:1, 14–61.

WARSHALL, S. [1962]. A theorem on Boolean matrices. *J. ACM* 9:1, 11–12.

WARSHALL, S., and R. M. SHAPIRO [1964]. A general purpose table driven compiler. *Proc. AFIPS Spring Joint Computer Conference*, **25**. Spartan, New York, pp. 59–65.

WEGBREIT, B. [1970]. *Studies in extensible programming languages.* Ph.D. Thesis, Harvard Univ., Cambridge, Mass.

WINOGRAD, S. [1965]. On the time required to perform addition. *J. ACM* 12:2, 277–285.

WINOGRAD, S. [1967]. On the time required to perform multiplication. *J. ACM* 14:4, 793–802.

WIRTH, N. [1968]. PL360—a programming language for the 360 computers. *J. ACM* 15:1, 37–34.

WIRTH, N., and H. WEBER [1966]. EULER—a generalization of ALGOL and its formal definition, Parts 1 and 2. *Comm. ACM* 9:1, 13–23 and 9:2, 89–99.

WISE, D. S. [1971]. Domolki's algorithm applied to generalized overlap resolvable grammars. *Proc. Third Annual ACM Symp. on Theory of Computing*, pp. 171–184.

WOOD, D. [1969a]. The theory of left factored languages. *Computer J.* 12:4, 349–356, and 13:1, 55–62.

WOOD, D. [1969b]. A note on top-down deterministic languages. *BIT* 9:4, 387–399.

WOOD, D. [1970]. Bibliography 23: Formal language theory and automata theory. *Computing Reviews* 11:7, 417–430.

WOZENCRAFT, J. M., and A. EVANS, JR. [1969]. *Notes on Programming Languages.* Dept. of Electrical Engineering, Massachusetts Institute of Technology, Cambridge, Mass.

YOUNGER, D. H. [1967]. Recognition and parsing of context-free languages in time n^3. *Information and Control* 10:2, 189–208.

INDEX TO LEMMAS, THEOREMS, AND ALGORITHMS

INDEX TO VOLUME I